THE STORY OF
Bob Marley's
Wailers WAILING BLUES

D1760806

3 8014 07038 5809

THE STORY OF
Bob Marley's
Wailers WAILING BLUES

JOHN MASOURI

OMNIBUS PRESS

London • New York • Paris • Sydney • Copenhagen • Berlin • Madrid • Tokyo

Copyright © 2008 Omnibus Press
(A Division of Music Sales Limited)

Cover designed by The Design Corporation
Picture research by Sarah Bacon

ISBN: 978-1-84609-689-1
Order No: OP51656

The Author hereby asserts his/her right to be identified as the author of this work in accordance with Sections 77 to 78 of the Copyright, Designs and Patents Act 1988.

All rights reserved. No part of this book may be reproduced in any form or by any electronic or mechanical means, including information storage or retrieval systems, without permission in writing from the publisher, except by a reviewer who may quote brief passages.

Exclusive Distributors
Music Sales Limited
14/15 Berners Street
London W1T 3LJ.

Music Sales Corporation
257 Park Avenue South
New York, NY 10010, USA.

Macmillan Distribution Services
53 Park West Drive
Derrimut, Vic 3030
Australia.

Every effort has been made to trace the copyright holders of the photographs in this book but one or two were unreachable. We would be grateful if the photographers concerned would contact us.

Typesetting by Galleon Typesetting, Ipswich
Printed in the United States of America by Quebecor World

A catalog record for this book is available from the British Library.

Visit Omnibus Press on the web at www.omnibuspress.com

CONTENTS

INTRODUCTION

I FIRST fell under the Wailers' spell after seeing their television appearance on *The Old Grey Whistle Test* in 1973. However, the moment of
realisation, when everything clicked into place, didn't arrive until years
later, after Aston "Family Man" Barrett sat down at a piano and rattled off
a selection of what he called "half blues". A few of the other Wailers who
were there that night in the back room of a south London pub gave
knowing smiles as "Fams" worked his way through 'Easy Snappin'',
'Stand By Me', and a couple of Fats Domino tunes. The roots of the
band's music were laid bare and the differences between the seductive
rhythms of the Caribbean, the sounds of black and hillbilly America and
England's gospel and music hall tradition all blurred into one, causing my
head to spin. In a flash, I saw that categories are meaningless and that music
is an undying spirit which can never be confined by time, place, or genre.
It can however, carry a message. The way Family Man and the Wailers
used music to convey something so life-affirming filled me with wonder
. . . and still does.

Family Man taught me a great deal more in the nine years I spent
working on this book, as we travelled intermittently throughout America,
Europe, and Jamaica, or sat talking in an endless succession of tour buses
and hotel rooms. I came to understand that even Bob Marley, blessed as he
was with prodigious gifts of his own, would have struggled to craft his
songs of freedom without this affable master of sound at his side.

Fams feels he's been cheated out of his life's work, and has good reason
to. He poured his heart and soul into making music that succeeded in fulfilling all the ambitions he and his fellow Wailers harboured and that has .
touched millions of people, yet he's been forced to watch from the sidelines as others have stolen the credit and rewards, leaving him with an
increasingly empty feeling and a cult status that can't feed his large family.
While Marley was alive, Family Man felt protected and free to follow his
creative muse as he pleased, despite the political violence surrounding
56 Hope Road, or the complexities of the Wailers' recording contract.
The mission to glorify Jah was always at the forefront of the band's music
alongside a desire to comfort, educate and inspire all creeds, as well as

aligning themselves with black liberation. Theirs was a selfless undertaking and while the Wailers enjoyed the fruits of hard-earned success, they cared little for material gain. With Tuff Gong, they were intent on building a network of business enterprises that would have revolutionised the local record industry and helped many young people escape from Trenchtown's crime, violence, poverty and frustration.

If Family Man feels embittered, it's because some of the people who've now turned their backs once shared in this grand adventure, when the Wailers had spread their roots rock reggae gospel to the four corners of the earth. One of the things that struck me most about the bassist was his well-mannered conservatism, yet the rebel in him still burns brightly. Knowing what I know now, I blame his mother. The former Violet Marshall is descended from the Maroons, a community of escaped slaves who lived free in the Jamaican mountains. They remained at large throughout the reign of the Spanish, who called these escaped slaves "cimarrons", meaning "wild ones". Under the leadership of legendary figures such as Cudjoe, the Maroons developed early forms of guerilla warfare in eluding their pursuers and were never defeated, despite being confronted by superior numbers and firepower. The British were forced to sign a treaty in 1738, guaranteeing them self-governance. In return they would cease their raids on plantations, hand back any escaped slaves seeking to join them and, in the event of an invasion, fight on the side of the British army. At Cudjoe's insistence, he and the British commander signed the treaty in blood and the Maroons have continued to retain relative autonomy ever since.

It's their unique history that makes the Maroons so different from other Jamaicans. Family Man delights in tracing his ancestry back to the arrival of the British, reminding people there were Barretts in Jamaica "long before any Marleys or Blackwells". In a curious twist of fate, these same Barretts were also related to the poet Elizabeth Barrett Browning. It's an unlikely scenario, but from this mix of slavery and nobility came a character destined to play a central role in the life story of Jamaica's most famous musician, Robert Nesta Marley.

CHAPTER ONE

Early Days

JAMAICA was still under colonial rule in 1946, the year that Aston "Family Man" Barrett was born. Life on the island was rapidly changing and not necessarily for the better, since Jamaica's army of small-time farmers and plantation workers were experiencing grave hardship and large numbers of them had begun looking for work in the towns, swelling urban populations to breaking point. This in turn led to slums springing up on the outskirts of Kingston. Riots and strikes became commonplace – a situation the British government largely turned a blind eye to, since it was more concerned with rebuilding its own war-torn cities after the ravages of World War II than tackling problems faced by its colonies. Jamaica however, had contributed in no small measure to the Allied war effort and so would continue to receive limited financial assistance in return for increased quotas of local products such as sugar and bauxite. This helped the middle classes, but made little provision for the poor, who were faced with rising insecurities in the wake of their traditional farming economy being threatened with collapse.

Violet Marshall's family weren't alone in leaving the countryside for a new life in the city. They had lived near Mount James in the parish of St Andrew's before settling in Kingston. Violet married Wilfred Barrett, who was a blacksmith from Fletcher's Land, near George VI Memorial Park (now National Heroes Park) in central Kingston, although his family were originally from St Elizabeth. The couple had three daughters, Fay, Olive and Winsome, before Aston Francis Barrett arrived on November 22, 1946. Another son, Carlton, would be born four years later, on December 17, 1950. Winsome went to live with an aunt in St Mary's, so the rest of the family didn't see a great deal of her apart from during the holidays.

During the brothers' early childhood, the Barretts lived at 26 Beeston Street, on the corner of Chancery Lane in downtown Kingston. Beeston Street was one block away from Orange Street, which came to be known as "Beat Street" because of the many record stores and studios found in the immediate vicinity. The teeming, musical metropolis this downtown area of Kingston would become was still some way off, however, and the local recording industry non-existent. The sound of big band jazz and New Orleans dominated people's musical tastes, as well as native, Caribbean styles such as mento. Church music, too, resonated with poorer, religious families like the Barretts, as well as country & western artists such as Jimmie Rodgers, Marty Robbins, Jim Reeves, and Hank Williams, who sang of everyday life and hardships in ways ordinary Jamaicans could understand only too well.

The year after Carlton was born, the Barretts' roof was badly damaged after a hurricane swept across Jamaica, destroying thousands of homes and leaving the countryside decimated in its wake.* Aston remembers playing in the pools of water it left behind, but his fondest memories are of the music he'd hear at Christmas time, when his father would take up a harmonica and entertain the family during the holidays.

"When my daddy played that harmonica, it sounded like a piano," Family Man recalls. "I could hear the bass and the melody in there. In fact, it was like country & western, the way he played it. I remember him saying that my grandfather was a player of many instruments, so I must follow in his footsteps. He was a tinsmith and played bass, guitar, and everything. I only used to see my other grandparents when I was much smaller, because they died quite close to one another. And I didn't know my father's mother and father at all."

The Barretts' living quarters backed onto a communal space – called a tenement yard in Jamaica – for washing and recreation, shared by several other families. While most were part of government housing schemes, this one was owned by a Mr Davis, who was related to local saxophone player Val Bennett. Aston describes Bennett as "the King Curtis of Jamaica" and would watch entranced as he and his band rehearsed in the same yard where he lived. Bennett's rhythm section at the time comprised Lloyd Knibs on drums, Lloyd Brevette on upright bass and Jah Jerry on guitar (all three would later join the Skatalites), along with two other regular visitors to the Barretts' tenement yard: tenor sax player Tommy McCook and alto saxophonist Roland Alphonso. Bennett's daughter Fay was another occasional visitor. She later became known in reggae circles for her duets with Charlie Ace, but she was primarily an actress and would often perform

---

* This vengeful act of nature was later immortalised in songs such as ''51 Storm'.

with the comedians Bim & Bam at Kingston's Regal Theatre. Bim & Bam lived across the street from the Barretts, in the same building where Bob Marley would one day open a record store.

Music and performing made an impression upon Aston and Carlton from the beginning, but their early lives were also disciplined and, like their sisters, both were expected to attend St Patrick's Church on North Street and the Salvation Army on Sunday mornings. Aston's school, like St Patrick's, was affiliated to the Catholic faith and had separate facilities for boys and girls. Fay and Olive both attended St Aloysius Girls' School, while Aston followed in his father's footsteps and enrolled at the nearby Boys' School in Duke Street. St Aloysius had been a mixed convent school when Aston's father went there, but it was rebuilt as two distinct institutions after a fire razed the original premises. While attending St Aloysius, Aston first met Herman Chin Loy, who would later own the Aquarius record shop and label in Halfway Tree. By this time, the Barretts had moved from their tenement yard into a family house at 23 Upper West Street in Hannah Town, not far from Kingston Public Hospital. They also lived in the Franklyn Town area, while saving to put down a deposit on a property of their own.

To get to school from Upper West Street, Aston would cut onto Orange Street and head for North Parade before turning into Duke Street. After lessons, he and his friends would sometimes walk around the corner to Ocean Boulevard and watch the ships sail into the docks. Kingston's waterfront was a hive of activity and a centre for both commercial and navy vessels. Aston immediately took note of the sailors' uniforms and would often wear military style clothing in later years, explaining how he "favoured the rude boy look." There weren't too many opportunities for misbehaviour at either home or school, however, since the teachers at St Aloysius weren't exactly shy of using their canes to discipline unruly students, as the more rebellious Herman would discover. Aston, on the other hand, was among the brightest pupils in his class and a prefect too, for a time. He proudly recalls how his name was the first to be called out at assembly in the mornings, which meant he had to be punctual. There's little doubt that he was diligent and determined during his school years.

However, music was in the Barrett blood and there was little chance of Aston avoiding the growing number of sound-systems, or mobile discotheques, playing in the Kingston area throughout the Fifties. While he was too young to attend in person, these sound-systems, nicknamed "houses of joy", would often set up in open-air venues and, thanks to huge speakers, the music could be heard for some distance. As a child, Aston remembers Tom the Great Sebastian spinning the latest rhythm & blues tunes from America, and how policeman Arthur Reid's wife won the lottery and invested her winnings into the Treasure Isle liquor store. Her husband subsequently bought a white fishtail Chevrolet Trojan and earned himself the nickname of Duke Reid the Trojan after taking ownership of a sound-system. He would eventually build a studio above the store and produce some of Jamaica's best-ever rocksteady sides on his Treasure Isle label, but back then sound-system competition was his abiding passion and Coxsone Dodd (who owned a set called Downbeat) had become his greatest rival.

The late Fifties was a good time to enter the music business, since sound-systems were highly popular and record sales had boomed as small Dansette players came on the market. Federal owners Ken and Gloria Khouri became the first major players in the Jamaican recording industry after establishing an office at 129 King Street, cutting a tune called 'Skokian', which many consider to be the first-ever Jamaican recording. Local radio had also made its appearance by then, since JBC had started in 1959 and RJR was certainly in existence by 1960. Island Records' supremo Chris Blackwell once rented an office above JBC, where artists such as Wilfred Edwards and Owen Gray would visit him and wait to hear their songs played over the air. The US stations WINZ and WGBS proved more popular, since they played a wider range of music, including hits from London and Latin America, as well as the United States.

Family Man Barrett: "They'd play all kinds of music, so we'd hear rhythm & blues from Chicago, soul, jazz, and also this style they called merengue. The latest sound back then was this Caribbean music they call soca now. It was like calypso and then there was this older type called the quadrille, which had faded out by the time I started playing. But we used to have this system called Rediffusion where you can just rent a box screwed into the wall and with wires attached, like how they run cable now. This was before my dad bought us a radio, which was a British make called a Philips. I never had a favourite programme, because I'd just listen to whatever song hit, then turn it right up!"

One of Aston's early favourites was Prince Buster, who opened Prince Buster's Record Shack on the corner of nearby Luke Lane and Charles Street in 1956. Forrester's Hall and Jubilee Tile Gardens were both popular venues for sound-system dances, and rivalry was keen between Buster's Voice of the People set and those owned by Duke Reid, Count

Bells, Tom the Great Sebastian, Coxsone, and King Edwards. Unlike his competitors, Buster couldn't afford to make trips to the US for records, so instead he championed whatever local music he could find, especially songs he produced for his own labels. Buster's early hits included 'Humpty Dumpty' by Eric "Monty" Morris, Basil Gabiddon's 'Put On Your Warpaint Baby' and his own 'Bad Minded People'.

In 1960, after Coxsone had lured away some of his key musicians, Buster brought the Folkes Brothers and Count Ossie's drummers into the studio for the first examples of recorded Rasta music. 'Chubby' and 'Oh Carolina', released in 1961 when Aston was just 14, marked the first time he or anyone else had heard the sounds of nyahbinghi committed to vinyl, but they were the exceptions in a field dominated by rhythm & blues and what Barrett calls "half blues". Prince Buster would soon become the king of ska or blue beat and also Jamaica's leading hit maker in Britain, where he spearheaded the craze for Jamaican music among white working class audiences.

"Some people have said that reggae music and ska came from pocomania or calypso, but it was nothing of the sort," explains singer Alton Ellis. "The ska came from American music. We used to dance to that music, because Coxsone used to buy rhythm & blues music from America and then make some specials for himself based on songs by people like Louis Jordan and Rosco Gordon. These were the artists who influenced us in making our own thing, because as soon as Coxsone play a Louis Jordan or whatever, another man would go jump on a plane and buy it the same day. That's why Coxsone began to make his own records using guys who came from the Alpha Boys' School and could imitate the American music.

"It was the New Orleans sound that was popular back then and that's what we followed. It's a shuffle; the left hand is playing on the beat and the right hand is playing just a little bit off. We copied our sound from that and called it the ska and that is how our thing evolved. Then it gradually developed into the rocksteady and the reggae from there."

In 1957 the Barrett family moved again, this time to 8 Van Street, in Rollington Town, Kingston 2. This was an area on the eastern outskirts of town, not far from Mountain View Avenue, which skirted the foot of Warieka Hill and the Long Mountain range. This upheaval meant that Aston had to change schools, since it was now too far for him to reach St Aloysius. His parents therefore got him transferred to Vauxhall School, which he attended for just a short time.

"In the first term you are a new student; just enrol and nothing done, so I don't get back the same marks again and I never get no form of justice from that school really. The vibes change because I was taken out of the scholarship class and I get downhearted, so I couldn't take any more school after that. I just couldn't get my head into the place, 'cause it was unfair to me, y'know? My father, he got hold of some encyclopaedias for me around that time, but that's when I get into the rude boy circles and get a little unruly and unfocused. But I was always a strong-minded guy. I knew the difference between good and bad and realised how it wasn't so good to go walking on the wild side."

Faced with the prospect of working in some unsatisfactory job or getting into further trouble, he joined the Jamaica Youth Corps. It was his sister Olive's friend Keith Young who recommended him. There were two Youth Corps camps in Jamaica at the time. One was in the St Andrew's area called Chester Vale and the other was in the parish of Manchester, in a mountainous district called Cobbler, midway between Christiana and Spaldings. Aston would spend the next 18 months of his life there, based in Block D, dormitory 10. During the day, he was expected to work hard, planting crops, feeding animals and breaking rocks in a nearby quarry overlooked by a steep incline dubbed Independence Hill. The camp consisted of 75 acres when he arrived, but soon expanded to well over 300 acres in total and is still used as a government training camp to this day. Aston felt at home living in such country surroundings, since the Barrett children would regularly visit relatives in places such as Mount James, St Mary's and Bangor Ridge, Portland, during their school holidays. He particularly enjoyed the clean air and fresh food and, while his time there was regimented, he discovered there were plenty of recreational opportunities on offer and not just football, cricket or lawn tennis.

"We form a little group called the Drive-In Cracker Boys!" Fams exclaims. "One of the teachers heard me playing around on the piano and started to encourage us from there. He even tried to make some arrangements to take us into town and into a studio to record. Well we didn't reach the studio, but we did some recording on his two-track tape machine and it was fun to hear ourselves played back, I tell you! This was the first time we'd had access to any instruments and there were five of us altogether. There was Marcus Wright, Winston Thomas and myself, but I don't remember the other two.

"I wasn't so good on piano at the time, but this guy Winston Thomas from St Ann's we call Duppy Ranch, he used to play it really well. He was teaching me some piano in the Cracker Boys and so it was at the camp I learn the basics of piano, bass and guitar, except I only play rhythm and pluck guitar and not the solo one. I never go too much into that part and I did love the singing too, except I never take it seriously and never sing lead, only harmonies. This Canadian guy, he get us to practise lots of songs from that time, old favourites like 'Stand By Me', 'Don't Play That Song For Me' and then hits by Fats Domino, Little Richard, and this Jamaican group called the Blues Busters. Sometimes we do some little shows in the country parts. Places like Christiana or Spaldings, and then we play at some church functions too."

Jamaica celebrated its independence from Britain while Aston was in the Youth Corps, and this caused a wave of fresh optimism to sweep the country. People's National Party (PNP) leader Norman Manley had called for a referendum the previous year and the electorate had voted strongly in favour of independence. Britain had recommended they join the West Indies Federation instead, but this was opposed by both parties and they were left with no choice but to grant Jamaica its freedom in 1962. Bustamante, duly installed as Jamaica's first prime minister, oversaw an immediate increase in foreign investment. Bustamante's government also declared a new public holiday called Independence Day, to be celebrated on the first Monday of August each year.[*]

Aston remembers seeing Jamaican national flags everywhere, even in the countryside. National pride now informed the social climate, especially among local musicians, who sensed the time had come for them to make their mark. After his brief spell with the Drive-In Cracker Boys, Aston felt the same way, although it would be some time before he could play music professionally. On his return to Kingston, he moved back into Van Street and became an apprentice welder at Chin's Welding Works on the corner of East Street and Laws Street. Just as importantly, he then set about getting himself a bass.

"We couldn't afford proper instruments," says Family Man, "because they were too expensive, but the pressure was still there for it, because I used to look in the showcase at Music Mart on Beeston Street, see that Fender bass in there and then trudge back to my house, I tell you. That's when I decide to make my own, because at Chin's they have a

---

[*] This would replace August 1, which had been celebrated as Emancipation Day ever since the abolition of slavery in 1834.

woodworking section round the back and that's where I get the materials to make my first bass. I get a nice piece of timber for the neck and then a broad enough piece to get the body. I then draw the shapes I want and take them to one of the guys in the woodwork shop and let him cut them out for me on the band saw. This is in the lunch break and then I put it all together, using a curtain rod for the one string and a small board under the bottom to ease the string off the fret. It was like a fretless, upright bass and my brother Carlton, he was getting so fascinated with music himself too. He made like a little drum riser and we got these empty tins of paint in different sizes, like quart- and gallon-sized cans. He might be walking somewhere on the street, then find himself half a little cymbal and he'd nail a piece of board on it and set it up so it would crash, so he'd have one cymbal to crash on the after beat.

"We're always there playing, then we'd use our mouths to blow the horns section like the Skatalites, with me playing ska blues on my little one-string bass. It don't have any hollow body to get that bass sound, but my back room near the back porch has a board floor with a little cellar below it, so when I rest it on the floor and pick it, the whole room vibrate and that's where I get that effect! So we there practising drum and bass. Putting down the roots and the backbone of the music although my original dream was to learn how to play the piano because the piano is so orchestral. It's like a full band to itself, because you can get bass, rhythm and you can play melody. And then the guitar is the next thing. I used to love seeing people playing the banjo with that high pitch. Then when I listen, I realise that the drum is the heartbeat of the music and the bass is the backbone. And I see that my brother is so gifted with the drum and I love drums too so I say, 'Well I'm going to be the backbone.' So if the heartbeat is right and the backbone is right, then the music should stand up and we can move forward."

It was after independence that Jamaican music really began moving away from the New Orleans, "boogie-woogie" type of beat that Alton Ellis talks about. Derrick Morgan, whose song 'Forward March' defined the era like few others, was among the forerunners of this movement. Derrick had the top seven chart positions inclusive on the Jamaican hit parade in the period following independence. Together with Jimmy Cliff, he was the main attraction at Beverley's Records, owned by Leslie Kong – a Chinese-Jamaican businessman who was still new to the recording business, but had the foresight to quickly sign up Desmond Dekker, who was studying engineering and working as a welder when chalking up his first hits for Beverley's. Dekker had bluffed his way into the studio and sang 'Honour Your Father And Your Mother' to Kong, causing in-house arranger Theophilus "Easy Snappin'" Beckford to race for the piano and immediately strike up a groove behind him.

Dekker began recording for Kong the following week and recommended Bob Marley to the label. Marley recorded 'Judge Not' and 'One More Cup Of Coffee' for Kong before Jackie Opel arrived in Jamaica from Barbados and took the local recording scene by storm, pushing Beverley's other artists into the shade. Encouraged by his friend Alvin "Seeco" Patterson, Marley went to Coxsone instead and formed a group, the Wailers, who debuted with the rowdy 'Simmer Down'. Other popular records that sold in their thousands during 1963 included Stranger Cole's 'Rough And Tough', Carlos Malcolm's 'Rukumbine', a handful of tunes by Lord Creator (including 'Don't Stay Out Late'), Baba Brooks' 'Watermelon Man' and tracks by Lord Tanamo, Byron Lee & the Dragonnaires, and the trombonist Don Drummond.

Since he was earning money from his welding job, Aston Barrett was another of the eager customers crowded around the counter in Randy's Record Store on North Parade, where he'd buy American as well as Jamaican releases.

"It was me who brought the first turntable into the family, which was one of those with the automatic arm where you can stack up the records on top," he says proudly. "My first hi-fi I made from this old jukebox that someone had thrown away and which I struggled to carry back to the house. I already have the treble, so I just need an amplifier and speaker, which I take out from there, patch them up and then it plays! That was the first stereo in my house and then I just build a cabinet for it out of what's left from the jukebox so I can take it outside and play all the tunes."

American stars such as Ray Charles, Sam Cooke, Ben E. King, and Chuck Jackson all toured Jamaica during that heady, post-independence era, a time when groups or singers were expected to dress smart and perform choreographed routines. While these shows were invariably packed, eyewitnesses claim they were never violent or disruptive. Yet, while the Jamaican public's love of American music would never diminish, there was also a need for local musicians to express their own identity, which they achieved by making that change in the music from "half-blues" to ska.

Coxsone Dodd had already been among the first to produce homemade recordings and many attribute the change in the beat to him and drummer Lloyd Knibs when both were experimenting at Federal studio one day. Knibs would open and close on the second and fourth beats on the hi-hat, then come down on the kick drum and the snare on the third, leaving the first beat empty. He would play the rim of the snare, rather than the open snare. Hence he developed a new style of playing which more established drummers like Drumbago subsequently followed.

Previous to this, Ken Richards and Easy Snappin' – both members of Clue J & the Blues Blasters – had been experimenting by heightening the emphasis on the second and fourth beats and creating a similar effect. Knibs heard what they were doing on guitar and piano and adapted it to his drums, although no one knows for sure. Coxsone had produced Easy Snappin's signature tune back in 1957 and also recorded these same musicians on many previous occasions, so it's not unreasonable to suppose he was a principal architect of ska. Despite fierce competition, he would also produce most of the Skatalites' best-ever work, which was the lightning rod for the new, exciting sounds of ska.

Aston says that he and Carlton's practice sessions were directly inspired by the Skatalites' rhythm section of Knibs and Lloyd Brevette. "When those musicians decide to form this band called Skatalites an' play the hardcore ska, the roots, everybody think this is a great change, because the band t'ing start get real popular like sound-system after that. Live music man!"

The Skatalites officially formed in June 1964, soon after Coxsone opened his studio on Brentford Road, although the various members had all played together before in various guises. Their line-up was a fluid affair, with drummer Knibs and double bass player Brevette at its core, accompanied by Drummond on trombone, Tommy McCook and Lester Sterling on tenor saxes, Roland Alphonso on alto, Johnny "Dizzy" Moore on trumpet, Jah Jerry and occasionally Ernest Ranglin on guitars and a teenage Jackie Mittoo on piano. They played regularly at venues like Gunboat Beach and the Bournemouth Club in east Kingston and recorded hundreds of tracks together before disbanding in the autumn of 1966. On one occasion Family Man saw the Skatalites play at the Rialto Theatre when they backed artists like Delroy Wilson, Ken Boothe, John Holt, Toots & the Maytals, Eric Monty Morris, the Heptones, and Three Tops.

Members of the Skatalites, like Drummond, were classically trained and had soaked up influences from jazz, latin, and Cuban music, as well as the usual mix of mento, calypso, country & western, pop, and American rhythm & blues. Cuban music was especially influential since McCook and Alphonso had both been born there, and hits like 'Peanut Vendor' and Mongo Santamaria's 'Watermelon Man' weren't alone in reaching a widespread audience during the early Sixties. Such diversity ensured the music was never dull and this had a galvanising effect on young players like the Barrett brothers, who were exposed to a wide range of styles from early on. Most ska bands featured vocalists (like child star Delroy Wilson, who Aston would try and imitate), while Toots & the Maytals – initially known as the Vikings or the Flames – were the first to incorporate gospel and sacred music with ska. Following on from the Folkes Brothers' 'Oh Carolina', there was even a Rasta presence thanks to the Mellow Cats (Zoot "Skully" Simms and Bunny "Skitter" Robinson) who recorded songs like 'Time To Pray' and 'Send Another Moses'.

The Skatalites created the most excitement in the Barrett household, tackling various genres including pop, television theme tunes, jazz, standards, and songs from Broadway musicals and film soundtracks, as well as the aforementioned latin tracks.

Ska had got popular after being aired on sound-systems at places like Foresters' Hall and the Chocomo Lawn. Byron Lee & the Dragonnaires then started playing it in uptown clubs around Kingston and introduced it to a wealthier and more influential audience. Lee's operation benefited from superior promotion and, since Edward Seaga had introduced him to the attorney Paul Marshall, he had made important connections in the overseas recording industry.

Before long, people like Ahmet Ertegun and Tom Dowd from Atlantic Records were visiting Kingston nightclubs such as the Glass Bucket at Half Way Tree. Lee's Dragonnaires were subsequently invited to play at the 1964 World's Fair in New York as part of a delegation including Prince Buster, Jimmy Cliff, and Eric "Monty" Morris. Lee's group also made several TV appearances and played at the city's Singer Bowl and the Peppermint Lounge, the scene of the Twist explosion. The Dragonnaires were the first to exploit ska's commercial potential and to recognise how important dance steps were in broadening its appeal to mainstream audiences. Celebrities like Jackie Kennedy were caught on camera doing the ska, which helped generate considerable media interest in the infectious dance beats coming from the West Indies.

The choice of those who'd represented Jamaica at the World's Fair was a cause of contention among other Kingston musicians. Neither Kes Chin & the Souvenirs or Carlos Malcolm and his Afro Jamaican Rhythms were considered well known enough, while the Skatalites didn't possess the right image, as by all accounts they didn't care what they looked like, or how they presented themselves. Certain members also smoked herb and were Rastafarians. In the words of Lee's right-hand man, Ronnie Nasralla, "the show element just wasn't there." This didn't bother the Barrett brothers, who were more concerned with the music than presentation, although Family Man was already beginning to express an interest in Rastafari by this time.

"The [Skatalites] bass player Lloyd Brevette, he's a Rastaman and he was the first dreadlocks musician in the studio. He wasn't the first I'd met, but them man stick to their roots and his playing was an influence on me too of course, because you know how one good artist always inspire another. That's because I realise this bass player is something else and how he's got such a unique style."

Practising their instruments while still living with their parents in Rollington Town proved a little difficult at times, but the Barrett brothers were determined to continue, despite having to make their livelihoods elsewhere.

"I wasn't playing professionally as yet, but it was starting to become a whole different venture," says Family Man. "Because after I leave Chin's, I get a job at Gauntlet Engineering at Last Street and then I go to Samson's Engineering Works on Rum Lane. I work at Samson's about three different times! And whilst I know I have to work, I need to have a job that I enjoy doing and that gives me some incentive. I mean I love engineering and things like that, but I don't want to be working in that kind of way forever. But I do welding, I do engineering and I even turn blacksmith for a while when I start making some of these gates and window grills that you see all over Jamaica. My father did blacksmith work and wanted me fi do that too. He was pleased to see me go to school, but him see me as his apprentice and he wanted me fi take it serious, y'know?

"But I used to do a lot of things like that, before I try to bring out the music full-time. I was still doing welding work when I see in the paper how local recordings were getting more popular and that was a step up for Jamaica now, because we could hear them on the radio. And I knew by then that to get your song on the radio, you had to put it on a record first, so I decide that when I'm ready to get involved, then I'll take it from there to the next stage, which I did. Except in the meantime I start to work from home, independently, because anytime you look in my front yard you'd see about a dozen bikes, like these NSU Quickly mopeds from London and also scooters like the Lambretta and Vespa. I loved how those bikes were constructed, because it's like those mechanics were made for us! It was nice, y'know?"

In 1964, the airwaves teemed with the sounds of young Jamaica and the hit roll call included Carlos Malcolm's 'Bonanza Ska', Justin Hinds & the Dominos' 'Carry Go Bring Come', Jackie Opel's 'Cry Me A River', Eric "Monty" Morris' 'Sammy Dead' and several tracks by Prince Buster, including 'Wash Wash' and 'Wings Of A Dove'. None, however, emulated the success of Millie Small's 'My Boy Lollipop', produced by Chris Blackwell, which would become Jamaica's first-ever crossover hit when it roared up the UK national charts, peaking at number two that March. The overseas ska and blue beat invasion had begun, but there were other, earthier and more rootsy voices starting to make an impact that had far greater resonance with the elder of the two Barrett brothers.

"There was a very young voice out there in the music belonging to Delroy Wilson that I liked very much. I hear the Clarendonians and Eric "Monty" Morris, also Stranger Cole, Ken Boothe, the Maytals, and Derrick Morgan, who I like for sure. But then I was at a party once when somebody sitting near me said, 'Come and hear this new group here.' And we went inside and punch the jukebox and guess what song it was. It was the Wailers and the song was called 'Simmer Down'! Well I tell you, I listened to that music so deep, I feel like I was a part of that group and that it was me and my brother who do that song! And believe you me, no other record played in that jukebox for the rest of the time we was inside there, because it was strictly 'Simmer Down' all the way! Hearing that record gave me my first real start to penetrate the music, because I think if these people are playing like this, then I can play it too. All I could think was, 'I've got to get involved, because it's my kind of thing.'

"But that record was a different kind of rap. It was a different kind of music and carried a different kind of harmony with expression, because no one does it like the Wailers. After that, I always hear their music on the radio and the jukebox and feel like I'm part of the syndicate, because when I hear them, it's like I fall into a trance! I never see them onstage or in the studio though, because I'm still finding my way at that time."

The Wailers' next hits included 'It Hurts To Be Alone' and 'Lonesome Feeling'. Both lacked the raw excitement of 'Simmer Down', but served to keep the group's profile reasonably high as they brushed shoulders with such groups as the Maytals ('Never You Change') the Techniques, the Blues Busters ('Wide Awake In A Dream') and the Paragons on the local charts. Alton Ellis' 'Dance Crasher' was also popular, as were the vibrant sounds of the Skatalites' 'Ball Of Fire', 'El Pussy Cat', and 'Guns Of Navarone'. Despite Millie Small's fade in popularity after 'My Boy Lollipop', ska managed to sustain its early success on the world stage and Byron Lee wasn't the only JA producer to begin sending tracks to New York for additional overdubs and final mixes in order to win a share of the rapidly expanding overseas market.

In 1965, the Impressions featuring Curtis Mayfield (who'd previously toured Jamaica with Jerry Butler) recorded in Kingston. Mayfield's clear falsetto was widely influential on local artists with Slim Smith, Pat Kelly, and Cornell Campbell all attempting to sing like him.* This was around the time Coxsone procured the franchise for Berry Gordy's Tamla-Motown label in the Caribbean and would regularly get his artists to cover the sounds of the Motor City. He even adapted Motown's slogan, 'The Sound of Young America' to 'The Sound of Young Jamaica'.

Coxsone recorded a session with a group called the Regals during this period, featuring singer Hopeton Lewis who came from Mountain View Avenue in east Kingston and who went to the same youth club as Sam Mitchell, who took him to Federal. After auditioning for Ken Khouri and being told to write his own material, Lewis returned a week later with the songs 'Take It Easy', 'Sounds And Pressure', and 'Music Got Soul'. All three became hits on Winston Blake's Merritone label, which Federal used for their own releases, since it was popular among Jamaica's middle classes. Lewis struggled to sing over the fast ska beats he was given at first, so session musicians Lynn Taitt and Gladstone Anderson slowed down the pace a little so he could voice the songs more comfortably. This arrangement promptly reaped dividends and 'Take It Easy' not only became a runaway hit but heralded a fresh change of direction in Jamaican music.†

With 'Take It Easy', arranger Taitt had brought the bass line of a song into focus for the first time. Aston's ears pricked up at the sound of Jackie Jackson's electric bass guitar, as prior to 'Take It Easy', most ska bass was played on the acoustic stand-up instrument, while the rhythm had been an accompaniment to whatever the horns were playing, simply holding down the chords. Taitt, from Trinidad, got his chance to go to Jamaica for the independence celebrations at the instigation of Byron Lee. He joined

---

* Mayfield's songs are the most versioned of all overseas artists in JA music and the Wailers recorded several, most notably 'People Get Ready'.
† 'Take It Easy' is now generally regarded as the first rocksteady record although others claim Delroy Wilson's 'Dancing Mood' deserves that honour.

the Sheiks and the Cavaliers before forming Lynn Taitt & the Comets. Family Man calls Lynn Taitt, "a wicked lead guitar player and arranger.

"He's not from Jamaica originally, but Trinidad, so the kind of music he played over there, he blended that with the Jamaica vibes and just floated on that. He put the Trinidad influence with the Jamaican sound and made it one and then it exploded. Yeah, I just used to keep my ears on top of the new sounds from Lynn Taitt, because his first band was called Lynn Taitt & the Comets, and with Lloyd Spence on bass. I used to follow them around a lot. In fact, I used to dress up like them, like I was one of the officers. Those were the days when my favourite parties were in session. You just warn me about a wedding and I'd say, 'Where?' Because we'd go to the place before the wedding party come from church and when the cars arrive with the bridesmaids and everybody, we'd put on our white gloves, open the car doors and the people them were shocked. They thought we were the ushers and they'd say 'I don't remember those people.' But we'd escort everybody right in and then set up a table for ourselves. The tallest one out of our group, he'd then go up to the caterers and say, 'You make a mistake with that table over there, 'cause it hasn't been dealt with as yet.' So, we'd be there drinking champagne and eating all these expensive treats, being well taken care of. We were the wedding crashers and we master the art of disguise so well, I think even the bride and bridegroom was tricked. It come like a surprise to find that we were behind it, but they just think we're part of the service . . ."

The Comets didn't make any recordings but were a popular live attraction. Taitt also recorded sessions with the Skatalites prior to forming Lynn Taitt & the Jets in 1966. The Khouris thought so highly of them they kept the band on a retainer, even supplying them with a van and equipment.

Federal was then Kingston's premier studio. This was right at the beginning of the rocksteady era, which coincided with the break-up of the Skatalites. McCook became musical director at the new Treasure Isle studio above Duke Reid's liquor store on Bond Street after the Skatalites split, while Alphonso based himself at Studio One, owned by Coxsone. Alphonso called his new band the Soul Brothers, while McCook formed the Supersonics, featuring organist Winston Wright, a.k.a. "Brubeck", who'd earlier played with the Comets. By then, rocksteady was fast gaining popularity thanks in part to Charlie Babcock of RJR ("the cool fool with the live jive") and other influential radio deejays such as Rodney Butler, Winston Williams, and Jeff Barnes.

Record producers like Coxsone and Duke Reid sponsored their own weekly radio shows. The Treasure Isle show was especially exciting as McCook led the island's top session musicians on a round of hits featuring Alton Ellis, the Paragons, Phyllis Dillon, the Melodians and many others. All of them were writing good songs with catchy, memorable lyrics that would ensure lasting appeal.

Family Man Barrett: "At that time, my brother and I were still practising and getting a little better. And of course, we used to listen to all the music we could. I even listen to Boris Gardner, 'cause he used to play a nice bass too, even though he was a tremendous singer as well. I listen to Byron Lee too, who had his own style, which is good! But I never used to hang out round the music too much, because I was still learning at the time. I just used to hang out with my brethren around the cabinetmaker's shop or in the gully bank, 'cause that's where we meet up a lot. We'd go there to reason and smoke the herb, because it was a cooler ghetto in those days and not so much like the Wild West! Those were the happy days, because you could just smoke and play music and the vibes was nice and smooth."

CHAPTER TWO

Rudie Don't Fear

AN estimated 100,000 people – one in ten being Rastafarians – welcomed Emperor Haile Selassie I at Kingston's Palisades Airport (later renamed the Norman Manley International Airport) on April 21, 1966. It was a wet and windy morning, but the rain had stopped as the Emperor's DC6 plane taxied to a halt on the runway. Thousands of people rushed onto the tarmac, which meant the Emperor was unable to leave the plane for over 30 minutes. Rasta spokesman Mortimer Planno finally led him down the steps, whereupon the assembled multitude showed their approval with an undulating sea of flags and banners. At least 60 Rastafarians were invited to official meetings with the Emperor during his four-day visit and it's said that he advised them to seek liberation before repatriation. He also spoke of the OAU (Organisation of African Unity) in his address to the Jamaican parliament and described Africans and Jamaicans as "blood brothers".

Aston says he heard people talking about Emperor Selassie in the Rasta camps. "I heard this and that, like how they were pressurising this man and heard how great he is and how his line is coming down from King David, because even the Bible tell you about it. I heard how he was of the highest rank and that every country recognised him as such.

"On the day itself, I heard of the big crowds at the airport, so I get on my bike and ride up Mountain View Avenue, and I'm having to skip over people, ride up on the banking and all that to follow him, because he's in this open back car. Mountain View Avenue, wasn't a dual carriageway like it is now. It was just a two-way, up and down road, and I see him trying to go through a whole mass of people. Then when I almost reach up to the National Stadium, I see him go to turn inside and me just stop on the bank and say, 'Bwoy, through all the confusion and excitement, this man can't get in the stadium.' There's no way he could get through all these people, 'cause it was way too crowded in there! I forget all thoughts of the National Stadium and just decide to watch everybody instead, so I sit down and just as I start to meditate, his car turn off from the stadium and head back too. I stand up on the bank now and as I'm stood there Selassie see me from out of the corner of his eye. I say, 'Look there. I've seen His Majesty in person.' And he was well dressed, sharp and neat with light skin and a little grey in his beard. Man, it was like he was speaking to me. It was like he said, 'Just relax. You don't have to follow the crowd. Just wait here and I'll pass by.'"

According to drummer Winston Grennan (as quoted in the book *More Axe 8: Mud Cannot Settle Without Water*), the night before Haile Selassie's arrival, Roland Alphonso and his band the Mediators backed the Wailers on an entire album's worth of material at Dynamics produced by Mortimer Planno. Grennan says he was rehearsing with Alphonso at a club on Orange Street called the Orange Bowl, when Planno and Bob Marley invited them to the session and recorded what Grennan calls "the original *Kaya* album" which included cuts of 'Rock My Boat' and 'Sun Is Shining'. Grennan also claims the Wailers were supposed to appear at the Ward Theatre that same night but didn't show up – much to the crowd's annoyance – because after a dispute with Planno, Marley took off for Montego Bay, where he stayed for at least a week before returning to Kingston with his hair cut short. However, all other sources state that Marley had left for the US in February and stayed in Delaware with his mother until October.

Aston hadn't met the Wailers at this stage and heard nothing about the session during the years he knew Marley.

"No, but Mortimer Planno was the mentor for Bob, Bunny and Peter though. For the Wailers, 'cause they were from the western part of Kingston and they go more deep in the Rasta thing than I do. I was just a spiritual man who is inspired from Jah. I never join any organisation of Rastafari. I'm just me, but Bob, he used to move with those people more, so I heard of him and I even see him once."

Alton Ellis wasn't privy to the Grennan recordings either, but knew the Wailers from their time at Studio One and attests to their relationship with Planno.

"Myself, Bob Marley and a lot of other Rasta brethren would gather in Mortimer Planno's yard at 35 Fifth Street," Ellis recalls. "We'd all go there and get ideas to put on record, because later down the line, that was Planno's quotation I put into words on 'Lord Deliver Us'. Planno was a man who was always fighting the system and he was saying, 'Let the people have food ta bumbaclaat and let the blind be led.' The man just cuss and every word 'im speak, it just record in my mind, so I get up and go into my yard, which was like five gates from his. I pick up my guitar and there's 'Lord Deliver Us'. But a lot of what Bob sing about also came from that circle and that teaching, y'know? Because we'd all sit around and read the Bible, eat some food and smoke herb. And somebody might be cooking cornmeal and callaloo or fish as we talk."

All three members of the Wailers embraced Rasta in the wake of Emperor Selassie's visit, as did a number of other local musicians. It was a time of great changes and social unrest and not just in Jamaica. In London, racial tension had led to riots in Notting Hill, despite the white population's growing fascination with Jamaican music, while the Civil Rights struggle in America was in full swing as black leaders like Martin Luther King sought to effect far-reaching reforms. Rastafarianism was yet to take hold of the popular imagination, although plenty had taken notice when Negus Tafari was crowned Emperor Haile Selassie I of Ethiopia, King of Kings, Lord of Lords, and Conquering Lion of the Tribe of Judah, on November 2, 1930 in Addis Ababa. Representatives of 72 different nations attended the ceremony, as Big Youth later sang on 'Dreadlocks Dread': "And he hath on his vesture and on his thigh, a name written King of Kings and Lord of Lords."[*] Selassie was therefore regarded as the Messiah, or "Christ in his Kingly character," as Garnet Silk would say.

Marcus Garvey, whom Burning Spear describes as "the first Rastaman", had lit the fuse by declaring, "Look to the East when a black King is crowned, for the day of deliverance is near." In the Twenties, Garvey had founded the United Negro Improvement Association, or UNIA, the largest ever pan-African organisation, whose slogan was 'One God, One Aim, One Destiny'. Garvey was later discredited and imprisoned before being expelled to Jamaica in 1929 but his legacy lives on in today's Rastafarian artists who continue to champion his ideals of economic self-reliance and self-determination.

The Ethiopian Coptic Church had first established links in Jamaica during the Thirties, soon after Haile Selassie's coronation. By the mid-Sixties, they'd established church premises at Four Miles on the Spanish Town Road. Their compatriots from the Ethiopian Orthodox Church (EOC) wouldn't appear in Jamaica until 1968. A visit by the

---

[*] Family Man played on 'Dreadlocks Dread' and the Biblical passage he refers to can be found in Revelations 19, verse 16.

Abuna, or head Ethiopian priest, caused a great deal of interest initially, but the fact that their philosophies bore strong similarities to Christianity and the leaders weren't wearing dreadlocks soon lost them support.

The EOC's aims just weren't revolutionary enough for some tastes, because while demonstrating little or no support for political and social change, they concentrated instead on prayer, personal discipline, Amharic language classes and the like. Selassie's divinity wasn't openly stated on the agenda, probably according to the Emperor's own wishes. Yet the EOC is one of the most ancient and historic of all African religious organisations. While essentially Christian, it has far stronger links to the Syrian and Coptic churches than the Protestants, since it does not accept the concept of original sin or purgatory. Legend traces its ancestry back to the Apostles. It also has a different bible to the Western churches, which contains numerous books omitted from other versions.

One of them is the Kebra Negast (Glory of the Kings), which traces the ruling dynasty of Ethiopia back to the marriage of King Solomon and the Queen of Sheba. This meant Ethiopia was the world's oldest monarchy during Selassie's reign and the Emperor represented an unbroken line of Ethiopian kings dating back to 900 BC. In fact, he was the 225th in line, according to the Kebra Negast. The EOC is also said to protect the Ark of the Covenant, with Emperor Selassie at the head of a group called the Nyahbinghi Order of Warriors, whose activities had been reported by the *Jamaica Times* in 1935, the year before Selassie appealed to the League of Nations against the Italian invasion of Ethiopia. Their vow of "Death to all black and white oppressors" is one that has been repeated in numerous reggae songs over the years and not only those by artists belonging to the Nyahbinghi Order.

Other breakaway figures were to emerge from the Rastafarian move-ment as Jamaican followers sought a suitable framework for their beliefs. One of the most prominent was Prince Edward Emmanuel, who founded a priest-like cult called the Ethiopian African National Congress whose members – known as "Bobo" or Ashanti dreads – dress in Biblical-style turban and robes. Prince Emmanuel had held an island-wide gathering or Grounation ceremony attended by thousands of Rastafarians in Kingston during March 1958 at the Coptic Theocratic Temple in Kingston Pen. Fifty years on Prince Emmanuel's influence is still strong.

Other so-called leaders weren't anywhere near as effective, or as honest. Seven years before Haile Selassie's visit, the Reverend Claudius Henry had pronounced himself "Moses of the Blacks" and declared that ships would set sail from Kingston for Africa. He sold tickets for this event and thousands of people turned up at his Rosalie Avenue headquarters expecting repatriation. Many had sold their land and belongings and were left destitute as a result of Henry's deception. This somewhat chaotic rush to embrace Rastafari persuaded Norman Manley's government to give serious credence to recommendations put forward in a study prepared by the University of the West Indies in 1960.

Their first recommendation was highly contentious and stated that the government should send a mission to African countries to arrange for the repatriation of Jamaicans. This proposal was initiated in 1961 and nine Rasta leaders, including Mortimer Planno, were duly sent on a tour of Ethiopia, Ghana, Nigeria, Liberia, and Sierra Leone. The findings of those who returned paved the way for Selassie's state visit to Jamaica five years later.

However, three months after the Emperor's visit government attitudes took a radically different turn, when Jamaican authorities decided to act against Rastafarians, whose influence was growing at a rapid pace among disenfranchised youths like the Wailers. People living in Kingston didn't exactly have to search far for spiritual and religious teachings, since pro-black organisations were plentiful at that time. Apart from the aforementioned, the Ras Tafari United Front, based at Liberty Hall in King Street, was where the Ethiopian World Federation founded their first Jamaican branch as far back as 1938. The EWF announced in 1955 that Emperor Haile Selassie was strengthening his merchant navy and that Ethiopian ships might sail into Kingston harbour, which was just a block away from the Rasta settlements in Back O' Wall, an area inhabited by Kingston's poorest sufferers.*

Soon after, Ras Sam Brown, who'd entered the 1961 election campaign as an independent candidate for west Kingston under the banner of the Black Man's Party, founded the Rastafarian Movement Recruitment Centre at 1000 Marcus Garvey Drive. Brown proved an inspirational figure to many young Rastafarians and especially those living in Back O' Wall. Prince Emmanuel's Ethiopian African National Congress also had its headquarters in Back O' Wall which had been a refuge for Rastafarians since 1954, after the police had destroyed a commune called Pinnacle near Sligoville, headed by Leonard Howell, another early Rasta pioneer. Back

---

* Jamaica is the land of the natural mystic, and yet it's shared with people so destitute, they're known simply as "sufferers".

O' Wall was thus a Rastafarian rallying place and red, gold and green flags would flutter from many of the squalid board dwellings and various cult headquarters, some of which had outer and inner gates for additional security.

"It was very militant then," Family Man confirms, "and I remember riding by there a night time, cah yuh can always get a good draw of weed from them. Prince Emmanuel's place, that was some herb camp man and it have this barbed wire fence cah it pure police and soldier 'round there. But even though I'd go there to buy herb, we'd pick up some knowledge from there at the same time, because at that time Rastafari was downgraded and discriminated against. That's through it's an ancient scene, taking the vow of a Nazarite which doesn't fit so well in the modern society, so you had to choose where to go, what to do and things like that. And worldwide, it's just like that up until today. But we'd go from there, sit in the park and then lick some chalice . . . Those Rastas from the camps were peaceful people, they'd just meet together to beat drum and smoke the good herb and then you begin to find this happening amongst musicians as well. Cah some of them musicians were rootsmen and people start to realise that Rastaman got soul. They got talent. We've got singers and players of instruments in the Rastafari and we bring them a different type of music called roots and culture and reality. Those times were nice in other ways too, cah anyone who left east to go west like me, he was well-treated, y'know? And whenever a man come east, him never have to worry about no shooting or war business."

A Rasta camp called Lennox Lodge, at the end of Sligo Avenue, at the foot of Warieka Hill in eastern Kingston was also popular with musicians as was Count Ossie's Mystic Revelation of Rastafari, or Rastafarian Repatriation Association of Jamaica, which the likes of Tommy McCook would visit for herb, music, reasonings, prayer and meditation. Three of the elders based there had visited Ethiopia as part of the government mission and a succession of local musicians became associated with them, including horn players Dave Madden and Cedric Brooks.

Yet not all Rastas were peace-loving people, and from the end of 1965 onwards, social tension, acts of vandalism and gang warfare marred any illusions of Shanty Town being a religious haven. The government attributed this unrest to the large numbers of Rastas living there and promptly arrested Ras Sam Brown. At the same time, the Jamaican police were launching offensives against the ganja trade by burning down fields in the country districts. The instigator behind such initiatives was Edward Seaga, a US-born Harvard graduate who'd returned to Jamaica several years earlier. He'd reputedly attempted to join the PNP, but ended up joining Bustamante's Jamaica Labour Party (JLP) instead, taking control of his west Kingston constituency in 1962. Seaga was feared for his links with revivalist cults, although he'd also studied musical anthropology and part owned WIRL (a.k.a. West Indies studio). Interestingly, his rival Dudley Thompson of the PNP had recently visited Kenya where he'd met Jomo Kenyatta and was calling himself "Burning Spear" – a name that Winston Rodney later adopted for a highly successful recording career from 1969 onwards.

Seaga ordered the razing of Back O' Wall, so that he could build housing for his supporters on the site renamed Tivoli Gardens. The destruction occurred on the morning of July 12, 1966. Some 250 police gathered at the nearby Denham Town police station, armed with bayonets, pistols, clubs and guns and attacked the Rasta settlements with no warning. Bulldozers appeared from a nearby gully, flattening the board huts within minutes. The ruins were then set on fire as the fire company looked on, leaving hundreds of people to sleep rough in nearby May Pen Cemetery. Two other camps were also destroyed over the next couple of days. Jamaica's leading newspapers – *The Daily Gleaner* and weekly *Public Opinion* – both condemned the government's actions and the music fraternity weren't slow to respond either. Desmond Dekker's '007 (Shanty Town)' was the most notable example. Dekker had written it after watching reports of a student demonstration on television, which found the demonstrators lining up on the Four Shore Road all the way down to Shanty Town. The dispute was over a plot of land close to the beach, which the government wanted to develop as an industrial complex. When the people resisted, the situation got out of control.

Industrial disputes involving the unions had also broken out prior to the Back O' Wall incident, whose demise was also documented in the Conquerors' 'What An Agony', produced by Sonia Pottinger. During this era the first evidence of government-sponsored gang activities became apparent among warring Kingston constituencies. Seaga was affiliated to the Phoenix gang, led by Zackie the High Priest and Frank "Bad Word" Gillespie. Claudie Massop – a future don of Tivoli Gardens – was a member of this group. In west Kingston, Dudley Thompson set up the Vikings led by Dillinger, who later shot and killed Zackie the High Priest and also the Spanglers. A street war erupted between the Phoenix and Vikings, in which displaced people from Back O' Wall united to fight against the authorities. This resulted in running battles down the Spanish Town Road, coinciding with news that armed gangs had started robbing uptown addresses. The government thus declared a state of emergency in the autumn of 1966, which lasted until the following year's elections.

Apart from '007 (Shanty Town)', 1966 found songs like Ken Boothe's 'The Train Is Coming', Alton & the Flames' 'Girl I've Got A Date', Delroy Wilson's 'Dancing Mood', and Prince Buster's 'Hard Man Fe Dead' gracing the Jamaican hit parade. However the emergence of the "rude boys" lit up the local streets and airwaves, as groups like the Wailers ('Rude Boy Ska'), and the Clarendonians ('Rude Boy Gone A Jail', 'Rudie Bam Bam') introduced a more aggressive feel to the ska and rocksteady beat.

"When the Wailers sing 'Rudie come from jail, 'cause Rudie get bail,' it was just a stage the music was going through," says Fams. "And yes, we danced when we listened to them, but we don't create things like those afterwards. It was just a young people's kind of thing really, 'cause it had all these connections with badness, but we laugh at the gimmicks for sure! People didn't see me as a rude boy or nothing like that at the time, but as a promising musician. I'm like a cat with manners and respect, 'cause they always teach me that from a kid. They say 'Manners take you far' so I keep it like that and live by the rules of both God and man."

Others played a far more central role in the rude boy phenomena, none more so than Derrick Morgan whose 'Rudie Don't Fear' was a classic of that era.

"When the rude boys get bad now, you have the Pigeon Gang, the Spanglers, and the Spade and Skulls," Morgan says, shaking his head at the memory. "These were the groups who would catch a fight and cut up one another if they met with one another. That song 'Rudie Don't Fear' caused a lot of trouble in Jamaica. I say in it 'Strong like lion, we are iron' and they would smash up bottles and yell 'Iron!' The crowds get so rough, I have to come out and make one called 'Cool Off Rudies'. But it was a bad guy named Busby who asked me to make a song for him and that's how I came to make 'Rudie Don't Fear'.

"Alton Ellis make a song called 'Cry Tough', then this guy Busby come to me and says he wants a rude boy song fi himself. Well them days you were afraid of those guys, so I give him a wax dub plate one Saturday night and him play it at a dance just 'round midnight. When 'im hear the line, 'Strong like lion, we are iron' he tell the deejay to stop and start it over and over again. Him start whip up people and get so bad that they kill him the following day. Then after Busby dead, this little youth named Johnny Buzz became a bad man too. It's him Jackie Edwards write about in that song 'Johnny Too Bad', 'cause the Slickers and him used to walk with two gun back then."

Prince Buster counteracted 'Rudie Don't Fear' with 'Judge Dread', sparking off a feud with Morgan, who quickly countered with lyrics asking, "Who gives my barrister dreadlocks?" Buster also sang 'Black Head Chineyman' about Morgan – a record that not only took a swipe at the singer's alliance with producer Leslie Kong, but also insinuated that his rival's tune was copied from Buster's own 'Better Must Come'. Morgan responded with 'Blazing Fire', which was responded to by Buster's 'Praise And No Raise'. Along the way, others like Shelly Duffus had attempted to join in but both Morgan and Buster ignored them. Both artists recognised the publicity advantages of their feud and revelled in the infamy it brought them, but eventually the local newspaper asked the two to pose for a photograph so the public could see they were really friends, when the rivalry was threatening to get out of hand. The pair even did two stage shows together at the height of the controversy; one in Montego Bay, the other in Kingston at the Palace Theatre, where the Wailers were among the support acts.

"When the rude boy thing really burst open is when Desmond Dekker come with '007' an' those lyrics about how, 'Them a loot, them a shoot, them a wail down in Shanty Town,'" says pioneer deejay Dennis Alcapone. "Because even I was a rude boy at the time and when we used to go to a dance, we used to gather up all the beer bottles in a corner. Then when certain tune a play we just throw them into the dancehall and yell 'Iron!' Cah we were 'tougher than tough' y'understand? That was an era, but most youths go through a similar phase, regardless of which decade it is. In those days when you hear of someone getting killed in a dancehall, it was either with an ice pick, knife, ratchet, or broken bottle. Then it move from that stage to when the gun and election business started and guns start to come into the dancehall. At first, it was just the police, the blue seam, who fire their service revolvers into the air. Well the rude boys never fear the blue seam so they jump them and take away their guns. And then some people used to have the original gun they make from a bicycle frame. A one-pop gun them call it, but you still had to fear the one-pop too, cah them say, 'It only one shot I have but one is enough. Now lay down!'"

Like the Barrett brothers, Alcapone would later record for Bunny Lee, Keith Hudson, Lee Perry, Duke Reid, Sonia Pottinger and Randy's as rocksteady turned to reggae. In the meantime, Alton Ellis had tired of the rude boys causing disturbances in the dancehalls and recorded 'Dance Crasher' for Duke Reid. This brought him into competition with the Wailers over at Studio One, which tested his popularity like never before. Ellis remembers being at a popular Trench Town nightspot and seeing two youths flashing their knives at him while dancing to rude boy songs. He knew then that the Wailers had gained the upper hand and reverted back to love songs. Ellis had performed 'Dance Crasher' with three harmony singers he called the Flames. He'd originally wanted Lloyd Charmers and Peter Touch (a.k.a. Tosh) in his group, but both declined the invitation. However, Charmers did lend deep-voiced vocals to the follow-up, 'Cry Tough', written about the same Busby that Derrick Morgan talks about. Ellis recalls how the local police held a party after Busby was finally shot and killed, although their celebrations would prove short-lived, as a succession of other gang leaders began to emerge from the Kingston ghettos.

Aston Barrett was just 20 years old when all this was happening and was still to make his studio debut. However, by late 1967 both he and Carlton were practising hard. In between working intermittently at Samson's and as a mechanic, Aston was fast developing his own, original technique on bass.

Family Man Barrett: "There was this friend of mine, who used to live the other side of this open land in between our two houses in Rollington Town called Robert Hemmings and he had a brother called Willie who was a Scoutmaster and also a real good artist. Willie was going to Excelsior High School where he learnt music, so he played the clarinet and saxophone. He'd often bring a friend with him who plays the trombone or trumpet and then we'd all jam together, or sometimes I'd be there fixing my bikes and listening to my brother next door with Robert and his other friend. They talk about drum and bass, but they should hear drum and horns! It was wicked, y'know? So then I build myself a new guitar after that, but it only carry two strings. The bass carry one string and the guitar had only two, but sometimes when he was out in the yard playing drums, I'm playing rhythm guitar, so you got rhythm and drums; you got drum and bass and you got drum and horns! Because Carly wasn't at work yet, then after a while he got a job as a decorator, 'cause he liked beautiful things. He liked to set up the place nice and he was very neat. He used to work in Wong Brothers' store in the Cross Roads area, doing their window display. He worked up there for a while and he was always well dressed, no matter whether it was morning time or what.

"But I have three set of friends at that time. One set, we just go and party, because we are the wedding crashers! And the next set we'll go to gym together, training and pumping iron, or going to the beach and keeping fit. Sometimes we'd go to the cinema as well and watch movies like *The Gladiator, Hercules, Ben Hur,* and *The Big Fisherman.* The next set of friends now is the one I play music with, because we'd smoke our little herbs and get some inspiration. This is with people like Webster Stewart, who we call Webby, and Max Romeo."

The Barrett brothers also knew the Gaylads' B. B. Seaton, who lived on Leaneral Street, just a few hundred yards from their home. Seaton, a talented singer, songwriter and guitarist who had started out in a duo with Ken Boothe, had a group called the Astronauts before forming the Gaylads with Maurice Roberts and Delano Stewart in the early Sixties. It was the Gaylads' hits for Coxsone (including 'Lady With The Red Dress On' and 'Joy In The Morning') and Miss Pottinger ('Hard To Confess') that really made Seaton's reputation. He introduced Jackie Mittoo to Coxsone and also worked as the A&R man at Studio One for a time. After Coxsone paid him a tidy sum on one occasion, Seaton invested it in musical instruments and the band he formed would back many of Coxsone's artists on live shows, including the Wailers. Seaton recalls how the Barretts would often stop by his house and watch the Gaylads rehearse, soaking up the vibes and occasionally trying out the instruments for themselves.

Jackie Jackson, who played bass on countless hits for Treasure Isle and Beverley's during the rocksteady era, also lived in Rollington Town around this time. He and Aston would meet at a local nightclub most Friday nights, although the older musician wasn't aware that his friend was secretly practising the bass in his spare time, and wouldn't hear him play for another six months at least. Someone who did know about Aston's growing proficiency on bass was Max Romeo.

"We were buddies and you don't see one without the other," Romeo says. "As a matter of fact when he started playing bass, I was working with this same guy Web Stewart, because we have a little band called the Astronauts. We had Maurice playing bass and Shan (whose real name was Winston Fallon) playing drums from the Gaylads' band, Web Stewart on guitar and then another guy, with me on lead vocals. Well we go on this gig one night and the bass player and drummer didn't show up. They said that they wanted more money, so they left the band. Family Man and

Carly, they were in the crowd, 'cause everywhere we go and play, they would be there. At that time, Family Man practise on a one-string banjo and Carly had these kerosene cans, which he'd set up like tom-toms and so on. He was playing on paint tins, but his timing was perfect and so were Family Man's ears for the bass so I say, 'Webby, give these guys a break' but he refused. Except I tell him that if we can play two songs, then the promoter can't say that we didn't make the gig and if them really couldn't manage it, then we could say the equipment broke down.

"Well, the first song we do was this Ken Boothe song that was popular at the time called 'Puppet On A String' and when those guys start playing, they sound better than the other guys who didn't show!"

Aston remembers it slightly differently, but agrees the outcome was the same. "I knew a guy named Webby, who was a cabinet maker and also played guitar. In fact, he'd got two guitars and I'd offer to help him do his woodwork. I'd do sanding and if it was Formica, then I'd use a t-iron and wipe off the gum. This would give him more time so we could jam together and then one Christmas season, he got a job to play out. He on guitar, a bass player and a drummer and the singer was Max Romeo. The job was on Christmas Eve, Christmas Night, and Boxing Night. On Christmas Eve, everybody turn up to perform, but on Christmas Day, no bass player turn up and no drummer. This was at a club on the eastern side of Jamaica called the Holiday Chalet and it was an embarrassment, so I say 'I will play the bass,' but Webby tell me I can't manage it yet. I told him, 'All you have to do is show me which key it's in and which chords you use.' I never know it called G, F, or C, but if him show me which key, then I know the rest will manifest.

"Max Romeo told him he'd play the drums and sing and that I will play the bass, but Webby have doubts so him bring a truck, take up all the equipment and take it over to his cabinet shop, where we plug into this bass amp and start to jam. Well, he's so pleasantly surprised. Him say, 'All the time I see you pick a little bass line pon a box guitar and I never know you could really get it.' Yet, all the time we're jamming, I'm trying to know where G is, 'cause I know where A, F, C and D is and I know where E is, so after a while I just learnt the first seven . . .

"After that, we always practise together, 'cause I play the bass while he play some box guitar and from there I believe I can make a career from it, if I really love it that deep. I used to look around and see this man who used to play music and see him relaxing on the street like nothing is happening. 'Cause them would think music people are people who would just go around, take drugs and drink and make a mess of themselves. But we say, 'No. That's not us.' We come to make a standard of consciousness in the music and set an example and become a role model. 'Cause we always discuss it and we feel it too and certain things you didn't mention but it's in the mind and how we approach this thing, y'know? And that's what keep us together, because we start the band soon after that. I meditate it and 'Bim!' It just came like that. Even when I was doing welding, my mind was always on music and getting a little band, because whenever I go to parties and see everybody dance, I tell them what I mean to do and I penetrate each and every instrument that's playing in there."

CHAPTER THREE

Hippy Boys

MAX Romeo was born in St. Ann's but grew up in Kingston with his grandmother. At 14 he left home and in his own words, attended "Sidewalk University."

Max Romeo: "Before I met Family Man, I was part of this little band from May Pen called Smokey & the Heroes. There were three of us in this band and we used to travel round to hotels, 'cause they used to have a lot of whorehouses in Jamaica where the sailors would go. We'd ask the boss if we can entertain them for some small money and they'd say to go ahead, y'know? Smokey travelled with his amplifier and his guitar. The drummer had just two pieces and a cymbal, which he carried in a bag on his shoulder and all I travelled with is a mic, which plugged into Smokey's amplifier. Sounds simple, right? But when we start playing, it was amazing! We start getting big-time now, becah we played at the Playboy Hotel and a few other big places, just by walking around talking to the entertainment managers and showing them what we could do. The question we'd get asked most was, 'Do you know 'Yellow Bird?'' 'cause they'd say if we only knew that one song, then everything was all right! And sometimes we'd get kicked out, but it was fun in those days and I learnt my stage experience from that time.

"The Emotions came after that, at the end of 1966, going into 1967 and Lloyd, the brother of Robbie Shakespeare, he was part of that group too. There was this gully . . . It was like a waterway with a bridge over it and I used to be under there with my guitar when I'm not doing anything, 'cause people would call me the gully singer and throw stones at me. Then Lloyd and Kenneth would start checking me and doing some ooh and aah type of harmonies and it sounded good, so I say we should start a group and that was the beginning of the Emotions. We went to Coxsone but he said we're not ready yet and Duke Reid said the same thing. Everybody say we're not ready yet, so we end up with Ken Lack and that's how we started. He and P. J. Patterson who became Prime Minister, they were road managers for the Skatalites at the time and that's when we voiced those tracks for the Caltone label."

Phil Pratt, the Pioneers, the Heptones, Roy Shirley, and Milton Boothe would also voice for Lack's Caltone label and so, too, future Hippy Boys' rhythm guitarist Alva Lewis, on a tune called 'Return Home'. After the break-up of the Emotions, Romeo tried his hand at solo singing and happened to be living in east Kingston when he befriended the Barrett brothers. Web Stewart introduced them to the singer and both would play an important role in Aston and Carly's early careers.

Family Man Barrett: "They were hip to music and deep into it before I come in. Then he told me that he hear us all the time practising and he's got a job at the Baby Grand up at Cross Roads, 'cause the people at the club ask him to go and get a little band. By this time, we'd been smoking and grooving together and he'd hear me plucking bass when I didn't even have any proper bass. Well there was this guy called Bobby Mack who was a guitarist and had a little band of his own. Him and his brother used to play at school dances and all that.

"Bobby Mack's father used to run a hardware store in Rollington Town, but when his band weren't playing, he'd rent out their equipment. He always had something and said, 'Yes, I can lend you a bass and an amplifier,' but the amplifier was a Check Mate and in need of repair, so I went out to Allman Town and got it fixed by this dreadlocks electronics guy. That amp, it carried two 12-inch speakers and two inputs. I was playing through one side, where was just one volume, treble, and bass. And then Web Stewart would play in the other side with mid-range, treble, and reverb, 'cause he played lead guitar, so both of us played through it together and that was the main drive for the band!

"It was at the Baby Grand where we blast off first. We play there on a Friday, Saturday, and Sunday night. Showtime! Three nights and the first time we play there, we take a break and we go towards the front bar and say to the people in there, 'Why are you here at the bar? Why don't you come around the back and listen to some music?' And them say, 'Yeah, we heard it, but we thought it was the jukebox!' We say, 'No, it's not a jukebox. It's just a band who play just like the records' and then there was nobody in the front bar any more! That was the Hippy Boys! And I tell you, when we played a song, we played it exact because we practise so hard. We go out to the club and practise like Monday, Tuesday, Wednesday, and Thursday evenings, because we were that serious about it.

"That's when Glen Adams and Reggie start to come around now and

Lloyd Charmers too, because there was an acoustic piano at the Baby Grand, so he used to play that with us. Delano Stewart from the Gaylads, he would sometimes play guitar with us as well and also B. B. Seaton, but he never stayed too long. Delano though, him play with us for a good little while, because he was there most evenings. He was a good singer, good musician and a very talented songwriter too, y'know?"

The band's stint at the Baby Grand took place during the early part of 1968, at a time when psychedelic rock and soul music were turning the international music scene on its head. Jamaica, inevitably, wouldn't lag far behind, although record buyers were still enthralled by rocksteady, and the rivalry between Coxsone and Duke Reid continued to be the source of the country's finest musical triumphs. This despite fierce competition from Leslie Kong and Prince Buster, who had moved their operations from Federal to WIRL to avail themselves of its newly installed four-track recording facilities. Byron Lee had bought WIRL from the receivers after it burnt down, renaming it Dynamic Sound Studios. Lee's right-hand man Ronnie Nasralla suggested they update the studio and he oversaw the construction of a new building on the same premises. There had always been a serious business rivalry between Federal and WIRL, and by late 1967 the former had also updated to four tracks. Treasure Isle (which had opened the previous year) wouldn't boast four-track facilities until 1970.

Producers such as Bunny Lee, Joe Gibbs, Sonia Pottinger, Ken Lack (real name Blondel Calnek), Lloyd Daley, and J. J. Johnson were all relatively new on the scene. They would soon be joined by Harry J, Lloyd Charmers, Phil Pratt, Herman Chin Loy, Glen Brown, Keith Hudson, Alvin Ranglin, Winston Riley, Prince Tony Robinson, Clive Chin, and Rupie Edwards as the local recording industry began to prosper and the overseas market for Jamaican music swelled beyond all expectation.

As well as Ken Boothe's version of 'Puppet On A String' – Coxsone having been in England when Sandie Shaw won that year's Eurovision Song Contest – other notable Studio One releases from 1967 included the Tennors' 'Pressure And Slide' and Alton Ellis & the Flames' genre-defining 'Rock Steady'. While Ellis gave rocksteady its name, Duke Reid gained the upper hand. A trio of hits by the Paragons ('Happy Go Lucky Girl', 'On The Beach', 'You And Your Smiling Face') were indicative of the timeless quality Tommy McCook & the Supersonics had brought to Treasure Isle productions and so too, the Jamaicans' 'Baba Boom' and 'Things You Say You Love'. American vocal groups such as the

Impressions, the Four Tops, and the Temptations were still immensely popular in Jamaica and among the Caribbean equivalents tasting local success that year were the Melodians ('You Have Caught Me'), the Techniques ('You Don't Care For Me', with Pat Kelly making his lead singing debut in place of Slim Smith), the Uniques, and the Wailers, whose self-produced 'Nice Time' was credited to 'Bob Marley and the Wailing Wailers'.

The more soulful and melodic quality to Jamaican music was down to the relaxed grooves of the new rocksteady beat, as typified by Roy Shirley's 'Hold Them' and the song that had sparked it all off, Hopeton Lewis' 'Take It Easy'.

Alton Ellis, Ken Boothe, Delroy Wilson, and Roy Shirley performed with the Dragonnaires on occasion, touring the island under the 'Rock Steady '67' (and 'Rock Steady '68') package banner, although the shows at the Carib Theatre, Kingston's most prestigious venue, drew the biggest crowds. The Carib Theatre was a favourite haunt of Aston and his friends, who would also visit the Majestic Theatre whenever Vere Johns hosted Opportunity Hour there. These were the stage equivalents of Johns' popular radio programme and bore comparison with New York's legendary Apollo Theater as audiences gleefully voiced their opinions of each act. Despite the joyousness of the rocksteady sound and the buoyant state of the local recording industry, the unease with which the authorities viewed Rastafarians remained and was further highlighted when two murders occurred on Jamaica's north coast during the latter part of 1967.

Alton Ellis: "Some Rastaman come out of the hills and chop up about three people. He chopped off a foreigner's head, chop off the gas station man's head and even chop off a dog's head. This happened in Montego Bay, and Bustamante, who was Prime Minister at the time, immediately announced that any man found with even a seed of herb is getting jailed immediately. He changed the law just because of that crime and he came down especially hard on us because a foreigner had been involved. Out of that now, Bunny Wailer, Lord Creator, and Toots from the Maytals all get 18 months' imprisonment for smoking herb, 'cause that's how Toots made his tune '54-46 Was My Number'. Bustamante, he was blaming what happened on ganja, but we all knew it wasn't that really."

Rastas said it wasn't the herb, but the pressure that had driven the Prime Minister crazy. While such violence was anathema to Rastafarian precepts, it served to highlight the growing unrest felt by many people during that time. In England and America, similar disillusionment with the system had given rise to the hippie or underground movement who, like the Rastas, were largely pacifists with a penchant for soft drugs like marijuana. They also wore their hair long, had liberal attitudes towards sex, and saw music as a vehicle for social change. Such thinking was in radical opposition to the conservative pop industry, which expected its artists to be well presented and entertain, rather than educate, their audiences. It would take a while for such ideas to gain momentum, although the first signs had developed in America a couple of years earlier, after Bob Dylan had trans-muted folk and protest songs into what people were now calling "rock", as opposed to rock'n'roll or rhythm & blues.

One of the emergent American West Coast groups, the Buffalo Springfield, whose line-up included Stephen Stills and Neil Young, had a sizable hit in 1967 with 'For What It's Worth' – a song that had been inspired by the Sunset Strip riots in Los Angeles the previous year. "There's something happening here, what it is, ain't exactly clear," Stills sang, going on to pinpoint how young people were being met with resistance and even oppression at the hands of the authorities, after exer-cising their right to freedom of speech. While Jamaican musical tastes generally reflected those of black Afro-Americans and therefore didn't usually stretch to the more bourgeois trappings of white rock bands, strong melodies have always been fair game and 'For What It's Worth' would prove no exception.

In the meantime, the Barrett brothers' embryonic band was beginning to jell, even though most of the members had yet to record in the studio. Webby Stewart, still working as a cabinetmaker in Rollington Town, was playing distinctive guitar licks, while Max Romeo was a charismatic front man, whose light tenor proved equally effective on either ballads or more up-tempo numbers. All they lacked now was a name, which Aston remembers arose quite spontaneously after the band auditioned for a residency at the Flamingo Hotel near Cross Roads and Half Way Tree one day.

"When the group first come out, we had two names in mind, because we thought we might call ourselves the Soul Mates, or become a new version of the Astronauts," he recalls. "What really happened now is that we were just practising and then as some time pass and we were sounding great, one night this little man pass and says he knows the woman who owns a hotel called the Flamingo and do we want him to arrange an audition? We say, 'Yeah,' and then sit around deciding what we're going to play, discussing it among ourselves and burning a joint or two. Then whcn we get there, there's only four or five people and them all sit down, but we turn the pressure pon them again, 'cause we play 'She Wears My Ring', 'Take Five', and 'Girl Of My Dreams' . . . A wicked selection of tunes me tell you! And we give them some favourite rocksteady too, like 'Perfidia'. All good stuff and vintage music from that time, but then when we stop the manageress say, 'You guys are good, but look at you, because why you dress like that? You people are so down to earth, you remind us of the hippies from the States, so you must be the Hippy Boys!' I say, 'What did you say?' Because that seem like a more international name and so we change the name right there!

"We heard the hippies wore long hair like the Rastas. Down to earth like the rootsman and that it was coming like Revelations for the white people. That's not to say our actions were like that, but we're like rude boys even though we're growing up in the church. We were more like soul rebels, even though we can still play wedding receptions and all of that. Anyway, so this lady buys some pretty, pretty shirt for us like we're calypsonians or actors from *Miami Vice* after that. It was a real little t'ing man . . ."

Max Romeo: "Before that, each individual just portrayed himself. One guy would wear a suit but another guy don't like that, so he would wear jeans and a T-shirt. But I like dressing up fancy, so I wear custom-built clothes all the time, 'cause I always find a tailor to cut my things. But in those days, bands usually wore uniforms with their name on it. Well we didn't bother with that. We were like more hippy style. Rebellious, y'know? Except not in music because we were playing a mixture of R&B and ballads. I was singing songs by Engelbert Humperdinck, Tom Jones, and Elvis Presley. Those kind of things and then some Caribbean material by people like Mighty Sparrow. Plus, we might interject a few of our own arrangements within the set and then the crowd would shower you onstage with coins. At the end of the night now, someone would sweep up the coins and bring them to us backstage. There was that and then some tourist might say he wants to hear a song like 'Delilah' and push 10 bucks in your pocket. It was fun!"

The Flamingo later became a nursing home but once hosted events attended by prominent society people, including visiting celebrities and local government ministers. By the time the Hippy Boys played there Aston had received his Family Man nickname. Contrary to popular opinion he wasn't a father yet, despite his best efforts. "I gave myself the name Family Man from my late teens because I was the one who loved to take care of things. That's because it would be me shouldering the roles of bandleader, engineer, and producer. I would set up the equipment and balance the sound, so I say to myself I don't want a name like producer, arranger, or stage manager, becah we are moving so happy and music is like a food that everybody can eat. As band members, we all share a name and play in E or G or whatever. We are a one family and I am the man in charge of that vibes, so I say, 'Well I am the Family Man,' and the name become a legend. But it was about taking care of the group and not about home life or anything domestic. Just Family Man taking care of these young boys called the Hippy Boys, Upsetters, Youth Professionals and then the Wailers and also all these other people we work with along the way.

"Music is an inborn concept," he continues, "and throughout the years I've been a producer, the man forming the band and the one who carries the instrumental section. I'm the man who chooses the instruments for the sound we put out and I'm the man who's taking care of the whole thing, so that's how I come up with that name, Family Man. It means I am a responsible person and we have to live and work together as a family. But I am a technician too, because if we have a piece of equipment and it's not working right, then I'll try and fix it up myself. I'll get parts for it if I can and then piece it together to make it work.

"I remember we do this gig at the Penguin Club one night and Max Romeo sing real good, but what thrill me so much was the mic. It was some old mic that somebody had thrown away, but I pick it up and play around with the wires until it sounding much better, then I solder it up and buy like some shield wire and lay it around there, y'know? And I so happy when I see the man wailing into that mic; believe me! Charlie Ace, he used to have a little discotheque what 'im used to keep birthday parties with. Then when 'im doing some other work sometimes, we'd just use his little discotheque for ourselves. He was always willing with t'ings like that. Well, his discotheque had these two twelve-inch speakers that we use on the bandstand. We just have the one little box on either side of us, but it sound good still. The equipment we use onstage, we have to line it up and balance it proper and that was my job, to make sure everything sounds just right, y'know? But Charlie Ace, he was my MC right up to Upsetters time and recorded his own tunes as well. He was one of Jamaica's first-ever talking artists, then 'im buy this British van called a Morris Minor and turn it into a mobile record stall."

Ace's mobile record store became a regular attraction around Kingston and photographs of his customised car with its gaily painted exterior and fitted speakers are often seen in books about reggae or Jamaica in the Seventies. He lent considerable excitement to the Hippy Boys' early gigs and recorded a number of duets with Val Bennett's daughter Faye during the late Sixties. During their residency at the Baby Grand, the Hippy Boys met Lloyd "Charmers" Tyrell who sat in on the venue's concert piano from time to time. A gifted all-rounder, he'd started out singing in a vocal duo called the Charmers, notching up a couple of hits as a solo artist before joining Alton Ellis & the Flames. Charmers then formed the Uniques with Jimmy Riley and former Techniques lead singer Keith "Slim" Smith, whose earliest hits were produced by Bunny "Striker" Lee.

Bunny, real name Edward Lee, had been a record plugger for both Duke Reid and Leslie Kong and, like Prince Buster and Derrick Morgan before him, used to run some of Reid's studio sessions on occasion. Slim Smith and Roy Shirley encouraged Lee to start producing in his own right, which he did once Reid gave him studio time in 1967. Lynn Taitt and his band did five tunes for Reid, including Roy Shirley's 'Give It To Me', which Ken Lack released on Caltone, and Lloyd & the Groovers' 'Listen To The Music' which became Lee's first hit.

WIRL then put out 'Shirley's Music Field' and asked Lee to produce sessions for them as Lee Perry, who'd joined from Coxsone, wasn't coming up with any hits. Bunny produced the Uniques' 'Let Me Go Girl' around this time, recorded the day Coxsone and Alton Ellis left for England on the Rock Steady tour. Charmers and B. B. Seaton (who'd written 'Let Me Go Girl') were both involved with the group at this point, although the very first Uniques' line-up had featured Derrick Morgan and Ken Boothe singing harmonies.

Lloyd Charmers: "Before I joined the Uniques, I used to rehearse at Alton Ellis' house in Trenchtown, because it was him who taught me how to sing harmonies. I used to go to Boys' Town School, but there was a place called Girls' Town School nearby, where Alton said there was a piano. Neither of us could play it, but that's where we wanted to rehearse, so we go up there one evening when it was closed, break the window and climb through it.

"Alton showed me the little he knew and then after he left, I sat there, just feeling my way around that piano and finding C, E, B, D, and also the chords that harmonise with them. Jeff Barnes, who used to be a deejay on JBC, had an uncle down in Greenwich Farm named Fish Head, so I started going to him for lessons after that, just to make sure what I was playing was correct. Fish Head taught me, but I didn't learn properly because I was quick and he was holding me back to earn money. I learn enough though, because Striker Lee came and gave me the opportunity to play, so that's where my opportunity came from. He called me, because I was living in Greenwich Farm near where he lived and he said to go with him and do some sessions. This was just before Striker formed the Uniques and recorded 'Let Me Go Girl' with Keith [Slim Smith], Martin [Jimmy Riley] and myself. Keith was in another group at the time called the Techniques. It was he and myself who started the group and then we got Martin to add harmonies later. In fact, most of those songs feature just the two of us, because we'd overdub the harmonies to make it sound like there were three of us."

In addition to being a talented singer and musician, Charmers also wanted to try his hand at production and from what he saw and heard at the Baby Grand, he knew Family Man had the right sound to help him start the ball rolling.

Max Romeo: "Lloyd Charmers, he was looking for a new type of rhythm, so he came by the Baby Grand one night to hear us and decided to jam with us on piano. He jammed with us a few times and then we got this residency at the Sheraton Ballroom near Kingston, 'cause we used to play there every Sunday night. But they were paying us little or no money, so we went to the union for assistance. Well the union guy was Sonny Bradshaw, who was a bandleader himself and he told us, 'You're lucky your band is playing, my guys need work!' Then the following week it was the Sonny Bradshaw Seven playing the gig. We were kicked out man and I'll never forget it! The band drifted apart after that and Lloyd Charmers had the idea of recording a song with them, but only using the bass player, which was Family Man, and the saxophone player. That was the first tune Family Man played on too."

"The first time I ever saw inside of a studio was the time I played on 'Watch This Sound' by the Uniques and my knees wobbled plenty, I tell you!" says Fams, laughing. "That was my first recording session and Slim Smith, Lloyd Charmers, and Jimmy Riley were the ones in the Uniques at that time. Before I go in, I saw B. B. Seaton from the Gaylads and said, 'I get this appointment to go in the studio and I don't know why they choose me instead of all these other experienced musicians.' But him say, 'Well if you don't go, how you ever gonna get it?' I say, 'You've got a point there!' I wasn't so nervous as I thought when I finally get there, even though I was the only amateur and I was playing bass, the backbone. This was in the early years of Dynamic Sounds, which Byron Lee rebuilt after the old studio had burned down, y'know? But once I'm inside there, I see players like Rannie "Bop" Williams and Lloyd Willis, 'cause we all get together for the first time on that session. The sound we put out that day, it move and it touch people, y'know? And it make us think, 'This is it man! This is the new stage!'"

Despite his understandable excitement, Family Man's grumbling bass sounded strangely exposed without the explosive rim shots of his brother Carly accompanying him. Instead, Shan, the drummer from the Gaylads band, played alongside Family Man. Fams and Shan knew each other from Rollington Town and Family Man also recognised a youth called Royal, who would later become known as "Tenor" playing sax with the Soul Syndicate. Royal occasionally played harmonica with the Hippy Boys and made his studio debut on 'Out Of Love' and 'Watch This Sound' (a cover of the Buffalo Springfield's 'For What It's Worth'), both recorded at this one session. The record was credited as a Lloyd Charmers' production when released on Winston Lo's Tramp label and became an immediate hit in Jamaica.

Jimmy Riley: "Winston Lo was a Chinese bookmaker in Greenwich Farm. He used to have this betting shop and one time, when things weren't happening with Bunny Lee and we needed money to finance a project, Lloyd Charmers talked him into loaning us a hundred pounds so we could record 'Watch This Sound' and 'Out Of Love'. 'Watch This Sound' was a cover song. I heard it in America by the Buffalo Springfield, but I couldn't remember all of it, so I put in what I could, took out the punchline and just record it! It was the second number one that we did, 'cause the first one was 'Let Me Go Girl'.

"In the Uniques I used to do all the writing. 'My Conversation', I wrote that. Also 'Love And Devotion', and 'Give Me Your Love'. I wrote 90 per cent of the Uniques' material, because the only song Lloyd Charmers wrote whilst he was in the Uniques was 'Out Of Love', for the Tramp label. Then again, Lloyd is the one who went to Mr Lo, so he's like the executive producer. He made it happen by going to borrow the money and naming the label Tramp. He played piano on the session too, but I found the song and Slim Smith help arrange the harmonies, so we do it together. We did a lot of our own production in those days though, 'cause Bunny Lee wasn't there during most of our sessions for him. It was just the musicians and us who arrange the sessions, but this is nearly always the case with reggae music. The bass man, he has a lot to do with making hit records, so any time you find a new bass man with a different feel and a different style, something bound to happen. Something changed that day and Family Man, he's been a year-to-year bass player ever since, because you might have a new one come up now and then with a different feel, but Family Man will always be there, with his own distinctive sound."

Lo's shop was located on East Avenue in Greenwich Farm, where Lee's family owned a food outlet. This served as a well-known hangout for local musicians such as Charmers and Adams, as well as the likes of Morgan, Romeo, and Cornel Campbell. Situated south of Maxfield Avenue and the Spanish Town Road, East Avenue was a thriving thoroughfare at the time, intersecting Marcus Garvey Drive at its southernmost point, ending right at the waterfront's edge. Despite the area being called "the Farm", the surroundings were anything but rural; the hot, dusty streets being flanked by a refinery and a disused railway line on one side and the run down shacks of Tinson Pen on the other. It was a close-knit community nevertheless and an integrated one, too. Charmers used to run errands for Lo as a youngster and had gone to see the Chinaman after he and Lee had fallen out over financial problems.

Lloyd Charmers: "I'll never forget it, because my son had just been born. I didn't have any money to buy some baby food, so I asked Winston for some because I was broke and Striker wasn't paying me. But I was a trustworthy person to Winston and so when I went to him, I knew he wouldn't turn me down. I told him I wanted to produce a record and so would it be all right for him to lend me something? He loaned me a hundred pounds and gave me three tins of baby food. I didn't have enough to pay everybody, but I called for Family Man and Delano Stewart from the Gaylads and this brother called Shan. Family Man, he said not to worry about anything, because he was glad to get the opportunity to play, y'understand? Anyway, we go and laid this track, but the drummer didn't have a hi-hat and so Linford Anderson and I went and cut out a piece of zinc from the fencing at Dynamic Sound. We bore a hole in it and then E. Q it until it sounded like some form of hi-hat. That song hit I tell you! Everything on Tramp is my production as well, because after Winston Lo saw what happened with 'Watch This Sound', he said, 'Lloyd, let me come in and help you,' because he'd watched me turn his investment into a hit record, y'know?

"After I'd paid for the session, I still didn't have a stamper though. I needed to press the record and I didn't have a penny, but I ordered it anyway and told them to start pressing. Then when they'd finished, I went back there, stacked up the records in the boot of my car, told them to make up the bill and drove out of there as fast as I could! I'm surprised they didn't send the police after me and put me in jail, but I went up to KG's at Cross Roads, sold them the records and then went back to Dynamic Sounds and paid them. That's how desperate I was. Striker had been saying I'd have to go back to him, but I was determined to make it on my own and so I was prepared to do anything to achieve my freedom."

The Hippy Boys, anchored by Family Man's bass, would play on a great many Charmers' productions in future, although for the time being they still didn't have a settled line-up, despite their regular stints at the Flamingo and Baby Grand, where the crowd would go wild whenever Charmers launched into Jackie Mittoo's 'Evening Time'. After they'd finished playing, the band members would get to share a box of fried chicken. Money was short, however, and Romeo's best efforts notwithstanding, it was becoming apparent the band would need proper representation if they were to realise their ambitions of turning professional.

Some time during 1968, the Hippy Boys came across their first manager, Bart Philips, who Family Man says was of Sicilian or Italian extraction and owned a car parts firm named Long Life Mufflers. These mufflers were widely advertised on Jamaican radio at the time – a factor that ensured Philips' business acumen went largely uncontested among the impressionable young musicians. His premises were situated close to the State Theatre, in front of Tops, a fried chicken concession which later became Kentucky Fried Chicken. Fams recalls that Philips' sister became Edward Seaga's first wife and that the Hippy Boys played their wedding reception, held at the Flamingo Hotel.*

Family Man Barrett: "When we first hear this man Bart Philips want to manage a band, we went up in the Halfway Tree area to this address we get for him and wait there until he come home from work. When we were there, we saw someone else waiting on him who said he was a keyboard player and his name was Bobby Kalphat. He told us the man needed a keyboard player for this band and when he asked us who we were, we said we were a little band from the east. It seemed the man wanted to manage two bands, so after him come, we talk to him and he

---

* There are some inconsistencies in this story, since Seaga had married Marie "Mitsy" Constantine some three years' earlier and other veteran Jamaican artists remember Bart's surname being Philigree, instead of Philips, although Family Man is certain that his own recollections are correct.

told us that the first audition was in Port Royal at the old hospital they have up there and this other band he managed called the New Breed would also be playing. We didn't have any uniforms, but he said we should all dress in black pants and white shirts. Well, everybody have black pants except Webby, who had dark brown pants but since he was the lead guitarist, it was alright for him to make a difference, y'know? Well, we go up to Port Royal early because we want to roll a little spliff and feel nice before the audition start, but we have to climb over the wall, 'cause this place was near the police training ground and everybody haffi hide. Then when we finish, we all come out from over the wall. The whole band! "Good herb me get them days Puppa!"

"But after we come back in, we drink two beers and then we're ready, cah it time fi the concert to start. This other group New Breed play first and them fix up nice man, 'cause they're wearing white pants, white shirt, white shoes and purple scarf. I say, 'Wow, the man really dress up 'im band.' Them have some ballads and were all right still but every song them play, everybody just clap their hands politely, y'know? Then when them finish playing, they just cool out with these pretty girls so we say we're going to make them flop now! So we tek the bandstand and Charlie Ace introduce us now and the first song we play, the whole place go quiet. You could hear a pin drop in there. It was that Solomon King song, 'She Wears My Ring' and everybody just a hold onto them girl, y'know? But the whole place was quiet like everybody's in a trance until Max Romeo hum like in the movie version of the song. That sound wicked me tell you and after that, we just play 'Drum Song' and it tear up the place! We'd got the same Bobby Kalphat playing organ with us that time and after 'Drum Song', we play 'Darker Shade Of Black'. We just rough them up with some instrumental, y'know? Max Romeo come in now and sang some wicked Alton Ellis songs. That shook them up again and then him sing, 'Oh, what a rocking vibration, Baby, what a sweet sensation.' A so we tear up the place, but we 'affi finish now and everybody applaud us.

"The owner, he thinks we're great and the next job we get from him was opening the Glass Slipper Plaza on Cross Roads. We were supposed to start early in the morning because it was being broadcast on the radio, but the amplifiers all blow. The bass amp go, the organ amp go, the guitar amp go. They all burn up, y'know? I tell the manager I know a little dreadlocks electrician round the corner, so I jump in my car and go over there an' say, 'Bwoy, yuh 'affi come now, cah we have a problem over deh so. Everyt'ing get fry.' Him just deal with that while I run go see the man with the parts, but by the time everyt'ing was working, it past the time we were supposed to come on the radio. We still perform though and it was a roadblock. Every bus that passed by that morning stopped and Cross Roads was rammed yet still the guest stars don't arrive.

"George Dekker, he always want to sing, but nobody ever tek 'im serious. He later joined the Pioneers, but they don't form yet and he had these songs called 'Mama Look Deh' and 'Laugh And A Ki Ki'. He go up first and Desmond Dekker came on next, 'cause he was the biggest artist on the bill but then as Desmond took up the mic, he fainted! He had two brethren with him, the Aces. One held him by the left hand, the other by the right and 'im just faint right there in the middle of them. I didn't know what was happening, y'know? He was just pretending, except it come like a surprise to me, then yuh just hear the man a sing, 'Wake up in the morning looking for bread sah, so every mouth can be fed.' That song tore up the place, me tell you! Because when he fainted, it was like him never get any breakfast from morning! That was a day to remember for sure, but the venue had a problem with equipment too, cah it was the last time anyone play there and them break it down and turn it into Skateland after that."

George Dekker was joined by Adams, Romeo, and Alva "Reggie" Lewis on the studio versions of 'Mama Look Deh' and 'Laugh And A Ki Ki', which Joe Gibbs would credit to the Reggae Boys and Soul Mates respectively, even though the band had recorded them as the Hippy Boys. Whoever paid the bills had the final say, but since the singers all profited from these songs ('Mama Look Deh' stayed at number one on the local charts for over three months), no one particularly minded. Reggie even bought his first car with the proceeds, which he purchased from radio deejay Winston Barnes for the princely sum of £350. He, Adams and the Barretts would later open Skateland as the Upsetters, with Dave Barker as their featured vocalist.

In the meantime, the Hippy Boys continued playing at clubs like the Baby Grand, the Green Basket, and the Blinking Beacon on Mountain View Avenue. They also underwent changes of personnel as some of the musicians Family Man played with on sessions were drafted in to duplicate the sound they'd found in the studio. Web Stewart was more concerned with his woodworking business than music and soon found himself being replaced by Ransford "Ranny Bop" Williams on lead guitar, who was also a member of Tommy McCook & the Supersonics.

Ranny Bop Williams: "I can remember going into the studio and playing with Family Man on 'Watch This Sound', but I was still playing with Tommy McCook and doing other sessions. We were doing lots of rocksteady at that time, because reggae wasn't born yet. When I came, I played in-between ska and rocksteady on the guitar and that brought about reggae, but no one wants to identify with that, or acknowledge the truth in what I say, but it comes right back down to me and I cannot count the number of records that I have played on in Jamaica. It's impossible, because there were so many hits for Bunny Lee with singers like Slim Smith, Delroy Wilson, and John Holt, and I played with Toots & the Maytals on most of their songs for Leslie Kong as well. You have greater guitarists than me like Ernest Ranglin, and my good friend Hux Brown was just ahead of me also, but I was the one who made the most money off sessions at that time."

Hailing from Spanish Town, where his mother was secretary for a local Seventh Day Adventist church, Ranny learnt guitar from a man called John Mack and played in a band with two doctors, Dr Charles and Dr Wright, before he was spotted by an acquaintance of Duke Reid, who invited him to record at Treasure Isle.

Ranny Bop Williams: "I was always fooling around musically and it was whilst I was playing and learning in Spanish Town that this brown-skinned man approached me and asked me to go to Kingston and play for him. I just said yes and didn't even get the man's name, I was so enthusiastic! I told him where I lived and so he came for me one Monday morning and took me to this studio at 23 Bond Street. It was Duke Reid's studio and I was asked to play on this session by a group called the Jamaicans, who were singing 'Baba Boom'. Well, they get me to play the guitar but I was so nervous, I wasn't able to play it properly, so they say it must have been someone else the man saw that day and not me. By this time I was teaching a guy named Evan Murphy, so Duke Reid say to me, 'You go back and bring him to me, because it can't be you.' So I went back to Spanish Town feeling all down to go find Evan Murphy, bring him back up there and they were still playing this same song, 'Baba Boom'. But when Evan started to play, they saw he was not ready and him say I taught him all he knew. That's how I get to play on this song eventually, but it was actually my second time in the studio because my first song was 'Good Manny' with the Pioneers, except we were just little boys from out of town and still under a parental situation and all that, so the song never reach anywhere.

"After that first session, I played for so many different producers and with so many different musicians that it's hard to call all their names. And whilst Tommy McCook was our bandleader at that time, I'm a member of everything where there's music and I play with almost everyone. I was leader for the Hippy Boys as a matter of fact, even though they were together before I joined them, because Webby, Family Man, and Carly were all there first. It's just that because I was in the Supersonics, everybody looked to me for leadership and I remember one night we played when Max Romeo was singing. Sonny Bradshaw had a contract at the Sheraton I believe and one Sunday his band couldn't make it, so he asked us to play instead and we tore that place apart. People were cheering us on the stage and that was real sweet!

"The band hadn't really done any recording yet; maybe individually for one or two producers, but not as the Hippy Boys. The single that actually made the Hippy Boys' name was 'Doctor No Go', but Hux Brown played on it and not me, because I was on tour with Tommy McCook at the time. People knew of me more than Family Man and the rest of them though and that's why they say I am the leader for the Hippy Boys. Then after a while, some of the other members start to get jealous and the Hippy Boys get a bad write-up in this weekly music paper saying I wasn't in tune and that create a bad impression. Well I was vexed, so I decide I'm not going back and that's when I left them to form this band called the El Dorados, but we still play together sometimes, meet up in the studio an' t'ing and they'd still call me for sessions."

The El Dorados made an impact at the Tunnel Club, deputising for Byron Lee, but they never got to record and when drummer Winston Grennan and organist Winston Wright both left the group, it soon folded. In the meantime, Ranny's lead guitar would continue to embellish tracks featuring various Hippy Boys until he moved to London in the early Seventies. Ranny wasn't the only significant addition to the Hippy Boys. Adams took over from Bobby Kalphat on keyboards and "Reggie" Lewis provided choppy rhythm guitar in the style of Jimmy Nolen, whose playing had proved a revelation on James Brown's recent soul hit, 'Cold Sweat'. Adams had been a member of the Astronauts, as well as early line-ups of the Heptones and the Pioneers, and was known as "Capo". He'd already recorded as a vocalist for Coxsone ('Wonder Thirst') and also doubled as a pianist and part-time A&R man for Duke Reid. He alternated on piano with Charmers at the Baby Grand and switched to organ as the Hippy Boys became more of a live attraction around Kingston.

"We also played a few gigs up Stony Hill as Hippy Boys, as well as places like the Golden Club," says Adams, speaking from his studio in Brooklyn. "We also played at several school dances and wedding parties as the band was getting established. I was playing organ by then, but I'd first learnt piano at school before getting to know Duke Reid and watching Gladstone Anderson play. That's where I get some of my early learning. I was playing a boogie, rhythm & blues type of thing back then and I become the arranger for that song by Don Drummond's girlfriend, Marguerita, called 'Woman A Come', which Duke Reid released in 1964. Nobody else could understand the song or interpret it, so they just left her to me. That was in the same period I was singing with Ken Boothe and hanging out with Stranger Cole and Joe White."

Adams had introduced Ranny to Treasure Isle, while Lee recruited Lewis after a recommendation by Derrick Morgan, who'd spotted him playing guitar in a Greenwich Farm bar. Alva was quickly dubbed "Reggie" by the other musicians, because of his resemblance to the comedian Reggie Carter. The presence of these additional musicians would give the Hippy Boys fresh impetus, as well as helping the Barretts to raise their own levels of performance.

"After we start to record now, people hear the music and ask, 'Who played guitar? Which drummer is involved?' But most of all, 'Who's the bass?'" says Fams proudly. "I start moving with the music people around the studios after that. Because it was Max Romeo who first took me to the western part of Kingston and let me know producers like Bunny Lee and then I get to know these other musicians like Ransford Williams, who we know as Ranny Bop. Also Hux Brown, Lynn Taitt, Hugh Malcolm and then horn players like Tommy McCook, Lester Sterling, Roland Alphonso, Herman Marquis, Headley Bennett as Deadly Headley, Bobby Ellis, Vin Gordon, Glen DaCosta and the trumpeter Dave Madden."

The Hippy Boys also decided to change their manager around this same time. While Bart Philips was getting the band regular work at places like the VIP, the Glass Bucket, Sombrero, Mavis Mercury Bank, and the Rainbow Club, the band's growing reputation wasn't reflected in their earnings and some members began to express their dissatisfaction. This came during a period when they were being booked for the occasional barbecue party on Long Lane or at the girls' school near Torrington Bridge, just below Sabrina Park, and were expected to play for refreshments only. Adams introduced them to Eddie Wong, whose family owned the Capital restaurant in Princes Street. Wong later became the

Hippy Boys' new manager and in Fam's own words, "did nothing wrong," as the group took the local recording scene by storm.

'Watch This Sound' rubbed shoulders with several other classic late Sixties' Jamaican sides on the JBC charts that year, such as Toots & the Maytals' '54-46 Was My Number', Desmond Dekker's 'It Mek' and 'Intensified '68', all of them produced by Leslie Kong. The Ethiopians ('Everything Crash'), Cables ('Baby Why'), Beltones ('No More Heart-aches') and the Heptones ('Baby', 'Why Did You Leave?') also notched up big hits that year, as did Larry Marshall with 'Nanny Goat'. Coxsone Dodd credits 'Nanny Goat' with ushering in the reggae era thanks to Eric Frater's distinctive rhythm guitar playing and few local musicians – including Family Man – dispute this.

The Barrett brothers and various band members played on a succession of tracks for Lloyd Charmers and Bunny Lee before 1968 ended, including Stranger Cole & Lester Sterling's 'Bangarang', which Lee maintains as the song that truly heralded the transition from rocksteady to reggae (and not 'Nanny Goat'). Just prior to this, Lee called Family Man in to play on Derrick Morgan's 'Hold Your Jack'. Drummer Leroy "Horsemouth" Wallace received some prophetic news from his rhythm partner as they were setting up in Treasure Isle studio. "I told him my brother is coming soon and 'im say, 'How you can know that?' But less than a month after-wards, he was there, 'cause Carly work at Wong's store as a decorator in them days and yet I knew he was ready for this."

Carly made his debut on 'Bangarang', and for the first time the Barrett brothers' drum and bass double act was committed to tape. Lee was again the producer and had asked Family Man to get Carly because he couldn't find either Horsemouth or Lloyd "Tin Leg" Adams.

"I'll tell you what happened to Tin Leg," says bassist Sidney Guisse, who later recorded under the name Junior Dan while a member of the Twelve Tribes band. "We were in Treasure Isle playing on 'Boom Shack A Lack A' by Hopeton Lewis, which has this wicked piano on the intro. That wasn't there originally, so when Duke Reid come now, he said he wants us to put this piano in it, but we were struggling to do it. He says, 'So what happen? You can't play the music?' We said it was hard and we weren't ready yet. We said, 'Just give us a little more time,' and there was this fly on the wall, right by the piano. Duke say, 'Mr Lindo, come on out of the way,' and 'Blam!' He let off the shotgun and a big hole appeared in the wall. He said, 'You get the sound yet?' And Tin Leg, he was like,

'Come on now, let's do it!' He's all agitated and as soon as we finish, Tin Leg says, 'I soon come back,' and disappears.

"We were wondering what's going on and somebody comes from downstairs so we say, 'Has anyone seen Drummie?' He say, 'He take the corner about 90 miles an hour!' This other drummer named Leroy come, so we say for him to come finish the session, because the other drummer gone and when he sit down on the drum stool, he leap back up saying, 'Shit!' The drum seat, it was soaking! Tin Leg took off and he wasn't seen for about two or three weeks! Next time I see him and he says he's working on the north coast in a hotel . . ."

Wallace told *Black Echoes* journalist Penny Reel he wasn't at the session because he'd been thrown in jail after demonstrating on behalf of Guyanese writer and activist Walter Rodney, who used to lecture at the University of the West Indies. Hugh Shearer had taken over leadership of the JLP after Bustamante's retirement in 1967 and soon experienced difficulties of his own, as demonstrations and unrest followed his controversial decision to ban books promoting civil rights and also to bar potential "troublemakers" like Rodney from visiting Jamaica.

Horsemouth Wallace: "They say no black man can come to Jamaica and I was upset, because from those times I'm a patriot to the system so I decide to fling stone and riot and I get caught in jail. This was October 28, 1968. I supposed to do a session for Bunny Lee, and Bunny Lee used Carly, Family Man's brother instead, 'cause Family Man and me used to play together before that. We played a tune named 'Wet Dream' and Max Romeo sing on the said version, but Derrick Morgan was the man who did it first. We used to do those sessions for Bunny Lee at Duke Reid's studio but that's the first tune Carly play on."

The session for 'Bangarang' also marked Adams' debut as an organist. He'd actually been summoned to play piano, but Gladstone "Gladdy" Anderson was still smarting after being owed money from a previous session. His piano lines didn't sound right, however, and so Lester Sterling took over while Charmers showed Adams what was required on organ. Lewis was another raw recruit that day, having only played guitar onstage prior to recording 'Bangarang'. Wilburn Cole's vocal contribution occurred almost by accident simply because Cole (given the nickname "Stranger" by his parents, as he didn't resemble anyone else in his family!) just happened to be passing by Treasure Isle while the session was in progress. Cole had started recording for Duke Reid in 1962, although his songs were initially covered by other artists such as Eric "Monty" Morris. Reid then introduced him to Millicent "Patsy" Todd, with whom he recorded a number of successful duets, including 'When You Call My Name'. Cole would also voice hits with Ken Boothe at the outset of his career.

While Alton Ellis claims he wrote some of the lyrics to 'Bangarang', it was Sterling's sax breaks and the churning rhythm track that proved so mesmerising, introducing something new and different to the Jamaican scene.

Lloyd Charmers: "That was a killer man! We did it as a joke and yet the joke turn out good, because we come up this line, 'Woman a want no bangarang,' and you can't help but wonder where we get such foolishness from! That was just creativity in motion and it comes from this desire to stop from doing the same things every day. That's the joy of being in the studio sometimes, because whatever mood you're in, that microphone picks it up. The studio vibe is like a ghost, y'know? It's a spirit and whatever vibe you feel when you go in the studio, that's what's going to come out in the music. You have to believe that, because that's coming from within you and it's a vibe, so if you go in there with a good vibes, then you'll get a good sound. Those things are beyond us, because we can't understand those things. It's God's work, because when I go into the studio, I have no idea what I'm going to do. I depend on my inner spirit to bring out my innovation, so that whatever's inside me can come out."

Bunny Lee: "The musicians at that time were young, so I told Lester Sterling to turn the song into a two-chord thing and it was him who came up with this expression 'Bangarang'. I told Lester to let's go try it and that was the first reggae tune, because reggae comes from the organ shuffle. Family Man, he played on another of those very early reggae tunes with the same organ shuffle, which is Derrick Morgan's 'Seven Letters'. That's what distinguishes reggae from rocksteady, because rocksteady was just plain and if an organ was there, it just played the solo and didn't shuffle like in those particular songs."

Lee had an enviable success rate for a newcomer, which is why he'd soon earn the name of "Striker". Family Man and Carly played on innumerable tracks for Lee in the wake of 'Bangarang', starting with Slim Smith's 'Everybody Need Love' and instrumental versions of 'Blowing In The Wind' and 'On Broadway'. One of their earliest and biggest hits was Pat Kelly's 'How Long (Will It Take)', which Charmers again claims credit for. 'How Long' received a lot of airplay in England throughout 1969; in fact, it was unlucky not to chart that year.[*] Apart from Kelly,

---

[*] 'How Long (Will It Take)' still gets reissued on a regular basis.

who'd made his reputation singing lead vocals on the Techniques' 'You Don't Care', Lee's main artists at the time included Derrick Morgan, Max Romeo, and Slim Smith, who'd record for the producer both as a solo act and as a member of the Uniques. Smith's light alto was already well loved in Jamaica and he followed 'Everybody Needs Love' with a beautifully understated cover of the Temptations' 'Ain't Too Proud To Beg', voiced over a typically unrelenting shuffle from the Barrett brothers.

Bunny Lee: "Niney was the one who really produced that song. He worked with Scratch and Clancy Eccles first but they didn't treat him good so I take him over and give him a bike and he became one of Jamaica's greatest record salesmen. But I put him in the studio and get him to produce tunes too, after I'd said to him, 'Niney, go down there and show them that you can make rhythm.' He and Ansel Collins, they came up with this other Slim Smith song too, called 'Slip Away'. I give Scratch a cut of that rhythm and he put Dave Barker on it for 'Prisoner Of Love'. We recorded those songs at Federal and then voiced them at Coxsone, because it all depended on how the studio time would a run in those days."

'Slip Away' had been a sizable hit in America for Clarence Carter during the autumn of 1968 and its theme of urgent sexual need suited Smith's delivery to perfection as the pleading in his voice reached fever pitch. That said, the soul original is far more laid back and has none of the drama and excitement invested in it by Slim and the Hippy Boys. Niney (real name Winston Holness) went on to a long and successful career in record production after learning the ropes from Lee.

"I was a salesman for at first," he confirms. "Then after moving with Bunny around the studio, I became a producer for him. In those days, Bunny was working with Pama Records so he had to fly out to England quite often and I was the man who continued with the production. Even when Bunny was around, he would just leave everything to me, cah he have to do the bigger part of the business. Shortly after that, he hooked up with Scratch and the music kept on blooming.

"It was around that same time version come in, because when Bunny Lee sight what Coxsone is doing, he said, 'I'm going to make some trouble,' and start to hit Coxsone real hard. Bunny Lee was the first person to do that, because from Coxsone have part one, Bunny Lee have part two as a version. After that now, the real version come in when Bunny make one rhythm and put 10 singers on it, then pick out the best one. I'm the man who went to the dances and gave U Roy the songs to play, 'cause he was deejaying on King Tubby's sound-system at the time.

"That's so we could see which one the people were rocking to, and every week we'd cut one like that. Bunny might have six, seven singers on the one rhythm, but U Roy would say to give him more version again, so that's what turned it into version."

'Everybody Needs Love', like the Uniques' 'My Conversation', inspired an album's worth of "versions" using the same rhythm and has been reworked endless times since, by many different reggae producers. The shuffle Lee talks about can be heard to dazzling effect on 'Everybody Needs Love', with its alternately wheedling and stabbing organ phrases and quietly pulsating rhythm. With Slim again sounding at his most anguished, it's little wonder the song was such a big hit in Jamaica, just as rocksteady turned into reggae. The original versions included Family Man and King Tubby's 'Ten Thousand Tons Of Dollar Bills', as well as Val Bennett's '1,000,000 Tons Of TNT', Roland Alphonso's 'Roly Poly', and Dennis Alcapone's 'Two Of A Kind'. Family Man plays organ on his and King Tubby's cut, reprising skills he'd first learnt some years earlier, as a member of the Drive-In Cracker Boys.

Family Man Barrett: "I play a lot of different instruments from those times, like rhythm guitar, piano and organ, as well as bass. I played organ on this instrumental album for Bunny Lee and I know it was released in England, 'cause I get a test press from Pama when we toured there as Upsetters. It was called *The Disintegrator* and has rhythms like 'Everybody Needs Love', 'Bangarang', and 'Ain't Too Proud To Beg'. Some of Bunny Lee's greatest early reggae tunes were on it and I play them using this strange tone to match the melody and the mood of each rhythm. The sound of it was so cool man! 'The Disintegrator' was the first track on it and Bunny Lee do this talk where he say, 'Introducing to you, the new musical explosion, the Disintegrator!' I'm scream and we repeat the voice two times and then the rhythm and the organ just a fire out, man! He recorded a version at Treasure Isle with Roland Alphonso too called 'Roly Poly', where we speed up the tape a little, y'know?

"Bunny work for himself at the time and he also run the odd session for Dynamic, 'cause 'im 'ave his little sound and 'im have the musicians and the artists, but 'im still do things like that. Bunny give us all a chance; 'im support the talent 'cause 'im sensitive to music too, y'know? And that was important. Yeah man, him know when a man can play and he was great at that."

Island Records' Dave Betteridge was a man with his ear to the ground and had wasted no time licensing some of Lee's productions to Chris

Blackwell's label. At this point, the company were based in Cambridge Road, London. Island then merged with Lee Goptal of Blue Cat to form Trojan Records, whose offices were in Neasden Lane, north west London. Graeme Goodall, who also ran the Doctor Bird label, set up Trojan subsidiary Attack and began issuing Bunny's productions thereafter, although not exclusively.* Undeterred by Lee's existing arrangement with Trojan, Pama created the Unity label in 1968 for his releases, including such hits as Roy Shirley's 'Hold Them', Slim Smith's 'Everybody Need Love' and Max Romeo's 'Wet Dream' – a song sharing the same rhythm as Derrick Morgan's 'Hold You Jack' (previously released on Island) but now featuring a radically different vocal. Although Romeo had sung backing vocals on several of Lee's productions (including 'Bangarang'), 'Wet Dream' was his first solo recording. Pama rescued the song from its flipside status and turned it into a runaway hit.

Songs with lewd or suggestive ("slack" in Jamaican parlance) lyrics had grown in popularity since the emergence of American comedian Blowfly, and Jamaican producers were quick to take note. However, while Lloyd Charmers and Prince Buster gleefully racked up hits in this vein, other artists were reluctant to voice this type of material, including Slim Smith, Roy Shirley, John Holt, Derrick Morgan and even Romeo himself.

"No, I didn't want to sing that song 'Wet Dream', but I was threatened by Bunny Lee, who said that if I didn't sing it, I couldn't come back in the studio! So, I say 'Alright,' and we go to Coxsone's studio to do it and Coxsone Dodd himself was the engineer, but when I went round the mic and the riddim start, Coxsone lock off the tape and say 'Bunny, I'm not a part of this! You can't come in here with this foo-foo singer and this idiot song. Me nah engineer them t'ings there. Me nah want no dutty music like that inna my studio, y'understand? Me is a man who deal with perfection!' Bunny say, 'Listen man. You can't tell me what to do. I rent this studio from you. If you don't want to engineer the song, let the apprentice sit round by the board.' So, Coxsone get up and go away and Errol Thompson do it instead. He was very young then and that was his first song as a professional engineer. It was the first rhythm that Leroy Horsemouth the drummer play on, too."

"Horsemouth used to work for Coxsone as a janitor and a printer," explains Bunny. "We couldn't get a drummer that day and so we try him

* Dandy Livingston was working for Pama Records at the time and told the Palmer brothers that he and Lee were cousins.

out for the first time, but Ranny Bop said, 'Bunny. Where did you get this foolish drummer from?' I said we have to try and work with him and that was the session for 'Hold You Jack', which become the same rhythm for 'Wet Dream' and some other songs."

'Wet Dream' stayed on the UK charts for 26 weeks, peaking at number 10 towards the end of May 1969. BBC deejay Tony Blackburn played it on Radio 1 twice before realising the lyrics weren't about a leaking roof at all and the corporation duly banned it. Because of this, Romeo never got to perform on *Top Of The Pops* and spent most of his time in the UK fielding questions as to what the words really meant, rather than getting journalists to focus on his talent. Ever the entrepreneur, Lee got Derrick Morgan to revisit the same rhythm for a cleaner version, 'I Love You'. There was also an instrumental cut, 'Day Dream', credited to the Bunny Lee All-Stars. Hardly surprisingly, in the wake of 'Wet Dream', Romeo opted to forego singing other suggestive songs and would be among the first wave of singers to embrace Rastafari as it made its presence felt in Jamaican music circles during the late Sixties.

CHAPTER FOUR

Liquidator

ALTHOUGH nowhere near as prolific, the Hippy Boys were beginning to rival Beverley's All-Stars and Tommy McCook's Supersonics as Jamaica's most in-demand session musicians, with 'Everybody Needs Love', 'Watch This Sound', and 'Bangarang' all selling well. Lee and Charmers were not the only producers to call upon the band's services. Harry J and Lee Perry were also drawn to the Barrett brothers' rhythm section and both would be rewarded with international success in return.

Sonia Pottinger, introduced to the Hippy Boys by Delano Stewart, remains the best known of a tiny handful of Jamaican women producers after recording hits by the Melodians, the Gaylads and Ken Boothe during the rocksteady era and, later, Marcia Griffiths and Culture once Pottinger assumed control of Treasure Isle in 1976, after Duke Reid passed away. Back in the late Sixties, she began releasing music on the Gay Feet label after her divorce from Lindon Pottinger, who ran Tip Top, a record and distribution outlet on Orange Street. (The pair separated after Sonia's affair with a local radio deejay called Al Plummer and people have referred to her as "Miss" Pottinger ever since.)

After leaving the Gaylads in the spring of 1968, Delano Stewart recommended the Hippy Boys to play on several tracks for Pottinger, including 'Stay A Little Bit Longer'. Stewart and B. B. Seaton had sat in with the Hippy Boys on guitar at places like the Flamingo Hotel, and both provided early encouragement as the band members strove to make a reputation for themselves.

"B. B. Seaton, he never stay too long, but Delano play with us for a good little while, 'cause he was there most evenings," says Fams. "He was like another Bob Marley type of artist, short the same way and a very talented songwriter too. He was a good singer, musician and good everyt'ing. When I first meet Bob now and start to work with him, it was like a step up for me, because I'm used to that type of vibe from Delano Stewart. Most of the other songs he do for Miss Pottinger, they were before my time, because I just a practise back then, but 'Stay A Little Bit Longer' was a big hit for him before he moved to America.

"It was shortly after that, we do this song for Miss Pottinger by Max Romeo and another guy named Artist, whose real name was Lloydie. That's the track which become 'Doctor No Go' and put the Hippy Boys on the map."

'Doctor No Go' was a nagging instrumental that only lasted two minutes, but with its languid piano, churning organ and scuttling backbeat, it still made an indelible impression upon first hearing. It didn't chart in England but enjoyed widespread popularity among reggae audiences, who couldn't get enough of this new and exciting sound from Jamaica. As with American soul-jazz and prototype funk (typified by James Brown and New Orleans group, the Meters), the emphasis was now on groove and rhythm and the Barrett brothers' syncopated drum and bass on tracks like 'Doctor No Go' fitted this bigger musical picture to perfection.

"Sonia Pottinger distributed 'Doctor No Go' on the Gay Feet label, but it was my production really," claims Max Romeo, who had by now left the Hippy Boys to pursue a solo career. "When I abandoned the band, I just leave everything for the new guys who take over. I didn't take anything from them. Audley Rollins took over as lead vocalist just after me, but 'Doctor No Go' is my rhythm, because it was made for 'You Can't Stop Me'. That was the original song on it, but then the rhythm was used as an instrumental and the title inspired by all these doctor films, because you had *Carry On Doctor* and all these other movies and that's what inspired the doctor thing in the music. In those days, everyone went to the cinema in the evenings, because we didn't have any other form of recreation, except for the dances at the weekend. We'd go to all the cinemas in Kingston; the Rialto, Palace, Majestic, Queens . . . You name it, and we'd go there."

Film adaptations of Richard Gordon's *Doctor* books had been made since the mid-Fifties, but it was the 1969 television sitcom *Doctor In The House* that sparked off the doctor craze in England, and its popularity soon spread to Jamaica. Charmers also produced tracks by the Hippy Boys named after doctor themes and so too Lee Perry, who had hits with both 'Medical Operation' and 'Live Injection'. Jamaican ska legends the Skatalites had also experienced success employing cinematic methods, the best example being 'Guns Of Navarone', which breached the UK Top 40 in the summer of 1967. The trend was by no means confined to Jamaica, since Memphis instrumental group Booker T & the MGs often weaved references to television or movie themes into their music ('Hang 'Em High', 'Mrs Robinson'). As already noted, the rhythm of the song now took precedence, rather than vocals and conventional structure and the melodies, if not original, could be borrowed from anywhere, so long as they struck a note of familiarity to the listener.

In the wake of 'Doctor No Go', Miss Pottinger released *Reggae With The Hippy Boys,* an album of instrumentals that was virtually indistinguishable from Charmers' productions and was clearly recorded around the same time. Already, the sound of the rhythm section is unmistakable, whether skanking lightly on the more laidback numbers, or rocking all out boogie-woogie style. Some of these tracks border on rhythm and blues with their "walking" bass lines and juke joint piano playing, while others chug along in classic Upsetter/Hippy Boys' fashion, with Reggie's scratchy rhythm guitar well to the fore. The band also cut a version of 'Drum Song' for Pottinger that captures all the spiritual majesty of Jackie Mittoo's original and must sound just like how the band used to play it onstage. Snatches of familiar melodies – including Scott McKenzie's '67 hippie anthem, 'San Francisco (Wear Some Flowers In Your Hair)' – gurgle in the mix, most of them picked out on either guitar or Charmers' acoustic and electric pianos. Yet it's Carly's crisp drumming and Family Man's dancing basslines that give these tracks edge and prevent them from sinking into MOR territory.

The Hippy Boys played on several Miss Pottinger-produced hits including Delroy Wilson's 'Put Yourself In My Place', but in 1969 their instrumentals definitely caused the most excitement. Charmers issued dozens of Hippy Boys' singles that year, including 'Zylon' (a Jamaican number one), 'Love', 'Michael Row The Boat Ashore', 'Hog In A Me Minty', 'Confidential', 'Cat Nip', 'Ling Tong Ting', 'Chicken Licken', 'Reggae Pressure', 'Follow This Sound', and 'Safari'.

Lloyd Charmers: "I'd already been recording for Miss Pottinger's husband as the Charmers, because we made a few songs that never did too bad for him, like 'Best Friend' and 'Never Seen A Girl Like You'. This was before 'Doctor No Go' and I automatically become part of the Hippy Boys then, because it was me who put it together and played on it with them.

"That was during a time I was doing a little thing on the side as Lloyd Tyrell, and it was working out too, because when I left the Uniques I went out on my own and did my little instrumentals. I'd still share the money with the other two, even though it wasn't the group who did it.

That's just how I am, but all of those instrumentals we did, they were an innovation, because when we go into the studio, we don't know what is going to happen, or what we're going to record. We just group together and see what happens. A man might say, 'Charmers, what are we going to do now?' and I'll say, 'Follow me.' I'll just start playing something and then the band will fall in behind me, argument finished!"

'Piccadilly Hop', 'Shanghai', a cover of the Meters' 'Look A Py Py', 'Voodoo', and 'Doctor Jeckyl' also tumbled out of such sessions. The Hippy Boys gained valuable experience and confidence recording in such a spontaneous manner, bringing out the humour in their music and helping them to become more creative. Such qualities reflect Charmers' personality, since he's a man who brims with optimism and positive ideas; the sort of character who can pluck something out of the air and make it a hit, no matter how silly it might seem, as he did when recording 'Pop A Top' with Lynford Anderson – inspired by the sound of a beer bottle being opened. The result was strikingly simple but original and typical of the work younger producers like Charmers, Lee, and Perry were doing, creating a musical climate where innovation could flourish and they could genuinely compete with more established labels such as Federal, Studio One, and Treasure Isle.

Charmers went on to produce at least three albums' worth of tracks with the Hippy Boys, most of them recorded at Dynamic, featuring himself (and not Glen Adams) on either piano or Hammond organ. A handful of Hippy Boys singles also appeared on subsidiary labels such as Bullet, after Charmers licensed them to Pama Records in London. Like the tracks produced by Miss Pottinger, most were tight, catchy instrumental sides, led by Charmers' churning organ and propelled by lockstep drum and bass, with scrubbing rhythm guitar from Reggie. Some again featured melodies borrowed from popular movie themes or television shows; others were alternative cuts of reggae hits like 'Everybody Needs Love' and 'How Long', which they'd originally recorded for Bunny Lee. Because of the organ sound, a lot of this music hasn't dated well, yet there's no mistaking the Barrett brothers' capacity to groove hard on any beat they were presented with, no matter how corny the melody. 'Cat Nip', released on the Camel label, was typical in this respect. Other hits for Charmers included 'Cloudburst', 'Cooyah' and the inevitable 'Psychedelic Reggae', which sounded decidedly tame compared to what contemporary rock groups like the Doors, Jimi Hendrix Experience, and the Mothers of Invention were doing elsewhere.

Instead of fusing their music with Eastern influences, using excessive distortion, or attempting to simulate LSD trips, Caribbean musicians favoured a more conservative approach and the Hippy Boys were no exception, despite sounding radical by Jamaican standards. Gimmicks, and not sonic pyrotechnics, were utilised to make the instrumentals more interesting, something Lee Perry would excel at whenever the Hippy Boys cut sessions for him as the Upsetters. It's Perry who provides the weird, repetitive "A hit cha" on 'Five To Five', for example, while that's Family Man's old school friend, Herman Chin Loy, belching on 'African Zulu'.

Lloyd Charmers: "I remember when I did 'Five To Five'. Man, that was serious! Scratch came to the studio and when he heard it, he said it was short of something. I said, 'Short of what?' He asked me if I understood about pocomania and I told him, 'Yes', so he came and put in the pocomania style and that was the touch! That made the song, because when he was finished, he said, 'There you go Lloydie. There's spirit in it now.' He was right too, because it had a vibes to it, and it was happening. I remember this deejay from JBC radio in Jamaica used to play 'Five To Five' every evening at five to five. You'd hear the clock alarm and then you'd know it was five to five. Every evening he used to play it, so you could set your clock to that song. The song did well and that deejay, he really loved it!"

Primitive dub effects courtesy of engineer Sid Bucknor were another feature of these early Charmers' productions, some of which appeared on the Hippy Boys' own label. Charmers now managed the Hippy Boys' affairs following Romeo's departure. The group gained more autonomy as a result, since they could now do deals with distributors for themselves, without going through other producers. It would be a short-lived arrangement, however, once Charmers launched another label called Splash and the Hippy Boys started to branch out on their own, becoming increasingly drawn into Lee Perry's orbit.

Lloyd Charmers: "I started Splash because you have to try, and I'm always trying. I did all those instrumentals because I needed to live and if the singing wasn't working, then I had to try something that was. It's simple. The bottom line is, go with what works. It doesn't matter whether something's in fashion or not. If it works for you, then do it and that's how I come to produce so many of those early Hippy Boys recordings, and do the first rude songs as Lloyd Tyrell, or Lloydie & the Lowbites, because everyone start to follow me after that."

The tracks Charmers is referring to featured 'slack' lyrics, the best-known examples appearing on an album titled *For Adults Only* which Charmers put together using a dozen or so rhythms played by the Hippy Boys. Family Man wasn't alone in expressing surprise as his friend turned the air blue with a ribald take on the old Doris Day hit, 'Que Será Será'. "Yes, because he changed the words to 'kiss me rass', but when we play the rhythm, we had no idea what the comedian have in mind!"

Tracks by the Hippy Boys had appeared on several compilations by this time, including 'House In Session', 'Reggae Is Tight' and 'Reggae Charm'. Although the band members weren't yet aware of the fact, their debut album had also begun to attract healthy sales in the Caribbean and England, where they'd become a favourite of the skinheads. These were British style rude boys who shaved their heads and wore a uniform of Ben Sherman shirts, braces, short-length trousers, and Doctor Marten's "bovver" boots. Working class thugs for the most part, they wedded their love of Jamaican ska and early reggae with affiliations to far right political organisations and a dislike of hippies which, ironically, didn't seem to matter one iota when it came to their appreciation of the Hippy Boys.

Reggae now became the buzzword, rather than rocksteady or blue beat, and the Hippy Boys were among the spearhead of this new development, although since most producers other than Charmers and Miss Pottinger insisted on renaming them, the band weren't receiving anywhere near the recognition they deserved. Charmers and Bunny Lee continued to call upon the band regularly for session work, not only for instrumentals, but also backing a wide variety of singers, including Pat Kelly, Derrick Morgan, Slim Smith, John Holt, Delroy Wilson, and many others. Family Man gained invaluable experience playing with other, more established musicians on these sessions, including forming a brief partnership with drummer Winston Grennan and guitarist Bobby Aitken of the Caribeats and this line-up played on several tracks by the Uniques.* Both Barrett brothers appear on their cover of Curtis Mayfield's 'My Woman's Love', as well as Pat Kelly's 'Try To Remember' and 'How Long', which Lee licensed to Gas in the UK.

Lloyd Charmers: "I did everything on those records. Everything! But when 'How Long' became a hit in England [in 1969], they put Bunny Lee's name as producer and they did the same thing with 'Try To

---

* Grennan claims to have taught Carly how to tune his drums, although Family Man has no recollection of this.

Remember', yet I am the producer and not Bunny. I was working for Bunny at the time, so as far as I'm concerned it's not a big thing. Bunny helped me to exercise my ability and showed me what I had and that's why I give credit to him, but at the same time, I did all the work. I was the producer and the arranger on those records, as well as a singer and musician and a lot of people don't know these things. For instance, I played the piano solo on 'How Long' and that was Pat Kelly's biggest hit!"

Despite such assertions, Charmers speaks of Lee with fondness and more than 35 years later, both men are still good friends. "I saved Striker's life one time because this singer brought some bad man to come stick him up. That's because when you sang for Bunny, sometimes you'd get no money, so this guy never take it so lightly as me. He went for his bad man cousin and they kidnap Bunny one night as we left the studio. They come to Dynamic Sounds, jook him down, and push the gun into his neck. They bundle him into this car, but they carry me along at the same time, thinking I'm going to go with what's happening, but I'm not into that, so when the guy take out the gun and cock it to shoot Bunny, I say, 'Gentlemen. If you're going to kill Bunny then you'd better kill me, because if Bunny dies, then I am not going to act as if nothing has happened. I am going to say that it's you two who kill him.' The man asks what kind of foolishness I'm talking, but that is what saved Bunny. They rough him up and t'ing yes, but at least they never kill him. They would have shot him otherwise though, because they shoot and kill someone else, just a couple of months later."

Lee is only too happy to credit Charmers for the work he did in the past and can take obvious pride in having fostered such a stellar line-up of Jamaican talent. As his music's popularity grew among overseas audiences, Lee began spending increasing amounts of time in London, overseeing licensing deals for his records and obtaining finance so he could keep the operation afloat back home. This meant he came to rely upon people such as Charmers or Winston Niney Holness, to organise sessions in his absence. While Lee got the credit and most of the monetary rewards, his assistants learnt how to produce hit records without too much interference and, more importantly, without having to worry about funding. It was an apprenticeship system of sorts and while open to abuse on both sides, it gave a lot of talented individuals the opportunity to make their mark in an industry that was expanding out of all recognition. Hits could now explode from nowhere and not just strike big on the local market, but also in places like England, the Netherlands, and France, where artists like

Desmond Dekker, Jimmy Cliff, and Prince Buster were representing the music's commercial appeal.

One of the most notable examples of a hit appearing from nowhere was Count Prince Miller's 'Mule Train', which can neither be described as vocal or deejay, but more like a crazed, Caribbean form of country & western. It sounded as if a cowboy had been let loose in a Kingston ginhouse but it was wholly in keeping with the times, when experimentation was at its height.

"I never intended to do it," says the Count, whose reputation largely rests upon these three minutes of happy mayhem. "I went to the studio with Jackie Edwards, because he was doing a session for Bunny Lee and I was leaving the following day for London. This was at Federal, because I'd been one of the first artists to voice there, with a group called the Downbeats. Anyway, as we walked in, Family Man, Lloyd Charmers, and all these other guys were sat around waiting for Bunny Lee and as soon as I walk in, they shout, 'Mule Train!' and start to play the song, so I joined in. They record it live, just like that, one take! They play it in the right key and everything, because 'Mule Train' was a popular song in Jamaica and I was one of the leading entertainers at that time. I used to tour all over with Byron Lee, performing in places like Trinidad, Barbados, Antigua, and all that, singing 'Mule Train'. I never had any intention of putting it on record though. It was just a showpiece, y'know? Bunny didn't even turn up until after I'd gone and I don't even get to know when they were releasing it, because soon after I get back to England, Derrick Harriott phoned me and said I was number one in Jamaica. I said, 'Which record is that?' He said 'Mule Train' and I never get a penny for it up until now.

"Mind you, Family Man and the band never got paid for playing on it either. They got paid for playing on the Jackie Edwards album, but that never sold too many copies really. The one that sold from that session was 'Mule Train' and we did a lot of shows with it afterwards, like on the BBC in England and all over. We even went to Australia with it."

The Barretts wouldn't learn of the single's success for some time. Just another in a never-ending succession of instrumentals, it had been recorded in a spirit of fun and with few expectations of it ever becoming a major hit. Other sessions carried more weight, especially one involving Toots & the Maytals, featuring just Family Man and Ranny Bop from the Hippy Boys' line-up. The Maytals were a group with serious pedigree in Jamaica, as they'd recorded a string of hits for Coxsone, Prince Buster, Beverley's, and Byron Lee since making their debut in the ska era. Led by

Toots Hibbert's exuberant vocals, the Maytals' songs were fired by gospel fervour and sounded as if the rhythms could barely contain the group at times. Shortly after winning the 1966 Jamaican Song Festival with 'Bam Bam', Toots went to prison for possession of ganja.

He and his fellow Maytals were on their way to a show in Ocho Rios when they were stopped at a roadblock and told to dismount from their Honda motorcycles. Toots was sent to call their manager, and on his return was confronted with claims that herb had been found in his suitcase. Toots didn't smoke at the time and so pleaded his innocence but was sentenced to 18 months' imprisonment. The group's first trip to England, where the Maytals were scheduled to perform a series of dates with Millie Small and Jackie Edwards, had to be cancelled. Toots, wearing his prison identity tag like a badge of pride, has always maintained he was framed. As previously mentioned (in Chapter Three) he wrote '54-46 Was My Number' on his release – a song he would record three times and which became one of his biggest hits.

The Maytals recommenced voicing for Leslie Kong's Beverley label after Toots' release and promptly made history with 'Do The Reggay', since this was the first song to mention the word "reggae" in its title. Kong ran an ice cream parlour cum record shop on Orange Street and had been the first to record Bob Marley. 'Judge Not' and 'One Cup Of Coffee' resulted from those sessions but sank without trace. Fortunately, Kong's reputation for picking hit songs improved considerably. During the late Sixties, he produced some fabulous records by Jimmy Cliff, the Pioneers, the Melodians, and Desmond Dekker.

Kong's track record with the Maytals was just as notable, even though Toots and his group couldn't emulate the same kind of crossover success as some of the producer's other acts. 'Monkey Man' would graze the lower reaches of the Top 50 during the summer of 1970, but it wasn't until after their barnstorming appearance in Perry Henzel's 1972 film, *The Harder They Come*, that songs like 'Pressure Drop' and 'Sweet And Dandy' began to win Toots & the Maytals an audience outside of Jamaica.

"I only played the two songs with Toots, 'Pressure Drop' and 'Sweet And Dandy' and they end up being among Toots' best-loved classics," chortles Fams. "Jackie Jackson, Hux Brown and them man do the regular stuff with Toots, but I do two of his biggest hits! It came like a blessing, because they just send for me to do this session and I am the only amateur when I get there. The only beginner is the bassist who anchors the whole thing, but that session was well done for sure. Federal was run by the

Khouris at the time, but that was a Beverley's session, run by Leslie Kong. Ranny Bop played rhythm guitar, whilst Hux Brown and Lynn Taitt shared lead guitar between them. Most of Beverley's tracks had Lynn Taitt on lead and Hux Brown on rhythm guitar, 'cause Ranny Bop was at Treasure Isle more times. He did one or two outside sessions though and got a beating from Duke Reid when 'im start to come out too! Yeah man, him get slap!"

Reid may have had a propensity for bullying but his slightly built, Chinese Jamaican rival couldn't have been more different. Desmond Dekker had such respect for Kong, he recorded for no one else until after Kong's death of a heart attack in 1971, claiming him to be Jamaica's best-ever producer.

"He had a very good ear for music because if he heard a song and said it was going to be a hit, then it usually turned out that way," says Dekker. "And whilst you may give him ten songs and he liked them all, he'd only ever choose one at a time for release as a single. He'll say, 'I like that one,' and from there it's like you can bet on it, because it was like a racehorse that always come out the winner. But one of the main reasons I used to enjoy working with him is because there wasn't any pressure. He just let me get on with it, and when I've got music, then we'd just go into the studio and do it. Leslie Kong have a record shop which had lots of space so we could rehearse, and there was a piano in it too, which meant the artists could sit there and write their songs, and we'd all practise there before going on to the studio, which was usually Byron Lee's studio, Dynamic, or this other one called Federal.

"The way he do it, it's like he don't use a particular band, but take one or two musicians from the Upsetters and then one from the Skatalites. He'd do it like that because everyone wanted to create their own sound and come up with something a little bit different from the rest. That is one of the things that make the music of that time last so long. If you get to use just the one band, then there's a possibility that you're going to get the same sound as some other person, although when you mix it, then you can come up with something unique and of course that makes it more inter-esting too. Well that's the way Leslie Kong and some of those other producers cut it back then."

"Leslie Kong was a great person," agrees Toots. "I never get to know him so well because he died from such a young age, but he gave me the most money in those days, which was about three pounds, and that was to split between the three of us. That was good compared to some of these other people, who wanted to give me 10 shillings! But yeah, Leslie Kong always knew when a song sounded good. He'd tell you what he liked after you'd auditioned for him, and he was a professional guy in how he dealt with you.

"Jimmy Cliff and Derrick Morgan sang for him a long time before us and they turned me down when I first went there. They didn't like my voice, because they said it sounded funny, but when I went back the next day, Leslie listened to me and also this guy named Winston Wright, who played the organ. We used to call him "Winnie". He was the one who took the audition and he liked my songs, because he recognised they had spirit and I used cultural words, righteous words. Words that told a story and that had a true meaning for anyone, because I would write about things that happened and also what I'd read in the Bible.

"That's what I was doing in songs like 'Pressure Drop', which is talking about how pressure is going to drop on the wicked, because from they hurt innocent people, then pressure is going to drop on them hard, man. When we wrote that song, Raleigh, Jerry and myself had fallen victim to some bad people who had promised us money we needed for our survival and yet they didn't pay us anything at all. That's why we decided to write a song about them. I won't call any names, but it was the man we record for before Leslie Kong and up until today, we don't see anything from them."

Artists such as Willie Nelson, Robert Palmer, the Clash, and the Specials have since covered 'Pressure Drop', while 'Sweet And Dandy' became the title track of an album released on Beverley's in 1969 and also won the Jamaican Song Festival that year. Family Man laughs when he talks of "controlling" this particular Festival and with good reason, since he also played on the two songs that came second and third – namely the Jamaicans' 'Festival Spirit' and Pat Kelly's 'Festival Time'.

"We had four other big hits that year. As Upsetters, we had 'Return Of Django', we had Max Romeo's 'Wet Dream', and 'Doctor No Go' as Hippy Boys and then we were supposed to go on tour behind 'Liquidator' as well, because all of them became popular in England at the same time."

'Liquidator' will be immediately familiar to many football fans in the UK, since it's often played during half-time intermission at league games up and down the country. A simple guitar phrase first draws the listener into this infectious instrumental. A virtuoso organ performance from Winston Wright that blends long, drawn-out melodies with Jimmy Smith-style, stabbing riffs, then does the rest, together with a pulsating rhythm section that never lets up for an instant but is yet somehow wonderfully understated at the same time. 'Liquidator' was a feel-good track on a par with anything that came out of Britain or America during the same era. The Staples Singers clearly thought so and their adaptation, 'I'll Take You There', which became a US number one in 1972, uses a near identical arrangement to that laid down by the Hippy Boys at Randy's. The song, crafted at the Stax studios in Memphis, included a new set of lyrics from Alvertis Isbell, a wailing harmonica, Pop Staples' tasteful guitar-picking, and a powerhouse vocal display from his daughter Mavis, one of America's finest soul singers.

While he's proud of them appreciating his music, Family Man remains a little dismayed at how the band members were denied a share of the proceeds.

"Yeah, the Staples Singers ended up copying 'Liquidator' and made enough money off it, but nobody seemed to know anything about the circumstances," he says, somewhat ruefully. "I even heard that Alton made a claim for it too, 'cause 'im say it come off his riddim for 'Girl I've Got A Date'. His was a different concept though, because although our one starts off like that, it then changes completely, plus we have a different intro. Alton's right in one sense because we get the idea from it at first, but then we make it our own."

Alton Ellis: "No, but 'Liquidator' is 'Girl I've Got A Date' because mine was recorded much earlier and it come in the beginning of version now, when them start to cover people's songs. The Staples Singers' 'I'll Take You There' came from 'Liquidator' as well and any time you have the opportunity to play those two songs together, you can tell it's a complete copy! The intro is identical, and I'm told that Mavis Staples was in Jamaica when she first heard 'Liquidator' and that's where she got the vibes. Her musicians say they wouldn't change it completely, because it might throw her off, so they start to copy it directly from the introduction and the only thing they change is that running note to make it funkier, but both those songs came from 'Girl I've Got A Date' originally. The Staples Singers paid [producer] Harry J Johnson for it and that's how come he was able to buy all these things in Jamaica, like a hotel and a studio and yet up until today Harry J don't know anything about music and isn't musically inclined at all."

"Harry J was just a man who sold insurance and then he decide to get involved with the music scene," says Fams. "And he got lucky too, cah 'im get a hit with Bob & Marcia's 'Young, Gifted And Black' and the next thing 'im get now is 'Liquidator' and from there 'im build a studio. It wasn't his song though. It was a track called 'What Am I Do' by this little brethren named Tony Scott but 'im couldn't handle it, so he pass it over to

Harry J and sign this contract. I say to him, 'You 'ave a copy of it for yourself?' 'Im say no, so I say, 'You sell the man everyt'ing, and don't even have a copy for yourself?' Because he sold Harry J the master tape and all his rights along with it, so we decide to record it over fi 'im after we come back from tour. We finish it up fi 'im still; use the same organ sample on it and then put in another drum so 'im have his own cut. But the original 'Liquidator', that was programmed at Randy's, 'cause they have an organ there, but it a little foo foo organ, so Glen Adams struggle with it at first. It was the engineer Errol Thompson, who they call "ET" who found the right tone fi it eventually, and it sound like the best we 'ave, so that's the one we used."

Adams pays tribute to Winston Wright's organ playing on 'Liquidator' but claims the original singer of 'What Am I To Do' wasn't Tony Scott, who was the producer, but guitarist Noel "Sowell" Bailey, who later joined the Youth Professionals and Roots Radics. "Foo foo" or not, Adams would play Randy's out-of-tune Hammond B3 – which Carly christened "the creep organ" – on a number of hits for Bunny Lee and Lee Perry over the coming months, including the mesmerising 'John Crow Skank'. Vincent Chin and his wife Pat, who owned Randy's record store on North Parade, had originally built the upstairs studio for their own use but such was the demand for recording facilities, they began hiring it out in the spring of 1968. They christened it Studio 17, since the premises were situated at 17 North Parade, right in the heart of downtown Kingston's commercial district. 'Liquidator' was one of the first major hits to be recorded there and while artists and musicians may grumble about his credentials, it was Johnson's entrepreneurial skills that helped it on its way.

After buying the rights from Tony Scott, Johnson licensed the track to Trojan and credited it to the Harry J All-Stars. With the success of 'Return Of Django' in mind, he commissioned sax player Val Bennett to blow on a version called 'Tons Of Gold', but the Hippy Boys' instrumental cut, 'Liquidator' generated most response. After travelling to England with it, Johnson persuaded deejay Tony Blackburn to play the track on Radio One, which enjoyed a monopoly among British stations at the time, and was therefore hugely influential in determining record sales. 'Liquidator' duly spent five months on the UK charts during the autumn of 1969, peaking at number nine that October.* Trojan awarded Harry J a distribution deal and

---

* Liquidator' has been reissued numerous times since. Thanks to a live cover version by the Specials, it even scaled the UK charts for a second time in March 1980.

his own label the following year. The deserved success of the Staples Singers' 'I'll Take You There' also gained Johnson sufficient money to open his own studio in Kingston, where Island acts like the Wailers and Toots & the Maytals would record extensively throughout the Seventies.

The Hippy Boys' other major success of 1969, depending on who you talk to, was 'Return Of Django', which some band members say was recorded for Lee Perry as the Upsetters, while other sources credit the Gladdy All-Stars. A catchy instrumental, highlighted by Bennett's strident tenor sax, the single stayed on the British charts for 15 weeks, peaking at five during October.

It's no accident Scratch named his most celebrated instrumental 'Return Of Django'. As Max Romeo has already pointed out, Perry and his friends were keen moviegoers and Django was his favourite character. That's because Django was a rude boy and would always triumph over whatever bad deal had been dished out to him. It's easy to see how Scratch could imagine himself as a Django-type figure; wronged by more powerful figures in the local music industry and yet tough enough to turn the tables on them. The sheer force of his personality – allied to all that creative energy – provided the drive and determination to succeed. All Scratch needed were the musicians to make his vision a reality, who were adaptable enough to try out new ideas and could keep pace with his inventive outpourings. The funny thing was Perry only recruited the Hippy Boys because he could no longer afford bigger name musicians. Since he didn't exactly have an impressive track record at that stage, even a relatively inexperienced band wasn't in a hurry to record for Scratch.

"He was broke, and so had to ask Family Man and his brother to accommodate him, but though Clancy Eccles was too boasty, he stayed with those other guys, like Jackie Jackson and them, and him flop out in the end," says Bunny Lee, laughing at the expense of an old rival. "Yeah, but Scratch couldn't afford them and that's how come he start to use my guys now, because when I had some studio time, I would work first and then Scratch work after. That's how come we end up with the same set of tunes, but I would have to talk to Fams on his behalf sometimes, because Fams would say, 'Bwoy, Scratch nah have no money.' That's why he and Carly stick with Miss Pottinger for a while, because them start finding hits for her and those big-name musicians couldn't find any. That's how come the Hippy Boys play on so many hits to come out of Jamaica during that time, because they had this natural ear for music and would do things spontaneously.

"Glen Adams, he played good organ, but the most important man in the group was Family Man. He's brilliant! He doesn't like to show off, but he can play nearly every damn thing in the music. Lee Perry and I, we called him "the Butcher", because he's such a great bass player. Family Man plays keyboards good too though, because you'd think it was Jackie Mittoo playing sometimes. He's very versatile, because he plays guitar, piano, organ, and every darned thing.

"But 'Return Of Django' is actually my tune, because it was originally a vocal called 'Oh Babe' we recorded at Coxsone's studio one time. I still have a cut of it for myself, but Lee Perry and I used to work together in those days and share the same sessions and so whatever tapes him have, I have them too. But it was me who start off those musicians called Upsetters and I give him some hit rhythms as well, because Perry got plenty of things from me and then Pama release them in England."

The vocal side Bunny is referring to is Neville Grant's cover of Fats Domino's 'Sick And Tired' and there's more than a touch of New Orleans in the Jamaican version. The original, recorded at a time when rock and roll had taken over from rhythm and blues, was played at a much faster tempo than the funky, strutting 'Return Of Django', which has a rhythm cut so loose, it's almost anarchic. Whether they played on it or not, it's this kind of spontaneous, youthful creativity that distinguished the Hippy Boys' playing from the more conventional approach of Tommy McCook's musicians, many of whom were schooled in musical theory. The immaculate arrangements of many Treasure Isle productions bear this out and while such skills didn't rule out the possibility of finding (and keeping) a good groove, these musicians' temperaments wouldn't have necessarily proved all that compatible with Perry's more restless flights of fancy – or at least not on a regular basis.

This is borne out by what Bunny says when questioned as to why the new look Upsetters were branded "wrong chord musicians" by some of the more established names on the local circuit. "Ranny Bop and Winston Wright, who played on most of Duke Reid's tunes, they would argue how Treasure Isle music had more chords in it than say Coxsone's. Duke Reid's music, it would have all these diminished chords and sevenths and that meant other musicians had trouble finding the right notes sometimes. Well, the Hippy Boys didn't study music like that, but Family Man has played some of the greatest bass lines inna reggae music up until now and yet him couldn't read or write music at the time. That's why these other guys used to call him and Carly my "wrong chord musicians," because they couldn't compete with say Peter Ashburn, or some of these other musicians who were amongst Byron Lee. All those uptown youths came from university and were music graduates, y'know? But they didn't have the vibes, and reggae music is all about that."

Reggae is not too dissimilar to blues in this respect, since it is feel, rather than technical expertise, that defines the best blues music. Bunny Lee and Lee Perry both knew this, despite their radically different outlook and requirements. Bunny may not have been a musician himself but he recognised raw talent when he heard it and knew what the record-buying public wanted, whereas Perry would work with the Barrett brothers for a relatively brief period but inspire them to heights they could never have imagined while practising on the veranda of their parents' home in Van Street. Unselfish and gregarious as ever, Bunny recommended the pair to other producers whenever the opportunity for extra sessions arose and never stopped championing them, even when more established musicians attempted to fight them down.

"There was a time when I'd take Family Man over to Treasure Isle on a Sunday morning so he could record tracks like 'Lockjaw'," says Bunny. "I'd say, 'Duke, you have to give my little wrong chord musicians some work, y'know?' Duke Reid got Fams and Carly to make some funky, funky reggae tunes around that time. That's when Treasure Isle start to change direction and mix up its sound a little."

'Lockjaw' is a Hippy Boys recording by rights, although Lewis and Adams' contributions are barely distinguishable since the rhythm is little more than stripped down, raw funk, led by Family Man's pirouetting bass lines. It sounded nothing like the more sophisticated, rocksteady tracks McCook had orchestrated for Duke Reid a few years earlier that had brought an almost classical dimension to Jamaican pop music. With the advent of 'Lockjaw', the existing order was about to change. "From coast to coast, the sound of now, Lockjaw!" announces Dave Barker, who would soon continue this theme on 'Shocks Of Mighty', lending growing impetus to the craze for deejay records as he urges the musicians on with yelps and exhortations even James Brown could feel proud of.

Other tracks recorded for Reid around the same time, like 'Nightfall' and 'Bang Bang', combine the sound of jaunty Hippy Boys' organ instrumentals with the cultured horns normally associated with Treasure Isle productions, as if McCook was at least trying to meet this group of funky upstarts halfway. Not so on a chugging 'Psychedelic Reggae', splattered with fuzz box guitar, that's even wilder than the Lloyd Charmers' track of the same name.

One of Family Man's initial sessions for Reid resulted in a cover of Andy Kim's 'Baby I Love You' by Alton Ellis in early 1970, just a few months after the original appeared in the US charts. Fams also backed the Sensations on one of their best-known Treasure Isle recordings, 'Every Day Is Like A Holiday', during this period. As was the case with a lot of Jamaican vocal groups, the Sensations' line-up is best described as fluid, since individual singers would come and go, depending on whatever opportunities presented themselves elsewhere. Jimmy Riley, Cornel Campbell, Winston Riley's brother Buster, and Aaron "Bobby" Davis, (whose nickname was Deeper Sensation) were all members of the Sensations at the outset. The Techniques had introduced them to Duke Reid but when the Techniques broke up, Jimmy Riley left to join Slim Smith and Lloyd Charmers in the Uniques, leaving Cornel Campbell and the others to form the Eternals. By the time Fams played bass and guitar on their recordings for Winston Riley in the early Seventies, Jackie Parrish had replaced Jimmy Riley and Cornel Campbell, who both pursued solo careers.

Up until Duke Reid's death in 1974, Family Man would continue to play the occasional session for Treasure Isle, partnering up with Lloyd Knibs, the drummer from the Skatalites, on occasion. Carly also guested with some of Reid's musicians from time to time and even toured on cruise ships around the Caribbean with Tommy McCook and the Supersonics once or twice. Some 40 years later, Family Man has fond memories of Reid, who he describes as a fair man, despite the unscrupulous business practices of the time.

Family Man Barrett: "I can picture of him sitting there outside of his liquor store wearing this big sombrero with a gold star on it, because he was like some ex-sheriff in Jamaica during the early Fifties and still wore that badge. He'd have this big old 45 in his lap and a shotgun in a wrap, leaning against his chair. I'd pass by him and say, 'Alright Mr Reid?' And he'd just growl somet'ing. Some people were a little frightened of him, because when the man feels nice 'im lick shot; ping! And if you take too long pon a tune, you hear the man fire off shots from downstairs and then come up and start talking, me a tell you!"

While typically generous in his assessment of Reid, Alton Ellis doesn't share Fams' opinion, despite his love of Reid's studio and the sounds created there.

Alton Ellis: "Duke Reid was mainly thinking about the financial side and the contents of the music weren't too much of a bother to him.

Having hits just meant more money to him and he wasn't a social person like Coxsone was. Coxsone would come round to my house at night time when we sit down, 'cause it's my kitchen in Trenchtown where we usually rehearse and every artist in Jamaica used to visit there. I was the leading artist at the time and everybody would come there to get the vibes, even Coxsone, 'cause he used to pass through when he's finished work and leave us some money so we could start to cook, buy some herb and t'ing. That's because he knew everything we're doing there is going to come back to him in a day or two, y'know? It was a whole heap of singing and t'ing that we were going on with, but Duke wasn't like that.

"Duke was just into business with his monkey face, two guns and all them things there. Yeah, he wasn't a nice person, but Coxsone was, and that's why he got away with some of the things he did, because if we were keeping a dance or something like that, Coxsone would turn up and when Coxsone himself keep a dance, well then you'd see him socialising and enjoying the music. He wouldn't just be at the gate collecting the money, or in the bar, nothing like that. He was there amongst the guys them and with someone like Roland Alphonso beside him, 'cause at that time Roland was his close friend. Duke Reid shot two men in the back when he was a policeman and he told me that himself. That's why he always had those guns hanging off him, for protection. Coxsone didn't need to carry a gun in those times, but Duke Reid wear two guns on him side and have a rifle in his office, leaning against the wall. Even with all of that now, one day a drunken man just walk up to him, shove a gun in 'im chest and then take his guns off him. The guy was so drunk he just stood there until the police arrived, so it turned out silly in the end, but that all happen because of him killing those two people before, or at least that's what we all put it down to . . ."

If Reid had only been interested in money, it's doubtful he would have allowed Family Man and the other Hippy Boys to experiment in the way they did.

Family Man Barrett: "The first time he called me in for a session I got there early and saw Gladstone Anderson upstairs, 'cause he was always there for the auditions. I ask him what's happening and he said Duke had left to make a phone call and two other bass players were there also. One of them was Albert Griffiths from the Gladiators, 'cause him played a little guitar and can pick two bass lines, plus he's a singer too. Then after a while the great Tommy McCook come in and say, 'Has the bass player turned up?' And the man tells him they have three. Tommy says, 'Well let's test them and just use the better one.' So Gladdy say, 'Fams, come,' but Tommy look at me and say 'Who is him?' Gladdy say to him, 'You say you want the better one, so I call the man.' Tommy now, him don't know me and says he's never heard of me, so from me hear that, I just unplug my bass, put it back in its case, hook it over my shoulder and say to him, 'Listen man. I don't come here for any competition. I come here to work, but through you have two other bass players already, I'll just leave.'

"Me step to the door now, but here comes Duke Reid himself with Boris Gardner, who's a more professional bass player than me and him can sing also. I tell Duke Reid that I'm leaving, seeing as they have two other bass players there and one of them more professional than me, but him say not to leave, because he wants me to see what goes on. I tell him okay, take a seat, lean on my guitar and watch the session, because I don't mind learning one or two tricks too. Yeah, so I stay up there and watch as they lay about three tracks, then just take up my guitar, go downstairs and as I'm leaving Duke call me over to the cashier's corner and pay me just to sit down there for my time. Him says he wants me to come back next week Saturday at 10 o'clock and when I return there, Tommy McCook has arrived from early, so I sit in the corner as 'im blow his bugle and 'im flute. Him looking at me over the top of his dark glasses like him a wonder what I'm going to perform today and what's so special about me, y'know? He's introducing me to the other musicians now before the session's about to start, and then Duke himself comes in. I had my Hofner violin bass with me that I got from London through Dave Betteridge, from the original Trojan time with the Upsetters, 'cause we look for some equipment like the Beatles.

"When I straighten up now, Duke Reid say, 'No, use the studio bass,' 'cause him have this heavy duty Fender Jazz with some big string like curtain rod on it, so I put down mine and take up his instead. I lick it nice though, me a tell you! Him have some sound-system box to play it through too, 'cause this was in the days of mic bass and it sound nice and then Alton Ellis, he sing the song that goes like this 'Oh wee baby. Baby I love you.' It was a successful session! It was Rannie Bop playing rhythm with us that day and Hux Brown playing lead. We had Gladstone on piano and then Aubrey Adams on the organ, 'cause him play on enough of those Treasure Isle tunes and most of them were hits too. Tommy McCook, he was pleased, but him still want to know where I come from so I tell him I play on 'Watch This Sound' and he was well impressed, 'cause him think it was Jackie Jackson who play on it. But that band really did swing with the t'ing man! And that get them hip to me, because I start to get a lot of sessions after that and I usually go for Tommy McCook whenever we need horns on other sessions as well."

Before leaving Coxsone and forming the Supersonics, McCook backed the Wailers on many of their Studio One recordings.* Family Man got to know McCook a little better through keyboard player Earl "Wya" Lindo, who'd invite him and Reggie Lewis behind the scenes whenever JBC were filming a weekly music programme called *Where It's At*.

"Whenever you wanted to plug a tune, you had to get it on *Where It's At*," recalls Bunny Lee. "It was broadcast every Saturday around five or six o'clock. We used to get singers like Slim Smith on it with their new tunes and they used to have a jazz programme too. Everybody get a chance to showcase what they can do, but sometimes an act would play for two or three weeks straight if they had a big enough hit. It was something like that programme they had in England called *Ready, Steady, Go!* because it meant we could take the music to the uptown people. Television was only just coming in at the time, because it was still in black and white, and then we'd have *Teenage Dance Party*, which was on JBC radio and we used to vote for the songs we wanted to get power play for the week. Every week, the winning song got played at least four times, so it automatically became a hit. A guy called Desmond Elliot was in charge of that programme and then later on you had this other guy called Phanso Walker, who came with this television show called *Young World*. Bob Marley was just an ordinary guy in those times, and he couldn't even get his foot through the front door, much less get radio play."

Tommy McCook & the Supersonics would regularly back performers on *Where It's At* and Family Man took great pride in helping to set up the equipment, while taking in the atmosphere backstage. Recording with McCook and members of the Supersonics at Treasure Isle, home to some of Jamaica's finest ever rocksteady music, represented a real badge of honour to the young, amateur bass player. Having said that, Bunny Lee bought a lot of studio time from Reid and he was useful in other ways too. Having started out as a record plugger, Lee knew people on the panel of judges who would select hits for the local radio stations and he would flood these stations with calls requesting certain songs to ensure maximum

---

* This connection would last right throughout the Seventies, since McCook would also play on some of Bunny Livingston's solo projects, in addition to well-known tracks by the later edition of Bob Marley & the Wailers.

airplay. Having Lee on your side was clearly a good thing and it was because of his support that the Hippy Boys were able to make the progress they did.

Another early supporter was Lloyd Daley, who owned a label called Matador. In the liner notes of the Jamaica Gold album, *From Matador's Arena*, Daley recalls that the first time he heard the word "reggae" was when Hux Brown told Lewis, "You must learn to play music man, you and this little reggae-jeggae beat you have." Daley goes on to say that, "It was like a buck-up (accident). The musicians didn't know what they actually made. They were just experimenting with different types of beats."

The Hippy Boys started working for Daley in late 1968, when they laid down the rhythm for the Scorchers' 'Ugly Man', which sold a reputed 50,000 copies in Jamaica and put Daley's label on the map as he made the transition from soundman to record producer. He had earned the name Matador during his sound-system battles with the likes of Duke Reid, Coxsone, and King Edwards in the ska era, but began to despair of the violence attached to the dancehall scene and defrayed the costs of setting up his own label by working as an electrician and also building sound-systems. In 1967, Daley married Deanna, the daughter of bandleader Eric Dean, and based his operations from a two-storey building at 43 Waltham Park Road. There was a radio and television repair shop at the front, an upstairs beauty parlour run by Deanna and a club called the House of Fame to the side. As well as a beautician, Deanna was a singer and had sung in a duo with Lloyd Robinson as Lloyd & Joy.

By the end of '68, Daley had produced songs with the Caribbeans, the Coasters, the Hamlins, the Paragons, the Uniques, Winston Samuel, and the Viceroys, as well as the aforesaid Scorchers. Horn players Johnny "Dizzy" Moore, Karl "Cannonball" Bryan and Vin Gordon also recorded for Daley around this time, as did organist Jackie Mittoo, who'd been riding high with 'Evening Time' and 'Ram Jam' when he cut 'Dark Side Of The Sun' that June. Just over a year later, a fresh set of faces passed the auditions held at Matador's rehearsal place on Waltham Park Road, including U Roy, a revised line-up of the Emotions, and the Wailing Souls, who recorded just one track, 'Gold Digger', for the young producer. Not so lucky were the Wailers, who Lloyd's wife Deanna considered "too ghetto". This was in the autumn of 1969, before the trio began work on their Beverley's album.

"Matador's shop had this little room to the side with a piano and a fridge in it," says Fams. "Him had a little saloon too, like Scratch, but we used to rehearse there, in that room. We'd meet up with the artists them and the piano man and the guitarist would work out the song between them. We just burn two spliff; get feeling nice and then we'd be ready to leave for the studio, because in them days, everything happened quickly and there's no time to waste."

If any of the artists needed assistance, more practised musicians like Hux Brown or Gladstone Anderson would help out with lyrics and arrangements, since the Barrett brothers were still relatively inexperienced themselves. Once the sessions were over, Daley would then pay everybody after supplying them with food and drink and checking the engineer had everything on tape. Graeme Goodall, who'd left Jamaica for England in 1965, was a close friend of Daley's and began licensing various titles to Pama once his operation gathered momentum. Matador's productions subsequently appeared on many different UK labels, including Doctor Bird, Green Door, Explosion, Duke, Bullet, Camel, Crab, Escort, Gas, Pama, Punch, and Supreme.

It's been said that Boris Gardiner wrote the music for Little Roy's 'Bongo Nyah', as well as playing the piano on the intro, although it's Carly and Family Man playing the rhythm and Anderson who acted as musical director.

Little Roy: "I used to just sing my songs in those days. My songs were never rehearsed or nothing and I never even used to write them down. It's like I just know them, but I'd go to the studio and Gladstone Anderson, who we call Gladdy, he'd catch the chords and then decide what key it's in. He'd start playing his piano and then the other musicians just join in until the rhythm for the song is there. Gladdy would lead them on most of the songs I do for Matador, then we go down to Dynamic, which used to be called Federal, to record them.

"Gladdy was just a musician though. He wasn't the producer, because Matador did a lot of work in the studio, being around the engineer, producing the sound he wants and determining how he wants the rhythm to sound. What he did was very important, because lots of other songs were made in that same studio and yet the reason they all sound different is because of the man directing them. If you notice Matador's songs, they have a very distinctive sound, so that's him, right there."

Earl "Little Roy" Lowe grew up in nearby Whitfield Town. He'd cut his first tune, 'Cool It', for Coxsone in 1965 at the age of 12 before recording two further singles with Prince Buster (who named him Little

Roy) in an unsuccessful bid to become a child star. Four years later, Little Roy joined Daley's camp and would remain there for the next two years while studying to be an engineer at St Andrew's Technical High School.

"My school was on the Spanish Town Road and most evenings I would walk the five, six miles to Washington Gardens where I lived and have to pass right near Matador's shop on Chisholm Avenue, by the No. 3 bus stop. There was this friend I used to walk home from school with called Ewan Gardiner and we'd sing a verse or two from 'Bongo Nyah' together, in those early days."

Deanna helped Little Roy work these lyrics into a fully fledged song. Recorded during the same session as the Hippy Boys' 'Zylon', 'Bongo Nyah' became Little Roy's first-ever hit, after it flew to the top of the Jamaican charts in late 1969. Several other artists covered it and Daley himself recorded a cut by Rasta drummer Count Ossie, called 'I Dread Version'. This was the same Count Ossie who'd founded the Mystic Revelation of Rastafari and become one of the first Rastas to enter a recording studio in Jamaica after playing on the Folkes Brothers' 'Oh Carolina' for Prince Buster.

Little Roy says the local radio stations usually refused to play Rasta songs, although they made an exception in his case. "Yes, because you have certain Rasta songs that everyone can hold onto, and that aren't offensive to people," he explains. "'Bongo Nyah' was my first number one and it was classed as a Rasta song, yet the lyrics come across more like humour than a judgement, y'know? Because people who eat pork would play it the most and they'd be punching that song on the jukeboxes in these bars, taking that line, 'One for the pork eater,' for a joke! But when I was singing for Matador, it was the first time I take up Rasta now and he would say to me, 'Why you talk about Selassie and all them things there? Because I know you come from a decent family, and the Rastas are some dutty set of people.' That is how people like him used to talk, and me live to see artists from them times who used to say them is Rasta trim back their dreadlocks, and go back in the church, so that just show you the different stages certain individuals go through.

"But I was around Rastas from when I was about 14 and living in Washington Gardens. I'd come in from school and we'd lick some chalice and t'ing, 'cause we used to have nuff Rass reasonings and vibes, except I never embrace His Majesty just yet, not until 1970. There wasn't a conflict about that and they never pressure me, but I was always saying Rastafari from those times."

The most spiritual Rastafarian music of all was sung by the Abyssinians, who'd already recorded 'Satta Massagana' by the time they were ready to voice 'Yim Mas Gin'. 'Satta Massagana' was only available in strictly limited quantities and had yet to be recognised for the enduring, roots classic it would become. In Amharic, the phrase "Satta Massagana" is used when giving thanks to an equal, while "Yim Mas Gan," is more appropriate when thanking God. Accompanying Bernard Collins in the Abyssinians were Donald and Linford Manning. Their other brother, Carlton, led a group called the Shoes, who recorded for Coxsone, while Estifanos was a priest with the Ethiopian Orthodox Church in Jamaica and would officiate at the burials of Bob Marley, Peter Tosh, and Jacob Miller. Whereas Little Roy's 'Bongo Nyah' is almost whimsical, the sound given 'Yim Mas Gin' is deep as the Rio Cobre with its blazing horns, swirling organ riffs (played by Wya Lindo) and relentless rhythmic pulse. Above this backdrop, soar three majestic voices promising, "If we can't be good, then we'll be careful and do the best we can."

It was spine-tingling in its intensity and profoundly reverential. The release of these two records heralded the birth of the roots reggae era, and it's no accident Family Man would later play on cuts of both. Ironically, the Abyssinians had wanted to voice 'Yim Mas Gin' for Lee Perry, but settled for recording it with Matador instead, so long as they could work with the same musicians. With hindsight, this was an inspired choice, although Scratch would soon have glories of his own to consider, as he too, responded to the Hippy Boys' calling.

CHAPTER FIVE

Upsettin'

L EE Perry used Family Man and other members of the Hippy Boys on the majority of his recordings throughout 1969 to 1970, when his reputation as a musical maverick began to crystallise. Measuring barely five feet tall, the diminutive Perry had arrived in Kingston from Trelawny, on Jamaica's north coast. Coxsone Dodd taught Perry the ropes of the music business, while employing him as a singer, sound-system operator and A&R man during the early to mid-Sixties. Coxsone had a record shop on Orange Street when Perry first knew him, although he'd later establish his own facilities on Brentford Road, which he named Studio One.

'Prince In The Back', a stinging blow aimed at Prince Buster, heralded Perry's debut as a vocalist in 1963. His recordings were idiosyncratic to say the least, and delivered more in jest than with any serious expectations of them being appreciated for their musical qualities. Perry couldn't sing especially well for one thing, although there was a razor-sharp sense of humour at work and he did have a keen ear for what the local audience liked. It was therefore hardly surprising he should have most success with dance-orientated novelty sides like 'Chicken Scratch' (from where he got the name Scratch) or ribald material such as 'Roast Duck' and 'Pussy Galore'. The Wailers sang harmonies on the latter and Rita's group the Soulettes also shared the occasional session with Perry prior to them all leaving Coxsone in 1966.

All struggled to make their mark for a time. The Wailers made a few records with Rastafarian elder Mortimer Planno and also attempted to go it alone before recording an album for Beverley's, while Perry based himself at WIRL, but then went back to Coxsone once WIRL sacked him. He also crossed paths with Clancy Eccles, Prince Buster (who'd obviously forgiven him for 'Prince In The Back'), and J. J. Johnson, for whom he voiced the acrimonious 'Run For Cover', aimed at Coxsone. Such vengeful attrition would become something of a hallmark for the pint-sized Perry, who was certainly fearless, even if he didn't always necessarily pick the right targets. Perry then began producing hits for Joe Gibbs' new Amalgamated label, such as the Pioneers' 'Long Shot Kick The Bucket' and his own 'I Am The Upsetter', which was yet another attack on Coxsone. Gibbs had received help from Bunny Lee and Roy Shirley in setting up Amalgamated and got off to a flying start with songs from Shirley, Tyrone Taylor, the Versatiles, Derrick Morgan, and Errol Dunkley. Also the Soul Mates, whose 'Them A Laugh And A Ki Ki' was pressed back-to-back with an early Hippy Boys side called 'The Hippies Are Here'.

Perry left Amalgamated in 1968 and the circumstances were again rancorous, since he would make the scathing 'People Funny Boy' about Gibbs shortly afterwards – a record that borrowed the melody from the Pioneers' 'Long Shot' and used the sound of a bawling infant to express his unhappiness towards yet another former employer. Perry certainly had a sense of humour, but he was also vindictive, with a healthy dose of paranoia thrown in for good measure. His talent for producing hit records couldn't be disputed, however, because 'People Funny Boy' reputedly sold 60,000 copies in Jamaica and left both of Gibbs' answer versions, 'People Grudgeful' and 'Pan Ya Machete', trailing in the popularity stakes.

"WIRL had fired Lee Perry because they said he couldn't give them any hits, and that's why they offered me the job instead," says Bunny. "I told them Lee Perry must stay, but then him go back to Coxsone for a while before trying again fi himself. I get Pama Records in England to order some records from him and he started to produce for himself after that. Then he, Pama, and I start up a thing between us. This was in late 1968.

"But Perry really start off as an engineer for a guy named Barry Lambert and Lynford Anderson was there too. They called their label Upset at first and then Perry broke off and renamed it Upsetter. Well Lynford Anderson, he was upset! The name Upsetters come from Roland Alphonso though, 'cause he had a band called that from a longer time still."

Little Richard's band was originally called the Upsetters and they were regarded as being among the best live rock and roll acts throughout the mid-to-late Fifties. Perry wasn't the only one to have been captivated by Little Richard's brilliance, as Bunny's eyes light up at the mention of such an old favourite. "When I was a child, I used to make a shilling out of lead and go punch the jukebox just to hear Little Richard sing 'Send Me Some Lovin', 'Lucille', and 'Jenny Jenny'," he says excitedly. "He was a crazy man, but we all used to idolise Little Richard when we were teenagers, 'ducking back in the alley' ['Long Tall Sally'] and all that. We used to love the new style he came with, playing the piano like a madman, cocking up his foot on the seat and everything. Then you had a next crazy one called Jerry Lee Lewis with 'Great Balls Of Fire'. We know about those guys in Jamaica from before Elvis Presley, then a little after that Elvis bust wide open."

Little Richard's over-the-top theatricality and his capacity to shock and bedazzle audiences may have influenced Perry's decision to use Richard's old band's name. Also like Richard, Scratch was certainly no stranger to controversy and wasn't averse to burning a few bridges in getting his career off the ground. Around the time he was working with Anderson, Scratch opened the Upsetter Record Shop at 36 Charles Street, on the corner of Beeston Street and Luke Lane. Prince Buster had previously owned the premises, which had a room in the back that could be used for rehearsals. Scratch now had the foundations of a credible business in place and wasted no time in testing the market with a few recordings. Singles by Burt Walters, the Mellotones, David Isaacs and Val Bennett (with a cover of Ben E. King's 'Spanish Harlem'), were first out of the starting gate, together with the Untouchables' 'Tighten Up' – a song that would become synonymous with Trojan in years to come. With help from Bunny Lee, Scratch initially licensed tracks like these to Doctor Bird, as well as Pama Records in the UK.

"Scratch would have his record shop out the front and inside he would have this little bar that we call the Green Door Saloon," Fams recalls. "Scratch was driving one of them Jaguar cars from England at the time and that was green also. Then behind the record shop, we have the rehearsal room. It was once a woodwork shop, but they move out and Lee Perry leased or rented the whole scene, so we just set up the equipment in there and we were always round there, jamming and feeling good. The musical vibe was always there, because you could hire men who can play music, or if you want, there was this little sound-system as well.

"Scratch would keep just the one little man in the storefront, but it was always real lively 'round the back, cah yuh 'ave nuff bad bwoy pass through; nuff Spanglers, Junglists an' everybody. Everybody who passed through, them come in like a soldier!" Fams adds, laughing. "Cah there was a resident policeman who come there and drink juice, but 'im nah bu'n spliff, y'know? 'Im bu'n herb in a pipe and Jah know, them man go a Africa pon training an' bring it back with them. Me sometimes have a taste of it too, cah him would say, 'Come try a draw of African herb, man.' We'd go outside, sit in his jeep and bu'n a spliff and he'd say, 'Hold this fi me' and put this 38 special in my hand. This was around '68, '69, and that was the nicest time, me tell you. They come like the happy days, because rude boys had respect for artists and musicians. The consideration was there, cah them days the don controlled them and if a man were to step out of line, he'd get beaten. You couldn't rob or kill without a cause, like you can today. Everyt'ing have to be accounted for, but it crazy right now. Everybody is loose and even the politician give up on the don man now."

Bob Marley would later adapt Richie Havens' 'Indian Rope Trick' and call it 'African Herbsman' in tribute to this same policeman but Marley wasn't the only one to get inspiration from things happening around Scratch.

"I have to lift my hat to that man Lee Perry," notes Ranny Bop. "The reason being that I didn't even rate him at first, because we see him as someone just coming around and feel say he doesn't know anything. That's how we think about him at first, but then after a while, we realise this man has something to offer that's different from the rest. Because after playing a few songs for him, he say he don't want you next time, no matter how good you are. He wants something else all the while. I remember him saying to me, 'I feel the first thing,' 'cause Hux come up with a great line on his guitar. Scratch was the one who caused him to do that and then he'd want me to do something else entirely. He'd say, 'Ranny Bop. Don't play anything similar; play something different' and that moment right there is where reggae is born. I just hear it and fit something between. Because it was rocksteady and ska before, so I come with this 'chink, chink' style of guitar and that was it, the birth of reggae. But I give Lee Perry the credit for encouraging me to bring something like that out of me and that's why I take my hat off to him."

Coxsone has already claimed that Eric Frater should be recognised as the architect for reggae, and in his book *Bob Marley: Conquering Lion Of Reggae*, Stephen Davis claims the change occurred after Scratch became inspired by music played at the Pocomania church in Trenchtown. Davis also points out that it had been necessary for younger producers like Perry to create something different in the face of competition from more established men such as Coxsone and Reid. Marley was unequivocal about what anchored the new beat and told Rob Bowman, "Jackie Jackson controlled rocksteady, while Family Man controls reggae."

Family Man Barrett: "Lee Perry used to hold sessions with other musicians like Jackie Jackson, Hux Brown, "Gladdy" Anderson, Winston Wright, and Tin Leg before us. Cah we had our little package and we usually play for Bunny Lee except for one and two tunes for Duke Reid. But Scratch, he caught the vibe and said we should do a t'ing, so the first tune we do together was an instrumental. First up, drum and bass, and that's how we started."

In early 1969 Glen Adams visited New York where he heard the Meters for the first time. Their prototype funk was of a different variety to that played by James Brown and Sly & the Family Stone, since it originated in New Orleans and had the more lazy, laidback drawl to prove it. A cover of the Meters' 'Sophisticated Cissy' marked the Hippy Boys' debut for Lee Perry, except he renamed them the Upsetters and retitled the track 'Medical Operation', to fit in with the current doctor craze.

"That track was between Lee Perry and Bunny Lee really," Fams continues. "It was their joint production, because they come with this record and have someone take it to all these different sets of musicians to do it over, but none of them could do it. Scratch say, 'Are you sure you take it to everybody and not even one band in Jamaica can turn it into somet'ing?' The man tells them there's this other band, but though Perry never try us yet, he don't know. He tells Scratch we're some young musicians and he don't really know if we can manage it, but him say, 'Take it to the man them!' All them bring is this 45, and after them play it, me and Ranny Bop take it home and study it. I make him alone study the guitar part, and then me begin to play the bass. I remember saying to him, 'Oh, it just a simple thing. It just a syncopation funk,' and yet everybody get carried away, cah they don't see where the root of it's coming from. Me listen and get the feel, then take it to Glen Adams and him say it's easy, becah two notes and it done. That was 'Medical Operation'."

Perry released 'Medical Operation' on the flipside of the Ravers' 'Badam Bam'. The rhythm of that song formed the basis of 'Live Injection', which Trojan chose as the official follow-up to 'Return Of Django', which didn't prove anywhere near as popular. Tracks like 'Bad Tooth' and 'The Dentist' would further Perry's fascination with medical matters, but the music itself bore no relation to his choice of titles. The Upsetters were too busy to notice in any case as they fired off a succession of rhythms distinguished by lockstep drum and bass, Lewis' choppy guitar riffs and Adams' vocal interjections (as on 'Man From MI5'). Perry's endeavours in overseeing the final mix, as well as financing and organising getting the tracks onto vinyl and into the shops, were tireless, to say the least. Between 1969 and 1970, he would release over 70 singles, the majority of them appearing on UK Upsetter. Singers like Busty Brown, David Isaacs, Dave

Barker, and Winston Jarrett all queued for Perry's favours, as did a host of vocal groups, including the Mellotones, the Inspirations (who also recorded as the Untouchables), the Termites, the Gaylads, the Muskyteers, and the West Indians, with Eric Donaldson on lead vocals.

As well as the catchy instrumentals that made Perry's reputation and brought him most success at the end of the Sixties, when tiring of doctor names, he released records with a horror theme such as 'The Vampire', 'Return Of The Vampire', 'Wolfman', 'Haunted House' and 'Dracula'. Like his rivals, Perry had also been inspired by spaghetti westerns. Sergio Corbucci's film *Django*, with Franco Nero in the lead role, had proved wildly popular in Jamaica, and so too, the Sergio Leone films *A Fistful Of Dollars*, *For A Few Dollars More*, and *The Good, The Bad And The Ugly*, starring Clint Eastwood. 'Django Shoots First', the predecessor to 'Return Of Django', had been released in 1968. Within a matter of months, Harry J had served up Richard Ace's 'Hang 'Em High' and Lloyd Charmers' 'Vengeance'. Clancy Eccles and Derrick Harriott would also make records with spaghetti western themes, but Perry weighed in with a slew of them, including 'Taste Of Killing', 'For A Few Dollars More', 'Dig Your Grave', and 'Clint Eastwood'.

" 'Clint Eastwood' was the first drum and bass really," says Family Man. "That was the first tune we do with that kind of 'Pop A Top' flavouring, because it was something we did to counteract what Clancy Eccles had out at the time, that King Stitt tune, 'Lee Van Cleef'. The one where him say, 'These are the days of war, Eastwood. I am the Ugly One, and if you want me, meet me at the Big Gundown. I am Van Cleef, and you will die.' But we run him down now with the 'Clint Eastwood', and that was the end of 'Lee Van Cleef'. We use that stuttering line, 'Clint Eastwood is tougher than Lee Van Cleef,' and then the drum and bass come in right there."

That the Upsetters had been studying the Meters was clear, yet their own brand of syncopated funk differed greatly from the New Orleans model. The guitar and keyboards are minimal – instead, all the emphasis is on Family Man's walking bass and Carly's percussive beats. Dub had yet to be invented and other reggae instrumentals like 'Return Of Django' and 'Liquidator' still hinged around a virtuoso performance from a sax or organ player. What the Upsetters did on 'Clint Eastwood' was therefore revolutionary, plus it had the added attraction of Perry's taunting on the intro, which brought it bang into line with what was happening on the local scene. While the music was full of invention and humour, what was occurring behind the scenes wasn't as light-hearted, since Perry was neglecting to pay his musicians and rumbles of discontent began to be heard from within the Upsetters' ranks.

Family Man Barrett: "That was the time I was just about to leave my parents' house and try to make it on my own. It wasn't easy, but I hung on in there and moved into this place on Johnson Terrace with Ranny Bop. Scratch, he wasn't paying us properly for sessions and so we had to try and deal with him differently. Because when we did 'Clint Eastwood', we said to him, 'All right, we create some Christmas money now, so make sure we get it.' None of those producers understood the business too well at the time and I'm aware of that, but they must do the right thing now and stop pretending they still don't know."

Perry did give Family Man a Ford Anglia while he was in the Upsetters and Dynamic Sounds bought him a Ford Cortina for playing on two albums' worth of material for them, including a Toots & the Maytals' cover of Otis Redding's 'Try A Little Tenderness'. The usual session fee at this time was two pounds, 10 shillings a track, but just as in America, Jamaican producers would often buy artists and musicians cars, in lieu of paying them proper royalties, if they'd contributed towards the writing or arrangements of songs. Over in Chicago, Chess Records had a tradition of buying Muddy Waters a new Cadillac every year, rather than issuing statements or informing him of how much he'd really earned, and several reggae producers adopted a similar policy. Being a keen mechanic, it's hardly surprising that Family Man liked cars and he also invested in a Ford Consul while still with the Upsetters. Bob Marley called this car Fams' "hot rod", which must have been said with a certain degree of wistfulness, since, according to Family Man, Marley "didn't even have a bicycle at this time."

Perry licensed 'Clint Eastwood' to Pama and an album of that name, plus another called *Many Moods Of The Upsetter*, duly appeared in early 1970. This was indeed the era of the 'version' and Scratch recorded several other versions of 'Clint Eastwood'. One hosted Dave Barker's cover of the Coasters' 'Yakety Yak', while another, 'The Tackro', was overdubbed with the producer's own crazy outbursts, sounding as if a madman had entered the studio. In the meantime, Trojan released Perry's debut LP, *The Upsetter*, as a precursor to offering him his own label deal. The album contained little by way of new Upsetters material, since it had originally been scheduled for a summer release, and 'Return Of Django', then riding high in the UK charts, wasn't even on it. Busty Brown and the Muskyteers, who later became known as the Silvertones, provided a smattering of vocal tracks and Perry also included 'Night Doctor' – an instrumental produced not by him, but keyboard player Ansel Collins, featuring personnel from Collins' band the RHT Invincibles.

"The thing with 'Night Doctor'," Perry told Carl Gayle, "is that it started as a series, where I was basing the music on a hospital theme. I planned to write that the night doctor give a live injection and performed a medical operation, but before we could even finish the thing, a lot of people in Jamaica started riding on the idea and making hit records. Tip Top Records (owned by Sonia Pottinger), they came in and spoiled the whole idea, so I said, 'Forget it . . .'"

The Hippy Boys' 'Doctor No Go' thwarted Perry's conception, but since they'd originally recorded it as a vocal track and hadn't given it that title anyway, they were hardly to blame. What's notable about 'Night Doctor' is that it marked the debut of a young drummer called Sly Dunbar, who would become one half of the famous reggae duo, Sly & Robbie. *The Upsetter* album also contains an alternative version of 'Night Doctor' called 'Thunderball', co-starring Val Bennett, who doubled as Perry's chauffeur for a spell. Although credited to the Upsetters, these tracks are better described as tributes to them and shine amid the rather more mundane items on the LP. Typically, there were no musician credits, or any indication that a fresh and exciting young band from Jamaica might be supplying some of the rhythms. The glory was Perry's alone, so it was he who appeared on the sleeve, dressed in a green velvet jacket, flanked by two young girls in mini skirts. His latest Upsetters line-up wouldn't see a copy until they visited England some weeks later, by which time 'Return Of Django', 'Liquidator', and 'Wet Dream' had all peaked and were beginning to fade from the charts.

Family Man Barrett: "We'd heard rumours they were using 'Return Of Django' as some form of commercial and then when people start to hear it, they'd ring the radio station and ask, 'What's that tune? Play it all the way through!' That was before it became a hit, because it took a while to catch on, from what I hear. When it was really bubbling in the chart, that's the time we should have left Jamaica, but that was between Scratch and Pama. Well, Scratch get stabbed in his hand and have to be in the hospital, so we have to wait two months for him to get strong and that hold up the promotion, although it still got to number five. Yeah, so we haffi struggle to get to England from the beginning, but say we have to try."

A radio and television commercial for Cadbury's Fruit & Nut – a popular chocolate bar – helped propel 'Return Of Django' into the charts.

While now a well-established route for making hits out of old songs, in particular, this form of advertising was not so common back in late 1969, when reggae music was still in its infancy. Trojan had to re-release and re-promote 'Return Of Django' when the demand for it began to grow. Perry, meanwhile, was recovering from a serious knife wound inflicted by his "baby mother", Pauline Morrison, who discovered he'd been having an affair with a young singer called Melanie Jonas. It wouldn't be until the end of November that he and the Upsetters finally boarded a plane to London and, true to his reputation, there had been further upsets, once his injuries had healed.

According to Bunny Lee, Perry had wanted to take Tommy McCook's Supersonics with him to England, rather than the musicians he claims actually played on 'Return Of Django': the Hippy Boys.

"When 'Return Of Django' hit now, Perry was wanting to carry some other band and I disagreed with that, so when the promoter, Tony Cousins, come to Jamaica, I insist that he meet the other musicians. I tell him that my guys have to go, because it's them who play the tune. Well Scratch want to come on the trip with his girlfriend and that's why Val Bennett didn't get to come. Val, he got really despondent after that, and ended up driving a hearse before he died. Tony Cousins, he would try to book anybody from Jamaica who went into the British charts and carry them to England for shows. This was before he and Bruce White start work for Trojan, because they did a lot of work for Trojan after that."

Ranny Bop was another member of the Upsetters' inner circle who didn't accompany them on tour as he was playing with the Supersonics at the time. Lloyd "Gitsy" Willis was scheduled to take his place at one point, but Scratch ended up taking Melanie Jonas instead so it was just the basic quartet of Adams, Lewis and the Barrett brothers who went to the UK.

"The Upsetter weren't a band, because Upsetter was just a person and everyone who plays for Upsetter is called by that name," explains Ranny. "We as Tommy McCook's rhythm section always perform on Upsetter's songs before Family Man and Carly join, but then 'Return Of Django' took off in England and they wanted the Upsetters up there. Well, I couldn't go because I was with Tommy, so Upsetter had to get himself another band. It's still Upsetter because that's his name, but it's not the same musicians playing, because apart from myself, Val Bennett and Winston Wright didn't go either."

★   ★   ★

Bruce White and Tony Cousins had a booking agency, Commercial Entertainment, based in Gerrard Street, Soho, in central London, and it was they who organised the Upsetters' and the Pioneers' first UK shows. The latter's 'Long Shot Kick The Bucket' had entered the British charts in early October and demand was high for a vocal trio described in one press report as "the Jamaican Drifters." The Upsetters' appearance was highly anticipated. Aside from their studio work, this was a band that loved to play for a live audience, whether it was backing singers like Carl Dawkins, or going it alone as a four-piece instrumental outfit. After red-hot Kingston performances at the VIP Club in Half Way Tree, the Sombrero on Molynes Road and the Blinking Beacon, at the bottom of Mountain View Avenue, the Upsetters were certainly ready to impress. They even played an open air event in Tivoli Gardens – an area so torn apart by gang and political violence, a musician would have to be well appreciated just to get out in one piece. Clubs like the Green Miss, the Savannah, and the Rainbow all opened their doors to the Upsetters during this period, as well as the Sheraton Hotel in downtown Kingston, where Wendell Martin was in charge of entertainment at the Jonkanoo Lounge.

The Upsetters' British tour began in the north of England, reaching London over a week later with a show at the ABC Cinema in Kensal Rise. The Pioneers, Desmond Dekker, and Max Romeo all shared the bill that night, at an event dubbed 'Reggae Steady Go'. It wasn't especially well attended, maybe because the local Caribbean community were waiting to see the band at smaller venues for less expensive ticket prices. The following day, on December 7, the tour played the Bag O' Nails in Kingly Street, just a stone's throw from Carnaby Street. The club had been very popular with the British rock aristocracy in the mid-Sixties but its allure had been superseded by other London nightclubs such as the Speakeasy.

The Upsetters played several other shows in greater London, including an appearance at the Four Aces in Dalston and one-nighters in Streatham, Kennington, and Crystal Palace. In between, they travelled up and down to cities like Huddersfield, Coventry, Derby, Sheffield, and Birmingham, while visiting coastal towns like Bournemouth, Margate, and Torquay, where audiences were mostly composed of Mods and skinheads. Ford Transit vans were then de rigeur for travelling musicians and there would be many nights, driving back down the M1 motorway to London, that the Upsetters members would sleep slumped in the back, surrounded by instruments and amplifiers. A group called Noel & the Fireballs, who supported on some of the dates, had to loan the Upsetters some of their equipment, as well as providing the back line. If the visiting Jamaicans had visions of taking England by storm, then the reality was proving altogether different, as Adams remembers only too well.

"First of all, the promoters put us in this small hall. They told us we were going to get a big hotel suite and all those things there, but them carry us to some bed and breakfast place. It never looked good, so we had to turn it down, because we'd come from Jamaica where we had nice things, y'know? We were all driving cars and whilst none of us owned our own houses, we rented nice places, we had decent clothes on our back and our lifestyle was good. We were having fun and we were making music, so we couldn't come all that way, only to end up in that condition. Because when we came into the business, we set an example, Carly, Family Man, Reggie and I. We changed things around and started trying to get a better deal for musicians, y'understand? We helped set that trend, so that musicians could get more respect. We develop a thing where the relationship between these producers and the musicians changed around and after dealing with people like Scratch, we couldn't have it so the producer used us. In fact, it was the opposite in our case, because the producers would have to come looking for us and hang out with us. We nah had to leave our house until we were ready man!"

Commercial Entertainment, who'd organised tours with the Ethiopians and Desmond Dekker, had no illusions about the hardships successful Jamaican acts could expect to face in England. The two countries were still worlds apart, despite the presence of so many Caribbean migrants and the growing popularity of their music among white, working class English youths, many of whom had first been exposed to "blue beat" after Millie's 'My Boy Lollipop' five years earlier. In the late Sixties, rock music had attained significant social importance and was now being recognised as an art form, in contrast to the lighter sounds flooding out of Jamaica, which were considered "primitive" in certain quarters. Radio 1 deejay Tony Blackburn was a notable exception, at least for the time being, as were Johnny Walker and Emperor Rosko. The offshore pirate station, Radio Caroline, also played an important role in helping reggae breach the mainstream. By late '69, it was no longer strange to see Desmond Dekker, Jimmy Cliff or the Pioneers in the charts or on *Top Of The Pops*, singing hits like 'Wonderful World, Beautiful People' and 'Long Shot Kick The Bucket'.

Trojan and Pama Records were home to many of the best Jamaican recordings and while albums by Caribbean acts lagged far behind their ιοck counterparts in terms of concept, presentation and sales, there was no doubting the popularity of singles. Trojan were quick to spot the potential of mid-price hits compilations and duly launched their *Tighten Up* series in early 1969, named after the Untouchables' cover of Archie Bell & the Drells' US hit. The second *Tighten Up* volume appeared just a few months later and went to number two in the UK national album charts, after which the powers-that-be decided to eliminate budget price albums from the listings.*

Members of the Upsetters played on several tracks on *Tighten Up Vol. 2,* including the Soul Mates' 'Them A Laugh And A Ki Ki' and their own two selections, 'Return Of Django' and 'Live Injection'. While Trojan were unarguably the dominant force in the UK reggae market at the time, with several UK chart hits to their credit, Pama also released a wealth of material featuring the Barrett brothers' rhythms, including albums by Max Romeo (*A Dream*) and Pat Kelly (*Pat Kelly Sings*). Slim Smith's album *Everybody Needs Love* was a big seller, as was Derrick Morgan's *Derrick Morgan In London*, which opened with another of the Hippy Boys', alias the Bunny Lee All-Stars', early successes, 'Seven Letters'. In 1969, Pama's best-selling compilations included *Unity's Great Reggae Hits* (featuring Bunny Lee productions), *Reggae Hits '69* (containing Max Romeo's 'Wet Dream', Pat Kelly's 'How Long' and Lester Sterling & Stranger Cole's 'Bangarang') and *Gas Greatest Hits*. The latter appeared on the label's Economy Series, while the Various Artists' set *Bullet: A World Of Reggae, Ska, Rock Steady And Blue Beat*, included the Hippy Boys' 'What's Your Excuse' and 'Hog In A Me Minty', as well as Ranny ("Bop") Williams' and the Hippy Boys' 'Summer Place'.

In addition to these albums, the Upsetters had played on Lloyd Charmers' 'Zylon' and 'Fire To Fire', Delroy Wilson's 'Put Yourself In My Place', Roland Alphonso's '1000 Tons Of Megaton' and Little Roy's 'Bongo Nyah', which all ranked among the year's most popular releases. It's no wonder that Adams talks of the Upsetters' comfortable lifestyles back in Jamaica and how they were so in demand with local producers.

Pama Records were owned by two brothers, Jeff and Harry Palmer, who started the label in late 1967 after licensing US soul tunes from their small office in South Harrow. They then moved to 78a Craven Park Road in Harlesden and by mid-1968 had created several subsidiaries for reggae

---

* Reggae would rarely feature in the UK album charts from that point onwards, or at least not until the Wailers released *Catch A Fire*, some years later.

music. Nu Beat was the first, launched in July with 'Train To Vietnam' by the Rudies. By December their Crab, Unity and Gas labels were up and running, followed by Bullet, Camel, Punch, Escort (dealing mainly with Harry J productions) and Success. Pama would stay "ethnic" until late 1970, by which time Trojan had scored several national hits by watering down the raw, authentic Jamaican sound and adding ornate string arrangements. By way of illustration, Pama released the plain, Jamaican mix of Bob & Marcia's 'Young, Gifted And Black', only to see it eclipsed by Trojan's orchestrated version, which roared into the UK charts the following March. Pama later metamorphosed into Jet Star after the Palmers' younger brother, Carl, previously involved in real estate, took over the business and remodelled it as Europe's leading reggae distributor. When the Upsetters passed through London in late '69, Family Man approached the Palmers about borrowing a record player so he could hear some of their latest releases.

Family Man Barrett: "I went amongst the Palmers and asked if they could lend me some test press I can listen to in the hotel, so them send someone round with this record player and the amount of test press that I personally play on, I was surprised! I remember this album track I do for Bunny Lee, an organ instrumental called 'The Disintegrator' on the same riddim Slim Smith use for 'Everybody Needs Love'. That was the title track, and it had the 'Bangarang' riddim on it too. We don't hear those in Jamaica yet. Then I went to this party and I hear some instrumental music I do for Randy's. That's for Vincent Chin himself, but he told me he wasn't using it and yet there it is, kicking up all over the place!"

This practice is still a familiar experience for many Jamaican artists while touring overseas, but it was even more common in the late Sixties and early Seventies, when fewer artists were able to tour, and producers knew they could license tracks in relative secrecy. The UK market had become vital to them, as it was where the most money could be made. There was certainly no shortage of sales outlets, especially in London, with shops in Balham (Record Corner), Clapham Junction, Lewisham (Musik City and Beverley's) and Tottenham. Brixton was particularly well served, with Desmond's Hip City in Atlantic Road and Musik City and Joe's Shack in Granville Arcade. Musik City also had branches in Kensal Rise, Balham, Shepherd's Bush Market, Deptford High Street and Dalston. Outside the capital there were well-established shops in Birmingham (Don Christie's and Brian Harris), Manchester, and Leeds, as well as an army of small-time entrepreneurs scattered around the country, who would furnish the many sound-systems and blues party deejays with all the latest tunes from Jamaica.

Britain even had its own elite band of reggae producers, including Joe Mansano, Lambert Briscoe, Dandy Livingstone, and Count Suckle, who owned the Q Club in Praed Street, near where the Upsetters stayed during their first London visit. "We were staying at the Hotel Edward near Paddington station, and you have a great bar over there too, with fish and chips," notes Family Man. Other band members have less happy memories. In an interview with *Grand Royal*, Adams said the tour, "started out cheerful, but it ended up rough. Mostly because of the company and their arrangements. We had bad times on the road because we didn't have any experience of travelling out there."

Perry, who'd appeared onstage a few times to milk whatever applause was forthcoming, disappeared back to Jamaica soon after the tour started and was of no help to his band whatsoever. "Scratch just came up there, collected some money, and then went back home," said Adams. "He just left us stranded up there with nothing." Reviews of their early shows suggest Perry's only contribution was to play occasional percussion, although he'd certainly kept busy behind the scenes, by conducting deals with both Pama and Trojan. He felt that Pama should have done better with the 'Clint Eastwood' single, but maybe it was simply ahead of its time and just too different from other, contemporary reggae releases, with the possible exception of Andy Cap's 'Pop A Top'.

Harry Palmer had visited Kingston two months before the tour began and his company's first Upsetters album, *Clint Eastwood*, bore traces of funk, reggae, Rastafari and soul, yet had an identity all of its own as the Upsetters stretched out like never before. Count Sticky's 'The Return Of The Ugly', 'Taste Of Killing', the title track and a riotous 'For A Few Dollars More' were all named with spaghetti westerns in mind; 'Selassie' and 'Earth's Rightful Ruler' blazed a trail for black consciousness, while 'Prisoner Of Love' and 'Ain't No Love' married sweet vocals to the Upsetters' pulsating rhythms.

Trojan also released an album within weeks of the Upsetters' arrival and while *Return Of Django* reprised several tracks from *The Upsetter*, it sounded a lot more vibrant. Like 'Return Of Django' itself, 'Cold Sweat', 'Live Injection', and 'Medical Operation' were all former singles. 'Cold Sweat' was an instrumental cut to the Reggae Boys' 'Ba Ba' and not a cover of the James Brown hit. "Take off your jacket and sock it," says Perry on the intro and the band does exactly that, as the Barrett brothers lock chords and Adams gets busy on his trusty Hammond. He had to make do with a Farfisa on the UK tour, but that would be the least of his worries.

"We were ripped off, because back in Jamaica, we'd been making plenty of money playing sessions, and that trip to England broke our rhythm," he says, ruefully. "[The agents] were paying us like £30 a week, but we have to feed ourselves and take care of everything out of that. [The record label] were supposed to be close to us, but when we turned to them for help, they took us to this music store and promised to buy us some instruments, but only if we did some work for them in return. We do an album, *The Good, The Bad And The Upsetters*, but we never got any proper guidance when we were doing it and everybody was just looking to make a quick dollar off us. Nobody was looking at the welfare of the artists or anything like that. That was the difference with Chris Blackwell, because he had more of a relationship with his artists at that time."

Adams' statement speaks volumes about the cutthroat nature of the Jamaican music industry. While some memories run deep, others fade quickly and the various members of the Upsetters are left with conflicting impressions of their six weeks in England. Family Man met his longtime girlfriend Vyris Edgehill on this trip and so has personal memories to cherish. Among the collective highlights was a flight to Holland, where the band appeared on a television programme called *Shoo Be Doo*. Family Man recalls how they all dressed in different coloured outfits for their performance which was recorded in just one take. This same footage was subsequently shown on *Top Of The Pops*.

The Upsetters were then invited to appear on the BBC show in person to plug 'Return Of Django', with an unknown horn player miming Val Bennett's part. They also appeared on singer Matt Munro's variety show around Christmas time and were interviewed at the BBC's studios in Cardiff, where they met Tom Jones. Or at least Glen, Reggie, and Carly did – Family Man having found other distractions back in London. Adams mentions how Eddy Grant of the Equals was a keen Upsetters' fan and so too the Cimarons, who appeared with the band at a send-off party at Harlesden's 21 Club, owned by the Palmer brothers. "That was one hell of a show, man!" says Family Man. "We had no knowledge of tape in those days, otherwise we really would have something to remember!"

During the tour the band first met Larry Lawrence, who took various members shopping or partying. Lawrence, who worked for the agency, was of a similar age but wasn't blamed by the band for the treatment meted out by his employers, who grew increasingly wary of Adams in particular.

"[The agency] didn't like me because I'm too aggressive when it comes to certain things," Adams explains. "I'm not a follower, y'understand? Because I took control, that's how we got the money to go back home, because every night I collect the money. A man would come backstage and say, 'Who is the governor?' And I would say, 'It's me.'

"We usually drink whisky and lime on that tour, so every morning we used to go into this liquor store up by the Hotel Edward in Paddington and buy a little bottle to drink in their office, which was by Piccadilly Circus. We go round there one day and we're complaining that £30 a week can't hold we and we want to go home. They said that can't happen, because Scratch is signed to them, but I say that has nothing to do with us and we want our passports. My blood run right up into my head and me just broke my whisky bottle on the desk and told this guy Alex [Hughes, who later made records as Judge Dread] that I'm going for his boss and if he makes one wrong move . . . First of all, I ask Bruce White if he knows where our passports are. He says no, so I search his office drawer for them and this is while him, Tony Cousins, Judge Dread, and a lawyer were surrounding me . . . All of them is in there, but I back them up with my whisky bottle, 'cause it have this wicked point on it and I just go straight up to the man sitting behind the desk, open the drawer and take out my passport. Everybody just came and took out their passport after that and we go outside now and sit in this restaurant across the street, where we can see them come and go, but they can't see us. That incident happened before we did *The Good, The Bad And The Upsetters* album, because we recorded that just a couple of days before leaving for Jamaica."

The Good, The Bad And The Upsetters* was recorded in one sitting at Chalk Farm studios in north London, with Vic Keary engineering. The Upsetters sound so lacklustre in places, many listeners thought the tracks had been recorded by English imposters rather than Jamaica's most exciting rhythm section. It's as if the band were simply going through their paces and while some point to the absence of Perry's creative genius by way of explanation, it's the sound of musicians, having endured six weeks of badly planned one-nighters, who feel threatened and cheated by those entrusted with their care, having been abandoned by their mentor. The covers of 'Guns Of Navarone' and Toots & the Maytals' 'Monkey

---

* The title, of course adapted from *The Good, The Bad And The Ugly* film. An excerpt from the soundtrack by Hugo Montenegro & his Orchestra had been a hit in 1968.

Man' fail to catch fire but still the rhythms snap and crackle with taut energy at times, especially on 'Straight To The Head', with its flurries of echo, 'Oney (Happy Clap)', and a track named after the Upsetters' bass player.

Commercial Entertainment's sister company, Commercial Artists, announced the release of *The Good, The Bad And The Upsetters* during February 1970, just weeks after the band returned to Jamaica. White and Cousins credited the fictitious Bruce Anthony as producer and were supposed to sign the album to President Records, but cut a deal with Trojan instead, who previewed the album with two singles, 'Family Man' and 'Capo'. Both disappeared without trace and while the album didn't exactly sell, it served as the launch pad for White and Cousins' latest venture, Creole Music. At least the sleeve was impressive; Dezo Hoffman's photo depicting the band members dressed like Mexican extras from a spaghetti western, complete with ponchos, sombreros, and firearms.

Perry was bitterly unhappy with *The Good, The Bad And The Upsetters,* describing it as the only disappointing work he'd ever been involved with. Which, of course, he hadn't been! He later released a line-up of different tracks using the same title and even the same artwork in an apparent bid to erase memories of the original, although another theory suggests Perry did this in order to deflect attention (and sales) from the band's own productions.

Family Man Barrett: "[We were] stranded in England, so we decided the only money we were likely to get was if we did something for ourselves and that's how we come together and do that album *The Good, The Bad And The Upsetters*. We thought Scratch was going to stay there with us and make sure that everything went down okay with the promoters, but it seems like he just collected the money and then went back to Jamaica. He left us and so the only way we could make any money was to keep on touring and then make a deal with Tony Cousins and Bruce White. The little money that we did make, we bought shoes and took them down to Jamaica for the sufferers them. It was like Santa Claus when we arrived back home, but then when Creole shipped the album to us, they sent it to Scratch instead, who covered up our credits on the back and put out a different version, so it's like we take another beating."

The Good, The Bad And The Upsetters wasn't the only album to appear that spring, since Trojan released two others, *Scratch The Upsetter Again* and *Eastwood Rides Again*, shortly after the Upsetters' return to Jamaica. Resourceful as ever, Perry had been doing brisk business in England and would enter into an alliance with Trojan that, while by no means exclusive, brought him significant exposure (and no shortage of financial reward) as the new decade began.

The sleeve for *Scratch The Upsetter Again* carried a photo of a gleeful Perry, taken at one of the Upsetters' British shows, about to hit a cowbell. The music was a lot less unbridled compared to previous tracks like 'Return Of Django'; the exceptions are Count Prince Miller's 'Mule Train', which came from a Bunny Lee session and 'Touch Of Fire', combining Adams' dark, psychedelic organ riffs with R&B style sax from Bennett, which had previously appeared on the *Return Of Django* album. Lewis' mournful lead vocals on 'She Is Gone Again' add a dash of country & western to the Upsetters' *oeuvre*, while 'Will You Still Love Me (Tomorrow)' is another vocal effort – this time by Dave Barker, who'd become the main singer in Perry's stable by this time. Barker sounds a little like Slim Smith as he tackles the Shirelles' 1961 hit.

The other key tracks were 'Bad Tooth' (a cut to Count Sticky's 'Return Of The Ugly') and the quirky 'One Punch, The Dentist And The Result', on which the chugging rhythm is almost drowned by languorous, sustained organ chords which, when suddenly disappearing from the mix, has an ear popping effect. However it's *Eastwood Rides Again* that contains the most thrills and captures Perry and the band with all guns blazing. Tracks like 'Baby Baby' and 'Django (Ol' Man River)' did not feature the current Upsetters line-up but Gladdy's All-Stars. In truth, they sound a little staid by comparison, which leaves the listener realising just how Perry's music benefited from the input of his untutored, yet brilliantly receptive young musicians. The title track in particular has everything you'd expect from this classic edition of the Upsetters. The bottom end bubbles, yet is rock solid; Carly's drums fizz with an irresistible mix of delicacy and propulsive energy, while Lewis fastens onto the groove, not shifting an inch. The finishing touches, as always, come from Adams, as his organ glides over this bedrock with just the right balance of menace and melody.

It's fascinating to hear the Upsetters' take on Booker T & the MGs ('Knock On Wood') while 'Popcorn' is jagged, raw funk, lacking only a frenzied James Brown vocal to give it that authentic, soul stamp of approval. It's a recipe repeated on 'Catch This' and 'Power Pack', which weaves traces of the Temptations' 'Cloud Nine' into the mix, thanks to Ranny Bop's wah-wah guitar. *Eastwood Rides Again* also included 'Tight Spot', which later resurfaced behind the Heptones' 'Revolution'.

Perry's penchant for recording different versions of his rhythms gave rise to some phenomenal early reggae sides and yet it made good business sense too, since producers in the same position paid musicians just the one session fee for recording these rhythms while offering them no share of the proceeds from subsequent versions. Alternative cuts therefore represented pure profit, apart from studio fees. This practice hadn't gone unnoticed by the Upsetters and after what had transpired in England, they were often in two minds about working with their crazy, but crafty Svengali. On the one hand he gave them unrivalled freedom in the studio to express themselves, but on the other he couldn't be trusted regarding practical matters. The number of releases pouring out of England also gave the band cause for concern, since the members often weren't present when these alternative versions were being recorded. The first they would hear of them was after the cuts in question were included on yet another Upsetters' album.

Pama meanwhile, weighed in with *Many Moods Of The Upsetter*. This was again a largely instrumental set with Carl Dawkins (on a full vocal cut of 'Cloud Nine'), David Isaacs, and Pat Satchmo (sounding just like Louis Armstrong, hence the name) providing the only vocals. Among the highlights was a cut of the 'Selassie' rhythm, 'Ex Ray Vision', which Adams was aware of as he overdubbed wild organ phrases on top. The original version, and also another cut featuring U Roy, Peter Tosh, and Rasta drummer Count Ossie, 'Rightful Ruler', had been included on the *Clint Eastwood* album. 'Selassie', their tribute to Emperor Haile Selassie I, (credited to the Reggae Boys – the name Adams, Lewis, and Max Romeo chose when singing tracks like 'Mama Look Deh' for Joe Gibbs and 'What Is This?' for Perry) was a master-class in lyrical economy, chanted over a rhythm that was brutally insistent and yet matched the triumphant and also righteous nature of their message to stunning effect. "Selassie, ah go burn them with fire. It's hot, it's hot, but we not gonna die . . ."

An extraordinarily powerful track, 'Selassie' arrived at a time when even well-mannered, conservative types like Family Man were beginning to deepen their interest in Rastafari. From now on, songs like this would inspire the Upsetters to even greater efforts as they sought to bring more depth and meaning to their music. They would find no shortage of accomplices along the way.

CHAPTER SIX

Black Progress

MEMBERS of the Upsetters weren't alone in answering the call as Jamaica responded to the sense of impending social change sweeping America in the late Sixties. Events happening on the mainland would irrevocably alter many Jamaicans' hopes and expectations of what might lie ahead, especially since the island had only gained its independence just a few years previously. At the heart of the US Civil Rights movement were two men, Malcolm X and Martin Luther King, both of whom proved widely influential among people of the Caribbean. The fiery Malcolm X, who'd risen to prominence from within the ranks of Elijah Muhammad's Black Muslims, had been assassinated several years earlier, yet his image could still be seen staring defiantly from walls in Kingston, as well as black ghetto communities in the US.

The popular perception of Malcolm X was of a black man who'd stood up for his rights without either fear or compromise. He'd taken on the white-controlled power structure and been demonised by it and yet was unyielding in his determination to obtain freedom "by any means necessary". By the end of the Sixties, his legacy of black pride, strict moral codes and organised resistance was beginning to unravel, and leaders of the group he'd inspired, the Black Panthers, were falling on the urban battle-fields, while the casualty rate in Vietnam continued to spiral out of control.

Whereas Malcolm X appealed to warriors in a carpe diem spirit, Martin Luther King represented a more acceptable version of racial reform. In June 1965, King had visited Jamaica to give an address, 'Facing The Challenge of a New Age' at the University of the West Indies campus in Mona, on the outskirts of Kingston, where he praised Marcus Garvey for "giving Negroes in the US a sense of dignity, a sense of personhood, a sense of manhood, a sense of somebodiness" – a statement that didn't go unnoticed among the Rastafarians, who also heeded the fact that King had visited Garvey's grave during his brief stay on the island. This southern preacher-turned-social-activist would become transformed into a beacon of hope for so many hardworking, God-fearing black people in America and beyond, and like Malcolm X he, too, was cut down before he could witness any of his more far-reaching ambitions being realised. His assassination in April 1968 (at the same Memphis motel where Steve Cropper and Wilson Pickett had written 'In The Midnight Hour') would radically alter the dynamics of race relations in America, and rioting and looting occurred in over a hundred US cities in its aftermath.

In the wake of Dr King's assassination, the Chambers Brothers (with the apt 'Time Has Come Today'), the Impressions, Sly & the Family Stone, and Aretha Franklin were also among those black American performers expressing the late Sixties zeitgeist and their efforts to effect lasting social reform would not go unheeded in the Caribbean, where deep-seated, collective memories of rebellion still lingered among the sufferers. Thanks to the label's new in-house producer, Norman Whitfield, even Tamla-Motown had nailed its colours to the mast with Edwin Starr's 'War' and the Temptations' 'Cloud Nine' and 'Ball Of Confusion'. James Brown best symbolised the struggle for racial equality after freeing himself from the shackles of poverty, earning his share of the American dream by dint of sheer will and determination, allied to prodigious musical talent and some of the most explosive, rhythmic backdrops in all of popular music. In triumphing over adversity, Brown had set an example to others disadvantaged by race or circumstance and, like Marcus Garvey, he was a fierce advocate of black ownership and economic self-determination.

Brown's overwhelming success in the R&B charts had certainly won him the ears of the black masses and yet he shared their collective weaknesses, as well as aspirations, which made him vulnerable to political machinations. First, he attended a White House dinner as a guest of President Lyndon Johnson and while he took obvious pride in the socially progressive leap this represented, it invited virulent criticism from Brown's ghetto constituents, many of whom felt that he'd sold out. After performing for the US troops in Vietnam (which again proved contentious), he then promised to endorse Senator Robert Kennedy, just before he, too, was assassinated, in June '68. Brown's next move was to switch his allegiance to a Republican, Vice President Hubert Humphreys, and campaign on his behalf in the Los Angeles black stronghold of Watts that summer, when racial tension was at its height.

Humphreys had opposed Kennedy, and Brown's stance proved unpopular with a lot of Afro-Americans. During this trip to Los Angeles Brown recorded his most overtly political song, 'Say It Loud, I'm Black And I'm Proud'. Legend has it that a grenade with Brown's name daubed on it was left outside his hotel room the night before he and his band went to the studio and that most of the kids they'd rounded up off the streets of Hollywood to sing on the chorus were either white or Hispanic and not black at all! Despite being erroneously – or perhaps deliberately – labelled as a black power record by the media (when it was really a rallying call for equal rights and opportunity), 'Say It Loud, I'm Black And I'm Proud' became Brown's latest R&B number one that August and even entered the Top 20 pop charts.

"It was absolutely the right time to make that statement," said Maceo Parker, who played tenor sax in Brown's backing band the JBs for many years and there were plenty who agreed with him. 'Say It Loud, I'm Black And I'm Proud' sold a reputed 750,000 copies in the States alone and its impact among black listeners was incalculable, yet Brown would later claim the record cost him his crossover audience, just as the pro-capitalist 'America Is My Home', recorded a week after King's death, had jeopardised his black following. At least some of his peers were still on side, as the Impressions proved with the challenging, yet dignified 'This Is My Country', 'Choice Of Colours' (which the Heptones would reiterate to stirring effect at Studio One) and the even more insistent 'We're A Winner', which promptly got banned by several radio stations due to its controversial lyrics.

Neither James Brown nor Curtis Mayfield were content to be puppets controlled by their respective record companies. Like Sam Cooke and Ray Charles before them, both wanted full control of their careers. Mayfield would put these ideas into practice and make them work for him right up until his death in 1999, yet it was Brown – now dubbed "the Godfather of Soul" – who enjoyed the most profile at the time and was fêted as an icon in the mainstream media, while coming under increasing scrutiny from pro-black organisations.

The Upsetters were summarily struck by Brown's charisma and celebrity status, but the stylistic, as well as lyrical, changes happening in his music interested them more. The Godfather's development had been keenly debated among Jamaican musicians for years, especially since he'd shifted the boundaries on prototype funk anthems like 'Out Of Sight', 'I Got You (I Feel Good)' and 'Cold Sweat'. The format of blending dynamic rhythm, a serious lyrical agenda and pop sensibilities into one crucial package, proved a revelation to Jamaican musicians like Bob Marley and the Barrett brothers. As soon as they heard 'Say It Loud . . .' they immediately recognised its potential to change people's lives and the possibility of it serving as the platform for significant social reform in Jamaica. The fact it had a funky beat that made dancers go wild helped, too.

When the Wailers adapted 'Say It Loud . . .' in the autumn of 1969, Brown's records were being played daily on Jamaican radio. The energy, drive, and lyrical messages of his songs permeated all corners of society, as did those of other artists promoting black pride. Sly & the Family Stone offered the confrontational 'Don't Call Me Nigger, Whitey', while Nina Simone extolled the virtues of being 'Young, Gifted And Black' – a song Bob (Andy) & Marcia (Griffiths) would soon turn into Harry J's next international hit. At the same time reggae was coming of age, rivalling soul and rock in terms of its social importance, despite receiving far less promotion. Desmond Dekker became the first-ever Jamaican artist to breach the US charts with 'Israelites', produced by Leslie Kong. What's more, 'Israelites' was no watered-down attempt at a pop hit, but an authentic reggae track about the economic hardships endured by ghetto people. "Get up in the morning, slaving for bread, sir, so that every mouth can be fed . . ."

The scene was thus set for a new, more culturally aware form of Caribbean music that not only shared many of the ideals and characteristics expressed by black American artists, but also reflected the concerns of its local audiences in terms of language, musical styles and topics. For instance, Rastafarianism and the back to Africa movement had a far stronger foothold in islands like Jamaica than mainland America, while Caribbean music was infused with the sounds of mento, calypso and burru drumming or Jonkanoo, as well as ska and rocksteady. Out of this synthesis roots reggae developed, which ultimately allowed artists like the Wailers, Burning Spear, and Culture to spearhead something of a cultural revolution.

'Say It Loud . . .' was the first Wailers cut to feature the Barrett brothers, although it was by no means a straightforward cover version. Instead of repeating Brown's assertion that "we'd rather die on our feet, than be living on our knees," Marley changed it to, "we stop living on our knees, and we start living on our feet." A declaration of intention thus becomes reality and what was once but a threat is put into immediate effect. Marley made changes elsewhere, too, by omitting "now we demand a chance to do things for ourselves. We're tired of beating our heads against the wall and working for someone else," in favour of "I've worked on jobs with my feet and my hands, but all the work I did was for the other man, children. We demand a right to do things for ourselves, instead of standing here, and working for someone else." Only the chorus of "say it loud, I'm black, and I'm proud" remained the same.

The music was never intended to merely duplicate the original. It is transformed into a groove that springs directly from the brothers' own inner dynamics. Family Man's bass bubbles and dances as if in joy, Carly's drums sputter, while Peter Tosh's guitar slashes against the beat, lending the track an aggressive edge that provides balance as well as substance. Tosh, Marley and Neville "Bunny Wailer" Livingston are joined on the chorus by the Soulettes – a group comprising Cecile Campbell, Hortense Lewis and Bob's wife Rita, who styled themselves after Aretha Franklin's backing singers, the Sweet Inspirations.

Family Man had already met Tosh by the time the rehearsals and recording sessions for 'Black Progress' got under way. Little was happening for the Wailers at the time and so Tosh would look for work as a session musician in between writing and recording alongside his old friends Marley and Livingston.

Family Man Barrett: "I used to see [Tosh] walking around with his box guitar and his little melodica. This was on Beat Street, which is called Orange Street and then near this place on the corner they call Idlers Rest. He would pass through there and I would hail him up. That was right by Randy's on North Parade, long before they even build the studio upstairs. Reggie first introduced me to Peter, because I remember Reggie telling him that if we get any recording session, then he can join us. I say, 'But I thought you were a singer?' so him say, 'Yeah I sing, but I can play music too.' So one or two times we'd take him on a session to play guitar, or maybe even melodica, because he could play that good too. Yeah, but he was more like a comedian to me really, walking around making jokes and with this Black Power fist made out of cardboard hanging round his neck. He was always very revolutionary, even from early, except his hair would blow and roll up like black pepper greens at that time, because 'im never dread yet. 'Im not so versy as a musician in truth, but 'im did 'ave a vibes, for sure . . ."

Tosh wasn't originally from Kingston, but Westmoreland, on the western tip of Jamaica. He was christened Winston Hubert McIntosh and had learnt piano and guitar while singing with his church choir. An aunt looked after him when he lived in the coastal town of Savannah-La-Mer. Like Marley, he was raised without a father and had learnt the virtues of self-reliance from a young age. The tall, lanky youth then moved to Denham Town as a teenager before relocating to Trenchtown where he befriended Marley and Livingstone. Bob was the only one of the trio to have recorded by the time he took them and two other members of the Wailers for harmony practice to the home of Joe Higgs, who had featured on hits by Higgs & Wilson in the late Fifties and ran informal music lessons from his yard in Trenchtown.

Tosh was more musical than either of his new-found friends and, in addition, had a warm, deep tenor that could also handle baritone duties well enough, given the right material. He had accompanied the Wailers on guitar when they auditioned for Studio One and had taught Marley his first few guitar chords. Coxsone would often praise Tosh for his melodic sense, as well as his jovial sense of humour, and first recorded him as a musician back in 1964 on the Wailers' 'Amen'. Tosh played on numerous sessions at Treasure Isle and Joe Gibbs and also familiarised himself with a wah-wah pedal, but while at Studio One as a member of the Wailers, his dual career as both sideman and lead singer first evolved. The folksy 'Hoot Nanny Hoot' was his debut, which he'd written after watching the popular US talent show on television. Tosh sang or shared lead on several of the Wailers' recordings from this period, including 'Teenager In Love', 'Lemon Tree', 'Jumbie Jamboree', 'Making Love' and a cover of the Temptations' 'Don't Look Back', which he would later re-record alongside Mick Jagger of the Rolling Stones.

Like Marley, Tosh would restlessly search for the best possible expression of certain songs, revisiting 'Maga Dog', 'When The Well Runs Dry', 'Can't You See?' and 'The Toughest' in years to come. Those he'd penned himself clearly had greater significance for him, and Lee Perry even credited Tosh as being a better songwriter than Marley, despite their obvious differences in style and presentation. Other tracks sung by Tosh had their roots in traditional material. 'Amen' and 'Sinner Man' were spirituals he'd first learnt in church, while 'Shame And Scandal' was a bawdy calypso backed by members of the Skatalites, which the Wailers invested with infectious humour and energy. Tosh's most overtly cultural song from the Studio One era was 'Rasta Shook Them Up', a track announced by the Amharic greeting "Selah", which tells the story of Selassie's visit to Jamaica. "We got one day of freedom," Tosh sings, and memories of this never deserted him, since the guitarist devoted much of his recorded output to singing about truth and rights after the Wailers left the label in late 1966.

Tosh sang lead on 'Funeral' (a.k.a. 'Burial') which he and Marley wrote about Coxsone, after inevitable financial disputes. Like the earliest versions of 'Stepping Razor' and 'Mus' Get A Beating', 'Funeral' was a Wailers' self-production, first released on their own Wail 'N Soul 'M label during 1968.* 'Stepping Razor' was written by the diminutive Joe Higgs, in which the line "Don't watch my size, I'm dangerous," applied to the towering figure of Tosh, who also sang lead on 'Love', produced by Danny Sims, and a Randy's production, 'You Can't Fool Me Again'. Tosh teamed up with Lee Perry and the Upsetters in the summer of 1969 for 'Earth's Rightful Ruler', voiced over the same rhythm as the Reggae Boys' 'Selassie'.

Tosh again talks in Amharic on the introduction to 'Earth's Rightful Ruler', although the first part was voiced over a different rhythm and spliced into the Upsetters' track by Perry at a later date. Glen Adams claims that 'Selassie' was really his production, but then Perry used it for U Roy's recording debut after the deejay's impressive performances on King Tubby's sound-system and, prior to that, while holding a mic on Dickie Dynamics in Jones Town. U Roy continues Tosh's invocation to Emperor Haile Selassie I in a speaking voice, trying to ride the rhythm with the same melodic brand of jive talk he'd perfect on records for Treasure Isle and Keith Hudson.

Within a year or so, U Roy would be the toast of Jamaica, whereas the Wailers were in the doldrums, searching for an outside producer while still struggling to make headway with their own recordings. Despite having served their apprenticeship with Coxsone, the group certainly had no intention of returning to him, no matter how hard it was trying to make it on its own. They were also saddled with the reputation of being trouble-makers, since Tosh and Livingston had both spent time in jail, while Marley was hardened by life in the ghetto and determined to achieve success on his own terms.

The Wailers' first record store was actually a home-based operation situated at 18A Greenwich Park Road – where Bob and Rita lived after getting married – situated at the top end of Trenchtown, near the Calvary cemetery. They had launched Wail 'N Soul 'M from there in 1967, soon

---

* Tosh and Prince Buster were allegedly jailed for a short time that year after joining a demonstration against Ian Smith's regime in Rhodesia.

after Bob's return from America, where he'd been staying with his mother in Delaware while working on an assembly line, saving as much money as he could. The earliest Wailers self-productions included 'Freedom Time', 'Bend Down Low', 'Mellow Mood', 'Nice Time', 'Bus Dem Shut', and 'Stir It Up', although the latter two wouldn't be released until more than a year later, in August 1968.

By then, Bob, Rita, and Peter had already begun rehearsing songs at a house in Russell Heights rented by Danny Sims, who shared a label called JAD with Texan singer Johnny Nash and arranger Arthur Jenkins. This reduced line-up of the Wailers recorded songs for JAD like 'Falling In And Out Of Love', 'Splish For My Splash', 'Wings Of A Dove' and 'What Goes Around Comes Around'; also reworkings of 'Nice Time', 'Mellow Mood' and 'Bend Down Low'.*

"Bob and Rita used to live in a place we called 'Armshouse', close by the cemetery," recalls Bunny Lee. "This was before Concrete Jungle was built. After Bob left for America, every time I pressed up a record, I'd drop some off round there for Rita to sell, so they could make ends meet. I used to carry Joe Gibbs round there as well, so he could buy copies of songs like 'Nice Time'.

"I used to pay Peter Touch £20 a week in those days, and that was big money back then. He'd be a singer, a musician, and an artist. He used to sing harmonies on some of my tunes and I have quite a lot of instrumentals with Peter as well, because Bob was still in Delaware, so every day Peter come down to the shop, or we go over to Randy's and work. He was a rebel in his ways, but he was very versatile. He could play keyboards, melodica, guitar, or sing harmonies. He was brilliant as a musician, because he play terrific organ on tunes like 'My Elusive Dreams' by Ernest Wilson."

Tosh's proficiency was also lauded by Sims, who told Marley historian Roger Steffens that he and Nash used his guitar "on practically every track we did. He held our rhythm together. Peter was the teacher, along with Paul Khouri, for that rocksteady sound. Peter directed us, and we spun off Peter Tosh. I saw him as the Rock of Gibraltar with that rhythm."

"He could do anything," Bunny concurs, "but as a singer now . . . I had Derrick Morgan, who would become my brother-in-law. He wasn't married to my sister as yet, but he and I were very good friends and he

---

* These tracks were later remixed by Joe Venerri in New York and overdubbed using top American session musicians like Chuck Rainey, Bernard Purdie, Eric Gale, and Richard Tee, whose list of credits included Aretha Franklin dates for Atlantic.

helped bring me in the business, because I'd started going around with him and Prince Buster in the early days. This was when I used to plug records for Coxsone and Duke Reid, and Derrick direct my first session with Lloyd & the Groovers as well. To me, Peter wasn't as good a singer as Derrick, and that's why I never use him as one too much.

"After that, Bob return to Jamaica and I was in charge of West Indies Records, so I'd give him and Mortimer Planno studio time to work, because Bob never had any money like myself. Bunny Wailer, he wasn't there, because he was in prison at that time, so Bob and Peter used to come with Planno and one or two other little guys instead. I remember him playing with Count Ossie and sometimes Bob used to play the guitar, with Planno the Rasta sitting in on piano, and Rita singing harmonies. Byron Lee has tapes of these sessions in his vaults somewhere, because there's at least half an album's worth of material that don't come out as yet. This was before they worked with Danny Sims; when Rita would be at the studio with her big belly, pregnant with child, and she and Bob can't find food fi eat. Rita, she knows what hardship is about, because she used to sell records for Bob, when no one wanted to know about Wailers."

Niney the Observer concurs with Lee, saying that, "sister Rita is the foundation of Bob Marley. She is the financier, 'cause she's the one who carry the records on her head, selling to the jukebox people them, and selling to the shops, 'cause in those days, you didn't get paper money for records. You get silver, which she'd lug around in her thread bag whilst Bob Marley was in the studio, working and making records. Sister Rita, she was a qualified nurse and go to good school, but through the love of Bob, she started to wear all these long frocks and say Rasta, which was a hard thing to do in those days."

Danny Sims was born in Mississippi and had started out in the restaurant business. In addition to his music interests, he ran Sapphire's on West 47th Street in New York, near Times Square, which he loved telling people was, "the first black-owned club south of 110th Street." Sapphire's was a popular hangout for entertainers like Harry Belafonte, Sidney Poitier, and a young Johnny Nash, who'd been signed to ABC Paramount and had appeared in two films, *Take A Giant Step* (filmed in Jamaica) and *Key Witness*, starring Dennis Hopper. From 1961 onwards, Nash had entered a series of short-lived record deals and experimented with jazz and soul, but was going nowhere before meeting Sims in 1965. Sims had recently assumed control of the Queen's Booking Agency, which had been owned by the late Dinah Washington. Once Sims had agreed to manage Nash, the pair formed a label called JoDa and debuted with 'Let's Move And Groove', featuring the arrangements of Arthur Jenkins, with whom they would eventually form JAD. Nash had been a frequent visitor to Jamaica since filming *Take A Giant Step* and had relatives there.

'Let's Move And Groove' quickly found favour on local Jamaican juke-boxes and after a promotional visit, Sims, Nash and Jenkins returned in 1967 to record at Federal, where they befriended the Khouris. These sessions resulted in 'Hold Me Tight', 'You Got Soul', and 'Cupid', all three of which achieved Top 10 success in the UK between August 1968 and August 1969. 'Hold Me Tight', with 'Let's Move And Groove' on the flipside, also went Top 5 in America. In the autumn of 1969, with 'Cupid' high in the charts, Nash was invited to perform alongside Jimmy Cliff and Desmond Dekker at the Caribbean Music Festival in Wembley, London. Cliff was enjoying crossover success with 'Wonderful World, Beautiful People' at the time, while Dekker had scored two Top 10 UK hits that summer with 'Israelites' and 'It Mek' and was already making inroads into the American market.

By now, JAD had assigned Bob Marley to write songs for Nash (reputedly paying him $100 a week) and had ambitions of establishing him on the overseas market. Nash's 1969 album, *Soul Folk*, had found him covering a disparate choice of songs, including Bob Dylan's 'Blowing In The Wind', Harry Belafonte's 'Island In The Sun', Elvis Presley's 'Love Me Tender', and another Sam Cooke cover, 'Chain Gang'. Nash was definitely in need of original material – an opinion another 1969 release, *Let's Go Dancing*, did nothing to dispel.

"When Danny Sims and Johnny Nash came to Jamaica, that was 1968, because I had 'Bangarang' and they come to find me down in Greenwich Farm," says Bunny Lee. "They were asking me which studios to use and so I carry them to Duke Reid's place and also Randy's. Johnny Nash's career started to move up from there, because this ex-policeman named Bagsy, he pirated Johnny Nash's tune, 'Cupid'. Johnny Nash go look for him and give the guy $500 and said, 'Thank you man, because you make the tune big and if you never press it up on white label, it would never get so popular.' A little after that, Johnny wanted some herb, so I go carry him over by Planno, because in those days, Planno used to sell the best herb in Jamaica. They strike up a friendship now and Bob used to be around there too, so them and Bob start work together."

Sims commissioned a New York deejay he knew called Magnificent Donahue, who'd since moved to the West Coast, to make a radio ad for 'Let's Move And Groove'. In his enthusiasm to boost the track, Magnificent Donahue inserted the line "burn baby burn" and put it on heavy rotation just as riots broke out in Watts and other black ghettos across America. Sims has since claimed he came under pressure from the US authorities as a result and this is he why he and Nash moved their operations to Kingston, not because of the cheaper recording costs, as suggested elsewhere.

"We went down there because we thought we were going to get killed by the CIA and the FBI," Sims told Justine Ketola of *Jah Works*. "For 'inciting a riot' as they called it. Detroit went down, Chicago went down and LA went down. The country just went up in flames and we were right in the midst of that. Jamaica was a place to get away from the shooting. I didn't even know Bob Marley then. We had a distributor at Federal Records, but the biggest studio was four tracks. We had to bring equipment down there. We brought our whole production crew down there. To us it was like paradise, but we never intended to stay because we had hit records in America. We had Gloria Gaynor, Lloyd Price . . . We were a hot little independent company . . ."

Sims says that Nash met the Marleys at a Rasta grounation in west Kingston and invited them to their house at 43 Russell Heights the following day. JAD signed Bob and Tosh soon after. According to Sims, this took place some time during 1966, although Planno didn't assume his managerial duties until after the Wailers had left Studio One in November of that year and Bob had returned from America. The grounation Sims refers to may have been called to celebrate the Ethiopian "Christmas" in January 1967. Jamaican radio deejay Neville Willoughby reportedly accompanied Nash to this Rasta gathering. Other sources, including Bunny Lee, suggest that Marley didn't sign to JAD until 1968, by which time Planno's Divine Theocratic Temple of Rastafari on Fifth Street in Trenchtown was in full swing and Marley and Tosh had begun to weave cultural themes into their recordings, as heard on 'Selassie Is The Chapel'.

In June that year, the Wailers, temporarily without Livingston who had been charged with possession of ganja and was imprisoned between July 1967 and September 1968, recorded 'Selassie Is The Chapel', produced by Planno at JBC studios. The song was an adaptation of the Orioles' 'Crying In The Chapel', although since Elvis Presley had had a major hit with it in 1965, it was probably his version that Marley and Tosh's cover was based on. Neither original rendition can touch the Wailers' for sheer feel and emotion, even if the simple backing track, using just acoustic guitar and Rasta drums, is ramshackle by comparison. Bob's lead vocal is full of expression and Rita's harmonies – twinned on this occasion with those of Constantine "Dream" Walker – soar heavenward, as you might expect from a woman who'd recently converted to Rastafari and assumed the name of Ganette Mander (or "Paradise").

Sims produced an early version of 'Soul Rebel' with the Wailers that autumn, although rumour has it he tried to steer the group away from recording too many cultural songs, preferring to concentrate on commercial material instead. Also in 1968 Johnny Nash invited journalist Cornelius "Lee" Ivory Jnr to Jamaica to report on the 'discovery' of a new music form, i.e., reggae. Ivory met Marley and Tosh on this trip and was introduced to the philosophies of Marcus Garvey and Rastafari. A former public relations director for Motown, Ivory had represented the media interests of Aretha Franklin, Mahalia Jackson, Jerry Butler and other music legends before co-founding black entertainment newspaper *The Word* with comedian and social activist Dick Gregory. While working for a Los Angeles-based weekly called *Soul,* Ivory travelled to Jamaica.* The following year he helped out with the Watts Summer Festival and, in collaboration with Nash, co-founded the Compton Crisis Intervention Team, aimed at tackling gang warfare in south central Los Angeles. That the Marleys and Tosh gravitated towards such company speaks volumes about the scope of their musical, as well as social, ambition.

According to Sims' estimate, the three ended up recording over 200 tracks for JAD, the publishing rights of which were assigned to Cayman Music and administered by CBS. The principal objectives were twofold. Marley (and also Tosh) would keep Nash supplied with material, while JAD would do their best to help the Wailers get international hits. There's little doubt that Sims, Nash and Jenkins were the first people to recognise Marley's potential in cracking the UK and American markets, even if their focus was understandably on the more established and commercially viable Nash at the time. Nash would cover several Marley compositions over the next few years, including 'Guava Jelly', 'Rock It Baby (Baby We've Got A Date)', 'Mellow Mood', 'Nice Time', 'Comma Comma', 'Stir It Up', and 'Reggae On Broadway', while co-writing 'You Poured Sugar On Me'.

---

* Danny Sims invited Muhammad Ali and Elijah Muhammad to Jamaica around this same time but both were denied entry by the Shearer government.

None of these would add to Nash's tally of bestsellers on either side of the Atlantic and there's definitely an argument to suggest it was Marley, not Nash, who prospered most from this part of the arrangement.

As regards the Wailers' own recordings for JAD, even their most dedicated fans would have to admit this material isn't among their best and that the group might have been trying just a little too hard for mainstream success, at the expense of their own identity as Caribbean soul rebels. They did have some scruples, however, since Marley was reluctant to record at Federal, on the grounds it was a "Babylon studio." According to Vincent Chin's oldest son Clive, this is what led to the JAD team booking Randy's for two months straight, after being introduced to the family by WIRL and Randy's engineer Bill Garnet. Vincent and his wife Pat had opened their first shop on the corner of East Street and Tower Street some 10 years previously. They'd named it Randy's Record Mart after a US record outlet, but then relocated to 17 North Parade in 1961, two years after Vincent had tried his hand at production with local mento and rhythm & blues acts. They'd originally built the upstairs studio for their own use, but then looked on in disbelief as South African trumpeter Hugh Masekela and jazz composer Quincy Jones arrived for sessions.

Family Man Barrett: "At that time, Randy's only had two tracks. Drum and bass go on one track and the rhythm pon the other and then we mix it down onto one track and voice. This is before Wailers come with Lee Perry, when we do songs like 'Liquidator'. It was a little after that, we hook up with Bob, Bunny, and Peter for 'Black Progress'."

The first time Family Man saw Bob Marley was after a friend pointed him out one day, sitting in the park opposite North Parade, close to the heart of bustling, downtown Kingston. Family Man was surprised to see that Marley had already started growing dreadlocks, since Rastas still hadn't gained the same levels of acceptance they'd enjoy in the Seventies.

"Bob hear me dismantle the bass on the Uniques' 'Watch This Sound' and shortly after that now, he appoint Reggie to fetch me for this session, so Reggie come fi carry me round Bob at this rehearsal place in an alley off Orange Street, near where them 'ave the traffic court now. Once I'm in there, Reggie leaves and I see Bob and the other man them rest easy, sipping on them chalice, so I just build up my lickle spliff and look pon 'im. After a time, Bob look back and sight me, cah 'im never know me yet, but me just stand in a corner and never speak. Me say to myself, 'Let me just rest here an' watch the man,' y'know? Reggie, he come back in now and Bob turn round to him and said, 'Reggie. I asked you to do me a favour, so what happen man?' Reggie says, 'But you ask me to bring you this musician and here he is, 'cause that's him over deh so.' Bob looks at me and said, 'Is your name Family Man?' Me answer him yes, so he said, 'Bloodclaat! Me never know, but you are the right man then.' He thought Family Man was an elder and didn't realise I was just a youth like him. That was the session for 'Black Progress', 'cause the three of them a sing it together. Bunny, Peter and Bob on vocals, myself and my brother playing rhythm and from that point on, we never give up, no matter the crisis."

According to Family Man, they recorded a cover of Junior Walker and the All-Stars' 'Gotta Hold Onto This Feeling' at the same session as 'Black Progress'. This has been contested in certain quarters, since the original didn't chart in the US until late February 1970. In actual fact, Motown had released it the previous November and there's every possibility Marley had access to an advance copy, due to Sims' industry contacts. The track found Junior Walker's quartet exploring a more sophisticated sound in collaboration with Johnny Bristol, rather than pursuing the raucous rhythm & blues style heard on their earlier hits like 'Shotgun' and 'Road Runner'. The Wailers' version remains reasonably faithful to the original, with Bob and Rita sparring on lead vocals with a directness rarely heard before. The rhythm is a lot more subdued than on 'Black Progress', but typically Upsetter-ish, while Lester Sterling and "Deadly" Headley Bennett lend colouring on alto and tenor saxes respectively.

Thoughts of how he'd been captivated by the Wailers' 'Simmer Down' drifted through Fams' mind as he leant against the wall of that cramped rehearsal studio and watched as Marley, Livingston, and Tosh began to navigate the songs they were going to sing at Randy's. Bob Andy, a former member of the Paragons, whose own stint at Studio One coincided with that of the Wailers, has memories of watching them rehearse.

"From as far back as the Sixties, the Wailers were feared as much as they were admired. They were a very strict bunch of guys and always had screw faces. They would keep anyone away from them with just a look. They didn't accommodate anyone. The Paragons liked and admired them, but were sort of scared of those looks, which protected them from any kind of intrusion or invasion of their privacy. They would mix because they were brethren, but they also had a very elitist attitude.

"There was a room where we used to listen to records. Coxsone would give artists music to listen to on this turntable and speakers, but there was another room between Coxsone's inner office and the music room where you could go and lock yourself in and no one else could enter. The Wailers had access to that and I did too. One particular day, I was the witness to a very special performance. It was like being let into a secret. I was very high from smoking and they were always high too. It was the first time I had seen each of the Wailers with a guitar and each time I remember this, it's like remembering a dream. I sat there and they were just messing around with various songs for a while, but finally it climaxed with a song called 'Ten To One', which I later found out was a Curtis Mayfield song. I realised how much the Impressions had influenced Marley in those times, since they were both trios and Curtis played guitar too.

"Bob sang the first line, then Bunny came in on the second and all three came in on the next line. Peter sang a line and then all three sang in harmony, then Bob and Bunny sang solo again. When they started that song, I saw a side of the Wailers I felt no one else had seen. It was like my own personal revelation. I've never heard music so beautiful and I've never seen such love and camaraderie in all my life. I knew then that the Wailers were special people, but they were special by being the Wailers, as a unit. When I reflect on that occasion, it was divine. It was like being on a spaceship, listening to the music of the spheres. I was spellbound and that memory will stay with me forever."

Family Man and Carly hit it off with the Wailers straight away, but after playing on 'Trouble On The Road Again', they wouldn't feature on the group's next few recordings because they were on tour with the Upsetters. Since their deal with Sims and Nash wasn't exclusive, the Wailers decided to record an album with Leslie Kong. Kong's hits with Desmond Dekker, Jimmy Cliff, the Pioneers, and Toots & the Maytals proved he had the capacity to deliver the crossover success Marley craved and while Bob harboured few fond memories of having recorded for the Chineyman in the past, there were precious few alternatives. The way the Beatles had made such spectacular use of the LP format in 1967 with *Sgt. Pepper's Lonely Hearts Club Band* had revolutionised music industry thinking and so the idea was to make Jamaica's first-ever concept album, using only Kong's own musicians, i.e., Gladdy's All-Stars, rather than the Upsetters. Gladdy Anderson, Jackie Jackson, Hux Brown, Winston Wright, and Mikey "Boo" Richards all played on these sessions, which took place at Dynamic Sound during the spring of 1970.

The results are far better than the Wailers have been given credit for since, whereas their Studio One material was uneven, the *Best Of The Wailers* album is consistent throughout. 'Soul Shakedown Party' was its biggest hit and Kong also released 'Stop The Train', doubled up with 'Caution' on a single. Good as these songs were, however, there was nothing to match Toots & the Maytals' '54-46 Was My Number', the Melodians' 'Rivers Of Babylon', or Desmond Dekker's 'Israelites'. What's interesting is that four of the ten tracks feature Tosh on lead vocals, which suggests he had a far more prominent role within the group than many people realise. On 'Can't You See', Tosh revisits a song they'd originally recorded for Coxsone, except the vocal arrangements now reflected those heard on rock tunes by American groups like the Byrds and Buffalo Springfield, whose work contained traces of folk and country. Another Tosh composition, 'Soon Come', strikes a balance between pleading for his girl's affections and asserting masculine pride by stating, "I don't like hanging round, or to be pushed around. I don't like soon come." (Tosh revisited this song after signing to the Rolling Stones' label in the late Seventies.)

Johnny Nash also sang 'Go Tell It On The Mountain', a traditional American folk song, which had been part of Tosh's repertoire since childhood. The dignity and authority he brings to this track is reminiscent of what one might hear listening to Leadbelly or Big Bill Broonzy. Tosh's other track, 'Stop The Train', also has a traditional feel. The Wailers later revived it for *Catch A Fire*, but this version contains more than a hint of blues and country as Tosh wraps himself in the image of an itinerant teacher, an outsider who realises he's been wasting his time and now must fulfil his own destiny. His vocal strength and presence is in contrast to the more haunting, fragile qualities expressed on Marley compositions like 'Caution' – a tale warning of making too many false moves, interspersed with Bunny's chants of "Hit me from the top, you crazy motherfucker."

There are further vocal interjections on 'Soul Captives', demonstrating a James Brown influence. The Wailers' more feisty side shows on 'Back Out', as Bob tells the lead character to back off and shut their mouth. A raunchy but understated 'Do It Twice' is among the other highlights, but it's the nagging, insistent 'Soul Shakedown Party', which Kong initially pinned his hopes on, that got the most airplay in Jamaica. Local success didn't translate into anything greater however, leaving the Wailers still searching for that elusive crossover hit.

When Beverley's released *The Best Of The Wailers* several months later, the title annoyed the group immensely, despite being a true enough description at the time. There's a possibly apocryphal story of how Livingston went and expressed his disapproval to Kong, telling him that since the best of Wailers is yet to come, this means Kong couldn't have long to live. The apparently healthy Kong died of a heart attack soon afterwards – an event that only reinforced impressions that the quietest and most withdrawn member of the Wailers had mystical powers and wasn't above using them whenever the occasion demanded it.

CHAPTER SEVEN

Soul Rebels

"THE Wailers moved from that shop in the alley off Orange Street to one in Beeston Street, right in front of where I born and grow," says Family Man. "I'd go there to buy one or two records after we'd played on 'Black Progress'. Bob would be there more times and we'd share ideas about the music, or maybe drink a water coconut when we were standing outside in the road. We were always there hanging out at the front of the shop, playing music, or maybe sitting upstairs, where Keith Hudson had an office for a while.

"Other times, we'd buy some food or eat a breadfruit around the back of the shop, and discuss this brethren Danny Sims, who'd come to Jamaica and lived up by Russell Heights. After a while, we start to hook up and go visit him together and rehearse, 'cause we do enough music and recordings at his house. We'd just lay down some demos on this tape recorder they had up there and then go record them at Federal or somewhere like that. Johnny Nash, he wasn't around at that time, although Bob had already written one or two songs with him by then. We did more than an album's worth of songs with Danny Sims. I don't know all of the releases, but I understand some of them have come out on the JAD label, like 'Chances Are'. Those tracks came from before we worked together for Lee Scratch Perry, because Bob was mostly on his own back then, and we were rehearsing a new concept of lyrics with melody and music, trying to catch a particular riff and a tempo that we could take on the street. That's because from Danny Sims have this international artist called Johnny Nash in the camp already, we were hoping to turn it into two, although it didn't quite work out like that."

The material Marley voiced for Sims might have been intended to help him find the same audience Nash was reaching, but the arrangements and production sounded lacking in something, even if Marley's songs weren't. On most of these JAD tracks, there is an uneasy compromise between the loose-limbed sound of early reggae or rocksteady and the more polished approach favoured by Sims, Jenkins, and producer Joe Venneri, who recalls Marley telling him that he wanted to be a soul star, "just like Otis Redding." The idea of this ever becoming a reality seems highly far-fetched, since Marley's voice had none of the authority and emotional range of singers like Redding, Wilson Pickett, or James Brown. If anything, Tosh's more expansive tones sounded better suited to this type of material, although it's doubtful the fiercely proud guitarist would have stooped so low as to sing lead on the Archies' 'Sugar Sugar', as Marley did for a session produced by Vincent Chin at Randy's in early 1970.*

The song's blatantly commercial, pop aesthetic couldn't be further removed from the rebel image the Wailers would pursue in tandem with Lee Perry and the Barrett brothers, confirming Family Man and Adams' assertion that the Wailers lacked direction and were at a definite low point during this stage of their careers. Marley's strengths as a songwriter weren't in question, nor the magic that ensued when he, Tosh, and Livingston gathered around the microphone to share harmonies. It was more that they sounded out of synch with the current music scene, since their soul or pop material wasn't convincing and even the reggae sides they made, including the beautiful waltz 'Send Me That Love', had so far failed to connect with audiences at home or abroad. In the meantime, reggae fans were lapping up hits by Derrick Morgan ('Moon Hop'), Boris Gardiner ('Elizabethan Reggae'), the Melodians, the Pioneers, Jimmy Cliff, Harry J All-Stars and, of course, the Upsetters.

The Upsetters played on Tosh's 'Oppressor Man' (credited as a Wailers' self-production) which reworked 'Sinner Man'. It was by no means the first time Tosh had recorded with the Upsetters or, indeed, the Hippy Boys, since he'd also recently overdubbed organ on a handful of their rhythms for Bunny Lee. These sessions, again held at Randy's, resulted in instrumental tracks – like 'Selassie Serenade', 'Crimson Pirate', 'The Return Of Al Capone', and 'Sun Valley', a cut of Slim Smith's 'Everybody Needs Love' – that would remain curios at best, bringing to an end Tosh's parallel career as a session player.

The contrast with 'Oppressor Man' couldn't have been greater, as the song heralded a new chapter in Tosh's personal odyssey with its booming bass sound and loping rhythm, decorated by Lewis' scrubbing guitar and Adams' nimble piano runs. There was a sense that Tosh was growing

---

* Wilson Pickett had transformed it into a Top 5 R&B hit that April, but it was the Archies' bubblegum number one from the previous October that audiences were most familiar with.

impatient with playing second fiddle to Marley and was already thinking of going solo while keeping his options open as a member of the Wailers. Tosh, along with Marley and Livingston, joined the Barretts on another session at Randy's soon afterwards, when they played on a track called 'Field Marshall', named after Carly. The Barretts also contributed towards two tracks by the Soulettes, 'My Desire' and 'Bring It Up', featuring Hortense Lewis on lead vocals, around the same time. These were among the last tracks recorded by members of the Wailers before they decided to rethink their whole musical strategy.

"There were a lot of things going on after we'd got back from England, and not just celebration," says Adams. "After a while, Scratch team up with Bob, Peter, and Bunny and ask if we'll play with them. We said, 'Okay, why not?' And they had a track recorded already, so we did some overdubs. That was 'My Cup', but we get a feel for what they were doing and then call a session. Everybody was glad about it, because it was quite something for the Wailers and Upsetters to get together like that. They'd been making some monstrous tunes like 'Hypocrites', but they were on something of a down at the time, because after 'Simmer Down', and Bob go away and then come back, he'd turned Rasta and the people weren't so fond of that. I remember when Bob first start to grow his locks, because Mortimer Planno and him were moving at that time, but then Bob cut his hair again. That was the last of them I saw, until one day I run into Bob on Spanish Town Road. He'd just come back to town from the country and he was selling some brooms. He had a whole heap of them on the top of the car and then I didn't see him again until after we'd got back from England and decided to work."

Both music critics and fans have voiced the opinion that the music Lee Perry produced with the Wailers is the best they ever did, even allowing for the more celebrated works issued by Island throughout the mid-to-late Seventies. It's a view not necessarily shared by the many buying budget-priced Bob Marley compilations listing familiar tracks like 'Kaya', 'Sun Is Shining' and 'Keep On Moving', only to find that they are earlier versions, recorded at Randy's with Lee Perry, and not the subsequent Marley recordings so beloved of an international audience. Yet there's no disputing the groundbreaking nature of these recordings, or the fact that they turned the Wailers' fortunes around.

Bunny Lee contends he was the one who recommended the Wailers work with Lee Perry, but that Marley had responded with, 'Who?

Chicken Scratch?' Marley thought he was still working with Coxsone, but Bunny assured him otherwise and pointed towards songs Perry had produced with Dave Barker, as evidence. Perry wasn't all that keen on working with singers, since they would keep asking him for money. He therefore decided to concentrate on instrumentals, bar the odd recording with Busty Brown, the Inspirations, and his girlfriend Melanie Jonas, whose version of Blood, Sweat & Tears' 'Spinning Wheel' would later achieve notoriety after being included on the *World's Worst Record Show* album, compiled by British radio deejay Kenny Everett. "Love is blind," they say, and in this instance, tone deaf as well, although Jonas was obviously an inspiration in other ways.

In early 1970, Perry was on an artistic high, full of creative energy and busy exercising his wizardry in the studio by stripping down and remodelling old tracks, splicing different rhythms together and overdubbing wild effects and bizarre vocals on top of them like a man possessed. Even the musicians were amazed at times, as a straightforward backing track would transform into a riotous outburst of comic mayhem or a dangerous slice of drum and bass, bristling with mind-blowing invention. By way of illustration, a listen to 'Kill Them All', 'Kinky Mood', 'Son Of Thunder' and 'Sipreano', or even 'Sound Underground' and 'Granny Show Parts 1 & 2', featuring Dave Barker, reveals Perry's eccentric genius.

Despite his reluctance to work with vocalists, Perry had taken a liking to Barker, who was his principal artist before the Wailers. Like the Barretts, Barker (real name: David Crooks) used to live in Rollington Town, near Franklyn Town where he was born. He and Glen Brown sang together as Glen & Dave in the rocksteady era, recording songs like 'Lady With The Bright Light' and 'Show Me The Way' for Coxsone. Barker was with Brown the day he dropped in on an Upsetters session at Randy's, which is how he came to voice 'Prisoner Of Love', after Perry had set Bunny Lee's 'Slip Away' rhythm into motion. After being badly beaten as a child, Barker had a stutter but his performance on this track had an immediacy Perry simply couldn't resist. It must have threatened to lift the roof off Studio 17 during this impromptu session where Perry renamed Crooks "Dave Barker". On 'Prisoner Of Love', and also a matching cut 'I Was Wrong', Barker sounds every inch the soul singer Marley wanted to be. His vocals caress or excite in equal measure and he could deejay too, as he'd soon prove on 'Lockjaw' and 'Shocks Of Mighty'.

'Prisoner Of Love' was licensed to Pama in late 1969, after Perry had travelled to England with the Upsetters, although the pair wouldn't achieve another hit until the following March, when 'Shocks Of Mighty' exploded out of Randy's after Barker first voiced 'Set Me Free' over the same rhythm (which Perry had again "borrowed" from Bunny Lee). Whereas 'Set Me Free' is a Slim Smith derivative, 'Shocks Of Mighty' opens with Barker proclaiming "this is upsetting. Shocks of mighty. Hit me back!" and then finds him screaming, James Brown-style, over another unrelenting Upsetters' groove centred around the Barretts' inimitable drum and bass. Trojan and Pama both had hits with the song, as Perry continued to sell them the same tracks, in the same fashion Bunny Lee did.

As the excitement surrounding 'Shocks Of Mighty' spread, Barker was kept busy recording songs for Bunny Lee, Sonia Pottinger, Lloyd Charmers, Jimmy Riley, Duke Reid, and Vincent Chin, as well as Perry. Bunny even teamed him with Family Man on the aptly named 'Hot Sauce', but Barker's Upsetter releases brought him the most exposure that year. Trojan followed 'Shocks Of Mighty' with 'Some Sympathy', sung Stax-style over a grumbling, Upsetters' backbeat, and 'Sound Underground', on which he again testifies but to less ebullient effect than either of his previous efforts. 'Sound Underground' had a somewhat moribund cover of Gerry & the Pacemakers' 1964 hit 'Don't Let The Sun Catch You Crying' on the flipside, for which all three Wailers contribute backing vocals.

When Barker talks about the Wailers, it's with a reverence born out of professional and spiritual kinship rather than hero worship. He describes them as having "a oneness" and says the Barrett brothers – whom he credits with possessing unique qualities as musicians – would put their whole selves into the recordings. Indeed, their skill and dedication had attracted Marley and the rest of the Wailers in the first place. Barker puts the early criticism they received from other musicians down to jealousy at them getting the lion's share of available session work. At the time the Barretts joined forces with the Wailers, the Upsetters were Jamaica's most in-demand rhythm section and they revelled in the fact. While not rich by any means, they all drove nice cars, wore decent clothes and had no trouble attracting female admirers. The chemistry between the young musicians was turning virtually every song they played on into hits and they were already beginning to produce tracks for themselves. Having stumbled across the Upsetters by default, Perry was having to fend off their growing discontentment over money and was secretly scouting around for other musicians he could exploit more easily. His main priority, however, was to keep Marley and the Wailers content, since it was only a matter of time before they would begin to happen. All they needed was the right material.

Barker says the Wailers' songs were always thoroughly rehearsed beforehand, so as to get them sounding exactly right and not waste any studio time. It was a radically different process from how the Barretts had been used to working with Bunny Lee and Lloyd Charmers and it helped instil them with discipline. As a former Youth Corps cadet, Fams responded to this more regimented approach quite happily, as did the neat and fastidious Carly. Barker admits he wasn't privy to the Wailers' inner sanctum, but would share the odd session with them, or exchange greetings whenever they met in a back room at Perry's shop on Charles Street, where the Wailers rehearsed prior to recording. Marley, who stayed at Perry's house in Cardiff Crescent for a while, allegedly took his producer's advice to stick with Tosh and Livingston for the time being, rather than entertain thoughts of going it alone. While respecting Marley's individual talent, particularly as a songwriter, the wily Upsetter recognised just how special the three sounded in unison and still cherished memories of their triumphs at Studio One, during the days when he too worked for Coxsone.

Barker witnessed Marley exchanging ideas for lyrics with Perry on several occasions, thus confirming the producer's claim to have co-written several of the Wailers' biggest hits from this period. Family Man, too, admits that, "Scratch always bring a vibes and some brand new approach towards any song," whereas others give him credit for influencing Marley's vocal style as the pair searched for a formula that would shift the Wailers' music into focus.

Barker claims Marley always knew what he wanted, but that getting it was dependent on the musicians he had around him. According to the singer, the involvement of a higher power had brought about the union of the Wailers and Upsetters and their alignment was intended to fulfil a spiritual purpose. This had nothing to do with the power of man, but was done for the love of the music and the mission that was revealed to them through the songs they were creating.* Barker points out how the Wailers and Barrett brothers became soul mates during their time with Perry and their dedication to the music was more important than anything else,

---

* It's interesting to note here that many years later, Marley's son Ziggy would make similar claims about his own music.

including, unfortunately, any attendant business matters. They fervently believed what they were doing was for the good of humanity and that money simply didn't apply at that stage; the joy came from knowing they were part of a force the whole world could share. Trust, however, was important, because if any money did result from such endeavours, then the singers and musicians expected it to be shared fairly between themselves and the producer, i.e. Perry. This trust, mixed with the love they had for the music, powered their creativity to fresh heights and enhanced the comradeship kindled during their initial sessions together.

Family Man Barrett: "When Bob and I first join forces, it wasn't just like any other artist and musician work together on one or two sessions. I wasn't a session musician for the Wailers, because I become part of a thing. We become the Wailers band and part of a long-term journey because all of us were young and aware of the work that we had to do in taking this music internationally. Bob, he had a family to support, because Ziggy, he was just a baby in his pram and the rest of them weren't born yet. It was from there that we start writing, arranging and producing music together and setting the standard for reggae music not only in Jamaica, but also the world. That was the talk right from those Beeston Street days and then Scratch, he started talking about us doing some things together, through we have the package in place already. That was when we do 'My Cup', 'Duppy Conqueror' and all of those other revolutionary sounds as soul rebels, because the music had changed by then, from what the Wailers had been doing with Leslie Kong.

"That was just a one-album deal and I wasn't involved with that. I liked a couple of tracks from it [*The Best Of The Wailers*], like 'Soul Shakedown Party', but it just had the regular Jamaican sound, the regular reggae sound and it never did anything for them either, because it was only after the Wailers join forces with the Barrett brothers, that they begin to have any real success. You can hear the difference if you listen to some of their earlier tracks, but we went out there and paved the way and opened those big, iron gates so that the rest of Jamaican music could rush through."

Listening to Family Man and Adams, you become aware of how peripheral a figure Perry was during those Wailers sessions. While feeding off his creative energy, Marley kept a tight rein on the producer's excesses and the material Perry recorded with the Wailers bears no trace of the gimmickry he'd employ elsewhere. It's the band that provides the most significant contribution, since the Wailers were already skilled in working out harmonies, merely needing a different framework for their musical

Neville "Bunny" Livingston, Robert Nesta Marley, and Peter "Tosh" McIntosh in an early publicity shot of the Wailing Wailers taken at the time they were recording for Studio One, circa 1964. **(LFI)**

Emperor Haile Selassie I of Ethiopia. (HULTON ARCHIVE/GETTY IMAGES)

The Upsetters during a session at Randy's Studio 17 in Kingston, 1968/69. From left to right:
Aston "Family Man" Barrett, Carlton Barrett, Alva "Reggie" Lewis, and Glen "Capo" Adams. (MICHAEL OCHS ARCHIVES/GETTY IMAGES)

(Above and bottom left) Peter, Bunny, Rita, and Bob rehearsing around the time they were recording for Danny Sims, Arthur Jenkins, and Johnny Nash's JAD label, 1968/69. **(URBANIMAGE.TV/TRAX/ASTLEY CHIN)**

Bob Marley on stage circa 1970, soon after recording *The Best Of The Wailers* album for Beverleys.
(URBANIMAGE.TV/TRAX/OSSIE HAMILTON)

An example of Coxsone Dodd's earliest sound-system equipment, as first used during the late Fifties. **(URBANIMAGE.TV/RON VESTER)**

Legendary Jamaica sound-system owner and record producer Clement "Coxsone" Dodd, proprietor of the Studio One label, and the Wailers' first-ever producer. **(URBANIMAGE.TV/BRIAN JAHN)**

An early publicity photo of American singer Johnny Nash, who first popularised the songs of Bob Marley to audiences outside of Jamaica, prior to the Wailers' own international breakthrough. **(HULTON ARCHIVE).**

Jamaican instrumentalist/record producer Augustus Pablo, at Channel One recording studio in Kingston during the late Seventies. **(URBANIMAGE.TV/JEAN BERNARD SOHIEZ)**

Bob and Rita with Sharon, Ziggy, Cedella, and baby Stephen in 1972. (URBANIMAGE.TV/TRAX/OSSIE HAMILTON)

The Soulettes, performing in Kingston, circa 1971. (URBANIMAGE.TV/TRAX/OSSIE HAMILTON)

Peter Tosh in reflective mood outside Dynamic Sound Studios, Kingston, 1970. (URBANIMAGE.TV/TRAX/OSSIE HAMILTON)

The Observer, producer of classic hits by Dennis Brown, Big Youth, Gregory Isaacs, and many others from the early Seventies onwards. (DAVID CORIO/GETTY IMAGES)

Max Romeo, original lead singer with the Hippy Boys, on stage during the late Seventies. (URBANIMAGE.TV/ADRIAN BOOT)

Bunny "Striker" Lee, Jamaica's most prolific record producer of the Seventies, and the man responsible for fostering the Barrett brothers' talents on a string of hits from the late Sixties onwards, including their 1968 joint debut, Lester Sterling and Stranger Cole's' 'My Bangarang'. (URBANIMAGE.TV/TIM BARROW)

A publicity shot of the Wailers, including the Barrett brothers, taken soon after the band signed with Island Records in 1972. (MICHAEL OCHS ARCHIVES/GETTY IMAGES)

Chris Blackwell with Junior Marvin in the late Seventies. (URBANIMAGE.TV/ADRIAN BOOT)

"Family Man" Barrett with chalice. (URBANIMAGE.TV/LEE JAFFE)

endeavours, rather than anything more dictatorial. Livingston in particular was suspicious of Perry right from the start and the friction between them would slowly fester like an open wound, despite the early promise of tracks like 'My Cup', 'Try Me' and 'Man To Man'.

'My Cup' was an adaptation of another James Brown song, 'I Guess I've Got To Cry, Cry, Cry', recorded at a time when Brown was breaking in a new set of musicians anchored by Phelps "Cat Fish" Collins and his younger brother Bootsy. The only known copies of this single are white label affairs bearing the stamp "Power Label", which could well be a Wailers/Perry collaboration or even a bootleg. Whatever the story behind the release, the record itself is an unusual mix of emotive singing and foot-tapping rhythm, confirming Adams' assertion that the Upsetters had already recorded the backing track before Marley poured his heart out on lead vocal, with the other two Wailers adding counterpoint harmonies. Family Man's bass joyfully gurgles away, detracting from the pain and loss in Marley's delivery, while Carly shuffles for all he's worth. As an opening salvo, it was radically different from their work with Kong and nowhere near as cohesive, yet there was an undeniable energy that hinted at greater things to come.

'My Cup' was recorded at Dynamic, where the Beverley's sessions had taken place. A photo of the Wailers from this period shows the group posed against the studio's perimeter fence in their hippy gear – Marley in patchwork denim flares and Tosh wearing brightly patterned trousers and a paisley shirt. None have dreadlocks as yet, Marley having cut his off since the occasion Family Man's friend pointed him out in the park. The three bear the look of men burdened by their dreams, but who have yet to fulfil them. Marley's face, especially, has an earnest expression, containing both impatience and steely determination.

The most notable change in approach concerned the arrangements. Whereas Kong was making quality, Jamaican-sounding product for the international pop market, Perry was just a small-time operator whose budget didn't stretch to using horn sections or strings, despite the success generated by 'Return Of Django'. Perry's biographer David Katz estimates the Wailers spent eight months recording for him in total, beginning with those initial Dynamic Sound sessions. 'Try Me', 'Small Axe', 'More Axe' and 'Man To Man' are all said to have been recorded there, together with Glen Adams' 'Never Had A Dream', a couple of songs by Dave Barker, plus three by Carl "Ras" Dawkins, including a cover of the Temptations' 'Cloud Nine'.

Thanks to Norman Whitfield's searching reality lyrics (co-written with Barrett Strong) and inspired production featuring slashing rhythm guitar, almost claustrophobic arrangements, and harmonies that contrasted deep bass with a stratospheric tenor, 'Cloud Nine' was a revelation when released at the beginning of 1969. Other unconventional yet commercial songs, like 'Say It Loud I'm Black And Proud' and Sly & the Family Stone's 'Everyday People' ushered in the funk era, whereupon soul and rock converged and the spirit of black power – allied to the hippies' freedom-loving ethics – served to liberate black music from its shackles.

Perry, the Wailers, and members of the Upsetters all loved 'Cloud Nine' and its influence pervades a fair percentage of their material from this period. You can hear it in how Tosh and Livingston harmonise on 'Try Me', as Marley first pleads for some girl's affections, but then subtly changes tack by declaring, "If you need satisfaction, listen baby I've got the action. Where I am, that's where it's at." The Wailers also make reference to 'Cloud Nine' in 'Rebel's Hop', blending it with lyrics from 'Rude Boy' (a.k.a. 'Rude Boy Ska' or 'Walk The Proud Land'), a track they first recorded for Coxsone, but which was now driven by funky guitar licks and stubborn bass. Livingston shines on this one and it's easy to see why he insists that ska and reggae have the same, rhythmic heartbeat at their core when you hear the Upsetters putting a (then) contemporary spin on music made several years earlier. There's a warmth and depth to 'Rebel's Hop' that shows the band settling in to the task of reinventing the Wailers, as evidenced by the chugging backdrops accorded 'No Water' and 'Reaction'. These songs are again led by Marley, whose voice aches with feeling, even though it sounds disembodied at times, as it floats above the rhythms.

'No Water' is another song about sexual need, offset once more by Tosh and Livingston's almost comic scat harmonies. "I'm in a bed, send me a nurse," Marley sings, with possible reference to Rita, while 'Reaction' casts a spell that's shrouded in mystery as Marley informs us that for "every little action, there's a reaction." It's one of the most haunting songs in the entire Wailers' catalogue and one can only imagine whether anyone but Perry would have allowed them to record a track this esoteric, since its chances of commercial success were clearly limited.

If clarification were needed of where the Wailers were at, or indeed, headed, then 'Soul Rebel' provides it. Adams says the Soul Syndicate played on the track, after the Upsetters had fallen out with Perry over money. Other sources suggest only Family Man is missing from the line-up and that Lloyd Parkes deputises on bass (as he does on 'It's Alright' and '400 Years'.) Regardless, it's again hypnotic as the first few bars draw the listener in, but then stop dead before the singing starts. Marley's plaintive vocals are framed by cooing harmonies, while his lyrics speak of the highs and lows of following his chosen path – his strength, derived from remaining steadfast to his goals, balanced out by a deepening sense of alienation. 'Soul Rebel' became the title track of the Wailers' first album for Perry, an apt choice since it's a starkly definitive statement from a band in transition. This kind of darkly introspective sound, plumbing the innermost recesses of the human psyche, shaped by Marley's Biblical teachings under Mortimer Planno, helped usher in the roots era of Jamaican music.

Marley blends Biblical references and romance on 'Corner Stone', a bouncy, philosophical ditty that shares a similar rhythm to 'Keep On Moving'. "The stone that the builder refuse will always be the head corner stone," he sings, while warning, "The things people refuse are the things they should use." The lyrics possibly refer to childhood issues (since Marley was abandoned by his father), as well as the neglect Marley had suffered through his music, but the wisdom in this song is far-reaching and by no means confined to his own situation. The remaining three tracks from *Soul Rebels* were recorded at Randy's, as opposed to Dynamic Sound. A version of 'It's Alright' appeared on the JA release of *The Good, Bad And The Upsetters* album. Tosh's percolating lead guitar is funk personified, but it's a groove song, and not a message carrier like the mournful 'No Sympathy' or '400 Years', both of which feature Tosh on lead vocals. The former is a song about desolation, yet in the midst of the gloom, Tosh announces he's on his way to happiness, where he can "find peace and rest" – a theme akin to that of 'Soul Rebel'.

'400 Years' decries how so many African descendants suffer from the after-effects of slavery. "Four hundred years of the same philosophy and black people, they still can't be free," Tosh laments, yet his lyrics also call for a collective awakening, since the time has now come for them "to make a move." Songs like '400 Years' have prompted comparisons between Tosh and John Lennon, who was renowned for being the most outspoken and non-conformist member of the Beatles. It's certainly an anthem (later reappearing on *Catch A Fire*) while 'No Sympathy' would be reworked during the *Burnin'* sessions but remained unreleased for more than three decades.

An instrumental cut of '400 Years', showcasing Uziah "Sticky" Thompson's intuitive feel for percussion, brings to a close one of the most beguiling albums in the history of Jamaican music, since no one had ever heard anything quite like it before.

Glen Adams: "After we do that first album for Scratch, I bring it to England and take it to Trojan. We mastered it up there before I left to return to Jamaica and that was May 1970. I remember I go back up to England after touring there in January, early February, so we took about four months to record that album *Soul Rebels*. That was the type of sound we were coming with at that time and yes, it was different to what everyone else was doing back then, because it was a big change from 'Liquidator' to 'Duppy Conqueror', y'know?"

"Reggae was a new concept at the time," adds Family Man. "I was the one with my brother who developed reggae, as it is known today. It was our drum and bass that formed the unique sound of the Hippy Boys and the Upsetters and it was this same sound that introduced me to Bob Marley and made the Wailers become international. This beat is what we called "one drop", and the basic reggae music we were creating represented the heartbeat of the people. The drum is the first instrument in the music so it must be outstanding and the bass was the backbone, so if either of these two weren't right, then the music itself couldn't be right. Without a good backbone and a strong heart, the music just wouldn't work.

"When we were working with the Wailers, singing and instruments come together as one, with each of us bouncing off the other's abilities. We'd listen to every man's part and then we'd come to the conclusion that maybe Bob should be the one to carry the vocals or whatsoever. Looking back, it seems like we co-produced a lot of those tracks, because we'd always be discussing how each particular track should go and what they needed to sound better. I was more involved than many people realise, because they call me 'Maestro' and I have to pass everything, even though I was so young at the time. But I used to look forward to those sessions and I looked forward to the responsibilities as well, because working with the Wailers come like a thrill to me and I was always wondering what was going to come next at those sessions."

Marley admitted to the *Jamaica Daily News* that the Wailers had "found their roots again," while working with Perry and the Upsetters. "Jamaica is such a controlled place," he later told Rob Bowman. "At that time, you have bands out there. You never think about getting instruments. You think about singing go a far way, especially if you get harmonies. It was just singing, y'know? But I find while we were singing, we were writing so much songs and find that the songs didn't turn out the way I write them when we go into the studio to do them with other musicians. It sounds slightly changed because of the other musicians. So we say, 'No. I don't feel that that is right. I want to do the music our way. The way how we feel like saying it.' So, we started learning to play things and getting other musicians such as Aston Barrett and Carly Barrett, getting a group together. You can't deal with music if you don't have the music. You have to control the music so it all falls into place so you can control what type of music you're getting. What type of music you want."

Glen Adams: "I remember Bob saying to someone how no one had rated us in Jamaica at one time. Then he said that despite being under-rated, we were the 'most bumbaclaat creative musicians in the world!'"

Perry arranged a handful of shows to promote *Soul Rebels*, the first of which was held at the Sombrero Club on Molynes Road, timed to coincide with Nicky Thomas' farewell celebrations. After his 'Love Of The Common People' had entered the UK Top 10 in June, the singer everyone called Nigel was preparing to leave for England. Approximately 300 people turned up for the Wailers' two-hour set, which led to further dates in Negril and Kingston. The band were keen to showcase the new, rebel style they'd forged with the Upsetters and with such strong songs in their armoury, as well as so many favourites from their Studio One days to draw from, anticipation was running high both onstage and off. The Upsetters played live gigs very rarely during their time with Perry, unlike when they were the Hippy Boys, so the band members were all looking forward to performing in front of local audiences again.*

Despite the growing closeness between the Wailers and the Barrett brothers, their relationship still hadn't developed into the closed circle it would become during the Island years. Members of the Upsetters con-tinued to play sessions for a growing number of other producers, while the Wailers persisted with recordings for both JAD and themselves. By the time they'd booked Randy's for 'Trouble On The Road Again' the studio had installed four-track equipment, although it's significant that Family Man would later be asked to remix and overdub this track before it became one of the last releases on the Wailers' Wail 'N Soul 'M label.

---

* Family Man recalls backing the Wailers at the VIP Club and a place on Orange Street called the Psychedelic Shop around this time, but since they're also reported to have per-formed at Skateland, the Silver Slipper, Prime Time, and the Glass Bucket at Cross Roads during 1970, it's possible the Soul Syndicate backed the Wailers on these dates.

Perry too, was busy working on side projects with Dave Barker, the Upsetters, and Junior Byles, whose 'What's This World Coming To' and 'Live As One' were beginning to cause a stir under his *nom-de-plume* of King Chubby. As well as Barker's debut album, Trojan released the Upsetters' *Eastwood Rides Again*, which in the absence of a group shot, had a photo of a Jamaican rude boy brandishing a revolver on the cover, in grand pseudo-Western tradition. The material therein was varied to say the least, with Val Bennett's 'Baby Baby' revisiting a sound first popular-ised by Fats Domino, while 'Red Hot' and 'Tight Spot' hinted at the emergence of dub as Perry stripped the rhythms to little more than just drum and bass.

James Brown would have thought his musicians had been moonlighting had he heard 'Popcorn' and 'Catch This', while 'Knock On Wood' and 'Power Pack' are pared down, tightened reggae instrumentals of Eddie Floyd's hit and the Temptations' 'Cloud Nine' respectively. It wasn't a great album and sounded as if it might have been put together while Lee was otherwise preoccupied, which of course he was. Barker's album *Prisoner Of Love* had similar flaws and the singer himself has never felt it did him justice; hardly surprising considering the other songs he recorded during this period. Furthermore, Trojan credited it to "Dave Barker meets The Upsetters", which reveals a lot about the group's selling power at the time. Among the highlights are the title track and its companion, 'I Was Wrong', 'Shocks Of Mighty', 'Set Me Free' and a cover of the Temptations' 'Runaway Child, Running Wild' complete with the now-obligatory wah-wah guitar. As on other Perry-produced soul covers, the aim wasn't to identically duplicate the sound and arrangement of the original, but to reconstruct it, giving it an entirely Jamaican twist. Barker does much the same thing with Bob Dylan's 'Blowing In The Wind' (taking the same musical backdrop Bunny Lee used for 'Reggae On Broadway') and also the Wailers' 'My Cup', which he sang over a different rhythm.

Interestingly, *Prisoner Of Love* and *Eastwood Rides Again* generated most attention in some quarters of the British music press, since the Wailers had yet to re-establish their overseas popularity. The music they were making was way too downbeat and introspective for skinheads intent on doing the Moon Hop all night. The song that really cemented the Wailers' involve-ment with the Upsetters was 'Duppy Conqueror', which Perry and Marley wrote in the Green Door Saloon after the producer had sent for Marley, telling him he wanted to write a song using the lines, "Yes me friend, me friend. Them set me free again. Yes me friend, me friend. Me deh pon street again."

'Duppy Conqueror' was an immediate hit after being released on single in Jamaica and on Trojan's Upsetter label in England. This version wasn't the original, however, and its success was only made possible after Perry had eaten a little humble pie and mended his relationship with the Upsetters, who'd refused to play on it initially, after the producer had again avoided payment for previous sessions. Thinking he could cut corners, Perry drafted in the Soul Syndicate, but Marley didn't like the rhythm they laid down for 'Duppy Conqueror' and insisted the Upsetters re-record it, just like they'd practised in rehearsals. His instinct was spot on, since the liquid skank they played that night at Randy's is among the most life-affirming of the entire Wailers/Upsetters oeuvre, with its dancing bass line, slice and dice rhythm guitar and mesmerising drum patterns by Carly. It starts quite slowly, with Marley's vocals framed by cooing harmonies, but the captivating rhythm undergoes a change of pace as Family Man breaks into a canter, the organ licks gain in intensity, and Livingston and Tosh's backing vocals unexpectedly dissolve into trilling bird noises.

The song itself casts Marley in the role of a returning outlaw who has righteousness on his side and therefore must win over adversity. It's the cry of a sufferer, borrowing a storyline derived from spaghetti westerns and fuelled by Biblical prophecy, but which also strikes deep at the heart of local superstitions. The singer has been wrongfully accused and imprisoned, but has freed himself thanks to the power of the Most High and is now heading for Mount Zion. Marley plays this spiritually charged, action hero with such conviction, it's as if he'd been born to the role, which of course, he probably had. 'Duppy' means ghost, or vengeful spirit in Jamaican patois, and those practising "obeah", or black magic are much feared in ghetto communities especially. Yet Marley announces he also has powers over the unknown and that good must always triumph over evil. He's therefore St George, Django, Peter Cushing, and King David all rolled into one, with the wickedest rhythm bubbling underneath him.

It's right there, on 'Duppy Conqueror', where the legend of Bob Marley really begins and it's little wonder the song sold so well, becoming a JA number one. It was even issued in America on Shelter Records the following year, but the version that was included on *Soul Revolution*, the Wailers' second album for Perry (or at least his own pressing of it), has an entirely different vocal mix, with Marley's lead dropping out for lengthy periods. It's nowhere near as bright or compelling as the single, but the rhythm's still a good deal more convincing than the Soul Syndicate's attempt.

Glen Adams: "Soul Syndicate were called Soul Mates originally and that was a group we help train. We show them things when they start to form, because Chinna, Fully, and Tony Chin were living behind my street in Greenwich Farm and they have a little band. Through we are in the music and we hear them practising, we go look for them and start to show them things. I never interfere with the instrumental part, but then after a while they want a singer for the group, but I have Upsetters work to do and things like that. They were just coming up at that time. They weren't really doing anything yet, but when we return from England, Bunny Lee try a thing with them and them never sound too bad. Scratch got interested then, because we were always unhappy with him over money and things.

"It was us who were supposed to record 'Duppy Conqueror', but we had another of our disagreements with Scratch and so he talked Bob into going with Soul Syndicate instead. Their track eventually became 'Mr Brown' because when Bob listened to it, he said he didn't want it and so we just go back and do 'Duppy Conqueror' the way it was supposed to be done. If you listen to that rhythm, you can hear a lot of grievance in it. It's as if we're saying to the man, 'You can't get around us!' 'Duppy Conqueror' and 'No Sympathy', they're two of my favourite tracks we do with the Wailers, because it's like I'm listening to another person playing, and 'Duppy Conqueror', it still give me a vibes, even now . . ."

As Adams states, the Soul Syndicate's original rhythm track was revived for 'Mr Brown', which he was going to sing before Perry suggested giving it to Marley. The story of 'Mr Brown' was inspired by sightings of a coffin on wheels, manned by talking crows dressed in top hats and supposedly containing Mr Brown's corpse. The rumours had started out in the countryside before spreading to Kingston, and for a three-day period during the autumn of 1970 they were the talk of the island. Livingston suggests it might have been a publicity stunt devised by Brown's Funeral Parlour, which was rivalling Madden's for custom at the time. If this was the case, it worked a treat since apart from all the news coverage, several artists and producers rushed to capitalise on it, including Niney, who later acknowledged how the Wailers, with Perry behind them, were the stronger force and therefore got the biggest hit.

Glen Adams: " 'Mr Brown' is the Wailers' music still, because it's from 'Duppy Conqueror' and shares the same progression. That's myself and

Peter Tosh playing the organ, which is this Wurlitzer they had at Randy's. The only thing Bob put into the song was that line, 'Call him duppy conqueror, the ghost catcher,' but the single of 'Duppy Conqueror' was already out on the street at the time and so it was magic. We said, 'Yeah, duppy conqueror come!' and we just put it on the track right away. 'Mr Brown' came out just two days after they'd recorded it, that's how quick it happened, but then it cause all kind of problems later on. Bob's company said it was Bob's song and I should accept a settlement but I said, 'No. You can't do that, because it's my song, and I wrote it.' After that, I got a series of affidavits from people like Bunny Wailer and Fams, but the company get this woman called Diane Jobson to say they don't have time to deal with me. They tell me to call this other lawyer, Michael Hylton, but every time I make an appointment with him when I'm in Jamaica, he's out of the country.

"I get upset after that and so put this lawyer on the case. I then discover to just take it over myself. I write letters and send something to *Billboard* that I fax over to Blue Mountain Music in London, together with all my affidavits, telling them we have to come to a sensible agreement, because they're not supposed to just push something down my throat like that. As a matter of fact, they start to tell me that Bob Marley's estate will just wait it out and then someone from Chris Blackwell's office in New York contacts me and says, 'Well Glen, it's not a lot of money on that song.' Except the first payment I get is the biggest cheque I ever receive from out of reggae music! And yes, it was a lot of money, but I just wanted the little bit I deserved, nothing more, and I've had to fight all kind of companies about it so far."

Back in 1970, Adams was happy to have written and played on another hit and was looking forward to the next as Scratch and the Wailers planned further sessions at Randy's over the Christmas and New Year period. As for the Soul Syndicate, they also played on the Wailers' 'Sun Is Shining' and continued to rehearse occasionally with Marley, Livingston, and Tosh at Sims' house in Russell Heights, as well as backing them on live shows. Adams makes it clear they and members of the Upsetters were friends, not rivals, although they must have felt disappointed when 'Dracula', their instrumental cut of 'Mr Brown', was credited to the Upsetters. According to Dave Katz, guitarists Tony Chin and Cleon Douglas, bassist George "Fully" Fullwood and drummer Carlton "Santa" Davis played on the original 'Duppy Conqueror'/'Mr Brown' session and not Earl "Chinna" Smith or drummer Leroy "Horsemouth" Wallace, as others have suggested.

Soul Syndicate had formed in 1969, calling themselves the Riddim Raiders for a time, before becoming the Soul Mates and, finally, Soul Syndicate. Drummer Max Edwards had passed through their ranks and also Reggie Lewis before Chinna joined. Bunny Lee baptised them in the studio and Phil Pratt gave them their first hits after he'd hired them to play on John Holt's 'My Heart Is Gone' and 'Strange Things'. They then played on sessions for Randy's and Niney the Observer, as well as Lee Perry. After a year or so, Horsemouth left to join the Vikings, but brought in Santa as his replacement. Davis had grown up in Trenchtown and, like Carly, had practised on empty pans before getting access to a proper kit. In Santa's case, this meant joining a drum corps on Waltham Park Road and playing with a band called the Graduates, who mixed a little jazz, soul, and pop in with their reggae. Santa played with them for a year before replacing Wallace in the Soul Syndicate. He later toured with Jimmy Cliff and Peter Tosh, in addition to the Wailers.

Soon after Santa's arrival (and thanks to Niney's recommendation), Dennis Brown became their lead vocalist for a year before handing the reins over to Freddie McGregor, who took his first trip to the US with the band. Rehearsals would take place at Fully's house on the corner of Delamere Avenue, where Tony Chin, Sugar Minott, Tristan Palmer, Al Campbell, and Barry Brown all lived at the time. Soul Syndicate were thus very much part of the Seventies' reggae fraternity and would play on a great number of hits throughout the roots era. Tyrone Downie played with them sometimes and also Augustus Pablo, but the group's main axis was Chinna, Fully, and Tony Chin, whose rhythm guitar playing caught Family Man's attention right from the start.

"Yes, because it's the sound of the country comes to town," Fams says, "and I always like that calypso, mento type of sound. You never hear too much of it any more but in the early days it was the foundation of our music and it was there when we were creating all these new sounds in the reggae era. Our original guitarist from the Hippy Boys, Web Stewart, he used to have this similar kind of style that was a mix-up between rocksteady and calypso. We used to call it "rocklypso" and one time we were onstage when he requested we play something like that, but nobody could start it! Everybody had forgotten the magic of it, and where to go, which made us all laugh, and even the audience too . . ."

You can hear Chin's rhythm guitar on several other Wailers recordings from the Upsetter period, including 'Dreamland' and 'Small Axe'. He would later play with the Aggravators, Joe Gibbs' Professionals, and also US chart-toppers Big Mountain, yet still cites Bob Marley as being his biggest inspiration and has often relayed his joy at being picked up by Marley and driven to Johnny Nash's house for sessions with the Wailers.

Working with Nash had certainly raised Marley's profile. In fact, he'd already come to the forefront by the time 'Duppy Conqueror' and 'Mr Brown' were released, as evidenced by the name "Bob Marley & the Wailing Wailers" on some of the promotional material used for those records. Even the *Soul Rebels* album was credited to "Bob Marley & the Wailers", as were certain Wail 'N Soul 'M releases, although Leslie Kong always referred to them as "the Wailers", as had Coxsone for the most part. God-given talent and personal charisma were the deciding factors, however, and not anything more underhand. Also, Marley was singing lead vocals on the majority of the material because he was writing most of the songs and so there was little room for dispute. "Argument done" as they say in Jamaica. Marley had displayed his leadership qualities from early on and would continue to exert a dominant influence over the Wailers' affairs.

CHAPTER EIGHT

Soul Revolution

AS 1970 drew to a close, American soul artists were still leading by
example, showing their Jamaican counterparts how to make political
statements. Curtis Mayfield's first solo album *Curtis* was a tour-de-force in
this respect, with such tracks as 'We People Who Are Darker Than Blue',
'Move On Up' and 'Miss Black America'. Edwin Starr's anti-Vietnam
protest song 'War' went to number one on both sides of the Atlantic, the
Temptations released the equally gripping 'Ball Of Confusion (That's
What The World Is Today)', while Donny Hathaway sang of urban
realities in 'The Ghetto'. Others like Diana Ross, Smokey Robinson, the
Jackson Five, the Detroit Spinners, and the Four Tops continued to
maintain the kind of traditional values that were rooted in gospel, rather
than protest.

Most outspoken of all were the Last Poets, a group of angry poets from
the streets of New York, whose self-titled debut album may not have sold
many copies, but caused shock waves with tracks like 'Niggers Are Scared
Of Revolution', 'Wake Up Niggers' and 'When The Revolution Comes'.
A young jazz poet Gil Scott Heron also made a splash by pointing out
'The Revolution Will Not Be Televised' and wrote other songs that
mocked the establishment ('Whitey On The Moon'). While relegated to
the underground, such modern-day firebrands stripped black consciousness down to its core, exposing all of its beauty and imperfections. Even
the inveterate, pro-black activist Nina Simone may have balked at such
confrontational tactics, but as Vietnam continued to blaze under a hail of
napalm, and the threat of riots still hung over many American cities, anger
and resentment were bound to surface in the music.

A tall, gangly construction worker from Kingston called Manley
Buchanan absorbed all this and, after polishing his mic technique on
Tippertone Hi-Fi, reinvented himself as Big Youth. He would be the first
Jamaican MC to chat social commentaries, but U Roy, famed for his
crowd-pleasing interjections on King Tubby's 'Hometown Hi Fi', totally

popularised the deejay art. When the likes of Sir Lord Comic, Count Machouki, and King Stitt talked on records, their lyrics never stretched the full length of a tune. Their objective was to spice up the rhythm and keep dancehall revellers happy, neither storytelling nor delivering a message. U Roy had broken new ground in 1970, as 'Wear You To The Ball', 'Wake The Town', and 'Rule The Nation' – all voiced on vintage rocksteady rhythms from Treasure Isle – went to first, second and third on the Jamaican charts. U Roy was duly hailed as a phenomenon and a flood of other deejays emerged in his wake, beginning with Dennis Alcapone ('Spanish Town', 'Lizzie').

The Melodians' 'Rivers Of Babylon', Ken Boothe's 'Freedom Street', John Holt's 'My Heart Is Gone', Alton Ellis' 'You Make Me So Very Happy' and Lord Tanamo's 'Rainy Night In Georgia' bagged the remaining chart places. Two songs by Carl Dawkins, 'Satisfaction' and 'Get Together', endorsed his reputation as a soul stylist; Jimmy Cliff was 'Sitting In Limbo', Derrick Harriott's 'Psychedelic Train' put a Caribbean twist on the soul/rock sound, while Delano Stewart's 'Stay A Little Bit Longer' (featuring the Hippy Boys) continued his run of hits for Miss Pottinger.

None breached the international charts, however, and there were signs of a rift developing between the kind of reggae doing well in Jamaica and that getting exposure in territories like England, where mainstream radio gave precedence to lavishly produced records with strings, or those demonstrating a more highly developed pop aesthetic. Nicky Thomas, Jimmy Cliff, Horace Faith, and Desmond Dekker (with a cover of Jimmy Cliff's 'You Can Get It If You Really Want') all passed the test in the latter half of 1970, as did Bobby Bloom's 'Montego Bay'. The latter wasn't proper reggae by any means, yet it still went to number three on the American charts.

Within this musical climate, where most black acts preaching social reform were being forced underground and only diluted reggae was getting onto mainstream radio, the Wailers commenced recording *Soul Revolution*, their second album for Upsetter. Marley's ambitions of becoming a soul star had clearly been re-evaluated and in common with Tosh, who'd been militant almost right from the outset, he was now ready to put his career on the line and make music that actually stood for something, in between romancing women or making the occasional dance record. 'Soul Almighty', with its references to doing the funky chicken and mashed potato, is a good example of the latter, although Perry wisely omitted it from *Soul Revolution*, since it's good natured generic froth with none of the lasting appeal that characterises the best Wailers songs.

Another track recorded but not used on the album was a cover of the Impressions' 'Long, Long Winter', written by Curtis Mayfield. The Wailers' affection for Mayfield's poetic lyrics and aching melodies was well known, but this song was a throwback to the type of material they were recording at Studio One and had little bearing on the more cultural stance they'd already begun to adopt elsewhere. 'Man To Man' is another discarded effort, despite hosting a combined Marley and Perry lyric that speaks eloquently of man's inhumanity to man, sung with ghetto wisdom. The rhythm, based around a cuffed rhythm guitar, sounds as if it's on the brink of falling apart, which might have been one reason why the track didn't make the grade, although a version of the song did appear on Perry's own Jamaican issue of *The Good, The Bad And The Upsetter* album.*

He was not the first to fall victim to the ironies lurking within 'Man To Man' which opens with the lines, "Man to man is so unjust, children you don't know who to trust". Marley was guilty of unjust behaviour in the wake of 'Duppy Conqueror' and 'Mr Brown', after mounting a vicious attack on Winston "Niney" Holness. Niney had a falling out with Bunny Lee and Perry, who resented his closeness to Joe Gibbs and Coxsone. The tribal divisions between these cocky newcomers and Kingston's ruling music hierarchies ran deep, and it took diplomacy to navigate the local scene. After making hits for other producers, including Bunny, Niney was eager to make a name for himself, which is why he'd cast his net further afield in the first place. After a short-lived venture with Coxsone, he started his own Observer label with two releases by Dennis Alcapone and Lizzy. One of them, 'Mr Brown's Coffin', was a rival to the Wailers song, but offered little by way of competition, since Niney had neither the finances nor reputation to promote it. However, his next recording would stir up a great deal more interest and put him on the map in ways he could never have imagined as 1970 came to a close.

Niney Holness: "Before I start to produce for myself, I used to be around Scratch, Bunny Lee, Clancy Eccles, Joe Gibbs, and Lynford Anderson, but whenever them man meet up it was pure war! It wasn't anything dangerous; man just mouth up each other, that's all. Bunny,

* Marley and the Barrett brothers would restore the inner glories of 'Man To Man' quite magnificently on the *Rastaman Vibration* track, 'Who The Cap Fit', five years later.

Scratch, and myself, we curse each other, we create a lot of things and sometimes we don't talk 'cause one would make a song off the next one and all that. We'd go somewhere and it might be war between the three of we, y'know? Then Joe Gibbs come in now and everybody war with each other. I was the one who try and make peace, 'cause I go between each of them, although sometimes they turn against me too, so I have to run when I see a man coming. It was nice though, because we have the music and everyone is creating something, even if he is sending a tune straight to somebody's head.

"After I get success with Bunny Lee now, they start cuss me and all that, so I go to Coxsone and he say I should start my own label. This is whilst I was still working on hits for him, but that's when I come with this label named Destroyer, based at his studio, but using my own musicians. Coxsone said to do it that way so the beat don't get mixed up with his and I'll have a different style, so I get Family Man, Reggie and those guys, 'cause nothing was happening for them yet. Like Upsetter just hold them, so I get them, go into Studio One and do tunes like 'Musical Police' and 'Cocaine Doctor'. Coxsone say his place on Orange Street can be my office, 'cause nobody ever use it, so I was there one day and Scratch come and turn over the desk, kick over everything and say, 'What you doing with that man up there?' because they know it was going to be trouble now. He said I shouldn't deal with Coxsone and that's when Scratch and I start to move. Coxsone say I didn't know what I was doing and Beverley wanted me to work as well, but I go around with Scratch and then Bunny said, 'Okay man, drive this car fi me.'

"The whole ah we is one company now, with Scratch, Bunny, and I working by day, but I used to go to Joe Gibbs at night-time as well, producing songs by Ken Parker. War start again between us because of this and I say, 'Listen, I'm getting vexed now. I'm going to make my own things as Niney the Observer and create a label for myself. They say I start with some big talk now and they're trying to guess what I'm up to because Max Romeo and I join forces, 'cause neither of us was working with Bunny Lee any more. We're on our own having to survive, so Max and I, we sit down in the house we share with Family Man and say we have to come with something hot to pay rent. Robbie Shakespeare was a man who love to read. We see him with a book and Maxie take it and say, 'Niney, come here. You know what kind of book is this? It's a Bible man! The Maccabee!' And when we start to read, we find all these powerful words in there, so we come up with a song named 'Maccabee Version'.

"After we voice the song, it was out there playing up a storm on dub, y'know? But Maxie, he never understand what's happening, because he's moving with Derrick Harriott by this time and Derrick wasn't a street person like we. He was light-skinned and always had nice, smooth girls around him, so through Maxie have that same colour, he was trying to be with them. Scotty would be round there mouthing Maxie, saying, 'Oh, what type of singer is that? The voice raw!' If you don't speak proper English in those days, a man would turn his back on you, y'know? Well, Maxie got influenced by that and sell out the song and stamper for a hundred pounds and man, that was a bad thing for him to do, because that same week, the guys start press up the record and it sell out the place. KG's come downtown to buy every copy of it they can find and when Bunny Lee see that now, him jump on it with Derrick Morgan and get him to sing this horse race song. When I see that now I say, 'Bwoy, I can't take this,' 'cause we're still struggling, so one night I come up with this song 'Blood And Fire'.

"I book some time with Byron Lee, but then when I go there, I'm told there's no studio time for me, so I run go to Randy's with the Soul Syndicate, and Hux Brown tells me he wants to play something for me, 'cause he could see that I was trying. I never have any money to pay for the tapes at first, but finally I was playing the dub and that's when Scratch heard it now. He say, 'Hey! You come pon the street!' And the next thing I know, Bob Marley and the rest of the Wailers were looking for me because Glen Adams went and told them that I was versioning their song 'Let The Sun Shine On Me', which has a similar sounding rhythm to that on 'Blood And Fire'. Lee Perry, he'd got drunk and told them they have to find Niney, so they were driving up and down trying to find me. The thing is, I didn't have the money to press 'Blood And Fire' at first and some of these people said they didn't want it, because it's a drug man tune.

"Anyway, I master it, get the stamper and then I go round to see Mr Wong, who have a pressing plant called West Indies Records in Chancery Lane. He said to press any amount and he'll pay for it. Well the day I go round there, they take the stamper off the press after a hundred copies or so 'cause there was some fighting going on outside and this guy who'd been stabbed came running into the place for rescue and it the same press him hide behind that have 'Blood And Fire' on it. Mr Ray, him get shy now, 'Cause it's Christmas Eve, so him say, 'Lock up the press!' and when I come him say, 'Take away your stuff. Take away your record. I don't want it in here.' I go into Randy's now and also Joe Gibbs, Aquarius and KG's, and they all say they don't want any. The lady at Randy's said she can't understand it and some say it's bad blood, but then Clancy Eccles take it up and pretty soon everyone have a copy of 'Blood And Fire'. Lynford Anderson took it up to the radio station and it's playing by night-time. The next day, he and Charlie Babcock were talking about how so many people had rang in, saying they'd never heard a record like this one before."

'Blood And Fire' was revolutionary all right, chanted by a desperado who wasn't even a proper singer or deejay. It's easy to hear why some people thought it was "a drug man tune", yet despite them being the outpourings of a man with nowhere to turn and nothing to lose, there was truth in the lyrics. From where Niney stood, the only solution was to cleanse everything with fire, let judgement take its course and then start afresh. "There is no more water to put out the fire," he warned. "Let it burn. Let it burn. Let it burn."

Niney (now Niney the Observer) got his nickname after losing a thumb in an accident some years previously. His altercation with the Wailers resulted in him being stabbed in the shoulder. This wasn't the only time he'd aroused their ire, since Marley also attacked him on a record called 'Mr Chatterbox'.

"With my contacts, I used to get things from the pressing plant," chuckles Bunny Lee. "I'd come out of there with 50 copies or so and of anybody's record, right? You might say they fell off the back of a lorry, but I'd take 25 round to Bob's shop. A producer might go round there, hear it playing and say, 'Ah, where yuh get this?' The man would say he get it from Bunny Lee and he'd come to me now, so me can explain to him. I'd say, 'Bwoy, Niney. It ah the runnings,' y'know? Bob and Niney have a disagreement and so that's how 'Mr Chatterbox' came about. They had a fight over it, but Niney used to get records from the same source as me too, because when your records are pressed, them guys know about it and they reserve a few for them hustling. If it valued at say a hundred dollars, you'd give the man twenty dollars and they'd just pocket that, but them do the same thing with my own as well. It was just a hustling thing, because when someone brought you 50 copies of a next man's record, you're going to buy it, knowing he's doing the same thing with some of yours.

"Anyway, Niney, Bob and myself had a little misunderstanding over that and so we decide to tease him on a tune, y'know? Niney wasn't working for Coxsone or Joe Gibbs any more, because he was working for himself that time, but we just rough him up a little still."

If a budding producer struggled to raise the money for studio fees, the artists, musicians, and a stamper, then paid for the records to be pressed, only to find that copies had disappeared out the back door, he was bound to be justifiably upset, especially if it was their first release. Niney kicked up a fuss and paid the price, although it certainly didn't put him off, as he would become one of the most highly respected reggae producers of the Seventies.

Glen Adams: "It wasn't really anything negative, because sometimes those things are meant as a tease. They're like theatre and I guess it helped Niney in so much as there was a connection between him and the world's greatest reggae singer, because for Bob Marley to sing a song about you, you have to be important, y'understand? But we were all roommates at that time. Niney, Reggie and I, we used to live in a rooming house and everyone used to come over there to play music and hang out. That was in Washington Gardens and the vibes, they were real nice otherwise."

'Mr Chatterbox' is a revamped cut of 'Mr Talkative', which the Wailers originally recorded for Coxsone. It tells the tale of a neighbourhood gossip, although Marley changes the lyrics to warn his victim that he'll be "battered around" and then describes the blows he's going to give him with obvious relish. "Biff, baff, boof . . ." It was a scathing attack on the unfortunate Niney, who's clearly identified on the introduction as Livingston declares, "Who that a come? Niney? Bwoy, is a Mr Talkative that, y'know? Man afraid of him like puss." Recorded at an impromptu session at Dynamic, it was never intended as a hit, although it's been reissued both with and without that incriminating intro many times since.

Through Niney, Family Man played his first-ever session at Studio One. He, Rannie Bop, Wya Lindo, Reggie, and another guitarist called Lennox laid more than half a dozen tracks at Coxsone's famous "musical academy" on Brentford Road. One of them was Alton Ellis' 'What Does It Take (To Win Your Love)', which later surfaced on 'Sunday Coming'. Family Man also recorded an album of organ instrumentals at Studio One, again produced by Niney on behalf of Coxsone.

Family Man Barrett: "The great Jackie Mittoo himself was sitting there in the engineering room, listening alongside Coxsone, and when I finished playing those tunes, he came out and said, 'You are the only man I ever hear play a minor melody, but in a major key, and it right!' Because I use Jackie's same tone, but with different licks."

Mittoo was the architect of so many reggae landmarks recorded at Studio One throughout the Sixties, and so to receive praise from him meant a great deal to the young Upsetter, especially since the organ wasn't even his main instrument.

Family Man, like Adams, had moved into the rooming house in Washington Gardens after returning from England. Rannie Bop was on tour with Jimmy Cliff and had left their flat in Johnson Terrace without any prior warning, so he wasn't part of the nightly activities at the new place, as Fams sat around playing his guitar or bass, working on new songs with Niney and Max Romeo.

The Wailers' first release of 1971 was 'Kaya' (the follow-up to 'Mr Brown'), which Bob and Scratch wrote on a trip to Perry's mother in Hanover. That Marley could indulge in his love of marijuana so freely and so happily, just two years after the harsh penalties imposed by Shearer's regime, is a sign of how confident Jamaican artists now felt in challenging the system. The lyrics are as tender and poetic as any love song – "I'm so high, I even touch the sky. Above the falling rain" – and there are signs, too, at how pleased Marley was to be back in the countryside or in his "neighbourhood", as he puts it (although Marley was raised in St Ann's further to the east and not Trelawny, where Perry was from).

Singer and producer capture the relaxed atmosphere of time spent away from the hustle and bustle of Kingston to heady perfection on 'Kaya'. The listener could almost imagine the early morning mist drifting over the hillside and the lush foliage surrounding the farmhouse. Rannie Bop's flamenco-like guitar ripples beneath Marley's languid vocals, as Lewis scratches away on rhythm and Livingston and Tosh coo in the background.*

The flipside of the Trojan single opens with Tosh being woken from his bed by knocks on the door and a request for ganja. "Seen, Jah," he responds, before the rhythm track unfurls and a cowbell competes for attention with freshly laid, scat vocals from Marley. If Trojan were any more enamoured of the Wailers by this stage, they certainly weren't showing it, since Lee Goptal declined to issue the *Soul Revolution* album, after Perry travelled to England with the tapes for mastering. Trojan was already heading in a more commercial direction, as illustrated by inoffensive party records like the Pioneers' 'Let Your Yeah Be Yeah' and the strings-drenched version of Bob & Marcia's 'Young, Gifted And Black'.

The tougher, visceral side of reggae was having to compete with the

---

* Marley would later sing 'Turn Me Loose' over the same rhythm, and eventually rework 'Kaya' in 1978.

glut of commercial pop in Britain (encompassing sentimental balladeers such as Andy Williams and Perry Como) so there seemed little hope of a chart breakthrough for an unruly bunch of Rastas from Kingston, who sang in praise of the herb and Biblical vengeance. *Soul Revolution* was a far more accomplished set than its predecessor *Soul Rebel*. The songs were stronger and the rhythms more organic somehow, as if inseparable from the Wailers' expression. Included were the hit singles, 'Kaya' and 'Duppy Conqueror', but there were other songs that would become just as popular like the opening 'Keep On Moving', which became a vital component of Marley's worldview (and one that he would re-record several times in future). All three Wailers share lead vocals on this Upsetter cut, as first Marley, then Tosh, and Livingston take turns in yearning for a place of refuge, both literally and in the mystical sense. "I've been accused of a killing, Lord knows I didn't do," opines Marley, before Tosh mourns abandoning his family as they flee from the hangman's noose. "Lord forgive me for not going back," pleads Livingston; except in the Wailers' canon, outlaws have a habit of triumphing in the end, no matter the odds, as one is reminded on the imperishable 'Duppy Conqueror'.

Soul Revolution also contained early versions of 'Don't Rock My Boat' and 'Sun Is Shining', as well as 'African Herbsman', adapted from Richie Havens' 'Indian Rope Man', from Havens' double album *Richard P. Havens, 1983* that Perry's assistant, Jubbie, would often play in the Upsetter's shop. Family Man says 'African Herbsman' was inspired by a soldier who smoked high grade marijuana from Angola and would stop by the Green Door Saloon sometimes. The real life African Herbsman would pull up in his Jeep, give Fams his gun to look after while he rolled a spliff, and take in whatever musical vibes were happening. Marley and the rest of the crew all loved him, but no one remembers the Herbsman's name. 'Don't Rock My Boat' is a delight featuring joyous bass progressions, swinging drum patterns and cajoling vocals. Marley had sung the same song when recording 'Chances Are' almost three years earlier, but it's this version that convinces us he really does feel like "a sweepstake winner," and is "happy inside, all of the time."

The rocking 'Fussing And Fighting' appeals for world peace, while 'Put It On' is delivered at a pace that's midway between a skank and nyahbinghi chant. Livingston's higher register carries the tune. "I rule my destiny, Lord I thank you," he croons, as Marley reminds us he's "put it on already and it was really, really steady." 'Put It On' was called 'I'm Gonna Put It On' when the Wailers first voiced it for Coxsone, back in February

1966. Two years later, they re-recorded it for JAD, and would return to it on *Burnin'* for a fourth attempt. However this 1970/71 version, recorded at Randy's for Perry, seeps into the furthermost recesses of the soul and had Goptal running for cover.

If 'Reaction' cast the deepest spell on *Soul Rebels*, that honour went to 'Sun Is Shining' this time round. Adams and members of Soul Syndicate alike swear to having played the languorous rhythm, brightened in places by Peter's melodica and a wonderfully uplifting lyric from Marley, whose optimism is in sharp relief to the music.*

The most surprising aspect about *Soul Revolution* was how little Tosh contributed to it, in comparison to *The Best Of The Wailers* and *Soul Rebels*. He wrote none of the songs and didn't sing one lead vocal. Admittedly, his melodica dominates 'Memphis' – a funky reggae instrumental reminiscent of tunes by the Mar-Keys and Booker T & the MGs – and his piano playing can be heard on 'Riding High', one of two tracks led by Livingston. The other, 'Brainwashing' – a bizarre litany of nursery rhymes that never quite gets to the point – Livingston sang as if it was a dance record by James Brown. Like the doleful 'Stand Alone', it promises more than it delivers.

Perry cut stampers for *Soul Revolution* on his trip to England but declined to release it there. Instead, he issued it on his own Maroon label in Jamaica as well as compiling an album, *Soul Revolution Part 2*, from the rhythm tracks. Since the rhythms weren't drastically altered, this wasn't a dub album per se. There was no use of effects, echo, reverb, or wild mixing techniques; more that certain instruments were brought to the fore and highlighted, giving the tracks a slightly different feel. Any remaining doubts the Upsetters weren't Jamaica's finest rhythm section were firmly laid to rest with this album, which Perry must have worked on in secret, since Family Man says the Wailers didn't know anything about it until copies surfaced in record shops. The vocal set said *Soul Revolution* on the label, but both albums had *Soul Revolution Part II* printed on the sleeve. This was not only confusing, but also fuelled speculation Scratch had lost heart for the project. Either that, or he was just being a skinflint, since the cover art was done on the cheap too, featuring an Adams' snap of the

---

* 'Sun Is Shining', also known as 'To The Rescue' and later reworked on Marley's *Kaya*, was the first single issued on the Wailers' new Tuff Gong label, but got pressed on Escort in the UK, after Bunny Lee had given it to Pama, along with 'Duppy Conqueror' (released on Unity).

Wailers cavorting about in Perry's back yard (with Scratch dressed as Huey Newton) brandishing toy pistols. The presentation of both albums was lacking and while the music had progressed, not much else had.

The Wailers' tenure with Perry was drawing to a close, although there were still a fair few gems left in the bag. Trojan released several on singles throughout 1971, including 'Small Axe', 'All In One' and 'Dreamland'. 'Small Axe' was issued in Jamaica at the same time as 'Concrete Jungle' – a song named after a government-housing scheme (the real life Arnett Gardens), produced by Sims. Adams remembers rehearsing this track shortly before he left for New York. Whereas 'Soul Rebel' had stated Marley's spiritual ambitions, 'Small Axe' proved a sensation, laying bare his and Perry's musical objectives for all to see. Derrick Morgan claims that Perry wrote the lyrics, borne out by Clancy Eccles' recollections of Scratch disappearing into the toilet of his shop, clutching a scrap from a paper cement bag before emerging with a satisfied look on his face some two hours later. Other sources claim Marley helped Perry finish the song, which seems most likely.

It begins with a phrase lifted from the Bible, contrasting the acts of those "working iniquity", with the everlasting goodness of Jah. Then comes the war cry, "if you are the big tree, we are the small axe, sharpened to cut you down." In Jamaican patois, "three" becomes "t'ree" and these lyrics left nothing to the imagination where the local music industry was concerned, since the big three were immediately recognisable as Studio One, Dynamic, and Federal. Marley, who had already expressed his dislike of these "Babylon studios" to Sims, must have been delighted with the sentiments of 'Small Axe' because Federal and Dynamic were the main distributors for local recordings and wielded disproportionate power over the ranks of smaller producers such as Perry and himself. Jackie Jackson apparently played bass on the first cut, but then Family Man replaced him on the second, slower one, retitled 'More Axe'. In an act of supreme irony, both versions were recorded at Dynamic, with a horn section comprising Tommy McCook, Vin Gordon, and Deadly Headly Bennett. Perry says the beat changed again at this point, giving them the vibes to go and create an album, although 'Small Axe' wouldn't be released until early 1971 in the UK and failed to stake a place on either of the Perry-produced Wailers albums.

'Small Axe' was followed by a medley of Wailers hits past and present that was probably intended as a reminder to Jamaican audiences in readiness for the group's live performances. 'Bend Down Low', 'Nice Time',

'One Love', 'Simmer Down', 'It Hurts To Be Alone', 'Lonesome Feeling', 'Love And Affection', 'Put It On', and 'Duppy Conqueror' would all have featured in their stage act, plus there was a spate of other reggae medleys released around the same time – most notably by Ken Boothe, the Gaylads, and the Heptones. 'Copasetic' was a version of the Wailers' medley featuring just one or two lines from U Roy on the intro and Rannie Bop's scything guitar. The flipside, 'Don't Cross The Nation', augmented by Tosh's guitar and Livingston on percussion, was shared with Little Ian Rock a.k.a. Ewan Gardiner, as Little Roy joined the Upsetters. After his success with 'Bongo Nyah', Little Roy remained determined to write songs inspired by the teachings of Rastafari and Marcus Garvey, despite misgivings from his regular producer, Lloyd "Matador" Daley. This might have been why 'Don't Cross The Nation' was first credited to Bob Marley & the Wailers, followed by Mark & Luke, rather than Little Roy himself.

"Me and Ewan Gardiner sing 'Don't Cross The Nation' from going to school," Little Roy explains. "Me and Lee Perry live two houses from each other, because I live in the second to last house in Hampton Crescent and his own is just around the corner, in Cardiff Crescent. I was singing for Matador in those times, but there were many evenings I'd be round at Lee Perry's house, singing songs like those. We were close, y'know? Bunny Wailer lived in Washington Gardens, as did Bob Andy and Marcia Griffiths, so Bob and Peter were always around as well. A lot of musicians lived in Washington Gardens, like Max Romeo and Prince Buster. Also Niney and Family Man because they lived in Pembroke Hall at that time."

Matador responded by recording 'Hard Fighter' with Little Roy and the Barrett brothers, using the same rhythm section to revive the fortunes of Alton Ellis, whose popularity had slipped a little as the music veered away from the sweet vocal sound of rocksteady, having taken on a more roots feel. 'Hard Fighter' is written from the perspective of someone determined to succeed against all odds by emphasising their originality, instead of imitating others. It's still recognised as being one of Little Roy's best-ever tracks, so it was little wonder Matador called the Barretts back into the studio for that session with Ellis. The two songs Family Man and Carly played on, 'Lord Deliver Us' and 'Back To Africa', not only returned Ellis to centre stage, but also invoked the admiration of Coxsone, in a roundabout way.

Alton Ellis: "When I get the offer from Matador to do those two tracks, I asked Coxsone how I should approach it. He said I should ask Matador for a certain amount and then gave me information regarding the business side, but he believed it was two little soft tunes I'd done there. He didn't think they were good enough for his label, but then when both of them went to number one, he say to me, 'Jackson. I want a piece of the action.' That means you have to sing it over for him but Matador, he was mad because those songs were two of the biggest hits to come out of his stable, apart from 'Bongo Nyah'. Well Matador's still mad at me today because after Pama had released those songs in England, they told him I gave them permission. But I did nothing of the sort, so I guess the record company wasn't paying Matador or me, but dealing with some form of piracy."

Ellis lived just down the road from Mortimer Planno in Trenchtown and the opening lines of 'Lord Deliver Us' were directly inspired by a sermon Planno had given to the Rasta faithful gathered in the courtyard of his house one night. "Let the naked be clothed, let the blind be led. Let the hungry be fed and the aged be protected . . ." The emotion Ellis put into this song bridges the same kind of gap between church and dancehall. Hip as ever, the musicians hungrily fed off this energy, as Family Man's bass strikes up an irresistible groove, and drums, organ, and rhythm guitar lock effortlessly into his changes. The melody and meaning within it, coupled with such fine singing and playing, ensure 'Lord Deliver Us', voiced without the slightest shred of self-pity, wouldn't leave the Jamaican charts for months. 'Back To Africa' surely qualifies as one of the most joyous songs ever written about repatriation. "I'm going to tell the world about it and I'm going to tell the world to shout it," he promises, as the harmonies swoop and holler in support, and the Barretts' rhythm revs into motion.

Alton Ellis: "The Rasta influence was gradually spreading at the time we did those songs. We were seeing and hearing the culture spoken every day on the street, so hearing it on record now was just a next step in that direction. But it wasn't really a surprise; it was just an extension of what was going on back then, because in America, Marvin Gaye and James Brown were singing about those black t'ings too. It was just the timing of it all really."

Ellis was so impressed by the Upsetters he was soon calling them to play on a session produced by himself with Dennis Brown. "The biggest hit I made in Coxsone's studio was 'If I Follow My Heart' with Dennis Brown, and it was taken away from me," he laments. "Coxsone was in England at the time and I rented the studio from his wife. This was in June 1971. I'd written that song in Neasden, but after I produce it now, Coxsone came back from England, heard the tape and immediately tried to take it from me. The costs he wanted to charge me for studio time went sky-high and everything gone up to the ceiling. We fall out for maybe a month or two. I didn't go to the studio, then one day now in the ghetto, I get bruck and want money so I go to him and say, 'Mr Dodd, hear what you do. Just pay me for the tune and keep it,' because that's what he wanted to hear all along."

The Upsetters didn't play any more sessions at Studio One after that, although Adams would renew his friendship with Coxsone after moving to Brooklyn. The veteran producer made 'If I Follow My Heart' the title track of Dennis Brown's second album for Studio One, but never gave Ellis credit for it, let alone proper royalties. With its sparse but elegant beats, the track proved how effective the Barretts were at backing balladeers, as well as acts like the Wailers, who were fusing funk, nyahbinghi and the sounds of rebellion into their music. They had learnt such versatility while recording for Bunny Lee and would continue working with him as their relationship with Perry slowly fizzled out. Their biggest hits for him during this period were recorded with Delroy Wilson (including 'Better Must Come' and 'Cool Operator') and John Holt, whose 'Stick By Me' turned into a monster record.

" 'Stick By Me', that was the longest number one hit in Jamaica," says Bunny, proudly. "Shep and the Limelights did the original, but Delroy Wilson sang the first reggae one and then after that now, we got the young Dennis Brown to sing it. Delroy, he was showing Dennis how to phrase it and that's why he used to call Delroy Wilson 'teacher'. Dennis Brown's version didn't come out at the time, because he was singing for Derrick Harriott and Derrick come and start quarrelling with me, saying how I was trying to take away his artist. I start back off now and Dennis, he was vex with me when the John Holt one hit, saying that I was stifling him, but I showed him how Derrick Harriott had caused it and through I had so much singer around me already, I didn't need that kind of problem. Dennis and I remained friends though, because Family Man play drum, bass, and piano on Dennis' version of 'A Whiter Shade Of Pale' and he play on the 'Stick By Me' with Rannie Bop and Carly as well. Those rhythms still can't finish, even up until now, but that's around the same time Hux Brown come join we, because he play on enough sessions with Family Man, Carly and myself, including 'Stick By Me'."

The All-Stars' guitarist had been quick to describe the Barretts as "Bunny's wrong chord musicians" in the past, but their strike rate was now beyond question, so Brown was soon welcomed into the fold. While he had played on the Wailers' Beverley's album, 'Stick By Me' required a similar kind of stop/start rhythm to Eric Donaldson's Festival-winning song, 'Cherry Oh Baby', which Bunny also produced. 'Stick By Me' would be Holt's biggest ever hit in Jamaica, staying on the Jamaican charts for a record number of weeks. The secret of its success wasn't just in his creamy tenor and smooth delivery or Bunny's relatively sophisticated arrangements. Carly's drumming is explosive in what would later be termed a lovers' rock tune, while Family Man's rolling bass line has been versioned endless times since. What they created was a prime slice of "rub-a-dub" (or "John Crow skank," as Bunny would call it) and this, coupled with Holt's flair for romance, meant 'Stick By Me' just couldn't be shifted from either sound-system or the airwaves for months.

The song's popularity didn't go unnoticed by the Wailers, who adopted a tender approach themselves on 'Dreamland', which Trojan credited to Bunny Livingston & the Wailers on its UK release. While it has the feel and sound of a love song, 'Dreamland' is also the story of a utopia or Promised Land and therefore entirely in keeping with Rastafarian thinking (despite starting life as 'My Dream Island', a doo wop side by the El Tempos.) The Barretts are again in rub-a-dub mode as they breathe new life into a song the Wailers first recorded for Coxsone, and which Livingston would later revisit on his *Blackheart Man* album. Junior Byles' 'A Place Called Africa' is another Upsetter production mixing a ballad style with roots and culture, and this blend of influences would become a hallmark of the Barretts' work with Marley, whose impatience with Perry had now reached breaking point.

Bunny Lee: "Mikey Faith used to have a sound-system called Emperor Faith, and he was Bob Marley's accountant in those days. If any of the records were damaged after they'd been pressed, then Scratch had to show Bob, y'know? That's how little trust there was between them. Scratch had to account for everything and one day I see it good, man. When 'Stick By Me' reach number one, I give John Holt a new car, which is a Ford Cortina GT. Well Bob see that and start say things like, 'Look how we have 'Duppy Conqueror' and get nothing and yet Striker Lee give Peter nuff money and buy John Holt a car.' That same day, Bob get a nice cheque from performing rights. I think it was from when Johnny Nash record 'Stir It Up' but the Wailers hardly do anything for Scratch after that."

Family Man Barrett: "Scratch didn't realise we'd got hip to the music industry by then and had an idea as to what goes on with the international scene. But he wasn't the only one who'd been travelling up and down making deals because there were plenty of other Jamaican producers doing the same thing. These people, they don't bank the money in Jamaica, but in England, so nobody can see them with it."

Perry and Marley later patched up their differences and occasionally recorded further tunes together. Family Man also visited the producer's legendary studio Black Ark to record after Perry assembled a new generation of Upsetters at his home studio in Washington Gardens. The experience of working with the Wailers would bring Perry enormous cache over the years and there's no doubting the brilliance of his creative input on the songs they made together. Bunny and Peter, however, wouldn't go near him, and after suffering yet another false dawn, Marley, too, would finally free himself from the shackles of an outside producer.

CHAPTER NINE

Trenchtown Rock

AT the height of his fame, Bob Marley looked back on his early musical experiences and told UK journalist John Williams, "We never knew much about our rights in the music, which means to say it gave a guy a chance to exploit. To how me see it, Downbeat (Coxsone) gave a lot of youths who people label as rude boys the chance to make something of themselves, and those who never knew they could sing, turned singer. We were just doing Jah works, night and day. When I was a youth, I was too young to observe certain things. I just kept on trying to make something out of very little, or nothing at all. It's only now one can check back and say, 'Yeah, me love the way how this sound and how me reach that note there, or this producer allow that to go on. Certain guys wanted us to sound his way, but we know how Wailers is supposed to sound so we just kept on through the struggles, preaching the message until mankind know and appreciate the ways of the Most High, Haile Selassie, Jah Rastafari."

Marley went on to say that Sims and Nash allowed him the time and the space to work on songs and Nash in particular showed respect for his talent, unlike other producers who sought to exploit him.

"I and I have to sing and fight against that," he continued. "I've seen too much oppression in my life for me to turn so and not mention it. We have to lash out, let it be heard and no matter how smart a guy tries, you can't run from reality. How can someone tell me that because of the colour of a man's skin or eyes, that determines where or how him fi live? Jah say mankind was made to have dominion over the animals, plants and those things. Not destroy it, but also live in harmony with them, so why should man have dominion over another man?"

B. B. Seaton, who later chaired the Musicians' Union in Jamaica, points out that hardly any of the local artists and musicians knew how to properly secure their futures back in the Sixties. He says they were all caught up in the process of creating "this phenomenon called reggae" and that nothing was done on a professional level to protect their interests, or with an eye towards the music having any lingering value in years to come. Local producers would pay their musicians a one-off recording fee and were often slow in coming up with that. Producers would either try and avoid paying altogether, or reduce the fee if the musicians had been especially prolific. Making a living playing sessions wasn't easy, and to earn money the musicians would not only have to play the rhythms, but work out the chords and produce the songs as well, as artists often came to the studio with just a few lyrics or a melody, with no idea about actual song construction.

The producers who financed the sessions either issued the tracks on their own labels, or licensed them for release overseas while claiming the publishing rights for themselves. The musicians weren't paid royalties, nor were they credited with additional songwriting and production duties. This dubious practice has left a good many Jamaican musicians bitter and disillusioned after seeing their work continually selling over the years, making other people wealthy. In their defence, Jamaican producers had only just begun to gain a foothold in the English market and no one could have imagined how the music's popularity would spread around the world on such a lasting basis. There certainly weren't many lawyers in Jamaica back then and none who specialised in music. Also, few people knew about publishing or production points, and yet in the studio, musicians like the Barrett brothers, Jackie Mittoo, and Gladdy Anderson were essentially co-writing and producing music they were only getting paid session rates for. It never occurred to them to insist on being credited for these additional contributions, and the producers who did have an inkling about how much money was at stake weren't in any hurry to tell the artist.

Alton Ellis is another of those artists who've never received their due rewards from the business. He blames Jamaica's politicians for allowing producers to continue exploiting local musicians. "Yes, because the same way Bustamante changed the laws regarding herb, he could have come down on the record producers and said, 'Look here, every artist has to sign a contract and you have to pay them x-amount and get the t'ing in order. Make a minimum wage for the singers,' but they didn't do that. They lay back and watch the producers disadvantage the singers and musicians them and up until today, none of the old guys get anything out of it, because we didn't know anything about publishing rights in those days, nothing at all! All I know was to go into the studio and sing the song and I don't know what happen afterwards. It was like there was a blank space.

"All I know is that it was out on vinyl, but the process from singing it to getting the master or the stamper cut, all of that was kept hidden from us, because it was in the producer's interests to keep us stupid. Yet at the same time you have people who come along and tell the producers how to run their business, because a lawyer might come to Coxsone and say, 'Look here, you better get these guys to sign that or this, because otherwise it can come back on you in five years time.' They would tell him how to do it and then get paid for giving him that knowledge, but we artists didn't have the money to pay anyone to come and tell us what to do. Not like Coxsone and Duke Reid."

It's interesting that while Marley gives Downbeat credit for allowing the Wailers an opportunity to become recording artists, he gave no acknowledgement to Lee Perry, or at least not by name. The Wailers were still recording for him when Dave Barker left for England in March 1971, although their association with the maverick producer would soon end. Barker didn't return to Jamaica for many years afterwards and still feels the injustice of being deprived of proper recompense for his music. He responded to the success of 'Small Axe' by voicing 'Shocks Of Mighty '71' (shared with Charlie Ace) on the same rhythm, and 'Upsetting Station', which again borrowed from the Temptations' 'Runaway Child, Running Wild' and was a cut of the Wailers' 'Duppy Conqueror'. Barker and Ansel Collins' two hits for Winston Riley, 'Double Barrel' and 'Monkey Spanner', paved the way for their overseas success with both songs becoming Top 10 hits in England. 'Double Barrel' hit the number one slot in March, while 'Monkey Spanner' reached number seven the following June.

"We opened Skateland as the Upsetters with Dave Barker before he left Jamaica," says Family Man, referring to the popular skating and concert venue owned by Jingles in central Kingston. "Charlie Ace come out and introduce him by saying, 'This is the man who did 'Double Barrel' and 'Shocks Of Mighty', so let's hear it for the one and only Dave Barker!' Dave, he run out and grab the mic, turn his back to the audience and say, 'This is Upsetters, shocks of mighty. Hit me back!' And that's how we start off. It was magic, I tell you!"

Perry continued to release singles by Dave Barker throughout the coming months, although none could match the dynamism achieved on 'Shocks Of Mighty' or 'Double Barrel'. One of them, 'What A Confusion', featured backing vocals from Livingston and has the feel of a protest song with its powerful reality lyrics. Barker's singing has rarely sounded so magisterial and, not for the first time, Family Man's bass lines bring joy to an otherwise sombre message song.

★   ★   ★

Soon after Barker's departure, Marley left Jamaica for New York and Stockholm, staying in Sweden approximately two months, and only returning to Kingston in June or July, after helping Nash write the soundtrack to a film called *Vill så garna tro.** On his way back to Jamaica, and still clutching Nash's guitar, he stopped off in London and found the *Soul Rebels* album on sale in some of the specialist shops dotted around the capital. Marley later accused Trojan of pirating the *Soul Rebels* and *African Herbsman* albums but Perry had sold them the rights and there was nothing the Wailers themselves could do about it. According to Livingston, the Wailers and Perry agreed a 50/50 split in their dealings with each other. If this is true, then the producer had clearly failed to honour his part of the arrangement by licensing tracks without the others' knowledge. Livingston also claimed Perry was broke when they made those albums and so the Wailers chose to forego payment initially, which only exacerbated affairs.

Family Man admits there was "a little falling out" with Perry, but denies there was a serious rift, although it's significant that neither Tosh nor Livingston would record with Scratch ever again and even the Barrett brothers steered clear of him for the most part.

Family Man Barrett: "It was just like leaving from Coxsone to Beverley's, try it on your own, realise that you need a little help and then come over here and we do a little t'ing. Then after that, we realise we have to take it to the next stage. Except all of those movements are for Jamaica alone, because they get three local deals – Coxsone, Beverley's, and Upsetters, different from what they tried on their own and that's still not it."

Adams has a more forthright view of what happened, and when his family invited him to go and live with them in America he had no hesitation in packing up and leaving for Brooklyn.

"That's right, because I didn't like the vibes in Jamaica when I left. It was so hard to make a living because those producers weren't paying us properly and we weren't getting any rewards. The whole situation was chaotic and when I left for America, it was because I was very upset with Lee Perry's behaviour and not just him alone, because we didn't have a system in place where we could get money and yet these producers would keep coming to us for work. Because of that, I sent my wife away and then I travelled up here myself a couple of months afterwards. Everything I had, I just gave it

---

* A light-hearted romance, produced and directed by Gunnar Hoglund, starring Christina Schollin and co-starring Nash as Robert, it closed immediately after its premiere on September 4.

away and said I wasn't going back, but the last tracks I play on with Upsetters before coming up to New York were for Bunny Lee, because we did John Holt's 'Stick By Me', Delroy Wilson's 'Better Must Come' and 'Jordan River' by Max Romeo. In fact, it was me who wrote that tune with Maxie and I was credited as one of the two artists on it until it became a hit, then I hear they change the label and my name disappeared!

"Maxie wanted the song for himself, but it was also us [the Upsetters] who played on 'Let The Power Fall On I' and 'Maccabee Version' and both Maxie and I sing on those tunes as well. 'Maccabee Version', that wasn't for Niney, but for a brother named Willy. I have the tape for that and also a tape Bob Marley put into my hand with 'Nice Time (Version)' on it, which Carly overdubbed drums onto, to give it a more up-to-date feel. The Wailers, they sing behind me on this tune called 'Never Have A Dream Come True' around that same time, but the last session I did with them was for Danny Sims, because we play on a whole portion of songs for him before I left. I remember practising 'Concrete Jungle' on one of his sessions. That was in 1971, because Bob stepped out of Jamaica around the same time, when he left for Sweden. It was directly after that I played on some tunes for Herman Chin Loy as Augustus Pablo, like 'Aquarius One'. The original rhythm track to that was called 'Old Kent Road'. Fams and Reggie played on it for Jimmy Riley, but it was 'Aquarius One' that start the name Augustus Pablo and I played on 'East Of The River Nile' as well."

Adams and Lewis had been hoping to get a deal with Pama Records after recording a series of duets as the Reggae Boys for Harry J and Joe Gibbs. The latter released several of these on his Pressure Beat label, including 'Me No Born', 'Reggae Train', 'The Wicked Must Survive' and 'Fly By Nite'. Gibbs also produced the Hippy Boys' 'Death Rides', which appeared on yet another of his labels, JoGib Records. Like Family Man, the keyboard player and guitarist had concentrated all their efforts on making hits and earning a living playing music. They kept telling themselves that a breakthrough waited just around the corner, but had grown impatient with the poor rate of return and were eager to try something else. Adams' name had appeared on a succession of organ instrumentals released on Camel, Nu Beat, Bullet, and Gas in the UK, courtesy of the Palmer brothers, while Harry J teamed him with Dave Barker in a bid to emulate the latter's success with Glen Brown. Lewis continued recording the occasional vocal tune (mainly for Bunny Lee) and all three Upsetters were becoming increasingly interested in production.

Family Man and Lewis started a label, Rhythm Force, while Adams named his Capo, after the nickname given to him for wearing oversized caps like those favoured by American soul stars. The resourcefulness with which producers like Bunny Lee and Scratch Perry hustled their licensing deals was rubbing off on those close to them, but singers and musicians in general were beginning to realise the benefits of self-sufficiency rather than relying upon unscrupulous producers.

The first serious attempt to buck this trend was made by Delroy Wilson, Ken Boothe, the Gaylads, and the Melodians in late 1968, after they had pooled resources and set up their own label, Links, "as in the strengthening links of a chain," according to B. B. Seaton. All of them had previously recorded plenty of hits for Coxsone, Miss Pottinger, and Bunny Lee, yet still had to endure financial hardship. The handful of singles they released under the Links' banner were fairly unsuccessful, however, and it wasn't until much later they discovered how their former paymasters had sabotaged them.

Glen Adams: "Rita used to have her little group, the Soulettes, with Hortense Lewis and Cecile Campbell. She would do that in between looking after the children. She would only come downtown every so often and the vibes used to get nice, y'know? But Scratch never recorded her, so it was Reggie and Family Man who started to record her on this label called Rhythm Force. Bob had a little store with his brethren Selwyn in there and sometimes Johnny Lover and Django would be there too. It was just a small-time operation, but basically, the women used to stay at home, and that includes Rita."

"Rhythm Force was a record label me and Reggie put out," Family Man concurs. "That was from when we started to produce some little tunes with U Roy, like the King Tubby Skank. We hold the vibes as the rhythm force, so we just create that label and call it that, y'know? And for the label design, we put a guitar and a bass pon it and it carry an "R" and an "F" as well. A rhythm guitar sign for Reggie and the "F" stand for Family Man. Rhythm Force! Yeah, man and we put out a tune by the Soulettes, 'cause one time we were trying to form a group with Rita and them, so we get them to cover one of the Beatles' songs, 'Let It Be'. I do that myself and just to help Rita really. We were with the Wailers too, of course, but everybody a move like one family and one camp."

Bunny Lee: "All of us used to move as one, because if we had just one banana, then we would share it. The whole of we was involved in the same thing, because Rhythm Force started at the same time as the Aggrovators and then Glen had his own label called Capo. But if they had some tracks they'd produced for themselves and couldn't put them out, then I'd release them and come up with the money. Fams' and Glen Adams' first cars, they get them from me because of things like that."

Like Coxsone, Bunny had recorded Rita Marley and the Soulettes early on, but by 1970 Family Man and Lewis had assumed stewardship of their recordings, giving the Soulettes that distinctive Upsetters/Wailers' sound. Both played on all their other recordings from this period. Whereas Scratch had issued 'Someday We'll Be Together' on Upsetter, '(You're) My Desire' and 'Bring It Up' were released on Tuff Gong. The latter has a lot in common with 'Stir It Up', except for slight differences in the lyrics and chorus. Carly's powerful drum rolls seem to dominate 'Bring It Up', whereas 'Let It Be' is a non-starter compared to Aretha Franklin's version, but delivered in a pleasant enough, folksy style over finger-popping bass runs from Family Man. Had it received Trojan's orchestral treatment, 'Let It Be' could well have been another hit to rival Bob & Marcia's 'Young, Gifted And Black', except Rhythm Force was a new label, and Family Man and Lewis had little or no influence with labels from overseas.

The Soulettes experienced little success thereafter, apart from when Richard Khouri cut a few sides with them at Federal and Perry released their cover of the Staple Singers' 'This World' on his Justice League label. Apart from Beverley Kelso and Ermine "Cheryl Green" Bramwell's early contributions at Studio One, the Soulettes first lent female harmonies to Wailers recordings, most notably on 'Lick Samba'.

Aside from working on sessions and producing tracks with Lewis, Family Man also recorded songs with Ranny Bop, including a version of Larry Marshall's 'Nanny Goat', but inexperience with business matters would ensure Caribbean Distributors on Orange Street profited from the proceeds. Family Man had at least two other labels, Danger Zone and Star Apple, before launching Fams and Cobra, followed by Atra Records. He would also use Niney's Defender label to issue certain tracks like 'Reasons', featuring Seeco Patterson. The list of tracks attributed to Family Man from the late Sixties and early Seventies is a lengthy one. Most are organ instrumentals, like 'Ten Thousand Tons Of Dollar Bills', 'Instalment Plan', 'Herb Tree', 'Sly Mongoose', 'Deep River', and 'Family Man Mood', although none have the immediacy of 'Return Of Django' or 'Liquidator'. It's as if Fams had been amusing himself in the studio with the results immortalised on plastic, reinforcing the theory that while an excellent musician, Family Man's creative gifts don't really come into play until he can bounce off others, sculpting an individual sound for them.

Ultimately, his ideal foil was Marley, who had directness as well as an extraordinary talent for lyrics and melody. That said, the Barretts also worked well with Tosh, as evidenced by songs they recorded with him at Joe Gibbs' studio in Duhaney Park during Marley's absence in Sweden. 'Rudie's Medley', which contains snippets of two Desmond Dekker songs, '007 (Shanty Town)' and 'Rude Boy Train', is the real curio among them. Tosh even imitates Dekker's thin, high vocal style before the pianist quotes 'Evening Time' and Tosh reprises 'I'm The Toughest'. The result is engaging, if hardly original, leaving 'Them Haffe Get A Beaten' and 'Maga Dog' as the choice tracks from this session. Rita and her Soulettes accompany Tosh on both and are especially effective on the latter with its refrain of, "Sorry for maga dog. Maga dog turn round and bite you." 'Maga' is a patois term meaning skinny and undernourished and anyone who has visited Jamaica and seen such dogs scouring for food by the road-side will understand the song's sentiments, even if it is written about a girl!

There's an element of calypso in the chorus and arrangement, while 'Them Haffe Get A Beaten' is more uptempo and finds Tosh lamenting the rise of the wicked, even as he predicts their downfall. "Them can't get away," he promises, as an organ chimes out behind him and Family Man's bass skanks in the background. Tosh also recorded 'Black Dignity' in the summer of 1971, a jerky nyahbinghi on which he again chants in Amharic. None of these tracks were made with a wider audience in mind, even if Dekker's '007' had scaled the British charts a few years earlier. Tosh, like Marley, wanted hits, although the tall, lanky Wailer was insistent on achieving success on his own terms and wasn't about to compromise for the sake of money or popularity. Taking this kind of stance meant all three Wailers were often short of money and, since they were also raising a family, Bob and Rita felt such hardships even more than the others.

Bunny Lee was able to help them out from time to time by licensing Wailers' productions to record companies in the UK, but the group were hardly household names and sales weren't always encouraging.

Bunny Lee: "No, but when I get £150 from Pama for a single and carry it back down to Jamaica with a contract, it was a joy! That's because Bob and them weren't making any money from anywhere else and used to look to me, just like everybody else, to bring them some money from Pama and Trojan. Pama used to give them a little more money than Trojan and so Pama and myself started to work more closely together. We set up a label together in Jamaica and my brother used to run it. If a record hit in Jamaica, Pama Records would just get it automatically, the contracts would be signed and Pama would send the money to my brother. It was a stepping stone and Pama became big, because they would release everybody's records at that time. They released a lot of Bob Marley & the Wailers on labels like Punch up in England."

The previous year, Bunny had struck deals with Pama for 'Duppy Conqueror', 'Sun Is Shining', and 'Pour Down Sunshine'. Pama issued the latter on Bullet, whereas 'Downpressor' and 'Small Axe' both got released on Punch and would be joined by 'Screw Face' once Bob had returned from abroad. Ever the willing entrepreneur, Bunny would also facilitate the release of 'Lick Samba', 'Guava Jelly', 'Grooving Kingston 12', 'Trenchtown Rock', 'Redder Than Red' and 'Lively Up Yourself' throughout 1971, the majority of which appeared on Trojan's Green Door label. Having severed their ties with Perry, the Wailers were determined to go it alone once more, even if they did face opposition from Jamaica's musical elite. The fact that the band members were ghetto people and intent on making Afro-centric music with few concessions to middle class tastes meant they were always going to struggle in getting their songs heard on the radio, or appearing on certain stage shows.

Bob Marley later told Rob Bowman that, "the wrong people used to have reggae in control. You still have the Wailers in that time but the only people who get the chance were Byron Lee & the Dragonnaires, except they never work it. It wasn't a talent thing. It was just that Byron Lee & the Dragonnaires, they couldn't make a reggae record. That's what delayed the music for such a long time, because you have guys who only play the music for money. The money part of the music, instead of going and create. They don't play until they get the money. They can't understand what I really try to say. I really sit down and create some music. Every song them guys play, people have sung, they've been played already. Nothing new. That's money. They control it."

One of the first things Marley did after returning from Sweden was to book some studio time. The new-look Wailers, minus Adams, meant business and their bold determination in challenging Jamaica's hierarchy would soon have repercussions throughout the industry, as artists like Gregory Isaacs and Errol Dunkley also started their own labels and pressurised the local radio deejays to play their records.

Family Man Barrett: "After those two albums for Scratch, we decide to make a move and check for our own business, and that inspired all these other artists to start singing for themselves. You see what happens when singers and musicians get together?"

Family Man wasn't present when the Wailers recorded 'Trenchtown Rock', 'Screw Face', 'Redder Than Red', 'Concrete Jungle' and 'Guava Jelly', which all feature Bunny Livingston on bass.

"No, because the flu had got me, so Bunny have to play bass on those tracks," Fams acknowledges. "I always rehearse them though and I guess everybody know them parts and t'ings like that, so it was easy for him to get around still, as a Wailer. Wya Lindo and one other keyboard player played on those sessions too, because we were still the Upsetters at the time. It was Lloyd Charmers and Gladstone Anderson who were playing piano with us, because they were the regular session men."

Lindo disputes this while other sources point towards Winston Wright as the organ player on those tracks. Lindo, who met the band through Tosh at Treasure Isle, says there was a difference between "sessions", meaning rehearsals and then "recordings", which took place in the studio. This is why Lindo's friend, Sidney Guisse, can claim that he, Lindo, Tin Leg, and Sowell (Noel Bailey) were the "first Wailing Wailers band," since the Upsetters obviously backed a great many artists for Lee Perry and others and weren't exclusively bound to the Wailers as yet.

Sidney Guisse: "Bob, Bunny, and Peter came to us and said, 'Look. We need a band to come and rehearse.' They had a record shop then, in Beeston Street, and we used to rehearse upstairs. This is long before the world had heard of Bob Marley and we played on quite a bit of their stuff, like 'Sun Is Shining', 'Kaya', and 'Bus Dem Shut'. We did all those original cuts in the early days. This was a different band from the Generation Gap, who I used to work with at Randy's and Treasure Isle mainly. During that time, I'd started to outgrow them, because Generation Gap was a band that just used to rehearse on Saturdays and we get one and two gigs here and there. That's when I joined another band called the Hell's Angels and most of the members went on to join Chalice. It was Wayne Armond's band and they had Clive Hunt on trumpet, Courtney Rob on keyboards, Richard Daley was the lead guitarist and the drummer was Bentley Ray. Some of these guys didn't go on to play music professionally, but that was the band that started to back the Wailers on shows on the road.

"We had the little band downtown, with Wya, Tin Leg, and Sowell, who would practise with them, but the Hell's Angels got a gig with

Derrick Harriott's Musical Chariot and we were doing this gig at the VIP Club every week. All of these other artists used to join us and especially Bob Marley, so our closeness developed from that, except I'd known him from when I was very small. My first spliff came from him, so I used to hang out with him all the time."

Lindo and Guisse both remember rehearsing 'Trenchtown Rock', although neither played on the actual recording. The song would become a Wailers' anthem and a staple of their live act for years to come. Rhythm guitar, drums, and bass mesh irresistibly on the opening bars before Bob declares, "One good thing about music, when it hits, you feel no pain." Lyrically, it's a feelgood tune, mixed with a little righteous teaching ("If you a big fish or sprat, you reap what you sow") and the singer's pride in his ghetto community, meaning the people rather than the actual environment. The way Marley calls for the music to "Hit me harder, brutalise me," again betrays the influence of James Brown, who'd recently signed to Polydor. Family Man would eagerly visit Randy's and buy copies of every James Brown single he could find on that familiar red label, including the Godfather's then current hits, 'Escape-ism' and 'Hot Pants'. "Uh. That's where it's at, S-M-O-K-I-N-G," exclaimed Brown on the latter, as the groove locked down around him.

If ever an example were needed of the impact Brown had on Jamaican music, and Marley and the Barrett brothers in particular, 'Hot Pants' was it. It's interesting to note that in West Africa, Fela Kuti was also busy assimilating James Brown's sound, injecting greater emphasis on rhythm into his music, while growing ever more vocal about social conditions in his native Nigeria. James Brown, Bob Marley, and Fela Kuti . . . between them, this trio of black icons formed a musical and cultural axis with roots in Africa, America, and the Caribbean – a geographical triangle echoing the main points on the slave trade route. All three recognised the importance of strengthening people within their own communities. Heard in this context, 'Trenchtown Rock' is a clarion call for pride in self and nationhood, as well as an invitation to party.

Lloyd McDonald of the Wailing Souls told David Katz that he, Winston "Pipe" Matthews, Norman Davis of the Tennors, Rita, Bunny, Bob, and a guy called Oswald "Saboo" Downer all sang harmonies on 'Trenchtown Rock' and that the song was initially conceived and rehearsed in Saboo's government yard on First Street in Trenchtown, hence the title. McDonald also states that the Wailing Souls' 'Back Biter' was recorded at the same session and the rhythm was later used for the Wailers' 'Baby We've Got A

Date'. He confirmed the Wailing Souls sang harmonies on songs like 'Redder Than Red' and 'Lick Samba' and remembers the police raiding Saboo's house on one occasion, whereupon they confiscated some of the Wailers' equipment. Tosh damaged his guitar jumping over the fence in his escape attempt. Escapades like this would cause Marley to redouble his efforts to leave Trenchtown, even though he was celebrating the ghetto in his music.

'Trenchtown Rock' promptly flew to number one on the Jamaican charts and stayed there for months. It would eventually make Trenchtown the most famous ghetto in the world, although it failed to chart in England and made next to no impact in the States, where Gary Hall, a friend of Skill Cole's, issued it on the G & C label. While its success was only local, as an expression of the Wailers' pride in their roots and an anthem for those transformed by the power of music, 'Trenchtown Rock' was a real milestone. A photo exists of Marley receiving an award from Red Stripe, after 'Trenchtown Rock' had sold 3,000 copies in Jamaica, wearing trousers that look like carpet material with their gaudy patterns. It must have been a proud moment for the young singer, who was still living in the poorest section of town and already carrying the hopes of Kingston's sufferers upon his slender shoulders.

U Roy, fresh from his triumphs at Treasure Isle, voiced over a stripped-down version of the same rhythm, and counters Marley's chorus with exhortations to "Keep on rocking and swing." The Wailers called his cut 'Kingston 12 Shuffle' and Tosh overdubbed a melodica onto it, to give it additional flavour. In the summer of 1971 they also recorded songs with Johnny Lover (most notably on a cut of 'Sun Is Shining' called 'Heathen's Rage') and Big Youth, as well as the Wailing Souls. The latter were also known as Pipe & the Pipers and sang both 'Harbour Shark' and 'Back Biter' at those sessions. A trio composed of Winston "Pipe" Matthews, Lloyd "Bread" McDonald and George "Buddy" Haye, they'd rehearsed alongside the Wailers in Joe Higgs' yard before following them to Studio One.

Whereas 'Trenchtown Rock' was the obvious hit resulting from that session without Family Man, the other tracks were by no means inferior. 'Guava Jelly' soon became a favourite of Johnny Nash and even Barbra Streisand took a shine to it, which must have pleased Sims enormously, since he owned the publishing rights. Together with 'Pour Down The Sunshine', 'Guava Jelly' is the most commercial of Marley's Tuff Gong compositions from this period and sounds as if it was written for Nash, rather than the same band of soul rebels who announced they were "dreader than dread" ('Redder Than Red') or painted a haunting portrait of ghetto life ('Concrete Jungle'). The version of 'Concrete Jungle' the Wailers recorded in July 1971 aches with the despair of living in a place like Arnett Gardens (and was a moody prototype for the cut that would later appear on *Catch A Fire*).

Built along similar lines as a Sixties British council estate, only using concrete instead of brick, Arnett Gardens was a housing project in west Kingston where violence and poverty had come to dominate people's lives and opportunities were so limited as to be virtually non-existent. The slow, meandering rhythm of 'Concrete Jungle' unwinds like a drowsy rattlesnake, accompanied by eerie, chanted harmonies, a wheezing organ and Vin Gordon's mournful trombone, before Marley begins singing. His bleak commentary is so full of powerful imagery and voiced with such emotion, the listener's left in no doubt as to the stark reality of his vision. This was music of an altogether different calibre to what Byron Lee & the Dragonnaires or, indeed, any other Jamaican acts were producing at the time. It's nothing short of musical alchemy and the poetry in the lyrics, vocal delivery, rhythm and arrangements is all-persuasive, like the very best of Bob Dylan's output from a few years earlier (and which had already influenced the Wailers, as demonstrated by their cover of 'Like A Rolling Stone'.) The line, "I'm always laughing like a clown" is tragi-comic genius, while the assertion there's "no chains around my feet, but I'm not free," points an accusatory finger at the system.

The rhythm of 'Screw Face' is a little livelier, with a message similar to that of 'Duppy Conqueror' in the way Marley exalts in the power of righteousness. Shadowed closely by Tosh and Livingston, he announces that while screw face, "know who fi frighten", such antics can't scare Jah Jah children, who remain safe, even though they may enter "ungodly waters", or meet "the pestilence that crawleth by night." 'Screw Face' bristles with attitude and yet has spiritual values at its core – a compelling duality that had become a Wailers trademark. 'Screw Face' was played a lot by sound-systems like Coxsone in London, paving the way for the Wailers' later popularity as part of the Island roster.

Bunny Lee: "Bob used to say to me, 'Why can't I go a England?' and I'd tell him he'd go as soon as he got a whole heap of hits. Bob just a struggle on his own up until then, because the first time he started to raise some proper money is when Allan Cole take them over. Skill Cole, he was a famous footballer that everybody like, and from he join up with Bob he start to make a difference, because everybody would play the Wailers' songs regular after that. Bob couldn't get his records played like myself before that, y'understand? They wouldn't play a Bob Marley tune at all and it was only after Skill Cole came on the scene that it changed."

Friendships between singers and sportsmen were nothing new and Marley's closeness with Jamaica's most famous footballer – a player with dreadlocks and who'd played in Brazil, home of the international world champions no less – bore echoes of how Muhammad Ali and Sam Cooke had bonded in the mid-Sixties. Both were aspiring black men blessed with an awareness of the cultural importance of what they were doing and intent upon excelling in their respective fields. Both, too, were brimming with confidence, filled with the realisation that their time had arrived. Cole's arrival from Brazil and his de facto role as the Wailers' manager coincided with the Wailers moving from the Soul Shack, in the alley off Orange Street, to new shop premises at 127 King Street, which is often referred to as being on Beeston Street, because of their proximity to each other. Singer Roy Shirley claims to have rented the place before the Wailers and says they broke in while he was overseas and "captured" it from him, except there's no evidence to support this. What is known is that the Wailers' tenure of the King Street shop, coupled with Cole's presence and the formation of the Tuff Gong label, heralded a new chapter in the Wailers' affairs.

The Barrett brothers were already dedicated members, and while musicians such as Glen Adams, Reggie Lewis, and Ranny Bop (who'd left to go on tour with Jimmy Cliff) no longer played an active role on Wailers' sessions, there were other, promising youngsters gravitating to their circle, like, for instance, Tyrone Downie.

Guy Coombs, who designed the Tuff Gong label, claims the name was his suggestion, and that "Gong" came from a conversation he and Marley had about Africans who'd use gongs for communication. Lee Perry also claims authorship, while others point out that "Tuff Gong" was Marley's street handle. Whatever its origins, Tuff Gong was launched with the release of 'Sun Is Shining' and, much to the band's delight, the first pressing sold out relatively quickly. The musician credits on 'Sun Is Shining' have again been hotly disputed over the years. Members of the Soul Syndicate claim to have played on it, while Livingston gives the nod to the Barrett brothers but also Downie, which Family Man disagrees with. It's a fine line between "sessions" and "recordings" (as already evidenced) and then there's the question of why the Wailers should launch their new label with a Perry production, when they had more than enough new material of their own.

What's not in doubt is the quality of the songs, and the Wailers' ambition to succeed with a brand of music representing their cultural perspective that could be ranked alongside the work of their US contemporaries. The basic trio of Marley, Tosh, and Livingstone had been together for almost a decade already and had learnt the business the hard way, with little to show for it. Worse still, they'd had to remain on the sidelines and watch as other local acts scored big hits on the English pop charts, yet the desire to express truth and reality in their songs burned more brightly than ever. They weren't alone in this of course, as manifestations of black pride had already permeated Kingston's bustling downtown scene. None of the Wailers had dreadlocks at this juncture, since Marley had cut his off and grown an Afro instead, like his friends Bob Andy and Marcia Griffiths, who'd followed 'Young, Gifted And Black' with another UK Top 20 single, 'Pied Piper'. Both had pedigree making hits for Coxsone, but were now recording for Harry J, who had ambitions of building his own studio.

It was an era of contrasting, but not necessarily conflicting, influences. The impact of revolutionary Black Panthers like Eldridge Cleaver and Huey Newton was just as strong as that of Emperor Haile Selassie I or Martin Luther King, and apart from listening to James Brown and Sly & the Family Stone, the Wailers were also interested in rock music, as well as jazz and folk. In some respects, they could be considered Jamaican hippies, since they were actively searching to make a difference to society and the mindset of people around them. They wanted to try and educate others, not only in their music, but also in the way they presented themselves. Downie remembers the Wailers' shop in Beeston Street selling a range of African-style artefacts. He particularly liked the picks and combs Tosh would carve out of wood and then paint in bright Rasta colours, while Lindo describes the Wailers as being "funky, psychedelic people, who used to make their own shoes."

Family Man Barrett: "Jean Watt, she was the girlfriend of Bunny Wailer, and she made all of his clothes, and also those in the shop. She used to have this little dressmaking shop behind the alley on Orange Street. Peter Touch had a shirt she made for him with a wicked African print on it. All of us liked that style at the time and so we'd go in there, choosing material and getting shirts made up. She made me a chocolate brown shirt once and it fit me like His Majesty's jacket, I tell you! Clancy Eccles' wife also made good shirts too, though she had better equipment and all that. Clancy Eccles himself was a tailor and he would make trousers for Carly and I when we were in the Upsetters, although Glen Adams would make his own, because he was a tailor himself and would make suits for lots of the musicians living in and around Greenwich Farm at that time."

Family Man backed Tosh on sessions at Randy's (recording 'Arise Blackman' and 'Leave My Business') before rejoining the Wailers to work on an alternative cut of 'Screw Face', which duly profited from his intuitive feel for rhythm, sounding more polished as a result. 'Arise Blackman' is a revolutionary recruitment drive, while 'Leave My Business' is a sufferer's declaration, devoid of all shame or thoughts of being less worthy than others. Tosh was growing noticeably more militant and his solo outings more frequent at this juncture since Marley had sung lead on the majority of recent Wailers recordings, including 'Satisfy My Soul Jah Jah' and 'Satisfy My Soul Babe', both of which share the same, lurching rhythm, although the overdubs differ and their lyrical themes couldn't be more dissimilar. Marley sings 'Satisfy My Soul Jah Jah' as part-invocation, part declaration of faith, whereas his delivery on its secular counterpart is filled out by harmonies and bears more spark.

These tracks are among the deepest and most profound in the entire Wailers canon – in a sense they are closely related to Yabby You's 'Conquering Lion', which Family Man also played on around the same time – and heralded the arrival of a new style of reggae music that oozed spirituality, and epitomises what Rastas call "word, sound and power". After playing all those syncopated rhythms for Lee Perry, the Barretts were now seeking ways in which to make the music sound "dread" and to convey the power of Jah, as described in the Book of Revelations. Family Man approached this task scientifically, in the manner of a consummate craftsman. He decided which sounds carried the right vibration in getting message across and this in turn determined what notes and chords he would use when constructing the rhythm tracks for songs by Bob Marley & the Wailers, Augustus Pablo, Yabby You, Burning Spear and others. We can hear the sound of deep, roots reggae music being born on some of the records he and Carly played on during 1971 and an entire genre would spring up in their wake, making Jamaica forever synonymous with Rastafari and the symbolism that surrounds it.

The session for 'Satisfy My Soul' took place in late summer, as did another at Randy's resulting in 'Lively Up Yourself', 'Craven Choke Puppy', and 'Lick Samba'. All featured the Barretts, together with Reggie

Lewis, the horn players Tommy McCook and Vin Gordon, members of the Soulettes, and two guest keyboard players.

Family Man Barrett: "Those were the sessions that Gladstone Anderson and Lloyd Charmers played on. They were Wailers self-productions, because we decide to stick together, and not do so many sessions for outside producers after that. We wanted to hold onto the roots and, at the same time, highlight ourselves internationally with those tunes there. That's what Bunny was trying to do on Dreamland and also Peter with songs like 'Maga Dog' and 'Legalise It'."

'Lick Samba', allegedly co-produced by Perry, although Family Man disputes this, is a lilting refrain about sex, led by Marley who can't resist the woman at the heart of the song, even though she's hurt him already. "It's not that I'm weak," he assures us, as the very Caribbean-sounding rhythm sways and shimmies behind him, presumably because he's feeling especially horny! Not unnaturally, it's the Soulettes' backing vocals that feature most prominently in the mix, rather than those of Livingston and Tosh. 'Craven Choke Puppy' has a more down home feel and restores the other two Wailers' cooing harmonies to their usual supporting role. Lyrically, it's written in the style of a parable as Marley sings of the inevitable consequences of greed. "Want all, lose all," he points out, using the example of a dog that loses its bone attempting to bite onto something else at the same time. The rhythm is a delight with its shuffling backbeat, swirling organ, and soulful sax passages.

Although recorded before the Wailers' international breakthrough, 'Craven Choke Puppy' could have graced either of their first two Island albums and the same is true of 'Lively Up Yourself', which at least became a mainstay of their live act; hardly surprising since the song is the perfect Jamaican dance record. It's exultant, life-affirming and joyous, and the ideal follow-up to 'Trenchtown Rock'. The Barretts' playing on this track is so infectious, it's impossible not to physically respond as the rhythm kicks in. Family Man's tumbling bassline is simply irresistible, Carly's snare and cymbals sizzle as if on the point of bursting into flames, while Lewis anchors the beat with carefully understated rhythm guitar. Again, McCook's sax playing is the model of eloquence as he answers Marley's call for the listener to abandon their cares and lose themselves in the music.

For once, Marley's lyrics are almost inconsequential and it's the rhythm that captivates, although his delivery is both urgent and well-timed, in the manner of a preacher's sermonising. The pocomania and kumina religions were based upon dancers being transported to some kind of spiritual ecstasy, and songs like 'Lively Up Yourself' operated on much the same level. The Wailers' Jamaican audience would instinctively make this connection, even subconsciously, as Marley sings lines like "you dip so, you dip so," a reference to the movements made by kumina dancers.

'Lively Up Yourself' and 'Trenchtown Rock' both featured on the Trojan album *African Herbsman*, released after the Wailers had signed with Island. The album was a cash-in, rehashing tracks from *Soul Revolution* along with singles licensed from Tuff Gong, that were intended to signify the Wailers' break with Perry, as opposed to giving people the impression they were still working together. This clearly wasn't the case.

As the Wailers were launching Tuff Gong, Scratch was recording acts like Neville Grant, Prince Tallis, and the Classics, as well as a former fireman from Jones Town, Junior Byles, who'd previously recorded for Joe Gibbs as a member of the Versatiles. His earliest release for Scratch, 'What Is This World Coming To', had been credited to King Chubby. He then recorded 'Got The Tip', which Pama released on the flipside of Peter Tosh's 'Downpresser'. Neither tune proved a success, although 'Got The Tip' featured harmonies by the Wailers, which made it highly sought-after in years to come. Tosh re-recorded 'Maga Dog' as 'Once Bitten' for Tuff Gong shortly after the triumph of 'Lively Up Yourself', as well as voicing 'The Lion' and a cover of the Beatles' 'Here Comes The Sun'. 'The Lion' is especially noteworthy, as Tosh points out the differences between genuine Rastas, and those Bunny Lee calls "beard men". "There are lots of guys who wear dreadlocks and are one million miles away from Rasta," Tosh proclaims on the intro. He goes on to accuse them of preaching love every day and yet killing by night. "I only hear your words, but I don't see your works," he tells them, after explaining how "the concept of Rasta is righteousness."

Marley meanwhile, was invited to crown Miss Musical Chariot at the Sombrero Club in Molynes Road in August 1971, around the same time that Miss Jamaica was crowned at the National Arena. After the success of 'Trenchtown Rock', he'd become quite the local celebrity, although he was hardly known for seeking attention and would always consider himself equal to the other band members. Occasions like this would help prepare him for the demands of the media and having to deal with life in the spotlight, but there's little to suggest that fame changed Marley's character or deflected him from his main concern, which was making the best music possible and remaining steadfast to the ideals he and the Wailers held so dear. The struggle to establish Tuff Gong was paramount, although old enmities still simmered under the surface, as Dennis Alcapone was to discover.

"Bob wasn't too pleased with me going to Coxsone back then, because he had a go at me and Lizzie one day at Randy's. He apologised after a while, but at the time he was saying how we shouldn't do any recording for Coxsone. I said it wasn't a matter of working for Coxsone. It's just that Coxsone had the ammunition we wanted and we needed to be there because U Roy was working with Treasure Isle, and since it's two big guns in town, I need to be there for my own development. He didn't like that, because he didn't want anyone doing anything for Coxsone. He was all right with the things I did for Lee Scratch Perry, but at that time everybody was doing their own thing, and I never had any beef with Coxsone back then. I just wanted to get on those rhythm tracks and get on with my own stuff, y'know? Studio One, it was the university of the music industry in Jamaica, but Bob had his beef and that was it.

"When we walked into Randy's shop that day, he had his back to the counter and Lizzie and I, we headed for the album rack and when we pass him, he said, 'See them bwoy there a work for Coxsone?' We didn't pay him any mind at first. We just continue looking at the albums on the rack, but then when we walk past him again he said, 'Alcapone, I shouldn't work for the man Coxsone, y'know?' Bob, he was a rebel, y'know? People look pon him now as a prophet, but he was a rebel. He did some very good work on this earth, but he was a rebel. He wasn't a soft touch. He was a man who could defend himself and stand up for what he believed in."

Alcapone had recently celebrated his first British Upsetters' release 'Well Dread' on the 'Cherry Oh Baby' rhythm and was rivalling U Roy's popularity with hit after hit in Jamaica at the time, recording for many of Jamaica's leading producers, including Keith Hudson and Bunny Lee. This was during a period when deejays were in the ascendancy and the influence of sound-systems was proving crucial in creating hits, since reggae was ill-served by radio. Alcapone, who would become the first-ever deejay to win an award (sponsored by the *Record Retailer*) in Jamaica, had made his reputation with 'El Paso', named after the Marty Robbins' country & western hit. Lizzy and Dillinger also shared a mic on 'El Paso', while Tippatone hosted Big Youth, and U Roy had left Coxsone to rejoin Tubby's Hometown Hi-Fi. This presumably met with Marley's approval, as demonstrated by the invitation for U Roy to come and voice 'Kingston 12 Shuffle' for Tuff Gong.

Bunny Lee: "The Wailers didn't really have a reputation for being troublemakers. It was through Mortimer Planno that the Wailers take up Rasta and people used to say how Rastas are troublemakers and undesirable. If an uptown youth did turn Rasta, they would ban him. They wouldn't want to know him, because when a man smoke ganja for the first time, the old-time people wouldn't want to know him, y'understand? They used to call Rastas "blackheart man", which is the equivalent of calling someone a paedophile nowadays. People said that Rastas would eat up children but I grow up around them, because you have some very decent Rastafarians, separate from those we'd call "beard man". That's because some murderers grow beards to hide from the police, but more time it was decent Rastafarians who get the blame. For instance, Woppy King was a Rastaman, but he used to go out at night-time and kill people, y'understand? And that would make him a beard man, not a Rastafarian. The Wailers though, they were Rasta and they weren't into anything bad like that."

Sharon Gordon knew the Wailers while they were still struggling to make in-roads into the music business and can also bear testimony to their good character.

"I've always loved Bob Marley from the first time I heard him speak, standing in front of my yard on Van Street in Rollington Town, Kingston, with the brothers Carly and Family Man, cautioning a group of bad bwoys notorious for terrorising the neighbourhood," she wrote on her website. "My family and I lived directly across the street from the Barretts. As fate would have it, my mom's maiden name was also Barrett, so there was a closeness developed between our families. Mom had a clothing factory on Beeston Street in downtown Kingston, close enough to Bob's little record shack up the street. We had repeated warnings that they were Rastas and so-called "blackheart" men who stole children and cut out their hearts. Of course, nothing was further from the truth and I would always find myself peeping through a hole in the zinc fence, hypnotised by the most beautiful melodies and harmonies. No wonder they were called the Wailers, because that's what they did all day long, just wail and wail.

"I spent many afternoons observing the way they interacted with each other. Their banter and jibes possessed a comfortable familiarity but, as always, some Bible-quoting adult would show up and shoo me away, promising to 'lodge a complaint' with my moms so she could know 'how bad I was.' Though only a little girl, I remember thinking how ridiculous it was that both Rastas and the Bible-quoting adults relied on the use of scripture as ammunition against each other."

Bunny Lee: "Rastas were undesirable to the uptown people. They didn't want their kids associating with people like that, in case they rob and steal and do everything bad. From a man start smoke weed and turn Rasta, a lot of people would think he'd gone mad and run him out the place. They'd think the boy had mashed up himself and say, 'Look how much money me did spend pon him. He should have gone to university and now him turn fool.' When Michael Manley start campaign, that's when the Rastas came forward, when the PNP came to power in the Seventies, with Tony Spaulding and some other men who want to show how rootsy them is. That's the way they got more votes, so he could build up them garrison."

Jamaica wouldn't go to the polls until February, but the run-in to the election lasted several months and was defined by the campaign of Norman Manley's son Michael, who not only consolidated his role as the island's most charismatic politician, but also used Rastafarian iconography in establishing the PNP on the side of the poor and needy. Music, too, played an important role in the 1972 election and, again, Manley chose wisely by selecting as his theme song Delroy Wilson's 'Better Must Come', a track produced by Bunny Lee, who was fast becoming Jamaica's most prolific producer. Bunny and his posse would travel in a convoy of up to three or four cars and more than one eyewitness has likened them to something out of an Al Capone movie! Unlike some of his competitors, Bunny embraced all forms of Jamaican music, whether it was light, Nat 'King' Cole-style balladry as practised by Jackie Edwards, or rude boy songs like 'Mr Chatterbox'.

A lot of the artists in his stable – including Cornel Campbell, Horace Andy, Dennis Brown, Alton Ellis, and Jackie Mittoo – had defected from Studio One and would re-record some of their best-known hits for Bunny, although his two most successful acts of 1970/71 were John Holt and Delroy Wilson. Wilson was two years younger than Family Man and had made his debut for Coxsone aged 13, after unsuccessful trials with King Edwards and Prince Buster. His earliest records, like 'Joe Liges', 'Don't Believe Him', 'Prince Pharoah', 'Remember Your Nest', and 'Back Biter', were all released within a year of Wilson joining Studio One, and were apparently aimed at Buster, who'd recently left Coxsone. Wilson spent more than five years at Brentford Road and yet it was Bunny who released his debut album, *Better Must Come*, and turned him from child star into an established hit-maker with a mature vocal style that some have likened to Marvin Gaye, but which is readily identifiable as his own.[*]

Roy Shirley says 'Better Must Come' originated from a song of his called 'Who God Bless' that he'd recorded with a band from Mandeville led by a bass-playing barber named Mr Chambers. According to Shirley, he'd taken them to Randy's to cut the tune; Delroy heard it and collaborated with Bunny Lee on his own version. Bunny disputes this, although there's no arguing who played on the track.

"It was Family Man who originated the bass line on 'Better Must Come', and Carly wasn't there, so Tin Leg played the drums. We call that beat the John Crow Skank, because that's when we were moving away from the rocksteady era and the shuffle come in that was played on Randy's organ, because it was out of key. Randy's wouldn't fix it, so we just touch it and that's what gave us that creeping sound. Bob have it in that tune, 'Duppy Conqueror'. Those songs weren't rocksteady or reggae. That was the 'John Crow Skank' and 'Mr Brown' has it too. You have to say it was Glen Adams who bring that in from Randy's studio, the creep organ thing, because Winston Wright and everybody start to do it after that, except it never came out all that good from Byron Lee's studio. That's because their organ wasn't out of tune and sounded different! It was there though, because those tunes like 'I Get My Kicks' and 'Grooving Out On Life', you can hear the creep organ in them too."

Tin Leg, who tended to accent the beat more than define it, partnered Family Man on an increasing number of sessions once the Upsetters slowly began to unravel. He drummed on 'Riding For A Fall' (which John Holt and Delroy Wilson both sang for Lee) and also 'The Clock', sung by John Holt, again recorded for Bunny in the early Seventies.

Bunny Lee: "That song 'The Clock' has one of the greatest bass lines Fams ever play until now! Fams find it on the bridge and then Pablo play the same rhythm and call it 'East Of The River Nile'. But we do a whole heap of Johnny Ace songs from that time, because apart from 'The Clock', there was 'Never Let Me Go' and 'Anymore'."[†]

---

[*] Wilson would later record for Sonia Pottinger, Lloyd Daley, Niney the Observer, Lloyd Charmers, Jack Ruby, Sly & Robbie, Gussie Clarke, and many other different producers until his death in 1995.
[†] Lewis played rhythm guitar and Adams, organ on 'The Clock' session, although it's Tin Leg on drums and not Carly.

Johnny Ace was an American singer and pianist who'd died at the age of 25 after shooting himself in the head during a game of Russian roulette, played with a loaded gun backstage at a show in Houston on Christmas Day 1954. He recorded fewer than two dozen songs during his career, and 12 of them were included on the *Memorial Album* that Bunny Lee played to the Upsetters prior to the session. Family Man claims they recorded the entire Johnny Ace album but that Bunny Lee only released 'The Clock'. This means there's a tape in the vaults somewhere containing 11 reggae cuts to songs like 'Pledging My Love', 'My Song' and 'How Can You Be So Mean', all faithfully transcribed from Ace's melancholy, R&B originals.

Since Bunny didn't have exclusive use of the Upsetters, he used a number of different musicians on his sessions. For instance, he got the Inner Circle band to play on Eric Donaldson's 'Cherry Oh Baby', after he heard them back Donaldson at his audition for the Jamaica Festival Song competition. 'Cherry Oh Baby' was a massive hit in 1971 for the producer people were starting to call "Striker", due to his unfailing success rate. Bunny's other big hits that year were 'Better Must Come' and John Holt's 'Stick By Me', which he recorded six times before finding the winning combination. Delroy Wilson sang the first version, followed by Dennis Brown, the Cables, and David Isaacs, who sang 'Island In The Sun' for Lee Perry. Holt's version was so popular the Khouris approached Family Man and asked him and the Upsetters to play on a track for Federal.

Family Man Barrett: "The Khouris, they first call me to play with Ernest Ranglin and then the next session I can recall was the time when they send over this 45 named 'Stagger Lee' (by Lloyd Price) and say they want us to turn it into a hit. They ask us to choose either John Holt or Delroy Wilson, so we give them John Holt and it was a hit!" At this point, he burst into song with the lines, "I was standing on the corner, when I heard my bulldog bark. They were barking at the two men who were gambling in the back. It was Stagger Lee and Billy."

Like a lot of Jamaicans, Fams has a deep-seated love of American R&B and country, as well as indigenous Caribbean music. He and Striker are alike in this respect and their appreciation of traditional music styles underpins so many of the tracks they've worked on together, although they are also willing to experiment and try out variations on old themes. True to form, 'Better Must Come' bridges two styles with its rollicking, bar room piano and churning dub mix. It's where New Orleans meets Jamaican reggae and Family Man's bass line is again aimed squarely at the dance floor. The other musicians sound muted by comparison, as if in awe of the way Fams' bass swoops and plunges throughout the track, while the song itself is masterful and a hymn to all those feeling hard done by, which was just about everybody in Jamaica during the summer of '71. "I've been trying a long, long time, and still I can't make it. Everything I try to do seems to go wrong. It seems I have done something wrong. Why they're trying to keep me down. Who God bless, no one must curse. Thank God, I am not the worse. Better must come. Better must come one day," sings Wilson, who follows the chorus with a line of pure defiance. "They can't conquer me," he warns. While he may be down on his luck, he's definitely not to be underestimated or written off.

Little Roy was at the session, waiting for his turn to voice the same rhythm, but Lloyd Daley the Matador arrived with a policeman and escorted him out of the studio, claiming the singer was contracted to him. No such mishap befell Alcapone, whose 'It Must Come' switched the meaning of the song and transformed it into a dance record. It's still bubbly and infectious, but it doesn't have the serious, social overtones of Wilson's version, or the same heartfelt expression of striving against the odds.

Bunny Lee could have been compromised by this, since people didn't know he hadn't agreed to his song being used by the PNP, and in such a politically volatile climate, where hopes and expectations rode so high on both sides, it wasn't wise to openly nail your colours to the mast.

"It didn't really cause me too much embarrassment," he says, "because if they use one of your songs, you just have to go with it and let the power fall as it will. Manley got this staff from Emperor Selassie. He said he had the rod to lead the people, the Rod of Correction, and he was Joshua. They come up with some gimmick, but then politics is all about who can fool the people most. Before this gun business start, the politicians hired strong-arm guys who didn't like to hit anyone with their hands through they were heavyweight boxers and that's where the gun violence come in. One of them was JLP and then Kid Ralph was a PNP. They were on the opposite sides of the fence, but it's all a front, because these politicians live like brothers and sisters and there's no way they're going to go out and fire a gun after one another. They cover each other's backs instead."

Apart from using 'Better Must Come' as one of their campaign songs, the PNP also approached Bunny about organising a tour of the island featuring some of Jamaica's best-known artists, whose job was to keep the people entertained before Manley gave a speech, rallying them to vote for him at the forthcoming election.

Bunny Lee: "I make Phantom, who was my apprentice at the time, get Clancy to organise it. The artists were supposed to get some houses built and that, because you have all these places named after artists now. You have Bob Marley Boulevard and Ken Boothe Avenue and all of that. But Clancy Eccles, his behaviour wasn't right. Hugh Shearer was in power and Manley beat him, but he and Manley were family. Well, Clancy go up there and start mouthing off about "dutty Shearer" and all of that and so Michael Manley start to shun him after that. Manley said to him, 'We pay you the money to pay the artists and you did a job, that's all.' They cast him aside after that, because he was too ragamuffin."

Bunny later released 'Take The Rod Offa My Back', which must have annoyed the PNP hierarchy. His brother-in-law Derrick Morgan was another producer to get caught up in political chicanery, after the PNP used Max Romeo's 'Let The Power Fall On I' to promote their campaign. Not that Romeo minded, since he was a PNP supporter and willingly participated in their Musical Bandwagon shows, which toured Jamaica throughout October. Artists like Ken Boothe, the Wailers, Dennis Brown, Alton Ellis, Tinga Stewart, and Judy Mowatt all performed on various dates which took place every weekend and perhaps two or three times during the week.

Max Romeo: "I was actually the one who wrote most of the lyrics for 'Better Must Come'. I was also the leading person on that Bandwagon thing, because I started out at the beginning, but then everybody else got scared and jumped off and left me! It made me feel like the bravest man on the island, because most of the guys who get the glory just do a few stints, but then get frightened off. In the beginning, you had Bob Marley, Ken Boothe, Delroy Wilson, the Chosen Few, and the whole works, but then it boiled down to just Clancy Eccles and myself. We succeeded in establishing what we set out to do though. It worked to a point and then the same thing as befell Marcus Garvey happened to Michael Manley. But the people love the Bandwagon and those were Michael's times. There was money around, but there wasn't much to buy because America was stopping everything from coming in and so we were singing those kind of songs in order to get the people's minds away from that type of livity."

Sidney Guisse played in the band supporting Manley and the PNP road show, and was onstage when shots rang out during Manley's speech at Black River in the parish of St. Elizabeth. "When they start firing, I pulled this Fender bass amplifier on top of myself and that's when I realised that the man hiding right next to me was Michael Manley!" Guisse says, laughing. "He was cowering behind the same box! Ken Boothe was up there, singing, 'We gonna walk, we gonna walk, down Freedom Street' and he had Manley up there with him, but from he went into the chorus, all we heard was pure gunshot!"

Guisse decided to concentrate on studio work after the incident and formed a group, Solid Foundation, who would play on the earliest hits recorded at Lee Perry's Black Ark, including Junior Byles' 'Curly Locks'. He and Pablove Black would later team up with Earl "Bagga" Walker and drummer Albert Malawi in the Twelve Tribes band, who backed artists such as Fred Locks, Little Roy, and Israel Vibration. Clancy Eccles, who'd bought the rights to 'Nice Time' and 'Hypocrites' from Rita Marley during the Wail N' Soul 'M era, says the Wailers did six shows on the PNP's Musical Bandwagon tour. Others suggest just Bob and Rita performed and that Tosh and Livingston refused to involve themselves with politics, no matter how Rasta-friendly they might seem.

"Even up until today, people are asking if better really will come," says Bunny Lee, reflecting on the Manley years. "Because we had PNP guys who would go out and kill people for nothing, but though the government protected them and made them look good, they were like vigilantes. They used to do enough things and get away with it and the police, them nah bother with them at all. Then on the other side, you had politicians who used to protect Jim Brown, but they can't protect anybody any more and we all have to protect ourselves now. If you look to live off another man's strength, then he's going to deny you, y'understand? These guys used to get a big house and give out some big contracts, but from you're given a job and you don't do it, they'll send some men to come kill your family. They'd build some big mansion for themselves, but then do things and have fi go run to America or England. Except they can't do that again, because they have to get visa and if it proves the man is running from Jamaica, then he's got problems."

Such things had yet to manifest in those heady days of Manley's rise to power and the optimism generated by his promises of social reform. After the more repressive stance of the JLP, Jamaica was preparing to embrace socialism and, to outward purposes at least, seeking solutions to the inequalities that had created widespread poverty among the island's working class. Not everyone was getting swept away quite so willingly, however. Especially not the Wailers, who chose to release 'Screw Face' as their Christmas single.

CHAPTER TEN

Youth Professionals

BY the time Marley left for Sweden, the Wailers were among the most popular acts in Jamaica. 'Duppy Conqueror' and 'Mr Brown' were still riding high, but 'Trenchtown Rock' and 'Lively Up Yourself' finally dispelled all doubts and proved these soul rebels had selling power, as well as artistic integrity. In many ways, Marley couldn't have left at a worse time, and yet the possibilities of working more closely with Nash and Sims were just too good to resist and the other Wailers knew he'd return for them should the right opportunity present itself. It was just a matter of *when* things would take off, not if, and since Marley was bound to gain further knowledge and experience on his travels, the entire group stood to benefit in the long run.

In any case, the Barretts were busy elsewhere, having played on so many hits in 1970. 'Stick By Me', 'Lord Deliver Us', 'Mule Train', 'Let The Power Fall On I', 'Cool Operator' and 'Better Must Come' were just some of the more visible records that bore their stamp. Eric Donaldson's 'Cherry Oh Baby' may have sold more copies, and the Chosen Few's version of 'Shaft' come closer to emulating an American sound, but the Barretts tapped into the Jamaican zeitgeist to best effect. Good session musicians need to be versatile and the Barretts took pride in diversity as they continued to weave strands of rock, folk, calypso, and funk into their music. At the same time however, and mostly in tandem with the Wailers, they were pursuing a new sound that was Jamaican by birth, yet had its roots in a more ancient and therefore African past. It stimulated them on a personal level and was a good deal more progressive than the majority of work they did for other producers. Working with the Wailers was inspirational and the songs Tosh and Marley were writing fuelled Family Man's imagination like no others.

More importantly, being a member of the Wailers felt like being part of a brotherhood. There was an aura about what they were doing that felt like destiny, no matter the practical considerations. Not unnaturally, the

Barrett brothers wanted to dedicate themselves to the group, yet despite the success of 'Trenchtown Rock', their dream of breaching the mainstream with an act as seemingly unmarketable as the Wailers seemed a long way off. Although their hearts and long-term ambitions were bound up with the Wailers, neither of the Barretts could afford to give up their freelance work as studio guns for hire, and while the rewards weren't that great, there was no shortage of job offers. Local producers circled like sharks and their rhythms began appearing on a bewildering number of releases – especially since "versioning" was now so widespread. To some degree, their popularity was due to their personalities, as well as their prowess. Both brothers were pleasant, easy-going characters and had a professional attitude that ensured good quality results. They were responsive; quick to grasp what was expected of them, and full of ideas. Family Man in particular was diligent and hardworking and would spend hours above and beyond the call of duty in getting the music to sound its best.

One of the Upsetters, first tasks after returning from England was to fulfil a promise they'd made to Tony Scott, by re-recording 'What Am I To Do'. It was a wasted effort, in truth, since Scott still had no proper means of promoting it and then had to watch in dismay as Harry J reaped both money and acclaim from the original version in the wake of 'Liquidator'. Family Man and Carly also played on the Ethiopians' 'Rub Them Down' for J. J. Johnson around the same time and laid down backing tracks at Treasure Isle for Hopeton Lewis & Dennis Alcapone's 'Judgement Day' and the Tennors' 'Weather Report'. Family Man's bass dips and wheels like a ghetto ballerina on the latter, as Ranny Bop's guitar slices through the rhythm with an action that's the very essence of the reggae shuffle. The Tennors were a trio composed of Clive Murphy, Norman Davis and the late Maurice "Prof" Johnson, who'd recorded hits like 'Pressure And Slide' and 'Ride Yuh Donkey' for Coxsone during the rocksteady era. 'Weather Report' was the tune that brought them back in the limelight and it probably would have crossed over too, had Duke Reid not stalled in releasing it for so long and Trojan or Pama declined to put some serious promotion behind it.

The Barretts also played on tracks for Phil Pratt towards the end of 1969 and early 1970 – sessions that resulted in songs by Ken Boothe (including 'Give To Me' and 'Morning'), Keith Poppin, Horace Andy ('Let The Teardrops Fall'), Errol Dunkley ('Running Child'), Al Campbell ('When The Grass Is Green' and 'A Game Called Love'), and Reggie Lewis. Keith Poppin's 'Envious' – a classic tale of envy delivered over simple bass, drums, and piano – still gets spun at reggae revival dances from time to time, along with its deejay version, I Roy's 'My Food Is Ration'. Ken Boothe's 'Artibella' brought Pratt's label to prominence with its throbbing rhythm, pleading vocals and haunting keyboard phrases. It soon hosted a classic deejay version, 'Keep Your Dread' by Big Youth. "Black people, we have been stripped and robbed of our names, our language, and our culture," he chants, by way of introduction to a song that packs more reality and righteous affirmation into two minutes than others twice as long.

The deep roots sound of this track has definite similarities with what the band were playing for Lee Perry and the Wailers, as they searched for a sound that embraced the militancy of black pride, yet retained enough commercial appeal to make the record a hit, which is what producers were paying them for. Just as he did for Bunny Lee, Family Man played organ, as well as bass, on some of these tracks, including the rocksteady style 'Victory' by the Phil Pratt All-Stars.

Phil Pratt: "Sometimes we never managed to get the whole band together, so it was just a case of using whoever was available. You might end up with a couple of musicians from one band and then a couple more from another. That's why we end up calling them All-Stars, but we were all learning and practising together, just trying to create some things for ourselves at the time."

It was Bunny who recommended Pratt use the Barretts, although Soul Syndicate would play on most of his hits thereafter. Real name Philip Choukee, and dubbed Pratt by Ken Lack while voicing songs for Caltone, the producer had the foresight to spot the potential of reggae superstars like Dennis Brown, Big Youth and Horace Andy from an early stage in their careers. By 1969, Pratt was renting a shop on Orange Street and producing tracks for his own Sunshot label with help from keyboard player Bobby Kalphat, who already knew the Hippy Boys through Bart Philips. It's Kalphat's melodica decorating 'Artibella Version', and his piano would later feature alongside Family Man's bass on the second version of 'Talk About Love' by Pat Kelly and Dillinger – a record dating from the mid-Seventies, and one of the first 12″ disco mixes to be released in Jamaica.

Other sessions recorded soon after the Upsetters' return yielded two songs for the Melodians' Tony Brevette, who was also attempting to go it alone. B. B. Seaton played lead guitar on the hypnotic 'Don't Get Weary', featuring a rhythm Family Man says "delves deep into Jamaican musical tradition" and possesses a deliciously poised swagger. Tapper Zukie later revived it for 'Don't Get Crazy', but it's Brevette's original that again showcases the Barretts' versatility.

"We just returned to those mento vibes, that nobody else wanted to play at the time," says Fams with a chuckle. "People around us said, 'No man, that can't work' and me just haffi smile, 'cause when singers and players of instruments come together, they must make the right play, y'know? And if you listen to the syncopation of the beat and how Gladdie Anderson plays piano on it, you can tell that's real, Jamaican country music. The one we did after that is called 'Took You By Surprise' and they used the drum and bass version of it as a commercial in Jamaica. The rhythm is more up-tempo and when they play it on the radio, the deejay would shout, 'Dub wise!' It was happening, I tell you!"

It was around this same time that Family Man formed the Youth Professionals. The Upsetters weren't playing too many live gigs, and Fams was being paired with other musicians in the studio, since more daring producers like Niney and Bunny Lee would often switch personnel on their records, in the hopes of stumbling across something fresh and different.

Bunny Lee: "That's because Fams knew all about chords and everything like that. Fams used to give everybody a break. Take drummers for instance. He'd bring in these different people and try them out and then rotate people we already knew on the sessions because he used to make Carly play a set, Tin Leg play a set and then a guy named Benbow, who's very good as well. Carlton Davis, who we call Santa, Fams would encourage him, and he was teaching Robbie Shakespeare as well."

Family Man says that Shakespeare, who lived on the border of Rollington Town and Vineyard Town, had a reputation as a troublemaker before learning bass. Fams met him though Robbie's older brother Lloydie, who used to sing in the Emotions with Max Romeo. Lloydie was no pushover, having once taken on five men single-handed – an encounter that left him with a bad back and a permanently swollen hand.

Family Man Barrett: "He used to carry this gun with a white chrome handle, but him always talk about Robbie so I say, 'Easy man, I will teach him fi play.' And him want fi buy Robbie a new guitar but I say I'll lend him one and all he should buy is some new strings, because I want 'im to know the difference between two strings. I say, 'I just want you to practise that' and then when I see him again, he's mastered that so I show 'im the next part now and him g'wan real good. 'Im can hear the sound, so then I show 'im what is E and G and that yuh 'ave minor and major, meaning you phrase it so. Him started to gain control now."

Shakespeare's first drum partner was called Benbow, who Carly taught at the same time Family Man was tutoring Robbie. The two youngsters had wanted to start a club in the Red Hills Road area and Family Man remembers taking a set of speakers up there in readiness for their first gig.

Family Man Barrett: "I also start Tyrone [Downie] and Touter, 'cause Touter, him a student in this t'ing. I found Touter in McGregor Gully, on the border of Rollington Town and Vineyard Town. He was still in school. I say to Robbie, 'I start this band, but over a period of time I'm going to pass it over to you.'"

The owner of the Green Mist, a nightclub on Langston Road midway between Rollington Town and Vineyard Town, invited Family Man to put together a band to play at a place some claim was a strip joint, but which Fams describes as being "a little rough sometimes".

Family Man Barrett: "We start out first with Reggie playing guitar, I on bass, Carly on drums and Tyrone on keyboards, but then I go for some different musicians."

Tin Leg had already played with Fams on sessions for Treasure Isle after leaving Now Generation and became the regular drummer in the new band once Carly found he didn't have any spare time between working his day job and playing sessions.

"I use a man called David on guitar," Family Man continues, "and the same little Tyrone, then we have Carl Dawkins and Touter and then we had this guy called Winston from Fourth Avenue, singing backing vocals as well. We'd rehearse like about three times a week, trying to get a vibes and they're all looking towards me for a name for the band, so I tell them not to worry, because the name will come. I say, 'Let's just get the music together first,' but at the second to last rehearsal, it sounded so good, every man get nice and then someone says I have to tell them the name that day. I laugh and then say, 'It's simple. I and I are youths but the people coming to the club they are expecting to hear some professional musicians, so let's call ourselves the Youth Professionals.'"

The Youth Professionals were designed to bring in extra income, as well as serve as a platform for new talent.

Family Man Barrett: "[Touter] was learning the keyboards in his spare time, because he'd come early and try and get some practice even though Tyrone was playing with us. The final line-up was myself on bass, Tin Leg on drums, Tyrone Downie on keyboards, David on rhythm guitar, Webbie Stewart from the Hippy Boys on lead guitar and Carl Dawkins on lead vocals, with Winston and Touter on harmonies. I have Trommie, which is Vin Gordon, playing trombone, and Royal on tenor sax. The Youth Professionals, they were just a little band really, but I still love my horns!"

The Youth Professionals played at the Green Mist every Friday, Saturday and Sunday night, although they also moonlighted at the Globe and Queen Theatres in central Kingston, where they kept the crowds happy for half an hour or so during intermissions. One New Year's Eve, they shared a bill with the Skatalites, who had reformed specially for the occasion, but it was rare for the band to venture too far from the Green Mist, despite having such a dynamic performer as Dawkins fronting them. Family Man says his stagecraft was electrifying, while others have called Dawkins "the Otis Redding of Jamaica". This isn't hard to understand after hearing him cut loose on hits like 'Bumpity Road', 'Get Together', or 'Satisfaction'. Family Man backed Dawkins on tunes for the Wailers and J. J. Johnson and regrets that Dawkins never made a bigger name for himself.

Family Man Barrett: "If Carl Dawkins just kept on the right track, there's no telling what could have happened, because the man could dance, sing, and perform real good. It's just that him drink too much and that slow 'im right down and upset everybody. Whether him used it with the Youth Professionals, I don't know. Me suspect 'im, but I know he was extra different from the rest. Either that or someone mix his drink with two lick or somet'ing, 'cause he used to sing and dance and gwan bad, like James Brown! And he'd sing all kind of songs, from soul, funk, blues, reggae, and ska, because we were a dance band, y'know? We'd play at all these wedding receptions, private parties and them things there. As a little band from Jamaica, it was a classic group really."

Dawkins' biggest ever hit, 'Satisfaction', sold over 80,000 copies in Jamaica alone on its release in 1970. The producer was J. J. Johnson, whose father owned Johnson's Drive-In on Maxwell Avenue, close to where the Hookim brothers would soon build Channel One. Carl's father was a drummer with Sonny Bradshaw's group and his son grew up around musicians such as Lester Sterling and members of the Techniques. Slim Smith had introduced him to J. J, who produced his earliest hits, 'Baby I Love You' and 'Hard Times'. Dawkins later wrote a protest song, 'Dr. Rodney', in support of activist Walter Rodney, whose ban by the Shearer government had caused riots in October 1968. Just like those of the Wailers, Dawkins' revolutionary credentials weren't in doubt. He embraced Rastafari after his release from Richmond Farm Prison, where he'd served time for a ganja rap alongside Bunny Livingston.

His stint in the Youth Professionals began soon after he joined Perry's circle for the second time, voicing a handful of songs as Ras Dawkins. The most well-known of these were 'Picture On The Wall' – a gutsy, uninhibited cover of the Freddie McKay hit, with all three Wailers contributing harmonies; and 'Cloud Nine' – taken at far slower pace than the Wailers' own cut, featuring Val Bennett's sax, as well as Tosh and Livingston's intrusive backing vocals.

None were hits on the scale of 'Satisfaction', although Trojan did release 'Picture On The Wall' on their UK Upsetter label in 1971, following singles by the Wailers, Dave Barker, Little Roy, and Junior Byles.

It was Errol Dunkley, rather than Dawkins, who profited most from the Youth Professionals in the studio once they'd got into their stride during the latter part of 1970. Dunkley was from Denham Town and had lived with his father after his parents separated, although he'd often hang out at his mother's bar, soaking up hits on the jukebox. He'd recorded for Prince Buster as a teenager, although it wasn't until Joe Gibbs heard him sing at a talent competition and produced hits like 'Please Stop Your Lying' and 'You're Gonna Need Me' that his career really took off. Dunkley then voiced for Bunny Lee and Coxsone before Gregory Isaacs took him to Rupie Edwards for 'Three In One'. It was this medley of Joe Gibbs' hits, skilfully reconstructed by Family Man, that put him back in the Jamaican charts during 1971.

Errol Dunkley: "I actually started out with Junior English when we were kids. I was about eleven, twelve at the time, and that's when we did those couple of songs for Prince Buster. He called us the Schoolboys, but then Junior left for England and I start recording for Joe Gibbs, even though I have a contract with Prince Buster, so Joe Gibbs have to buy out that before he could release 'You're Gonna Need Me', 'cause Buster never wanted him to put it out. But I go to Joe Gibbs 'cause nothing was really happening with Prince Buster and it was Bunny Lee who introduced us, 'cause he was working with Joe Gibbs at the time. I had three big hits for Joe Gibbs – 'You're Gonna Need Me', 'Please Stop Your Lying Girl' and 'I'm Going Home' – which I later did with Family Man as a medley. That was the 'Three In One' for Rupie Edwards. But before I work for Rupie Edwards, there were people like Coxsone, who I record for after I leave Joe Gibbs.

"Leroy Sibbles of the Heptones, he was the one who took me to Studio One at the same time Dennis Brown was there and also Horace Andy.

180

Then people like Burning Spear come along and the Wailing Souls, who'd been around a long time still. Carlton and the Shoe, he played guitar as a session musician while writing a few songs for himself like 'Love Me Forever'. But t'ings wasn't happening for me at Studio One and Gregory Isaacs, who was my good friend, he was singing for Rupie Edwards at the time. We used to spar 'round in the music industry, so he took me to Rupie Edwards and I did that tune 'Three In One', which was an immediate hit. After that now, I did 'Darling Ooh' for myself, 'cause Gregory and I team up at the same time and produce 'Movie Star', which was the first song we do on the African Museum label. Gregory Isaacs and I were the first two artists to really go out and produce ourselves. We used to put our money together, rent the studio, pay the musicians and everything, but I later sold 'Darling Ooh' and those other songs to Miss Pottinger and regretted it, 'cause they were big hits! And that's when I start gettin' some recognition again."

Family Man didn't play on Dunkley's first recordings for Gibbs, but was more than happy to test his skills on the new versions.

" 'Three In One' was a medley of [Dunkley's] greatest songs, and you really couldn't hear the difference, or tell whether it was the original tape or what," Fams says, proudly. "That's because when we rehearse those songs, we fit them in like piston rings, so tight were those rhythms. After that now, I play on some cover songs like 'Movie Star' and 'Darling Ooh', 'cause I produce that album for him with Miss Pottinger and Tip Top Records called *Darling Ooh*. And that was a smash! In fact, I play on that whole album *Darling Ooh* by Errol Dunkley. I arrange all of the songs and I call the sessions, bring in the musicians and everyt'ing. We record some of the tracks at Treasure Isle, some at Randy's and, I think, at Dynamics too, y'know? That was the last thing I do for Miss Pottinger, because all those times I deal with Bob, I don't see her. I just picture her in the early years."

Whereas Miss Pottinger took care of the local market, Trojan Records released *Darling Ooh* on their Attack subsidiary during 1972. This album is so cohesive, it's best described as a suite of songs, which is surprising considering there were at least three different studios involved. Dunkley was no supreme stylist and couldn't dominate a song like Dawkins. His vocals are reminiscent of Delroy Wilson's and even a young Dennis Brown's in places, except he doesn't share the same finesse of either. Instead, his voice has a mournful quality, no matter what he's singing about, as the Youth Professionals lay down a succession of sparsely arranged, homogenous beats that rarely intrude and yet are taut with inner dynamics.

The album opens with 'You Never Know', which tells of a man whose heart has already been broken and yet is convinced things will work out better with the same girl next time. You just know he's fooling himself – "riding for a fall" as they say in Jamaica – and the way the band keep it tight and simple, yet create such a wistful atmosphere in support, is nothing short of masterful. 'Movie Star' opens with melancholy horns, but the rhythm itself is anything but passive as Tin Leg plays all over his kit and the guitarist slashes at, rather than strumming the chords. The song itself is a cover of Delroy Wilson's 'I Don't Know Why', yet there are shades of William de Vaughn's 'Be Thankful For What You've Got' in the lyrics, as Dunkley professes his love for a ghetto girl.* Dunkley's version is definitive, and so, too, 'Created By The Father', as covered by Dennis Brown on his *Wolves And Leopards* album. Dunkley also sang 'Created By The Father' for Randy's. The original cut of 'A Little Way Different' features a majestic arrangement as Dunkley calls for tolerance and mutual understanding, irrespective of colour, creed, or faith. (The later version was re-recorded in London with Dennis Bovell). Tyrone's organ playing stands out especially.

'Like To Be Boozed' is a more up-tempo discourse on drunkards. 'Darling Ooh' is a cover of Delroy Wilson's 'Your Love Is Amazing', featuring a kind of lurching rhythm that appears to stumble at times, yet, of course, never does. Dunkley's voice is again tinged with sadness, even when expressing overwhelming affection, and this is also true of 'Baby I Love You' – the same song Alton Ellis recorded at Treasure Isle during Family Man's first ever session for Duke Reid. Ellis' version is brighter and more immediate, whereas the emphasis in Dunkley's is on feel and rhythm. It still fits within the concept of the album, as does a reworking of the former Joe Gibbs' hit 'You're Gonna Need Me', on which Family Man's bass dances with joy and the whole band locks into the groove as if their lives depended on it.

Errol's vocals notwithstanding, there's no question that Family Man is the dominant musical presence on these tracks. His bassline on 'I'm Not The Man For You' is as ruthless and insistent as the one he plays on Big Youth's 'Screaming Target', but then every one of the album's 12 tracks is full of subtle interaction between bass and drums, organ and chinking rhythm guitar, interspersed by occasional trumpet and trombone. The latter really come into their own on 'Hi-Lite Parts 1 & 2' – a foot-tapping

* Buju Banton and Wayne Wonder successfully revived it in the early Nineties.

instrumental that has a country feel with its honky-tonk piano and skanking guitar. It's like nothing else on the album but is great fun and shows off the talents of both horn players to deserved effect. Trojan left it off the album's 1979 reissue but it's a delightful example of what the Youth Professionals were capable of when in a playful mood.

While adept at playing popular hits for club audiences, Family Man knew the Youth Professionals would provide him with something different when it came to studio work and so it proved. Although they wouldn't play on Wailers projects, Fams enjoyed the chemistry generated by this particular set of musicians, and took pride in hearing them develop their own identity. This was compounded by his own slight variation in sound, since by the time sessions for the *Darling Ooh* album started, he'd changed instruments, passing his trusty Hofner violin bass on to Robbie Shakespeare.

Family Man Barrett: "That was the one I give him, because another bass came by me, an Epiphone, but it didn't have enough bottom to it. I think it was something to do with the circuit, so I carry it down to the shop and ask if I can buy a substitute part. Them say no, so I take it back home and solder it up myself. Clean it properly with some filing paper so it don't make any noise when I'm in the studio and fit it up back and then I mark on it, "The Sound Of Now." That's the bass I use on some great licks for Errol Dunkley. Songs like 'Black Cinderella', 'Movie Star' and 'Darling Ooh'.

Dunkley left for shows in Nassau and the Cayman Islands soon after the release of 'Movie Star'. When he came back, robbers had broken into his record shop and plundered his jukeboxes. Although still only young, he was resilient, but when the very same thing happened the following year, he sold up and left for London after accepting an offer to join Count Shelly's Third World label. Whether he or Family Man was the producer of *Darling Ooh* is a moot point. Fams was certainly experienced enough to produce the album himself, whereas Dunkley was still relatively new to the business, or at least as a label owner. He was ambitious, though, and continued making hit records long after leaving Jamaica. He even scored a UK Top 20 hit in 1979 with a cover of John Holt's 'OK Fred', and made history by becoming the first promoter to take a Jamaican sound-system to England. The arrival of Ray Symbolic, with Ranking Joe at the control tower, would cause an explosion of interest in dancehall overseas, thus laying the foundations for today's ragga music. In a simple twist of fate, the track that lit the blue touch-paper of Jamaica's digital revolution was Wayne Smith's 'Under Mi Sleng-Teng'.

Family Man Barrett: "When the rockers sound was going on, Jimmy Radway wanted it for some recording, so that's how we come up with this song, 'Black Cinderella'. These Japanese people caught onto it later and put in this Casio machine. That was the setting they discover when making that track, 'Under Mi Sleng-Teng', because it's my bassline they design it from originally.

"We do some other long time, bad man sessions for Jimmy Radway. That was the band where I bring in Tyrone and it was the first band for Robbie Shakespeare too, but he never join them yet. Radway did those tunes like 'Mother Lisa' by Leroy Smart. They used to call him One Foot Jimmy. He was a cool guy, but nothing extravagant; a politician and some kind of relative to Tyrone Downie. I think maybe he was Tyrone's uncle, because Tyrone did some work for Keith Hudson and when Keith never paid him, Jimmy go down to Dynamic Sounds and tears a rassclaat strip off a Keith Hudson, saying, 'Don't you take this here youth for a fool, or I'll find a stick and beat you from morning 'til night!' Well, Keith is a bad man and he has this bad man friend as a sidekick called Stamma, y'know? But One Foot Jimmy, he never worry too much about that."

Lloyd "Jimmy" Radway came from Allman Town although, like Dunkley and Gregory Isaacs, he grew up in Denham Town, before training as an upholsterer. 'Black Cinderella' was the debut release on his Fe Me Time label, which he'd set up in 1972 after being loaned a hundred pounds by a local timber importer. The session took place at Dynamic, with Carly replacing Tin Leg, and Reggie playing rhythm guitar. Powered by Family Man's relentless bassline and underpinned by Tyrone's (making his studio debut) stabbing organ riffs, it's a magnificent track. The Youth Professionals' horn section is at its searing best on the bridge and Dunkley's vocals are more haunting than on anything recorded with the band so far. The lyrics were apparently written about a girl from Allman Town who was desperately trying to carve out a decent life for herself, despite her mother's entreaties to become a prostitute like her two sisters. Big Youth was at the session and stepped up to the mic to deliver 'The Best Big Youth' on the same rhythm straight after Dunkley had finished. Radway later recorded I Roy on it for 'Sound Education' and got Augustus Pablo to blow melodica on an instrumental cut, 'Cinderella In Black', although it was Dunkley's version that proved the biggest hit after reaching number one on both the JBC and RJR charts.

Its success encouraged Radway to continue as a producer before he eventually became disillusioned with the local music business and stopped making records altogether. The Barretts again play on Vin Gordon's 'Zion Youth', a moody trombone instrumental containing strong echoes of 'Black Cinderella', and Hortense Ellis' dark as night 'Hell And Sorrow', featuring Alton's older sister. They also reputedly backed Anthony "Sangie" Davis' group the Gatherers on an unreleased track for Lee Perry, recorded before their epochal 'Words Of My Mouth'. Tyrone recorded instrumentals of his own for Fe Me Time, including 'Organ D', which gave rise to his first nickname. Both were released in 1972, while Tyrone's 'Movie Star Version 3', a cut to the Errol Dunkley hit, appeared on *African Museum*.

Tyrone had been raised in the Vineyard Town area by his mother, Gwendoline Edwards, but was living in Cockburn Pen when Family Man enrolled him in the Youth Professionals at the age of 14. Gwendoline therefore insisted Tyrone could only play at weekends, so as not to interfere with his studies. Family Man, who was 10 years older and living in Pembroke Hall, was a guiding influence on the youngster during his teenage years, as were Bob, Rita, and the other Wailers. By the time he was asked to participate on an album, *In Memory Of Bishop Gibson*, recorded at Kingston College using Randy's studio equipment, he was already proficient on keyboards and clarinet, attracting the attention of Vincent Chin's son Clive, Randy's engineer Errol Thompson, and Augustus Pablo, who had all attended "KC" before him.

As Organ D, Tyrone recorded a handful of instrumentals before growing disenchanted with the Kingston scene and headed for the north coast with Jo Jo Bennett & the Fugitives. On his frequent trips back to Kingston, he recorded sides for Bunny Lee, Munchie Jackson, Blacker Morwell, Rupie Edwards, and Clive Chin, who recorded Tyrone on *Blackman's World*. He also played occasional sessions for Augustus Pablo's Hot Stuff and Rockers labels before joining the Wailers in 1976.

Another old friend of Family Man's had made his first forays into record production. Herman Chin Loy was Leslie Kong's cousin and worked for Beverley's before pooling resources with his brother Lloyd and opening the One Stop record store on King Street, which Derrick Harriott later took over. Chin Loy stayed in the King Street area for three years until it became a war zone for rival Phoenix and Vikings gangs. He then left to work at KG's, the music store and record distributors in Half Way Tree, moonlighting as a deejay before opening the Aquarius Record Shop in 1969. His first few releases included Bruce Ruffin's near-UK hit 'Rain', and instrumentals he'd bought from various other producers and licensed for his Aquarius label. Some of them, like 'African Zulu' and 'Shang I', featured Lloyd Charmers and the Hippy Boys, whereas others, including 'Reggae To The Fields' and 'Old Kent Road', were provided by Family Man, who played on a number of Chin Loy's earliest productions, including those featuring Augustus Pablo.

"Herman always made sure him come get me, because we sit on the same bench at St Aloysius Boys' School when we were young. That's where we spring up from, then I go to the Jamaica Youth Corps, before I return like the prodigal son, turned into a GI or something!" says Family Man, laughing. "But I play on lots of tracks for [Loy] like 'Sing A Song' by Richie Mac (MacDonald), who later sing lead vocals with the Chosen Few. I do some serious work with Richie touring around Jamaica, 'cause we used to include songs by Dennis Brown, the Gaylads, and Abyssinians, like 'Satta Massagana' as part of our act; also Errol Dunkley's 'Black Cinderella', and 'Skylarking' by Horace Andy. But those early songs for Herman were done at Dynamic, with Mikey and Geoffrey Chung playing guitar, Tin Leg on drums, myself on bass, and the same Augustus Pablo on piano, as well as the melodica."

Chin Loy had made up the name Augustus Pablo and used it for a sequence of organ instrumentals, irrespective of who'd played on them. Tracks featuring Lloyd Charmers and Glen Adams (including 'Aquarius One') were originally credited to Augustus Pablo until Horace Swaby, an accountant's son from Havendale, walked into Chin Loy's shop one day clutching a melodica. Peter Tosh also played melodica of course, and so too Bobby Kalphat, although the sound of it was still a relative novelty at the time, since they were manufactured primarily as children's toys. Swaby however, got such feel and expression out of it that Chin Loy immediately felt compelled to record him. From thereon, the name Augustus Pablo would stick with him and the humble melodica become transformed into a vehicle for some of the most uplifting and spiritual music of the entire roots era.

Family Man Barrett: "Pablo was like a little uptown man turned ghetto. That's how him want to be and him sight up the roots t'ing right away, 'cause some of them come in pon it on a different level, but it even surprise me when 'im dread. I guess he don't know what 'im get into! But he was from an uptown area and I hear 'im get a fight from his family about coming into the music, 'cause maybe them have other ideas fi 'im and he get caught in the middle of that. It was Clive Chin who introduced me to him still, 'cause I think he was from Clive's school. But the man was sick for years. I don't know whether 'im have diabetes or something, but 'im always need treatment."

Pablo, who later died from a rare nerve disorder, shared a sound-system called Rockers with his brother Garth, and despite his middle class background had already developed a preference for the heavier, downtown sound he heard coming out of studios like Randy's. He therefore knew what style of recordings he wanted to make, although he saw himself as more of a pianist than melodica player, when first playing sessions. Chin Loy asked him to audition right there in his shop and promptly invited him to overdub some rhythms. Pablo's 'Iggy Iggy' duly appeared in late 1971, although it wasn't exactly an auspicious debut. Swaby's melodica playing was uneven and the rhythm itself a somewhat laboured cut of the Heptones' 'How Could I Leave'. The best thing about the record was Chin Loy's deejayed intro, delivered in the style of a newsreader, made up of pure jive talk. Better by far was 'East Of The River Nile', which had an unusual rhythmic structure and is so captivating, it could be used to charm snakes were it not for some crashing cymbals and animated bursts of percussion.

The Upsetters recorded it the night before Adams left for New York, and a more beguiling coda to their partnership couldn't be imagined. Loy would soon revisit it for a deejay cut, 'Soul Vibration', but it's Pablo's version that casts the greater spell and provided him with his first notable release. Chin Loy called it 'East Of The River Nile' because of what he describes as "its Far Eastern sound." This was another of Family Man's innovations, although he's quick to point out that it didn't necessarily arise from studying music, but from being receptive to whatever he heard around him.

Family Man Barrett: "It wasn't me who invented it. It came strictly through a higher power, like when I did 'Eastern Memphis'. Sometimes when I listen for those kinds of sounds, I find them in unlikely places. For instance, I don't hear too much from records, but through watching certain movies and especially the historical ones. I hear these inspirational sounds in the background where they're riding on a camel, or have about six guys playing trumpets in movies like *Ben Hur* and that's what gives me the vibes for transferring them to reggae, and creating that Far East sound."

Pablo would later re-record 'East Of The River Nile', but failed to emulate its magical beauty on other sessions for Chin Loy, despite titles such as 'Song Of The East'. The closest they came was on 'The Red Sea' and 'I-Man', a prototype of the rhythm Family Man and Pablo would use behind Jacob Miller's 'Baby, I Love You So', included on their classic *Rockers Meets King Tubby Downtown* album. What's notable about Pablo's recordings for Aquarius is that they contain the blueprint for his subsequent success and far from sounding cheap or disrespectful, his melodica playing actually enhances the magisterial feel of the rhythms. The combination introduced something new to reggae and heralded a more spiritual approach to recording instrumentals.

Chin Loy later issued *Aquarius Dub*, widely regarded as the first-ever dub album, and pioneered Jamaican soul music with Zap Pow lead singer Beres Hammond, as well as recording the likes of Dennis Brown, Alton Ellis, Ernest Ranglin, Harold Butler, Boris Gardiner, and Little Roy. The latter describes Chin Loy as the best producer he ever worked with in Jamaica, and credits him for successfully bridging the divide between Kingston's uptown and downtown music fraternities.

"City sound-system music is a rebellious music which portrays dissent from authority as well as having sexual overtones in the rub-a-dub style," Chin Loy once told David Rodigan. "Ghetto rebel music explains the sorrows of four hundred years to the present enslavement and exploitation of a people. City disco music is business-orientated and, like country reggae music, is influenced by our radio stations, which the city rebel music is not."

In other words, artists and musicians weren't primarily concerned with financial rewards or airplay when making roots music. Instead, they were looking to express a common heritage and protest about the hardships facing those who'd been disenfranchised from mainstream society. Rebel music was the voice of the sufferers and the Wailers were being joined by an increasing number of other acts with a similar agenda, including uptown youths like Pablo.

Pablo later recruited Family Man on material produced for his own Rockers' label, including 'Skankin' Easy', although it was Robbie Shakespeare, the bassist who replaced him in the Youth Professionals, who would play on tracks such as 'Frozen Dub' and 'Cassava Piece'. Those sessions were some way off, however, since Pablo still lacked what it took to become a successful producer and had yet to establish himself as a session musician, let alone have a hit in his own right. His breakthrough track, 'Java', produced at Randy's by Clive Chin, provided a wonderful illustration of the early rockers' sound with its driving rhythm, ethereal melodies, and dubbed up vocals.

Family Man Barrett: "This man from Canada gave me a 45 and said, 'I want you to study this good, 'cause I want a hit out of it.' He said he didn't want the horns, but just the rhythm, so I go home and listen to it and then call for some musicians to do this tune, 'Java'. I get Earl "Chinna" Smith to play rhythm guitar and I find another bass man fi it, which is Fully [George Fullwood] from Soul Syndicate, because I played piano, with Santa on drums. It's a guy called Jackson playing that long time kind of melody on lead guitar and then we do the intro with the Chosen Few on vocals before Pablo come in and tear it up. And you see that horn section from the original 'Java'? You know what I did with it? That was the horns playing on Errol Dunkley's 'Black Cinderella', except I play back the bass myself that time."

The Canadian in question was Dennis Wright, who was a friend of Chin's, who later worked for Blue Mountain. Wright was supposed to sing on it but Chin didn't like his vocals and so had to improvise.

Clive Chin: "Dennis Wright was a schoolmate of mine from KC and the man couldn't hold the tune! I took him into the studio to audition him and there was this one song he had about some woman he'd met. It was a love song but he couldn't manage the vocals, so instead of wasting a good rhythm . . . What actually happened was, it was recorded during a session held by my uncle Keith and when Dennis came in and auditioned the song, Family Man was the one who really orchestrated it, because he was playing piano and it's always the piano player who determines the chord structure and the arrangements. The lead guitarist, Jackson Jones, he migrated to Canada in the early Seventies. Ossie Hibbert played the organ, Fully Fullwood was on bass and this light-skinned guy called Tony King played percussion. This was even before Sticky. I think it was just tambourine he played on the session, but he used to play the bongos as well.

"Errol Thompson the engineer, he wanted us to put out the rhythm track the way it was, but Pablo happened to be there when we were deciding what to do and so he ended up playing on it. Then I brought in the Chosen Few to do the introduction, because we needed a catch to it. I wanted them to sing the lyrics to the Impressions' 'East Of Java' but it didn't fit, so we just said, 'Java' in the end.*

"Errol had been an apprentice at Studio One under Sylvan Morris

---

* Errol Thompson, also known as "E.T.", was Randy's engineer until 1974, when he left to work with Joe Gibbs. He was one of Jamaica's most prolific and influential studio engineers, in addition to being a major pioneer of dub.

before being introduced to my father, but I knew him from choir school, which was facing Kingston College on the corner of South Camp Road and North Street. It was funded by the church and intended to be this place where they raised choirboys. Tony Gregory, Dobby Dobson, Delroy Wilson, and all of those guys passed through there. It wasn't just a place you'd learn to sing though, because they'd teach you to play instruments as well. They had pretty strict tutors, but that's where I met Errol. This was in about 1967, but he came to Randy's through Mr Galbraith, who used to look after the instruments in the studio."

This was the same choir school Tyrone Downie attended, although he was two years younger than Thompson and Chin. During their regular Sunday evening sessions at Randy's, the two friends recorded several other versions to 'Java', including those by Tommy McCook, I Roy, and Dennis Alcapone. Various dub mixes of it also formed the basis of an album called *Java Java Dub*, featuring vocal snippets by deejay Crutches, Bingy Bunny, and Thompson himself. A spark of genius thus went a very long way and 'Java' – which was only Chin's second-ever production – soon heralded Pablo's debut album, *This Is Augustus Pablo*, released by Randy's in 1973. 'Java' had been voted Best Instrumental of 1972, by which time Chin and the young melodica player had been truly baptised into the downtown scene, thanks to Family Man and the procession of other characters passing through 17 North Parade. Chin had known the Barretts ever since the studio first opened and had seen producers like Lee Perry and Bunny Lee in action on a daily basis. His father, uncle and aunt had their own labels and it was only natural that the bright and inquisitive Clive should wish to follow them, although it wasn't just making hit records he was interested in, but becoming part of a movement.

Those references to the Impressions' 'East Of Java' had been no accident, since Chin was a keen fan of American soul artists such as James Brown, Curtis Mayfield, and the Temptations, and readily identified with the outpourings of black pride emanating from Jamaica and the US, despite being light-skinned and of Chinese extraction. There was revolution in the air and young people like him wanted to be a part of it. A short time earlier, Chin had watched entranced as Perry produced the Wailers at Randy's, and was fully aware of the differences between what they were trying to achieve, compared to other, more commercially minded Jamaican acts. In deference to Isaac Hayes, who'd taken to wearing chains in reminding people about slavery, he'd named his sound-system Black Moses, which played a mix of soul and reggae between 1970 and 1971.

Clive Chin: "Black Moses didn't play out all that often. I played at the J.C. headquarters up in New Kingston and then I played out another time with Pablo, but these motorbike guys came and caused a disturbance. I'm sure I played out another time, right where Seaga did have his residence, but when the sound became obsolete, we put it in the dub room. The turntable, speakers, and the E Q equipment in there were from Black Moses and we used it to mix plenty of tunes during those times. A lot of Niney's tracks were mixed in the dub room using that same equipment. Dennis Thompson used to do a lot of mixes on it, because we hardly ever mixed inside of the studio. We'd just run the tracks through that E Q and cut it straight from there. Dennis Thompson, he was bad in them ways there, and what he did really added to the creativity that used to come out of that place. That was the thing about Randy's studio because it wasn't just about the sound you'd get from the desk itself, but what you got when you were cutting the tracks during the mastering process."

Dennis Thompson – no relation to Errol – needed to be exceptional in order to be entrusted with mixing down Family Man's music, and he was. His mixing techniques at Randy's – and also the explorations of King Tubby's in west Kingston – were part of the wholesale changes happening in Jamaican music. Dub, version and deejaying had all sprung up as if from nowhere over the past year or so, although such innovations had made reggae more saleable than ever as it enjoyed another run of success on the UK charts thanks to Dave & Ansel Collins, Bob & Marcia, and the Pioneers. Yet local musicians continued to get ripped off, even if they did play on endless sessions, or secured themselves a production deal with a company from overseas. Despite their popularity at home and abroad, the Barrett brothers were still struggling to make a decent living playing music, and with Marley away for at least two months, their prospects weren't looking too good by the end of '71.

Family Man: "Carly, he was still working at KG's in Cross Roads. Although sometimes he'd be invited to tour with Tommy McCook and the Supersonics when them fly out to some of the small islands and do some shows over there. This was after the Upsetters, but we'd still do sessions regularly just the same. Bob, he was in Sweden and taking time out to plan some things on the business side at that stage, but I stay with the music vibes, every time! Then, when we're ready, we can easily merge . . ."

Family Man handed over the Youth Professionals to Shakespeare before leaving to play on the MS *Starward*, a ship owned by Norwegian Cruise

Lines that ferried holidaymakers around the Caribbean.

"We were travelling between Jamaica, Miami, and Haiti. In between playing bass in the Wailers and on all those other sessions, I was playing calypso music for the tourists at the quayside and then we'd play on the ship too, although I had seasickness most of the time. I'd just stare at the floor, looking at the same spot, I tell you . . .

"There were just two of us from Jamaica in that band, Tin Leg and myself. The other two guys were from Barbados. The lead singer, he played congas and the next one guitar. Him played good too, but I was just making up time really, 'cause Bob say he was going over to England to discuss business and I need to be earning in the meantime. I remember applying for my visa and they say, 'How long you going to be working on this ship?' I say, 'Forever,' so I get a visa for four years! But then every time the boat came back to Jamaica, I say to Carly, 'Has Bob come?' And he say, 'No, Bob don't come yet,' and we keep doing that until the fourth time, when I see Bob himself. Bob say, 'I'm ready.' I say, 'Well this is my last trip then!' Yeah, so I wait 'til the boat reach Haiti and then the next stop is Kingston so I say, 'I'm resigning this work right here.' The man ask me what's wrong, knowing it can't be the money, because he'd just given me a pay rise. I say, 'No, it's not the pay. It's just not my kind of t'ing,' so they take back the ID and return my passport."

Family Man occupied his time by making himself available for session work in Jamaica. On his return home, Marley told Fams that Sims had arranged for the Wailers to go to London and tour with Johnny Nash. It was just the kind of opportunity the group had been waiting for and one that would finally herald their breakthrough outside of Jamaica.

CHAPTER ELEVEN

The Harder They Come

PEOPLE still argue over where Marley actually went when, with 'Screwface' still riding high in the Jamaican charts, he boarded a plane from Kingston during December 1971. Some claim he returned to Sweden before travelling to London, while others point towards the handful of shows Marley, Livingston, and Tosh performed in America over the holiday period as 1971 gave way to 1972. Family Man says the Wailers used pick-up bands for these dates, since there wasn't enough money for band members to accompany them and, in any case, he was still entertaining tourists on the MS *Starward*. It would be the last time any of the Wailers toured without their own musicians, which suggests the experience wasn't to their liking, something Glen Adams confirms.

"Bob, Peter and Bunny come in for shows. First we have a vibes and go through a thing, because when they performed at the President's Chateau in Brooklyn, it was just the three of them. I played onstage with them at that show. I wasn't in any band at the time, but I was at the concert and the keyboardist wasn't playing what Bob wanted. He saw me there and said I had to come up onstage, so me just go up there and play, but some rude boy come and upset it. He wanted Bob to sing 'Screwface' and through him nah sing it, the man start to fire shot inna the place. The police just come and shut down the dance after that, but the Wailers, they'd just come over to do two shows for Tony Spaulding, one at the Concourse Manor [sic] and one in Brooklyn."

The Wailers' arrival in New York for shows promoted by Spaulding, who was a high-ranking member of the PNP, suggests favours were extended to Marley in return, especially since the Wailers had performed as part of the PNP's Musical Bandwagon only a few weeks earlier. The New Year's Eve show at the Concord Manor on East 161st Street in the Bronx* marked one of the few occasions when the three original Wailers

---

* The venue was later renamed Concourse Plaza and turned into a multiplex cinema.

performed together in the US. Legend has it they also played gigs in Manhattan, Pennsylvania, Queens, and Delaware throughout January 1972, although by the end of that month Marley was back in London and Tosh and Livingston had returned to Jamaica. Once in London, Marley rejoined Sims and Nash as they put the finishing touches to Nash's latest album, *I Can See Clearly Now*. Marley spent over three months in England. He, Sims, Nash, Texan keyboard player John "Rabbit" Bundrick and Rabbit's Swedish girlfriend shared an apartment at 333 King's Road, Chelsea for a while before moving to a third floor flat at 34 Ridgemount Gardens, off Gower Street, near Tottenham Court Road, where they stayed until April. Marley had befriended Bundrick in Stockholm and schooled him in reggae time and rhythm, despite Bundrick noticing how Marley's guitar was always out of tune (presumably because there was no Family Man around to tune it for him.)

Rabbit described the house they all shared in Stockholm as "a songwriting factory", since music could be heard coming from every room. Marley and Bundrick worked together on the soundtrack to a film Nash had starred in with well-respected Scandinavian actress Christina Schollin. Unfortunately, the film flopped after its Swedish premiere in Stockholm, which meant bad news for Nash and Sims on yet another front, since they'd also bought the music rights. Nash was trying out Marley compositions when the musicians were informed the money had run out and they wouldn't be paid unless Sims won a card game he'd set up with a Swedish gangster. Sims duly lost all the money and then got angry when cornered by Bundrick and friends, who were depending on him for money and their tickets home. Tempers became frayed, but even the hard-bitten Sims had to back down after threatening Marley, who stood his ground. The altercation cost Nash his guitar and tape-recorder, since both disappeared with Marley back to Jamaica.

All hostilities seemed to have been forgotten once the final sessions for *I Can See Clearly Now* got under way. It transpired the album would contain several Marley songs including 'Stir It Up', 'Guava Jelly' and 'Comma Comma', plus 'You Poured Sugar On Me', a Marley-Nash co-composition.* By the time 'Stir It Up' charted in April, Nash was signed to CBS in the UK and Epic in the US. 'I Can See Clearly Now' went Top 5 that June followed by the release of the album in August,

---

* Another Marley composition, 'Nice Time', written about his daughter Cedella, appeared on Nash's follow-up album, *My Merry Go Round*, in 1973.

which received good reviews, despite it only just scraping into the Top 40 album chart. 'There Are More Questions Than Answers' became Nash's second Top 10 hit of the year, in October, marking a welcome return to the British charts since his run of success with 'Hold Me Tight', 'You Got Soul' and 'Cupid', three years earlier.

In March '72, Marley recorded a number of tracks for CBS with members of Bundrick's band, Sons of the Jungle, including 'Dance Do The Reggae', 'Gonna Get You', 'Stay With Me', 'Oh Lord I Got To Get There', and a re-recording of the Wailers' Studio One hit, 'I'm Hurting Inside'. CBS released 'Reggae On Broadway' as a single in May. Sims was hoping that CBS would sign Marley as a solo act, but the response to 'Reggae On Broadway' wasn't good and so they didn't take up their option on him. This was understandable, since the material and production hardly did Marley justice and there was nothing that could match 'Trenchtown Rock' and 'Lively Up Yourself' for sheer excitement. Ironically enough, it was Paul Simon's 'Mother And Child Reunion' – a record made at Byron Lee's newly opened Dynamic Sound Studio in Kingston – that had provided one of the year's biggest hits, and its success on the UK and US charts would attract considerable interest in Jamaica's latest, state-of-the-art recording facilities. Another coincidence was that Simon's hit featured none other than Ranny "Bop" Williams on rhythm guitar, who happened to be living in London while Marley was recording for CBS and accompanying Nash on his promotional gigs up and down the country.

"Bob Marley called me to play sessions with him when we were both in London, although I'd played on some of his songs with the Wailers before then," says Ranny. "'Trenchtown Rock' was the first one in rocksteady times, the original version, and then I go on tour with Johnny Nash and I was accompanying them both when Johnny said to me, 'Ranny Bop. Right now Bob Marley call yuh name.' He was saying I should go back to Bob and so I became the first Jamaican musician in a foreign country to play for Bob Marley, then when they came back to England later that same year, they asked me to join with them one more time. I was going to do it but I'd already started playing with Jimmy Cliff by then and just couldn't break away like that, so they just stick together and form the band without me. But I am one of the original members of the Wailers band and I was there before most of them."

There were two sessions at CBS Studios during Marley's London trip, although on this occasion he recorded material better suited to his

Jamaican audience, namely alternative cuts of 'Stir It Up', 'Concrete Jungle', 'Slave Driver', '400 Years', and 'Midnight Ravers'. He had either recorded these tracks first and been told they weren't commercial enough, or he'd started off trying to voice songs he considered more chart-friendly and recognised (or been told) that they were unrepresentative. At the very least, it illustrates how Marley was unsure of which direction to go in without the counsel of the other Wailers, or input from his trusty musical accomplices, the Barretts. Sims was involved in the production of both sessions and Ranny Bop says he played guitar on one, together with members of the Cimarons. 'Slave Driver' and 'Midnight Ravers' were both new; the latter mixed Biblical imagery of "10,000 chariots" with what some have interpreted as a commentary on the unisex fashions he saw in London. "Can't tell the woman from the man, 'caused they're dressed in the same pollution. Their minds are confused with confusion," he sings, before bewailing how such problems were ever going to be solved.

Family Man Barrett: "That song came from walking around Portobello Road and in Harlesden and then coming back into the West End and taking a look at Piccadilly Circus, where Bob once ran into Marcus [Wright]. It was different for us, seeing how people moved and how they were dressing. Hearing how they were talking and what they were listening to, because the hippies were still in and the skinheads were still around, too. There was still a lot of fuss being made of the Beatles and also the influences coming from Jamaica and America, where they had the soul and the rock music going on. It was the era of Led Zeppelin and Traffic and also the Rolling Stones. The Jackson Five, they were trying to make a breakthrough too, and we run into them a lot of times when we were in London. The Jackson Five had a great sound and the fans were already going crazy over them, y'know? They were part of the great Tamla Motown stable at the time and, of course, we were listening to the Godfather of Soul, James Brown, and people like Quincy Jones. We'd be there, soaking up all these different kinds of music whilst working on our own style of roots rock reggae, and that was a great feeling, y'know?"

'Midnight Ravers' was good, but 'Slave Driver' is even better; a smouldering, one-man revolt against the horrors of slavery, both past and present. "Every time I hear the crack of a whip, my blood runs cold. I remember on the slave ship, how they brutalised our very souls." Marley then identifies poverty and illiteracy as the new chains that bind, while warning of how the tables have turned and the slave masters are about to "catch a fire". While the production could have been improved (and he would re-record both tracks before the year was out), Marley's choice of songs was impeccable. However, there was still no indication that anyone from CBS was listening.

Family Man Barrett: "Rannie Bop come up to London before us and met up with Bob, Danny Sims, and Johnny Nash. Them try to do a thing and call it Wailers, but Bunny and Peter weren't there and nor my brother and I, so it coming like them try a test and Bob know from that test that t'ings couldn't work unless him have his band, so him come back and say, 'Boy, we haffi go and do a t'ing, y'know? And build up this band here serious.' I say, 'Okay,' so he go and check out a building for rehearsal, 'cause this was soon after I come back from the MS *Starward* as a boatman . . ."

Just prior to Marley returning to Jamaica in May, the Johnny Nash entourage – including Rabbit and his girlfriend, as well as Nash and Sims – had decamped to 12 Queensborough Terrace, just off Bayswater Road in central London. Marley, Livingston, Tosh, and the Barretts all stayed there later that summer, although Fams wasted no time in making himself available for session work in the meantime.

In March, Michael Manley had stormed to victory in the country's election with a record number of votes and was dominating the local media, with his third wife, the actress, model, and radio announcer Beverly Anderson, by his side. Manley's personal charisma and his socialist agenda had raised hopes of much-needed reforms on the island and there was even a sense of relief among normally apolitical Rastas, who'd long despaired of the repressive Shearer government. Manley, with his Rod of Correction at the ready, might prove a different proposition and his success was widely celebrated, as in Ken Lazarus' hit 'Hail The Man', written and produced by Ernie Smith, who had just won the Tokyo Song Festival, and had a hit of his own with 'Pitta Patta'. Prior to the election, economic and political power had rested with white and mixed race Jamaicans, yet Manley had won power thanks to a majority of black voters, and he was now expected to deliver.

This honeymoon period wouldn't last long, but lyrics devoted to cultural or reality matters now became more widespread, as artists like Big Youth arrived to shake up the scene. While influenced by U Roy and Dennis Alcapone, Big Youth had spurned the use of gangster names and spoke of everyday trials and tribulations in his songs, as well as more revolutionary topics. Downtown people loved him, not only for what he said, but the way in which he said it, since rather than string together rhyming couplets, he'd chant in a style that later became known as "sing-jaying". During early 1972, he had a massive hit with 'S90 Skank' for one-time ghetto dentist-turned-producer Keith Hudson, but then Prince Buster called for the Barretts, and recorded 'Chi Chi Run' with him straight after. These two tracks chased each other up and down both Jamaican charts all summer, together with Big Youth's cut of 'Movie Star' (which Family Man also played on). He and Carly filled a tape of rhythms for Buster around this time that was later released on an album called *The Message*.

This was in addition to playing sessions for Glen Brown, whose releases that year included cuts of 'Two Wedden Skank' and 'Dirty Harry' (most notably by horn player Richard "Dirty Harry" Hall, Prince Jazzbo and Richie MacDonald); Big Youth's brilliant 'Opportunity Rock'; and the prophetic 'This Ya Year Fe Rebels'. Brown's rhythms were of the deep, heavy roots persuasion, although his melodica playing on 'Merry Up' is supremely lyrical and the dub mixes of his tunes – engineered by King Tubby, for the most part – were positively symphonic on occasion. The Barretts received scant recompense for their contributions, since the producer struggled to keep his various labels afloat and could barely afford to press up more than a couple of hundred copies at a time. It was the joy of playing music and laying the foundations of a new, more cultural style of reggae that drove them – feelings that members of the Skatalites had experienced just over a decade previously when pioneering ska and gifting Jamaica with its own musical identity.

Led, though not exclusively, by the Barretts, there were far-reaching changes taking place within this shared identity that would entirely alter the face of Jamaican music. In England, mod and skinhead audiences were growing dismayed at how the new Jamaican releases featured slower rhythms and lyrics that were no longer simple or even nonsensical but dealt with weighty issues such as slavery, black history or religion. Reggae wasn't as fun, and a lot of these fairweather fans would drift into the northern soul scene as a result, or embrace predominantly white, home-grown UK acts that were highly unlikely to rail about African repatriation. If this was a talking point among Jamaican musicians, it barely concerned them for long, especially not those, like the Barretts, who were actively seeking ways in which to expand their vocabulary in such areas.

Both stayed busy playing sessions between rehearsing for the Wailers' forthcoming UK tour dates. Family Man in particular nearly always responded to Bunny Lee's promptings whenever the wily producer had something up his sleeve. Bunny's friend and rival Lee Perry had concentrated on producing Junior Byles after losing the Wailers, and their first hit, 'Beat Down Babylon', had stayed in the local charts for weeks on end and would eventually get voted Jamaica's Record of the Year. Junior had sung 'King Of Babylon' and 'Joshua's Desire' in the build-up to the election, and scorned Hugh Shearer on 'Pharoah Hiding', issued shortly after Manley's victory, although none matched the impact of 'Beat Down Babylon'. Perry would release an album's worth of cuts to this rhythm over the next few years, while Freddie McGregor sang it for Coxsone. However, it was Bunny Lee who was quickest off the mark, with a version by Delroy Wilson.

Bunny Lee: "'Beat Down Babylon', that's Family Man again. It's not Scratch's tune originally, but a track from Canada that E T hear and make Family Man do over, then Junior Byles sing it, so that was Errol Thompson's tune really."

Perry, who was preparing to move into new premises at 5 Cardiff Crescent, off Washington Boulevard, wasn't in the mood to contest the point. In the meantime, Bunny reciprocated the favour to Family Man by releasing U Roy's 'King Tubby's Skank' on Jackpot and licensing it to Trojan, who issued it on Green Door in the UK. Fams had produced the track – a tribute to King Tubby's sound-system – with Reggie Lewis for Rhythm Force, although it was a lot more convenient to pass it to Bunny and let him deal with the pressing and distribution than struggle with such costly matters themselves. 'King Tubby's Skank' is delivered by a deejay facing stiff competition from younger rivals. "My name is not Alcapone," he says by way of introduction, "but I can tip them tone, y'know?" This last line is a reference to Tippertone, the sound-system that had spawned Big Youth, which he and Family Man would soon honour in 'Tippertone Rock'. The elder Barrett brother was typically even-handed and generous with his time, as Bunny Lee recruited him and Coxsone's cousin, Sidney Bucknor, for a trip to Maxfield Avenue in a rough part of Kingston, where the Hookim family had set up recording facilities.

The premises at 29 Maxfield Avenue had housed an ice cream parlour, liquor store, and jukebox concession before Joseph ("Jo Jo") Hookim and his three brothers built their new studio. Hookim was a friend of John Holt, who took him to see the newly refurbished Dynamic Sound. The Chinese born Jamaican was suitably impressed and officially opened

Channel One in the summer of 1972, shortly before the Wailers left for England. Bunny Lee had been the first producer to test the API console, after taking Delroy Wilson there to sing over the Tyrone Davis soul hit, 'Can I Change My Mind'. Dennis Alcapone was another early visitor; he voiced 'Cassius Clay' over Bunny's cut of 'Drum Song' there, although the rhythm had been recorded at Harry J's new 16-track studio at 10 Roosevelt Avenue. Harry J's would become one of the most popular recording studios on the island, especially once Johnson hired engineer Sylvan Morris, but it was Channel One that yielded the most hits during the early Seventies. Hookim didn't charge Bunny for the first session, since he considered it a trial run. The sound wasn't great, which is why Bunny took Family Man with him second time round.

"When Jo Jo set up his studio at first, it never sounded right," confirms Fams. "Bunny Lee and I, we carry an engineer up there to rewire the board and set it properly. That was Sid Bucknor, who worked at Harry J's for a while before moving to London. We tell Jo Jo it would improve the sound and the first big hit drop out of it was Delroy Wilson's 'Better Must Come', but then I return again and get Gregory Isaacs to sing this Bob Andy song, 'The Sun Never Shines For Me' and that was the first hit for Dillinger too, the 'CB 200'. Every time I go there, Jo Jo say, 'Here comes the man who mek the bass talk!' Well you see them songs there? They help build Channel One and then they have this guy called Ranchie who used to play some bass and also guitar fi them as well. This was when Barnabus join them programme and things take off after that, but I play on a portion of songs fi them for sure."

Winston Grennan claims that it was he, Jackie Jackson, Hux Brown, Gladdy Anderson and Winston Wright who went to Channel One and did the first test to make sure the equipment was working properly. They didn't go back because they weren't being paid and the studio was in a ghetto area, which meant their fancy cars and motorbikes were at risk!

Family Man Barrett: "The people in that part, them harass the artists too much. They buck them up for some money and most musicians and session man haffi give them money all the while. Music haffi make though and the Hookims were nice people. I remember this one time we were at Channel One soon after it opened and Jo Jo came up with a pretty guitar and say, 'Who want this guitar?' Everybody say, 'Me!' But I say, 'Give it to Chinna,' cah them times me just a bring Chinna Smith inna it and he need a better guitar. I say we have to give Jo Jo a hit for it and Chinna say, 'OK, OK,' so everybody gather round me now and the only person who don't is Tommy McCook, 'cause him stand off waiting to hear the result. Everybody look pon me for the tune we're going to play and then I say, 'Do you remember this Coxsone song called 'In Cold Blood'? And everybody say 'Yeah.' I say, 'Well this one named the new 'In Cold Blood.' I look over and see Tommy McCook smile at that, like I hit the right spot and about 10 weeks later it was a number one! We just do it as an instrumental and then out of the blue Tommy McCook play on a version, 'cause him say he want a touch off it long time. It kick off too, 'cause him just heat up the rhythm with his big horn, I tell you!

"Tommy loved to play with me, cah we want to show him what we can do and yet we want to learn at the same time and it was a good feeling. After a while, he realise how me stay, 'cause me is not a selfish kid, y'know? Me want to learn and me genuinely love it. We do a lot of work together over the years, including a good few tracks with Bob."

In 1972 the Jamaican government commissioned a report that recommended the decriminalisation of marijuana – another reason for the Rastas to feel optimistic about Manley. It also prompted Family Man to release 'Herb Tree', another of his instrumentals, which first appeared on Studio Sound, then on the Downtown label. It featured harmonica by the Youth Professionals' horn player Royal and sounds as if it dates from a Hippy Boys' session, since the skipping rhythm has none of the dread-fuelled gravitas Family Man was recording elsewhere.

The most haunting example of this was to be found on a track he'd recorded prior to taking the job on MS *Starward*. 'Conquering Lion' was credited to Vivian Jackson and the Ralph Brothers, although few people in Kingston knew who they were, least of all those sold copies by Jackson himself. Once demand for the rhythm had intensified, Big Youth voiced Yabby Youth on the same track and Tommy McCook and Don D Jnr (Vin Gordon) combined for a horns version called 'Fisherman Special'. Jackson also released a mix by King Tubby called 'Big Youth Fights Against Capitalism'.

The original release of 'Conquering Lion' was Jackson's debut recording, which arose from a vision he'd had some time previously. The son of a politician, Jackson was unusual in that he was a Christian, like his mother, and had no liking for Rastafarians, despite wearing dreadlocks. This earned him the name of "Jesus Dread", as well as considerable scorn from Rastas in west Kingston, where he was living at the time. Horsemouth, the drummer with Generation Gap when Jackson first told him about the song, was sufficiently intrigued to gather up several instruments and invite Fams and Chinna Smith to meet with Jackson on the gully bank in Waterhouse. After he described what he wanted, they told him the song could work but they'd need to book a studio. Jackson had no money and so returned to his job in a nearby furnace. He'd already had to leave the job once due to ill health and was eventually hospitalised with a range of ailments, including an ulcerated stomach and pneumonia. Finally, by the end of 1971, Jackson had recovered enough strength to buy tape and book studio time at Dynamic for the recording of 'Conquering Lion', featuring Chinna on guitar, Horsemouth on drums, and Family Man on bass and organ.

Jackson later voiced the rhythm at King Tubby's, after recruiting Alric Forbes and Bobby Melody to sing harmonies as the Ralph Brothers. It then took Jackson another six months to find enough money to have the record pressed, although it became a steady seller from thereon, especially once Big Youth had blessed his tape. "Lightning clap, and a weak heart drop," he warned, as Yabby and the Ralph Brothers' harmonies ebb and flow among his own revelatory verses. Thanks to its inclusion on Big Youth's *Dreadlocks Dread*, it was this version that so captivated overseas reggae fans, although Jackson's own take is powerfully uplifting and the rhythm itself extraordinary, with a dread factor that is clean off the scale. After Smith strums a few chords on the intro, he, Family Man and Horsemouth lock into an insidious groove that buries its way into the deeper reaches of consciousness, aided by undulating organ riffs and chanted, celestial backing vocals that have a profoundly otherworldly feel to them.

Yabby Jackson: "If you notice, all the music I do from that time on, we try and build a new Bible. Like the first one was revolution, where they say man shall rise, but what I am trying to do is build a new Bible for the generation coming by using the same wax and stone and the same Dead Sea Scrolls. And my message is that man shall not die, but live forever. I don't learn from books though. I learn from exercising my brain and by communicating with the spirit that is within me, and the system cannot control that. That's why I can tell you how it was like from that time until this time, because the truth, it doesn't change. But them claim me have a gift for music because every thought has a different chord and a different range. It's a marvel. It can dance and go wild like barbarian, but I keep hearing things inside of my thoughts I have to put into music. Me just try sleep under tree and feel it was some madness until I begin to communicate with musicians and them start agree these things have to go pon record. Family Man is roots music and somehow encouraged me. He reach into the earth and also my thoughts, then join Bob Marley, but all other Rastas turn against me, die, and then come back.

"No prophet has honour in his own land and amongst his own people. Only the false prophets, but if you notice, when you hear my music, even the tracks where I'm not singing, you can still feel the message inna it and that's real reggae music to the bone. It will put you in the right frame of mind for the things that are conscious and belonging to the truth, and it will draw your attention to whatever can be described as oppression. But it's nothing to do with any church or religion. Instead, I use music to teach black history and to remind the world of what it takes to be a human being, so anyone hearing it will get the opportunity to see those things. That's what I try to do, highlight black history as I see it, and to show my people that we are all one nation, coming from ancient Africa. Because we stem from such a strong root and by immersing ourselves in that, we can emerge as peaceful people and with love in our hearts. But I can only reach people by music and doing it any other way would have been impossible, because I couldn't get a passport and when I try to do other work, nothing else work out for me.

"The situation I go through with the hospital and all the hatred I meet from the Rastas, all I end up with is a country doctor, who look pon me and say I'm going to die. They say I have a rare complaint they only just discover and that my heart is too small. That's when they start putting me on steroids, and I discover that no man can live on steroids for longer than two years without experiencing serious side effects like high blood pressure and heart failure, yet with me, everything stay normal and they couldn't understand that at all."

'Conquering Lion' had a mesmerising effect on people, but when they asked who the artist was, Jackson would plead ignorance, telling them that he was selling it for King Tubby. This was around the time Tubby first dubbed Jackson "Yabby You" and the name has stuck ever since. 'Conquering Lion' was and is utterly unique, because there's still no other record quite like it. Family Man remembers that initial recording session at Dynamic also marking Errol Brown's debut as an engineer, although other sources suggest it was Karl Pitterson who did the honours.

The second track Family Man arranged and played on for Jackson was 'Love Thy Neighbour', which the singer credited to Yabby You & the Defenders. Right from the onset, Yabby urges listeners to heed his voice and love the word of God, while loving their neighbours as themselves.

Yabby Jackson: "Family Man, when him see that I'm ill, him come every Saturday and cook food and thing. He bring a little bush, buy ganja, but any time him up by Bob Marley and Peter Touch, him stay in the background doing his work, but that is the significance of the tune 'Love Thy Neighbour' and Family Man have nuff creativity."

Yabby wasn't a great singer but his vocals are utterly without guile, and by his own admission he was far more concerned with delivering a message than creating an artistic impression. Voiced one night at King Tubby's as gun warfare raged in the streets outside, 'Love Thy Neighbour' is another striking roots hymn, voiced over a drunken, but hypnotic rhythm Fams had recorded at Randy's with Robbie Shakespeare on bass, Carly on drums, and himself on rhythm guitar. The horn arrangement is unusual too, since it blends Vin Gordon's trombone with the clarinets of Herman Marquis and Dirty Harry. Family Man did not stop there, since he used this same rhythm for 'Distant Drums', which had the added attraction of the three Wailers playing percussion, just as they might do at a Rasta grounation. Marley and Tosh play repeater and Livingston the funde, but it's the air of reverence they create, more than the actual music, that's so compelling.*

As the Wailers prepared to board a plane to London, there was still no obvious replacement for Glen Adams and the band was also missing a guitarist.

Family Man Barrett: "When we decide to get moving together with Bob now I say, 'Are you ready Reggie? Let's go again.' Well he didn't want to move, so we have to leave him behind and he's got nobody to blame but himself when it comes to that part. Carly tell me that Reggie don't want to go on tour again, so I'm left thinking, 'What's he in this thing for?' Him just wanted to drive up and down and spar with us. Drive and talk and sell records. Well it never sounded too bad. That was the time when I give him the four-track with 'Nanny Skank' on it and rhythms like 'Old Kent Road'. We'd recorded it at Dynamic soon after the place just open and it have a sound to it, I tell you, like some great old vibes . . . I mix it down once and say I have to go buy a mix tape, a quarter inch on a

---

* 'Distant Drums' was later issued on the Fams label as were two other tracks, 'Trouble Dub' and 'Dub Feeling', cut with the Wailers around the same time. Originally titled 'Feel Alright', 'Dub Feeling' was recorded at Randy's with Lloyd Brevette on bass. Family Man simply replaced the bass line with one of his own and put the record out to please grassroots fans, rather than with any commercial expectations.

small reel, but this guy called Blacker asked me to loan it to him so he can record another tune on there. I remember leaving the tape at his place and that was the last I see of it. Later on, I hear a version of it by Leroy Sibbles produced by Joe Gibbs singing something about our day will come. Well mine never did, 'cause I never see even a half penny yet, yet it was my music!"

It was Prince Buster and not Joe Gibbs who released the Heptones' 'Our Day Will Come', but the end result was academic as Family Man was again left with nothing to show for his creativity. The fact that the generous and trusting 26-year-old had never completed his schooling and therefore avoided dealing with paperwork only increased his chances of being taken advantage of. At least he felt secure in the company of his brother, Marley, and, to a certain extent, Tosh. Livingston, however, wasn't a warm, open person by any stretch of the imagination, but Family Man always respected his talent and the fact that he and Marley had close family ties.*

When the three Wailers and the Barrett brothers arrived in London in July, English reggae aficionados were still reeling from the impact of Perry Henzell's *The Harder They Come*. This low-budget Jamaican action movie, with Jimmy Cliff in the leading role, had caused a minor sensation on its release to art house cinemas and colleges. It also held the distinction of being the first film to be subtitled when all of the characters spoke English, which serves to illustrate how many Brits were familiar with patois at the time. Cliff's character attains fame after becoming Jamaica's most wanted outlaw *and* a successful singer, while on the run from the police after a tune he voices for a local producer starts selling in droves. With package holidays to the Caribbean still practically unheard of, Henzell's film also gave foreigners their first glimpse of what life on the island was really like, with poor people scavenging for food on garbage dumps and scenes from a typical Kingston ghetto with its maze of alleyways lined with zinc fence, just like the one where Marley, Tosh, and Livingston had lived.

One scene illustrated how the Jamaican record industry worked, as fictitious studio owner/producer Mr Hilton puts pressure on local deejays not to promote Cliff's record, making sure the shops won't stock it. He buys out the singer's rights for just $20 as another bunch of hopefuls gather outside the gate.

* The union between Bob's mother and Livingston's father produced a daughter called Pearl. Tosh would also have a child with Livingston's sister.

Island released the film's accompanying soundtrack that summer. Songs like the title track and 'Many Rivers To Cross', 'Sitting In Limbo' and 'You Can Get It If You Really Want' made Jimmy Cliff a major star, although he would soon leave Island for EMI, citing irreconcilable differences. The two Toots & the Maytals songs Family Man played on – 'Sweet And Dandy' and 'Pressure Drop' – were included, although it was Jackie Jackson, Hux Brown, and friends who backed the Maytals in the film scenes. The group's studio performance was truly explosive, even eclipsing that of Jimmy Cliff, although neither of these "live" cuts made the album. The Melodians' breathtaking Jamaican spiritual 'Rivers Of Babylon', Desmond Dekker's 'Shanty Town', and deejay Scotty's 'Draw Your Brakes' were also included on the soundtrack, together with 'Johnny Too Bad' by the Slickers.

Family Man Barrett: "We were friendly with these other brothers who form this group Slickers and we used to do shows with their bigger brother too, from out of the east. We'd go out there and perform with them; jam a little and they don't pay, but it was fun. We'd just get together and play music, y'know? We'd pack up the equipment in these two cars and then squeeze inside surrounded by amplifiers, guitars and a drum set before heading out east. It was fun doing that, I tell you, but that's where the Slickers come from, 'cause it was after that now they do this song 'Johnny Too Bad', written by Delroy Wilson's brother, Bat. His real name was Trevor I think, but 'im get shot, 'cause he was into some bad boy business."

This claim is confirmed by a note printed on the album jacket that reads, "When the lawyer was getting copyright clearance on that tune, one of the writers was underground. The other was on death row." The liner notes went on to mention the incredible outpouring of new releases from such "a small section of a small city in a small island in the Caribbean," and how two actors were killed during the making of the film. Here, at last, was the reality behind a music that was still derided by certain mainstream radio deejays and print journalists in the UK and yet was rapidly redefining itself as a symbol of struggle and rebellion in the minds of young record-buyers, who were beginning to tire of rock star excess. Reggae music was no longer seen as the preserve of skinheads, but had begun to reflect the struggle to survive in a world riddled with crime, violence, and post-colonial neglect. It spoke directly to the sufferers, and what uplifted them was pride in their royal ancestry and the expression of black culture, of which reggae music now formed a significant part.

Where black music was concerned, America still reigned supreme, not just in record sales, but also cultural impact and influence. In August some 90,000 people attended Wattstax – an outdoor benefit concert hosted by Stax Records in the Los Angeles district of Watts, seven years to the day since riots had torn the area apart, featuring the Staple Singers, the Bar Kays, Rufus Thomas, Albert King, and the self-styled Black Moses, Isaac Hayes. Wattstax has been billed as the Woodstock of American soul music, and it coincided with the *Shaft* movies – events that inspired many young black Londoners to sport Afros and big collared shirts, gradually replacing the revolutionary chic of Malcolm X and the Panthers. For the first time, black artists were being asked to score movie soundtracks, and Curtis Mayfield (*Superfly*), Marvin Gaye (*Trouble Man*), and Bobby Womack (*Across 110th Street*) rose to the occasion magnificently. All combined a street vibe and their social conscience with musical ability of the highest calibre.

Meanwhile, just as BBC Radio 1 announced they would soon be broadcasting around the clock, the average British teen and pre-teen punter was buying hit singles by Alice Cooper, Donny Osmond, Slade and T Rex, while their elder siblings preferred the more cerebral progressive rock of Yes, ELP and Pink Floyd, or singer/songwriters like James Taylor, Cat Stevens and Joni Mitchell. *Top Of The Pops* catered for the singles market, while the latter genres were well covered by *The Old Grey Whistle Test*, hosted by 'serious music' deejay, "Whispering" Bob Harris.

When the five Jamaican musicians arrived in London that summer, they headed for Sims' apartment at 12 Queensborough Terrace, just off Bayswater Road in central London.

Family Man Barrett: "Johnny Nash and Danny Sims were living in this area of London called Queensway. They had this big flat there and that's where we used to hang out before we decided to leave, because Danny needed his space and we needed our space too. He asked us if we wanted a hotel and we said, 'No, we don't want to be in a hotel. We want our own house,' and that's how we ended up in Neasden."

Freelance publicist, Brent Clarke, whom Sims hired to promote 'I Can See Clearly Now', found the Wailers a rented house in the north London suburb.

"At the time, they were working on this big construction called the North Circular," Fams continues, "and there were road works everywhere. That was the time I run into Brinsley Forde one Friday night. He was pushing his car trying to start it. It was a '65 Ford Cortina, so I help the man and get it rolling. We had to get it moving and off the road because it wasn't taxed, so that meant we could only use it at the weekend!"

Forde was just 19 when he met the Wailers and would later form Aswad, in addition to starring in the Franco Rossi film, *Babylon*. The British-born son of Caribbean parents, he knew of the Wailers and couldn't believe his luck when they moved into his neighbourhood. He learnt to play guitar on his visits to their house, and every weekend they would pile into his car and head for Caribbean nightspots like the Four Aces in Dalston, Mr B's in Peckham, or the Roaring Twenties in Carnaby Street, where Lloydie Coxsone's sound-system had a residency for a while. Fams loved watching the selector Festus at work, especially when he'd drop some of the deep roots music he and his brother had been playing on back home. The Barretts met up with Larry Lawrence again and of course Ranny Bop, who was working for Pama Records in Harlesden. Marley, too, already knew quite a few people from previous visits including one or two from Trenchtown, like Delroy Washington who says that Fams taught him keyboards on that trip. Marley also requested Washington's help in rephrasing his lyrics for European audiences. It was also thanks to him that Fams got reacquainted with Vyris Edgehill, whom he'd romanced on the Upsetters' tour.

Soon after arriving, the five Wailers posed for photos on the Thames embankment, basking in London's sunshine. Tosh wore the obligatory string vest (topped by Che Guevara beret), Marley, a patchwork denim jacket, and a bare-armed Family Man combined a floral shirt with fringed, buckskin waistcoat. Marley's Afro isn't the backcombed model favoured by models in *Ebony* magazine, but a nest of baby dreadlocks, while the Barrett brothers still have conventional trims. As the days grew shorter, the novelty of the British capital palled and none of the Wailers enjoyed being in London that autumn. Family Man says it was the treatment they received from Sims that angered them.

"Danny Sims never did anything for us," he exclaims. "Danny Sims used Bob's talent to get hits for Johnny Nash and said he would give us £20 a week pocket money, but I said, 'Pocket money? Do you think we've just left school? We are some big session men back a yard and Carly and I, we've left that to come up here and £20 a week can't replace that.' He just have us rehearsing for the one show anyway, so I say, 'If we plan to be here for a week, give us some cash in advance, otherwise it's best for me to be in Jamaica doing my regular sessions.' That's when my brother and I decide we need to talk to him, since he's supposed to have a plan for us and we think he should give us some form of advance. The next Friday we get the envelope again and it looked healthier this time. It looked fatter and yet when we open it up, it's full of paper with just the same £20 in there. We say, 'What kind of thing is that?' We start to lick out and Bob took it personal, saying how he'd invited us to England, but that Danny Sims isn't acting fair.

"It's coming like some war business, because Bob say to him, 'Is it war yuh want fi deal with? Well, let us go out into the street then.' But them nah want fi war and things just cool off for a little while. Bunny Wailer, he don't like how there's trouble between we and Danny Sims and Johnny Nash, but me tell him we've been up in London already and we have an idea what goes on. I tell him you have to be like a soldier on guard but he don't say too much to me, so me and him don't stay so chatty chatty after that."

Apart from unsuitable living quarters, one of the other hassles the band faced was the long journey each day to Rondor Music's rehearsal facilities in Surrey. Since Sims hadn't provided a car, the five of them had to travel by public transport from Neasden.

Family Man Barrett: "Every day we have to take about three trains to go to this place called Kingston-upon-Thames and then we'd be there in this small little room, whilst Johnny Nash was in a big room rehearsing with his band Sons of the Jungle across the hall. We never play with Johnny Nash directly, but we did a nice little section of our own and Bob, Bunny, and Peter, they were singing some songs, man. We used to do this song 'Reggae On Broadway' that went, 'Hey, hey mama, hey. Get down on the floor.' It was like a crossover t'ing and then we used to do songs like 'Oh Lord, I've Got To Get There' and 'Concrete Jungle' also.

"The one show we did do with Johnny Nash. I don't recall whereabouts it was exactly, but I was there with Bob Marley, Peter Touch, Bunny Wailer, and my brother, and some English musicians did play with us, too, like the drummer, guitarist and keyboard player from the Cimarons. That's because I'd been sent to get them, through I had experience of being in London the year previously. We were going to start out with two drummers, like the Godfather of Soul, James Brown, and we had three guitar players too, because we had Guichy from the Cimarons on rhythm and Peter on lead, plus Bob would play rhythm guitar now and then, once I'd shown him the riffs and the vibes. This was around the time Johnny Nash had that hit 'I Can See Clearly Now' and the Wailers were from foreign, just coming up. Extra!"

The show that Family Man refers to took place at the Commonwealth Social Club in Croydon, Surrey. According to Livingston, people began leaving after the Wailers' set and Nash began hitting the wall with his fist in despair when the show ended. Family Man hadn't seen Nash's performance and so can't verify whether many people left early or not, but he remembers a crowd of eager fans gathering round them as they stepped outside the venue. If this had been the case, then Sims certainly wouldn't have wanted the Wailers upstaging his headline act, no matter how much they both valued Marley's songs. 'I Can See Clearly Now' was taking off in the US, which had been his and Nash's gameplan all along.

Family Man Barrett: "Brent Clarke and I, we talk a lot. We move together more times, take in a blues and go to shows at Acklam Hall and them places, so I say, 'What's happening in the music?' He say he heard Chris Blackwell, the head of Island Records talking about how they'd love to get that group the Wailers on his label and that band the Upsetters. I said, 'Well, that could be possible. Do they know we're here?' He say, 'Yeah, they know you're here,' so I say to organise the t'ing, because we'd had disagreements with Danny Sims, and Brent Clarke knew that. I told him I'd explain what's happening to Bob and the rest of them, which I did, and then I tell Brent Clarke to talk to Bob about it as well, but they meet with Island whilst my brother and myself were out and we didn't know the meeting had been set up so quickly! Carly and I, we went out to see people like Vyris and that's why we didn't get to see Chris Blackwell, or sign that first contract with Bob, Bunny and Peter, 'cause there was supposed to be the five of us on it, but it's just those three sign instead.

"We still have respect for the brethren them as vocal, but from we move out of Jamaica, there were five of us. It was like an army, a battalion, and we were all there together, so if one man got wounded, then you're not supposed to leave him. You're supposed to pick him up and bring him in and I am the mastermind for that meeting with Island."

Bunny Lee disputes it was Clarke who set up the meeting with Island, claiming a spot of ganja smuggling had been the catalyst for the Wailers' arrival on Island.

Bunny Lee: "It was Dave Betteridge who took the Wailers to Chris Blackwell after Johnny Nash had sent for them. A man from Jamaica called Jah Lights used to send up herb and the police raid the house where the Wailers were staying. The police lock up Bob them and it was Dave Betteridge me haffi go to and also Larry Lawrence so we could arrange for them to get bail. A guy named Rennie, who was a cousin of mine, he take the charge instead and say the herb was for him. Him get bail and run go a Liberia and then Jah Lights say Wailers can't come back to Jamaica because them sell out his weed, so I have to explain and say, 'No, it's not them and it's not your brother's fault either.' But that's how the connection was made, because Dave Betteridge, he was working for Island at the time."

Family Man struck up a deal of his own with Clarke (for shared production), while Marley started to fret about his contractual obligations to Nash and Sims, since these had to be resolved before signing with Island. Blackwell knew of the Wailers' rebel image and in the wake of *The Harder They Come* (and also Jimmy Cliff's defection to EMI), he felt sure this would translate into sales if marketed properly. He therefore granted the Wailers creative freedom to make an album and Marley was desperate to begin work on it as soon as possible.

In the meantime, Rabbit Bundrick had briefly left Nash's circle to tour Japan with Island rock group Free, supporting labelmates Emerson, Lake & Palmer. Traffic's Rebop Kawkuba (also signed to Island) had played Bundrick's demo tapes to Blackwell, who suggested he audition for the Free job. Following the tour, Bundrick continued to play the occasional session with Nash, which is when he first heard Sims and Marley arguing over the fact the latter wanted to sign with Island. This altercation took place in August, shortly before Sims and Nash left to promote 'I Can See Clearly Now' in the US, where it eventually topped the *Billboard* chart in November. Legend suggests the Wailers were left stranded by Sims and they'd gone to Blackwell for help, seeing that Island had originally issued Marley's debut single for Leslie Kong in the UK. What's more likely is that Blackwell offered the Wailers a deal with a £4000 advance, but advised Marley to talk with Sims about resolving his commitments to JAD.

CHAPTER TWELVE

Catch A Fire

ANTICIPATION among the Wailers was high when the *Catch A Fire* sessions began in September 1972.

Family Man Barrett: "We were proud to get a deal with a major company, so we were enthusiastic for sure. We were ready to take the thing to a different level and soon as we get back to Jamaica, we couldn't wait to start work on the new album. That was when everyone's soul was together. We just book some studio time and get right in there man. Boom, boom, boom and it done! We didn't have to rehearse those songs too much either, because they were there in our heads already. That's because we'd been rehearsing a programme, like an album and showcase, when we were in London with Johnny Nash. We'd be running through all of those *Catch A Fire* tracks in that basement studio, so we were definitely well-rehearsed and that's how we were able to record them so quickly."

In the aftermath of 'Reggae On Broadway', which had flopped, the Wailers' approach towards achieving their breakthrough on the international scene had changed. Pop success certainly wasn't something Island Records were all that concerned about, since Blackwell had visions of the band crossing over to rock audiences. He correctly surmised the hippies would relate to the band's rebel philosophy, their unconventional appearance, and liberal attitudes to sex and drugs, but knew the promotion had to be right. Reggae had a reputation of being cheap dance music appealing only to skinheads, so Island would have their work cut out in presenting the Wailers as a credible alternative, despite the radically different nature of their music. The express intention was to make a 'proper' album, just as the Wailers had done for Beverley's, and one that would engage the attention of overseas listeners in ways beyond the more commercial likes of Desmond Dekker or Jimmy Cliff.

Cliff, though, had been the catalyst for this change, which is why Blackwell was sorry to lose him to rival EMI. Thanks to *The Harder They Come*, a growing number of hippies and young black kids in the UK received their first glimpse of Rastafarians and readily identified with their struggles against authority. They'd also become fascinated by the sight of a Jamaican underworld teeming with larger-than-life characters, and were now ready to further explore this music reflecting life in Kingston's ghettos. The harsh romanticism of Jamaican life – a tropical paradise populated by hustlers, outlaws and prophets of every description – would soon prove irresistible, as would the fact that such esoteric glories could be encapsulated in songs containing the same kind of poetic lyricism heard from the likes of black American soul singers such as Curtis Mayfield.

"Bob, Bunny and Peter had brought the music to the first stage, which was making it known on the Jamaican market, so now we had to make it known on the international stage," Family Man points out, citing Mayfield's *Roots* and *Superfly* albums as seminal influences on the Wailers during this period. "We know the grassroots bottom already and then we get the vibe of the international scene from going up to London and sampling the European side. We were trying to uplift everything when we did that first international album, *Catch A Fire*, and it was a great trailer for us. We had this great feeling inside, like our time had come at last, and we wanted that to come out in the music."

Marley collected Island's advance from Byron Lee, who was acting as the label's intermediary. This arrangement meant that Dynamic would be an obvious choice of studio and ensured the Wailers spent at least part of the money on recording costs. Legend has it that Blackwell gave the Wailers the advance on trust, but had cleverly taken precautionary measures, just in case they absconded. The Wailers were also encouraged to use Harry J's new studio, since Blackwell had helped finance it, therefore acts signed to Island had priority. Randy's might well have been the Wailers' first choice had it not been for the Chin family's difficulties in getting the same sound heard on the recent Upsetter productions.

Clive Chin: "That's because my father took certain parts of the studio, like the console, to the garrison up by Up Park Camp. That was so he could record an album with Bishop Gibson by the KC Choir. The sound changed after that and it took the longest while to get that shit back together. It almost cost Errol Thompson his job, in fact. This was in 1972, because I'd left K. C the previous year, but Tyrone Downie was still there and he was in the choir singing on that album. It was one Rassclaat mission to get back that sound, I tell you! You can imagine them just taking the equipment up there as a good deed, since it was a worthwhile project, except then when they bring it back to the studio, they couldn't find that deep, bass register everyone love so much. That's what inspired Lee Perry to move on and build the Black Ark and then right after that, we upgrade to 16-track, which changed the sound again. That's when they get the one-inch tape too . . ."

The musicians credited on the sleeve of *Catch A Fire* were Family Man and Carly on bass and drums respectively, Tosh on piano, organ, guitar, and vocals, Livingston on congas, bongos, and vocals, and Marley on lead vocals and acoustic guitar. Just like their rock roster, Island wanted to project the Wailers as a self-contained unit. However, they also recruited additional musicians for the sessions, including Reggie "Alva" Lewis, pianist Gladstone Anderson, organist Winston Wright and the Lewis brothers from Inner Circle. Robbie Shakespeare played on a couple of tracks including 'Concrete Jungle' and 'Stir It Up'.

Carly and Shakespeare had played together on the session for Bunny Livingston's 'Bide Up' at Randy's earlier in the year. Tyrone Downie played organ and Tommy McCook, flute.* In a documentary filmed by Jeremy Marre, Blackwell offers fulsome praise of Shakespeare's playing on 'Stir It Up' without mentioning Family Man's contribution at all. Yet it was Marley's musical right-hand man who created those bass-lines and who recruited Shakespeare in the first place, fetching him from his parents' home in Jacques Crescent.

However, Roger Lewis claims it was he and his brother Ian who played guitar and bass on 'Stir It Up', with Sparrow Martin on drums. Inner Circle had recently played on Eric Donaldson's hit 'Cherry Oh Baby', and although the members were only youngsters, it's easy to see why Marley might consider trying them out, especially since they'd backed him onstage several times. The Inner Circle band also worked a lot at Dynamic, which meant they were often to hand whenever Fams and Carly were late for a session or otherwise occupied. When it came to recording, Marley liked to strike when the iron was hot. The immediacy of his music depended on capturing a particular expression as he felt it, and if any of his first choice musicians weren't there, then he was not above trying out someone else, just to get proceedings under way. This practice diminished in later years after the Wailers' music became so readily defined and the Barrett brothers stopped doing outside sessions.

Still, it wasn't as if Marley had to look far, since Tosh played guitar and

* Carly and Shakespeare also played together on Bunny Livingston's 'Pass It On', written by Jean Watt.

keyboaids and Livingston could play bass if necessary, as he had done on 'Trenchtown Rock'. After being present at so many rehearsals, Livingston knew Family Man's parts inside out and so had no hesitation filling in for him when the band cut 'Midnight Ravers', for instance. The original bassline, however, was again Family Man's creation and so the sound Marley wanted to hear wasn't affected, despite occasional changes of personnel.

Sylvan Morris was the engineer at Dynamic, and by Jamaican standards he was more technically skilled than most, which helped with what the Wailers were trying to achieve in taking the music forward to compete with what was happening in Britain and America. Morris says the recording of *Catch A Fire* was relatively straightforward, since the Wailers were accustomed to studio work and were clearly well-rehearsed. The sessions were recorded on eight-track tape, with the drums mixed on one track and guitar and piano together. All the recording took place in the same room, which gave the sound coherence. The result was music with a hard, driving backbeat, with R&B overtones, derived from American soul music influences.

Morris describes the Wailers as being "very spiritual . . . godly even." Shakespeare says that Livingston never made jokes or smiled and that Marley was serious also, although Tosh was always cracking jokes and laughing. This observation concurs with what Bob Andy and others have said about the Wailers as a tightly knit group and something of a closed shop to outsiders. Livingston talks of the Wailers being "musical brothers" and how a member was rarely seen without the others, whether they were working or not. The bond shared by the three of them was therefore more than just friendship or shared ambition. They were virtual family members who also thought alike about many issues and shared a militancy few other Jamaican groups had.

"That's how we lived, and how we survived," Livingston told Jeremy Marre, going on to say that in Trenchtown you had to excel at whatever you did and to stay tough, because "if you were soft, you were thrown overboard."

In late '72, it wasn't yet fashionable to chant Rastafari and wear dreadlocks. According to Family Man, Livingston was the most vocal of the three Wailers when it came to espousing Rastafari. All had begun reading up on Haile Selassie I and Marcus Garvey, studying the Bible, and learning what they could about black history. All except Family Man, who listened attentively, but was unable to engage on the same level as the others due to his poor education. The Wailers' bass man had little time or inclination to seek assistance. Instead, his important contributions came in a more musical form, as he strove to translate into sound what he heard around him. He and Carly still hadn't begun growing locks by this stage, unlike Livingston, Tosh, and Marley, whose hair resembled an unruly Afro, giving him the look of a Caribbean Jimi Hendrix.

More than ever, the Wailers were identifying with the Israelites, who'd been cast into the wilderness and forced to seek the Promised Land. Even the name "Wailers" conjured up images of sufferers, crying out for salvation. It was no surprise to them that the descendants of African slaves had been blessed with the power of music, since this was their gift from God – an in-born concept to be revered, but also mobilised, in their quest for freedom. Together with other Rastafarians, they viewed chanting and drumming as not only a form of communion, but also a weapon of peace – one designed to bring down the walls of Jericho and unlock the chains that Babylon still used to enslave them. Music was thus a holy, religious mission, as well as a means of educating and recruiting other like-minded souls. That it could also bring about fame and fortune didn't hurt, since Marley in particular saw nothing wrong with success, provided you didn't lose your integrity and used it to help the less fortunate.

To realise such ambitions meant selling lots of records, performing to widespread audiences and, improbable as it may seem, taking the sound of nyahbinghi beyond the ghetto and elevating it into the public consciousness. Such an aim might be acknowledged as one of the founding precepts of roots reggae today, but it was little more than a ganja-fuelled pipedream at the time.

Finding material for *Catch A Fire* wasn't difficult, as Marley and Tosh both had plenty of songs to hand. Some, like 'Concrete Jungle', weren't exactly new, except previous versions didn't share anything like the same level of intensity. This was also true of Tosh's '400 Years' and 'Stop That Train', while 'Baby We've Got A Date (Rock It Baby)', bore a slight resemblance to the Wailing Souls' 'Back Biter', recorded a year earlier at the 'Trenchtown Rock' session.

Family Man Barrett: "Some of the songs had been recorded before, yes, in different studios and with different musicians, but we gave them that strict timing and brought the feeling out of them more."

Neither Fams nor Carly had played on the original versions of 'Concrete Jungle' and 'Stop That Train', so the two brothers relished the opportunity to put their own, unique stamp on the tracks. It was a happy

Bob Marley, 1972. The Afro hairstyle was soon to give way to Rasta dreadlocks. (URBANIMAGE.TV/TRAX/OSSIE HAMILTON)

Wya Lindo, Tosh, Marley, Carly (obscured), Livingston, and Family Man perform on BBC TV's *The Old Grey Whistle Test* in 1973. **(ALAN MESSER/REX FEATURES)**

Glen Adams, former keyboard player with the Hippy Boys, Upsetters, and early Wailers pictured circa 2001.
(URBANIMAGE.TV/DAVID KATZ)

Tosh and Livingston share a smoke. Marley's increasingly prominent profile lead to their departure from the Wailers. **(URBANIMAGE.TV/ADRIAN BOOT)**

Island Records publicity image issued to coincide with the Wailers' US tour of late 1973 with Joe Higgs having replaced Bunny Wailer. **(MICHAEL OCHS ARCHIVE/GETTY IMAGES)**

Marley manager, Don Taylor (left) with recent Wailers recruit, Al Anderson, 1975.
(URBANIMAGE.TV/ADRIAN BOOT)

56 Hope Road, as it was during the mid-to-late Seventies, when Bob Marley and members of the Wailers lived and recorded there. (URBANIMAGE.TV/ADRIAN BOOT)

Family Man, Bob Marley and Bunny Wailer welcome the mother of the Jackson Five to 56 Hope Road, 1974. (URBANIMAGE.TV/LEE JAFFE)

The studio partnership of Sly Dunbar (right) and Family Man's former pupil, Robbie Shakespeare, circa 1980. (URBANIMAGE.TV/ADRIAN BOOT)

Tyrone Downie, the original keyboard player for the Youth Professionals, who was recruited into the Wailers by Family Man, at home in Kingston, 1976. (URBANIMAGE.TV/LEE JAFFE)

Peter Tosh, pictured onstage shortly after recording his debut album, *Legalise It*, 1976. (URBANIMAGE.TV/LEE JAFFE)

Burning Spear on stage in London, 1977, shortly after signing to Island Records and releasing the classic *Marcus Garvey*. **(URBANIMAGE.TV/ADRIAN BOOT)**

Lee "Scratch" Perry, producer of the Upsetters' hits and the Wailers' *Soul Rebels*, *Soul Revolution*, and *African Herbsman* albums, depicted at Black Ark studio, circa 1976. **(URBANIMAGE.TV/ADRIAN BOOT)**

Marley in full flight on stage. **(DALLE/IDOLS)**

The I Threes on stage at London's Rainbow Theatre during the Exodus tour of 1977. Left to right: Judy Mowatt, Rita Marley, and Marcia Griffiths. (GRAHAM WILTSHIRE/GETTY IMAGES)

Marley, flanked by politicians Michael Manley and Edward Seaga at the One Love Peace concert in Kingston, Jamaica, 1978. (URBANIMAGE.TV/56 HOPE ROAD MUSIC/ADRIAN BOOT)

Marley in characteristic pose, playing football during the late Seventies. An injury resulting from a robust tackle was to lead to his cancer. (URBANIMAGE.TV/56 HOPE ROAD MUSIC/ADRIAN BOOT)

Cindy Breakspeare is crowned Miss World in London on November 18, 1976, at the time her relationship with Marley became news. (HULTON ARCHIVE/GETTY IMAGES)

The Wailers' entourage photographed during the Rastaman Vibration tour, 1976. Alvin "Seeco" Patterson is third from left, while guitarist Donald Kinsey is stood between Rita Marley and Marcia Griffiths. (LAURENS VAN HOUTEN/FRANK WHITE PHOTO AGENCY)

time for them, as they were still in demand as session musicians while enjoying the experience of remodelling the Wailers' music to their own style. It was a measure of their commitment that both cut down on their activities elsewhere, despite feeling slighted at how Marley, Livingston, and Tosh had excluded them from the Island deal. Family Man says they had confidence "that singers and players of instruments shall be there," just like the Bible promised.

"Darkness has covered my life," Marley sings on 'Concrete Jungle', asking, "Where is this love to be found?" He's bound in captivity, "where the living is hardest" and not only in the individual sense, since his own life and the broader culture he represents are one and the same. Marley was speaking on behalf of the sufferers, and his identification with them is total. As an opening statement, 'Concrete Jungle' couldn't be bettered. It was also skilfully executed, with Carly's drums investing the track with pace and dynamics. Marley's lead rarely sounded so evocative, while Livingston's harmonies lend the track a lightness that's wholly at odds with the lyrics.

The contrast with Tosh's mournful declaration that "no sun will shine" is palpable. Tosh's low baritone chants "Rastafari" towards the fade – an impromptu ad lib that's almost buried in the mix.* 'Concrete Jungle' may be bleak in terms of subject matter, but it's a stunning track for 1972; a year in reggae otherwise defined by songs like Errol Dunkley's 'Black Cinderella', Clancy Eccles' 'Rod Of Correction' and Dandy Livingstone's 'Suzanne, Beware Of The Devil'. Studio One released a slew of majestic roots tracks on the reggae underground, including Burning Spear's 'Creation Rebel', the Gladiators' 'Bongo Red' and Horace Andy's 'Skylarking'.

In November, Marley flew to London with the master tapes to supervise the overdubs and final mixing alongside Blackwell, who took a co-production credit. (Marley once denied Blackwell was his producer, preferring to describe him as his "translator.") Work took place at Island's studios in Basing Street, west London, a converted church that was a hubbub of activity during the early Seventies. Working in shifts, engineers Carlton Lee, Stuart Barrett, and Tony Platt oversaw the transfer of the original eight-track tapes onto 16-track. Various overdubs were added including additional vocals from Marley, plus Moog synthesiser, clavinet and electric piano parts played by "Rabbit" Bundrick, whose contributions,

---

* It's deleted completely from the remixed version of *Catch A Fire*.

spread over two days, earned him just £30.* Despite having spent time with Marley in Sweden, the Texan wasn't all that familiar with reggae and so was happy to follow direction. Marley couldn't find the notes or chords but made rhythmic actions with his hands and, in true Rasta fashion, instructed Rabbit to "play from the heart."

Guitarist Wayne Perkins, another American, was more or less left to his own devices, responding to the soulfulness of songs like 'Stir It Up' with a delicacy that proved ideally suited to the Wailers' cause. Hailing from Birmingham, Alabama, Perkins replaced the late Duane Allman as session guitarist at the famed Muscle Shoals studio and played on sessions by Joe Cocker, the Soul Children, Steve Winwood, and Jimmy Cliff, among others. Shortly after, he formed Smith, Perkins & Smith who Blackwell signed to Island, and they toured Europe with labelmates Free and Fairport Convention. While in London, Perkins' group recorded tracks at Island studios.

"You would constantly run into people in the hallway like Jeff Beck, Steve Winwood and Cat Stevens," he recalled. "The Eagles were doing *Desperado* with Glyn Johns downstairs while we were upstairs doing our second album. I shared an apartment building with the Eagles and Joe Cocker at 333 King's Road [where Marley, Bundrick, Johnny Nash, and Danny Sims had stayed].

"Anyway, while working on the album, I ran into Blackwell in the hallway and he asked me if I'd like to try my hand at reggae. I said, 'What the hell is that?' He said, 'Jamaican music.' I said, 'What kind of guitar do you want?' And he said, 'The kind you play, rock'n'roll blues, that Southern thing . . .' I said, 'Sure, I'll give it a try,' so I took my Les Paul and a twin, went downstairs to meet Bob Marley, and ended up playing on he and the Wailers' very first album . . ."

Because the Wailers' music wasn't anything like the R&B, gospel, country, or rock'n'roll Perkins had grown up with, Blackwell advised him to be guided by the bass, rather than the melodies. Thankfully, Perkins' tasteful solos were exactly what the Wailers needed in attracting a rock audience. In the wake of Jimi Hendrix and Eric Clapton (following on from the jazz tradition), rock musicians had become revered as virtuosos. This occasionally resulted in overblown histrionics as guitarists, keyboard players, and even drummers embarked on marathon solos, causing their music to lose all sense of balance. No Jamaican act ever ventured down

---

* Bundrick had recently played on albums by John Martyn (*Solid Air*) and Free (*Heartbreaker*).

that route, since there wasn't an audience for it there. It's doubtful this style of playing would have suited the Wailers' purpose in any case.

"You've got to remember, at that time, when people were always discussing solos and how musicianship was important, these reggae guys were novelty music," Blackwell told Vivian Goldman. "But I wanted people to view the Wailers as being really great music."

Ultimately, it was the subtle interplay between the singers and each instrument that made the Wailers' sound so special. Their musical credibility came from a growing appreciation of the band's sticky, homogenous grooves, centred upon the Barretts' rhythm section. Just as Family Man had promised, it was a different musical concept. Rarely did the two worlds of rock and reggae meet, but for many in the former camp, *Catch A Fire* would be their first introduction to reggae.

Perkins went on to play with Leon Russell and journeyed to Jamaica with Eric Clapton. In 1975 he unsuccessfully auditioned for the vacant guitar role in the Rolling Stones (he appears on several tracks on their 1976 album *Black And Blue*). While his legacy as a guitarist and songwriter is considerable, it's arguable whether anything in Perkins' catalogue has had the same impact as his work on *Catch A Fire*. His playing helped to launch an entire genre, namely roots rock reggae, making it influential once *Catch A Fire* began to be heard in wider circles.*

Family Man never got to meet Perkins, although he describes the Southerner's guitar sound as "cool".

"It dropped in properly, y'know? His guitar has a good feel, but then Bob was there to make sure it was done correctly, so we expected that and even Chris Blackwell himself played a part, because he's very sensitive to music. He knows the music t'ing and he loves it. He's not a musician, but he knows what's right and he recognises what can work for sure."

While he was pleased with Perkins' guitar work, Fams was not that impressed with Bundrick's contributions. The bassist was a keyboard player himself and so had a more informed opinion about Bundrick's decorative arrangements. He also disapproved of what Blackwell and Marley did with the backing vocals on most of the tracks, as they were a good deal lower in the mix than on the original Jamaican cut.

Family Man Barrett: "I wasn't there, because otherwise I could have told them that everything has to be in harmony. The harmonies have to stand out and be in harmony with Bob's voice, so they could never be

---

* In 1995, Perkins finally received a platinum CD for his contributions – some 23 years on!

hiding into the rhythm like that if I'd have been there. That's why you hear the difference in terms of sound quality on albums like *Natty Dread*. You can hear the harmony between the music and the melodies on those later albums, because the melodies created by the voices and lead instruments should come out to the front part of the mix and the harmonies aren't supposed to be in the background like that. They must be out there, close to what Bob was doing, and the only things that are supposed to be in the background are the fills, like if you use horns. The Wailers use a different concept of harmony. It's music using harmony, melody, and expression, created by three voices in unison.

"The Wailers' harmonies, they were unique and that's thanks to the teaching of the Jamaican Godfather of Soul, the late, great Joe Higgs. That's the man who taught them the gospel harmonies they use on their songs and he really didn't get much credit for that. That's what made him so miserable in later years, because his works weren't properly recognised and that's what frustrates most artists from Jamaica. His teaching, it was properly strict, because he always listened to the great sounds on the radio and learnt from that. We would all learn about music from listening to the radio in those early days, before we could afford to buy the latest records from America and Jamaica at places like Randy's."

The fact that some tracks were speeded up didn't worry Family Man unduly, as he is quick to admit the Wailers often used studio "tricks" to enhance what they were doing. Fams says Tosh and Livingston were in broad agreement with what they heard when Marley returned to Jamaica with copies of the final mix, since all five members shared the same intention.

Of the album's tracks, 'Concrete Jungle' and 'Stir It Up' featured the most additions, but there is little doubt that the former greatly benefited from Perkins' interventions. The remix features a more arresting intro thanks to his sublime guitar work. Shortly before flying to Europe, Perkins had visited Manny's music store in New York and bought a sustain pedal that could hold a note for up to three minutes. The lingering atmospherics this created was quite magical, especially since the notes would feed back at a whole octave higher towards the end of their cycle. Tony Platt put additional echo on the device during Perkins' solo and Marley was delighted with it (except Perkins couldn't understand a word Marley said to him!) Marley's and Livingston's vocals are brighter and sharper, especially as the song heads towards its exuberant finish.

When the Wailers first voiced 'Concrete Jungle', Marley was living out the lyrics, both literally and metaphorically, yet by the time he was overdubbing his vocals in London, he felt more confident about escaping the ghetto and it showed in his vocals. Things were changing for the better as Tosh, too, was making plans to leave but then he and the other Wailers felt as though they were on the verge of something bigger.

Family Man Barrett: "Things were changing, but Bob was still living in Trenchtown. From I know Wailers; they were always living in Trenchtown. Everyone was still in that area and then Bunny come out when him move in with his father in Washington Gardens. At that time, I was moving between my parents' home in Rollington Town and Pembroke Hall, where I live with some other musicians like Niney and Max Romeo. We used to rent a house from a fisherman near Washington Gardens and then one of the guys had a room in Patrick City, too, which is just the other side of Washington Boulevard. We were just moving around that part of north-west Kingston at the time. Marcia Griffiths was living in Washington Gardens with her family, and Prince Buster, Lee Perry and Little Roy all lived in that same area as well.

"Just before then, that's the time Bob tell me he's living in the worse place and I say not to worry, because we'll soon get him out of the trench."

The Wailers' exodus out of the ghetto had begun, since Tosh, too, was making plans to leave, but the reasons why poor black people like themselves had ended up there would never be forgotten. It was colonialism that created poverty, since all of the island's wealth was in the hands of a privileged few and their former slaves were left to struggle for survival amid political corruption, police brutality and record levels of unemployment and violent crime. Despite the emergence of a black middle class, the social order at top and bottom of the economic scale had changed little. As far as the sufferers were concerned, it was as if slavery hadn't been abolished, but had simply taken on a newer and more insidious form. Such observations formed the basis of 'Slave Driver', which, despite its lamenting sentiment, is a victory song of sorts. "You're gonna get burned," Marley warns the powers that be, telling it like it is over a chugging rhythm, pointing out how ghetto people are "chained in poverty" and also illiteracy, since they could not afford a decent education.

As on most of these early tracks, Livingston's harmonies are the perfect foil, his contributions invariably overshadowing those of Tosh. Fams' bass is more prominent, and handclaps are added to accentuate the rhythm, as well as sound effects to accompany the phrase "crack of the whip", leaving the listener in no doubt as to what the song is about. 'Slave Driver' conveys the horror and injustices of slavery and it's still one of the most uncompromising songs in the Wailers' armoury. '400 Years' and 'Stop That Train' were substantially reworked from their initial appearance on *The Best Of The Wailers* and *Soul Rebels* albums. Both tracks have more complex rhythmic structures than most of the other tracks on *Catch A Fire*, although the message in each is crystal clear, with Tosh's vocals and lyrics typically unrelenting. He preaches revolution on the former: "Why do they still fight against the youths of today? Let's make a move. The time has come and if fools don't see, the youths are going to be strong," he warns, before describing a utopian land of liberty, where his people can "live a good, good life" and be free.

Tosh then tempers such optimism with the observation that while black people have been waiting 400 years for their freedom (since the advent of slavery, in fact), they were still struggling to free themselves of the philosophies that bind them. The remixed speeded-up version featured a different intro, which has additional guitar and electric piano, and a more baroque feel as Bundrick tries to turn the arrangement into the kind one might expect to hear from late Sixties' West Coast groups like the Doors or Iron Butterfly. Family Man was not alone in thinking that the carnival atmosphere created by Bundrick's playing detracted from the song's hard-hitting message.

It may well be that Bundrick felt more at home on Tosh's songs, which tend to be closer in feel and structure to American music than those of Marley. Noticeably different from the album's other tracks, 'Stop That Train' is another of the guitarist's rousing, "we shall overcome"-type songs, with its roots in the US folk scene and Tosh's early love of Hootenanny. One could imagine Pete Seeger or Bob Dylan singing it, or perhaps The Band, whose album *Music From Big Pink* (1968) heralded a return to more traditional forms, around the time Tosh wrote the song. The lyrics are about a good man's search for happiness; a seeker after truth who's grown disillusioned with those around him. It's a very visual song, with a moral at its core, like many of those found in folk and country music. The remixed version lends even more drama to Tosh's vocals, particularly when his cry of "all my life" is mixed semi-a cappella amid a flurry of organ. Bundrick's playing isn't quite so obtrusive this time, apart from on the intro. With 'Stop That Train', it's intriguing to think how Tosh struggled to get his songs featured on Wailers' albums, and surprising that he stayed in Marley's shadow for as long as he did.

Tosh's slashing rhythm guitar is all over 'Baby We've Got A Date', along with high, falsetto harmonies from Livingston and another of Perkins' inspired performances as his exquisite lead guitar swoops and soars, as if gliding on unseen air currents. Everything about this track is near perfect, from Marley's joyfully seductive lead, to the Barrett brothers' delightfully skanking drum and bass. The remixed version is less languid and the harmonies much changed from how Tosh and Livingston first sang them. The original is more compelling, but there's no denying the suggestive power of that snaky lead guitar, or the feelgood qualities of the song itself.

In its Jamaican guise, 'Kinky Reggae' opened with Marley's laugh. He confesses how he had to "hit and run" and didn't want to settle in "a kinky part of town." After presumably having his way with a woman, he tells her he has to ride on and that she's got to ride on, too. It's a lewd song, "kinky as kinky can be," but at the same time gloriously tongue-in-cheek, recalling previously ribald efforts like 'Shame And Scandal', which the Wailers recorded at Studio One. Songs like this are an extension of the calypso tradition and belie Marley's reputation as a "screw face," since they're a tease and voiced with a disarming, yet knowing sense of humour. Marley revoiced large sections of 'Kinky Reggae' in London, adding vocal interjections like "Give it up" to a commentary that already had plenty of spice, making it sound even more exuberant.

The lockstep drum, bass, and rhythm guitar on 'Stir It Up' is pure Upsetters, no matter that Fams was not playing the walking bass part.* The original recording is like a sketch compared to the overdubbed version, which contrasts Marley's laidback vocal with an irresistible, skanking backbeat. Although seductive after a fashion, it's as if Marley is singing more in hope than certainty on 'Stir It Up'. He sounds unsure and this impression remains, despite him voicing additional harmonies to fill out those of Livingston. The most arresting part of the song is Perkins' restrained guitar playing, which is again outstanding as he navigates a path through various sustain and wah-wah effects. He and Bundrick trade solos over several bars and, taken as a whole, it's difficult to understand why Blackwell came to prefer 'Stir It Up' in its original form.

A cry from the heart, 'No More Trouble' is delivered with compassion, avoiding any hint of sloganeering as the listener is urged to "make love, not war" and to "look down if you are above, help the weak if you are

---

* It's therefore interesting to conjecture what Family Man would have done with the track if he had played on it.

strong." 'No More Trouble' is a deeply political message song, sounding like a companion to Edwin Starr's 'War' in many ways. Among the earliest of Marley's Island recordings that could be termed classic, it's easily the best song from *Catch A Fire* in terms of lyrics and musical accompaniment. Family Man's playing is sublime while his brother's timekeeping borders on the surreal. There are dramatic changes of pace and chord structure throughout and the harmonies are positively choral, like the Temptations or any other top-level American soul act. Livingston's high falsetto frames Marley's lead, offset by Bundrick's burbling, electric piano. It's as if the Wailers had been studying Tamla producer Norman Whitfield, which of course they had, except with no loss of their own, uniquely Jamaican essence.

The re-recorded 'Midnight Ravers' contains a good deal more power than its initial incarnation and the interplay between drums, bass, and rhythm guitar is simply wondrous, as if the Barretts can scarcely disguise their delight at breathing new life into the track. The remixed version is relatively unchanged, with no lead guitar or extra organ fills. Blackwell and Marley seemed to have taken an altogether more subtle approach, apart from lowering the backing harmonies and adding handclaps in places. 'Midnight Ravers' is quite scary enough in any case with its quasi-Biblical imagery and almost Gothic portrayal of London's nightlife.

'All Day All Night' and 'High Tide Or Low Tide' weren't included on *Catch A Fire*, but were recorded at the same sessions. Both are love songs, which may well have swayed Blackwell's decision to omit them. 'All Day And All Night' sounds more like a soul record than anything recorded in Jamaica. Island might have considered that romantic songs cut in an R&B style didn't fit with the image of Rasta revolutionaries, even though they'd been a part of the Wailers' *oeuvre* since the beginning. Marley professes his undying love, while Tosh and Livingston plead, "God guide and protect us. When we're wrong, please connect us," as the topic switches from romantic to divine love.* Blackwell has since admitted that 'High Tide Or Low Tide' probably should have been included on the album, but it really wasn't that essential.

Family Man Barrett: "Deciding which songs were to be used on *Catch A Fire* wasn't my department at that time. It was my early years of

---

* The song became a favourite of Bob and Rita's youngest son Stephen, born in April 1971. Thirty-five years later he performed a live version of it on his MySpace website, as one of his sons danced around the stage with him.

concentrating on the band and the music itself. I was ever ready when it came to making and playing the music, but not anything else at that time. We were always looking to be creative, though, and always trying to cover the mileage that no one else did before. Those songs 'All Day All Night' and 'High Tide Or Low Tide' came from the beginning stages of going for international success and I did think it might be a little too early to release them. They didn't fit the marketing strategy we were aiming for back then.

"They were songs we thought might get us in the *Billboard* charts and bubbling under the Top 100, just like a mighty dread, y'know?" he says, with a chuckle. "It didn't hurt to try these things, because we wanted to make an album that had all these different concepts of music in it, such as international rock and, of course, Jamaica roots, which is the heartbeat of the people."

While the Wailers were busy trying to crack the rock market, or at least get their foot in the door, one of the industry's most visible groups was taking the opposite route and heading for Kingston. The Rolling Stones' Mick Jagger and Keith Richards were already long-time reggae fans by the time they arrived at Dynamic Sound in November to record *Goat's Head Soup*. Richards had the soundtrack to *The Harder They Come* on heavy rotation in his room at the Terra Nova Hotel, and shortly after arriving he paid Tommy Steele US $147,000 for a luxury villa called Point of View overlooking Cutlass Bay near Ocho Rios.

"Jamaica is the most musically conscious place I've ever been to," he told Victor Bockris. "It's the only place that's come out with a really different kind of new music which still has that basic simplicity of rock'n' roll. All they've done is turn the beat around and they seem to have a limitless supply of talent."

It wasn't a particularly happy time in the Stones' career. The two songwriters hadn't been getting on and joint writing sessions at Richards' Swiss home near Montreux had proved tense affairs before the band arrived in Jamaica. A more important factor was the band's choice of engineers. Instead of locals such as Sylvan Morris, the Stones' regular pairing of Jimmy Miller and Andy Johns sat behind the mixing board.

"They've got this very informal attitude [in Jamaica]," Richards told Bockris. "In the US and in England and Europe, they've got their own completely idiotic rules about what you can do and can't do with those machines, you know, and you can never turn something off, you've gotta touch this and focus that knob and get this light flashing. There's all this sort of etiquette. It's like watching etiquette at the table – that's where the knife should be and the dessert spoon there and you wonder what the fuck it's all about. But they don't know anything about this in Jamaica and they just say, 'With this machine you can do this.' And they just play it like another instrument, so the guy behind the control board is like another musician."

There wasn't much respect being shown to the Stones outside of the studio, judging by Bunny Lee's recollections.

"When the Rolling Stones came to Jamaica, Mick Jagger had a girl with him and about 30 men go with her," he recalls, laughing. "That was round the back of Dynamic. Peter Tosh was there and everyone, and Mick Jagger come charging out of the studio, mad as hell! Byron Lee made a studio especially for them when they were recording that *Goat's Head Soup* album, but they didn't like the sound in there. I am still the only man to get hits out of that studio in Jamaica, y'know? Because records like Delroy Wilson's 'Riding For A Fall' and 'Rain From The Skies', they have a different sound to them if you notice. Some of the later versions of 'Cherry Oh Baby' were done there as well, but the others were done in the bigger studio, where the Wailers recorded *Catch A Fire*. The one built for the Stones was different. It had a weird kind of sound and it never work for everybody."*

Home for Bob, Rita, and the children was still 18A Greenwich Park Road in Trenchtown, where they lived with Viola (a.k.a. "Aunty"), the sister of Rita's father, Leroy Anderson, who the others called "Papa Roy." Rita had moved back there after returning from Delaware, where she worked as a nurse. She and the children had stayed with Bob's mother Cedella, while Bob travelled to Sweden and London with Sims and Nash. Rita wasn't singing at the time and hadn't made any records since Family Man and Lewis had tried to get things moving with the Soulettes more than a year earlier. In her autobiography, *No Woman No Cry*, Rita says it was a Rastafarian elder named Gabby who told her about the new housing project in Bull Bay, situated some eight miles east of Kingston. Rita originally thought it too far out of town, but changed her mind after Gabby took her there to look round. Gabby urged Rita to persuade her husband to use his influence with PNP Minister of Housing Anthony Spaulding to secure a move, but she chose instead to speak to Skill Cole, who wasted no

---

* Released in August 1973 to general disappointment, *Goat's Head Soup* contained no obvious reggae feel, despite its recording location.

time in making the arrangements in late 1972, shortly after Bob's return from London.

Bob gave Rita $3000 as a down-payment on the newly built two-bedroom house at 15 Windsor Lodge, which at the time was little more than a concrete structure, with no electricity, water supply or telephone. It was close to the beach, though, and had enough land attached for a vegetable garden. Rita made it into a home for her and the children with no real help from Bob, who would still visit often, despite his relationships with other women. Rita writes of how Lewis would visit her in Bull Bay and run errands with her until she tired of his inattentive driving and cursed him for suggesting she ask for Bob's help in teaching her to drive. Like Bob, Rita was proud of her independence and hated the idea of appearing weak or unable to cope. Family Man claims it was he who finally taught her to drive. In any event, Rita got her licence soon afterwards and became a regular commuter between Bull Bay and Kingston.

Carly, too, was undergoing changes, since he'd become a father for the first time in December, after his girlfriend Carol Berry gave birth to a son, Errol.

Unlike Marley and Family Man, Carly did not have lots of children with different women. He and the other Wailers were already viewed as celebrities in downtown Kingston, although their warrior reputations made them feared, more than loved. They still weren't easily approached, or at least not Marley and Livingston in particular.

Island and the Wailers tested public reaction just prior to the arrival of *Catch A Fire*, with the appearance of 'Baby We Got A Date', 'Midnight Ravers' and 'Concrete Jungle' on Tuff Gong singles. The album followed amid a blizzard of publicity just before Christmas, initially attracting attention for its striking cover, designed to look like a Zippo. These chunky metal lighters were popular with dope smokers, since the flame would stay lit, even in windy conditions. The lid when flipped open revealed a wick and serrated wheel used for making sparks. The Island design team cleverly replicated this so the vinyl slotted inside a painted, flaming wick, while the top half of the sleeve formed the lift-up lid. It was a brilliant, if expensive piece of marketing and its appearance in British record stores made people take notice. Island reportedly spent over £30,000 on promotion, an unprecedented amount for a reggae record. *Catch A Fire* duly became the first reggae album to be marketed and promoted in the same way as a rock title, and to underline the feeling that something special was taking place,

Island advertised in all three of the UK's major rock publications, namely *Sounds*, *NME*, and *Melody Maker*.

These weekly papers were highly influential at the time, in the absence of pirate radio or a more liberated music policy from the BBC, which still operated severe restrictions on the amount of needle time given to new releases. To see a reggae album so widely promoted was highly unusual, which served to strengthen the impression that *Catch A Fire* marked the beginning of something new and exciting, or at least intriguing, that demanded further investigation by music fans. Musicians, too, were compelled to check out what the Wailers were doing and discovered that *Catch A Fire* signified the emergence of a new phase of reggae far removed from the gimmicky, Caribbean pop tunes that had found their way into the UK charts. None of the tracks on *The Harder They Come* soundtrack dealt with dread themes as did 'Concrete Jungle', 'Slave Driver', or '400 Years'.

Many grassroots fans, sensing that Island had an altogether different agenda in mind, didn't take to the album immediately. For one thing, most of the songs were brand new; there was no 'Screwface', 'Trenchtown Rock', 'Lively Up Yourself', or 'Lick Samba', and the production wasn't as sparkling as that heard on records from Beverley's or Treasure Isle. There were also those who claimed the Wailers' music had somehow been ruined by the additional overdubbing, and such rumours intensified after original Jamaican pressings of *Catch A Fire* went on sale in London. Ray Hurford of *Small Axe* magazine remembers seeing copies of the JA press on sale in Camden market for £20, an extortionate price for those times. The record was being sold in a cheaply printed sleeve that looked similar to the Island release, except it didn't open up like the familiar Zippo design.*

Despite its groundbreaking qualities, *Catch A Fire* only sold a disappointing 14,000 copies in its first year of release. Bringing the Wailers to the attention of a new market had required major investment and the next round of expenditure would involve tour support. While the Wailers were gaining interest from discerning rock fans, they lacked the added cache of chart hits. But was the established British reggae audience ready for a Jamaican group singing about oppression in Trenchtown, depriving them of a chance to do "the Moon Stomp"? The Wailers were about to divide opinion like never before.

---

* Marley collectors would hotly dispute this album's existence until Island finally made the Jamaican mix available as part of the *Catch A Fire* Deluxe Edition, released in 2001.

CHAPTER THIRTEEN

Midnight Ravers

AROUND the same time Island issued *Catch A Fire*, Johnny Nash's *My Merry Go Round* – the album his record company was hoping would capitalise on the success of 'I Can See Clearly Now' – was released in America. Marley flew to New York in January 1973 and confronted Sims backstage at a Nash show, demanding a release from his contractual obligations with JAD. In return, Sims insisted Marley sign a new publishing contract with Cayman Music, and that Island pay him £5000 towards what he'd spent on Marley's career thus far and grant him a two per cent over-ride on the Wailers' first six albums. Blackwell apparently agreed to these terms and a deal was struck, meaning the Wailers were now solely contracted to Island, with no remaining loose ends.

It was during this same New York trip that Marley met filmmaker Lee Jaffe through Blackwell's friend Dickie Jobson, whose sister Diane would eventually become Marley's lawyer. Jobson invited the singer to a party at the Windsor Hotel on West 56th Street and Sixth Avenue. It was at this party, in the room of Traffic drummer Jim Capaldi, where Marley also met actress Esther Anderson, who had starred in *A Warm December* with Sidney Poitier and was rumoured to have had affairs with both Blackwell and Marlon Brando. Although Jamaican by birth, Anderson had lived in England for long periods where she moved in rarefied social circles. She and 22-year-old Jaffe had met in Paris, shortly before the latter saw *The Harder They Come* at an art house cinema. Both Anderson and Schneider had agreed to appear in his next film, based on the life of sculptor Gordon Matta-Clarke. Filming was due to take place in Chile, where the political situation was already growing volatile because of opposition to President Salvador Allende's social reforms.

Marley thus found himself in bohemian company, but if the sufferer from Trenchtown felt at all out of his depth, he didn't show it. Being around Sims and Nash had already inured him to showbiz behaviour and the ease with which Jaffe and Anderson moved in such circles was something he needed to develop if the Wailers were going to achieve success outside of Jamaica. Meeting Capaldi gave Marley an opportunity to learn something about Island, too, since Traffic had experienced more than their share of ups and downs with the label. After Steve Winwood contracted peritonitis, Capaldi had spent the best part of 1972 recording his first solo album, *Oh How We Danced*, featuring contributions from several of his Traffic bandmates and guitarist Paul Kossoff. Capaldi had then rejoined Traffic for their latest album, *Shoot Out At The Fantasy Factory*, recorded with session musicians from Muscle Shoals, which the band were currently promoting in the US.

Marley spent time with Jaffe at his loft on Greene Street in SoHo. There was an art gallery downstairs where New York's art intelligentsia congregated and copious amounts of herb were available, thanks to Jaffe's connections. The filmmaker told Roger Steffens that for the week he and Marley were together in New York, "the *Catch A Fire* album became the soundtrack for what was, at that time, the center of the art world," and that Marley had walked into an environment "where being a poet and musician was regarded without suspicion."

"It made him comfortable to be in my world from the start," Jaffe said. Marley's week in New York only strengthened his resolve to make it in the music business. It was a far cry from how artists and musicians were ruthlessly exploited in Kingston. Before he left, Marley, Jaffe and Dickie Jobson visited Manny's Music Store on 48th Street. The Wailers were going to need some decent equipment for the string of UK dates Island had planned.

Rehearsals began in earnest once Marley returned to Jamaica. Apart from running Island Records, Blackwell also dealt in real estate, both with and without the involvement of Jobson. Blackwell allowed the Wailers to use the back yard of a sprawling, slightly run-down colonial house he'd bought at 56 Hope Road in uptown Kingston, not far from the Prime Minister's residence. Blackwell named the place Island House and used it as a base for his various business interests. Esther Anderson, who'd invested money in Island, stayed there after her break-up with *Bertolucci* screenwriter Mark Peploe, and Jaffe also resided there for a while. An elderly English lady called Miss Gough rented an adjoining outbuilding around the back of the house, near where Rennie the handyman lived. It was the downstairs offices that saw most activity, however, except for in the evenings, when, according to Livingston, the Wailers spent the first three months of 1973 rehearsing and trying out new songs.

Alongside tracks from *Catch A Fire*, the band also ran through older songs like 'Duppy Conqueror' and 'Small Axe', as well as songs being considered for inclusion on their next album. Island knew the band would have little time to write and record new material while on the road, as they hoped to release a second Wailers album by the end of the year.

Marley often spent time hanging out in Trenchtown, playing football with Skill Cole during the day and driving out to Bull Bay after rehearsals when he wasn't seeing Anderson, now the two of them had begun a relationship. Cole was Marley's closest friend and was still performing managerial duties for the Wailers on occasion, as was Jobson, who acted as go-between for the band and Blackwell whenever the latter was off the island, which was often. Occasionally Marley would climb in his battered old station wagon and go and visit his family in St Ann's, where he'd write songs, smoke herb and meditate. Family Man, too, would take trips out to the countryside, although he and Carly were still active on the local recording scene, whenever they weren't hanging out at the Wailers' shop in Beeston Street. They could often be seen standing in front of the doorway, smoking a spliff, drinking a juice, and listening to the music coming from inside, while chatting to whoever happened to drop by. Tosh was also a regular visitor to the shop and would even serve behind the counter whenever Rita or Selwyn weren't there. Jean Watt still had her dressmaking shop around the corner, so Livingston, too, was often in the vicinity.

Prompted by Cole, all three singers adhered to a rigorous fitness regime, placing great value on eating proper foods, since Rastafarians believed in following an ital, or natural diet, and looking after themselves physically, mentally, and spiritually. While agreeing with this, Family Man and Carly didn't exercise with the other Wailers all that much and tended to socialise with their own friends more. They still regarded themselves as "warriors in training", however, and took pride in keeping fit. "We were like gladiators," Family Man says, proudly, "and ready for anything."

Jobson acted as unofficial tour guide for Island personnel or contacts visiting Jamaica from time to time, and therefore knew all the best places. He would sometimes drive the Wailers party to Hellshire Beach, near Kingston, where Marley's friend Countryman lived. They would swim and idle on the beach, eating freshly caught fish cooked over a wood fire by the water's edge. Other days they headed out east where Rita was putting finishing touches to 15 Windsor Lodge. Bunny and Jean now lived in a nearby Rasta community near Cane River Falls at the foot of the

Dallas Mountains, where the black sands sparkled in the sunlight and the waters were rumoured to have healing powers. After driving to Bull Bay, Jaffe, Marley, and Cole would travel to see Livingston on foot by running along the beach and then circling around the mountainside. Cane River Falls was once a haven for bandits, the most famous being Three Fingered Jack, who terrorised local plantation owners and the British army in times gone by.

Such tales must have delighted Livingston, who'd entered the most creative period of his life so far and found a gifted and sympathetic song-writing partner in Jean Watt. The two worked together on 'Hallelujah Time', 'The Oppressed Song' and 'Reincarnated Souls', although Livingston would later claim sole credit once their relationship was over. 'Reincarnated Souls' was one of the songs recorded during the *Catch A Fire* sessions and was chosen as the flipside of 'Concrete Jungle'. It was the working title of the Wailers' next album, which was taking shape just weeks after the release of *Catch A Fire*, with Marley, Livingston, and Tosh constantly writing new material. Tosh had recently recruited Family Man and Carly for a session at Treasure Isle that produced 'Mark Of The Beast', while inspiration poured out of Marley ever since meeting Esther Anderson. Fired by her angry, informed brand of socialism, he was working on songs like 'Burnin' And Lootin'' that bristled with righteous indignation, but were wrapped in striking melodies.

The Wailers relished being signed to Island, since it brought them a welcome sense of security. They no longer had to scrabble for studio time. Instead, they could develop and record their songs in relative peace, while being encouraged to explore new avenues of expression. Such freedom came at a price, however, as the Wailers now had more professional responsibilities. Large amounts of money were being invested in their careers and the expectations placed on them were greater than at any other time during their 10-year history.

At the beginning of March Blackwell, who wanted to visit Trinidad for the Carnival, arranged to charter a plane for the trip. Anderson suggested he invite Marley and Jaffe, whose plans to visit Chile had fallen through. Blackwell, Jobson, Marley, Anderson, Jaffe and his Brazilian girlfriend Liani do Rosario, Capaldi, and American entertainment attorney Abe Somers and his wife Phyllis were among the party who boarded a DC3 at Kingston airport. En route to Trinidad, they stopped off in Martinique and Tobago, but then ran into difficulties when landing in Haiti on the return leg of their journey. Planes travelling to Haiti were supposed to give 24 hours' notice before landing and so instead of a welcoming committee, Marley and friends were met in Port-au-Prince by members of the Ton Ton Macoute pointing machine guns at their heads. After a night under house arrest, the revellers were finally escorted back to their plane and allowed to take off, but not before Marley became separated from the main group. Jaffe witnessed him getting angry for the first time. "How could you leave me surrounded by deranged fascists, speaking some foreign language?" he thundered, as the others looked on helplessly.

Soon after returning from Trinidad, Marley wrote 'I Shot The Sheriff'. Some theories state the lyrics refer to the system and were written at a time when Jamaicans – especially those living in Kingston – were subject to an endless round of curfews, roadblocks and police harassment like Marley had just endured in Haiti.

The song was later finished in England with help from Esther Anderson, who told Steffens that Marley was very proud of his powers of impregnation and had expressed surprise that she had not yet fallen pregnant. He was not happy when she told him that she was using contraception, which in turn prompted the line, "Every day I plant the seed, you kill it before it grows." The sheriff is therefore the doctor who supplies her with contraceptive pills.

Family Man agrees with Anderson's account. "Yeah, she highlight it and that's why he have to go and write about it, because I remember we were all someplace, and I bu'n some weed whilst listening to him and Esther Anderson arguing. Those times there, Esther and Bob were grooving man, and so she's supposed to be a co-writer for that song."

Anderson was good for Marley since she, too, was of mixed race, and knew what it was like to feel estranged from both camps. Her father was a Scottish architect and her mother a woman of East Indian descent who lived in the parish of St Mary. Anderson may have been a movie star, but she'd grown up in relative poverty and so had more in common with the aspiring Rastaman from St Ann's than might be imagined. The couple were fast becoming inseparable, but to allay Rita's suspicions, Marley told her Anderson was Jaffe's girlfriend, and that she worked for Island. This was at least partially true, since Anderson was a talented photographer and had already taken shots for the Wailers' next album sleeve. What Rita didn't know was that Bob's consort was planning to accompany the Wailers to London.

Reggie "Alva" Lewis could have joined the Wailers' rehearsals at Hope Road, had he been prepared to tour with them. Tosh and Marley could cover his parts, but finding a keyboard player posed a bigger problem. Winston Wright was too busy playing sessions or backing Jimmy Cliff, and Tyrone had gone off to the north coast with Jo Jo Bennett & the Fugitives. Marley didn't think either musician was quite ready yet, despite their growing potential. One night, Family Man went to the Sombrero club on Molynes Road and watched as a local band, Now Generation, blazed through a selection of pop and reggae hits, including 'Trenchtown Rock' and 'Screwface'. He was especially impressed with Wya Lindo and asked him to come to the Wailers' rehearsal the following day. The way Lindo's rhythmic keyboard lines meshed with the Barrett brothers' reminded Family Man of when they'd played with Glen Adams in the Upsetters, except this young hot shot, who'd just turned 20, was even more gifted technically and had just the kind of creative flair the Wailers had been looking for.

Lindo felt at home duplicating Bundrick's lines on *Catch A Fire*, welcoming the opportunity to test himself on more outward-looking material. Local producers invariably frowned upon too much experimentation, even when they had the means. Dynamic and Federal both had mellotrons but no one could play them except Lindo, who worked out how to strike the keys so that the tape loops which imitated various musical instruments moved into the right positions at the correct acceleration rate to give the desired effect. This was musicianship on an altogether different plane to what usually took place in Kingston's studios.[*]

The Wailers' three frontmen already knew Lindo; Tosh especially, since the two had played together on sessions, including tunes for Duke Reid and Joe Gibbs. Shortly after that, Tosh had asked him to jam on a few Wailers songs at Randy's. No recordings resulted from those sessions, but Lindo loved the Wailers' freedom of expression and remembers Tosh encouraging him to innovate and "not just go with the trend". Lindo even attended one of the Wailers' Lee Perry-produced sessions, but remembers little other than peering through thick clouds of ganja smoke that enveloped the room.

Like Tosh and Marley, Lindo was a country boy. His family came from Trelawny and he'd been raised in a strict, Christian household, which he later admitted made him rather spoilt. Lindo got the nickname Wya at school after showing off his skills as a footballer, although his main passion

---

[*] Al Anderson later claimed the other members – particularly Tosh and Livingston – found Lindo's talent rather overwhelming.

was music and the piano in particular. Jazz became his first love, especially the soul jazz sounds of Lee Morgan and Jimmy Smith, whose Blue Note sides could often be heard on US stations beamed across the Gulf of Mexico. After moving to Kingston, Lindo attended Excelsior High School, where the different houses would regularly compete against each other in end of term musical "clashes". He entered one such competition as a bass player and won, but his primary instrument was still the piano, which he'd practise in the lunch breaks and after-school classes. It was at Excelsior where he joined his first band, the Meters, named after the renowned New Orleans funk outfit.*

Lindo's first experience of being among working musicians came when Coxsone invited him to overdub a few tracks at Studio One. This was around the time Coxsone was releasing Jackie Mittoo's *Evening Time* album, after the Skatalites' former pianist had taken up organ. Tommy McCook then invited Lindo over to Treasure Isle, where he met professional keyboard players like Aubrey Adams, Winston Wright, and Keith Sterling. (The latter was also approached to join the Wailers, but turned them down because he didn't smoke herb and therefore wasn't sure he'd fit in.) The emphasis at Treasure Isle was on written music, and amateurism wasn't tolerated, as Family Man and Carly had already discovered, yet the gifted teenager from Waltham Park had no such problems. Aubrey Adams helped him with his sight reading and U Roy introduced him to some of the more colourful characters on the local scene, including Perry and Tosh. McCook even invited him to play with the Supersonics whenever they appeared on *Where It's At*, although Lindo would have to try and stay out of camera shot, since he was still a student at Excelsior.

It was at JBC's television studios where Lindo first sat down at a Hammond C3 organ. His friend Joe Cooper helped show him the rudiments, since the Hammond had four draw bars operated with the feet and therefore demanded more co-ordination than most other keyboards. Before long, Lindo was the featured soloist on several instrumental hits for Treasure Isle, including 'White Rum And The Ball', which used the same rhythm as the Paragons' 'Wear You To The Ball'. Alton Ellis had recently defected from Studio One and Lindo was astonished that he'd chosen Treasure Isle over Coxsone's famous label. Lindo played organ, and Gladdy Anderson piano, on the majority of Ellis' Treasure Isle releases,

---

* It was the (Jamaican) Meters who played on Bob Andy's 'Games People Play' and Dennis Brown's 'Money In My Pocket', as well as the early Peter Tosh sides for Joe Gibbs.

including 'Remember That Sunday' and 'I Can't Stop Now'. By then, Aubrey Adams' style was growing stale, so Lindo's playing brought a sparkle to Duke Reid's productions, although he certainly wasn't the sort to rest on his laurels. Lindo felt creatively stifled at the limitations in Jamaican music, where rhythm and feel were considered far more important than technique or experimentation. He was therefore determined to try and expand his horizons, especially after hearing the innovations coming from overseas.

Like a lot of organists, he'd recently heard 'Superstition' (from Stevie Wonder's 1972 album *Talking Book*) and discovered the clavinet, a Hohner electronic keyboard that Billy Preston featured on his latest hit, 'Outa Space' (and that Bundrick played on 'Concrete Jungle'). Lindo was also listening to progressive rock groups like ELP and Yes, who incorporated symphonic grandeur and sweeping, jazz-like improvisations into their music. It was this kind of restless ambition that compelled him and guitarist Mikey Chung to enrol on a course at the Jamaica School of Music, supervised by Jamaica Defence Force bandleader Joe Williams. As members of Now Generation, Lindo, Chung, his brother Geoffrey, bassist Val Douglas and drummer Mikey "Boo" Richards, were in demand for sessions and had gained a reputation for themselves after playing on Junior Byles' 'Beat Down Babylon' and hits for Matador, including the Abyssinians' 'Y Mas Gin', by the time Family Man saw them play.

Lindo still had a lot to prove. The spring '73 UK dates represented the Wailers' first professional tour and it afforded them an opportunity to show what they were made of to British audiences, without riding on Johnny Nash's coat tails. (Nash had just entered the US Top 20 with his version of 'Stir It Up'.)

Jaffe didn't accompany them to London, since the additional expense wasn't justified. Jobson would be far more useful to the operation. Island staff had worked hard in arousing interest in the Wailers by booking slots on BBC radio, as well as *The Old Grey Whistle Test*. To describe the tour as low-budget is an understatement. The Wailers squeezed into a Ford Transit van and since there were few main highways in Britain at the time, travelling between concerts was a laborious task, with the band having to navigate a network of back roads, passing through villages and small towns. There was no money for a road crew, nor sound engineer, so this meant the band were at the mercy of whoever the venues employed. Family Man would help out as best he could, as few of these people had any experience at mixing reggae music, but the sound quality was often far from ideal. Some of the early gigs weren't exactly well attended, and audiences were mainly white (as expected from English college crowds in 1973). Not only that, there was only a handful of Jamaican food outlets in the entire country, which made obtaining the band's desired food difficult and the rainy weather was colder than what they were used to in Jamaica.

Blackwell had rented Pink Floyd's keyboards for prog fan Lindo, who was delighted to be playing the same equipment as Rick Wright. He remembers the Island people being helpful, but says the Wailers were adamant that commercialism shouldn't be allowed to interfere with their spiritual and social aims, something that Tosh was even more committed to than Marley.

The tour began on April 27 at Nottingham's Coleman Club. From there, the band headed to Lancaster University before returning to London to play at Mr B's in Peckham, where they got a lively response due to the large number of Caribbean people in the audience. Three days later, the Wailers' debut appearance on British television would prove a milestone for reggae in the UK.

Bands didn't need a hit single to get on BBC2's *The Old Grey Whistle Test* – which immediately distinguished it from BBC1's chart-based show *Top Of The Pops* – making it the sole showcase for album-oriented rock acts. The Wailers were the first reggae act to appear on the programme, which was an event in itself, and their riveting performance would seal the band's reputation as Jamaica's most compelling reggae act. Domestic VCRs weren't widely available in 1973, so reaction to the Wailers' slot spread by word of mouth. Most of the *Whistle Test*'s viewers had not heard reggae, let alone seen people with dreadlocks. *The Harder They Come* still hadn't secured widespread distribution, so it's impossible to overestimate the effect of seeing Bunny in a fez, hunched over his conga drums, or Marley framed by a halo of baby dreads, solemnly intoning the words to 'Concrete Jungle' and 'Stir It Up'.

The Wailers mimed to pre-recorded rhythm tracks for the taping, with only the vocals "live", but the "live" illusion was convincing as Fams rocked back and forth, with Carly riding his kit like a champion jockey, his arms and feet locked in perpetual motion.

Family Man Barrett: "The t'ing was to get the roots culture and reality message across. Even in the rehearsal, we knew we'd got a magic different from the other top groups who were around at the time, and all the other acts on Island's label, like Traffic or whosoever."

The Wailers opened their gigs with 'Rastaman Chant' and a version of this – with Marley, Tosh, Livingston and Carly all playing drums – was included in another important session for John Peel's radio programme, taped that same day.* A string of university gigs followed, to audiences comprising mainly young, white rock fans, many of whom had been mesmerised after seeing the Wailers on television a few days earlier. Appearances at Hatfield Polytechnic, York University, Manchester University, the 67 Club in Wolverhampton, Essex University in Colchester, Boobs in Bristol, North Staffordshire Polytechnic in Stoke-on-Trent, and Teeside preceded a return to Mr B's on May 13. The Wailers were then booked to play four nights at the Speakeasy, a small, dimly lit basement club in Margaret Street, just north of Oxford Circus in London's West End. Since opening in 1966, the 'Speak' had become the watering hole of choice for London's rock aristocracy, including members of the Beatles, the Rolling Stones and the Who. Jimi Hendrix had performed there, as had Deep Purple, Thin Lizzy and a host of other top bands. Even Johnny Nash had played the club a year or so earlier.

The crowds filing into the Speakeasy for the Wailers' residency included several music journalists, who'd been notably resistant to reggae's novelty aspect in the past. However, this music was nothing like they'd seen or heard before. What the Wailers played over the course of those four nights, and the intensity with which they performed, confirmed how reggae had taken on a whole new dimension since the joyful abandon of 'Double Barrel' and 'Return Of Django'. The music of the Wailers wasn't just out to entertain, but to connect on a whole deeper level with its listeners; the soul, the spirit and the diaphragm felt the vibration, before articulating what else might be happening. The music still lacked a name at this point, as the term "roots rock reggae" wouldn't emerge until later. For now, the Wailers' music seemed beyond description, and audiences were reacting as if hypnotised by its other-worldliness. Word of this Biblical-looking troupe of Rasta prophets from the Kingston ghettos spread even faster after the Speakeasy showcases.

Family Man Barrett: "There came a point where we just knew how we were going to set it and that come when we were playing at the Speakeasy. The Speakeasy was the most prestigious club in London at the time and that was our breaking point. That was when we first began to get the attention of the media, because they were all there that night, just waiting

* The session, also featuring 'Concrete Jungle' and 'Stir It Up', was broadcast on BBC Radio 1 later that month.

to see what we could do. One reviewer, he said we cast a spell over the audience and after that it was like magic . . ."

This was just the effect the Wailers wanted; to transport their audience into a state of reverie and elation, where their inhibitions would fall away and they would become reborn as righteous, fighting for truth and rights, and living according to Rasta precepts. The parallels with how members of the congregation would testify in church back home was uncanny, except the Wailers were promoting a brand of religion free of the shackles associated with slavery. Marley, Tosh, and Livingston may have substituted Rastafarianism for Christianity, but it was the spirituality in their music that captivated people.

Dennis Morris, a 14-year-old interested in photography, met the band during one of their soundchecks at the Speakeasy. Morris took time off from school in Hackney, east London, to attend a couple of Wailers shows in the north of England. The Blackpool crowd consisted of only about a hundred punters. According to Morris, the band's Rasta philosophies were often perceived as "a black power thing" by many black people in Britain, which is why the Wailers found acceptance amongst whites initially. This may well have been true where older black people were concerned, but it was more likely to have been the choice of venues that kept younger black fans away.

Also, the Wailers' alliance with Island had caused a certain amount of suspicion from within the black community, with claims the band had sold out after allowing rock overdubs on *Catch A Fire*. With this in mind, and to coincide with the Wailers' presence on UK shores, Trojan released *African Herbsman*, which basically consisted of *Soul Revolution*, plus earlier tracks such as 'Trenchtown Rock', 'Lively Up Yourself' and 'Small Axe'. (Trojan later repackaged *Soul Rebels* as *Rasta Revolution*, again including 'Trenchtown Rock' and 'Lively Up Yourself' as bonus tracks.)

Whether Lee Perry, now based at the Black Ark, his home studio in Cardiff Crescent, near Washington Gardens, was consulted about its release is a moot point. Having bought the rights, Trojan were at liberty to do what they liked with the tracks. Needless to say, the Wailers had no prior knowledge of these releases and could only look on in anger as they distracted attention from *Catch A Fire*.*

---

* Perry was far more interested in his current work. His next album, *Blackboard Jungle Dub*, was a collaboration with King Tubby that made radical use of remixed rhythm tracks, including those first heard behind 'Dreamland', 'Kaya', and 'Keep On Moving'.

Island arranged additional studio time at Basing Street, so the band arranged to finish off their next album during days off. 'Get Up, Stand Up', a song co-written by Marley and Tosh, was completed shortly after British workers marched in protest on May 1, with the rhythm inspired by War's 'The World Is A Ghetto', which had recently scaled the American charts. As well as being the album's opening track, 'Get Up, Stand Up' was the most powerful, lyrical statement on *Burnin'*. It's as if the Wailers shifted into top gear while in England, as the tracks finished at Island would be among the strongest on the entire album. Family Man played keyboards on 'Get Up, Stand Up', since Lindo's probationary period wasn't quite over, despite his confident displays onstage.

British reggae deejay David Rodigan was present when the Wailers played at the Fulham Greyhound, on May 20. After the show, Rodigan remembers seeing a cloud of smoke billowing from a nearby doorway and was amazed to discover it was Marley, taking a well-earned spliff break. Dates followed at Northampton's Fantasia and Leicester Polytechnic, before the band returned to London to perform at the Paris Theatre on May 24, recorded as part of the BBC's *In Concert* radio series. The band then played in Exmouth, east Devon and up to Bristol again, where they gigged at the Bamboo Club, owned by Tony Bullimore. There were more black faces in evidence there, and so, too, at the Sundown Theatre in Edmonton, north London, where the Wailers played on May 27, sharing a bill with Matumbi who, together with the Cimarons, were one of Britain's most popular reggae bands. Matumbi filmed a section of their show, featuring Blue Mink vocalist Madeline Bell, which they dedicated to Ethiopian Famine Relief. The Wailers' performance was also filmed, and judging by the footage, it seems they thoroughly enjoyed themselves.

Marley is a vibrant, charismatic figure with his wild hair and tight trousers. He's full of smiles as he strikes rock poses, playing around with the phrasing of certain songs and joining Tosh on a highly charged, semi-a cappella rendition of 'Get Up, Stand Up'. Livingston is again hunched over his congas, and Lindo's playing is more freeform than Bundrick's studio embellishments. It's a joy to see him dancing behind his twin keyboards as the Barretts anchor proceedings with transcendent drum and bass. The sound quality is good too, which must have made a welcome change.

Hugh Francis, who played guitar with 90% Inclusive on the same bill, still has vivid memories of the Wailers' appearance. "The Sundown was an old theatre. It was the kind of place you'd go to see Saturday morning shows and then they'd turn it into a music venue by taking out the seats. Like the Wailers, we were unusual, since we were a self-contained unit who wrote our own songs and played our own instruments, and most other reggae bands were usually just there to back the singers. Marsha Hunt was the MC that day, and she had her little girl with her [Karis], who was Mick Jagger's daughter. We set up our equipment and we had all this Orange [amplification] gear, which was new at the time. We looked bad! I can't remember whereabouts we were on the bill, but the back line belonged to us and instead of changing the equipment over, we let the Wailers use it as well. I remember going backstage and opening their dressing-room door, and the smoke that came out of there was like a fog! Anyway, we played our set, and then the Wailers came on. The crowd were bursting with anticipation, because this was a massive gig.

"The place went dark and I heard this steady pulse, this drumming coming out of the darkness. It was so dramatic and then this chanting started, 'I hear the voice of the Rastaman say . . .' This wasn't normal for reggae and it really did feel like something new. The set they played that day just blew the place away and I was hooked. It was soon after that gig I began hearing more people talking about Bob Marley & the Wailers. There was a buzz around them from that moment onwards and the next time I saw them was when we were invited by Chris Blackwell to play a gig at the Island studios in Hammersmith. They had this reception room downstairs and Bob and some of the band were there.

"After we'd performed, Chris Blackwell thanked us for coming, and then for some reason I had to go into one of the offices. In those days, every group would spray their name on the equipment, so the roadies could identify it quickly. Anyway, I went into this office and there was a photo of the Wailers performing at Edmonton with this equipment behind them, bearing the name 90% Inclusive . . ."

Francis' group had been signed to Vertigo, a subsidiary of Phonogram, on the recommendation of Eddie Grant, who ran a label and production company (Ice Records) from his house in Stamford Hill. Grant liked the way 90% Inclusive blended Jamaican influences with rock and soul and noted how Francis had drawn inspiration from Jimi Hendrix, Steve Cropper, Albert King, and Big Jim Sullivan when forging his own style of playing, despite people questioning him, "Why are you guys messing with lead guitars and fuzz boxes? What are you trying to do? That's not reggae."

Hugh Francis: "They didn't understand there was a new movement going on, but all we knew was that guys like Jimi Hendrix had changed things round and we wanted to be part of whatever was developing out of that. That's why we played all the universities and that's what made us different. We weren't doing the reggae clubs and those students loved the Fender guitar, the fuzz box, and our whole approach . . . After I heard the guitar playing on *Catch A Fire*, I couldn't believe someone was thinking along the same lines as we were, although the Wailers didn't have that same sound when they played at Edmonton. The guys who'd played those overdubs weren't there, but I knew something big was about to happen after the release of that album, because there was no way we could all be soaking up these different influences and not break new ground by combining it with that Jamaican reggae sound. We were heavily influenced by rock, and for the Wailers now to be heading along the same road was significant. We started to see how the press and the media started getting behind them and people on the street could see how it was bringing some pride back into black music. Not just in terms of how it related to people in the Caribbean, but to blacks in the UK as well.

"I was really feeling it and whilst I knew we were different, it was an extension of what we were doing as well. We were in tune with the same frequency and whereas we were criticised for blending rock with reggae, there was no way of stopping what was happening. The momentum was just so strong and the way the guitar was coming through on those tracks from *Catch A Fire* was awesome. But there was another thing about the Wailers. It wasn't just the fact that Bob Marley was a fantastic lyricist, but he also had the knack of writing wonderful melodies. Put all that together with this great rhythm section who'd once been called the Upsetters and it was the meeting of real giants. I remember listening to the bass on those first two Island albums and thinking it wasn't so much the notes that Family Man played that made his music so compelling, it was the notes he didn't play. It was the gaps! It's almost as though he'd written the gaps first and then the notes are what's left. That sound was truly revolutionary, and people should be more aware of this, because all too often, the emphasis is only on Bob . . ."

While signed to Grant, Francis met another innovative Jamaican musician with ties to the Wailers during this same era.

"I used to jam with friends from X-Press and that's how I met Rannie Bop. He was their guitarist, and his finger-picking on Ginger Williams' 'Tenderly' was unique. I used to think, 'How does he do that?' It was like a hovercraft. It didn't go in the water but glided over it. Rannie became quite a force in British reggae and then just disappeared after a while. We had no idea where he went, because he didn't say goodbye or anything like that and he didn't talk about what he'd been doing back in Jamaica either."*

Like many of his contemporaries, Jamaican-born Francis grew up around Rastafarians, and yet he only started growing locks after bands like the Wailers had begun instilling cultural pride into the music. He says that thanks to them, Rastas began to be viewed differently and with a lot more respect than he remembered back home in Rocky Point, Clarendon. The Wailers thus not only brought about regeneration where reggae music was concerned, they also furthered the cause of Rastafari among people hungry for cultural identity and who were no longer afraid or ashamed to align themselves with a cult once thought to be composed of murderers and madmen. Black people in England had already had their eyes opened to the horrors of slavery by Alex Haley's book *Roots* and its accompanying television series. They were aware that not all Africans were uneducated savages, as they'd been led to believe, but some were cultured people from highly evolved societies, led by royal families who'd overseen significant achievements in the realms of art, architecture, and science. They hadn't learnt this in British schools where colonial thinking still prevailed, but through less official channels of expression, such as music, film, and literature.

This was a generation who'd rejected the subservience of their immigrant elders and were either too young to remember Malcolm X and the Black Panthers, or longed for a rekindling of the same, rebellious spirit. It's not difficult, therefore, to imagine the shared pain they felt when hearing Marley sing about how the slave masters, "brutalised our very souls", or the sense of empowerment that coursed through their veins when they were urged to "get up, stand up" for their rights. The Wailers' music pulled no punches and while more mainstream British reggae fans weren't that enamoured, there were plenty of black radicals, anarchists and white, middle class liberals who were thrilled to hear Tosh declare they were "sick and tired of the bullshit" and that as soon as the table, meaning the system, is overturned, the oppressors are "gonna get burned".

After five weeks of concentrated touring and recording, the Wailers reached the end of their first British jaunt with shows at Birmingham's Top Rank and Southampton's Coach House.

* Rannie briefly resurfaced at Lee Perry's Black Ark before moving to Canada. While he continued to meet up with the Wailers from time to time, he grew increasingly distant from them.

Lindo was viewed as family by this stage, and so he definitely wouldn't be rejoining Now Generation on his return home. No other keyboard player could play in that same rock style and Marley loved how his classically trained approach dovetailed with the Barretts' instinctive genius.

One person who would not be accompanying the Wailers on their forthcoming American tour was Bunny Wailer. Roger Steffens maintains that Livingston objected to a quote from Blackwell, who'd announced the Wailers would be playing "freak clubs" – i.e. rock venues – in the States. Other reports suggest that he was scared of flying. Family Man disagrees, claiming that rifts had developed between Livingston and the others while in England.

Family Man Barrett: "When we get maybe two-thirds of the way into the tour, I start to hear and see evidence of some strange attitude from him. I can't exactly pinpoint when it started, but it came like he was spoiling the thing and this wasn't what we'd discussed back in Jamaica, because we were going to tour the world and spread the message to the four corners of the earth. We were going to show what could happen when singers and players of instruments come together and each would get paid according to his works, which was Jah works. Bunny, he was one of those who'd been talking a lot more than the rest of us. In fact, he was reciting that kind of talk a lot more than even Bob himself, because Bob was a man who'd take note of something and then meditate on it before reaching a decision, but then once he'd decided on something, he'd say, 'This must be done by all means!' That's because you've got theory and then you've got practice. Both of them are nice, yes, but they have to work together, in harmony, and Bunny wasn't practising that.

"I remember we'd be on tour, sat in the van, and he and I would often have a little falling-out. I'd buy some comics to read while we were travelling and one time I see how he's well interested. Well, we weren't speaking to each other at the time and yet I see how he's reading my things, so after a while, I touch his arm and drop two comics next to him. The man gets real vexed, saying not to touch him and that any man who touches him will get *sick*. I say, 'Sorry sir, I thought you might like to see two new comics and I never knew you were reading your Bible.'"

CHAPTER FOURTEEN

Burnin'

MARLEY would tell Jamaican broadcaster Dermot Hussey that Bunny Wailer left the Wailers because he didn't like touring. "If you don't want to work, that's your business and I don't care," he said, adding that if someone sang on one of his records but then wouldn't promote it, they're wasting his time and them "nah defend nutten." Marley also announced that whoever played with him "is Wailers", meaning he now thought of the group as a collective, rather than being limited to the original trio.

Family Man Barrett: "Bunny didn't want to travel with us, it's true, yet he knew the Wailers had to tour, because with music we get to understand that you have to go out there and promote your product. It's not only about the producing of it, because we have to go out there and perform. If you're a musician, you're going to have to play for people live too, but it seems like Bob, Bunny and Peter have a little friction developing between the three of them at that time and I don't know the details behind it, but it was plain enough for me to see. And whilst I wasn't privy to what was being said between them, actions speak louder than words and I could see the cracks begin to develop in their relationship, for sure. Peter, he was still recording his own songs in between the sessions for *Catch A Fire* and *Burnin'*, and Bunny start to do likewise. Myself and Carly, we're not on the contract, but we're still there, working with all of them the same way."

True to form, Fams returned home to 14 Anglesey Avenue after the tour and kept a low profile, apart from when the band would gather for rehearsals at Hope Road. The Wailers' one-time mentor, Joe Higgs, had agreed to fill in for Livingston on percussion and backing vocals on the US dates, beginning in July. The rest of the band either knew Higgs by reputation, courtesy of early hits like 'Manny Oh' and 'There's A Reward, or from seeing him at Hope Road, where he'd been staying while trying to secure an album deal of his own with Island. Astute as ever, Blackwell had already released a handful of songs Higgs had recorded for Harry J on the Sioux and Blue Mountain labels (including 'Wages Of War' and 'World Upside Down'), so the arrangement was of mutual benefit.

Blackwell installed Jaffe at the Windsor Hotel in New York and put him to work securing gigs for the Wailers out of an office Island rented from Capitol Records' East Coast operation, conveniently located across the street. Jaffe marched into Max's Kansas City on Park Avenue South, off Union Square, with a copy of *Catch A Fire*, flipped opened the Zippo cover and played 'Concrete Jungle' to manager Sam Hood, who remarked it sounded like "the Drifters with raised consciousness." Hood offered the Wailers a four-night slot at the club, beginning on July 18. The arrangement represented a real coup for Jaffe, since Max's attracted a fashionable crowd and had strong connections with the downtown, New York art intelligentsia.

Jaffe acted as road manager for the duration of the tour, after being given a crash course by former Mountain manager Gary Kurfirst. Jaffe's expertise in this area didn't get off to a particularly good start when the band's work permits didn't arrive in time, which meant they had to fly from Jamaica to Toronto, drive to Niagara Falls, wake up a lawyer in the middle of the night to sort out the paperwork and then drive another eight hours to New York in time for their first Max's appearance. Other Marley sources state that the Wailers' 1973 US dates began with a five-day residency at Paul's Mall in Boston, Massachusetts, from July 11–15. These remain Family Man's favourite shows of the entire tour, not only because of the especially receptive crowd, but also because the band lived relatively communally.

Family Man Barrett: "We had an especially good time in Boston. That's because they had two basement clubs, one in the St Paul's Mall and another called the Jazz Workshop, and the atmosphere was good in both of them. The band playing the Jazz Workshop, whenever they take five, we play and vice versa, t'ings like that, y'know? We used to make like two breaks a night, then one night after we'd finished performing, there was this old guy waiting for us outside and when he saw us he said, 'Man. I'm 72 years of age and I've been listening to a lot of noise, but I like your noise, even though it's something strange to me.' He said it was a pleasure and a blessing to have heard us and we all felt good about that.

"It was around that same time we run into Alan James, who later became a driver for the Marley family. He brought this record player from out of his home and we string it up there in our rooms at the hotel, which was like a motel really, so we'd be there cooking every day, listening to music on some decent equipment and smoking herb, because we could always get some strong Columbian when we were there. Boy, it came like we did legalise it, except we didn't get trouble from anybody. It was so cool, I tell you, and the vibes just flow, because we wrote a good few songs during that time as well. It was like we were just foresighting them really, 'cause it wasn't long after that we recorded songs like 'So Jah Seh', 'Talking Blues' and even 'Natty Dread', too."

The Wailers preferred the more relaxed atmosphere of Boston to the relentless pace of New York. Jaffe booked the band into the Chelsea Hotel, on West 23rd Street, where the likes of Janis Joplin, Joni Mitchell, and Leonard Cohen had stayed, so the arrival of several dreadlocked, Jamaican musicians would not cause undue fuss. It was also inexpensive, which suited Island's purposes, and was relatively close to the venue. More importantly, at least where the Wailers were concerned, some of the rooms were self-catering, which meant they could cook their own food. Family Man has fewer recollections of playing Max's, despite the Wailers supporting Bruce Springsteen, the artist rock journalist (and future Springsteen manager) Jon Landau would describe as "the future of rock and roll."

Family Man Barrett: "He was only just getting popular at the time, because I remember the name more than the man himself. But we knew him of course and recognised how he'd got himself established before we do, but then when we come on the scene it's with another kind of blues entirely . . ."

Springsteen was playing for $1,500 a night in 1973, but probably got less for his Max's residency. The upstairs club only had a capacity of 350 or thereabouts, although it was packed for the five nights he and the Wailers appeared. This was due to the buzz surrounding the New Jersey-born artist and the fact that his label Columbia had bought a lot of tickets for media people, who were unexpectedly rocked off their heels by the sight of Marley leading the Wailers through the likes of 'Concrete Jungle' and 'Get Up, Stand Up'. There were early and late shows each evening, mainly to white audiences, although there was a handful of Jamaicans in attendance, including Glen Adams.

"When I first came to New York, I used to go around to people and ask them if they'd heard of Bob Marley & the Wailers, but no one had at that time," says Adams, smiling at the memory. "Then in 1973, Island Records brought them there and I went for them that Sunday afternoon, took them back to Brooklyn, minus Bob, and we did this recording for Brad Osbourne called 'Macka Dub'. We just lick a session, because it was a long time since I'd played with them and when I knew they were in town, I just called a session right away. That was the way we'd always done it, because we just work, but when we returned to Manhattan with the band, which was Fams, Carly, Wya, Peter Touch, and myself, Bob screw pon me and said, 'How come you just take away the Wailers and record?' I said I'd never taken the Wailers and it was the Upsetters I'd been moving with. But him screw, saying I'd been carrying them away to take part in some hustling and then right away, Chris Blackwell came in the room and broke up the discussion."

"Chris give Bob $500 to take his mind off it, but I see how serious it was between them and then that same night, when we go down to Max's Kansas City, I took along my movie camera, right? Because I move up now from the stills camera, but when I try and take some footage of them, Chris Blackwell is there telling me I can't shine any light on them, so I had to stop what I was doing, because I couldn't see. On account of what Bob say to me that day, I could see the kind of moves they were making and we all take heed of the changes in the sound from *Catch A Fire* onwards as well. I start to respect the label and the movements from that time onwards and so I just go on my own merry way after that."

Adams later played with Crown Heights Affair and the Rockit Band, who won a Grammy in 1984 with Herbie Hancock for their ground-breaking electro hit, 'Rockit'. He also recorded with Billy Ocean ('Caribbean Queen') and Freddie Jackson before working on the sound-tracks of *New Jack City* and *What About Africa?* The Brad Osbourne session was the last time Adams played with the Barretts during Marley's lifetime.[*]

Thanks to the exposure afforded by Island's publicity drive, the American rock fraternity were now beginning to show an interest in Marley and the Wailers. Roots reggae had a slow, hypnotic beat and this new sound, coupled with the kind of arresting lyrics and melodies Marley, and to a lesser extent, Tosh, were coming up with, was hard to resist. Although the Wailers had recorded 'Get Up, Stand Up' in London a couple of months earlier, Marley had a nagging feeling that something was missing and so arranged for it to be re-recorded at A & R studios in New

---

[*] Springsteen, too, would remember his one-time opening act with affection. Eight years later, while touring the UK, he received the news of Marley's death and dedicated 'This Land Is Your Land' in tribute.

York around the time of the Max's shows. The original version was slower with far less dramatic impact than either the unreleased single version (which has the feel of a soul record), or the final album cut, which is taut with menace and sung with just the right quota of exuberance. Marley's delivery was initially almost wistful but there is no mistaking the urgency in his and Tosh's voices on the final cut, which transforms the song into a protest of heady, persuasive power.

'Get Up, Stand Up' is capable of standing alongside any of the defining, political pop and rock songs, including the Beatles' 'Revolution', the Rolling Stones' 'Street Fighting Man' and Bob Dylan's early protest folk. Like these artists' best work, the song's sentiment is universal in urging all, irrespective of race, to recognise their self-worth; to heed the strength of collective action, cast away dependence on religious brainwashing and to marshal their individual resources in resisting an increasingly oppressive system. That said, the lyrics would have particular resonance with Jamaican listeners familiar with the work of Marcus Garvey, as Marley warns, "Most people think great God will come from the sky. Take away everything and make everybody feel high. But if you know what life is worth, you will look for yours on earth and now you see the light, you stand up for your rights."

Family Man agrees that the lyrics are more typical of Tosh than Marley in many ways, and recalls the jubilation the band felt when everything fell into place on the final version. There was a sense that the Wailers had just recorded their best-ever track.

Burnin' was released on October 19, just a matter of days after the band recommenced touring in the US. The most obvious difference between the album and its predecessor was the lack of any overdubs aimed at ensnaring rock fans. Instead of pandering to young, white music lovers directly, the Wailers absorbed what had made *Catch A Fire* so distinctive, and took up the baton for themselves. There might have been a lack of guitar solos, but the arrangements on *Burnin'* were a lot sharper and lessons had clearly been learnt.

Family Man Barrett: "When it came to recording *Burnin'* now, we said we are glad to know we lay the tracks in Jamaica, or at least the bottom, the roots, and then we leave from Jamaica and get that top mix to go with the hard bottom, and it worked."

Family Man distinctly remembers recording certain tracks for *Burnin'* at the same time as *Catch A Fire*. Other sources suggest they were recorded after Marley's trip to Trinidad before the Wailers left for London. Just to confuse matters further, Livingston has claimed the *Burnin'* sessions took place in April, after the band's first UK dates but before the band left for the US. This isn't the only grey area connected with the album. While Island engineers Tony Platt and Phil Brown are mentioned, no musician credits appear on the original sleeve of *Burnin'*. According to the notes in Island's 2004 Deluxe Edition reissue, Lindo is credited with playing keyboards but Fams disputes this.

Family Man Barrett: "When we were recording *Catch A Fire*, we'd done a few extra tracks and those were the ones we end up overdubbing in England at Basing Street. Then when we were promoting *Catch A Fire* on that first tour, we had a day off to go into the studio and do the second album, *Burnin'*. Each and every one of us was contributing when it came to producing and arranging: Bob, Bunny, Peter, myself and Carly, who'd come up with ideas for percussion and drum patterns. Wya was with us then, but he wasn't directly part of the band yet. I can't remember exactly when he came in, because when we were recording 'Get Up, Stand Up', I was doing most of the keyboard playing. I play the piano and this other keyboard they had, called a clavinet. I remember they had this upright piano and there was this little grand piano. It wasn't like a real grand. It was like an imitation and it sounded a bit dull, so I told them I like the upright piano and we end up getting quite a few tracks from it. We just lay the mic over the top and that gave us a better sound. It sound like a harp and it sound sweeter than the grand. Anyway, that was the one I use on 'Get Up, Stand Up' and it definitely wasn't Wya."

Lindo himself says his first studio session with the Wailers coincided with them recording 'Am A Do', yet the style of playing on tracks like 'I Shot The Sheriff' and 'One Foundation' suggests otherwise. Seeco Patterson is credited with playing percussion and, again, Family Man disputes this and says while Seeco might "beat a drum and lick a chalice" with band members from time to time, he was their roadie when *Burnin'* was being recorded and wasn't performing onstage with the Wailers as yet.

In Anderson's front sleeve photo, Lindo's face appears alongside those of Marley, Livingston, Tosh, and the Barrett brothers, underlining his official status as a Wailer. Although the album is credited to the Wailers (as opposed to Bob Marley & the Wailers), Marley's head is depicted slightly larger and more centrally on the front cover, which was designed to look as if the title and photos had been burned into the wood. There is no mistaking the fact that Marley was the central character, since the rear sleeve features a large, close-up photo of him smoking a spliff, with no other Wailer in sight. It's a striking image, audacious in its disregard for then-current drug laws.* This was confrontational stuff, since not so long beforehand, members of the rock fraternity had been persecuted and even jailed for marijuana use in the UK. Attitudes were changing however.

Anderson's photo tableau printed inside the gatefold sleeve was equally evocative. Most are of Marley and friends clowning by the beach or in some rural setting. In juxtaposition, others offer a glimpse of the hardships of everyday life in urban Kingston, showing people toiling through the hot and dusty streets, or standing amid scenes of poverty. Another photo finds Livingston standing in front of a poster advertising a sound-system clash between King Tubby, Tippertone, and Emperor Faith. It was an image to get every reggae fan's heart racing if only in retrospect, since cassettes of live dancehall sessions would not become popular for another few years.

Burnin' was a more democratic affair than *Catch A Fire*, with Livingston contributing 'Pass It On' and 'Hallelujah Time'. The album would have been even more so had two other Livingston songs, 'Reincarnated Souls' and 'The Oppressed Song', been included. Livingston wasn't a prolific writer at the time and was dependent upon Jean Watt for lyrics. Watt wasn't a musician, which might explain why her lyrics are a little wordy in places, but there is a gentle spirituality to these songs that immediately distinguishes them from Marley and Tosh's efforts.

'Pass It On' and 'Hallelujah Time' are tracks that could have been written by Curtis Mayfield, since they're both couched in Biblical terms and voiced in the style of modern-day gospel songs. 'Pass It On' opens with lilting electric piano from Family Man, before he and Carly combine on a rhythm founded in nyahbinghi that would probably lurch horribly out of control in the hands of lesser musicians. Livingston and Tosh's harmonies are delivered straight out of the church tradition and so, too, the lyrics, as the former promises how "in the kingdom of Jah, man shall reign" and addresses the eternal question of how we behave towards our fellow man, particularly the underprivileged. "Help your brothers, pass it on . . ." 'Hallelujah Time' heralds the arrival of a new epoch, where freedom reigns and events are determined by destiny. The words are full of pastoral imagery as Livingston sings of dew-soaked grass, ploughing the

* The photo was taken at the same session as the image that appeared on subsequent re-pressings of *Catch A Fire*.

earth, the cane crop being watered by "the sweat from man's brow" and, again borrowing from Christian metaphor, sheep being scattered over rocks and mountains.

A churning organ shadows the rise and fall of Livingston's melodies, just as it does on 'The Oppression Song'. The effect is perhaps overdone on the latter, which is possibly why it was omitted from the album. Opening like a folk song before expanding into another stumbling rhythm, Livingston ruminates on the poor man's plight and hints at a broader interest in mysticism with the lines, "There's no rest in the west, so to the east he goes, where he can find peace of mind."

'Reincarnated Souls' is a beautifully written karmic history lesson. "We are reincarnated souls from that time. And we are living earth, heat, air, and water in this time," he begins, describing how man was formed by the manifestation of God's will, meaning we are all "word made flesh." Apart from such captivating lyrics, 'Reincarnated Souls' is also refreshingly melodic and a precursor of what would follow on Bunny's debut solo album, *Blackheart Man*, which included reworked versions of both 'The Oppressed Song' and 'Reincarnated Souls'. However, the more superior cuts are the *Burnin'* out-takes, with Marley and Tosh on backing vocals.

"I remember when we were recording backing vocals on 'Reincarnated Souls' and they were singing about water, I say we need a sound effect," recalls Family Man, in reference to the line, "Those who are thirsty, let them drink clear water." "The first thing you'd think of in those days would be a sound effects album, but the kind of sound I was looking for wasn't on any of those we had, so I called for some newspaper and a mic, spread the newspaper on the floor and stood there with two glasses, one full of water and the other empty. I was standing over all this with my headphones on saying, 'Run the tape!' and then just as he sang 'water', I emptied the glass on the paper."*

Family Man also suggests the original version of 'Iron Lion Zion' was recorded during the *Burnin'* sessions. There's something about the song's structure that certainly suggests it was recorded around the same time as 'I Shot The Sheriff' or 'Get Up, Stand Up', although the Seventies' cut is little more than a sketch compared with the posthumous remix, released in 1992. The outlaw theme fits too, as Marley sings about having to "run like a fugitive" and having no gun; yet he's quick to assert his fearlessness on

---

* This version of 'Reincarnated Souls' was completed at Basing Street during the UK leg of the *Catch A Fire* tour.

the chorus. "I'm going to be iron, like a lion in Zion," he boasts, echoing how the Jamaican rude boys would call out "Iron!" as they smashed their beer bottles on the ground in the Kingston dancehalls. Marley sings harmonies, while the rhythm surges forward as if swept along by some unseen, irresistible force. This original cut would have made a wonderful addition to *Burnin'* had the Wailers completed it.

'Burnin' And Lootin'' is a classic example of Marley standing up for the angry, disaffected youth he saw milling about in the Kingston ghettos. "How many rivers do we have to cross, before we can talk to the boss?" Marley asks. 'Burnin' And Lootin'' doest not advocate violence, but warns of reprisals if social inequalities are allowed to persist when there'll be "weeping and wailing tonight". It's addressed not only to the powers-that-be but also to the sufferers themselves, who are reminded of what can happen if they stray from the rootsman's path. Not only will hard drugs slow you down, Marley counsels, but "this not the music of the ghetto."

'Burnin' And Lootin'' was akin to 'Concrete Jungle' and 'Slave Driver' in its subject matter of hard-hitting reality, but it was the closing 'Rasta Man Chant' (which opened the Wailers' live act from the time) that provided the most valid expression of Marley's solidarity with the Rastafarian faith. With Family Man, Marley, Livingston and Tosh regularly attending nyahbinghi sessions, apart from a few, wistful organ phrases, 'Rasta Man Chant' was a close approximation to the music heard at a grounation up Warieka Hill, or in some tenement yard in the ghetto. It's essentially an invocation, powered by Rasta hand drums, and resulted from a slightly later session at Harry J's, with Sylvan Morris at the mixing board.

Marley welcomes Babylon's demise at the hands of the Almighty and eventual repatriation for the righteous. "One bright morning when my work is over, I will fly away home," he promises. The origins of 'Rasta Man Chant' are buried in the realm of spirituals, although it sounds as though it was based on 'I'll Fly Away', written by Albert Brumley, which a multitude of gospel and country & western singers covered over the years (including the Five Blind Boys of Alabama, Jim Reeves, and the Stanley Brothers). 'Put It On', which the Wailers first recorded at Studio One as 'I'm Gonna Put It On' and then revived for sessions with Perry and Sims in the search for the authoritative cut, also has its roots in the church tradition. "Feel that spirit, Lord I thank you," Marley intones on this latest version, assuring us he's "not boasting."

The reason why the Wailers reworked so many old songs for *Burnin'* isn't difficult to appreciate. For one thing, only a small minority of people had heard *Soul Rebels* or *Soul Revolution*, let alone any of the Wailers' more obscure (and poorly distributed) sides for Studio One. To the band's growing army of rock-oriented fans, these songs were brand new, prompting some of them into seeking out the originals. Also, signing with Island had given the Wailers access to better equipment and recording facilities. The standards of production were now higher and the musicians more practised than they were three years earlier. Family Man, in particular, had new ideas he wanted to incorporate into certain songs, whether this meant introducing up-to-date instrumentation like clavinet, or altering the arrangements in some way. It's his improved artistry that makes the difference to 'Small Axe', which has a looser feel than the version the Wailers sang for Lee Perry. Tosh's baritone sums it up perfectly. "Well sharp," he drones, and the same is true of 'Duppy Conqueror', another remake of a Lee Perry production.

The *Burnin'* version isn't so exuberant and the harmonies are less striking, but Marley's lead is definitely more soulful. Both songs stand up to their changes well and if the intention was to supersede Perry's versions when recreating them for the Wailers' new-found audience, there's little doubt they succeeded. The Wailers also recorded a new version of 'No Sympathy', written and performed by Peter, during the *Burnin'* sessions. (The original appeared on *Soul Rebels*, and Tosh returned to it a third time for his debut album *Legalise It*.) It's not hard to see why it was left off *Burnin'* as, while sounding more modern than the Upsetter cut, Tosh doesn't voice it with anywhere near as much feeling, even when lamenting he's received "not one word of advice from my so-called friends."

Tosh's sole contribution to *Burnin'* was 'One Foundation', which conveys a simple sentiment that's clearly delivered. "We've got to build our love on one foundation," he sings, but then neatly sidesteps the temptation to indulge in rose-tinted idealism by warning how "they've got to put aside their segregation," otherwise there'll be no truth and no real direction. Another line makes direct reference to the church, as Tosh warns, "got to put aside their denomination, otherwise there'll be no love." The chorus is also uncomplicated, except the point is made well enough, without any of the sloganeering that can blight material of this kind. Not for the first time, there is a folk influence in Tosh's music; unsurprisingly, given his listening habits.

Family Man Barrett: "We listen deep to all kinds of music. Bob, Bunny, and Peter, they are all singers and so it's natural they should listen deeply to what is happening in the world of music, plus Peter is musical as well. Bob Dylan, he was a popular singer in all of the singers' minds in Jamaica from that time, and that's how Mr Robert Nesta took on that name, Bob, too. He got the inspiration from Bob Dylan and Dylan was definitely a favourite of Peter's, for sure."

On 'No Sympathy', Marley questions the integrity of his so-called friends, by asking, "What kind of love have they got for me?" The answer would come sooner than he thought, since there were cracks under the surface that he and Tosh would not be able to paper over for much longer. On *Catch A Fire*, all of the songs had been credited to Marley, despite Tosh's authorship of 'Stop That Train' and '400 Years'. Speaking in Jeremy Marre's documentary, *Catch A Fire*, Livingston remarked, "We never credit no individual. We made the songs together. All we did was put the songs in one individual name and then when we got the returns, we'd split it three ways."

This was not the case with *Burnin'* which credits Jean Watt ('Hallelujah Time', 'Pass It On'), Tosh ('One Foundation' and half of 'Get Up, Stand Up'), while Marley wrote the remainder, except for 'Rasta Man Chant', which is listed as being a traditional composition, arranged by the Wailers. 'Rasta Man Chant' marked the original Wailers trio's last-ever recording session.

Family Man Barrett: "It was like you had three big bulls in a one pen. All three were singers, but Bob's unique style and star was already beginning to shine. He had taken the lead in singing on *Catch A Fire* and on the new album, and this caused friction with Bunny and Peter."

Family Man went on to say that while laying tracks and jamming in the studio around the time of *Burnin'*, he and Carly's relationship with their charismatic frontman deepened. Both Barrett brothers were now essential to the band's musical identity, and Marley was already paying them handsomely for touring and recording.

Family Man Barrett: "I can't remember how much Bob paid us, but it was much more than session rates," he acknowledges. "We never received any money from Peter or Bunny, only Bob, although as far as I can recall, Bob, Bunny, and Peter were equal partners who split their money three ways. Bunny had told me this."

Presumably all three Wailers contributed towards recording and touring costs before Livingston left the group, even though it was Marley who was the paymaster. The picture of Marley that emerges is one of a team player who understood the value of having the right people around him and rewarded their loyalty accordingly. Livingston didn't treat Family Man and Carly particularly well after they played on his sessions, but the brothers still got on with Tosh, who didn't let his problems with Marley detract from their shared comradeship.

While the people at Island Records weren't always to Tosh's liking, they continued to work hard on the Wailers' behalf, securing the band a US tour supporting Sly & the Family Stone. While both trailblazing acts had crossed the divide between traditional forms of black music and rock, Sly & the Family Stone enjoyed a greater deal of mainstream success. As already illustrated, classic albums like *Stand!* and *There's A Riot Goin' On* proved a revelatory synthesis of funk, soul, and psychedelic rock, and their influence had not gone undetected in Jamaica. Songs like 'Dance To The Music' and 'Everyday People' exploded with such irresistible excitement, even the normally placid Family Man remembers dancing to them. Their latest album *Fresh* yielded the hit 'If You Want Me To Stay', but several key personnel had left the year before and Stone gained a worrying reputation for arriving at gigs late, or not turning up at all. He had become enshrined as the archetypal troubled genius in the minds of many music journalists, who flocked to gigs, if only to see Stone self-destruct. Touring with such an erratic genius looked an inspired match, on paper at least.

The tour was made up of 17 dates, scattered throughout the length and breadth of America, commencing in October with shows in Florida (Homestead and Tampa), then swung north-east through Lexington and Denver before heading south to Las Vegas. The Wailers were the first reggae band to tour in some of these cities where audiences were more accustomed to country, blues, soul, and rock acts. Some punters thought that they'd be watching the Wailers, a late Fifties-early Sixties rock'n'roll outfit from Tacoma, near Seattle, who'd had minor US hits with 'Louie, Louie' and 'Tall Cool One'.* Viewed from a perspective more than three decades later, it's hard to appreciate the incomprehension the Wailers encountered on this tour and the difficulties they faced in having to open for one of the most dynamic soul artists in America, albeit one that was hampered by a debilitating drug habit.

There was little contact between Stone and the Wailers and no camaraderie to speak of. It was therefore hardly unexpected when Stone let the Wailers go after the Las Vegas show and continued touring without them.

Higgs later told Roger Steffens that Stone had fired them because they

---

* The group still own the copyright for the name Wailers in the US.

weren't connecting with his audience. "They couldn't relate to us. He said our music was too slow, that people couldn't understand what we were saying and we didn't dress the way the audience expected us to dress."

Family Man Barrett: "Sly Stone's people left early before we got up. We were left stranded at the hotel, not knowing what was happening and without any money. There'd been some vibration coming from his quarters earlier on in the tour, so I figured something was going on in his mind, y'know? What we were doing, it was a different concept of music from what they were used to and it obviously didn't sound right to them. Maybe we were too rebellious for them and they weren't ready for the Rastaman vibration, coming from the throne of King David. Sly Stone took us for simpletons in leaving us high and dry like that. He didn't know we were the archangels, because his career just went downhill from there."

The Barretts had encountered problems like these touring England with the Upsetters, the difference being that there weren't too many West Indian communities in America during the early Seventies, especially Las Vegas. A Jamaican attorney, Gus Brown, came to their rescue and put the band in touch with a promoter in San Francisco, who booked two shows for the Wailers at the city's Matrix Club on 19 and 20 October. These were hastily arranged affairs and contrary to Island's official version of events, Family Man recalls the promoter did little more than break even, leaving the Wailers struggling to cover their bills, wondering how and when they were going to get home. The crowd's response had been promising, however. Word spread like wildfire about this electrifying new reggae band from Jamaica, and the same promoter took a chance by booking them into the Matrix for a further two nights on the 29th and 30th. This time, the San Franciscan audiences who'd been weaned on new music at venues like Bill Graham's Fillmore West and Winterland sold out both nights, prompting local station KSAN-FM to step in with the offer of a "live" broadcast the following day. Legendary KSAN deejay Tom Donahue had helped promote *Catch A Fire* on his show, and it was he who hosted the session from the Record Plant in Sausalito.*

There were only a handful of people present, although this proved deceiving judging by the audience reaction. Marley's insistence on regular rehearsals may have honed the Wailers into a tightly drilled unit, but they

---

* Seven of the songs from the Wailers' set finally surfaced on the 1991 Island album, *Talkin' Blues*.

sound wonderfully ragged in places. The band members seem determined to forget their troubles and enjoy themselves. Lindo's keyboard playing is brighter than ever, while Carly circles the beat like a man possessed on tracks like 'Burnin' And Lootin''. There was never a better reggae drummer on the planet when Carly was in this kind of form, with no trace of excess in his playing. While the rhythm section provides a platform for the others to express themselves, they also created space for improvisation, just as the best jazz players do. 'Slave Driver' opens with a slinky, loose-limbed jam, but avoids becoming soporific thanks to Tosh's slashing guitar and Lindo's darting organ riffs. Whereas the interplay between Adams' organ and Lewis' rhythm playing made such a difference to the Upsetters' sound, Tosh and Lindo are a more dynamic pairing and the tension they create on these live tracks would never be repeated on subsequent Wailers' tours.

Tosh spars with both Lindo and Marley on 'Get Up, Stand Up', which is again played almost freeform as the Wailers' two lead singers happily ad lib in between verses. It now seems inconceivable that Tosh wasn't granted additional space to perform his own material, or to take a more central role. He did get to sing 'Can't Blame The Youth', which Tosh, Family Man and Tin Leg had recorded at Treasure Isle shortly after completing *Catch A Fire*. 'Can't Blame The Youth' was released on Tosh's own Intel-Diplo label in between recording tracks for his first solo album, *Legalise It*.

Shortly after the KSAN-FM broadcast, the Wailers left for Los Angeles and another closed doors performance at the Capitol Records Tower in Hollywood, just north of the intersection of Hollywood Boulevard and Vine Street. Home to the label's recording and film studio facilities, the building was more used to the likes of Frank Sinatra and Nat King Cole than itinerant Jamaican musicians. The Wailers had been invited there by Shelter Records, who had recently launched a film company specialising in music called Shelter Vision. In addition to recording the band's performance on 16-track tape, Shelter Vision also arranged to film it in colour, using a three-camera shoot. Few, if any, reggae acts had been documented in this way, and bearing in mind the impact the Wailers' *Old Grey Whistle Test* appearance had caused, one can only speculate what the effect might have been had this footage received an airing at the time.

The Wailers ran through 18 songs, including three takes of 'Rastaman Chant' and 'Midnight Ravers'. Marley sang his heart out on 'Duppy Conqueror' and 'No More Trouble', while Tosh strode to the mic wearing a floppy woollen, yellow hat for 'Stop That Train' and 'Can't Blame The Youth'. Family Man, wearing a US Army helmet and impenetrable shades, was the epitome of inscrutable cool as he gently rocked to the waves of sound washing over him from his bass amp. To one side and slightly up front, Higgs sat or stood behind brightly painted red, green and gold conga drums, occasionally leaning forward to sing the higher register harmonies Livingston had originally voiced. Lindo and Carly were partly hidden by their respective instruments, although their contributions to the Wailers' sound were typically immense.

Higgs left shortly after the LA gig, leaving the rest of the band to fulfil a couple more shows without him before heading back to Jamaica. Their Californian adventures had left them exhausted but Island had already arranged further UK concerts to promote *Burnin'*, which had been enthusiastically received by the music press and public alike. Not that the climate or circumstances were to make them feel especially welcome. The rigours of constant touring made the Wailers' insistence on healthy food and exercise even more important, so it was no surprise when Tosh succumbed to bronchitis before the tour commenced. His illness meant the first five dates had to be cancelled, including those in Nottingham, Bradford, Birmingham, and Stafford, with the first show occurring at the Blackpool Locarno on November 22. The following day they piled into a Ford Transit and headed for Leeds, where they played a storming set at the local Polytechnic.

Island finally released a tape of this performance in 2004 as part of the Deluxe Edition of *Burnin'*, and despite the absence of Livingston and Higgs, it's thrilling from start to finish. With there being no time to rehearse anyone else before leaving, Marley and Tosh had to fill in vocally as best they could.*

Freed of Livingston's negativity and Higgs' stern authority, Marley sounds more liberated in Leeds than during any of the Wailers' previous, Island-era performances. The detached, soulful figure that had fronted the line-up earlier in the year was now recast as a charismatic performer, full of energy and unafraid to impose his personality upon both the songs and the crowd. The Bob Marley who became a superstar came into his own during this leg of the Burnin' tour.

Following the Leeds gig, the Wailers crossed the Pennines to Liverpool,

* While the other members were all formidable musicians, they couldn't be let anywhere near a microphone!

passing through Doncaster before returning to London for a radio broadcast hosted by John Peel on the 26th at Kensington House, Shepherd's Bush. Manchester was next, before the last gig in Northampton on the 30th. The weather had turned bitterly cold, with snow, so there was little complaint from the Jamaicans when the remaining dates, including Leicester and some all-important London shows, were cancelled after Tosh's bronchitis returned. Tales circulated in the music press about the tour being curtailed because of the weather – a first in rock history – and how Jah had created the adverse conditions in anger at the Wailers spending so much time in Babylon. This was all fanciful, given Marley and the Barretts' determination to succeed outside of the reggae market. Marley missed very few shows in his career, but the apocryphal notion of this quixotic band of ganja-smoking, Caribbean rabble-rousers quitting the rigours of a British winter because of their belief in some Old Testament demagogue made good copy.

The conclusion of this tour marked the end of a crucial chapter in the Wailers' history. Tosh became increasingly upset at how the emphasis was being put on Marley, though this was nothing new as Lee Perry had previously called them Bob Marley & the Wailers. In the wake of Tosh's resignation, Marley stayed behind in London for talks with Blackwell, while Family Man and Carly headed back to Jamaica.

Family Man Barrett: "Esther was the one who talked to Bob about getting the first option on 56 Hope Road. At the time, it was owned by Chris Blackwell and we were happy leaving Bob to deal with the paperwork, because we trusted him for sure and it was all part of the partnership we had, like this dream of turning Tuff Gong into a little Motown. That's when I got another job to go with those of bandleader, musical arranger, and producer, which was director for Tuff Gong . . ."

CHAPTER FIFTEEN

Pick A Dub

THE music scene in Jamaica was changing fast and the relatively new concepts of dub, roots, and deejaying spread like wildfire, despite Dynamic and Federal's best attempts to churn out more traditional-sounding pop-reggae tunes. Rasta music was on the increase and so, too, tracks expressing reality or cultural themes, like Ken Boothe's magnificent version of Syl Johnson's 'Is It Because I'm Black?', or the Heptones' 'Book Of Rules'. In the wake of *The Harder They Come* and *Catch A Fire*, tastes had begun to change and the music now had a new audience, eager to hear a more vibrant, "dread" sound from the ghettos. A fresh intake of producers emerged to challenge the "big three" mentioned in 'Small Axe'. As well as Bunny Lee and Joe Gibbs, the likes of Gussie Clarke, Leonard Chin and Clive Chin were youths barely out of their teens.

As prime architects of this new sound, the Barretts were in constant demand around Kingston's studios whenever they were back in Jamaica. Hardly a day went by without a producer calling for the brothers if they were seen hanging out at the Wailers' shop on King Street.

Family Man Barrett: "By that time, I was doing so many sessions with different singers that I learned to be sensitive to their voices. I had a gift for making the music sound different for each singer I worked with and it was from there I developed a skill for creating, writing, orchestrating and arranging music. What I'd do is follow the vocal lines and listen out for the melody and the concept of how the person sings. I try to build that around them and let them float so the whole thing swings and a sway, because I wasn't going to force no riddim pon an artist. That's deejaying stuff! Because you're supposed to create and a so we set the t'ing.

"The words, they're also very important of course, because I listen to the feel and expression of what they're trying to put across and then we try and bring it out. We just try to make that better each time and develop it, y'know? We try and take it to higher heights and then we get some deeper understanding for sure, as we go along."

The Barretts learnt the value of encouraging newcomers from Bunny Lee, who'd become the most prolific and successful producer on the island. Family Man introduced his pupil Robbie Shakespeare to Bunny, who let the boy play bass on certain sessions. If it's hard telling their playing apart on Bunny's productions from 1972–73, that's because Family Man would often show Shakespeare what to play. Family Man and Carly both played with Bunny's new studio band the Aggrovators on occasion, except the brothers' touring commitments with the Wailers meant they weren't so accessible as before.

Bunny Lee: "I get that name Aggrovators from Eddie Grant. He was in the Equals back then but Larry Lawrence and I were friends and Eddie would say to him, 'Oh Larry, stop causing me aggro.' I asked him what aggro meant and he said, 'Trouble.' That's when I decide to call my group the Aggrovators, because before that they used to play for everybody and weren't just called Bunny Lee All-Stars, but also the Joe Gibbs All-Stars and Harry J All-Stars, you name it.

"After Rannie Bop leave, that's when I start to bring in some different man like Chinna Smith. Rannie had been playing the picking guitar up until then, but a new sound developed once he'd gone. Family Man and Carly, we stick with them for years, even after they become the Wailers, because Family Man continue to play on a lot of my tunes . . .

"In those times, when certain guys want to catch up with some practice, they'd come right back to the old school, except Family Man and Carly never leave it, and right now, I could put out an entire album with the Wailers' band if I want. Family Man, he always has a peaceful vibe about him, because I remember one time we were in Treasure Isle and Coxsone take away this horn from Roland Alphonso. It looked like Coxsone buy it for him but then they fall out, because the man go upstairs and snatch away the horn. Family Man laugh and Roland went up to him, took off Family Man's glasses and stomp them into the floor. I say, 'Roland. What kind of stupidness is that? Because it's Coxsone you should be doing that to.' Family Man, he didn't react, but just said, 'True, true.'"

As a notorious "Mr Fix It" Bunny knew helpful people on both sides of the political divide, and in between doing deals with other record companies and distributors, he had a remarkable even-handed attitude towards the artists and musicians in his stable.

Bunny Lee: "You can't be treating one as a favourite, or putting one above another, otherwise that will cause problems. Every man is a man and you have to treat it as a wheel, because if a spoke gets loose and you don't tune it back up, then very soon that spoke's going to cause a next one to burst and lick the whole thing out of synch. That's how I used to run my organisation, like a wheel, so if one artist come and they want better treatment than the others, then it's better them go to a different producer, because the sun has to shine pon every man and not just someone like Johnny Clarke, who had a lot of hits at one time. I couldn't just pay John Holt and not Delroy Wilson. I wasn't like that, because even if you a swing, then everybody had to go home at the weekend with the same £20 and that's how I used to keep my thing together.

"If I don't have food in my yard on the Friday, then I have to go make a deal with Randy's and sell them some records cheap, so I can have enough money to pay everyone. That's why everything run smooth, because the thing with Coxsone now, is that if you get a hit and him give you a penny, when royalty time come, he's going to draw back his money. But with me now, if I have a tune and can't handle it, then I'll go sort it by some other means. I'll go give it to Dynamic, Miss Pottinger, or Federal, so they can distribute it for me and the artists can see some money out of it. That's why my tunes came out on so many different labels, because the artist and myself know that Miss Pottinger could get a whole heap of airplay and that would help break the song. You have to compromise and if you're supposed to get a pound, you might only get half, but it's a sacrifice worth making because if an artist's song is getting played, then he's going to get stage shows and especially if it goes to number one. Artists, they lived off stage shows back then, because it was a regular source of income for them.

"Coxsone, he used to pay his musicians weekly, so they weren't dependent onstage shows, but when I started, I didn't have any money, so I have to join up with West Indies Records, who paid the musicians for me. In that time, each musician would get paid 30 shillings per side and that's why I'd use each rhythm like about five times, because that way I'd only have to pay the one fee. It was me who bring that in. I'd dub on horns and put out an instrumental version of it and things like that. We just didn't have that kind of money, so when musicians start to come up now, like Family Man and Carly, I pass over my thing to Total Sounds, so they can get paid properly. Musicians and artists, from them inna the clique now, every Thursday they can go there and get a cheque. Family Man and Robbie Shakespeare would come and play any amount of tunes for me in a different spirit, so when money start to come in now, I have to look after them and all of them know they have a cheque to pick up on a Thursday.

"We used to run a session every Tuesday or Friday at Harry J's studio and we use any amount of studio time, so Harry J would get his cheque too. Every man was living good and it wasn't just about me. That's why I could go anywhere inna Jamaica, because people come from Matches Lane, Jungle, and Tivoli Gardens and if he don't get a money, then he get some records to go sell so he can find some food for the pot. Some of these men, we'd help them come out of badness and give them a few rhythms so they could start up as producers. We'd pay the studio time for him and press up the first few records, so I become popular amongst everybody."

Family Man also played guitar on the majority of Bunny's productions with Al Campbell, but the most influential track he masterminded from this time was Johnny Clarke's 'None Shall Escape The Judgment'. This groundbreaking record, based around a plunging "rockers" style bassline, featured a fresh kind of rhythm called "flyers", based on drummer Santa Davis' sizzling cymbal work. Clarke had only achieved a couple of minor hits for Rupie Edwards before teaming up with Bunny. The song not only launched the "flyers" sound but also Clarke's career as a singer.

Family Man Barrett: "The Johnny Clarke session, that was the time when I was bringing Robbie in this. I bring a bass fi 'im and carry Bob Marley's guitar, 'cause I play rhythm guitar and also some piano on those tracks. A typical session would find Robbie on bass, Santa on drums, I on rhythm guitar and Chinna on lead guitar, with Gladstone Anderson, Ossie Hibbert, or Bobby Kalphat on keyboards. That's how we start that series with Santa on the drums, playing that flying cymbal, because we use that sound on a whole heap of songs with Johnny Clarke, Linval Thompson, and Cornel Campbell."

Bunny Lee: "Fams arrange that song, because when Earl Zero come with this tune 'None Shall Escape The Judgment', them couldn't go no further. It was Fams who showed Robbie the changes. Him and Chinna work it out from there, but Earl Zero couldn't manage it at all."

Family Man Barrett: "That's right, because it wasn't even Johnny Clarke's song. It was some guys from the countryside and them come in with their box guitar playing this long-time calypso or madrigal kind of phrase. But Bunny nah like the sound when them sing over it, so we get the magic of it now and start to set the riddim; Santa on drums, Chinna on lead guitar, Robbie on bass and me on rhythm guitar. A so we set it now, except we put a little bridge inna it. 'Anyt'ing Jah say, I will always do . . .' And him came in and sings, 'As I approach the gate of Zion . . .' I say for

264

him to hold it the same way and let me swing it so, but that song rest upon the one chord, y'know? One chord, me a tell you!"

Santa had been inspired by MFSB drummer Earl Young's style and technique on the track, 'T.S.O.P (The Sound Of Philadelphia)', which the weekly television show *Soul Train* used as its theme music. Young helped create the "Philly" sound, playing on hits produced by Kenneth Gamble and Leon Huff at Sigma Sound Studios in Philadelphia during the early Seventies.

Johnny Clarke: "That's why it took off so fast, because there was like a slight change in the reggae as far as the drum pattern was concerned, y'know? It was completely different to whatever else was happening, because in those times we were so original. You could say we were original like 100 per cent, both in terms of the rhythm and the lyrics, because in those times, you couldn't introduce yourself as a new artist and get a hit with a cover song. You'd have to meditate on what you're doing and be creative, and that's the reason why songs like 'None Shall Escape The Judgement' and [its follow up, again arranged by Family Man] 'Move Out Of Babylon' were such big hits."

The established stars Bunny had in his stable like Delroy Wilson, Slim Smith, John Holt, Stranger Cole, Derrick Morgan, and Alton Ellis now faced serious competition as newer acts such as Cornel Campbell and Linval Thompson began having hits on flyers rhythms.

Johnny Clarke: "A producer like Bunny Lee, you might have to go there for months and you still can't get a chance, because he has so many big names in the camp . . . There were enough setbacks, but then one day you go to the studio, the producer hear you sing your song on an a cappella basis first and if him feel the vibes and say alright, he's going to leave it up to the musicians to work it into a hit. That's why the musicians were so important, because he'd go over to the piano man or someone like Family Man or Touter and Tyrone Downie, who Family Man was grooming at the time and everything happen from there."

Bunny Lee: "You know who else was brilliant in those days? Earl 'Wya' Lindo, who played on songs like 'You Are My Angel' by Horace Andy, because he found the bassline and did all the arrangements on that tune."

A bewildering amount of Bunny Lee material exists featuring various Wailers members, especially Family Man, who spent a lot of time in the studio with the producer, searching for hit melodies and arrangements. While Fams mixed some of these productions, much of the material was taken over to King Tubby's home studio in Dromilly Avenue, just off

Penwood Road in Waterhouse. Tubby, real name Osbourne Ruddock, was a little older than Family Man and had grown up around High Holborn Street in central Kingston, before moving to Waterhouse in the mid-Fifties. Despite his slim build, his mother had called him Tubby as a child and it stuck. He'd begun experimenting with electronics after graduating from Kingston Technical College, although he made his money by repairing electrical equipment. People were already dragging their old radios and televisions to Tubby's house by the time Fams and Bunny began knocking on his door with reels of tape in their hands.

Tubby's set-up didn't allow room for recording rhythms and he didn't even have voicing facilities there at first, until Bunny convinced him to put up soundproofing and invest in a decent microphone. The three of them started collaborating in the late Sixties, around the time Tubby was working at Treasure Isle as a dub cutter, launching his own sound-system, Tubby's Home Town Hi-Fi. Bunny gave Tubby exclusive mixes of hits like Slim Smith's 'Ain't Too Proud To Beg' and 'Everybody Needs Love', featuring the Hippy Boys' rhythm section. Tubby would also play a lot of Coxsone and Treasure Isle productions, including dubs to popular hits by Phyllis Dillon, the Melodians, and the Techniques, whose 'You Don't Care' became a regular showstopper once he'd transformed it virtually out of recognition by feeding it through his customised reverb and echo. Tubby's resident MC in the early days was U Roy, and the combination of U Roy's jive toasting and Tubby's on-the-spot mixing – not to mention his set's impeccable weight and quality of sound – was unrivalled in the early Seventies, when crowds would often break down fences to get into his open-air dances.

The response to what Tubby was doing was immediate. Randy's engineer Errol Thompson began mixing versions for Joe Gibbs from 1970 onwards, and two years later Tubby was working with Lee Perry (most notably on 'Blackboard Jungle Dub'), Augustus Pablo, Prince Tony Robinson and Glen Brown, who all began experimenting with dub there-after. The list was soon extended to Roy Cousins, Winston Riley, Yabby You, Carlton Patterson and, of course, Bunny Lee, whose flying cymbal sound dominated reggae dancehalls until the Revolutionaries developed rockers at Channel One in mid-1975. By then, King Tubby was the undisputed master of dub and driving around in a brown and beige Ford Cortina GXL4 with K TUBBY registration plates. Philip Smart, Pat Kelly, Prince (later King) Jammys and Scientist all learnt their craft at Tubby's customised mixing board, but none could match the master for the artistry he brought to simple two- and three-chord reggae rhythms. In his hands, dub reggae took on the air of a symphony as he drenched vocals in echo and expanded and contracted instruments in the mix.

Music journalists in England likened King Tubby's mixes to early psychedelia. They weren't far wrong, since it was the experiments of rock musicians like Jimi Hendrix and Pink Floyd that had first alerted Tubby and Lee Perry to what could be achieved by using more daring studio techniques. Perry first heard the Jimi Hendrix Experience's 1967 *Are You Experienced* album while he was in London with the Upsetters, and was immediately blown away by its revolutionary use of reverb and sound effects on tracks like 'Third Stone From The Sun'. Perry would furnish his tracks with mad experimentation in his quest for some cosmic transfiguration, but Tubby was an altogether different kind of dub sorcerer, and the finesse, dynamism, and sheer artistic expression he brought to his mixes were akin to jazz or classical music at times.*

Family Man Barrett: "King Tubby, he was so inventive. He was one of the good scientists from Jamaica and he was one of the best soundmen for pure sound, because he really knew how to play music in the open air. The man was so sensitive to music, too, because he started his own little dub thing, some mix t'ing, and give you a sound you could never get anywhere else.

"He turn that whole house into his studio eventually. He had his lab in there and him always have his transformer round the back, with a radio antenna. He was a well respected man in the area there. A couple of times we give him a tape of Bob's tunes to mix for some sound-system. I don't know whether it was Tippertone or Emperor Faith, because that same sound had three different names, y'know? At first, it was the same Sir Patrick that played with King Tubby. Then it became King Attorney, and finally Socialist Roots. I think it was King Attorney who first get specials by the Wailers, then when it turn Socialist Roots, we give them dub cuts of 'War', 'So Much Things To Say', 'Guiltiness' and 'Running Away'.

"There were three sounds I used to cut dubs of Wailers' songs for in Jamaica. Jah Love, Socialist Roots, and this police sound from Ocho Rios called Soul To Soul. I cut the Soul To Soul dubplates up at Channel One, when I Roy was monitoring things for them. I always give Lloydie Coxsone some exclusive music in those early days too, because all

---

* Rumours continue to abound that Tubby made his own remix of Miles Davis' *Kind Of Blue*, although no copies have as yet surfaced.

them specials me a talk of, me cut them off for him as well. It was Tubby who start it off though and become the first man to play the Wailers on dub."

Johnny Clarke: "King Tubby have this giant sound-system. He would have all these dubplates by people like me, Jacob Miller, Horace Andy, Cornel Campbell, and those guys. We'd go to his studio on the weekend, singing different lyrics to the same rhythm, so he can draw like three pieces of it. If you were a rival soundman, you might find yourself on your knees after hearing like four or five artists on the same rhythm. That was really something back then, as far as sound-system was concerned, except they take it too far after a while. But it was always on a Sunday that we'd go to Tubby's and sing around the mic, giving him all of these different versions . . .

"I never leave King Tubby's, to be honest with you, because even later tunes I produce for myself like 'African People', I do round there. That's because Tubby's come like a form of commotion and he had a lot to do with all those new songs and hits back in them days. His sound-system always have a big following as far as the massive is concerned, because he'd drop some of those tunes on dubplate months before they're released.

"It was like a form of radio station, because when the songs come on the market now, people would rush out to buy them. Those times, people would go a dance to hear pre-release, because there was a difference between the tunes they'd hear a sound-system play and what came out on single or album. It wasn't like nowadays, where the radio station is competing with the sound, because it's the same song them play now. You turn on the radio and then it flood the place 'til it come like nutten, but in those days, if you want fi hear certain selection, yuh haffi go a dance. Yuh haffi go like King Tubby's, because you couldn't turn on your radio and get that. You have some other, more commercial stuff playing on the radio and in discos, but the roots was like an underground music and could only be heard on sounds like King Tubby's Hi Fi. There was a difference between that and a disco, because a disco would mix American soul music with some reggae, only not the hardcore, roots rock reggae like the Wailers would play.

"When you want to hear that now, you'd go a King Tubby's, El Paso with Dennis Alcapone, Tippertone, Arrows, or maybe Emperor Faith. Even V J the Dub Master, who'd string up on the street corner near where I live, in Waltham Park. In those days when a sound was playing, they'd have a steel horn on top of a house or maybe up in a tree and they'd sometimes string up and test them sound from four in the morning. That's why a youth like me haffi get involved in those things, because I'd be sat up in bed, listening to some Alton Ellis or Studio One before me haffi get up for school, so having a man like V J living next door, you can imagine! An' through that, I usually follow his sound around and especially whenever he had a clash with some other man. Like on a Friday, we'd jump up on the truck and go out in the country somewhere, lift all the boxes, and then be ready to pack everything up in the morning. And in those days, we never had any entertainers on the mic either."

It was the response from London sound-systems like Coxsone and Lord David that persuaded Bunny to make Clarke his number one artist during the mid-Seventies. By that time, Channel One on Maxfield Avenue, owned by the Hookims, was the most popular studio in Kingston, and literally hundreds of hits poured out from there during the mid-to-late Seventies. Family Man and Carly didn't appear on sessions there all that often, although Fams did play a role in its early history.

Bunny Lee: "I made the first tune at Channel One, which was Delroy Wilson's 'Can I Change My Mind'. That was in 1973, except Jo Jo Hookim, he was just starting up in the business and so I just pass it over to him. But it was John Holt and myself who make Jo Jo build that studio. Jo Jo used to own a lot of jukeboxes before that and when Channel One first open, Sidney Buckner was their engineer, but he wasn't paying too much attention to the equipment they had in there. He thought certain functions were just decoration, so I carry Fams round there, to show him what can happen. Family Man, he played on 'Can I Change My Mind', but the rhythm was done at Harry J's and I just carry the tape round to Channel One when they were testing the studio, because that's where Delroy voiced it."

Family Man Barrett: "Because of what happened with Island and the fact that my brother and I weren't on the contract, me and [Island publicist] Brent Clarke get tight. I start to travel with my own tape after that and when we were in London for the Catch A Fire tour, I ask him to carry me to a small production studio where I can cut some dubplates. I wanted to make some extra money, because I'd just started to get kids at the time. It was a little after that Brent Clarke and I set up [record label] Atra, which means 'eternal life', because he'd been in London whilst I was in Jamaica and he'd always dreamed of getting involved with music, so I was his starter, y'know? My personal stake in the company was going to be 25 per cent, or that's what I was led to understand, because [Clarke] brought in his brother Sebastian as well, even though he alone was supposed to be involved with it . . .

"Anyway, the two of them came to Jamaica and that's when we went to the studio and recorded those tracks with Winston Jarrett from the Righteous Flames, and Horace Andy. The Khouris who run Federal, they were the ones who were supposed to release the Horace Andy tracks, because a couple of them were playing on the radio in Jamaica, soon after we finish working on the *Catch A Fire* album. We do some work with Keith Hudson, and then Brent Clarke bring in Hugh Mundell, but by then I was so busy, I couldn't do any more sessions again, but had to concentrate on Bob Marley & the Wailers. It was shortly after that I hear Hugh Mundell got shot up, and both of the Clarke brothers died also."

The Horace Andy and Winston Jarrett material, recorded at Randy's, first saw the light of day on an album called *Earth Must Be Hell*. The Mundell tracks would later surface on *Arise*, containing 'Rent Man', 'Mr Big Bad Wolf', 'Nature Provides', and 'Arise And A Shine'. In a bid to emulate *Catch A Fire*, Clarke got Rabbit Bundrick to overdub piano on some of the tracks and Downie and Lindo also contributed keyboards. After final mixing at London's De Lane Lea studios, the album was released in 1974 with production credits split between Brent Clarke and Ashton (sic) Barrett. *Arise* is a solid enough collection, split evenly between the two singers, but apart from the title track, sung by Horace, there's nothing on it resembling the dread roots sound found on recent Wailers' albums. Instead, Clarke and Fams went for a more commercial sound. Jarrett's 'Country Woman' might have even charted had it received better promotion.

Atra also released Keith Hudson's albums including *Flesh Of My Skin*, *Torch Of Freedom* and, most notably, *Pick A Dub*, which author Jon Savage once described as "the greatest dub album ever". It wasn't conceived as a dub album but had been pieced together from rhythm tracks Hudson produced during 1972–73. Family Man was again credited as co-producer, despite the Soul Syndicate playing on certain cuts. The sound of *Pick A Dub* would be hardcore drum and bass, with none of the gimmicks distinguishing dub sets issued by Joe Gibbs or Lee Perry. Apart from snatches of echoed vocals by Big Youth, Horace Andy, or Hudson himself, there's little else by way of decoration. If any evidence were needed that Carlton Barrett was the best reggae drummer in the world, then *Pick A Dub* is as good a place to start as any.

The most celebrated tracks are versions of the Abyssinians' 'Satta

Massagana' and 'Declaration Of Rights' and the manner in which Family
Man and Carly deconstruct them is spine-chilling in their intensity. The
more that is stripped away from the rhythms, the more power seems to be
generated. *Pick A Dub* isn't one-dimensional by any means, however, as
demonstrated on the delightful 'Depth Charge', which Hudson cleverly
saved until last.

Family Man Barrett: "Before we do anything for Keith Hudson, we do
a portion of tunes for Prince Buster, 'cause you know the style that everybody play now, the haul and pull up? We do a whole album like that for
him, where the groove is kind of scratchy. We were creating those things
like 10 years ahead! We used to call Reggie "Boop Man", and that style of
rhythm named after him too. That's when Keith Hudson have this hit
'Riot' by the Soul Syndicate with Fully and them, but me do one after that
called 'Cell Block 11'. Everybody love that movie *Riot In Cell Block 11* in
Jamaica, so when Keith Hudson draw for the Riot, me just draw for the
Cell Block 11. It's Chinna who play on both of them and me give him his
first car for playing on that 45 for me. Oh, and the same guy play trumpet
on the two of them as well, which was Johnny 'Dizzy' Moore, from the
Skatalites.

"Keith Hudson and I get friendly after that because he always had some
good ideas and a great feel for the music as well. He wasn't such a wonderful singer, but him have a good vibes for sure, and he always try hard to get
something different going on. When we did those tracks on *Pick A Dub*, it
was in between *Catch A Fire* and *Natty Dread*, and he had this place on
South Parade, across the square from Randy's. We try to give him a rebel
sound, more than just hits. Tracks with that deep feeling to them, but he
was trying to make it as a singer really, or at least that's what he used to
portray at the time. I play that track 'I Know My Rights' for him. That
was part of the last session what we did for him before he passed, but it
wasn't me personally in control of those sessions for *Pick A Dub*, because I
only produce them for him. They had a different vibes though, for sure."

"Keith Hudson, he was like one of the outcasts in that whole scenario,"
says Junia Walker. "They'd been something between him and Bob for
years, because basically they never talked, so whenever one of the Wailers
would associate with Keith, they took quite a risk, because maybe Bob
wouldn't trust you so much afterwards. That was Carly's situation. Not so
much Fams, even though Keith used to hire both of them in the studio,
but Carly maintained his connections with Keith no matter what, because
there were times when they'd come back from tour and the Wailers

would be on one side of the street and Carly would be on the other with us. Carly was always keeping in touch with everybody else, no matter how they and Bob were getting along. He'd still keep those connections, whereas Fams was more with Bob, but Carly would deal with everybody, just the same.

"Keith was the kind of person who always liked to introduce you to something. That was his attitude, because he was one of the first money-makers in the reggae business really. He wasn't big like Coxsone or Federal, but he started running his own show from early on and he was one of the first independent producers, when most people in Jamaica didn't even know what an independent producer was. He was willing to take his dentist's money and try something, and the more he earned the more he would try and do on a bigger scale. He gained respect from a lot of musicians by being like that and that's how he ended up getting so much good rhythms from them. Because people in the business admired him for what he was doing and every musician wanted to have a hand in it, because they figured that at the end of the day, he was going to bring back some returns and it was going to be uplifting for them. He was creative in his thinking and he was willing to go over to England and push open any door to try and get them more exposure.

"That's what happened with the Jah Woosh song 'I'm Alright', because Keith was getting ready to leave for England and Jah Woosh desperately wanted to get on the tape, since he knew that if Keith left with something, the exposure might bring him bigger rewards, which it did. Keith and Brent Clarke, they fell out after *Flesh Of My Skin*, which Brent Clarke totally financed, although I'm not so sure about *Torch Of Freedom*. Fams and Carly, they were like Keith's supporting team at the time, and I was the one who went to the bank and got the money to pay them after those *Pick A Dub* sessions. I remember Keith telling Family Man a story, just to get him on board in the recording of it, as if it was some kind of joint venture, but then I wasn't sure if the man got paid properly after that. Family Man said he did, so that gave me some satisfaction!

"I was working in Barclays bank at that time and really admired the work Fams and them were doing. And although I couldn't really approach them on my own for productions, Keith would front everything for me, like when I wanted a rhythm, or maybe a mix down at King Tubby's or something. That was how I get King Tubby to do an exclusive cut of 'Satta' for my sound, using the same rhythm Keith had on the *Pick A Dub* album. My sound was called Black Equinox. I played it at mainly parties, or at functions with Third World. This was the same year we both started out, which was 1974. I was the disco and they were the band, and it was their manager who taught me about everything to do with promotion."

Atra was never likely to be a great success, thanks to Clarke's lack of experience and Family Man's growing responsibilities with the Wailers. While working on *Pick A Dub*, Fams persuaded Clarke to license tracks from a young producer called Leonard Chin, who'd been among the first to record Augustus Pablo, along with his good friend Clive Chin. Big Joe's *Jah Guide* and *Down Santic Way*, Augustus Pablo's *Pablo In Dub*, and two sides by Horace Andy, 'Children Of Israel' and 'Problems', all appeared on the label in the period 1973–74, by which time Leonard had left for London and was preparing for a successful spell producing UK lovers' rock.

Leonard Chin: "I remember when Keith Hudson had this tune called 'True, True To Your Heart'. I used to go in there, dancing to it as a small youth and Keith would say, 'Hey, bumbaclaat Santic. I like how you dance man.' Keith and I were cool and a lot of his rough talk was like a joke where he's looking to impress you, but if you don't know him, then it might not seem like such a good act and could easily come like a war t'ing. I was this little youth who never used to mix with certain guys, but he used to have a way about him. A lot of people see him as a badman, but once I get to know him, we used to laugh all the time.

"Keith rented the upstairs part of the Wailers' shop. Family Man and Carly, they were still up the road, working with Upsetter when I first know them, but I'd often see Bob, Peter, and Bunny hanging around outside. This is before the Wailers grew locks and Rita, she was with the Soulettes, then you had the Gaylettes, with Judy Mowatt and two other girls, who were recording songs for Federal. All of them were around at that time, Bob, Peter, Bunny, Rita, Family Man, and his brother. Peter was doing tunes like 'Maga Dog' and 'Can't Blame The Youth' and I used to look up to those people with a whole heap of respect, as a younger youth. I was learning things from them I never plan for and that came just from being around them. I was hanging out at the shop and listening out for tips about recording songs, because that's what I wanted.

"I still remember when we all went to Randy's and recorded that track, 'Children Of Israel'. Family Man was on bass, Carly on drums and Easy Snappin', he played the acoustic piano. It was a good year after that I record *Pablo In Dub*, because I didn't have a rhythm guitar on the first cut. That was overdubbed after a year later whilst *Pablo In Dub* was still in the charts. Leroy Sibbles, he put the rhythm guitar on it for me and he played bass on some of my tracks as well, like the version of 'Harder Shade Of Black', Gregory Isaacs' 'I'll Be Around' and Roman Stewart's 'Peace In The Valley'. Tin Leg played on those and Reggie Lewis was around in those times as well. [Reggie] was still playing with the Barretts back then and these were the people who helped me, because I came into this thing with nothing, as a boy.

"When I was a singer, I had a little band called Umoja. Quite a few of the guys who played in that band used to go to the same school as me in Vineyard Town. The second record I did, I was hanging around with Clive Chin at the time. I was actually taking photographs of the band, because I was an apprentice with the *Gleaner*, but both of us get on well and I end up singing. I kind of pushed them to let me sing a couple of numbers onstage. It was soon after that I get Family and Carly to make me a rhythm, but the first cut of it was by a guy called Jah Mojo and it had an intro featuring this Chinese man talking! I don't know what happened to it, but then I get Pablo to blow some melodica, and call it *Pablo In Dub*.

"In those days, more time me go a session, I'd say, 'Bob, lend me your guitar now,' so Bob Marley would lend me his Gibson and then I'd go pick up Robbie and set off to do something like 'Screaming Target' or a bad set of tune for Bunny Lee."

Self-described "born entrepreneur" 'Gussie' Clarke, who grew up in downtown Kingston around the Beeston Street area, began selling records as a teenager. Before graduating from high school in 1971, Clarke built himself a sound-system, King Gussie's Hi-Fi. His next move was to set up a dub-cutting machine in a shop at 79 Church Street, which did brisk business among sounds like Tippertone and Gemini. While based at Church Street and still only 19, Clarke began producing tracks, beginning with 'The Higher The Mountain', the rhythm for which was used "off the shelf" from Errol Dunkley. For the follow up, Clarke recruited Family Man who took Robbie Shakespeare along with him.

Family Man and Carly played on several sessions for Clarke during this period which provided the backbone of three classic albums: *Presenting I Roy*, an instrumental set called *Black Foundation Dub*, and Big Youth's *Screaming Target*, referred to as "the sensation of 1972" by writer Lorna Cox in the album's liner notes. Big Youth grew up on Princess Street, near the harbour front, and trained as a mechanic after leaving school at 14. He'd been working as a labourer at the site of the Sheraton hotel before taking up the mic and replacing Jah Stitch on Lord Tippertone Hi Fi in March 1971, at I Roy's insistence. Black awareness and social consciousness were an integral part of Big Youth's lyrics and this is what made him so different from other deejays like U Roy, Dennis Alcapone, and I Roy. His emergence made the jive talking style popularised by MCs such as Count Machouki and King Stitt virtually obsolete. Big Youth's propensity for message lyrics, coupled with a preference for the hardest rhythms, would see his fame in Jamaica snowball unchecked for the rest of the decade.

Fams had played on Big Youth's first few releases, beginning with his cut of Errol Dunkley's 'Movie Star', taken from the 'Oh Darling' sessions, followed by 'The Best Big Youth'. This was Big Youth's cut of Dunkley's 'Black Cinderella', played by the Youth Professionals. The deejay then toasted over the Wailers' 'Keep On Moving' for Lee Perry and recorded two songs for Phil Pratt before teaming up with Clarke for 'The Killer' and 'Tippertone Rock'. His next release was 'Chi Chi Run' for Prince Buster, which Family Man also played on. By this time, Youth had recorded 'S90 Skank' for Keith Hudson and the race was on for the top of the Jamaican charts, which the latter finally won in the early part of 1973.

'Screaming Target' was a cut of K. C. White's 'No, No, No (You Don't Love Me)', which Dawn Penn first sang for Studio One, although the song itself originated in the American south, courtesy of R&B singer Willie Cobb. A friend asks Big Youth if he's seen the new Clint Eastwood movie *Dirty Harry*. Jah Youth answers in the affirmative then claims he's seen a movie even better at the Carib Theatre called *Screaming Target*. Just as you're drawn into the pair's drawled patois, Big Youth lets rip with some almighty screams, K. C. White croons the chorus and the rhythm kicks in, hard as nails. It's a piece of great theatre and an unforgettable record, produced by someone who'd only been out of school two years. Clarke produced some remarkable, alternative versions of 'Screaming Target', including a wild, gypsy violin cut by the Simplicity People, and Augustus Pablo's 'Oregon Style'.

Clive Chin and Errol "E T" Thompson produced Pablo's debut album, *This Is Augustus Pablo*, featuring Family Man on most of the tracks, including two licensed from Santic. His presence ensured the album had the required, deep roots sound to make it popular with young reggae fans, and Pablo's reflective meanderings were underpinned with music of real weight and substance. Most of Chin's productions were issued on the same Randy's label his father had started in the Sixties, although he would later form two of his own, Wisdom and One-Way Sounds. The family had switched to Impact around the time Java was released, and 'Too Late', 'Guiding Red', and 'Dub Organiser' were all issued on the distinctive orange label with its big exclamation mark while Fams was touring overseas with the Wailers. There's a free and easy charm to these productions that Pablo never quite recaptured.

Clive Chin: "Carly was an extremely nice person. That's my recollection of him, whereas Family Man was always fairly reserved by comparison and more quiet. They were two brothers with very different personalities, because Carly was creative in a different sense to Family Man. He certainly had the capability of doing it, but he just didn't exercise it in the same kind of way as Fams did. Take, for example, when I started with the rebel rock sound back in the early Seventies. I didn't use Carly, because I used Tin Leg. The reason I used Tin Leg was because the two of them had very different styles and to me, as an up-and-coming producer, I liked the different combination I got by mixing the sounds of Family Man's bass and Tin Leg's drums. They were very creative and innovative, and my recollection is that you could direct Tin Leg. You could prompt him as to how you wanted him to play, whereas with Carly, you just had to go with the flow."

Family Man also played on Errol Dunkley's 'Created By The Father' and Hortense Ellis' 'Woman Of The Ghetto', in addition to her brother Alton's 'Too Late To Turn Back Now', which Pablo also versioned. The original was by the Cornelius Brothers but the Randy's interpretation is wonderfully understated and sung with such grace by Alton.

Clive Chin: "When I used to cover the American songs, we always used to try and make them different. I mean there are some songs we did cover identically at Randy's, but I myself tried to do them differently, whereas when Derrick Harriott covered 'Shaft' with the Chosen Few, you couldn't tell it apart from the original! There wasn't a rhythm guitar on 'Too Late', the rhythm was a cheese grater, y'know? But that's what made the record so exciting."

'Too Late' also features a blast of reverb just as the vocals start to fade, that people used to cheer whenever sound-systems played it in blues dances.

Clive Chin: "Oh yes! And yet that was a mistake, because when we were doing the final mix, it was a Sunday evening and Errol Thompson and myself were there. 'Too Late' is running from the multi-track down to the quarter inch tape and the reverb was already set, but I just push it up more, so that's where that spontaneous surge of reverb came from. Then when me hear it, I just pull it back down real quick. I was listening to it on a big monitor and get the fright of my life!

"Those were happy days, really and truly. It wasn't like now, where you just programme something. We were dealing with creativity, because in those days we used to have to mic up everything. At one time, we'd use an overhead mic that would have to take everything. That was in the days of Lloyd Knibs and Drumbago when you had the voice on one track, and the rhythm on the other, so if anyone made a mistake, you'd have to re-record the whole thing. We go over to four-track after that. That was in the early Seventies, because you had drum and bass; you had rhythm, you have a voice track, and you have a horns track. That's why I always say that those times were the best in terms of creativity, because you'd record something and just release it straight away. Nowadays you tend to get a bit hesitant about it. You remix, revoice, and the by the time the song comes out, it doesn't appeal to you anymore. When we used to voice Dennis Brown, Alton Ellis or whoever, we would just get it done there and then. There was no coming back tomorrow or next week, because if they came back the next day, they'd have a totally different vibe."

Spontaneity was at the heart of what Clive calls "rebel music", which sought to make some kind of statement both lyrically and musically, as well as fulfilling the usual criteria of making hit records. The only trouble was that local radio stations didn't want to be seen promoting Rasta music played by "blackheart men", and were reluctant to play them. Bob Marley was nowhere near to being enshrined as a cultural icon and the few outlets that did play roots music were usually in rundown areas that tended to attract violence.

Clive Chin: "The music needed to change anyway, because right after rocksteady, there was a period of reggae where the music was really chopping. That was down to the Hippy Boys, not even the Upsetters, because this was in 1969 and virtually everything that came out back then was real up-tempo. After a while, some of us younger guys felt there had to be a change and so we started to experiment with something a bit different. Instead of all those fast beats, we went for a more down-tempo sound, based around two chords. That was the beginning of the rebel era and it was more of a Jamaican sound, because we began to get away from some of that American soul influence."

With a cavernous, grumbling bassline (from Family Man) and stripped-down arrangement, Horace Andy's 'Problems', produced by Leonard Chin, couldn't have been further removed from the sophisticated soul records being made in the US at that time. While the Wailers were heeding the emergence of War and absorbing Stevie Wonder's innovations, it was sweet soul songs like the Spinners' 'Could It Be I'm Falling In Love', the Stylistics' 'Break Up To Make Up' and Diana Ross' 'Touch Me In The Morning' that were most popular with local record buyers. While favouring the heavy roots sound, Family Man continued to play music in a variety of styles and took a keen interest in acts like Rufus, Labi Siffre, and the Pointer Sisters, whose 'Yes We Can Can' always got a good reception whenever the deejays at one of New Kingston's uptown discos gave it a spin. It was this open-minded versatility that ensured Fams' continuing popularity as a session man as well as being indispensable to Marley's vision of creating authentic roots reggae music for a crossover audience.

Shortly after releasing the original cut of Dennis Brown's 'Money In My Pocket' (produced by Niney the Observer), Joe Gibbs invited Family Man to his studio in Duhaney Park to start work on Brown's debut album for the label. The young singer was still attending St Stephen's College at the time, but had already become another Jamaican child star in the same tradition as Delroy Wilson. Seeco Patterson had stopped by Joe Gibbs' studio on the day Family Man was there and overheard some people talking at the gate.

Seeco Patterson: "Me hear the man them a talk and them say, 'Oh, see Bob Marley bass man deh pon a session with Dennis Brown? Bob Marley bass man!' Them just wave as them see this little brown car come fly inna the place and then every man gather round there that day. Man a eat food, drink coconut water and smoke herb, because they all say Bob Marley bass man is the greatest inna Jamaica . . ."

Family Man Barrett: "Them times we haffi let off money fi food and all that before we a work. I'd been there when they played the test press of 'Money In My Pocket', and my sessions with Dennis came right after that. I played rhythm guitar and I had Robbie with me on bass. I don't remember which songs we did, but I remember the cover, because him have on a vest and straight hat like a beaver turned to the side and you could see three pictures of him, side by side. It was the first album Joe Gibbs produced with Dennis Brown but when I first hear it I say, 'Why did they mix the guitar so loud?' I can recall the guitar really blasting, so I know it by the jacket, and I know it by the sound."

Gibbs released Brown's album, rather unimaginatively titled *Best Of Vol. 1*, shortly after the singer's first tour of England in late 1974. A mix of sentimental ballads and covers including 'The Poor Side Of Town' (a US hit for Johnny Rivers in 1966), Lobo's 'Don't Expect Me To Be Your Friend', Ken Boothe's 'Silver Words' and Nat King Cole's 'Pretend', Brown contributed 'Let Me Live', 'We Will Be Free', 'My Kind', 'Summertime' and 'Westbound Train', produced by Niney the Observer. Family Man's old flatmate would soon produce a slew of other hits for Brown, including 'Cassandra', 'I Am The Conqueror' and 'No More Will I Roam' which led to *Swing* magazine voting him Producer of the Year in late 1974. The following year Niney released *Live At The Turntable*, featuring Brown, Big Youth, and Delroy Wilson, Brown's album *Just Dennis*, and *Dubbing With The Observer*.

It had been Niney who'd taken Family Man to see Gibbs in early 1973, although the convivial atmosphere wouldn't last much longer.

"No, because at that time, I was working with Bunny Lee in the days and Joe Gibbs at night," says Niney, "but it couldn't work 'cause a man would say, 'What you do? Take a song and give it to Joe Gibbs?' Everybody work with Joe Gibbs though and not only myself but also Scratch and Bunny Lee, because Bunny was the man who start Joe Gibbs. But when Joe Gibbs first built his studio, I was with him every day. I bring Dennis Brown there 'cause I never produce him for myself yet and also the Heptones. And it was me who produced Franco Nero for him as well."

Brown was also a friend of Little Roy and had guested with him and Leroy Sibbles on 'Righteous Man'. Together with 'Nyah Medley', the tune had heralded Little Roy's return to the studio after the period spent hiding from Matador Daley after being dragged out of the Bunny Lee session at Matador's insistence more than a year previously. Little Roy had formed a Rasta label called Tafari with brothers Maurice and Melvin "Munchie" Jackson, who'd warmed to the task by producing the Heptones' 'Revolution'.

Tafari's first two productions were released on the Hepic label, owned by Leroy Sibbles and a disc jockey called David MacKenzie. Both tracks were recorded at Randy's with Family Man and Carly. One was Little Roy's 'Mr T' and the other was 'Free For All', an instrumental tune featuring Family Man on keyboards. Maurice Jackson initially helped finance the project although his brother Munchie, who'd recently returned to Kingston after working with Lloyd Barnes in New York, would soon join him. Like Little Roy, both Jackson brothers hailed from Whitfield Town but were living in Washington Gardens when Tafari started. The Jacksons' mother was contracted to supply food and drink to Kingston's hospital and prisons, and her house at 17 Coleyville Avenue became the label's unofficial headquarters. For obvious reasons, given the amount of boxes in the place, they called it the Packing House. The equipment wasn't particularly good but the brothers could experiment as the mood took them.

Most of the tracks they recorded there were little more than demos, except there was an inveigling spirituality to some of Little Roy's tracks, which were later released on an album called *Tribal War*. The idea was for Barnes to issue Tafari material in New York, and the Little Roy songs 'Prophesy' and 'Tribal War' duly became their first two releases in the US (or anywhere else for that matter). Munchie produced 'Tribal War', 'Blackbird', and 'Mr T', which Brown versioned as 'Set Your Heart Free'. After a while, Lee Perry, who lived just round the corner from the Packing House, also became involved with Tafari. He engineered 'Prophesy' at Randy's for the Jacksons and 'Tribal War' at Black Ark, which is where Little Roy voiced 'Jah Count On I'.

Little Roy: "Upsetter had given us the rhythms for 'Forward On A Yard' and 'Revolution', so I recorded 'Don't Cross The Nation' and another song for him in return. Munchie had a sound-system and a reel-to-reel tape recorder in there, so that's where it all started from really and then we used to keep our own dances some evenings. We had a sound called Tafari and Munchie used to play it up by Waltham Park Road occasionally. We weren't a competition sound. It was more like a home sound really but then when it came to recording, we'd have the rhythm all ready and then just voice on the reel-to-reel. It was a two-track, so we had the rhythm on one track and we'd voice on the other. Songs like 'Ticket To Zion' were voiced like that and there was more vibes in the Packing House than some studios, except we'd use Randy's for tracks like 'Free For All' and 'Mr T'. They were laid with Family Man, Carly, and Rannie Bop, with Leroy Sibbles on piano and Ossie Hibbert playing organ.

"The Packing House situation lasted about two years altogether. The line-up of people that passed through there was amazing really, because you'd get members of the Wailers, Lee Perry, Marcia Griffiths, Gregory Isaacs, Keith Hudson, the Heptones, Dennis Brown . . . They didn't all record there but people were always dropping by. I also sang a track for Lloyd Charmers around that time and which later appeared on the *Tribal War* album. Munchie and Lloyd Barnes put it out, but they only pressed 500 copies because I rebel, saying those songs weren't quite up to standard."

To capitalise on the interest generated by *Tribal War*, other labels were quick to produce their own versions of the song, just as they'd done with Little Roy's previous hit, 'Bongo Nyah'. They didn't always credit the rightful copyright owner either, which left Little Roy struggling to reclaim some of his songs in later years.

Little Roy: "That's why my career get in such a fight, because if certain people couldn't reap from you, they'd try and lock you from the radio. It's like they're paying guys to not play your one and if you have a good song, then they'll just lick it over with a next artist. Now that I'm older, I get to see that it's a syndicate of people who kept the door nailed shut from the inside. That's how they stayed on top as Jamaica's only producers and all of them carried guns too. That's why the business became so radical and a lot of us artists started to produce ourselves, except we weren't really aware of what we were getting ourselves into. People used to rate some of these producers highly but most of them had ties with the police and only certain artists were let through. That's why you haffi be a hard fighter, y'know? Yeah man!"

'Hard Fighter' was another stirring Little Roy/Family Man collaboration, produced by Matador, and just one of a string of gems sung by this little-heralded singer. Rasta people were searching for ways to harness that same cultural explosion Leonard Chin described, although cracks were already beginning to appear in the utopian vision of Rastafari portrayed in songs like 'Hallelujah Time', 'Pass It On', and 'One Foundation'. "You think it's the hair on your head, make you dreader than dread?" asks Junior Byles on 'Rasta No Pickpocket', going on to proclaim "Rasta nah dwell in sin," because "Rasta nah commit no crime, Rasta love divine." Byles wrote the song after he and Perry heard reports about some dreadlocked youths who'd been caught robbing people downtown. Family Man didn't play on the song but recalls it being commented on among the Wailers' circle particularly the lines, "Throw me corn, me nah call no fowl. You pick it up already. Who the cap fit, him haffi to wear it."

Tracks like 'Rasta No Pickpocket' and, later on, Dennis Brown's 'Wolves And Leopards' exposed a growing awareness among astute Rastafarians that not all who were drawn to the cause were heeding the faith's essential precepts or codes of behaviour. The ranks of wanted criminals, known as "beardsmen", who took refuge in the Rasta camps, were now swelling. Becoming a Rasta meant adopting the right moral code, yet there were plenty of youths who had seized upon the militant, dread look but were forgetting the message. As Byles points out, the good inevitably "suffer along with the bad."

CHAPTER SIXTEEN

Rebel Music

BY late 1973, the Wailers had transformed into a promising touring act with major label backing and a burgeoning reputation among overseas rock fans. Their records had been reviewed in mainstream publications like *Rolling Stone* and they had performed live on radio and television in both Britain and America, reaching audiences many of their Jamaican contemporaries could only dream of.

Marley returned from England accompanied by Lee Jaffe, whose plans to go to Chile to make a film had been stymied by the overthrow of Salvador Allende in September. Perry Henzell had offered to lend him the equipment but Jaffe couldn't find a backer so he decided to spend more time in Jamaica, being around musicians he considered, "articulate, powerful, focused on where they wanted to go and the message that they had and how to get it out there." What he encountered completely bowled the filmmaker over.

"I couldn't think that any other mission could be more important," Jaffe wrote in his book *One Love: Life With Bob Marley And The Wailers*. "I knew they were not going to compromise to get a hit record. It was the most fierce, pure attitude I had ever been confronted with and it left me very humble. I had always considered my work radical and to meet the Wailers and sense the enormity of what they were doing . . . Well, I just wanted to be a part of that."

Jaffe described Bob and Esther Anderson as "the most amazing couple, they were awesome! When you saw them together, the visual thing of it was so intense. They were just so compelling, you couldn't look at them and their personalities were so intense. You know, Esther never stopped talking. It was chic to be politically radical, especially in the circles that Esther was rolling in, because obviously she was always the outsider, so she had to be the voice of the people. So here was this guy, the poet from the ghetto, and it was just a natural thing for her to be with him."

At every opportunity, the couple would drive to Negril, where they were building a house made from local timber, thatched with palm fronds. Jaffe would often join them as they drove out of Kingston, through Spanish Town and May Pen, following the twisting country roads on their way to the west coast. Reading Jaffe's book one gets the impression he was very close to Marley, and yet there are those who recall Marley beating him and ordering him to do menial work.

Junia Walker: "Yeah, Bob used to treat him rough. It's like Lee Jaffe come to Jamaica thinking he was going to have this bed of roses and yet in the evening, Bob would just throw him the broom and tell him to sweep up the shop. That's how Bob handle the man, because he was some kind of hippy, I seem to remember . . ."

A number of people connected with the Wailers have said this was the happiest period of Marley's life, and there's certainly enough photographic evidence to support this. At Anderson's invitation, he was currently lodging at 56 Hope Road. "Cindy Breakspeare moved in with her brother Mike, who we call Reds," Family Man recalls. "I remember Reds used to ride a bike, because we used to joke about, 'There goes Mike on his bike.' But Dickie Jobson's sister Diane used to run the Island offices and we'd sometimes be asked to keep the door of the rehearsal studio closed because of the noise we were making. That's due to the fact it was uptown and the whole area was so quiet."

Chris Blackwell never actually lived there and often stayed elsewhere when he was on the island. Rita and her four children never lived there either, as Bob kept his family life separate, although Rita would occasionally drive into Kingston from Bull Bay, just to be a part of what was happening. Bob had spent time with other women before but Anderson was an altogether different kind of threat, since she was beautiful, intelligent and famous, nothing at all like Rita's previous rivals in Trenchtown.

Anderson's brother, Winston, was a Rasta as well as a farmer and had devised an early form of vaporiser used for smoking herb. The smoke would be drawn through a bamboo water pipe and whoever inhaled on it received a concentrated blast of strong Jamaican collie that even Marley found heavy going. Family Man recalls Livingston and Lindo using it a lot and claims the latter often couldn't handle it, which caused arguments between Marley and Livingston. Marley was concerned that Lindo should cut down on smoking herb, whereas Livingston defended the keyboard player's right to smoke as much as he liked, without interference from anyone, let alone a Rasta. Family Man had noted Lindo's fondness for drugs during the Burnin' tour and recalls how they'd sometimes go to a club or party but would leave as soon as any cocaine ("nose candy") was passed round, except Lindo would slip out of the hotel and head back there when he thought no one had noticed.

Lindo duly parted company with the Wailers around the same time as Tosh, saying he'd received an offer to join Taj Mahal's band and was off to San Francisco with American percussionist Larry MacDonald. With hindsight, Fams realises that Lindo's mental condition wasn't stable even then, although it would develop into something more troubling when he returned to the Wailers' fold.

As relations between Marley, Livingston, and Tosh broke down, the bond between Marley and the Barretts strengthened. While he was in need of support, the Barretts were earning good money as session musicians and commissions were plentiful. Not having their names on the Island contract still rankled but Marley had treated the brothers well, both on a business and personal level and the musical chemistry within the band was solid enough to override this detail for the present time.

"Esther Anderson, she was the one who who talked to Bob about getting the first option on the property at 56 Hope Road for us," Family Man recalled in 2006, "so that was a good thing which come out of it . . . The deal involved Bob, and then me and my brother . . . we were happy leaving him to deal with the paperwork, because we trusted him for sure and it was all part of the partnership we had, like this dream of turning Tuff Gong into a little Motown . . .

"Chris Blackwell came to Hope Road one day in late 1973, or maybe early 1974. Bob was talking with him and my friend Gladstone 'Gabby' Williams and I heard Chris say he didn't know what the future would hold, now that Peter and Bunny had left. Gabby then said to Chris, 'Don't worry, Family Man and Carly will put the band back together.' Soon after this, I was with Bob and Carly at the back of Island House in the courtyard, in the shade of the mango tree. We were discussing what had happened and Bob asked me what I thought we should do. I said we should form a new band, the three of us, because this is the power of the trinity. Bob asked me what our first move should be and I told him I would rearrange the music room to make it into a demo studio, so that we could record our new concept of lyrics and music and then listen back to it before going in the studio. Bob and Carly agreed that we should form a new band and I should get on with setting up the demo studio.

"After our discussions, I installed a cassette deck and two reel-to-reel tape machines in the music room to create demo tapes. We also had an early form of drum machine called a Rhythm King I had bought on a trip to America. Shortly afterwards, Bob went and booked some studio time and that's when we begin to write, rehearse and record the tracks we later include on the *Natty Dread* album. This wasn't with Peter Tosh or Bunny Wailer, but with Aston and Carlton Barrett taking their place as Wailers. That was when we started writing songs like 'War', 'Talkin' Blues', 'Them Belly Full', 'Want More' and 'Rebel Music (3 O'Clock Roadblock).' Those songs came to us quickly and they come to us just at the right time because the blessings were flowing and people around us, they could see what we were trying to do. We had this feeling that nothing could stop us at that time, because Jah will must be done, even though we were being watched by many different eyes, whether it was Island, or people who'd already dropped out. It was then we realised there is really no end to this music and that nothing could really stop us as we worked to get the music established and to find its rightful place."

The Barretts' experience of the international market and expertise in musical arranging ensured Marley's songs mainstream appeal. Yet Rita Marley and Chris Blackwell would later decribe the brothers as "hired sidemen" of little importance. "Following Bunny and Peter's departure, the band comprised Bob Marley and a group of backing musicians which changed from time to time," Blackwell stated in a court affidavit. "The backing musicians were not equal members of the band in the same way that Bunny and Peter had been and they did not contribute to songwriting and recording in the same way either."

Blackwell did admit that Family Man was an important member of the band, "because he played the bass guitar, a key element of reggae music." He also admitted that Marley trusted Fams' ears, and so the bassist was often present at the mixing of the Wailers' recordings. He denied, however, that Family Man was regarded as the band's foreman or musical director. "It was Bob's music and he was in charge."

"Bob told me he'd spoken to Chris and told Carly and I we were going to do a new album," said Family Man in 2006. "Bob booked the studio and, as far as I'm aware, he paid for the studio time and the tapes from money paid to him by Island Records as part of our advance. We started laying down tracks for this album at Harry J's studio, after having done the original creative work on the lyrics and the melodies for the songs in the music room. As we were working on these songs, we agreed that we needed to get a fuller sound and we also needed someone to play instead of

'Wya', who we couldn't find. We also agreed to bring in some extra backing musicians to help complete the recording. Bob asked me to find two musicians, so I introduced Gladstone "Gladdy" Anderson to play piano and Winston Wright to play organ. Bob brought in Tommy McCook and a musician known to me as "Bubbles" to play tenor sax and trombone respectively. They were all brought in and paid by Bob as session musicians.*

"Bob later told me he'd again spoken to Chris and said they'd decided to call our new group Bob Marley & the Wailers. Carly and I were happy with that name. Bob, Carly, and I then had further discussions in the music room at Island House and agreed we would split all the money we earned together as Bob Marley & the Wailers equally; that Bob would look after the business side of things and deal with Island Records and that I would be responsible for the band and the music. Bob said that Peter and Bunny had their names on the contract and yet the two whose names weren't on the contract had stayed. Because of this, he said he would negotiate a new contract with Island Records with all three of our names on it. We also agreed that the royalty payable on each new album should go up."

In the New Year, Family Man set up the recording equipment in the rehearsal room and began balancing the sound levels while Marley drove downtown to West Indies studio where he met up with Lee Perry and an English journalist called Chris Lane. Scratch had invited the teenager to Jamaica after being interviewed for *Black Music* magazine and had clearly re-established his friendship with Marley, who overdubbed vocals on two Upsetter rhythms. Lane, who would later run the Dub Vendor record shop and the Fashion label with John McGillvray as well as becoming one of Britain's most successful reggae producers, recalls the session as being good-spirited and while the tracks recorded ('Turn Me Loose', 'Keep On Skanking') weren't anything special, there's a coded message to Tosh and Livingston on the latter. "You can't get the truth out of our hearts," he tells them, "and you can't make the finish, if you didn't start."

Bunny Lee: "Peter and Bunny couldn't wait to become stars, because they used to call Chris Blackwell 'Whitewell' and were always looking for

---

* Much to their chagrin, Anderson, Wright, Bubbles, and Dennis "Ska" Campbell weren't officially credited for their contributions to *Natty Dread*, and nor were McCook and Vin Gordon, who are also believed to have played horns on several tracks.

him to give them some money whenever he came to Jamaica. After they left, it was Fams who encouraged Bob to get some people and form the Wailers."

As signatories to the first contract, Tosh and Livingston were still receiving money from Island which the Barretts found irksome, since it was they and Marley who continued to provide the two ex-Wailers with an income.

Family Man Barrett: "When Bunny and Peter depart from the group, that's when we start laying the tracks for *Natty Dread*. We step it up in every way too. Not only musically, but also in the lyrics, because they became more political. It's like we make that step up not only on the outside, but also on the inside, and that's down to the other two having left as well. It's like the fire was burning from the inside out, because Peter and Bunny thought we were making a mistake by being around this white man's place but we were there because of what we wanted to achieve and get done. We had our focus on that.

"It's like the three of them had a long-term problem from Trenchtown. Not a problem exactly but a vibes. When the split happened, it had been coming for a while and the reasons for it were beyond my knowledge, since I didn't concern myself with their arguments, except I still watch to make sure Bob come through safely. All I can say is that the others were supposed to know what we started out to do and yet they seemed to forget about it, because both of them stopped along the way. It helped clear the atmosphere once they'd left, but when those three was quarrelling, it get me real downhearted. It's like them give up the struggle and so we haffi say no way, our will must be done."

"Me no want to say this but me little bit tense with the Wailers we have first time, with Bunny and Peter," Marley was quoted in the book *Bob Marley: In His Own Words*. "Is like them don't want understand one can't just play music for Jamaica alone and you can't learn that way. Me get the most of my learning when me travel and talk to other people. That was a kind of worry me have and why me never so loose before."

Sometime in January 1974, Tosh went into the rehearsal room at Hope Road and started dragging an amplifier out the door when Marley stopped him, saying that if he was planning on going it alone, then he must leave everything behind. The atmosphere was strained, yet despite the imposing Tosh physically having the upper hand he eventually backed down and left, carrying his guitar and mumbling obscenities. While Tosh and Marley remained friends and even performed together a few times after this incident, Tosh ceased to be a Wailer and neither his nor Livingston's name would appear on the revised Island contract.

Junia Walker: "Peter used to call Chris Blackwell a vampire. He'd curse him bad and it was that that break up the whole Wailers, because Peter decided he couldn't abide him. The way Peter told it, it was like Bob just wanted to get ahead and he'd sold his soul to gain the whole world. It came like that. There was a big blow-up downtown, because Peter was so adamant about not dealing with Blackwell, but it seems that Bob decided, 'Hey, this is my future,' y'know? But it was a big controversy at the time. Peter was cursing Blackwell in the worst kind of way and yet few of us even knew who he was at that time . . .

"It shouldn't have happened though. They should have all stuck together from day one, throughout all the ups, the downs . . . Just Peter, Bob and Bunny and I think it's like a partial curse to the whole world of reggae that this didn't happen. By the time they broke up, Peter and Bunny were gradually starting to get themselves out of it in any case. Bunny had started Solomonic and Peter had his own Intel-Diplo label and the two of them were selling their own records through the Wailers' shop anyhow. Because of this situation now, it was like two different camps . . .

"It's like Bob had to make a new following and so he started to make new friends, because he'd lost his original crowd when he decided to go off with those [Island Records] people. Because you had people who loved Peter and who loved Bunny and them could never take onto what Bob was doing with Island. To a lot of people, it looked as though Bob was just into making a lot of money and he'd deserted them."

Fams doesn't necessarily blame these outside influences. The way he sees it, Tosh and Livingston lacked the flexibility, discipline and determination required in continuing with the Wailers' original vision. However, it's difficult to imagine the lines in 'Talkin' Blues', "Your feet is too big for your shoes" and "So who's going to stay at home, when the freedom fighters are fighting?" being directed at anyone else.

Family Man Barrett: "The words to 'Talkin' Blues' are so true to life, because after Peter and Bunny left, they didn't realise how hard it was for us. They left us lying on the ground as 56 Hope Road wasn't under our control then. It was still owned by Chris Blackwell, so we'd crash round the back more time in between rehearsals. We'd spread some crocus bags on the floor, or sleep on the roof in those days. We'd lie on our backs, looking up at the sky and the stars, meditating. Either that or we'd sit around, playing our guitars and working out new songs. We were glad to be there still, as it was a place where we could smoke herb in peace and safety, since no police would come around there. But that's where lyrics like, 'Cold ground was our bed last night and rock stone was our pillow' came from, because there was nothing of ours there at that stage."

'Talkin' Blues' was one of several songs whose authorship was contested in the court case Family Man brought against Universal-Island Records Limited and the Marley estate in 2006.

"Bob, Carly and I jammed together in the music room to develop the melody and lyrics and bring out the sound," he stated in his court testimony. "Then the other musicians joined us at Harry J's, where we laid down the basic tracks. When we were in the music room, a friend of Bob's, Leghorn Coghill was there too and also [keyboard player] Ian Winter, who was living at 56 Hope Road and who I allowed to join in playing the music sometimes . . . Carly's songs were 'Talkin' Blues', 'Them Belly Full' and 'Revolution'. I was with him when these were first created in the music room and taped there. He sang the words and melody for each song, which was developed through the jamming process by the three of us and then later at Harry J's studio with the full band, where the master tapes were made ready for final mixing and overdubbing."

Winter, a young musician who Fams invited to Hope Road after a chance meeting at Robbie Shakespeare's house, claimed in his evidence to have been present in the music room when 'Talkin' Blues' was written. He recalled Family Man and Carly talking about Tosh and Livingston leaving the group and confirmed it was Carly who originated the phrases, "Talkin' blues," and "Their feet is too big for those shoes." At first he stated Marley wasn't there when it was written but then changed his mind and said Marley and Carly worked on the song together.

Lee Jaffe, on the other hand, remembers Marley writing the song at Rita's house in Bull Bay, after Jaffe had slept overnight on the porch. Marley woke him early the next morning singing the first few lines of the song, "Cold ground was my bed last night and rock stone was my pillow too." Jaffe then got up and started playing his harmonica. He says Marley worked on the song for some weeks before it was finally recorded. Jaffe also claimed that he'd been trying to interest Marley in blues music and had made him cassettes of various tracks, including a song called 'Walkin' Blues'. It's not known whether Howlin' Wolf's 1969 recording 'Hard Luck' was on that tape, but with lyrics like, 'Well rocks is my pillow, cold ground is my bed," the Wolf might well have been the inspiration for 'Talkin' Blues'.

According to Jaffe, Rita was up and about, getting the children ready for school by the time he and Bob worked on the song, but neither she nor any of the Marley children have ever verified this account.

'Talkin' Blues' wasn't the only song inspired by the Wailers' changed circumstances. Family Man says 'Them Belly Full' was also written in response to Tosh and Livingston's departure and that it was Carly who came up with the words. Winter remembers Carly philosophising about political events in Jamaica while tapping out a rhythm as he talked. Two years into Manley's tenure as Prime Minister, economic hardships were affecting rich and poor alike. Revolution was in the air and as the lyrics of 'Them Belly Full' explain, "a hungry mob is an angry mob," since "pot a cook, but it nuh nuff." Winter and another Hope Road regular, Legon Coghill, a.k.a. Leghorn, an artist who used to help distribute records for Tuff Gong, contributed to the song's basic outline as the Barrett brothers began to jam, while Carly kept repeating the phrase, 'Them belly full, but we hungry." Winter asserted that Marley hadn't arrived by the time he, Leghorn, Carly, and Family Man completed the song's basic structure.

Junia Walker: "Leghorn was the guy who painted the inside of Bob's shop on Beeston Street. The last time I saw Leghorn, he told me he'd never received anything for that song, but in those days, if you wrote something you'd take it to Bob, because he was the singer and he'd take care of you. And whilst Bob himself was alive, it was easy for him to point out these people and then reward them. When him not around, then it's a totally different thing, because you need the original people around to say what really happened . . ."

Rita Marley disputed Leghorn was a musician or songwriter, regardless of the fact that he and Carly were credited with co-writing 'Talkin' Blues', 'Them Belly Full' and 'Revolution' on *Natty Dread*. Leghorn would later claim sole authorship of 'Them Belly Full' while Skill Cole swore in an affidavit that he co-wrote it with Marley. In his evidence, Jaffe claims Marley wrote the song after they'd been discussing the division between Jamaica's rich and poor on their way home from Port Royal. He says the song had nothing to do with Tosh and Livingston leaving the band and, indeed, they were still members of the Wailers when it was written.

The judge Mr Justice Lewison preferred Jaffe's evidence and found that Marley composed and authored 'Talkin' Blues', 'Them Belly Full' and 'Revolution'.

★   ★   ★

Now that they were able to record demos, Marley and the Barretts would tape their impromptu jam sessions and distil whatever developed of interest. This refining process was left up to Family Man, who would work on the arrangements, deciding what instruments to use in bringing the songs to life. Marley was a primitive musician and therefore couldn't match the Barretts in this respect.

Family Man Barrett: "We always start off recording the bass and drum and then the acoustic piano, because we have to get those instruments right before we start overdubbing synthesisers and all that. We get an original sound doing it that way and then we can bring in other stuff. When we record *Natty Dread*, Wya wasn't around, so it was mainly Touter who played keyboards. I'd invite him up to 56 Hope Road, although on songs like 'Talkin' Blues', I myself play piano and Bob plays rhythm guitar and then I get this horn section man from the Skatalites, Ska Campbell and have him right between the rhythm guitar and keyboards. 'Revolution' has that same combination too. One time Sly Dunbar saw me at the studio and asked me how I get that sound and I say, 'That's Mr Campbell on the baritone sax,' because it a grumble and go 'round it. Yeah and these modern musics need some of that treatment too."

While the Wailers were not opposed to working during daylight hours, they preferred recording in the evenings at Harry J's. This wasn't only because they were nightbirds, but also due to other, more practical reasons.

Family Man Barrett: "Night was when all the factories and the businesses close down and so we get a more steady flow of current. We might get power cuts or power surges otherwise, so we are always there, working on the night shift. Or the graveyard shift, as some would call it, like rat pack patrol! I remember one time the whole place shut down, so after that now, Harry J set up a generator and them did have it set pon automatic, so any time the main power supply get cut off, that chip in. The only thing is, this wasn't so good for the equipment, so we always turn it off the automatic and then start it up if the power goes, before switching it back on. Because when it shut off and the other one start up, it would come in with such a heavy force that nuff people get frightened, me tell you! Yeah and them haffi make sure to stabilise that transformer, unless it get burnt out too . . ."

Harry J's wasn't the best studio in Jamaica but, power cuts aside, it provided the right sound for what the band wanted. They also liked the fact that they could work there in relative peace. Wailers sessions weren't casual affairs and so people were disinclined to visit the studio unless they had a reason to be there or had been specially invited. This was not the case at other Kingston studios like Channel One, where there was always a mass of people gathered in the control room. Marley and the Barretts were far too disciplined to suffer that kind of arrangement and apart from Sylvan Morris and assorted session musicians they had Harry J's to themselves for the most part.

'Natty Dread' was not only the first track to be recorded for the album but also the first Wailers track to be graced by the harmonies of the I-Threes, consisting of Rita, Marcia Griffiths and Judy Mowatt. Griffiths came up with the name "I-Three" because, in her words, the I-Three, "became like one, mentally, spiritually and emotionally. We shared a lot of things together as sisters and found that we grooved beautifully."

Rita, along with Skill Cole, are credited as the song's writers, and while both were admittedly well versed in Trenchtown's realities, it seems doubtful they possessed the poetic genius needed to pen such a remarkable song in which Marley journeys through a Trenchtown steeped in metaphor. Following the colonial model, Kingston, like New York City, is built according to a grid system. The streets mainly run parallel to one another and are often named in sequence. Heading south from Greenwich Park Road, where the Marleys stayed with Rita's Aunt Viola, the streets descend in numerical order, beginning with Fourteenth Street, and ending with First Street, running parallel to the Spanish Town Road. Marley's words are clearly aimed at Rastafarians as he talks of being "one thousand miles away from home" (Ethiopia) and urges them to get their culture. "Don't stay there and jester, or the battle will be hotter, and you won't get no supper," he warns, before promising that, "I and I gonna have things our way." Once again, Marley outlined the plight of the sufferer, or in this case, the Rastaman, and turned it into a song of eventual triumph.

Family Man Barrett: "After 'Natty Dread' itself, we record 'Talkin' Blues', 'Revolution' and 'Rebel Music (3 O'Clock Roadblock)'. 'Rebel Music' was very special, because when we first work on it, we approach it like a ballad, but then we just rope in that and get the soul and the depth going instead, so that when we go to the studio we can do another t'ing with it now. That original version was never released, but the first instrument I play on the finished one was the clavinet, which have that certain tone and feel to it. I'd asked Wya to do it for me originally, but he'd gone off by then, but you can hear where that magic was coming from. I try to capture that built-in reality, so they can feel the message, y'know? And Bob smile, because everything was in full control . . ."

Family Man later claimed in an affidavit that, "the idea for 'Rebel Music' was inspired in me by a song called 'Soul Rebel' that we recorded as the Upsetters for Lee Perry on the first Upsetters album, which was also called *Soul Rebel*. Bob had written the original song. I thought up the new lyrics and melody and played and sang these in the music room, where we jammed together to make demo tapes. These demos were recorded onto cassette and reel-to-reel tapes, which were later stolen."

Family Man adds that 'Rebel Music (3 O'Clock Roadblock)' started out as a ballad and was credited to him and Bob's cousin, Hugh Peart, during Marley's lifetime, although he would later deny having heard of Peart in the 2006 court action. This is because he only knew Peart as "Sledger". This wasn't the only inconsistency in Fams' story, since he also recalled Marley contributing lyrics to the song, once he'd ascertained the melody and chords during the jamming process. Winter claimed he witnessed Family Man writing the words but didn't mention Sledger at all, while Jaffe says the song was written during a long car journey when he, Marley, Peart and Esther Anderson were returning to Kingston from Negril late one night. Everyone in the car was smoking ganja, despite the danger of them being stopped by the police. Jaffe says this is what inspired the lyrics that Marley wrote over the four or five hours he and Jaffe were sittting in the back of the car, playing guitar and harmonica, making up songs.

Again, the judge ruled in favour of Jaffe and found Marley to be the sole composer and author of 'Rebel Music' despite Family Man's musical arrangements. Gilberto Gil described 'Rebel Music' as "a rebel cry in every sense," and said it "holds all the issues; the question of power, public freedom, civil liberties, and feelings against the establishment . . ." The song's main thrust revolves around the concept of freedom and Marley's own integrity as a righteous Rastaman. "Why can't we roam this open country?" he asks in the opening verse. "Why can't we be what we want to be? We want to be free . . ." In a magnificent show of strength, he then invites the listener to, "Take my soul and suss me out. Check my life if I'm in doubt." He wasn't just addressing ganja-toting dreadlocks driving around Jamaica. As in many of his songs, 'Rebel Music' told of Marley's own life and culture in detail, while revealing something profound about the human spirit. The writers Franz Fanon and Jean Paul Sartre were among those formulating the notion that true revolutionaries must possess honest intentions and Marley obviously felt the same. Fear, desire, strength, and determination intermingle as he lends visionary expression to the Barretts' unshakeable rhythms. With the "pure heart and clean hands" of the Rastafarians, anything was possible.

Tek Life and Frowser, two bad boys from Trenchtown, were in the control room the night 'Rebel Music' was recorded. Marley was hoping to steer them onto the straight and narrow. Jaffe was also there that night and was asked to play harmonica on both 'Rebel Music' and 'Talkin' Blues'.

Family Man Barrett: "Lee Jaffe, he was never too deep in like the studio part back then . . . I have to tell him what key his harmonica has and how to find a G or an A. And then in the studio when he play, I have to stand behind him and say, 'When I squeeze your shoulder, you blow and then when I squeeze again, you stop.' It was me who tell him all of that, otherwise the style what him have, he would have played all the while from top to bottom, like a madman."

Despite their differences Jaffe later wrote in his biography how Family Man's "unique, innovative style and authorship of brilliant new rhythms directly or indirectly influenced a whole generation of players in Jamaica and far beyond."

The other *Natty Dread* track that gave rise to contention was 'No Woman No Cry', which Marley credited to his old friend Vincent "Tatta" Ford – a man who'd given him guidance, solace and also shelter when he lived in the ghetto. Bob and Rita had been regular visitors to Ford's house soon after they'd first met, although by the time the song was recorded the quietly spoken Rasta had lost both legs and was confined to a wheelchair. There's no evidence of Ford ever writing anything else apart from 'No Woman No Cry', but then the history of popular music is littered with similar instances. This is the more charitable view, since others have suggested Marley merely gave the song to Ford to ensure the latter would receive an income. If Ford did write 'No Woman No Cry', then the line about the lead character's feet being his "only carriage" is especially potent.

Using evocative images of Marley and his brethren huddled in a government yard under the Trenchtown night sky, one can picture them reasoning about current affairs, or perhaps reading aloud from a dog-eared Bible by the fire's flickering light as people drifted in and out or gazed impassively from the sidelines. While the children slept and the gathering became more intimate, laughter and song would ring out in the darkness as Marley's friend Georgie served up cornmeal porridge from the pot placed in the embers. "In this refuge, you can't forget your past," sings Marley, and in such an environment, where comradeship was crucial to survival, a man had to know his friends from his enemies as a matter of urgency. The character might be poor and without a woman to console him, but he's going to push on through regardless.

While *Natty Dread* remains the most revolutionary set of the Wailers' recording career, among the first tracks recorded was a new irreverent version of 'Bend Down Low', the first Wail 'N Soul 'M single released in 1966 and re-recorded two years later for Danny Sims. The band continued to feature it in their stage performances and the Barretts, who hadn't played on either of the earlier versions, were keen to put their own stamp on the remake. As well as bass, Fams played piano and clavinet, while Lindo played Fender Rhodes.

The album also included an uptempo recut of 'Lively Up Yourself', a highlight of *African Herbsman*, although since this new version differed relatively little from the one recorded for Perry, one can only assume the Wailers wanted to reclaim the song for themselves. The *Natty Dread* version is a little slower with the vocals less pronounced, since Livingston's harmonies are absent. Marley's vocals are gloriously uninhibited, however. "Lively up yourself and don't be no drag," he exhorts, promising that we'll soon be rocking, like we "never did before." The song is an invitation to party but because "reggae is another bag," it's the newness of the genre (at least to crossover audiences) that was being celebrated. Marley leaves space for the rhythm to percolate beneath him, alongside the guitar and Tommy McCook's tenor sax solos which provide this exuberant remake with its main instrumental focus.*

The final track, 'Revolution', was decidedly more introspective than the other songs on *Natty Dread*. Echoing black activists such as Angela Davis and the Panthers, Marley informs that, "It takes a revolution to make a solution," although his goal isn't assuming power, but winning freedom. For all his rhetoric about burning churches, and the use of imagery borrowed from the Old Testament when evoking "lightning, thunder, brimstone, and fire," Marley's revolutionary stance is unconvincing. He comes across as wary and streetwise, sleeping rough in places where you "can't trust no shadow after dark" and warning "never make a politician grant you a favour. They will always want to control you forever". Marley didn't like the fact that Rita and Skill Cole had gone to Anthony Spaulding for help when arranging the purchase of the house in Bull Bay and felt sure there would be repercussions further down the line.

* The ribald 'Am-A-Do', recorded during the sessions, was shelved.

"Bob practised what he preached," recalls Ian Winter. "He lived how he talked and he was unique in that regard as well. What make it happen is simple, because he had a universal love and no matter where you come from, he would treat you with the same dignity as his own, right there besides him and even more so if you is a man who say Rastafari. Whenever he saw someone like that, he'd say, 'Who's that? Come in man and let we reason and spread the word.' Bob was a very disciplined person. He was very disciplined regarding his music and also in terms of his life-style, because every day he used to get up in the morning and go for exercise and then eat some natural food before going into the studio for rehearsal. That was how the programme set up and the band members execute just what they plan, no matter what. That means if there were five days set aside for rehearsal and only two people come, the rehearsals still go on. We all used to live this way, and combine music with keeping fit, so every time them finish playing football, them just ready to start play some music. And then when Bob's gone again, Family Man is there, playing back what they did and adding to it, 'cause we love to record what we do."

In addition to regular exercise, Family Man says they'd eat fresh fish bought at the beach, as well as fruit and vegetables, making their own juices, and drinking a fermented concoction of herbs he calls "tonic and bitters", but which other Jamaicans often refer to as "roots". Good health was vital, but so, too, were the Wailers' spiritual concerns. They would always start a recording session by smoking some herb, reciting a psalm and giving thanks and praise.

Family Man Barrett: "We work on structuring our minds and our souls, and we do it physically, spiritually, and mentally. We weren't studying any war or wickedness and that's why we leave ourselves open in some ways, but now we learn and hopefully the younger artists coming up today won't make the same mistakes. Because when I look back and see how we do tracks like, 'Your enemy could be your best friend and your best friend your worse enemy,' I realise how true those lyrics really were."

At the end of May, the Wailers took a break from recording and supported American soul star Marvin Gaye at two concerts in Kingston. Jamaican promoter Stephen Hill, of Celebrity Concerts, had phoned impresario Don Taylor in Los Angeles, requesting help in finding a name artist for a benefit to raise funds for the construction of a much-needed sports facility in Trenchtown.

Taylor suggested Gaye, whom he knew had sympathy for worthy causes as the singer had recently appeared at a similar event in Chicago called Operation Push, organised by the Reverend Jesse Jackson.

Hill announced the shows in March after he and Taylor accompanied Gaye and Anthony Spaulding on a tour of Trenchtown. The arrival of an internationally renowned superstar such as Marvin Gaye became a major talking point for weeks, and did wonders for Spaulding's standing in his ghetto constituency. Spaulding recommended Marley as the support act, and in the light of hits like 'Trenchtown Rock', it was a hugely popular choice.

Gaye returned to Jamaica two months later with his mother, two sisters, brother Frankie, and various Motown executives. A press conference was held at Kingston's Sheraton Hotel, where the Motown singer confessed to being an ardent sports fan, and even spoke about the possibility of retiring from live performances altogether, having recently endured a miserable show in front of 18,000 people at the LA Forum. However, he was looking forward to performing in Jamaica, where he felt people understood his music better, or at least the more cultural shift in direction he'd taken since recording *What's Going On*. Hill told the assembled media representatives "it was through the efforts of promoter Don Taylor that Mr Gaye's visit to Jamaica had been made possible."

The first concert took place on May 21 in front of a packed and wildly enthusiastic audience at the 2,500 capacity Carib Theatre. Zap Pow opened the show, followed by Marcia Griffiths, who was joined by Rita Marley and Judy Mowatt for a medley of Sweet Inspirations numbers towards the end of her set. A 45-minute delay spent readying the Wailers' equipment was obviously worth the wait since the *Gleaner* reported how "Bob Marley's performance was superb, bettered only by the star of the show, Marvin Gaye," who was accompanied by a 30-piece band.

The three original Wailers put aside their differences to perform together for the first time since the UK Catch A Fire tour almost exactly a year before. Despite having played piano and organ on the ongoing *Natty Dread* sessions, Touter's age precluded him from appearing on stage so Marley approached Tyrone Downie, who performed his first Wailers gig playing clavinet and keyboards. The home crowd's welcome was enthusiastic to say the least. Whereas Gaye, despite his increasingly radical beliefs, was trapped by his audience's expectations, the Wailers had no such limitations and delivered a set brimming with committed message songs.

Jaffe played harmonica on 'Rebel Music', while both Tosh and

Livingston were allocated solo slots. The former's 'Can't Blame The Youth' had been a staple of the Wailers' live act (although Marley never attempted it alone), while the latter's 'Arab Oil Weapon', co-written by Jean Watt and recorded at Randy's with the Barretts, made reference to the OPEC oil crisis.

On Labour Day, May 31, the Wailers and Gaye performed at the National Stadium, not too far from Harry J's studio on Roosevelt Avenue. Before the show began, the Mayor of Kingston, Ralph Brown, presented the soul singer with the keys to the city and praised him for his outstanding contributions to music. Michael Manley was in the audience that night, together with Governor General Florian Glasspole, and Berry Gordy's sister Esther Edwards. Cedric Brooks, Big Youth, and Al Green and Cynthia Richards, backed by Skin, Flesh & Bones, were among the opening acts.

"Bob Marley & the Wailers certainly didn't let down the thousands of fans who turned up at both the Carib Theatre and National Stadium," trumpeted the *Gleaner* correspondent. "Jamaica has produced in Bob Marley & the Wailers an aggregation that can create ripples with any of the international rock superstars of today. Bob Marley, with his locks flying in different directions, his uncontrollable feet constantly dancing, and his acoustic guitar giving off some real, heavy vibrations, was really saying something."

As if in response to what he'd seen at the Carib, Gaye scaled down the size of his band to give a more down home performance.

Family Man Barrett: "He did another good show, although he didn't bother changing into some pretty, pretty clothes anymore. He just came out on stage and sing all those tunes like 'What's Going On'. First, we see him in a shiny suit and then after that him turned rootsman! Because if you notice, what he did after those shows was put away his tuxedo, put on a tam and start showing himself all natural. You can tell he caught our vibes right from deh so and him keep that same rootsman image all the while after that."*

Marley didn't get to meet Gaye during that May '74 visit, although when visiting the Sheraton Hotel the next day to collect his appearance fee, he encountered Don Taylor. Taylor was Jamaican and, as a youth, had worked

---

* While he doesn't recall Gaye ever visiting Marley at Hope Road, Family Man says the two singers did strike up a friendship after the concerts and spent time hanging out whenever Gaye was in Jamaica, particularly after he bought some land on the north coast.

as a valet for visiting US stars like Fats Domino, Ben E. King and Little Anthony & the Imperials. After a short spell in the Bahamas, he returned to Jamaica before being invited to America by Jackie Wilson. Taylor subsequently joined the US army and after being discharged, he became Little Anthony & the Imperials' manager. He obviously impressed Marley with his knowledge of the music business and the two agreed to stay in touch.

The sound of Jamaica made an impact on another major artist from the Motown stable. Stevie Wonder, who was no stranger to Jamaica, having first visited the island in 1969, included a reggae track on his latest album *Fulfillingness, First Finale*, released in July '74. 'Boogie On Reggae Woman' wasn't quite like anything played in Kingston, but there was no mistaking its influences and the source of that funky, undulating groove.*

In the eight months before the Wailers performed again, and with the basic tracks for *Natty Dread* laid down, the Barretts killed time by playing the occasional session (most notably with Tosh) and working on new material. According to Family Man, a week after completing work with Martha Velez on her *Escape From Babylon* album at Harry J's, he and Marley (with Cole and Jaffe) left for San Francisco to collaborate with Taj Mahal, who was primarily a blues artist, but incorporated Cajun as well as Caribbean influences into his music. However, this account doesn't tally with that of Sire Records' A&R man Craig Leon or Velez herself, who claims she first met Marley in April 1975 and that her Jamaican trip didn't take place until a month after.

Also, despite the inclusion of 'Bend Down Low' and 'Get Up, Stand Up', Velez's album sounds as if it dates from slightly after the *Natty Dread* period. The style of production is different, but then the mix of disco and reggae tracks heard on the album would naturally differ from the arrangements heard on Wailers recordings.

Taj Mahal, who'd been listening intently to *Catch A Fire* and *Burnin'* and was no doubt aware Marley had written Johnny Nash's US hit 'Stir It Up', had phoned Marley to request help with his next album *Mo' Roots* at CBS Studios. According to Marley, the two men had developed a form of "telepathic contact" before meeting up on the West Coast.

"He said he was going to do 'Slave Driver' so I went to meet him," Marley told an interviewer in 1975. "He's good and he's strong and he's got a West Indian thing." Family Man says he and Marley changed the

---

* Stevie Wonder requested the Wailers as his support act when performing in Jamaica towards the end of 1975.

song from how Taj had initially recorded it, to "make it a little more heavier than what they first had in mind," but it remains faithful to the Wailers' arrangement in virtually every detail. As well as overdubbing piano (playing it ska fashion) on 'Slave Driver', Fams mixed 'Big Mama' and 'Cajun Waltz'. Taj's own band played on the remaining tracks, including two other reggae covers, 'Desperate Lover' and 'Johnny Too Bad', as well as 'Clara (St. Kitts' Woman)', a song dedicated to Taj's grandmother.

Marley spoke of the Wailers' business situation with Taj, who recommended they should consult Ray Tisdale, whose practice was based in Los Angeles. Tisdale agreed to a meeting and so Marley, Family Man, Cole and Jaffe flew to LA as soon as work was finished at CBS.

Family Man Barrett: "Bob told me he wanted to see Island Records to get some money and to get legal advice. He said the legal advice he wanted was about publishing and other legal issues he had with Danny Sims and also because Bunny and Peter had left the scene and he wanted to make sure that they didn't continue to benefit from our work."

Things were happening fast, but the Wailers' new partnership still hadn't signed a replacement contract, and in the absence of an advance they were struggling for cash. Jaffe claims Marley instructed him to search around for another label, as at one point it didn't seem likely that Island would retain the Wailers. After Jaffe discovered the Grateful Dead had started their own label, using independent forms of distribution, he contacted rock promoter Bill Graham while in San Francisco. According to Jaffe, Graham invited him and Family Man to a Grateful Dead concert at the Fillmore West, where they discussed the possibility of signing the Wailers. Jaffe says Marley later pulled out of the deal because Rastas didn't deal with death and Dead guitarist Jerry Garcia had drug problems. Graham would more than likely have become the Wailers' manager.*

Family Man remembers the Grateful Dead concert although he says it took place in Los Angeles at the UCLA, rather than the Fillmore West, which seems more plausible considering Graham closed the latter venue down in 1971. He has no recollection of any business dealings with the Dead, except for when Garcia offered to loan the band's sound-system to the Wailers.

Family Man Barrett: "I'd told Bob, although I can't remember when,

---

* There is no reference to this episode in *Bill Graham Presents*, Graham's autobiography (with Robert Greenfield) published posthumously. Neither is there a mention in Sandy Troy's Garcia biography, *Captain Trips: The Life And Fast Times Of Jerry Garcia.*

that he should get some advice on our contract with Island, which he wanted to be a simple, two-page document. I think it was after our visit to Ray Tisdale that we talked about this. I was particularly keen that he should get advice for us, and I wanted to be sure that my brother and I would be paid by Island for our recording work. Bob said that he would instruct a lawyer for us."

CHAPTER SEVENTEEN

Talkin' Blues

SHELTER Records was a small company that had achieved moderate success over the past four years by the time the Wailers' entourage came into contact with them during the summer of 1974. After switching distribution from Capitol/EMI to MCA, the label was taking on new acts like Phoebe Snow and Don Preston, as well as reissuing their back catalogue.* Shelter had released several albums by Leon Russell, as well as blues guitarist Freddie King, J. J. Cale, Richard Torrance, and assorted friends of Russell's from the LA scene. Former Sly Stone backing singer Mary McCreary, who was married to Russell, had also been recording for the label. Her latest album, *Jezebel*, included reggae-tinged tracks such as 'Singing The Blues', which she'd recorded during a weekend session at the Treasure Isle studio in Kingston. Label co-owner (with Russell) Denny Cordell had fallen in love with Jamaican music while in England and even purchased the rights to distribute Studio One releases in the US, although nothing ultimately resulted from this, perhaps because Cordell arranged the deal with Junior Lincoln, who ran the Bamboo label, and not with Coxsone himself.

Together with his old friend Chris Blackwell, Cordell was very much interested in helping reggae gain a foothold in the States, but it was Don Williams, who ran a publishing company called Number Eleven Music, who took care of Shelter's reggae interests. Williams heard this new music coming from Cordell's office, and became further enraptured after seeing *The Harder They Come*. It was publicity generated by the film that enabled Williams to obtain funding for reggae releases on CBS' Special Projects label.

Don Williams: "Shelter was just a bunch of people who really loved music, so you get the money and put it out and that's exactly what I did.

---

* They'd also resolved their difficulties with DC Comics, since Shelter's logo design had incorporated a Superman-like "S" which was considered an infringement of copyright.

My life had changed after I'd heard one of the records Coxsone made with Toots & the Maytals called 'Never Grow Old', because when Denny came back from England one time and I heard those rude horn lines, it was just too much for me. I said, 'Can I go there [Jamaica]? Let me change my life.'"

Williams' photographer girlfriend had been hired to take stills on the set of *Papillion*, which Steve McQueen and Dustin Hoffman were filming in Jamaica, so he accompanied her to Kingston. He continued to travel back and forth between Los Angeles and Kingston on a regular basis, occasionally staying at 56 Hope Road in the back room directly above where the Wailers rehearsed. Williams signed Tosh, Livingston, and Joe Higgs to publishing deals with Number Eleven Music. The Barrett brothers weren't offered a contract, as Williams didn't consider them to be writers.

Family Man Barrett: "We'd gone over [to LA] to make sure everything is all right with some new business. Carly and I, we don't know about the business part, even though we are Bob's partners. It seems like Denny Cordell was trying to help Bob get out of some deal with Danny Sims, so these negotiations involve CBS and Shelter Records, and Chris Blackwell was just coming into the picture as well. At that time, Chris Blackwell had an office off Sunset Boulevard and Denny Cordell contacted him, so they can talk. The impression I get was that Island and Shelter Records were going to work together and share the Wailers, but then Chris Blackwell start to control the whole scene. We were glad for that though, because we didn't want to be in no tug-of-war, and that deal wouldn't involve Bunny or Peter, so it meant a break from that as well."

This is not how events are remembered by Williams, who had to negotiate with Sims on Marley's behalf.

"I'd been working with Peter and Bunny for I don't know how long, but then it got to the point where Bob was able to get out of his deal with Danny Sims. Lee Jaffe, who was hanging out with the guys one time, came into the office and said Bob finally wanted to make a new publishing deal, but he didn't want to sell his equity any longer. He wanted only to have someone manage his publishing company and Denny Cordell couldn't deal with that. He couldn't deal with me making a deal that did not require a portion of Marley's publishing, so that started a rift between the two of us and ultimately led to the break up of Shelter, since Denny and I got into an absolute, total fight after Bob announced what he wanted to do . . ."

As well as offices on Hollywood Boulevard, Shelter also owned a studio in Tulsa, Oklahoma (Russell's hometown) which was spacious and well-appointed with a 24-track mixing board, housed in a converted church. Russell had been a professional musician since leaving school. After backing Jerry Lee Lewis in a local nightclub as a teenager, he'd been invited out on the road with "the Killer" and eventually made his way to Los Angeles, where he joined the Wrecking Crew, a band of the city's elite session musicians, and started to write his own material including George Benson's 'This Masquerade', B. B. King's 'Hummingbird', and Joe Cocker's 'Delta Lady', before touring with Cocker in Mad Dogs and Englishmen. The engineer on that tour, Peter Nichols, who later moved from Los Angeles to Tulsa, worked in Shelter's studio for a time. Russell had co-written songs on Eric Clapton's first solo album, released in 1970, and several of the musicians in Clapton's new band, all recommended by Russell, were from Oklahoma.

Don Williams: "We got Eric to record 'I Shot The Sheriff' whilst the Wailers were hanging around in Los Angeles, because one of my best friends, Jamie Oldaker, was Eric's drummer. Another player from Tulsa, Eric's bassist, Carl Radle, got into reggae at that time as well. I guess we just got into it from early for whatever reason, so consequently everybody wanted to make records with the guys. It was musicians wanting to play with musicians."

According to biographer Ray Coleman, Clapton had been jamming with guitarist George Terry at Criteria studios in Miami when Terry played him *Burnin'*. Clapton was immediately taken with 'I Shot The Sheriff' and decided to record it. The people at Shelter were thrilled, since they knew what such an endorsement could do for the Wailers' reputation among the rock audience. Sessions for *461 Ocean Boulevard*, Clapton's 'comeback' album – his first in three years since overcoming a lengthy heroin addiction – took place during April and May, with the album following in July. On the strength of 'I Shot The Sheriff', a hit on both sides of the Atlantic, particularly in America where it reached number one in September, *461 Ocean Boulevard* became one of the biggest-selling albums of Clapton's career.*

Family Man first heard Clapton's version of 'I Shot The Sheriff', "the one with the rotary drum in it," in Tulsa. "We were pleased he'd done a

---

* Clapton and George Terry co-wrote a reggae-inspired tune, 'Don't Blame Me', for Clapton's next album, *There's One In Every Crowd*, which met with nowhere near the same degree of success.

version of it, and that people were listening to what we were doing. It was a next stage, because the first person to cover one of Bob's songs was Johnny Nash except after Eric Clapton did his, then every rock act had to do a reggae song!"

In *Bob Marley: In His Own Words*, Marley admitted the Wailers' own cut of 'I Shot The Sheriff' couldn't be a hit single, "but when someone do over a song, them can hear what you did and try and improve on what you do. Maybe they can make it a bit better than the first person who do it."

Clapton didn't meet Marley until well over a year later. When the guitarist asked Marley about the song's lyrics, he was cryptically told that some of them were true and some of them not, but wouldn't confirm which exactly. Marley later claimed (as quoted in *Bob Marley: In His Own Words*) that 'I Shot The Sheriff' is about wickedness.

"The message is a kind of diplomatic statement. You have to kind of suss things out. 'I Shot The Sheriff' is like I shot wickedness. It's not really a sheriff; it's the elements of wickedness, because people been judging you and you can't stand it no more and you explode. You just explode. I wanted to say, 'I shot the police,' but the government would have made a fuss so I said, 'Shot the sheriff,' instead; but it's the same idea: justice.

"Clapton asked me about the song because he didn't know the meaning of it. Him like the kind of music and him like the melody, so I don't know if he did it because Elton John say 'Don't shoot me, I'm only the piano player', or Bob Dylan say, 'Take the badge off me, I can't shoot them any more,' [from 'Knocking On Heaven's Door'] and this one man say, 'I shot the sheriff.' That song never fit anyone else but Eric Clapton, right beside Elton John and Bob Dylan."

According to Jaffe, he and Marley shared in the writing of the lyrics, pointing to the use of the word 'deputy', an American term, in support of his contention. Family Man scoffs at this.

"Lee Jaffe told us that he's the one who got Eric Clapton to do a cover version of it . . . Bob sometimes get angry and rough and he beat up on Lee Jaffe so bad one time I haffi say to him, 'Ease up man, or we going to have a big doctor bill to pay.' Even when we were in Tulsa, I say to Lee Jaffe that we need to get management or something when we were doing those tracks and he was supposed to be sorting out something, but things never work out as they should, which is why I back out of it and don't go any further with him after that."

★ ★ ★

With their profile now considerably increased thanks to the Clapton cover, the Wailers' next album would prove crucial.

Family Man Barrett: "I say I think I'll go back down to Tulsa and do some research, because I wanted to listen to as much as I could from the Top 10 and get some ideas and inspiration for the final production of *Natty Dread*. I told Bob I needed to go back down to that side to listen to some country music, because country music lyrics were coming next to reggae, due to the fact they always tell it like it is and how they're cut without being too commercial. After that, I just call the Island office in LA, told them I would like some money, about $2000, and they can take it from our royalties. When I reach the office, the money was waiting for me in an envelope and so Lee Jaffe and I, we rent a Ford Pinto, go to the beachside first and enjoy ourselves, and then after 48 hours, we head for Tulsa.

"When we get there, we do two songs with this guy named Peter Nicols, who was working in the Shelter office. He said he wasn't going to fly with us, but would drive from LA, and it was going to take him between two to three days, so he gave us his house keys and said there'd be a car waiting for us when we get [to Tulsa]. He'd made a deal with me to do two tunes, one of which was going to be my own production, so I get my own tape ready and recruit some session guys. I get this guitarist named Richie and the drummer was Jamie Oldaker. The song we did was called 'Cottage By The Seaside', with vocals by Maria Anderson."

Hailing from the Jungle area of Kingston, Anderson had met Family Man at a Bunny Lee session, where she voiced a song called 'Devil In Bed', although the studio time ran out before they could finish it. Her next session was with Family Man, recording 'Cottage By The Seaside' and 'Woman In Love'.

"I still have the rough mix of 'Cottage By The Seaside', except the vocals are all on one channel and the rhythm on another. That's how it was recorded, since [Maria] had voiced her part in Jamaica before I left for San Francisco. After I get back to Jamaica, I give it to this guy Mikey to put it out on a 45. He was living at 56 Hope Road and had this label called Micron with Ronnie Burke. Tyrone Taylor, he signed with them soon afterwards, and that's where he got the idea for that big hit of his, 'Cottage In Negril'. Maria Anderson wandered off to Germany after that and I've only ever seen her daughter since."

While the rhythm is top-notch on 'Woman In Love', Anderson's voice is pleasant at best, suggesting that Family Man was prone to sentimentality when the mood took him. 'Woman In Love' was issued as a single by

Micron and included on a compilation called *Cobra Style: Lost Productions* (credited to Aston "Family Man" Barrett), released by Heartbeat some 30 years later.

Family Man would later describe Micron as "some little bandulu business," although back in the mid-Seventies, he was happy to give a helping hand to people just starting out in the record business who were trying to make a difference. While in Tulsa, overdubbing 'Cottage By The Seaside', Family Man came across the kind of sound he'd been searching for and would adapt for use with the Wailers. It was more rhythmic and centred on the axis of drum and bass as usual, but with the main groove dominating every instrument, including lead vocals.

Family Man Barrett: "When I was about to mix *Natty Dread*, I was listening to everyt'ing hot in the charts. I listen to Rufus when Chaka Khan was with them and especially 'Tell Me Something Good' with that big, hard band behind her. I listen to some country music too, like J. J. Cale, and also Joe Cocker, because he's very musical and sings some good blues, but the man I learn most from was the Godfather of Soul, Mr James Brown. He had the sound they were talking about at that convention in LA, with the emphasis on the rhythm section, but he sight it long before they do, because he had this album called *The Payback*, and that's where we were at too, moving forwards as a band and not looking back. I remember putting it on cassette, and then laying down on the carpet with this little boom box, listening to it over and over and taking note of the separation of all the music. I think to myself, 'This is what I need to hear. I need a foot drum recorded just like that, where they place it off in the mix and the snare and the hi-hat the same.' The only thing centred was the lead vocal, so that's how I learn to separate the mono and stereo to get that *Natty Dread* sound."

With a pulsating, monster groove stretched over nearly eight minutes, 'The Payback' was written on the back of Brown's soundtrack for the blaxploitation movie, *Black Caesar*. Brown was unhappy that a follow-up project, *Hell Up In Harlem*, had been given to Edwin Starr and that 'The Payback' hadn't been considered funky enough by the film's producer. He was also in bitter dispute with Polydor, whom he'd accused of racist behaviour. "I need those hits," he demanded on 'The Payback' – a track which established Brown as "Minister of the New Super Heavy Funk."

Having found the key to the Wailers' new sound on *Natty Dread*, Family Man arranged to rendezvous with his brother and Marley.

Family Man Barrett: "Bob and I were going to London to finish the recording work for our album, but Bob wanted to go to New York first, which he did with Skill Cole. After we finish up in Tulsa, Lee Jaffe and I fly back to LA. Lee Jaffe say he better ring Bob, but when he phone New York, Bob had already left for London. I get the number for him and he say, 'What happen man? Yuh no come mix the album? Just come now!' He gave me the address of where he was staying, which was a house off the King's Road in Chelsea. I needed money for my travel to get to London and I went to Island Records' offices after telephoning them and they advanced me $2000, which I signed for. I can't recall the name of the person I spoke to, but we agreed that the money would be taken from my royalties under the contract we were going to get with Island and which I understood was going ahead from my discussions with Bob.

"Jaffe and I flew to New York, but I leave him there and me alone fly to England. Bob had phoned Carly in Jamaica in the meantime and asked him to come too, so that same night I arrive, we all go in the studio and listen to the tracks from *Natty Dread*. It was after that we decide what has to be done and where to put in overdubs and make cassettes of the tracks so we can meditate upon which direction to take and how we can add to that."

The Wailers arrived to an England under a form of siege, which made lyrics such as "feel like bombing a church" ('Talkin' Blues') and those heard on Burnin' And Lootin'' and 'Revolution' seem all the more relevant. The IRA were busy waging a bombing campaign on the mainland; earlier in 1974, 11 people had been killed when a coach to Manchester was bombed, and four months later another 11 were injured in a blast at the Houses of Parliament. In July, explosions at the Tower of London injured over 40 more. That same month, over 10,000 Greek Cypriots took to the streets, protesting at Britain's response to Turkey's invasion of their island, while mass arrests occurred at a rock festival in Great Windsor Park over the August Bank Holiday.

Marley and the Barretts had spent that weekend walking around Ladbroke Grove, where the Notting Hill Carnival was in full swing. Jamaican trombonist Rico Rodriguez, who played with a band called Undivided in the early Seventies, recalls seeing them at Carnival that year.

"We were playing at the corner of Lancaster Road and All Saints Road, and we were playing some Don Drummond music," he told David Katz. "I'd just finished my solo, the rhythm was still bubbling and the saxophone player was playing. We looked across the road and the Wailers were standing there. I touch my friend and say, 'Bwoy, the man them like the music across there,' because everyone was looking at us intently. Bob Marley, Carlton Barrett, and Family Man were really there with us and they didn't leave until we take a break."

Family Man had cut Lloydie Coxsone's sound-system some exclusive dubplates before Carnival started, and it was there, in the crowded streets of west London, where people first heard tracks like 'Knotty Dread' (the dub of 'Natty Dread') and 'Talkin' Blues' in stripped-down form, with Marley's vocals floating eerily over naked drum and bass.

Family Man Barrett: "The vibes were flowing and it's like we were at the beginning of something special, because that carnival in Ladbroke Grove was pure magic that year, me a tell you! Every carnival man a play Bob Marley, because if you don't hear 'Natty Dread', you hear 'Roadblock' in the place, and everywhere we look, we see people walking around and saying, 'Wow! What a change.' That because all they could smell was herb and the people them were so peaceful, just grooving to the music."

A month or so later, the British government issued a report stating that excessive cannabis use caused brain damage, although it's doubtful whether anyone from the Wailers' camp paid heed. There were more important matters to contemplate. Three weeks before Carnival, President Nixon had resigned because of the Watergate scandal, and disillusionment with the political apparatus was still widespread. The Wailers' alternative world view, based on Rastafarian teachings, now appeared more relevant than ever. Increasing numbers of British black youths were taking an interest in their cultural origins, growing dreadlocks and joining roots reggae bands. Nor did the Wailers' revolutionary sentiments go unheeded by representatives of an angry, white underclass, some of whom would later evolve into punks. As tastes in contemporary music continued to change, this groundswell of disaffected youth would provide the Wailers with much of their audience over the next few years.

The Wailers' old acquaintance from Jamaica, Sid Bucknor, sat behind the board while *Natty Dread* was overdubbed and mixed at Island's studios in Basing Street. The label had two work bases now that Blackwell had purchased 22 St Peter's Square in Hammersmith, which housed the Island offices and some additional recording equipment in the basement. Phil Ault took charge of sessions there. Family Man says Blackwell would often drop in while the Wailers worked in the studio, but he never directed them.

"Chris Blackwell, he'd sit in his little room and listen to every session, then he'd come out and say, 'That is a different concept of music you're doing,' or he'd ask me if I had any weed, because he always used to have a little draw when he was around us. He was a rootsman like that, y'know? We all felt as though we were at the start of something powerful though, because it was at that same time Bob met Julian's mother [Lucy Pounder], who was such a nice, sweet girl. Everything was going good, I tell you."

Marley's seduction technique, or at least an approximation of it, was captured on tape during that 1974 London visit, although these recordings would not surface until many years later. It's fascinating to hear him serenading two girls with his guitar, improvising lyrics along the lines of 'I'm loose.' He sounds happy and relaxed, making fun of the way he looks and punctuating certain phrases with James Brown-like screams of delight. Five minutes later, and both girls are harmonising along with him, as someone – possibly reggae singer Delroy Washington – accompanies them on percussion. Bob and another female voice can be heard on a song called 'Lonely Day', which is clearly unfinished. "Do you think I couldn't remember the things I've said?" he asks, before reminding us that, "things are not always the way they seem." It's a song of loss, yet it's delivered without a trace of self-pity. Neither song would ever be recorded; they were mercly compositional fragments, tossed off into the ether as Bob strummed his guitar, searching for inspiration. "Another day, another song" as he puts it.

Despite the I-Threes receiving credit on the album sleeve, two uncredited English women – perhaps the ones heard on the tape – sang backing vocals on several *Natty Dread* tracks, most notably, 'No Woman No Cry', which was recorded in its entirety during the Wailers' London stay.

Family Man: "That first evening I reach London, by the time we finished listening to all the tracks it was late, so it wasn't until the next night we start overdubbing. It was a different place to where we'd been staying in Chelsea before, because it was closer to the river this time. We were walking along the King's Road, hoping we would bump into a rootsman so we could get some herb, and then out of the blue we see this guy coming down the street with a bass guitar in one hand, and a six pack in the other. That was Al Anderson and we say, 'Hello, you're a musician and a bass player too?' He said, 'No, I'm really a guitarist but I love bass. Who are you guys?' We say we are the Wailers, his face lights up and then he asks us what we're doing in town. We tell him we're working on some tracks and just start doing it that day, but we need to get some herb. He says he knows where to get some real good shit, some Thai sticks, but they are very expensive. We tell him we don't mind and we'll buy a few, so he took us to a brethren of his in Ladbroke Grove, a small island guy called Bunny MacKenzie, who was also a musician.

"After we'd sampled two spliff, the man say his sister and cousin loved singing, so Bob said for him to bring them out and introduce them to us, because we'd been discussing where to find backing singers. After they come out, Bob asked them to sing for us, but they were both shy, and said they didn't know what to sing. Bob told them they didn't need to sing an actual song and that we just wanted to hear how they sounded. They do two short bursts of singing and then go back in their room so Bob asks me what I think of them. I say they remind me of this group from the US called the Pointer Sisters, who do this song that goes, 'I know that we can make it. I know that we can. We can, can . . .' I say that since they sound like the Pointer Sisters, we should appoint them.

"After we meet Al, we took him back to the place where we were staying. We played some tapes for him and then carry him and those two girls to the studio with us that same night, although Al had to go back home and get his guitar first. 'Am A Do' and 'No Woman No Cry' were overdubbed at the same session and then we finish some other overdubs later on. I never see either of those MacKenzie girls after that."

Anderson, who'd been living in London for a year when he encountered the Wailers, remembers the version of events differently. He claimed Blackwell originally suggested Paul Kossoff of Island act Free follow Wayne Perkins' example by applying lead guitar overdubs to *Natty Dread*. By 1974, Free had experienced great success with their blues-based rock sound, anchored by Paul Rodgers' powerful vocals and Kossoff's emotive guitar playing. However, successes like 'All Right Now', 'The Stealer', 'My Brother Jake' and 'Wishing Well' were in the past and Kossoff had left the group. Battling with drug problems while attempting to carve out a solo career with Backstreet Crawler, the troubled 24-year-old couldn't manage what Blackwell asked of him and so suggested his friend Anderson instead, who apart from being a talented guitarist, was an occasional tape operator at Basing Street and therefore already known to the Island boss. Paul's father was the well-known actor David Kossoff and the two guitarists would often stay at his house in Golders Green, talking about music late into the night.*

---

* In another twist of fate, Kossoff's band included drummer Conrad Isadore, who was a childhood friend of singer/guitarist Junior Hanson, a.k.a. Junior Marvin, who joined Bob Marley & the Wailers in 1977.

Anderson describes Kossoff as "a very intelligent man, an extremely good guitarist and a great guy. He was really good to me, because I substituted for him on *Natty Dread* and got the gig. It's all thanks to Paul Kossoff really."

Anderson already knew members of other Island acts such as Traffic before arriving in London with the Detroit Emeralds, who toured the UK during early 1974. The Emeralds, formed around the four Tilston brothers, were signed to Westbound Records in Detroit and had scored R&B hits with 'Do Me Right', 'Baby Let Me Take You In My Arms' and 'You're Getting A Little Too Smart'.

Al Anderson: "My mother used to take me to all these shows. She basically did everything so I could get out there, work, and make my own money. She encouraged me to be independent and God bless her for that. Although I'm from New Jersey, my family are basically from New York and Virginia and I was always in bands from school. I was in several talent show groups and we'd go touring, but I'm from a musical background anyway, because my father would play bass for James Brown and my mother was a piano player.

"Bud Parks invited me over to England to do some work with the members of Maynard Ferguson's band, and if I wasn't staying with Bud Parks or Maynard Ferguson's guys, then I was playing with Traffic or Free. Chris Wood [of Traffic] lived in Marble Arch and I was always crashing at his place. I was playing with a band called JR & the Steamrollers with Jerome Ribsen, the bass player from Detroit Emeralds. Chas Jankel was in that band and also Pete Van Hook, who sang with Mike & the Mechanics. He joined Van Morrison after a while, whilst Chas played with Ian Dury. These were the guys I formed my first band with over here. Pete Van Hook, he was a great drummer, but the Steamrollers used to play Ronnie Scott's for like £20 a night and were perfectly happy with that."

Anderson also played in a group called Third World, although they had to change their name because of the Jamaican reggae band (signed to Island) of the same name. By this time, he was sharing a flat in Putney with the Nigerian lead singer of Shakatu who played a blend of rock, soul, and African music and were considerably less commercial than fellow African fusion band Osibisa, which is why Anderson thinks Island passed on their album, despite the involvement of Traffic percussionist Remi Kabaka.

Anderson was used to working with musicians from different cultural backgrounds and enjoyed learning about other forms of music, provided they had soul and energy. As a teenager, he'd soaked up every style of music he could, and apart from being knowledgeable about rock, soul, and blues, he'd also listened intently to jazz musicians such as Larry Young, who he knew from New Jersey, and also Grant Green, Wes Montgomery, Joe Pass, Tony Williams, John Coltrane and Joe Henderson, among others. Anderson, who'd been living in London for a year when he encountered the Wailers, had already recorded with a disco band called Centurion.

Family Man Barrett: "Al was like a blues guitarist at the time, but he was quick to learn. He'd heard of us, but this was something different from what he knew already. He had an open mind and he did good in getting us those Thai sticks! I start to groom him from there, help him get a tone and see where he can fit in, where to come in and where to come out."

It's hard to detect Anderson's relative inexperience, as his playing on *Natty Dread* is economic, yet expressive, as typified by the solo on 'No Woman No Cry'. His wah-wah playing on 'Them Belly Full', 'Talkin' Blues' and particularly 'Rebel Music', simmers and writhes beneath Jaffe's harmonica before coming to a sudden stop, like a car suddenly being braked. The solo then starts up exactly where it left off, leaving the listener scrambling to regain focus. Family Man's use of dynamics on this track is superb and so, too, his arrangements on 'So Jah Seh', with the female harmonies mirroring the horn lines, delivered in the style of an R&B revue.

The McKenzie girls are at their most vibrant on this track, along with 'Them Belly Full', 'Talkin' Blues', and 'Revolution', and at their most suggestive on 'Am A Do', originally recorded just before Lindo left the Wailers.* The female harmonies, albeit a little naïve-sounding in places, made all the difference to *Natty Dread*, and such vocals would help define the Wailers' sound in future.

One can only imagine what *Natty Dread* would have turned out like had Kossoff played guitar instead of Anderson. The ex-Free axeman's anguished lead breaks might well have detracted from the Wailers' supple, rhythmic genius, with the session ending up becoming more of a showcase for Kossoff, rather than the band. While Marley handled guitar on 'Natty Dread', Anderson's bluesy licks on 'Lively Up Yourself' were again wonderfully understated with feel and sensitivity.

Family Man Barrett: "That second version of 'Lively Up Yourself' was done in London at Island's studio [in Hammersmith]. Tommy McCook and this trombone player, Bubbles, play the horns, because Tommy

* 'Am A Do' was eventually left off *Natty Dread*.

McCook does that wicked solo near the end. We make the rhythm part different, because the original version recorded at Harry J's doesn't have that same change in it. The second cut, that's the one with the step in it, 'cause everybody get more lively now. That's because we're working in a new studio and the feeling at the time was that Island's business is Wailers' business. Other acts on the label were leaving, and so we began to feel like we were part of Island by then."

Anderson was about to leave for Lagos with Shakatu before that fateful meeting with Marley and the Barretts. Although playing in Shakatu offered him the opportunity to learn something of African music, it wasn't necessarily what he wanted to do on a long-term basis. The young American felt an immediate rapport with the three carefree Jamaicans who were obviously dedicated to their music, so he abandoned his original plans once Marley offered him the chance to join the Wailers.

Al Anderson: "I knew Steve Winwood, Chris Wood and those guys, and they said, 'Don't go to Africa. Go to Jamaica because it's better.' It was a fantastic time for me. Chris Blackwell offered me royalties to be in the band and I accepted them. He offered me a three per cent royalty to be in the Wailers, and that should be worth hundreds of thousand of dollars today."[*]

Before heading back to Jamaica, Marley and the Barretts went to see some old friends at the Empire Ballroom in Leicester Square, where Dennis Alcapone was heading an all-star line-up of reggae acts.

Dennis Alcapone: "That was with me and Dennis Brown, and Desmond Dekker was on the bill as well. Halfway through the show, I called Bob onstage and introduced him to the crowd, but Bob wasn't really established in England as yet and so Desmond Dekker and I were the stars that night. Bob wasn't in his element back then. Bunny and Peter had already left the group, so he was there with Family Man and Carly, and also the boxer Bunny Sterling. The Wailers had recently finished *Natty Dread*, so I guess I played my little part in helping them promote it right there. It was a wicked show, too, and everyone was really pleased to see them."

Brown had recently made his UK debut with the Jamaica Showcase, touring with Toots & the Maytals, Cynthia Richards, Al Brown, and Skin, Flesh & Bones, featuring drummer Sly Dunbar. Reggae was experiencing a boom period in the UK; sales of records and concert tickets were healthy

---

[*] Evidence of such an arrangement still hasn't surfaced but Anderson insists that [future Wailers' manager] Don Taylor had all the relevant documents in his possession.

and to help keep up with the hits flooding out of Jamaica every week, Britain now had a profusion of specialist record stores and independent labels scattered throughout the country, including Third World, DIP, Ashanti, Tropical, Magnet, Black Wax, Lord Koos and Atra. The principal venues for reggae in London were All Nations in Hackney, the Apollo in Harlesden, Count Suckle's Q Club in Paddington, and the Crypt in Deptford. Marley and the Barretts attended a Coxsone dance at the Four Aces in Dalston. Once there, they discreetly built a spliff in a darkened corner and took in the atmosphere as Festus played dubplate mixes of artists like Marley, Brown, and Johnny Clarke.

Throughout 1974, it was impossible not to hear the sound of flyers in reggae circles or in a different fashion, such as Junior Byles' 'Curly Locks', produced by Lee Perry, telling of a dreadlocks bid to woo some high society girl; Delroy Wilson's 'Have Some Mercy'; Gregory Isaacs's 'Love Is Overdue'; Carl Malcolm's 'Miss Wire Waist' (produced by Clive Chin); and Toots & the Maytals' irresistible 'Time Tough'. Carl Douglas' 'Kung Fu Fighting', while not Jamaican (although Douglas was), could also be heard at reggae dances, as selectors lightened the mood with some good-natured pop. The Barretts also caught up with their old friend Larry Lawrence who was now running a record shop, Ethnic, in Kensal Green. Lawrence arranged to visit Jamaica so they could lay him some rhythms at Harry J's. These sessions resulted in tracks like Junior Delgado's 'Reaction', Sidney Rogers' 'People Living In Glass Houses' and Dave Barker's cover of the Temptations' 'Get Ready'. The Barretts were also pleased to see the Cimarons had released a debut album, although the tracks on it were no match for a version of 'Talkin' Blues' that the band would soon record for Tommy Cowans.

As work neared completion on *Natty Dread*, the Wailers met up with Ray Tisdale as arranged in Los Angeles. Tisdale spent about two unproductive weeks in London, negotiating directly with Chris Blackwell and lawyer Charles Levison, of the firm Harbottle & Lewis. At least one further meeting with Blackwell and Levison took place at Island's West Hollywood offices, some time later. At a 2006 court hearing, Tisdale claimed that the only person he represented or took instructions from during this process was Marley, despite the Barretts' understanding that Marley was acting on their behalf. In a statement dated February 14, 2006, Tisdale says he doesn't recall why the names of the Barrett brothers appeared at the top of the 1974 Recording Agreement (along with that of Marley) and said the

Barretts weren't parties to this contract, to the best of his recollections.*
Tisdale stated the agreement was signed on or around October 15, but was
backdated to August 27, which is presumably when he first met with
Blackwell and Levinson. He also confirmed the Barretts' names appear on
letters relating to this revised Island contract, and referred to these letters as
"side documents."

To complicate matters further, an undated handwritten note was
unearthed in Harbottle & Lewis' files that set out the proposed terms
between Island and Marley, making distinct reference to "Family" and
"Carly". Tisdale admitted Levison was under the impression the Barrett
brothers would be signing the 1974 agreement. There was also evidence
of Tisdale using the term "clients" in some of his correspondence with
Levison, yet he has no recollection of why he should have used this plural
form and says he made no attempt to obtain the brothers' signatures when
finalising the agreement. Parallel to negotiating this contract, Tisdale
was also negotiating an agreement for the purchase of 56 Hope Road.
He again claimed to have been solely representing Marley, although
the final agreement was between Blackwell and a company called Ten
Ambassadors Limited, owned by Marley. Tisdale suggests this could have
been why he used the word "clients", as opposed to "client", and recalls
turning down the opportunity to represent Family Man in negotiating a
deal with Shelter Music Publishing, since he perceived a potential conflict
of interest with his existing client (i.e. Marley).

Family Man denies making such a request, saying he never discussed
business with Tisdale when visiting his office with Marley, Cole, and Jaffe
in the summer of '74, but merely waited for Marley in reception. After
being shown correspondence relating to the 1974 Recording Agreement
taken from Island's own archives, Blackwell admitted Levinson clearly
believed the Barretts would also be signing it. He says he cannot recall the
details of that negotiation, but admits this could well have been the
original intention, since all three Wailers had signed the 1972 contract. He
says this was because the Wailers were relatively unheard of in 1972, that
reggae hadn't yet reached a global audience, and he didn't know whether
the group would be a success.

"By the time of the 1974 Recording Agreement," Blackwell said in his

---

* Tisdale later had a dispute with Robert White of Island over the payment of his fees
relating to this procedure (since they were to be taken from the Wailers' royalties) and had
to ask Chris Blackwell to intercede on his behalf.

testimony, "the situation had evolved as the band's popularity grew, and it became clear that Bob Marley was the sole creative and dynamic force behind the band, and the person whose services Island wanted to secure." Island viewed the Barretts as session musicians, rather than performers like Tosh and Livingston, and so it didn't make sense to sign them individually. Blackwell did, however, acknowledge that Levinson's meeting with Tisdale was to discuss the possibility of Island taking up an option to acquire the Barretts' future recording services, in return for meeting recording costs and paying royalty rates that matched those payable to Marley (although no advance would be payable.) Blackwell didn't recall whether this proposal went any further, but this confirmed (in his mind) that the Barretts were not intended to be parties to the 1974 Recording Agreement.

The ramifications would prove catastrophic for the Barretts. Despite him allegedly promising the Barretts they would be equal partners, the renewed Island contract gave Marley full entitlement. The brothers, who trusted Marley implicitly, were convinced they would own a share of everything their endeavours produced. With the divisions created by Tosh and Livingston behind them, there was a feeling of well-being in the Wailers' camp as Marley left for New York with the *Natty Dread* master tapes, while the Barretts returned to Jamaica.

CHAPTER EIGHTEEN

Fire Burning

FRESH from their exploits in America and England, the Wailers returned home to find that Jamaica, too, was in turmoil. Earlier in the year, Prime Minister Manley had introduced the controversial Gun Court Act. The legality of new, stricter measures for controlling gun crime had been tested in April, after four men were sentenced to indefinite detention for possessing unlicensed firearms. In a throwback to Jamaica's colonial past, their case had to be brought before the British Privy Council Judicial Committee, who declared the Gun Court constitutional, but said that mandatory sentences of indefinite detention were unlawful. Gun Court law was subsequently amended to life imprisonment without the right of appeal, which could hardly be described as a climb-down. Despite his liberal ideals (and as the victim of at least one assassination attempt), Manley had vowed to address gun-related violence and wasn't about to run scared from Jamaica's "shotters".

"Brothers have turned to crime, so they die from time," sang Bob Andy on his 1974 hit 'Fire Burning'. "We'd like to ask you leaders, what have you got in mind? I see the fire spreading; it's getting hotter than hot. The haves will want to be in the shoes of the have-nots. If the sign is on your door, then you will be safe for sure. But if you are in pretence, then you're on the wrong side of the fence."

Andy's message couldn't have been clearer. Insurgents were in the ascendancy and if the social reforms promised by Manley before the 1972 elections weren't going to be delivered willingly, then there was no shortage of people determined to seize them by force. This was not revolution but mob rule.

"Down here in the ghetto, we know the horror of the guns. We wear the scars of violence, so sons, turn in your guns," pleaded the vocalist on Broadway's 'Ghetto Guns', whose request went largely unheeded as the number of violent crimes, robberies, rapes, murders, and outbreaks of arson multiplied alarmingly. People everywhere complained of corruption which led to police stations being bombed, courthouses being invaded by angry mobs, and mass breakouts from local jails, as Jamaica suffered its worst cases of civil unrest since the slave rebellions. "Kingston hot," Big Youth declared.

Jamaica wasn't the only place to witness serious upheaval. Back in the UK, rioting prisoners set fire to the Maze Prison in Belfast shortly after Harold Wilson's re-election, and a fresh spate of bombings in Guildford and Birmingham left 23 dead and over 200 injured. Western and Caribbean societies alike were being engulfed in conflict and few believed the Rastas offered a credible alternative, not with stories being published in the *New York Post* linking them with drug dealing and organised crime, or other reports associating Rastas with gang wars.

New Jersey was a world apart from the one that confronted Anderson in Kingston, as he recalled. "When I reached Jamaica, Bob picked me up at Norman Manley International Airport. It was the evening flight from Miami and he drove me around several places. Apparently, there were no hotels available. I was expecting transportation and a place to stay."

The new Island contract still hadn't been signed so the band had no money to pay for such luxuries. The night the guitarist arrived he slept outside on a veranda in Bull Bay and ended up camping on a floor at Sledger's house among the narrow lanes lined with zinc fencing. He was woken every morning by the burning sun and a cacophony of voices as neighbours washed under the tap in the yard, chivvied their children, or went about their chores. Many had no food, starting the day with just a cup of tea made with condensed milk. The more fortunate ate cornmeal porridge.

Most days, Marley would call for Anderson and they would head for the downtown area to hang out at the Wailers' shop for a while, or pass by Randy's on North Parade, where music people would greet each other and lean against the counter, listening to all the latest releases. Other times, they'd visit Lee Perry's Black Ark, where Scratch would hold court in the yard, yelling expletives and cursing some poor onlooker before being engulfed by another wave of madness and heading inside, where he'd bark instructions to his musicians from behind the mixing board. Marley and Perry had fallen out several times, and Bunny Lee had no time for him whatsoever, but when it came to shaping words and music, Marley knew the diminutive Perry had few equals. Touter was also very helpful and, like Marley, introduced the young American to a lot of people.

Other times, Marley and Anderson might visit a character named Ital, who lived in a virtual war zone called Matches Lane. Bob used to take Ital food after the former footballer hit hard times. As their car pulled up, a group of youths would watch them warily, guns drawn. Anderson says people down there didn't care too much for Marley, who risked his life by visiting Ital in this way. Ital responded to this generosity by getting Rita pregnant. Marley was furious when he found out. Jaffe remembers the musician boxing his estranged wife to the ground and kicking her, on one of their trips to the house in Bull Bay. She was heavily pregnant at the time and the hypocrisy of Marley's behaviour wasn't lost on Ital, who managed to diffuse the situation before things spiralled out of control.

Anderson also claims Rita was beaten and kicked by Marley, especially after the child, Stephanie, was born. However, in her autobiography *No Woman No Cry*, Rita cited Stephanie's father as Tacky, a Rastaman who worked in an accountant's office. What's not in doubt is that Rita showed Anderson kindness soon after his arrival. Knowing he often went hungry, she took him cocoa bread and porridge. According to Anderson, Marley never gave him anything other than a taste of his ghetto upbringing. As he became more independent, the American befriended artists and fellow musicians such as I Roy, U Roy, Touter, and Jacob Miller, whom he backed on sessions for Inner Circle. Anderson recalls Marley being worried about Miller, who was full of energy, and would say things like, 'I'm the future and those guys are *old!*'

Al Anderson: "Bob used to take me to see Alton Ellis and Dennis Brown and they were selling more records than anyone imagined in those days. They were selling far more than the Wailers, because Bob had nothing going for him in 1974 and couldn't even afford to give me anything to eat. After staying with Sledger, I slept on the floor in Hope Road for six months to be a part of this band, but being in Jamaica was fantastic. I mean I got to eat the greatest food in the world, I was around some of the mentally strongest people ever, I was living in Kingston, and my dream had come true, because I got to hear some of the most dynamite music ever. I knew Robbie and Sly, Dennis Brown, Horsemouth, and Dirty Harry . . . I knew all of the musicians who came to prominence in Jamaica during that time, but for me, I didn't even need food. I had music, and I was doing sessions with these guys. Kingston and the local music scene were truly amazing then. It was unbelievable.

"They had a gully where sound-systems would play and all these deejays would do their rapping there, 'cause these guys hadn't broken out as yet. I saw I Roy, U Roy, and Big Youth . . . I went to Skateland, and all of these other amazing places."

Still in his early twenties, the American guitarist was eager to immerse himself in the island's music and culture. Untroubled by past grievances or politics, he could travel with a degree of freedom few locals could enjoy. If you were from an area affiliated with either the PNP or JLP, you ran the risk of losing your life by straying into the wrong territory. Anderson reiterates others' observations of how happy Marley was during this period, despite his recent altercations with Tosh and Livingston and a growing distrust of Blackwell. He confirms how Marley would hear a line or phrase, turn it around and make it his own, or come up with a verse and melody out of thin air. While having been around plenty of other singers, Anderson had never spent time with a songwriter so naturally gifted, or who could command such telepathic understanding from his musicians.

This was not achieved by issuing directions as to how the music should be played, but through sheer application. Marley took his music seriously and led by example in making every situation count, whether rehearsing at Hope Road or performing in front of audiences. The Wailers worked off vibes, but they were also highly disciplined, something Anderson had to quickly get used to, despite the distractions around him.

Al Anderson: "Well, I just did my thing and fitted in where I could, because Jamaica has a lot of great guitarists like Chinna, Stephen Coore, and Ernest Ranglin, and I was always aware of them. Ernest is the grand master, so we all bow down to him. I love watching him. You just can't touch him, but I had so much respect for all those guys. I was lucky to be around them, because they made me use my ears. They taught me such a great deal, because when I went down to Jamaica, that's where I learnt the most about music in my whole life. It was all about touch and so I had to be able to recognise this before I could understand what else was happening. I didn't know anything about that back home. In the States they'd write chords down and dictate patterns, but in Jamaica it was entirely different, because from the moment they started playing, they knew where all the chords were going, whilst I was just stood there, thinking, 'What the fuck is this?' It was like radar and it was incredible to see how their ears led them to what they were doing, as if it was the most natural thing in the world.

"But it was Family Man and Carly who showed me how to play reggae, and that's how it happened for me. They showed me what 'kotch' meant and how to watch the shuffle and to listen for when the music was dropping in or out so I just followed them and they taught me so much."

Tosh invited the guitarist to play on tracks he was recording at Treasure

Isle that would be released on *Legalise It*. According to Jaffe, an associate of his called Robbie Yuckman financed the sessions and the engineer only had one eye and part of his ear missing, although neither Anderson nor Family Man has any recollection of this.* Anderson scorns Jaffe's assertion of being producer, saying he just hustled some tapes and studio time. Also, none of the musicians got paid, which is why the guitarist refers to Jaffe as "an opportunist and a hustler." At the same time, Jaffe claims to have served as a buffer between Anderson and Marley, who didn't like how the two Americans "spoke the same language."

At the time of the sessions, Tosh was living in Spanish Town with his girlfriend Yvonne Whittingham, who'd accompanied the Wailers on the Burnin' tour. Tosh requested the Barrett brothers help because the three of them already shared an understanding, and Tosh considered them the best musicians in Jamaica. Jaffe hadn't been so keen, since he thought Marley would be displeased and certainly wouldn't let them tour with Tosh to promote his album. Marley knew Family Man's priorities better than anyone, even though the Barretts weren't legally bound to the Wailers, or Island. There was no trace of animosity as the brothers set up their equipment at Treasure Isle to record 'What You Gonna Do?' and 'Burial' (released on Tosh's own Intel Diplo label) and returned for further sessions, with the addition of Tommy McCook and Dave Madden on horns, that resulted in 'Why Must I Cry?', ''Til Your Well Runs Dry', 'Legalise It' and 'Igziabeher (Let Jah Be Praised)'. The remaining tracks on *Legalise It* were recorded later with a different line-up of musicians.†

Once finished, the album took an eternity to be released. Jaffe spent two years trying to get a deal for the record, since Tosh refused to deal with Island and alternatives were thin on the ground. EMI, who'd struggled in maintaining Jimmy Cliff's profile after *The Harder They Come*, were backing away from signing more reggae acts and no other label expressed interest. Jaffe thinks that either Blackwell had forewarned people, or they were scared of dealing with Tosh, who would later describe peace as "a diploma you get from the cemetery."

Tosh's quest for equal rights and justice would never leave him, and *Legalise It* left listeners in no doubt as to where his sympathies lay. The title

---

* Marley was rumoured to have lent Jaffe US $1,000 towards the funding of the *Legalise It* sessions.
† Al Anderson, Robbie Shakespeare, "Santa" Davis, and Tyrone Downie play on 'Iration', reworkings of 'No Sympathy' and 'Brand New Secondhand', and 'Ketchy Shubby'.

track is now regarded as a reggae classic, with its swooping harmonies and lurching backbeat behind a passionate defence of the herb. Tosh was at his best when proselytising, and the song's pro-weed sentiments would resurface on countless other reggae recordings. Anderson's guitar bristles on 'Burial', a warning to the authorities, featuring clever wordplay on "ginal", meaning a scoundrel and general. "Now we know the truth," Tosh admonishes, before declaring that "A rich man's heaven is a poor man's hell." The urban folk tale 'What You Gonna Do' tells how a young man's arrest has left his mother stranded without a breadwinner. 'Why Must I Cry' is a strongly articulated sufferer's lament, voiced over a joyous rhythm, typical of so much Seventies' roots reggae. The mood changes to one of ancient dread on 'Igziabeher'. Downie's swirling keyboards, Tosh's spoken word passages (in Amharic) and a battery of thunder and lightning effects combine to create a sound that's as dark and mysterious as a Pharaoh's tomb. It's the type of song Marley could never have written, due to its esoteric nature, shrouded in mysticism.

Tosh's political songs ram their message home with a directness that's far removed from Marley's impressionistic word paintings. Despite a mutual love of soul, R&B and gospel, their influences differ too. ''Til Your Well Runs Dry' is a Jamaican reggae-blues flecked with country overtones, distinguished by Anderson's weeping guitar. Tosh starts by describing his woman's infidelity, but then shifts gear after turning down her appeals for reconciliation, taunting her now she is alone. There's a mocking, almost gleeful, cruelty to his delivery, and with Livingston providing harmonies it would have made a great addition to *Burnin'*.

Family Man Barrett: "Peter and Bunny, they never leave no matter what and whilst they have their own feelings, they didn't lose the good vibes just like that. When they recorded their first two albums, *Legalise It* and *Blackheart Man* [respectively], they were just trying to show Bob what they could do by themselves, differently from the Wailers.

"Soon after those sessions [Carly and I] we slow down on doing music for other people and decide to strengthen our own thing [with the Wailers] and take it to the top. That was the meditation of that time."

Soon after the Tosh sessions, the Barrett brothers cut down on studio work for others, although Family Man continued to oversee recordings when he got the chance. During this period, he cut two tracks at Randy's, including 'Eastern Memphis', sharing the session with JBC announcer Errol "ET" Thompson (not to be confused with another engineer of the same name, who mixed the tracks).* 'Eastern Memphis' is an instrumental of majestic roots reggae, distinguished by uplifting horns, anchored by a rhythm that fair takes the breath away. The author was transported when hearing the song while gazing at the tide gently lapping against the shore on a moonlit night in Jamaica. Each musician lends an individual flourish to what proves an almighty, unspoken, clarion call. Little wonder that Family Man called his band the Rebel Arms and the dub 'Rebel Am I', since rarely has an instrumental stirred up such strong emotions.

Carly, Downie, Lindo (who plays organ, synthesiser and clavinet), and guitarist Eric "Rickenbacker" Frater accompanied Family Man and the horn players on the session, and the chemistry between them was remarkable.

Family Man considers Eastern Memphis as the jewel in his solo crown and the track that properly launched his own Cobra label.† Copies went on sale in the Wailers' King Street shop, where it competed for sales with 'Rebel Music (3 O'Clock Roadblock)' and other recent Wailers releases. Inspired by his love of the Skatalites, Family Man had planned to record an instrumental album called *All Horns Show Up*, highlighting musicians like Tommy McCook, Lester Sterling, and trombonist Vin Gordon, who was also known as "Don D Junior", since his style of playing favoured Don Drummond's, but this never happened.

Despite their growing reputation overseas, the Wailers were still struggling to get airtime on local radio in the autumn of 1974. More than one source tells of radio announcers being bundled into the trunk of a car by Marley supporters and then driven through the dangerous back streets of Kingston. "Would Bob Marley himself ever be implicated in things like that?" asked Sims on a television documentary made after Marley's death. "Of course not!"

Having written hits for Johnny Nash and Eric Clapton obviously wasn't enough to guarantee Marley exposure in uptown Jamaican circles, since there was still widespread resistance to the notion of promoting Rastafari and "ghetto music". The extent of the island's worsening social problems didn't help, nor did the fact that a more sophisticated form of reggae,

---

* The companion track to 'Eastern Memphis' remains unreleased, although Marcia Griffiths – who was living with E.T. at the time – inherited the master tapes after his death.
† 'Eastern Memphis' can be found on *The Cobra Style: Lost Productions* Heartbeat compilation released in 1999.

composed of well-crafted ballads drenched in strings, was proving so successful at home and abroad. Ken Boothe had a UK number one with a cover of Bread's 'Everything I Own' in September, produced by former Hippy Boy, Lloyd Charmers. He and Ken Boothe's follow-up, 'Crying Over You', raced to number 11 three months later, by which time John Holt's cover of Kris Kristofferson's 'Help Me Make It Through The Night' had also breached the UK Top 10. The smooth-voiced Holt would enjoy long-standing popularity with middle-of-the-road audiences in England, who probably shuddered at hearing righteous Rasta artists like the Wailers, Peter Tosh, and Big Youth.

This helps to explain why the Wailers' UK concert and media appearances proved influential, as not everyone wanted their reggae to be laden with syrup. Away from the major labels and BBC radio, the underground market was booming, independent labels flourishing and the dances overflowing. UK reggae bands like Aswad and Matumbi were on the rise and there were plenty of rock fans, having listened to Eric Clapton's *461 Ocean Boulevard*, now realising just how good 'I Shot The Sheriff' was.

Clapton wasn't the only renowned guitar player to cover the song. Eric Gale included a version on his 1975 *Negril* album, recorded in Jamaica with an eclectic mix of local and visiting musicians, including Family Man, who laid down a semi-instrumental cut at Harry J's led by Gale's wah-wah guitar. The version rocked just as assuredly as Clapton's but received little attention by comparison. Although born in Brooklyn, the 36-year-old session guitarist (who backed the likes of Herbie Mann and Quincy Jones before playing on US R&B and pop hits by Paul Simon, Aretha Franklin, and many others) was a regular visitor to Jamaica. His parents were Barbadian and so Caribbean influences were never far from the surface in his recordings, including the calypso flavoured 'Negril', 'Rasta', and a deliciously lazy 'Negril Sea Sunset'.* A review in the *Philadelphia Tribune* described *Negril* as "an exquisite fusion of Jamaican-American elements welded with superb, impassioned playing," claiming that it "can and will set a new direction in the music of the mid-Seventies." Soon after the album's release, Gale helped found Stuff, a group comprising renowned session players such as Cornell Dupree, Steve Gadd, Gordon Edwards, and Richard Tee.

---

* Negril was still relatively unspoilt in the early Seventies, and a hippy haven with its white sand beaches and palm tree-lined shore, which made it a favourite hangout spot for visiting musicians.

Micron preceded the release of *Negril* with a version of 'Talkin' Blues' featuring I Roy, produced by Pete Weston, and a handful of tracks licensed from Jimmy Radway, who'd built on the success of 'Black Cinderella' with songs by Leroy Smart, Hortense Ellis, and Augustus Pablo. Micron was conceived by Mike Breakspeare (Cindy's brother) whom Family Man had known for some time and so was happy to oblige him with material once the label was up and running.

"[Mike] was one of the tenants of 56 Hope Road, coming from the little Island office and living around the side there. Bob and Carly, they like him too and sometimes we all sit down and bu'n a spliff, reasoning about music and thinking about how to make it go somewhere, because the music never reach its international peak yet. We used to think he must be one of those kids who come from a rich family and him know the system is rotten but him love music, so if him see a set of man want go through, 'im say them haffi work together. But the two people he see come together and make something of Micron was Pete Weston and Ronnie Burke [who later became one of the principal organisers of the Reggae Sunsplash festival in Jamaica] and it get big very quickly after that. In fact, too big, too quickly, because they had a shop downtown and couldn't manage it, so Bunny Wailer take it over for Solomonic and then it change to Cash & Carry."

Micron issued Joe Higgs' *Life Of Contradiction*, with rhythms played by Lindo's band Now Generation. It was Higgs' first full-length album and contained several covers of his own hits from the Sixties, the best-known being 'There's A Reward'. Higgs, who died soon after being released from a Los Angeles hospital in 1999, was one of Jamaica's finest songwriters and a protest singer of understated power and depth. His influence on Tosh's songwriting was unmistakable. Tosh later returned the compliment by covering his mentor's 'Steppin' Razor', complete with the line, "Don't watch my size, I'm dangerous." Unlike the diminutive Higgs, the six-foot-plus Tosh still managed to deliver the line without laughing, even after being ribbed by the likes of Robbie Shakespeare.

Apart from recording with Bunny Lee's Aggrovators, Shakespeare was currently playing with Touter in a latter-day line-up of the Youth Professionals, backing Carl Dawkins. The band had a residency at a club called Evil People on Red Hills Road, not far from where Carly's girlfriend, Carol Berry, worked as a dancer. On his breaks, Shakespeare would lay down the Hofner violin bass Family Man had given him and wander across the road to go check Skin, Flesh & Bones at Tit-For-Tat, where the brilliant young drummer Lowell "Sly" Dunbar was already turning heads with his formidable technique and exquisite timing. Dunbar had absorbed what soul drummers like MFSB's Earl Young were doing and was adapting it to reggae, as demonstrated on the hit version of Al Green's 'Here I Am Baby', sung by Skin, Flesh & Bones' lead singer Al Brown. Such experimentation would soon result in the "rockers" sound, powered by militant, double-time drumbeats, and duly immortalised in song by Bunny Wailer (on the track 'Rockers').

Family Man Barrett: "Robbie asked me if I hear the Carl Dawkins tune him play called 'Satisfaction'. When I return from England now, Carl want me to play the next one for him, so we do this one for J. J. Johnson, 'Fire Burning'. J.J. had to come to me for that arrangement and I play organ on it too. It was a little electric organ, but I listen to the tone carefully, so I can get the best possible sound out of it. You have to blend everything in to get the best picture and that's how I found that melody. It's all about shade and colour you see . . ."

A similar thing happened with an old acquaintance of Marley's from St Ann's Bay called Winston Rodney, a.k.a Burning Spear. On Marley's recommendation, Rodney had recorded two albums' worth of songs at Studio One, including the classic 'Rocking Time', 'Foggy Road', and 'Creation Rebel'. Rodney's rasping chants and righteous lyrics were hardly guaranteed to set the dancehalls alight, but helped create the most soulful expression of dread, roots reggae in the label's history. After a while, Rodney became disillusioned with the poor financial returns offered by Coxsone and, once back in St Ann's, hooked up with Lawrence Lindo (alias Jack Ruby, named after the man who shot John F. Kennedy's assassin, Lee Harvey Oswald). A large, burly man with a thick, black beard, Lindo had been around sound-systems since a schoolboy and even played at independence celebrations after his family had moved from Kingston to Ocho Rios. His career as a producer got off the ground with songs by Delroy Wilson & the Heptones, but it was Ruby's work with Rodney that put him on the map and would finally bring Burning Spear to the attention of an international audience.

Rodney had taken his alias from Jomo Kenyatta, then President of Kenya. Kenyatta's political activities, most notably his alleged links with the Mau Mau, had resulted in him being jailed for several years by the authorities. He was made Kenya's first Prime Minister shortly after his release in 1961, and eight years later was busy implementing land reforms and resettlement programmes.* Like Marcus Garvey, Kenyatta was a major force in the struggle for black people's self-governance. These men weren't racists or black supremacists, but stood up for what they believed in and defended their own. They were nationalists in the process of helping build a nation and provided powerful role models for the serious and determined Rodney, who was 21 when auditioning for Coxsone. Not that you'd know it from the austere gravity of a song like 'Door Peep' (from 1969), which rivalled the Abyssinians' 'Satta Massagana' for sheer depth of spiritual feeling.

Despite the artistic merits of Spear's Studio One productions, Coxsone kept a lot of them under wraps, and even the songs he did release didn't sell that well. The closest he came to a hit was in late 1972 with 'Joe Frasier', voiced in tribute to the boxer, over the same rhythm as a righteous Rasta hymn called 'He Prayed'. Frasier was reigning heavy-weight champion of the world and was due to defend his title against unbeaten challenger George Foreman at the National Stadium the following January. The winner would then fight Muhammad Ali, who was already worshipped by black and white boxing fans alike. The excitement surrounding this event had consumed everyone's attention for weeks, and the island's musicians were no exception. Big Youth paid tribute to the fight and also Dennis Alcapone, who toasted over Spear's cut with suitably knowledgeable awe.

Rodney, who later referred to himself as "the man from the hills", lived in a fishing village on the north coast, well away from the hype surrounding the music industry and not too far from Garvey's own birthplace. Spear's focus has always been on educating black people about their history, encouraging them towards self-advancement, tempered by rightful behaviour. Three decades later, he is one of the few Jamaican artists to have retained their integrity, together with his original audience. Spear had originally asked Leonard Chin if he wanted to be involved in the production of an album, but the latter declined, since he'd already arranged to leave for England. Ruby proved a fair replacement, however. As a soundman, he knew people in the business, could organise sessions, and wouldn't interfere with what his artist wanted, since Rodney had had enough of waiting for someone else to release his music and making changes to it without consulting the artist. He wanted more control over what he was doing, and since he wasn't in a position of financing

* Kenya gained its independence from the British in 1963 – a year later than Jamaica.

everything by himself, his first option was to go into partnership with someone who would put up the money but take a back seat.

The pair's first production was 'Marcus Garvey', which Ruby released on the Fox label in 1974. Very few people knew who Spear was singing about, but the song was a revelation with its powerful message, mournful, cajoling vocals and a storming rhythm track in the new "rockers" style. He and Spear recruited Delroy Hines and Rupert Willington to sing backing vocals. Rehearsals had taken place in Ruby's yard in the thick, hazy sun of the afternoons and would often continue into the evenings. Like Marley, Spear was a strict taskmaster, insisting on perfecting his songs' arrangements before attempting to record them. Since there were no studios on the north coast, artists and producers who lived in the area had to visit Kingston to record. To get there, they would have to take the A1, past Bamboo and Claremont, before traversing Mount Diablo into Linstead and heading for Bog Walk, where the road twisted and turned through leafy glades. If thirsty, they would stop at a makeshift roadside stall for fresh fruit or a jelly coconut, before navigating the narrow bridge over the Rio Cobre, just wide enough for one vehicle at a time.

After that, the journey became relatively straightforward through Spanish Town and onto Kingston, where musicians would group outside Randy's or Harry J's, swapping tales and smoking a spliff or two in readiness for the session. It was a journey Marley knew well, although Nine Miles, where relatives of his grandfather Omeriah Malcolm still lived, was some distance inland from St Ann's Bay. Rodney and Ruby travelled down to Kingston several times during the making of *Marcus Garvey*, since it was compiled from tracks recorded at different sessions by a changeable line-up of musicians. Randy's usual engineer, Errol "ET" Thompson, started mixing some of the tracks, but then fell out with Vincent Chin over money and left to work for Joe Gibbs. Vincent had to call in George Philpot from Dynamics, who took over for a while before being replaced by Karl Pitterson.

Ruby's group of musicians came to be known as the Black Disciples. Shakespeare played bass on most of the tracks and Leroy "Horsemouth" Wallace drums, with Tony Chin and Chinna contributing rhythm and lead guitars respectively. Touter and Tyrone played organ and clavinet, while Bobby Ellis, Tommy McCook, Richard "Dirty Harry" Hall, Vin Gordon, and Herman Marquis made up the horn section [Wya Lindo was included among the Black Disciples' ranks before he moved to San Francisco]. Family Man flitted in and out whenever his schedule allowed, but would feature on most Burning Spear albums released over the next decade.

Family Man Barrett: "I used to sell Jack Ruby dubs to some of my earliest productions. This was from even before I started touring with Bob, but the first time I recorded for him was when we did Burning Spear's *Marcus Garvey* album. After we return to Jamaica, I hear this Burning Spear song, 'Marcus Garvey', played by Robbie Shakespeare. It get popular, but then Jack Ruby say to me, 'Well, your student nice Fams, but I'd like you to play the next one.' That's when we did 'Old Marcus Garvey', which had a different arrangement."

The rhythm is lazier on 'Old Marcus Garvey' and sways, more than rocks, as Spear intones his lyrics, mantra-like. "No one remembers old Marcus Garvey," he chants, amid horns that strike up a bold refrain, but then fade away to allow space for another highly evocative history lesson.

At his peak, Garvey was a visionary leader who'd forged trade links with Liberia and launched the Black Star Line, the world's first black-owned shipping fleet. He was finally discredited by reports that he'd defrauded UNIA (the Universal Negro Improvement and Conservation Association) and had been forced to watch from a jail cell as his constituency's trust in him evaporated.* Garvey's importance was little heralded, even in Jamaica, and his memory had been allowed to fade away there long before Burning Spear arrived to rekindle a reappraisal of his achievements.

"After we did *Marcus Garvey*, a lot of singers start to sing about Marcus Garvey and Black Star Line," Ruby told *Black Echoes'* Anna Arnone. "Awareness come to the people then, because no man tell you about black history before that. Black history is a mystery to we. All we know about is Christopher Columbus and them guys. You no go learn about no great black heroes."

Reiterating Ruby's view, Carly's son Akila Barrett agrees there's been a lack of black history taught in Jamaican schools.

"That's because we were all educated in European history," he explains. "We were colonials, remember, and had the British ruling us, then once we became independent, we started looking more into our culture and to lean more on the music, because the music was always the voice of the people. A lot of things our foreparents wanted to say, I guess they couldn't, otherwise they would have been arrested. That's why they had

---

* US government papers requested under the Freedom of Information Act have now proved his innocence.

to channel it through the music, because the music is the free speech everyone can absorb, but you don't have to listen to it if you don't want to. It's not forced on you, but the sound and the message is what hypnotise people and that's what the music of artists like Burning Spear and Bob Marley & the Wailers was all about. They hypnotise you with the sound and the message, and it put you in this state of mind and awaken you."

Rodney concurs, saying people who tried to spread the word about Garvey in his community were often looked down upon as if they were crazy. Not so Rastafarians, who honoured Garvey's accomplishments and his prophesy concerning the coming of Emperor Haile Selassie I.

"I myself was lucky enough to hear about Marcus Garvey from early on, from even before I was singing," Spear says. "Musically the vibes just a come and I start present the man through music. I was the first one to sing about Garvey, because so many people had never heard about him until the song 'Marcus Garvey' come out, and it cause a lot of tension because everybody start asking, 'Who was this man Marcus Garvey?' It's like I dig up something there musically, because it was finished, but then we go back and revive the whole thing.

"When we did those first records, it was the right time to speak out on his behalf, I think, because Marcus Garvey wasn't a bad guy, or someone involved with violence. He wasn't involved in stupidness, or trying to overthrow the United States of America. He was a man who stood up for equal rights and justice and who did a lot of important things for Afro-Americans. He showed them how to open their mouths and talk and ask for certain things. He showed them to stand up for themselves and how to think. He showed them how to be brave, to pray for guidance, and to create an aura of self-confidence. He showed them how to help themselves and gave Afro-Americans a lot of important information, even if they were scattered around the world and had no one else to represent them. They had no one else to speak with their voice, so you can see the importance of Marcus Garvey and let's not talk of a couple of little things which may or may not have taken place outside of that, because we don't have no more like him. We don't see any signs we'll have any more great leaders who are going to be there for black people, or represent us internationally, and I don't see anyone like that up until now.

"Marcus Garvey thought it was about time we black people looked upon each other as a nation, so we can assist our own development and get involved in world trading and stuff like that. To earn respect and help people identify their own movement, because there were millions of people in his organisation at one stage, and no other black man do what he do. That's why the government bring him down because the man was so strong and they were scared his movement would crash them. The chain of events he started, it would have continued to develop without them, so that would have been a problem. That's why they end up saying, 'Why should the law allow a man like that to continue on his journey and with his work, knowing that it gonna develop and reach places?' It was going to get so big and they don't really want that to happen. That's when the system start to bribe people, and get them to speak against him. It was as if they didn't want anyone to say there were African descendants.

"That was the last thing they wanted to hear, because they'd been working hard to get that out of you already, so when a man like Marcus Garvey leave Jamaica and come to the United States of America and say, 'Africa for the Africans,' that get to them. He came to open the eyes of black folks enough to be their speaker and become their voice. He was the one who straighten out black folks and put them on track and who set the pace for Dr Martin Luther King, Malcolm X and all those other men, so that they could go out there and let others hear their voice and help the concerns of black folks be recognised by the system."

Dancehall artists would later inform the reggae public of what was happening in their ghetto communities, but singers like Burning Spear, Dennis Brown, and the Wailers were informing them of their past to build themselves a better future. As their messages began to hit home, increasing numbers of other Jamaican artists began growing dreadlocks, learning about men like Garvey and Selassie, and writing songs containing more conscious, militant lyrics, infused with Rastafari, calling for unity and social change.

"Reggae music is black people's way of life," Ruby said. "It's our means of communicating to people in other parts of the world what is happening around the society of the people in Jamaica."

'Slavery Days' made considerable impact when following up 'Marcus Garvey' in 1974. "'Slavery Days', like the point of a needle on a naked ass, elicited a sudden reaction," wrote Carl Gayle in his liner notes for *Man In The Hills*. He described Spear as "a feeling of the age, a sign of the times. It's symbolic, it illuminates."

Island distributed the *Marcus Garvey* album outside Jamaica, except grassroots fans were frustrated by the tracks being sped up and remixed. That still didn't prevent the record being hailed as a classic upon its release in 1975. A year later, Island issued a dub companion, *Garvey's Ghost*, and arranged for Spear to tour England, backed by members of Aswad. As electrifying as these shows were, it would be the last time Rodney used pick-up bands, since on Family Man's recommendation he insisted on travelling with his own musicians. Rodney's life and career were thus actively shaped by Marcus Garvey's philosophies, especially with regard to self-reliance and self-determination. Spear and the Wailers were alike in this respect, since both wanted to make a difference and set an example by the way they lived, as well as what they preached in their music.

Family Man doesn't recall Spear and Marley discussing business together, but acknowledges the two men were friends. Both were mindful of the pitfalls awaiting the unwary when it came to dealing with producers and licensing their songs to other parties. Spear produced himself, and wouldn't sing for anyone else after splitting with Ruby in 1977, and Marley was determined to do the same, despite his ongoing friendship (and occasional collaborations) with Lee Perry.

On August 6, 1974, Marley had signed a letter authorising Island Artists Ltd to pay the sum of $3,000 to the law firm of Sanders & Tisdale, covering Ray Tisdale's trip to London to negotiate the Wailers' contract. This money was to be deducted from any future advance payable to the Wailers. Marley signed the letter, "on behalf of WAILERS." Family Man and Carly were also thought to have signed a letter (dated August 26) authorising Tisdale to represent them in any future negotiations. Four days later, Levinson sent Tisdale a draft agreement with a cover letter stating, "I enclose herewith a draft of the proposed agreement with Bob Marley & the Wailers. If the agreement is in order would you please arrange for it to be signed by Bob Marley, Family Man, and Carly, and return it to me in due course."

The draft agreement also gave Marley and the Barretts the option to buy 56 Hope Road. During the option period, they were entitled to live on the property, but wouldn't be entitled to use it after June 1, 1976, "or at any time if your exclusive recording agreement with Island Records Limited shall be terminated." On September 2, Levinson sent this draft option agreement to a lawyer in Jamaica for advice about security of tenure. In his covering letter, he explained that his client, Chris Blackwell, intended to grant the option to "some Jamaicans".

Tisdale replied to Levinson's letter on September 10 after returning to Los Angeles. In it, he suggested a number of detailed changes to the "new agreement between Bob Marley and the Wailers." One of them proposed that any solo albums by Marley or the Barretts should count towards the number of releases stipulated in the contract, although this suggestion was rejected. There was no mention of any changes to the listed parties. In fact, Tisdale's letter concluded: "our clients and I are most anxious to finalise execution of the subject agreements. It would be greatly appreciated if you can revise the agreements in accordance with our comments and transmit execution copies thereof to me for execution by our clients." Tisdale clearly understood his clients were Marley *and* the two Barrett brothers, and if Family Man is to be believed the lawyer had never been given reason to think otherwise.

"I remember that at some point in the second half of 1974, Bob phoned me," Family Man Barrett said in 2006. "I was in Jamaica, but I don't recall where he was, since we never spoke on the phone when we were both in Jamaica. He said that Chris had produced a contract similar to the first contract Bob had signed with Island Records and which contained clauses he was unhappy with. He said he was refusing to sign it unless it was changed so that Carly and I's names were also included on it. Island then returned with a new contract which he was pleased with and that now had all of our names on it and that he was going to sign on behalf of the three of us. Bob said that he would never sign anything unless it was on behalf of Carly and I as well, so I told Bob to go ahead. He rang back soon afterwards, within a day or two, and said that he'd signed the contract for the three of us."

In the middle of October, Marley alone signed and initialled every page of all the various documents relating to the Wailers' deal with Island. In the letter to the company written on his behalf by Tisdale, it stated that "pursuant to the terms of such an agreement, Island Records Ltd. will be paying me on behalf of the Wailers." It was signed "P/K/A Bob Marley, on behalf of the Wailers." The recording agreement itself, henceforth known as "the 1974 Recording Agreement," was addressed to Family Man, Carly, and Marley by name, and stated $15,000 would be paid on acceptance of the first album (i.e. *Natty Dread*), $12,500 on completion of the first US tour, and the same amount on acceptance of the second album. Fifteen thousand dollars would be payable on completion of the second US tour and also on acceptance of each album during the first renewal term. Twenty thousand dollars would be payable on acceptance of each album during the second renewal term. The Wailers' contract was slated to last until August 26, 1975, or 60 days later if they hadn't recorded at least two albums by that date.

Island also reserved an option to extend the period. This same contract also included a line stating: "the Artist shall mean the Artist or Artists whose names and addresses appear at the head of the Agreement." This included the Barretts, as both their names appear at the top of the contract.

In a letter sent on October 29 to Island, Levinson pointed out that, "Whilst Bob has signed, it still requires signature by Aston Barrett and Carlton Barrett before any money is paid." This means Island had accepted *Natty Dread* for release by then, but no advance had been forthcoming. A letter from Levinson (dated November 11) again noted he was still waiting "to receive the agreement signed by Family Man and Carly." Tisdale wrote to Marley and the Barretts several times, requesting that the brothers sign the contract, but to no avail. On March 27, 1975, Levinson, who'd now left Harbottle & Lewis and gone to work for Island, wrote to Tisdale again, saying, "I can now confirm we have not received a fully executed copy of the new Bob Marley & the Wailers agreement. Accordingly, the old agreement is still in force and as a matter of goodwill, we have been making certain payments to Bob Marley as advances in the spirit of the new agreement. This has been done entirely on an ex gratis basis and without prejudice to our contractual position."

The Barretts never did sign the revised contract. At the time, Family Man was too busy working on new tracks, setting up the music room at 56 Hope Road, tutoring newcomers like Al Anderson, and trying to provide for his growing family, to pay full attention to the legal ramifications. Because he didn't read or write too well and since the Barretts trusted Marley to make the right decisions on their behalf, why should he worry?

CHAPTER NINETEEN

Natty Dread

MARLEY and Esther Anderson parted company towards the end of 1974. Anderson had finally decided that the time was right to have a child with Bob, but after falling ill and undergoing an operation, she found she was infertile and the relationship petered out amid an aura of sadness. Despite their painful separation, she remained instrumental in the arrangements to buy 56 Hope Road from Blackwell.

If Rita hoped to reconcile with her estranged husband, she kept such thoughts to herself. In March '74, she teamed up with Marcia Griffiths, who had reverted to recording soul-tinged, MOR reggae tracks for local producers like Lloyd Charmers. Covers of Roberta Flack's 'Sweet Bitter Love' and 'The First Time Ever I Saw Your Face', Neil Diamond's 'Play Me', and the Three Degrees' 'When Will I See You Again' were among her stock-in-trade. It was music for the uptown crowd, and Griffiths' shows at the House of Chen in New Kingston, supporting Hezekiah Shojam, were more cabaret than roots reggae. Griffiths wanted to try something different during the House of Chen residency which stretched over three consecutive weekends, so she invited Rita and Judy Mowatt to perform a couple of numbers with her. Despite their lack of rehearsal, they got a tremendous reception. "We tore the place down! We had to encore continuously," Rita wrote in *No Woman No Cry*. "The audience would not stop calling for more! And from thereafter we knew that we could do a thing. And if you are not doing *your* thing, we could all come together and do *our* thing."

Rita rediscovered herself as a singer and as a Rasta woman she would have a profound effect on Mowatt, who began to change her life and appearance after spending more time with the two other singers. Born in Industry Village, Gordon Town, Mowatt's earliest musical experiences came through singing in school choirs, first at Holy Trinity, and then Kingston Commercial. While still at school, she became a member of a dance troupe, although she'd originally wanted to be a nurse. After touring the Caribbean as a dancer, in 1967 she formed a singing group called the Gaylettes (also known as the Gaytones) with two teenage friends, Beryl Lawrence and Merle Clemonson. Their repertoire consisted mainly of overseas soul hits by groups such as the Supremes and Gladys Knight & the Pips, although Mowatt's own favourite was Aretha Franklin. The Gaylettes finally disbanded in 1970, after Lawrence and Clemonson emigrated to the US. Mowatt recorded under a series of pseudonyms including Juliann, and a year later she had her first hit with a cover of Miriam Makeba's 'I Shall Sing' for Sonia Pottinger, followed by songs like 'Way Over Yonder' and 'Emergency Call'.

Some reports suggest it was Lee Scratch Perry who heard about the impromptu appearance at Chen's and recommended Marley hire the women to sing backing vocals (they had already sung on 'Natty Dread'). Rita only remembers Marley's driver turning up at Bull Bay a few days after the show, insisting she round up the other two and bring them to Harry J's, where Marley and the band were waiting. Family Man was won over from the minute the three started singing. The I-Threes provided the final piece of the recording jigsaw.

Island announced the break-up of the original Wailers in October just prior to the release of *Natty Dread*, which featured only Tony Wright's painting of Marley on the front sleeve. The portrait depicted Marley, framed by an unruly shock of dreadlocks, looking straight back at the viewer as thunder and lightning rages in the background. Even the back cover image was striking, capturing Marley onstage, bare-chested with head thrown back, eyes closed, his right fist held aloft in classic revolutionary pose. Last time out, he'd been photographed openly flouting marijuana use, but this was different. Marley was no longer seen as a rebel in the individual sense, but was being skilfully marketed as a torchbearer for Rastafarians, the underprivileged and the reggae genre as a whole. The overriding impression was of an artist unapologetically committed to his music and the social and cultural conditions that had inspired it.

Island had decided to change the title from *Knotty Dread*, substituting the word 'Natty' instead (usually taken to mean dapper or well-dressed.)

Al Anderson: "We had to beg Chris Blackwell not to spell *Natty Dread* like he did, but to use the word Knotty instead. Except he made it *Natty Dread*, because that was the way he saw it . . ."[*]

---

[*] Ironically, thanks to the success of the album, a spate of Jamaican releases using the word "natty" in their title flooded out of shops like Randy's over the coming year.

"The first two records, *Catch A Fire* and *Burnin'*, didn't do too well in Jamaica, but *Natty Dread* was a hit there and outside," Blackwell told Vivian Goldman. "*Natty Dread* was a killer record. It really delivered the goods. But it was a very different sound from the first two, with Peter and Bunny's harmonies. It was now a solo voice with vocal harmonies, and *Natty Dread* stands on its own.

"*Natty Dread* get everybody talking, and then *Catch A Fire* and *Burnin'* start to sell like never before, because it was *Natty Dread* that made those two albums more popular."

The critical response to the album was rapturous in places and fully justified Island's decision to stand by the group following Tosh and Livingston's departure. The new line-up had silenced their doubters and delivered a record that impressed on all levels. The only thing it lacked was a spin-off hit single, despite Island and Tuff Gong releasing 'Lively Up Yourself', 'Rebel Music' (a.k.a. 'Roadblock'), 'Them Belly Full', 'Natty Dread', and 'So Jah Seh' on the seven inch format.

Ironically, while Marley continued to aim for crossover success, Family Man and Carly were climbing the UK charts courtesy of Rupie Edwards. 'Irie Feelings (Skanga)' had reached number nine in November '74, followed by a second hit, 'Leggo Skanga'. In truth, there was little to these tunes beyond a simple vocal refrain and the Barretts' persuasive rhythm section, but British pop fans' love for the undemanding nature of gimmicky reggae songs they could dance to, remixed over the same happy beats, made them ideal choices for mainstream airplay.

Family Man Barrett: "We'd done some earlier tracks for Rupie Edwards as well, like that Errol Dunkley medley, 'Three In One'. After that, we do the last, greatest thing for him, the 'Irie Feelings', so 'im can leave out of Jamaica and fly to England to see Trojan, Pama and all those people.* He produced some good music in Jamaica, with artists like Gregory Isaacs and Johnny Clarke. Not too much. He would just do his own thing, but sometimes it was hard for him to get the big artists. We see him struggle and so we give him some nice songs, like that piece of drum and bass you hear there, and if I'm not mistaken, he did something else on the same rhythm too."

In late February '75, Marley finally received the balance of the Wailers' Island advance, minus the "ex gratis" payments mentioned in Levinson's

* The Cactus label released both Rupie Edwards singles.

(March 27) letter to Tisdale and the cost of Family Man's air travel from the US. Levinson confirmed Island's receipt of the fully executed 1974 Recording Agreement on February 19, which left Marley as the sole recipient for the Wailers. Family Man maintains he, Bob, and Carly were of the understanding that each member would receive a third once expenses had been deducted.

Marley had spoken intermittently via phone with Don Taylor since their first meeting in January '74. As well as managing Little Anthony & the Imperials, Taylor was looking after former Motown singer Martha Reeves, who was currently signed to Island. While negotiating Reeves' release to join Clive Davis' Arista stable, Taylor heard from Island President Charlie Nuccio that Marley was still in need of professional management. Marley had been trying to manage the band's affairs up to this point, with help from Dickie Jobson (who Family Man didn't entirely trust) and Skill Cole who, despite his nickname, lacked the requisite know-how. Jaffe's friend Robbie Yuckman was also touted as a prospective manager, although his qualifications for this role were unclear. (He was voted out after Marley called a band meeting.) After Taylor flew to Kingston, staying at an apartment in Worthington Towers on Worthington Avenue, Marley set up a meeting with Cole and Jobson and the parties agreed a 10 per cent management commission on Marley's earnings. Tisdale ceased to act for Marley and the Wailers once Taylor became their manager. David Steinberg, who'd been introduced to Taylor by Thom Bell of Philly International, took over as Taylor's legal representative.

Family Man: "I remember [Taylor] come to Hope Road and get down on his knees, saying, 'I want to work for you brother Bob.' And then Bob keep a meeting and tell us that two men want to work with us as manager. He say one of them is a black man and the other white and which one do we prefer? All I hear was this chorus of voices saying, 'Black man' and especially from Tyrone, who was there among us. Well me and my brother don't know about anything racial, or follow the business side of things too tough, so we leave the decision to Bob and don't need fi answer that anyway, 'cause I know Bob thinks we'll prefer the black man. Then I say to myself, 'Well I wonder if it was that same man I see pon him knee?' because that is not a good approach. It's like he was a ginal [a hustler] and if you're coming to do a works, then you're supposed to have a proper t'ing set-up. It was a little after that I discover its Don Taylor and him just float pon what is there already. The only thing he did was bring in David

Steinberg, 'cause Bob had already set up some publishing arrangement with a girlfriend of his called Yvette Morris.

"This was in '74, the same time I became a member of ASCAP myself, so these things were put into place well before Don Taylor came. After he started working for us now, and Bob introduce him to certain things, I see him trying to firm up this second contract with Chris Blackwell. I don't know the details or what percentage was agreed between him and Bob, but we needed someone to concentrate on the business side for sure, so we could carry on with our music. Don said he could get us increased royalties on future albums and we liked that idea, so he's supposed to make sure these things work out properly. Except when him do that, he credits all these other people [on *Natty Dread*] who are not pertaining to the band, such as Allan Skill Cole, Sledger, and man like Tatta."

Like Sims, Taylor was a fast talker and his arrival marked a shift within the Wailers' inner dynamic. He soon got the impression Marley didn't trust Blackwell, and also claims the former told Tisdale that Family Man and Carly would eventually sign the 1974 Recording Agreement, but then advised them not to, although that's not how Family Man remembers it.

Taylor examined the terms of the first Island contract. Marley still hadn't received any royalties as either artist or producer, and the Wailers had only got their $12,000 after hiring Tisdale. Island subsequently paid the Wailers $38,000 towards tour expenses for upcoming US dates during June and July. Marley alone had requested these payments since Taylor hadn't yet assumed stewardship of the band's affairs. In his book *So Much Things To Say: My Life As Bob Marley's Manager*, Taylor confirmed that after the break-up of the original Wailers, the singer had signed a new contract with Island "as Bob Marley and the Wailers, naming Family Man Barrett and Carly as the new Wailers, upon the signing of which he had received the aforementioned $12,000."

Blackwell couldn't understand how this could have been the case, but agreed there'd been an expectation the Barretts would sign the initial contract. "Initially, when Peter and Bunny left, I felt that perhaps the Barretts should be involved in the contract," he told the High Court in 2006. "When Don Taylor became involved later on, he was against that. Also, what happened was the stature of Bob himself had risen to such a degree that there was no longer the need really to present the image of a band. It was much more Bob Marley now . . .

"I wanted to continue the same thing I had started with the idea of the

Wailers. During this period, basically Bob emerged out of the Wailers as a solo artist. That was the first thing. The second thing was that Don Taylor became the manager of Bob Marley and had no interest in other people being on the contract."

Taylor claims Marley told him he'd done this so as not to be committed to the document's terms yet could still get his hands on the money, although if this was the case, neither of the Barrett brothers was informed. However, more importantly, because the contract wasn't completed by all the relevant parties it could be said to be of questionable validity.

On March 8, the Wailers appeared at Kingston's National Stadium with the Jackson Five. The five brothers from Gary, Indiana, led by Michael, the precocious and prodigiously talented youngest sibling, had already notched up a string of hits for Motown, including 'I Want You Back', 'ABC', 'The Love You Save' and 'I'll Be There'. By the time of the Kingston show, they'd expanded the line-up to include youngest brother Randy and sisters La Toya and six-year-old Janet. If the Wailers had reservations about sharing a bill with family-oriented superstars like the Jacksons, Family Man wasn't aware of any. Al Anderson, who was playing his first show with the new line-up, says no one clapped.

"There was, like, 200 people there, because nobody in Jamaica was interested in Bob Marley at that time," he recalls. "They were more into Peter Tosh, Jimmy Cliff, and deejays like U Roy, who were talking about what was really happening in Jamaica at that time. Then *Natty Dread* came out and everything started happening from there, because people began to realise that Bob, too, had made a statement, whereas everyone else had been pretty much afraid to. He went really far."

Family Man's memories of the concert differ from Anderson's although it was hardly surprising people began leaving, since the Jacksons went on first.

Family Man Barrett: "From what I remember, it was a huge turn out, because Michael had this song out called 'Ben' at the time. Bunny and Peter perform there with us too, because we always invite them to perform with us on the international shows. Bunny, he was wearing a suit made from crocus bags and Peter had on this martial arts gear, like white trousers with a white samurai top. It was cool, I tell you! Before the Jacksons come on, I set up this tape recorder backstage but every time I set it up, they plug me out and cut off the mic, which I'd placed in front of the monitor. When I went round to security to collect the mic, I was told they didn't want anybody taping their shows. I told them it was just for our own little personal t'ing so we could play it in our music room, but they insist on taking my equipment away and so all I get is pieces like 'ABC' and 'Ben'. But when I play them back, the quality of it is just like listening to the records!"

The National Stadium's capacity was 15,000 people, but only 2,000 remained when Marley, Tosh and Livingston took the stage, backed by the Barretts, Downie, Anderson, the I-Threes, and Jaffe, who played harmonica on 'Rebel Music (3 O'Clock Roadblock)', with Dirty Harry on sax and Bobby Ellis on trumpet augmenting the Wailers' regular line-up. The show, lasting six hours in total, started 90 minutes late and had to be stopped twice since the seating arrangements were badly organised. People at the front perched on top of stacked-up chairs, leaving those sitting behind unable to see the stage. This led to those in the £10 seats breaking through the police barriers to get into the £15 section, resulting in an uneasy tension that even the best efforts of MC Don Topping and comedian Rannie Williams failed to quell.

Family Man Barrett: "The Jacksons came and visited us at 56 Hope Road. There was this tree that fall down and make a great arch round by the back so only a small car could pass and I remember we had all these pictures taken with them right there, by that tree. I had to catch one of them – I think it was Jermaine – after he'd slipped trying to climb up there."

Photos of the Jacksons' visit to the Wailers' headquarters later appeared in Jaffe's book. Apart from the charismatic Marley, it's almost impossible to tell the American family and the Jamaican artists apart, although Michael is conspicuous by his absence. Family Man's dreads have fully sprouted and his beard is beginning to thicken, while Livingston has on a cap of the type favoured by hip African Americans.*

Island stepped up their promotional campaign and began sending media representatives around to 56 Hope Road. The interlopers would hang around like lost souls as Marley and friends played football on the grass at the front of the house. The Wailers' entourage cooked ital food, reasoning among one another while rolling huge, conical spliffs. Marley would sit near the entrance gate, from where he could vet who was coming and

---

* A craze for tams had started at the turn of the year and stalls in Kingston's downtown markets were full of them, especially black with red, gold, and green trimmings, which sold for between $5 and $7.50.

going. Family Man describes the scene around Hope Road as peaceful and welcoming, despite the occasional noise complaint and the odd comment about how the upmarket residential area was being colonised by Rastafarians. Although no longer part of the Wailers, Tosh and Livingston would often drop by, catching up on news, holding forth on a variety of subjects, and taking careful note of whatever Family Man happened to be working on in the music room. Livingston had been contracted to Island when Family Man and Carly played on 'Arab Oil Weapon' and 'Fighting Against Conviction' (both released on Solomonic) but he was now free to pursue his own deal and so was busy accumulating material for an album.

One of the first songs recorded was called 'Armagideon'. "There was this Rastaman who'd sit around the back of the yard each morning, chanting and beating the drums," recalls Ian Winter, "and he had this big bass drum that would ring out over the whole place. It was some real nyabinghi he was coming with and it kept reverberating around the yard, so Family Man heard this sound a couple of mornings and made up the bass-line from that."

Family Man Barrett: "It took about three mornings to put it together, 'cause none of them was the same. Every morning he'd play it different, but then I tune into what the sound was saying and figure out 'Armagideon' from there. That Rastaman did his share, but then Ian and myself play it on that same machine drum we use for 'No Woman No Cry', the Rhythm King. There was this deejay who call himself Black Skin the Prophet and after we record him on it, that track become one of the main dubs for this sound-system in Jamaica called Jah Love. The selector's name was Ilawi and Brigadier Jerry was the deejay, 'cause he voice his own cut of it after we give them Black Skin's version, plus the raw rhythm. Bunny Wailer told me he loved the track and he was going to write some lyrics for it, so that song 'Armagideon' really belongs to both of us, since I built the rhythm and he wrote the lyrics. A little while later, I arrange and produce it for him at Aquarius studio, as part of [Bunny's] *Blackheart Man* album."

Black Skin (real name: Sonny Washington) was a neighbour of Rita and Judy's in Bull Bay. Livingston issued a song of his, 'Single Woman', on Solomonic, while Family Man produced 'Jack Sprat' before supplying Black Skin with rhythms and arranging the horn sections on the singer's own productions. 'Jah Jah Children Lives' and 'They Never Love' (recorded under the alias of I Sings), remain among Black Skin's best-known tracks, but 'Black Skin', featuring the kind of horns that made Errol Dunkley's 'Hi-Lite' so entrancing, showcases him to best effect. "Hasn't your teacher told you that your poor foreparents were captured as slaves and forcibly removed from their homeland by the white man?" he asks. "And if you are a Jamaican, from Africa, then why do you have to stand here and fight against your black skin?" While not the best vocalist, Black Skin could certainly get a message across, and the fact he had Jamaica's best rhythm section backing him didn't hurt either.

Brigadier Jerry's cut of 'Armagideon' was recorded over a rhythm played by the Twelve Tribes band but would not be released for some years. While good, it's nowhere near as compelling as Bunny Wailer's version, which creates the impression of relentless, impending judgment but skilfully avoids sounding doom-laden thanks to McCook's dancing flute, Tosh's bursts of melodica and Downie's tinkling piano runs. Seeco's percussion and Livingston's funde drum join Carly in measuring the beat, while Tosh and Family Man duel on rhythm guitar. 'Armagideon' proved to be one of the outstanding tracks on *Blackheart Man*, once Island released it in 1976. The Barretts and Downie played on nearly every track, as did Tosh, who contributed backing vocals. Marley's only appearance on the album was on a recut of 'Dreamland'.

Blackheart Man remains Livingston's undisputed masterpiece. Led by the title track (again featuring McCook's flute), there's a pastoral feel unlike anything he recorded with Marley and Tosh, apart from tracks like 'The Oppressed Song' and 'Reincarnated Souls', which were left off *Burnin'*. Like 'Rastaman' ("that's the strangest man I've seen"), 'Blackheart Man' is a romantic portrayal of the Rastaman, opening with a warning not to go near him because "even lions fear him". The lyrics make reference to the widespread belief that Rastas are dangerous madmen who "give candy to children and then take them away." Once the myth is removed, the Rasta becomes a gypsy-like character without family or friends, but who has like-minded brethren all over Jamaica, and "even in the lonely parts of the country." Bunny turns our sympathies around in a manner that's both persuasive and subtle without preaching. "Wisdom can be found in the simplest of places," he sings.

'Fighting Against Conviction' was a return to the song (originally called 'Battering Down Sentence') Livingston wrote in jail while doing time for ganja possession in 1968. He renamed it when taking Tosh, the Barretts, Downie, and Robbie Shakespeare into Harry J's for the song's definitive treatment. Shakespeare also plays on 'Fig Tree' (a symbol of peace and safety) and 'This Train', which although credited to Livingston is anchored in the gospel tradition, as Bunny rides the allegorical train to Rasta heaven (i.e. Zion) over trance-like, semi-acoustic, nyahbinghi beats. "When I was just a kid, an old man used to sing a little song, but now I've grown to be a man, and it still lingers deep in my soul." While the framework of the song had been handed down through the generations, Bunny's expression is unique, especially when he picks up the pace and starts testifying over the final few bars.

Anderson says Livingston was frightening and that he never liked him, recalling an occasion when Marley, Tosh, and Livingston stood under a tree outside Harry J's, arguing over Livingston's claims that the American guitarist was a spy who'd been sent to Jamaica by Blackwell to drive divisions between them. Livingston had refused to let him play on the sessions ("Where's Chinna?" he'd demand) and said he didn't want his music to sound like Marley's, although since the Barretts played on most of *Blackheart Man*, this seems a flimsy excuse. Anderson never felt comfortable being around the three of them when they were together. An unspoken tension and rivalry existed between them that only a placid sort like Family Man could safely ease. Anderson also recalls an upset Marley storming around to the back of Hope Road while some of the band enthused over Livingston's album. He was plainly jealous, and it would be the last occasion any of the Wailers played on a Bunny Wailer session, at least during Marley's lifetime. Clive Chin tells of an occasion when he was doing a session at Harry J's with members of the Wailers. Livingston had booked studio time, but had to wait until Chin finished, since they were running late.

Carly became increasingly embarrassed and angry. "He got very emotional, stopped playing, and got up to start remonstrating," Chin recalls. "The last session I did with him, I ended up leaving the tape behind, because I had no money to finish it and we went over time on that session as well. Randy's was still functioning, but I had a relationship going with Harry J and he'd given me some studio time. Carly took exception to the fact that there were some other people waiting. Bunny Wailer had arrived and that made him feel very uncomfortable."

Most of *Blackheart Man* was recorded at Aquarius, a little-used studio in central Kingston, near Half Way Tree. The engineer, Karl Pitterson, had been an apprentice at Dynamic when 'Trenchtown Rock', 'The Harder They Come' and early hits by Toots & the Maytals had been recorded there. He also worked on sessions by Cat Stevens and the Rolling Stones at Dynamic before defecting to Federal for about nine months, followed by a period in Canada. After returning to Dynamic (and mixing Tosh's *Legalise It* album in New York), he then transferred his skills to Aquarius. Pitterson took the *Blackheart Man* tapes to London for final mixing, before being recruited by Island, engineering tracks by Robert Palmer, Aswad, Steel Pulse, and Rico Rodriguez.

The Barretts played on Jimmy Cliff's *Brave Warrior* around the time of *Natty Dread*. After leaving Island and signing with EMI, Cliff's career had lost momentum. The company didn't seem to know how to market him, and this, coupled with a lack of suitable film offers in the wake of *The Harder They Come*, had left him struggling to regain direction. Cliff was aiming for a different sound, just as he'd found when visiting Muscle Shoals in Alabama to record *Another Cycle*. Otherwise, Cliff used Jackie Jackson, Ansel Collins, Winston Wright, and Hux Brown, who'd played on the majority of his Jamaican recordings.

Jimmy Cliff: "Family Man and them had a particular sound they were known for and even though they were established and becoming exclusively linked to Bob, if someone like a Jimmy Cliff wanted them, they would still gladly come and do a session. That was a classical piece of music we did, with songs like 'Brave Warrior', 'Bandwagon' and 'Every Tub', and I was really happy with it. That team Family Man had around him, they were all such great musicians and especially Family Man, but the whole team were good."

Tracks like 'Bandwagon', 'My People', and the title track are scintillating examples of what could happen when the Barretts were given first-rate material to work with, since their rhythms seem to bubble with joy, especially on 'Brave Warrior'. Tosh, Touter, and the I-Threes, whose close-knit harmonies were now an indispensable part of the Wailers' sound, joined them on the sessions, which again took place at Harry J's, with Sylvan Morris as engineer. Working with Cliff reinforced Family Man's belief that the Wailers were now ready for the international market.

In 1975, disco broke in America. Deejays in the tourist nightspots were falling over themselves to play hits like Van McCoy's 'The Hustle', which McCoy and a group of session musicians (including Eric Gale) had hastily put together in response to the current trend. It was dance music, pure and simple, and tended to promote a joyful but measured narcissism. While considered anathema to more serious music fans, discos began to proliferate at an alarming rate and club owners welcomed the fact they had only a deejay, some lights and a PA to pay for, instead of a crew of people, as with a band or sound-system. Dancers didn't want interruptions either, so deejays would keep the momentum going by playing extended mixes pressed on the first 12″ singles or disco 45s. Prototype, electronic dance records from Germany (soon to be termed "Eurodisco") were making an appearance and, unbeknown to most, deejays in the Bronx were already chopping up beats on twin turntables, as hip-hop took its first, tentative steps. Family Man, like Robbie Shakespeare, was briefly interested in the galloping basslines used on many disco records because they reminded him of how Larry Graham slapped the strings on those early Sly & the Family Stone hits.

In April, Marley and Taylor flew to New York, where they met with Martha Velez and Sire Records' Seymour Stein, Richard Gottehrer, and Craig Leon. Hailing from Puerto Rico, Velez had performed with the New York cast of *Hair* before singing backing vocals for Van Morrison. Critics likened her to Julie Driscoll and Elkie Brooks and her first album, *Fiends And Angels*, had been recorded in London during the late Sixties with an incredible line-up of rock talent, including Eric Clapton, Jack Bruce, Chris Wood, Mitch Mitchell, and Paul Kossoff. Velez had an eclectic taste, having experimented with rock, blues, soul, and folk by the time she entered Sire's offices with a copy of Johnny Nash's 'Stir It Up', expressing a desire to cover it. Knowing Marley through Alex Sadkin, Leon phoned him in Jamaica. Marley was polite, but didn't seem all that keen. In the meantime, Leon kept playing Velez reggae while Taylor talked his client into discussing the matter further in New York.

Velez was living in Woodstock and enjoying a certain amount of cult recognition thanks to her second album, *Hypnotise*. Marley especially liked the track 'Living Outside The Law' and agreed to oversee the production of her next album, which Sire was hoping would capture a roots feel. The label was taking a gamble on Marley as a producer, since apart from one or two releases by local acts, he'd solely overseen his own records. Velez, on the other hand, was convinced she'd made the right choice, even though Marley's dress sense was questionable. "It was April 1975 and rainy, hot and humid," she told Marco Virgona. "Bob was dressed head to toe in leather. His manager Don Taylor was there too. I thought the leather was a bit weird at first, but then I went to Jamaica. It is always balmy and warm, and April in New York was actually 'cold weather' for Bob's tropical system. The truth is, we didn't talk. Bob never said a word and neither did I, but he looked at me and read my face and eyes, as I did him.

I knew we connected on an artist's level that has very little definition, but is powerful and unspoken."

Velez flew to Jamaica, staying at the Sheraton hotel for three weeks, before briefly returning to New York. She then flew back to Jamaica and rejoined the Wailers at Sea Grapes, a resort in Negril. Martha Velez: "One of my favourite stories is when we – Bob, the Wailers, Peter Tosh and I – drove out to Negril, Jamaica, to rehearse and write for the *Babylon* album. We were driving and singing. All of a sudden, a torrential thunderstorm came down, the way they do in the tropics, full, and noisy, and merciless. The car started to turn off the road. I think Seeco was driving. We swerved right around in one, two, three, four circles . . . The car wouldn't stop and Seeco couldn't get control . . . Everyone was screaming or holding their breath, but not Bob . . . Bob just laughed all the while and called to Jah and then when the car just stopped in a big mud puddle, we all got out and pushed. Bob Marley, music icon, pushing a car out of the mud and singing. He was always singing and always laughing. He was a beautiful soul. He called me Sister and that was the greatest honour of all."

Velez and the Wailers headed from New York back to Kingston where they recorded an album's worth of tracks at Harry J's. Marley had requested Lee Perry's help with production and Scratch, as always, was full of ideas. The Barretts provided the rhythm section, with Anderson and Chinna on guitars, Downie on organ, and Gladstone Anderson and Touter on piano, while trumpeter David Madden and saxophonist Glen DaCosta made up the horn section. In some instances Martha only laid down guide vocals but the rhythms were more or less nailed from the start. Marley and Velez shared a writing credit on 'Disco Night', which celebrates the joys of the weekend, and bounces merrily along as the horns punctuate the changes. It's the kind of track Kool & the Gang were recording at the time, with more of a Jamaican flavour.

Martha Velez: "We wrote 'Disco Night' together in a different way than how he worked with the Wailers. We did it in the American way of sitting down and hammering out ideas, lyrics and music ideas, hooks etc. He had to say that Rita Marley had written it with me because of publishing restrictions, but everyone knew that it was co-written by Bob and I."

Velez recalls how Marley would usually write songs by recording the Wailers' jam sessions, trying out different ideas before getting Seeco to play back the tape to see what was there. She refers to this, at times, inspirational process as "channelling". Velez's appreciation of Marley's songwriting skills was evident from her decision to feature four of his songs on the resulting *Escape From Babylon* album.* Velez is a forceful singer, almost aggressive at times, yet her interpretation of 'Get Up, Stand Up' is understated in comparison to Marley and Tosh's original, but no less soulful. The rhythm is more languid as the Barretts slow down the groove, allowing Velez's vocals to shine through. 'Bend Down Low' is transformed from a bacchanal into a sultry invitation. 'Happiness' was a cut of 'I'm Hurting Inside', an early Wailers production that Marley later re-recorded at CBS's studios in London. Velez opens up, describing the pain of a failed relationship. "I've done you no wrong," she wails, "reveal yourself to me." 'There You Are' ('Stand Alone' on the *Soul Revolution* album) was an inspired choice, as Velez's version has a sparkle that the original lacked.

Velez penned the remaining four tracks, with 'Wild Bird' being the standout, delivered over a delicious, one-drop rhythm that epitomises laid back, tropical soul. 'Come On In' is a testament to love and commitment, brightened by Anderson's guitar, while 'Money Man' tells the pertinent story of an unwary artist signing her rights away. "Take your hands right out of my pocket," she sings. "All I got left is my little heart and I ain't about to hock it."

"I mainly worked on the record once the tracks were done in Jamaica and Martha was back in New York," Leon told Marco Virgona. "It took a very long time for the record to come together in Jamaica; a lot of going to the beach and playing football for several months on and off. Martha went down and co-wrote a few songs during that time. Then there was a whirl-wind of sessions and all the tracks were done in about eighteen hours! Back in New York, we did some vocals at Plaza Sound and also Regent Sound. Bob was around in New York at the time, as he was doing some gigs with his band. At any rate, we did the work on the overdubs. Richard Gottehrer left the company, so I ended up doing the mixes at Plaza. Bob was on the road but got tapes and made comments on balances and stuff, and then I would go and change things if necessary.

"I had put the bass way up in the mix and it caused a bit of comment from Seymour and others at Sire when I played the mixes for them, as they thought it was too much. Bob's only comment was that the bass should be louder and heavier, so I went back and turned it up more! In retrospect I think it should have even been heavier."

Plaza Sound in New York had wonderful acoustics and was housed in

---

* Except, strangely, 'Stir It Up', which was Velez's original point of contact with Marley.

an old, art deco-style room upstairs at Radio City Music Hall (the exact location where Leon recorded the Ramones' debut album the following year). The I-Threes later overdubbed backing vocals on several tracks, most notably the Marley songs. Their input made all the difference, framing Velez's lead quite beautifully.

Although they were distancing themselves from playing on other people's sessions, as well as Velez's album the Barretts worked on the *Stingray* album by Joe Cocker, who was in the throes of alcoholism.

Family Man Barrett: "Yeah, it was like 'im been drinking beers, but bwoy, I love the man and when I see him, I know 'im can go with a t'ing. I say he's a true musician, 'cause him just bubble with it, y'know? I'd heard his music from the same time we started out with Island, 'cause Chris Blackwell used to have a lot of albums in his office, stacked right up to the ceiling and I buck up this one with Joe Cocker on it, singing 'Woman To Woman'. That song was happening, I tell you!

"Lee Jaffe told us a lot about Joe Cocker before we do the session and was there among us when Joe come to Jamaica. I remember we do maybe three or four tracks that night. We all just play together and then Joe come up with the lyrics and a melody, because him can find the right keys for sure. 'Im just hold a vibe in there and do 'is t'ing, y'know? I say 'Yeah man, you got the soul,' and my brother's there just watching me, waiting to see what we're going to do. He was on drums, I play bass, Tyrone the organ and Peter played guitar. Then there was this guy who say he was Joe Cocker's manager, but he wasn't disciplined, so 'im disappear pretty fast!"

Fams was referring to Reg Lock, who'd asked Jaffe to arrange for the Wailers to play on Cocker's cover of Bob Dylan's 'The Man In Me'. Cocker's version is different from the other tracks on the album, which consisted of laid back Southern rock and gospel-infused, raw-throated blues. Cocker happily ad-libs as Downie's jabbing, darting organ fills gambol around him, while Tosh's cuffed rhythm guitar dovetails with Family Man's bass and Carly's unmistakable way of accenting the offbeat on the hi-hat. The arrangement is basically the same as Dylan's original (on 1970's *New Morning*) but the feel couldn't be more dissimilar. It's now been reggaefied, inspiring versions by Matumbi and Freddie McGregor. While the lyrics say "storm clouds are raging all around my door", it's hard to picture it from the uplifting rhythm.

At the time of the *Stingray* sessions, Cocker was beginning to voice more torch songs and ballads, as evidenced by his then current US hit, 'You Are So Beautiful'. Several tracks on *Stingray* were recorded at

Dynamic, produced by Rob Fraboni, featuring members of Stuff, the studio band formed by Eric Gale. *Stingray* peaked on the *Billboard* charts at 70, the lowest placing of Cocker's career to date. Despite the low sales, the critics generally liked it and Cocker would later refer to it as his "after hours album". However a section of his audience was still hoping for another instalment of *Mad Dogs And Englishmen*, preferring him to sing out-and-out rock music.

While the Wailers were working in exalted company, other Jamaican musicians had to confront familiar indignities in their bid to make a living.

"I did a lot of work over at Harry J's," says Marley's friend Junior Dan. "This was in about 1975, when Jackie Brown, the Cables, Melodians, Bob Andy, Marcia Griffiths, and all of that was going on. Harry J had called me in and said he had all these albums to do, but could only give us a small amount of money. He said that he'd give us studio time instead, so we did it and at the end of about 13, 14 albums, I got my own album done, but then he took a mix of it without me knowing, went to England and made a deal with Chris Blackwell. That album was never released, and the only song people might know from it was one called 'Save Life'. It was a song Bob used to like and I was in Harry J's mixing it one day when Skill Cole came in saying, 'Is that Bob's tune you're finishing?' I said it was me, so he run outside to get Bob and Chris Blackwell to come listen, and Chris said he'd heard it already, on a tape Harry J had given me. I said, 'You can't have heard it. You're not supposed to have heard this before inna your life!' He said 'yes', so I walk right into Harry J's office to have it out with him.

"Before that, he'd said he wanted to promote me in England and had taken some photographs with me behind the microphone, playing my bass and singing. It was all beginning to add up now. Harry J said he took a rough mix and carried it up to England to see if Island would like it, so I said, 'But why you never tell me? You're trying to pull some stunt behind my back, so I'm taking my stuff out of here today.' He said, 'Well you can't take my tape.' I'd just played on 13 albums for him without pay and now he's saying I can't have my tape unless I pay him £50 or £60, when session musicians like myself were only getting like £10 a side, or something like that. I just go find a local bad man and say, 'Look, Harry J is messing me around and I need a gun.' He say sure, so I stick it in my waist, go back in his office, show him the gun and tell him I've come for the tape. He starts protesting, saying I can't have the tape and he's got security men outside, and I'm in there thinking I might have to shoot my way out except I don't want to do that, so I say, 'Alright. None of us is going to have this,' and he has a demagnetiser in his office, so I stick it on there and it's gone. The only thing left from it is that one song, and then a friend lets out a whistle to let me know the police is coming, so I run out the back and jump over the wall, and never went back."

CHAPTER TWENTY

All The Way From Trenchtown

AFTER Marley had "officially" hired Don Taylor by verbal agreement and a handshake, his new manager phoned Stu Weintraub of Associated Booking to begin planning the Wailers' summer '75 American tour. He also called Island's Charlie Nuccio, who'd been fretting about the lost opportunities in promoting *Natty Dread*, but was delighted to hear the Wailers would be touring once more. Now that he had help with the business side of things, Marley was more confident in going out on the road with a new Wailers line-up in place. Apart from Family Man and Carly, the band consisted of Anderson on lead guitar, Downie on keyboards, and Seeco on percussion. Rita and Judy would be the only backing vocalists, as Marcia was pregnant and couldn't travel. Touter didn't go, since Marley considered him too young, and in the continuing absence of Lindo, that left Tyrone as first choice. Jaffe claims to have persuaded Marley to hire the keyboardist, but Family Man says otherwise.

"Tyrone had come in the picture after the Youth Professionals split up, and Robbie headed off to do things for himself," he recalls. "Tyrone was playing at this hotel between Ocho Rios and Montego Bay. Me bring in some percussion with Seeco too, 'cause it was from there 'im take it more serious."

Prior to meeting Rita and moving in with her Aunt Viola, Marley had lived at 9 Second Street in Trenchtown. Seeco, who was several years older, lived at No. 20 and had first befriended Marley during a game of cricket. Bob bowled him two overs and Seeco had hit him all over the street, laughing good-naturedly as his young neighbour grew increasingly disconsolate. Marley would often sing in Seeco's yard, practising songs he'd heard on the radio. Although Joe Higgs lived just down the road, he and Marley had fallen out and so weren't on speaking terms at the time. Seeco had been an associate of calypso star Lord Flea before the latter moved to Miami, and was well versed in jazz, as well as calypso and mento. He'd also known Joe Harriott, who'd left for London and become a mainstay of the British jazz scene during the Sixties.

Soon after their friendship began, Marley called round to Seeco's yard, saying he was going to audition for Studio One and did Seeco want to come with him? Seeco said no, as he was cooking. Marley didn't have his own songs at that point, but went to see Coxsone anyway, sang two songs, but was told to come back in six months' time, since the producer didn't think he was ready. According to Seeco, this was before Marley visited Leslie Kong and voiced 'Judge Not'. Not long afterwards, Seeco's wife Willie nursed "my Nesta" back to health after a sliver of metal had lodged in his eye. Marley had received the injury while working as a welder alongside another future reggae pioneer, Desmond Dekker. Marley and Seeco wrote 'Simmer Down' together, just before Marley's second audition for Coxsone, by which time he'd made peace with Higgs and formed the Wailing Wailers. Seeco remained one of Marley's closest friends and mentors. His presence provided Bob with a continuing reminder of how far they'd come since those early days of struggle in Trenchtown and his counsel was therefore welcomed, even though he had no role in the Wailers' business affairs.

The 1975 Natty Dread tour was Taylor's first as the Wailers' manager, although according to Family Man, it was Marley who negotiated touring expenses from Island. Taylor appointed Tony Garnett as tour manager and hired two roadies, which pleased Family Man and Carly no end.

Family Man Barrett: "When my brother and I were out on the road with Bob, Bunny, and Peter, we were the handymen of the group, lifting up the instruments and things like that. We never allow them to lift up so much as a bag, and then because Peter and Bunny's names appear on *Catch A Fire* and *Burnin'*, they get money sent to them direct and that's how they could afford to set up their own labels, Intel Diplo and Solomonic. Peter said he is an intelligent diplomat and yet he had us as slaves until we get these two other guys, Harper and Benjamin Foot, to roadie for us. After they join, Carly and I ease off the lifting because Bob would say to us, 'Mind your fingers!' He didn't want us to damage anything that could affect our playing."

Blackwell had worked for Jamaica's Governor General, Hugh Foot, as a young man, so hiring his son Benjamin was clearly a reciprocal gesture. It was also Neville Garrick's first tour as the Wailers' lighting man. Garrick had earned his graphic arts degree from UCLA, where his cultural sensibilities had been stirred after seeing Angela Davis enshrined as a symbol of resistance for African-Americans. Wearing her hair in a large Afro, she remained resolute about her allegiance with the Black Panthers after being put on trial in February 1972, and was eventually found innocent of illegally procuring guns for them. Garrick had also been in Los Angeles during the Wattstax Festival that summer, and watched entranced as Jesse Jackson and Richard Pryor addressed the vast crowd. The black renaissance was fading; the momentum derived from the civil rights movement dissipated after the deaths of Malcolm X and Martin Luther King, as had the flurry of Black Nationalism fuelled by the Panthers and musicians such as James Brown and Curtis Mayfield.

The US government's sustained offensives against activists of all persuasions – both black and white – drove any semblance of organised resistance even further underground. As if from nowhere, heroin was beginning to flood the streets and this new mood of despair was compounded by the plight of returning soldiers from Vietnam, many of whom were unable to get work, suffered from trauma-related illnesses and were even looked down upon for having participated in such a shameful war. Gil Scott Heron's 'Home Is Where The Hatred Is' expressed a lot of what they were feeling, and there was growing unrest in the Middle East, too, as conflicts raged between Israel and Syria and Egypt, and also Jordan and Saudi Arabia. With the hippie ideals of peace and love lying in tatters, fresh hope was needed.

Garrick returned to Kingston and became art director at the *Jamaica Daily News* in 1973. One of his earliest assignments was to cover the Marvin Gaye concert at the Carib Theatre in May '74. Garrick met Marley at a post-show press party and the two became close friends. Neville eventually left the *Daily News* after being invited to work for the Wailers, or "Jah", as Marley told him. One of his first tasks was to design and paint a backdrop for the Wailers' stage performances that would visually define their Rastafarian beliefs. No other Jamaican group had done this before, but with such rich imagery to draw upon, Garrick's imagination was quick to ignite as he envisioned glorious tapestries using dread iconography. Some of his ideas may have been inspired by the Jamaica National Dance Theatre Company's production *Court Of Jah*, which was staged in April, featuring three songs from *Natty Dread*. Choreographed by Rex Nettleford, the dancers performed their routines in front of a brightly coloured painting of a Rastaman designed by local artist Colin Garland.

This striking image was later matched by Garrick's own designs, which depicted black heroes such as Marcus Garvey and Emperor Haile Selassie I.

The backdrops he created were suspended behind the Wailers as they performed onstage to further underline what the band represented, in the unlikely case audiences missed the significance of Marley's lyrics. Here was Rastafarian culture writ large, in colourful imagery 10 to 12 feet tall, measuring over 20 feet in length.

Garrick's time on the road started memorably when he was arrested at Miami airport.

Family Man Barrett: "I had two pounds of herb on me that day, stitched into a pillow, one pound of bush and one pound of sensimelia. I didn't get checked, but since the others were wearing army pants and had like army bags on their shoulders, the customs people didn't like it. They pulled Neville Garrick over, looked into his bag and there it was. Don Taylor, he turned to me and said, 'Family Man, get on the bus and we'll deal with the situation,' so I threw the pillow over my shoulder and walked away. Neville Garrick spent a while locked up in there, so we always tried to travel clean after that."

Noel "King Sporty" Williams was contacted to help bail Garrick out. The one-time Jamaican deejay had met Marley at Studio One but had subsequently moved to Miami, where he'd created a niche for himself as a producer with TK Records.

The tour opened at Miami's Diplomat Hotel on June 5. The Wailers then flew to Toronto, performing at Massey Hall (June 8), followed by two shows at the Quiet Knight Club in Chicago, where Bob, Rita, and Seeco were reunited with Junior Braithwaite. After playing Detroit and Cleveland, the Wailers were in New York, performing in front of 10,000 people at the Schaeffer Music Festival, held at the Wollman Skating Rink in Central Park, on June 18. Blues guitarist Roy Buchanan opened the festival and other acts on the bill included Rory Gallagher, the J Geils Band, Judy Collins, Journey, Dave Mason, Three Dog Night, Blood, Sweat & Tears, and Peter Frampton. Writing in the *Village Voice*, Patrick Carr described the Wailers' Central Park performance as "a true musical love rush" that left "Jamaicans and Americans giddy with glee." Other reports make mention of Marley's unintelligibility, although Griel Marcus called them "the best black band in the world," saying *Natty Dread* combined good beats "with a heavy dose of mystery which sneaks up on you, drops back, confuses your feelings and engages your mind."

Jaffe left the Wailers after the Central Park show, ostensibly to help Tosh put the finishing touches to *Legalise It* at Shelter Records' Tulsa studio. Jaffe and Marley hadn't seen eye to eye ever since an argument during a trip to Los Angeles to meet with Chris Blackwell. Jaffe was unhappy about the changed spelling of *Natty Dread* and also about Marley and Taylor's decision to allocate songwriting credits "to the wrong people". He couldn't understand why Marley had remained relatively unmoved by what Jaffe saw as record label machinations, and was upset at not being mentioned anywhere on the jacket. He and Marley started arguing in the Island offices on Sunset Boulevard and continued back at their hotel.

"I wanted to know if he was going to let [*Natty Dread*] come out like that and he started to go off on me about how I was too concerned with my own credit, but I wasn't buying it," he wrote in *One Love: Life With Bob Marley And The Wailers*. "I wanted to know how the album that was called *Knotty Dread* could be released with a title that meant exactly the opposite. It turned into us cursing at each other. It started with shoving, but I was not going to back down and then it turned into a fistfight. We were just about the same size, so nobody really won. It just ended in exhaustion, but it was not really over because nothing had been resolved. We stopped talking to each other and it wasn't until half a year later when I was in jail in Kingston Central [after being caught with herb at a Kingston roadblock] and Bob arranged for me to have money for a lawyer that I was able to forgive him, knowing that his being there for me was more important than any fight we could possibly have. For me, it wasn't the same any more between us because part of my desire to go play with Peter came from the fact that I felt I had contributed so much to *Knotty Dread* without any credit and that kind of put me in the same boat as Peter. We both had something to prove with *Legalise It*."

Jaffe alleged Taylor would occasionally stand in front of him onstage, blocking him from the audience, although Family Man says that since he wasn't supposed to be on the stage in the first place, "he was hyping up himself too much. It was Bob's stage, not his, and when it came to things like that, Don Taylor never interfered with any one of us in the music department. He was there to deal with the paperwork, but yes, he was always backstage or in the wings, because he and Tony Garnet would make sure we had towels and water, t'ings like that. Lee Jaffe, he had no right to be there." Since Taylor refers to Jaffe as a "gofer" in his book and Family Man calls him "a weasel", it's safe to assume his presence wasn't exactly missed.

Staying in New York at the Plaza Hotel, the Wailers played at the Spectrum Theatre in Philadelphia, and the following night at the Manhattan

Centre, a hastily booked show (by the Jamaica Progressive League) due to crowd reaction at the Schaeffer Music Festival. Anthony Spaulding, Martha Velez, various Sire Records' staff and eight finalists from a Miss Jamaica USA contest were in the audience, although the atmosphere was rather subdued, despite it being a full house. One reviewer, after noting the Wailers had played three encores "once the suits had left", likened Marley to "a young Mick Jagger". "That was one of the best live performances I have ever seen in my life," says Craig Leon. "The energy level was so high and the music spoke even better than the recordings. It really rocked."

The tour moved on to Hartford, Connecticut and a seven-night stand to enthusiastic crowds at St Paul's Mall in Boston, Massachusetts, between June 23–29. By now, the club was the band's home from home and so, too, the self-catering apartments where they could cook their own food and relax without fear of unnecessary attention. Thanks to local connections, good herb could be scored without too much trouble. The band then headed to the West Coast, first appearing on *The Manhattan Transfer Show* taped at the CBS Television Studios in Hollywood.

Manhattan Transfer, a four-part vocal harmony group whose nostalgic presentation and choice of material harked back to the Forties, had recently released their debut album to rave reviews. For four weeks over the summer, they were given their own syndicated Sunday evening show – the usual potpourri of songs and humour, typical of the light entertainment shown on Seventies' American television. Manhattan Transfer's brand of good-time revivalism inevitably stood in marked contrast to their Jamaican guests' militant, Rastafarian agenda. Rather than perform some of their repertoire's lighter material, the Wailers plumbed for 'Get Up, Stand Up' and 'Kinky Reggae', although only the latter made the final cut. One can only speculate what viewers in Middle America thought when Marley sidled up to the mic, shook his locks and sang of Miss Brown, who had "brown sugar all over her booga wooga."

The Wailers started a four-day residency at San Francisco's Boarding House, beginning July 4. The following day, Arthur Ashe becoming the first black tennis player to win Wimbledon was a cause for rejoicing. Even though none of the band played or followed tennis to any great extent, the fact that a black man triumphed in what had previously been a white, bourgeois pursuit appealed, giving Ashe's victory even more significance than the independence celebrations. While in the Bay Area, the band were driving through town when they chanced upon Wya Lindo walking

down the street carrying an instrument case. They immediately stopped
the van and began plying their former keyboardist with questions. With
his classically trained prowess, Marley readily offered to rehire him but
Lindo, who was studying music at Berkeley and residing comfortably at
Taj Mahal's house on the outskirts of San Francisco, declined.

Once the Wailers' residency at the Boarding House ended, the tour bus
headed for the Paramount Theatre in Oakland. Taylor's ex-client Martha
Reeves was support act, further strengthening the bond with Motown
artists. The show, booked by Bill Graham at short notice, was another
sell-out, just as he'd expected. The ripples of excitement generated by
these concerts quickly spread further down the coast, in advance of the
Wailers' prestigious shows at LA's Roxy Theatre between July 9–13. The
venue was co-owned by record executive David Geffen, and his celebrity
connections, coupled with the venue's location on Sunset Boulevard,
made it a magnet for music industry types living in Beverly Hills, or the
canyons above Sunset Strip. Joni Mitchell, Cat Stevens, George Harrison,
Ringo Starr and members of the Rolling Stones, Grateful Dead, and the
Band attended the Wailers' shows and the buzz surrounding the Roxy
concerts wouldn't begin to fade until Bruce Springsteen played the club in
October. Harrison told *Melody Maker* that Marley was the ". . . best thing
I've seen in 10 years. Marley reminds me so much of Dylan in the early
days, playing guitar as if he's so new to it. And his rhythm is so simple yet
so beautiful. I could watch the Wailers all night."

Harrison wasn't the only ex-Beatle interested in Marley. John Lennon
had asked to meet Marley in New York, but the singer sent Al Anderson
in his place. Anderson reported back after his meeting with John and
Yoko at a restaurant that the Lennons' interest was genuine, but nothing
came of it. The guitarist thinks Lennon was either too political for
Marley's liking or that the timing had been unfortunate since Marley was
actively seeking to disengage himself from being seen as a figurehead.*

Taylor and Steinberg arranged a meeting with Blackwell while in Los
Angeles. Marley's manager felt the 1974 agreement wasn't generous
enough to his client and made it clear that he wished to renegotiate its
terms – a common enough practice in the music industry when an artist's
popularity increased. While refusing to accept that the 1974 Recording
Agreement was unfair, Blackwell was willing to renegotiate it. Island

---

* Paul McCartney did record with Lee Perry but it's interesting to speculate what would
have emerged had Marley and Lennon ever ventured into a studio together.

and Marley therefore agreed to terminate and replace the previous agreement.

"I began to sense that Blackwell was using various persons and things to try and control the situation," Taylor wrote in his autobiography. "Later it became clear to me that what Chris was doing was feeling out the weak links in the chain, the people he could own either by employing them in his firms or hanging out the carrots of benefits and monetary reward."

The Barrett brothers played no part in these business discussions and Blackwell asserts there was no reason why they should have done. During one meeting, Taylor broached the subject of Marley purchasing 56 Hope Road, and asked for a million dollar advance for the Wailers' next three albums. Blackwell insisted it should be ten, pointing out that an artist's career was usually over by then, although this didn't allow for live albums, an oversight Marley would soon regret. While agreeing certain terms in principle, nothing was actually finalised during these meetings. Taylor and Blackwell agreed to meet again in London, where the Wailers were due to play shows.

The band arrived in England to find their old associate Johnny Nash at number one in the charts with 'Tears On My Pillow' while the remaining chart places were taken up with lightweight disco tracks, including Van McCoy's 'The Hustle', alongside novelty records like Judge Dread's 'Je T' Aime (Moi Non Plus)', a ribald version of Serge Gainsbourg and Jane Birkin's controversial 1969 hit. Family Man and Carly laughed in disbelief when they discovered that Judge Dread was a pseudonym for former bouncer Alex Hughes, who'd worked for Commercial Entertainment when the brothers had toured England with the Upsetters.

After witnessing the crowds' response at the Roxy (particularly their singing along to 'No Woman No Cry'), Blackwell arranged to record the Wailers' London appearances on July 17 and 18 at the Lyceum Theatre, just off the Strand, in London's West End. Steve Smith recorded the shows on the Rolling Stones' Mobile Studio, using two-track equipment, while Dave Harper was the sound engineer inside the venue which was packed to the rafters both nights. Third World, who'd also signed to Island, were the support act. Blackwell described the concerts as "sensational" and a turning point in Marley's career.

"It was the closest I have ever got to a religious experience," wrote deejay and filmmaker Don Letts in his book *Culture Clash: Punk Meets Dread Rockers*. "The venue was so packed that whenever anyone moved I was lifted off the ground. It was the single most exciting music moment of my life. We were thrashing around with this British black, Black British identity crisis and then the full impact and reality of what we had heard on [Marley's] records all came together in that show. It was no longer an abstract thing that you could interpret one way or another. Here was the man onstage, delivering it live and direct. It gave me the confidence to be myself. Bob Marley brought the politic to the forefront in reggae. It was a militant Rasta rebel vibe."

In December, Island issued the recordings as *Bob Marley & The Wailers Live!* Most of the tracks were taken from the second night and mixed by Phil Brown at Basing Street. Smith and Blackwell were credited with production of the record (as opposed to the music) which continues to be rated as one of the best all-time live albums. While not a classic Marley performance, it's certainly an archetypal one.

The crowd are in the mood right from the start as Tony Garnett announces: "This, I want to tell you, is the Trenchtown experience – all the way from Trenchtown, Jamaica, Bob Marley & the Wailers!" The band sound tight but loose. Downie's playing is noticeably more restrained and less obtrusive than Lindo's. 'Trenchtown Rock' is perfunctory but receives wild applause regardless, while Tyrone and Family Man combine to brilliant effect on 'Burnin' And Lootin''. Marley's vocals are heartfelt as he accentuates the lyrics with characteristic hand gestures such as putting his arm across his brow. "How many rivers do we have to cross, to speak to the boss?" he beseeches, as Rita and Judy coo in support, swaying in unison, looking the epitome of Rasta womanhood in their flowing robes and with their locks tightly wrapped in red, gold and green. Marley, clad in familiar denim, roams the length of the stage or jogs on the spot, his dreadlocks flailing under the arc lights as he summons the power of Jah.

Family Man stands impassive behind shades and a bowler hat. Like Anderson, he'd started to grow dreadlocks, while Downie still had a semi-Afro. Only Carly's hair is short but then he always did have a reputation for being neat and tidy. The band finally hit their stride on 'Them Belly Full'. Halfway through, Anderson lets rip with a snarling wah-wah solo, without ever detracting from the rhythm which was paramount to the Wailers' music. People start to call out requests but Marley doesn't respond. The band launches into 'Lively Up Yourself' which receives an ecstatic welcome. The crowd responds not only to what Marley's singing but also his charisma and command of the music. Like a modern-day shaman, he's caught up in the spirit of the music, dancing or gesturing, yet his command of the situation is total. James Brown had the same gift; capable of mesmerising an audience while rousing them to dizzy heights of musical communion.

'No Woman No Cry' is transformed from a reggae blues into a full-blown, ghetto melodrama. Marley's vocals are borne on a tide of emotion as the crowd sing along with him in as passionate a display of audience participation as was ever heard on record, particularly on the life-affirming "everything's going to be alright" chorus. The original *Natty Dread* studio cut pales in comparison to this seven-minute version featuring Downie's Bach-like organ phrases and Anderson's wonderfully poignant solo. 'I Shot The Sheriff' forcibly grabs the attention before turning into a loping skank, enhanced by powerful organ riffs and the I-Threes' bright harmonies. It's arguably the best track on the entire album and again surpasses the studio original. By this point, Marley still hasn't spoken to the audience, but then he doesn't need to, since he's communicating on some other level. The original album ended with 'Get Up, Stand Up', featuring a fatback groove on the intro and a chorus that sent shivers racing down the spine, with Marley's memorable theatrical cries of "A woy, a woy yo yo."

An additional track, 'Kinky Reggae', was issued as the flipside to the album's lead-off single 'No Woman No Cry' (and later included as a bonus track on the remastered version of *Live At The Lyceum*, as it would later be known, when reissued in 1981.) Marley introduces it and then calls out each band member in turn. "I want you to meet my brother Carlton over here," he says. Carly's timekeeping is unreal; he doesn't solo, but simply accentuates the beat, just like his brother. "I want you to meet my sisters," Bob continues, as he signals towards Judy and Rita, whose marital status was denied onstage and whenever the subject was broached in interviews. There is a sense that comments about Marley's enunciation in the US press might have had an effect, since his every word is crystal clear which came as unexpected when the resulting album hit the streets.

Family Man Barrett: "We didn't exactly know what Island had in mind. We knew they were taping it, but we hadn't been told anything else and I didn't work on the final mix, which is why the only track that came out any good was 'No Woman No Cry'. That's the one they played on the radio a lot, and after that people start talking about the I-Threes, who they think sang on *Natty Dread*. The rest of the tracks weren't so hot, but that album still went on to become a legend in its own time. It was a surprise when I see it for the first time though, I tell you. A good surprise in the sense that it helped us reach a little further; knowing we had a live album out and people were getting to hear our live performance. But no, we didn't take part in it at all, because it was mixed by these guys who were around Island at the time and who try and outshine those of us who play and arrange everything in the band."

Family Man further pointed out how the album wasn't representational because 'Rasta Man Chant', the Wailers' traditional concert opener, was left off. Anderson wasn't happy with the results either, saying the first (Friday) night show was great but the band were told to play looser on the Saturday.

While in London, the band stayed in South Kensington at 1 Harrington Gardens, not far from the Natural History and Science museums. After the final Lyceum show, Don Letts followed them back to the apartment and sat feeling slightly awed as Marley held court among a circle of visitors. Letts combined both his main interests of music and fashion by working at Acme Attractions in the King's Road. After they'd got to know each other a little better, Marley would sometimes visit Letts at Acme to buy herb. Future Sex Pistol and reggae fan John Lydon, with his close friend Sid Vicious, was also a regular visitor to Acme, in the days when glam rock was metamorphosing into punk courtesy of Malcolm McLaren, and Vivienne Westwood's daring fashions. Marley and Family Man both liked London and appreciated how the young people were quick to grasp new ideas in expressing themselves. Jamaica was conservative by comparison, hidebound by outdated conventions, stemming from what many Rastas referred to as a "colonial mentality".

The UK tour wound up at Birmingham Odeon on July 19 and Manchester's Hard Rock Café on the 20th. However, the upbeat atmosphere was spoilt by press reports of unhappiness within the Wailers' camp from Anderson and Downie, who complained they received less money than the others. An angry Marley viewed this as an act of betrayal to the extent of threatening them with expulsion. In all other respects, the Natty Dread tour was an unqualified success, giving Island a further push in capitalising on the Wailers' fast-growing popularity outside of the core reggae market. Marley now had more leverage with the label than ever and with Taylor's help, he could finally negotiate terms designed to bring him nearer to his dream of artistic and economic independence.

While in London he, Taylor, and Blackwell shook hands on the Wailers' revised contract, referred to as the 1975 Recording Agreement.

As was the case in Los Angeles, the Barretts played no part in these discussions. The brothers assumed their unofficial arrangement with Marley was still valid and were blissfully unaware of being ineligible for a share in the legacy they continued to work towards creating. Was this deliberate, or did the situation arise almost of its own volition, since the brothers hadn't signed the original contract when they'd had the chance? Blackwell insists Island simply responded to market forces. "The press totally embraced Bob Marley," he said in 2006. "There was a huge amount of press articles and imagery of Bob Marley. It all became Bob Marley."

In reality, this process was one of the primary reasons why Tosh had left the Wailers, but there were other reasons why Island were so keen to play ball with Taylor.

"We wanted to extend our period of working with Bob Marley for a longer period of time," Blackwell continued. "One of the key differences is that Don Taylor was able to get Bob touring. It was very important to get Bob touring because that was the best way to build his career."

The other contributing factor was that Taylor had generated a buzz around Marley and the Wailers from elsewhere. Clive Davis, head of Arista Records, expressed interest in signing the band just two or three days before they arrived in London. The news must have sent shock waves reverberating around 22 St Peter's Square, since directly after arriving in London, the band were met by Island's Denise Mills, who rushed them off to meet Blackwell for urgent business talks. Taylor reiterated how his client wanted to purchase 56 Hope Road and, after some hesitation, Blackwell agreed to sell the property for US $125,000. Two days later, when Taylor and Marley went to sign the deal, they were presented with a statement claiming the artist owed Island US $550,000, yet Marley only ever remembered receiving £8,000 for *Catch A Fire* and *Burnin'*, and $12,000 for *Natty Dread*, plus the tour expenses advance. Taylor requested a breakdown of the accounts and discovered the rest of the money had been paid to Island employees acting on Marley's behalf.

Shrewdly noticing how Marley, Tosh and Livingston hadn't signed authorisations for any of these sums, Taylor refused to pay and got Island to waive Marley's share. Between August 12 and September 19, the revised six-album contract was finalised, with Island delivering a $250,000 advance with half being deducted for the purchase of 56 Hope Road followed by $50,000 for the first album (*Rastaman Vibration*) under the new deal. This represented a stratospheric increase, underlining Island's increased belief in the artist, and Taylor's bargaining powers.

Family Man Barrett: "Chris Blackwell didn't want us to stray and we didn't want to wheel out of Island either, because we talk about that with Bob. We decided Chris Blackwell wasn't trying to hold onto us like how Danny Sims did with Johnny Nash. It was a different strategy at work and so we weren't looking to get out of Island and Chris knew that. That's what he'd planned I guess, because he was pleased that Peter was out of the way and he could therefore get more control over us."

During the recording of the Wailers' next album, Marley's contract with Cayman Music came up for renewal. Marley renewed it for another year on the condition that the recording and management parts of the contract reverted back to him. Sims and Nash had agreed to this in a settlement agreement drawn up in or around October 1973. Marley had been signed to them as a songwriter and the company was therefore entitled to a share of his songwriting revenues until October 1976. Marley acknowledged that "any or all songs which I have written to the date hereof and all the songs I will write during the next three years will be published by said Cayman Music Inc." As well as publishing and world copyrights, Sims' agreement also entitled him to all compositions Marley "wrote, composed, created or conceived, in whole or in part, by himself alone or in collaboration during the term of the agreement."

After signing the settlement with Sims, Marley formed Tuff Gong Music. As Taylor delved deeper into the Wailers' business affairs, he discovered Tuff Gong Music had been registered in the US, thus incurring taxes and that Marley's friend Yvette Morris owned 99 per cent of the company. Taylor corrected this and formed Bob Marley Music, which he registered in Tortola in the British Virgin Islands. At the same time, he set about restructuring Marley's accounts. He appointed accountant Marvin Zolt, who like Steinberg was an expert in offshore tax structures. Taylor had originally met Zolt through Little Anthony, although it was Jerome Kurtz who set up a tax plan for Marley and the Wailers, advising them to register a company in Tortola, so they'd be exempt from paying tax in the US and UK. A contact attorney in Tortola, Michael Regiles, sold Marley a company called Media Aides for $1,000 because a structure was needed to own the rights to *Live!*, initially only released in the UK, which wasn't part of the Island deal. Marley was eventually paid around $500,000 for the UK and European distribution rights, which were paid into Media Aides.

"After Don began to manage us, Bob told me he had regular meetings with him about business and how to best organise our affairs," Family Man recalled in his 2006 evidence. Don said he could arrange for offshore companies to be set up, which would help save tax. Bob, Carly, and I were concerned that when we started touring and the money was coming in big time, we always had some money put away for a rainy day. Bob asked Don to look after that side of things. Given the currency exchange controls and the fact that we were earning substantial sums outside Jamaica, we wanted to make sure that we always had enough money available when we were abroad and in particular, when we were in Europe and America. This was something Don set up for us because we always had cash when we needed it whilst travelling.

"Bob told me that he was going to arrange for an offshore account to put our money in and said he would bring in to Jamaica whatever was needed to pay expenses and for the band. He said that he, Carly, and myself would be signatories on that account, but I told him this wasn't necessary and that he should set up the account in his name, for the three of us. He set up the offshore account and he had the money paid from that account into an account at the Citizens Bank in Jamaica. The idea was that we could take out what we needed and leave the rest for a rainy day."

Those who actively participated in the Wailers' business affairs didn't agree this was the case. Thomas Hayes worked for the Island group of companies between 1965 and 1993, initially as a salesman, then as international director and business affairs director and finally chairman. He was directly involved in the day-to-day liaison between Island and Bob Marley from 1975 until Marley's death in 1981. In a statement dated February 10, 2006, he says he only dealt with "Bob Marley, his lawyer, or his manager in respect of legal or business issues. As far as I am aware, neither the Barretts nor any of the other backing musicians had a direct contractual relationship with Island." Hayes admits that he wasn't involved in the 1974 Recording Agreement, but confirms that from Island's perspective the company "did not regard the Barretts as parties to that agreement."

Hayes took part in negotiating the 1975 Recording Agreement dated August 5, 1975, between Bob Marley and Island Records Limited. He also signed the Media Aides Agreement between Island Records Inc and Media Aides Limited, dated August 6, 1975, and the 1976 Recording Agreement between Bob Marley and Island Records Limited, dated December 15, 1976, on behalf of Island Records Inc and Island Records Limited respectively. He says the 1975 Agreement was terminated and the Media Aides Agreement entered into at the request of Steinberg and Taylor. Hayes understands this was for financial planning purposes.

When asked about the 1974 and 1975 recording agreements, Charles

Levison reiterated it was Marley's services that Island wished to secure. In a statement dated February 13, 2006, he said he didn't recollect why the Barrett brothers' names were added to the 1974 Recording Agreement or recall dealing with Family Man and Carly about the matter – only Marley and Taylor. Nor does he recall why he believed that the Barretts would be signing the 1974 agreement, as evidenced by Island's original correspondence. He interpreted his own handwritten notes on one such document to mean that Island was interested in having an option to acquire the Barretts' recording services in future, and while no advance would be paid to them, their royalty rates would match those paid to Marley.

"I'm on the second contract with Island, cah that only involve Bob Marley, Aston, and Carlton Barrett," insists Family Man. "It don't involve Bunny Wailer or Peter Touch, cah that date from the first time and all of that get void by the time the second contract was signed. The only t'ing they were involved with was this Tuff Gong thing between Bob, Bunny, and Peter, and yet when Bob sign this thing here, them two wasn't Wailers, and not even Rita Marley. And when royalty time come round, Bob take out his investment and then split the royalty 50–50; 50 per cent for him and 50 per cent for the band. And when I work pon royalties, I take half of that 50 per cent for my brother and I and the other half I split between the other musicians. We do that and it not even the money they should get. It's a lot more, but we just do that to keep everybody happy.

"When we were on the road, the session musicians and road crew were paid from the tour support money paid by Island Records. Bob often handed out money from concerts, as Don did not always tour with us. There was no fixed arrangement or practice as to how the other 50 per cent would be divided. That depended on the significance of other band members' contributions and on how much work they put in. As other musicians became part of the band, they were paid on the same basis, taking a percentage that came out of the 50 per cent share Bob didn't take. This was the case with musicians like Junior Marvin and Wya Lindo, who were both band members at various stages. However, my brother and I always got the largest shares and our shares were equal. Bob would generally discuss with me how the other 50 per cent should be divided and we would agree on who should be paid what. I can't recall specific conversations in which we all agreed the arrangements I describe but that's what we did. Bob also used to give Carly and I money on top to compensate us for having given up our third way split, as contracted brethren. Carly and I

367

still got paid our royalties every three months, unlike the other band members, because they were session musicians, and just engaged for touring and studio work."

This system worked fine when the band was touring, but alternative arrangements were later made in the case of the Barretts.

Family Man Barrett: "I discussed with Bob whether Carly and I could get regular payments from Island Records. That's because when we were recording, we often had no money coming in, because we only got paid every six months. Bob told Don to arrange that, and after this, we started to get money from Island Records every three months. I called this 'royalty time'. It was money from our earnings, and this continued until Bob's death."

In fact, these weren't royalties at all, but payments made from funds Island advanced to Marley that were recoupable from his personal earnings, hence all the difficulties Family Man would later encounter when he began talking about "royalties".

On November 25, 1975, Taylor wrote to Blackwell requesting the Barretts be paid $1,400 per month when they weren't touring, and for these sums to be deducted from "session costs pertaining to your contract with Bob Marley." Levinson replied in a letter dated December 17, confirming he'd sent $8,400 to Taylor's account, and instructed the same amount to be paid each quarter until December 1976 "on the basis that Bob Marley can request us to terminate this arrangement at any time." Another stipulation was that Island themselves could terminate this arrangement, "if Bob Marley should agree to Carly and Family Man recording for an artist not on the Island label." He concluded by asking Taylor for a copy of Marley's agreement with Carly and Family Man "just for the purposes of completing our records when this is signed."

Of course, there was no written agreement between them. Taylor informed Levinson on February 26 that "Bob Marley's agreement with Carlton and Aston Barrett has nothing to do with his agreement with Island Records. In fact, Carlton and Aston are free to work with anyone Bob chooses without causing termination of Bob's financial agreement with Island Records."

Judging by Levinson's letter, there was still the perception that Island retained the Barretts' exclusive recording services, even though there was no hard evidence to support this. This clearly meant the Barretts were no longer contracted to Island, if indeed they'd ever been in the first place.

CHAPTER TWENTY-ONE

Dread Lion

THE Wailers returned to Jamaica from touring in August 1975. Marley arrived home separately as he stopped off in Delaware to see his mother. Accounts of the band's overseas shows had filtered through, with the August 10 edition of the *Sunday Gleaner* reporting how "entertainment writers in North America, Britain, and other countries have been reaching into their store of superlatives to describe the fantastic talent of Jamaica's reigning King of Reggae, Bob Marley . . . every reviewer has extolled the dynamism and talent of this young man, who has set the world of popular music aflame with his searing rhythms and lyrics, backed up by the compelling beat of Jamaican reggae."

Marley was quoted as saying that Jamaican musicians were handicapped by their unoriginality. "They tend to lean on other musicians' material, and that sometimes turns original ideas into mediocrity." He claimed to get his inspiration from "going in the hills to be at peace with himself and his God."

During that same month, the *Gleaner* reprinted an article Sebastian Clarke (brother of Brent Clarke) had written for the *New Musical Express*. "Bob Marley is only as good as his back-up musicians," Clarke wrote. "Marley is undoubtedly an excellent lyricist and possesses an ability to arrange, but it is Family Man's surreptitious role as bandleader and co-arranger that sustains the group's essential unity." The article made reference to "a youth named Robbie" (Shakespeare) heard playing on 'Concrete Jungle', and who Family Man says "played on this Johnny Clarke you hear about." Family Man also says he "gave a lot of coaching" to Alva 'Reggie' Lewis, crediting Jackie Jackson as his main influence, who Clarke says "has been noticeably associated with a middlebrow studio like Byron Lee's Dynamic." Fams admitted to Clarke that the Wailers were "more like a solo thing right now. Bob do the lead singing and you have the backing, so the music just stay so, to direct riddim. Bob and I put the music together. On certain tune, you might hear the guitar take a solo, but it's really vocal and riddim. If you do hear a tune with a solo, it depend on that particular tune, that feel, but most tunes is just riddim.

"Most times, I fit a line to the instruments according to the inspiration I get from the tune when we rehearse, when working out or jamming. Most times, too, Bob feel a t'ing and might just pick on him guitar and from there develop it." The feature was accompanied by an out-of-date photo showing the bassist with trimmed hair, playing his Hofner (whereas he now wore dreadlocks and had changed to a Fender).

Despite healthy reviews, the *Live!* version of 'No Woman No Cry' narrowly failed to breach the UK Top 20 in August, where it lost out to such milestones of popular culture as Jasper Carrot's 'Funky Moped'. The single didn't chart at all in America, where the likes of John Denver, Elton John, and the Eagles ruled the roost. *Natty Dread* didn't chart either and only managed to scrape into the UK Top 50 that November, with *Live!* peaking at 38 the following month. Thanks to a combination of union regulations and the BBC's monopoly of UK radio and television, it was difficult to make an impression upon the British charts in 1975.

To most record buyers, reggae was like music from another planet, especially hardcore dub by the likes of Augustus Perry, Lee Scratch Perry, and King Tubby. A lot of the vocal stuff was raw, infectious and soaked in revolutionary fervour, featuring characters with such outlandish names as Prince Jazzbo, Tappa Zukie, and Shorty the President, who told of cartoon-like escapades in a near-unintelligible language. It was out-rageous, mind-boggling, trance-inducing and hilarious, often at the same time. With rare exception, most of these recordings were only available in limited qualities, on badly pressed vinyl, in specialist shops located away from the average high street. Whereas Ken Boothe and John Holt's MOR brand of reggae got Radio 1 airplay, it was rare to hear roots music on national radio or in clubs, yet a growing army of fanatics emerged who would not listen to anything else. Together with audiences in Jamaica, these people revelled in I Roy's feud with Prince Jazzbo, and singers like Johnny Clarke, Cornel Campbell, and Jacob Miller.

Marley's songs were becoming popular in Jamaica as the year 1975 drew to a close. As lead singer with Inner Circle, Miller covered 'Rebel Music (3 O'Clock Roadblock)' and 'I Shot The Sheriff', Clarke versioned 'No Woman No Cry', and the Cimarons (under the guise of the Maroons) made a brilliant job of 'Talkin' Blues'. Clarke's 'Declaration Of Rights', 'Rock With Me Baby' and 'Joshua's Word' (expressing criticism of Michael Manley) were produced by Bunny Lee, who also masterminded such Cornel Campbell hits as 'The Gorgon'*, 'Conquering Gorgon', and 'Dance In A Greenwich Farm', which epitomised the transition between flyers and rockers, as well as a host of tracks by Linval Thompson, such as 'Jah Jah A The Conqueror', 'Ride On Natty Dread', and 'Long, Long Dreadlocks'.

As a budding producer, Linval recruited Family Man to play on sessions for his own Thompson Sound label which resulted in *I Love Marijuana*, a best-selling album for Trojan. Although Marley wasn't in favour of his bassist playing outside sessions, he nodded with approval when hearing his friend's lines underpinning tracks from Eric Gale's *Negril*, Max Romeo's *Revelation Time*, and songs by Gregory Isaacs ('Sun Shines For Me') and Dillinger ('CB 200'). The latter pair were recorded at Channel One, which the Hookim brothers had turned into a veritable hits factory thanks to songs by Junior Byles ('Fade Away') and vocal trio the Mighty Diamonds, who'd shot to prominence with 'I Need A Roof', 'Right Time' and 'Country Living'. Their song, 'Have Mercy', and U Roy's 'Runaway Girl' were among the first singles released on Virgin Records' Frontline offshoot. It wasn't the only new label to capitalise on the roots reggae boom. Three former Trojan staffers formed Klik to release Big Youth's *Dreadlocks Dread*.

Big Youth had been releasing hits on his own Negust Negast label, as well as voicing tunes for Yabby You, Randy's, and Prince Tony. Jack Ruby even unleashed him over the same rhythm as Burning Spear's 'Marcus Garvey', as songs by Pablo Moses, the Morwells, Itals, Michael Rose, and the Abyssinians brought cultural, roots reggae music to the fore. Literally hundreds of others followed, including the African Brothers, Twinkle Brothers, Fred Locks, Tyrone Taylor, Prince Lincoln's Royal Rasses, and Ras Michael & the Sons of Negus, whose 'None A Jah Jah Children' provided the perfect synthesis between nyahbinghi and Seventies-style dancehall. Ras Michael's *Dadawah* album, featuring contributions from both Peter Tosh and Robbie Shakespeare, was being distributed by Tommy Cowans' Talent Corporation, also home to Jacob Miller and Inner Circle.

1975 was also the year Rastafari took over Jamaica, with Jacob Miller scoring heavily with 'Tenement Yard', 'Baby I Love You So' and 'Tired

---

* Bunny recalls: "Bagga Walker played the bass on that and Fams the piano . . . A man we used to know would call out, 'That man a gorgon!' We like the talk and so Derrick Morgan wrote a song about it."

Fi Lick Weed In A Bush' – songs that left his allegiance in no doubt. While it had failed to breach the mainstream, the influence of the Wailers' *Natty Dread* and its success in capturing the zeitgeist of the Jamaican scene at that time was unprecedented. The band had already recorded many of the tracks that would appear on their next album when, on August 28, the front page of the *Gleaner* blazed the headline: "Haile Selassie Dies At 83." In a report from Addis Ababa, servants had found the Emperor dead in his bed the day before. Despite his advanced years, he had been under house arrest since the previous September, after being deposed by a military coup. Two months earlier, he'd had a prostate operation but his son, Crown Prince Asfa Wossen Haile Selassie, who was exiled in London, said his father had been in good health, and demanded an independent autopsy.

Michael Manley made a public announcement in which he stated "the world will remember Haile Selassie as an outstanding statesman and particularly for his efforts to free Africa from colonialism, racism, and all forms of foreign domination . . . we realise that the Jamaican Rastafarian community, for whom His Imperial Majesty was a unique symbol, will be especially distressed to learn of the passing of this great man."

To the Rasta community, Selassie's death was inconceivable. He was the Messiah, the Christ figure come again. Therefore the King of Kings and Conquering Lion of the Tribe of Judah, who'd drawn representatives from 72 different nations to his coronation over 40 years ago, could not die like any ordinary mortal. Elders shook their heads sagely, saying, "Jah can't dead." Younger adherents weren't so sure and confusion reigned as discussions raged back and forth in the tenement yards of Kingston and around the campfires of Rasta settlements in Warieka Hill and beyond.

The following day, the Wailers played at Kingston's National Arena, backing the I-Threes. The show, dubbed No Woman No Cry, marked Rita Marley's debut as a promoter. Other acts on the bill included Inner Circle and King Tubby's Hi-Fi featuring U Roy.

"Many people are scoffers," said Marley, shortly after. "Many people say to me, 'Your God is dead. How can he dead? How can God die mon?' These people, they don't think too clear. They have the devil in them and that devil is some trick devil. He smart their eyes and vex the brain. That's why me wrote 'Jah Live'."

The way in which Marley grasped the initiative and delivered 'Jah Live' amid such uneasiness was the mark of a truly great artist. Rastafarians who needed reassuring were presented with a rousing endorsement of Selassie's divinity that rang out like a clarion call. It was a tune of immense importance to Rastafarians and yet Island failed to promote the single when it appeared in January 1976, even stating that it wasn't the official follow-up to 'No Woman No Cry'. The irony was that the song is arguably the most relevant in Marley's entire catalogue, for which he had to dig deepest within his soul as he grappled – like so many other Rastafarians – with the enormity of what had happened in his spiritual homeland of Ethiopia.

The rhythm for 'Jah Live' had already been recorded in readiness for Marley's lyrics, which he voiced before a spellbound assembly of friends (including Lee Perry), hangers-on and band members at Harry J's. As the session drew to a close, Sylvan Morris was still trying to mix the song. When the results didn't sound right, Tyrone Downie signalled that Family Man should take over. Even though he was Jamaica's leading engineer at the time, Morris later admitted Family Man had directed all the music and that he'd learnt a lot from the bassist about balancing the sound.

Family Man Barrett: "When we work pon 'Jah Live', it's like Scratch and [Morris] come with some weird set of vibes, cah we used to work well together, but me gone past that now. I think [Morris] was under pressure at the time, so me just start help him out. I was there at the studio watching him try to mix it, but four times him have to pull up and start again. Everybody start to get ignorant, and him as the engineer feel embarrassed, because he kept saying, 'What kind of sound you want?' and all them t'ings. I say, 'Well you have 16 tracks, so I would like to hear it pon the 16 track,' but he say that if him put it on there, then some will cancel out. I say we have to tone each one properly and get the harmony, because it's like you're painting a picture and adding each separate colour. He said, 'I like how you sound. I like what you talk,' and then him ask me what I want to hear first. I say the drum is the first instrument in music and so to bring in the foot drum and then the snare and the hi-hat, left and right, until everyt'ing match up. Then we bring in the percussion track 'cause once you hear that with the drums and you still can't dance to it, then it's not right yet.

"As soon as he heard that, him felt pleased and ease off. The bass a bite now and we put the lead guitar over that. 'Cause Al play the intro on the solo, then we set the rhythm guitar and the piano 'til them just lock together as one. That's the Gong's sound right there, and it can't be no tinny business, 'cause it need to have a natural fire and the rhythm guitar and the piano, them have to mesh together. Anyway, that was how 'Jah Live' was mixed."

Marley's vocal sounds weary, as if weighed down by the task confronting him, and even the rhythm is somewhat sluggish. "The truth is an offence, but not a sin," he begins. "Yes, he who laughs last is he who win. A foolish dog barks at a flying bird. One sure thing people must learn is to respect the shepherd. Who says in their heart, 'Rasta, your God is dead?'" he asks in an affirmation that must have stiffened the resolve of all Rastafarians, replacing doubt with the sweetest of certainty. "But I and I know, Jah Jah, it shall be dread, dreader dread."

In the years after his death, Marley commentators tend now to cite this track to lend weight to their theories of the singer being a prophet invested with unearthly powers. Conversely, Marley has rarely sounded more human, and while 'Jah Live' all but disappeared after being released, it's a haunting testament to Marley's frailties, as well as his strengths. There are two versions, one with a war cry on the intro. Marley picked up on this sound after hearing Martha Velez do her vocal exercises, and he would adopt it on future tracks like 'Crazy Baldhead'.

Family Man Barrett: "It was Martha Velez who teach Bob to clear his throat and make that high-pitched sound, because when she was among us and we were working on her [*Escape From Babylon*] album, one morning she come outside at Hope Road and make that sound, but she do it in a more lower tone and you could hear it ringing around the whole yard! It was like an echo chamber and Bob take notice of that, yet him don't have that same deep voice as she have, so him reach for it a little higher. Martha Velez, she should get her credit for having made that sound, believe me! Bob was a great expressionist though. No one could express words like Bob, because whenever he used a term, he'd try to express it in the best possible way. He gave it meaning and feeling and so we tried to do the same thing when creating the music to go with it. That's what made it so special, for sure, but it was more than that, because it was the whole lifestyle. Every day he'd be running and making a lot of juices, because in those days, we all look like gladiators! Yeah man, 'cause all of us were well primed and prepared . . ."

A month after the recording of 'Jah Live', Marley gave a two-hour interview to Dermot Hussey which JBC broadcast in September 1975.[*] Marley was being accused of selling out because of his Hope Road address and a brand-new BMW, which he said stood for 'Bob Marley & the Wailers.' Such accusations pained Marley greatly, since he spent very little

[*] Extracts from this interview later appeared on the *Talkin' Blues* album.

on himself, and was renowned for giving money to those more deserving. After pointing out how he had lived in Ghost Town not too long before, he told Hussey he was "done with the suffering business" and didn't listen to his detractors.

"Plenty people ah just pure hypocrite," he said, defensively. Typically, he might have followed this with the phrase, "Who the cap fit, let them wear it," from one of the Wailers' recent recordings.

Also in September, Don Taylor, in association with American producer Karen Allen Baxter, announced "the Dream Show", a concert featuring the Wailers and Stevie Wonder at the National Stadium on Saturday, October 4. The Motown star, who had recently recuperated from a near fatal car crash and been nominated for no fewer than five Grammy awards, was being brought to Jamaica courtesy of National Sports Ltd and NASABA Artists' Management of New York, who organised a series of events between September 29–October 5, designed to restore confidence in the island's tourist trade after the recent civil unrest. One of these was the ATP Nations' Cup Tennis Tournament, featuring Wimbledon champion Arthur Ashe (although complaints were made about the lack of other big-name contestants). On September 30, Muhammad Ali and Joe Frasier took top billing in a sold-out, closed circuit telecast in the National Arena of their world heavyweight title fight in Manila.*

Wonder, who had recently professed a liking for Lee Perry's dub experiments and was friendly with members of Third World, who were booked as a support act, arrived at Norman Manley International Airport on the Friday afternoon and booked in at the Sheraton Hotel, where he ran a gauntlet of international media people. Some of them visited 56 Hope Road, where the Wailers were rehearsing over three nights in a room with a single plank bench resting on cinder blocks a foot off the plain, dirt floor. Red and green light bulbs cast diffuse shadows across the bare walls as the band ran through tracks from *Natty Dread* and also a handful of songs with Tosh and Livingston. Marley's feelings for his two former colleagues still ran deep, no matter the divisions between them, and his decision to invite them on to the bill was typically magnanimous.

Whereas Livingston spoke of the original Wailers working together spiritually, sharing the same message, Tosh was typically forthright when

---

* Ali duly won after Frasier's trainer Eddie Futch threw in the towel during the fourteenth round. The "Thriller in Manila" clash is generally regarded as the best heavyweight-boxing match of all time.

questioned by the *Gleaner* as to whether the trio would ever record again.

"The Wailers will always stay together because as it was in the beginning, so shall it be in the end," he said. "What really cause the rumour [that the Wailers had separated] is the fact that Bunny and I refuse to sing for Island because of its poor treatment of us after singing so many hits. We are still doing our thing together, but if there is a recording session for Island, we will be missing, because we will not record for Chris Blackwell again. Bob will find out some day that they are only using him, and Island Records are pirates as far as I'm concerned. They were the first to violate the contract we had. People think we have money but I don't even have a house. The contract said that we should have access to the receipts from album sales every three months, but one year after our first album was released, Island told us we owed them $41,000. That money was accumulated through expenses for accommodation and other things during our stays abroad. Yet we were performing free of charge to promote those albums."

The atmosphere at Hope Road was relaxed as the musicians talked and smoked, while children played around their feet or gambolled in the yard outside. The show itself wasn't that well attended, mainly because the organisers had crammed so many events into the week's programme that people simply couldn't afford them all. Harold Melvin & the Blue Notes failed to appear, allegedly because of financial reasons. This was a disappointment to many in the crowd, who applauded Third World as they ran through 'Satta Massagana', 'Sun Won't Shine' and 'Days Of Slavery',* but then started slow handclapping during a lengthy delay in setting up the Wailers' equipment. There were also further problems with security, as people in the front blocked the view of those sittting behind them, causing angry scenes. Don Topping was again the MC, and mightily relieved when the Wailers finally took the stage, opening with 'Rasta Man Chant' and 'Nice Time'. "It's been a long time we no have no nice time and I want you to think about that," Marley announced. Livingston sang 'Dreamland' and 'Battering Down Sentence', while Tosh launched into 'Can't Blame The Youth' and received roars of approval for 'Legalise It', which had been banned from the airwaves in Jamaica.

The Wailers also played 'Simmer Down' (apt in the circumstances),

---

* This part of "the Dream Show" was later broadcast on JBC television on New Year's Eve.

'So Jah Seh', 'No Woman No Cry', and 'Jah Live', which received tumultuous cheers from the Rasta congregation. Stevie Wonder's band Wonderlove played a set, before the main attraction was led onstage to a hero's reception and performed a set lasting well over two hours. After a rocking 'Boogie On Reggae Woman', Stevie stopped to welcome members of the Salvation Army onstage, who thanked him for the donation of his $23,000 fee towards their School for the Blind in Manning Hill Road, Kingston. As it was nearly two in the morning, much of the audience thought this was the end of the show and left. However, Wonder came back to sing 'You Are The Sunshine Of My Life' and 'Living In The City', before calling the Wailers back on for an encore, jamming with them on 'Superstition' and 'I Shot The Sheriff'.

It was a momentous occasion, and not just in the musical sense, since Marley – who'd already been embraced by the rock fraternity – had now been endorsed by one of America's leading black artists. Both understood each other's music better than many realised, being humanitarian singers believing in universal love and defending black culture while extolling racial harmony.* The concert was memorable in other ways. No one knew it at the time, but it would be the last time the three original Wailers performed together.

Having assumed ownership of 56 Hope Road, the Wailers immediately set about making improvements. At this point, Marley and Family Man were the only band members to live there on a more or less permanent basis, together with some Rasta brethren named Sticko, Barry, Ashanti, and Senior. The other members would come and go, depending on whether they were needed for rehearsals or informal jamming sessions.

Family Man Barrett: "All those years people were hearing about Bob and the Wailers, we was working to pay for the place . . . When Peter and Bunny left, it was still Island House and we turn it into Tuff Gong . . . That was the time Bob said we could move some equipment in there, because the place was supposed to belong to the three of us and we weren't just renting it any more."

In a statement dated February 15, 2006, Blackwell wrote that, "I never agreed to sell 56 Hope Road to Bob, Aston, and Carly. However, I did agree with Bob that he could live at 56 Hope Road and that although the

---

* According to Al Anderson, Stevie Wonder was enthusiastic in collaborating with the Wailers, but Marley's shyness ensured a joint recording venture never occurred.

house was worth (at that time) in the region of $125,000, he would only have to pay that amount if he ever left Island Records. Bob died before his agreement with Island expired so, as he never left Island, I decided to give the house to his estate."

Family Man's lawyers responded by unearthing a certificate of title under Jamaican law, dated December 18, 1975, claiming "Robert Nesta Marley of 56 Hope Road in the parish of St Andrew is now the proprietary of the estate." The deeds were later transferred to Mutual Security Merchant Bank and Trust Company Limited after Bob's death in 1981.

"Bob took care of business; I took care of the music," Family Man stated in his written evidence, going on to define his musical role at Hope Road. We do things ourselves. When Bob is around, we do things together, just the same. I was always in there, Bob never stayed there the whole day. More time he was out playing soccer with his friends. I set up the music room, got the band together, made the band rehearse and got all of us to work together. Without the band, there can be no music. This is where we created the lyrics, the melody, and the rhythms. If Carly was not in the rehearsal room, the first thing I would do was plug in the drum machine, which was that Rhythm King I'd bought in Los Angeles. That machine set the tempo and was used to create the concept of new riffs and feel, which is why the rhythm is so precise when you listen to certain tracks. I would do a lot of the overdubbing myself. I not only played bass, keyboards, piano, acoustic and rhythm guitar, organ and organ shuffle, but also percussion. If I was not happy with any of the sounds and the musicians had left or were no longer available, then I would overdub new parts using these instruments.

"I would arrange the structure of the music, the rhythm, and the chords. Carly contributed greatly to the rhythm, as you would expect. Tyrone also made great contributions to the rhythm and sound. I would do the mixing and I would sit by the side of the engineer as we mixed and see to it that each individual instrument is of the proper tone and in the right position within the rhythm. It's like painting a picture only instead of colours I would use instruments in creating the full sound. I'd help with the backing vocals too, because I was the person who would ensure the pitch was right and they expressed the true feeling of the lyrics. I would bring in the horn section and give them whatever arrangements each of them had to play. Those phrases had to fit in with the melodies and the melodies and phrases then had to fit in with the rhythm to achieve the proper sound."

Al Anderson confirmed Family Man's studio expertise in his own evidence: "Bob had been concerned that once Peter and Bunny had left, they may have tried to take the Barrett brothers away from him. He didn't want to give them the option of coming in and grabbing them, as he recognised he needed the Barrett brothers' rhythm section to write and orchestrate the music that complemented his songwriting so well. Their contributions were absolutely instrumental to the sound of Bob Marley & the Wailers, which was created by them. The combination of the Barrett brothers' skills as Jamaica's leading rhythm section meant they were in a unique position, because you could always hire a keyboard player, backing singers, other guitarists, or a horn section, but Family Man and Carly were the foundation for Bob Marley & the Wailers.

"In my experience, when Bob Marley came into the studio to record his vocals, he'd already created the lyrics and basic melody. He was never involved in producing, orchestrating, or engineering the song in the studio, since those were Family Man's responsibilities. Bob had the poetry, Family Man and Carly had the music and these were the elements that created the Bob Marley & the Wailers' sound. Bob knew very well that Family Man was also an amazing engineer and producer. He worked incredibly hard and was always sitting at the mixing-board with the engineer. Sometimes Chris Blackwell would be sat there as well, but Family Man was always the one to direct and orchestrate how the music should be recorded.

"From my own observations, he was in the studio 24/7. He produced, arranged and wrote songs. He was also very adept at tuning my instrument and tuning Bob's instrument. He taught Bob more chords than Bob knew. Bob did not know much about music, but had the poetry. Carlton and Aston wrote melodies and wrote rhythms, although we were never told what to play. Nobody told us anything about how to record. Family Man was an engineer. He was a producer. He worked with anybody that Chris brought into the studio to work on the records. He lived at Hope Road. He lived in the studio from 1974 when I met him and that's how it was."

Recording sessions continued throughout October 1975 well into the New Year. The majority of tracks on *Rastaman Vibration*, together with others such as 'I Know', 'Roots', 'Heathen' and 'One Love/People Get Ready' were written and recorded during this period. Family Man would oversee the taping of demos and rehearsals at Hope Road before he and the other Wailers made the short trip to Harry J's. After being fuelled by the response generated by the Natty Dread tour and having played with Stevie Wonder, Marley's creative powers were now in overdrive. He had his own home at last in Island House and his love life wasn't in such bad shape either. Jamaican table tennis champion Anita Belvanis was expecting his child and he'd become romantically involved with his tenant Cindy Breakspeare, who would replace Esther Anderson as his most influential muse.

Family Man was busy working on tracks that would later appear on the Heartbeat albums *Cobra Style* and *Family Man In Dub*. The best of these were also released on the Fams and Cobra labels, credited to Family Man & the Rebel Arms. Family Man played most of the instruments himself, including bass, piano, organ, rhythm guitar, and drum machine. For overdubs, he recruited drummer Hugh Malcolm, lead guitarist Eric Frater, pianist Ian Winter and the horn players Glen DaCosta, Vin Gordon and Dave Madden. 'Cobra Style' and 'Well Pleased' are among the best tracks to result from these sessions, together with Jimmy Riley's 'We're Gonna Make It' (a.k.a. 'Attitude'), and a virtual one-man cut of the Studio One instrumental, 'Who Done It?', named 'Guided Missile'.

Having worked with Martha Velez, both Family Man and Marley had ambitions of producing other artists. A Jamaican girl called Olive Grant, who also recorded under the names Senyah and Ta Teasha Love, crossed paths with Family Man soon after the move into 56 Hope Road. While Marley took little interest, there was something about her voice Fams liked. Since the recording facilities at Harry J's were expensive, he took her down to Randy's.

Clive Chin: "We recorded about four songs with Senya, but she was really young at the time. In fact, I think she was only about 16, but she went to audition for Bunny Wailer at first, and it was him who put her onto Family Man. After he brought her to the studio, we got Carol Nelson, who used to sing in a group called Roots, to sing backing vocals for her. The first tune she did for us was 'Oh Jah Come', which we recorded around the same time Bob did 'Jah Live'. Then we recorded 'Children Of The Ghetto' and 'Roots Man', which was the last session I did with Carly. He wasn't on all of them, because Family Man used a drum machine on some of the other tracks, which gave him a different feel. It wasn't a matter of him choosing it over all these great drummers who were around, because he was just experimenting and trying a thing. He's a genius on the bass, which is the foundation of this music as we know, but he sure got a feel from it, y'know? Because he'd record bass along with it and then play keyboards over it as well."*

Randy's dominance had begun to fade once Channel One and Joe Gibbs got into their stride. Lee Perry's Black Ark studio was now also functional, after being christened with Junior Byles' 'Curly Locks' and Perry's *Blackboard Jungle Dub* album, featuring several old Wailers rhythms. Eccentric as ever, Scratch released the stereo version of *Blackboard Jungle Dub* with his own mix in one channel and King Tubby's in the other. Marley and Family Man would both look in on Scratch from time to time, although the latter wasn't there when Marley took the Rhythm King out of Hope Road and voiced two songs at Black Ark, accompanied only by his guitar and the chatter of mechanical drumbeats. One of them, 'Rainbow Country', conjures up images of the nights he and the Barretts would sketch out songs on the roof of Hope Road. "Moon is rising," he sings, "if we're lucky, together we'll always be." It's a song of discovery and celebrating life in the here and now, since the Promised Land ("rainbow country") might just lie beneath our feet, rather than in some mythical afterlife. Music was, as ever, his salvation. "Hey, Mr Music, you sure sound good to me. I can't refuse it. What have you got to be? Feel like dancing. Dance 'cause we are free."

The other track was an early version of 'Natural Mystic'. Marley was obviously still hurting after the break-up of the original Wailers ("There's a natural mystic blowing through the air. If you listen carefully now, you will hear . . .") and there's sadness in his voice as he acknowledges the futility of living in the past. "Things are not the way they used to be," he admits, "don't tell no lie. One and all got to face reality now."

Like 'Rainbow Country', 'Natural Mystic' was never intended for release. Scratch later overdubbed both these tracks with additional instruments and backing vocals. His common-law wife Pauline Morrison then licensed them to Enzo Hamilton, who released them as 12″ singles on the Daddy Kool label.

Family Man Barrett: "Bob decide to do a thing down at Scratch's place, because he just a run the machine drum in a room by himself sometimes, when he's working on new songs. It's just that some of them things get mixed up and that's what they use to put out and try to promote those

---

* Chin released 'Oh Jah Come', 'Children Of The Ghetto' and 'Natural Woman' on the One Away Sounds label, and recorded Sweeny's 'Won't Come Easy' with the Wailers around the same time.

records. It was Bob's guitar alone and the machine box at first, and then they dub this other machine drum on there. Them try a thing for sure, because they want to create a sound that'll help them sell like the real thing. Well I wasn't into that. Those things are rude and they should never have come out like that."

Some sources claim an entire album's worth of material exists from these Black Ark sessions. One of the tracks is an instrumental – derived from 'A Get A Lick', Bumps Oakley's Studio One hit – known variously as 'Chim Cherie', 'Phase One' and 'Billie Jean'. Family Man would often make rhythms and if Marley then felt inspired enough to write lyrics, a new Wailers song was born. Unbelievably, given its impact upon the Jamaican dancehall scene, 'Billie Jean' didn't get Marley's creative juices flowing and so was left unused once Family Man had taped it on Scratch's four-track equipment.

Family Man Barrett: "I did four tracks during that session at the Black Ark, and by then I know this same little drum machine inside out. One was a cut of 'La Bamba', blending reggae and samba and then you have 'Dread Lion', but it was the 'Chim Cherie' that do best."

The instrumental would take on a new life in 1984 when American reggae artist Shinehead voiced three versions, one of the cuts being a cover of Michael Jackson's 'Billie Jean'. Born in Ashford, Kent, Shinehead spent most of his childhood in Jamaica before moving to New York, learning how to deejay on local sound-systems such as Downbeat. A rival sound-system, African Love, was owned by Claude Evans, who'd lived in the Waltham Park area of Kingston, before moving to Havendale to attend high school. Evans left for New York in 1967 and became a maths teacher but was also a keen record collector, forming African Love after amalgamating with Mikey Ferguson, another sound-system owner.

Claude Evans: "Shinehead was on Downbeat, but there was something about our system he liked, he came over to us, and of course, we accepted him. We started working together from there and did a lot of sound-system stuff. He had something different from most other deejays because he could sing, rap, deejay . . . He could do everything, so I decided to invest in him and make a single. That single was 'Billie Jean'. It was a classic song, performed over a classic rhythm and the two elements fitted together like a hand in a glove. It was a gift! As far as I knew, it had been produced by Scratch the Upsetter and was never voiced by Bob Marley or anyone else, but was one of the all-time, killer dancehall dubs. If you were a top sound-system, then you had to have it, and I grew to love it for that reason."

Shinehead had asked Evans to try and find the rhythm after hearing it played in a Kilimanjaro dance. Shinehead's mentor, Brigadier Jerry, was the deejay that night and had the Brooklyn crowd so excited that the selector had to "haul and pull up" the same rhythm several times over.

Claude Evans: "Shinehead started to experiment with it, because we actually did three vocals on it. He sang the two Michael Jackson songs, 'The Lady In My Life' and 'Billie Jean' on it, and then we did 'Mama Used To Say', which was by an English soul artist called Junior Giscombe. Originally I just had the dubplate and so when we decided to do the record, I went to Jamaica to try and get the master tapes and was told to go and see Danny Dread. He was a selector who used to play Volcano and different sound-systems, so I checked him, he had a copy of it under his bed in a box, and I bought it from him. We did the record, but then Scratch heard it and contacted the distributors, so of course we had to pay him as well!"

Evans later discovered that Danny Dread and Lee Perry had no rights to the track and it was Family Man he should have been negotiating with.

Family Man Barrett: "Shinehead's manager told me he pay Scratch for it. He's a good friend of my cousin Ken Clarke, who lived in the Bronx, and they would always come visit us in Bob's time. Bring us a little present and t'ing and if him don't come himself, he send it through someone else. It's our music them hear right from the early days, so them haffi get involved with it I guess, although I still got a surprise when me hear Shinehead sing, 'She was more like a beauty queen,' and then another version that starts with, 'My mama say, son be careful . . .'"

Despite having caused a sensation with the first edition released by Evans' own label, the two Michael Jackson songs weren't included on *Rough And Rugged*, Shinehead's debut album, because of licensing difficulties. In the meantime, Virgin Records released 'Billie Jean', backed with 'Mama Used To Say' on a 12″ single. The "Billie Jean rhythm", as it was now known, would be widely copied in reggae circles thereafter.

Claude Evans: "Why Bob didn't find lyrics for it I don't know, but I'm glad he didn't, otherwise our thing would never have happened! It's one of the best dancehall rhythms ever and I genuinely thought Scratch produced it. I never knew Family Man conceptualised it, although it sounds like a one-man thing, with him playing bass, the drum machine and guitar, and that's it. You can tell the bass is live because it changes and the groove is so wicked, which is why it's been versioned many times since, but to me no one gets that same groove as Family Man, because they don't change the notes like he does. All these years on and that rhythm still sounds current, because the younger generation of soundmen and record collectors still need it in their collection to show that they have some depth, just like we did."

Rastafarian men call their women "Empress" and Judy Mowatt certainly had a regal appearance on the sleeve of her 1975 debut album *Mellow Mood*, wearing a brightly coloured Rasta head wrap, like a Caribbean version of Frida Kahlo. Although credited as a Tuff Gong production – the first by any artist other than the Wailers – the album first appeared on Mowatt's own Ashandan label, formed with her boyfriend, Skill Cole, before being licensed to EMI in 1976. Most of the sessions took place at Harry J's, while several earlier tracks recorded for Miss Pottinger were included, alongside several Family Man rhythms and arrangements, including the title track which the Wailers originally recorded in 1968. 'You Poured Sugar On Me' was written by Marley with Johnny Nash in the late Sixties, 'What An Experience' had previously been released by Mowatt as an Ashandan single, while Joe Scott's composition 'Never Let Me Go' first appeared on the Royale label.

The remaining tracks were 'Love Seed' (written by Bunny Wailer), 'First Cut', 'Just A Stranger Here', 'My People' and 'Rasta Woman Chant', which Mowatt wrote in 1972, soon after embracing Rastafari. Her next single, 'Only Woman', also produced by Cole, attracted a fair degree of controversy, since some people thought it was allied to the women's liberation movement.

"Liberation means to be free and of course I am free because I'm not in bondage," she was quoted in the *Jamaica Gleaner*. "Everyone sees through his own eyes, so if one sees this as a woman's lib song, it's just a matter of opinion. The reason for writing it is simply because of the situation existing among my sisters."

The name for Mowatt and Cole's label, Ashandan, came through their membership of a Rastafarian organisation called the Twelve Tribes of Israel. Formed in 1968 by Dr Vernon Carrington, later known as "Prophet Gad", the Twelve Tribes was considered the most liberal of the Rastafarian groups, since it welcomed non-black members, and had less of an anti-female bias. Carrington felt his role was to reunite the lost tribes of Israel as mentioned in Biblical scripture. Members of his cult believed

Carrington to be the angel discussed in Revelations, who'd been gifted with the "seal of the living God" and had the "power to damage the earth and the sea." Adherents were named Benjamin, Issachar, Joseph, Reuben, Judah, Levi, Naptali, Simeon, Zebulun, Asher or Dan, according to the month they were born. Judy and Skill Cole's Twelve Tribes names were Asher and Dan, hence the title.

After establishing their headquarters just a stone's throw from 56 Hope Road, the Twelve Tribes spread to places such as the US, New Zealand, Europe, and Africa. Marley became a member during a concert he hosted for the sect at the Wailers' headquarters, where artists like Little Roy performed, backed by the Twelve Tribes' own band and members of Generation Gap. The musicians included bassist Earl "Bagga" Walker and keyboard player Pablove Black, who regularly guested on sessions for Coxsone. Junior Dan was another of their bass players, while Sangie Davis played guitar and Albert Malawi, drums. Junior remembers a table and chairs being set up in the yard at Hope Road during the concert and a line of people queuing to join. When it was Marley's turn, the clerk asked, "Name?". The singer laughed and looked around, as if sharing the joke, but the man remained deadly serious. "Name?" he demanded. "Robert Nesta Marley," came the sheepish reply.

"I am one of the Twelve Tribes of Israel," Marley later told a journalist, "and we are trying to unite the people so that we can move back to Africa. The Twelve Tribes are the twelve sons of Israel, representing the twelve tendencies of man from Reuben to Benjamin so that every man is born in one of the twelve months, and each month is represented by a tribe. I come from the tribe of Joseph, and Haile Selassie the conquering lion is of the tribe of Judah."

Having such a high profile member in their midst did wonders for Carrington and his organisation, since it made recruitment so much easier. The Twelve Tribes soon attracted a number of other leading reggae singers, including Dennis Brown and Freddie McGregor.

Family Man Barrett: "It was we and Bob who give them the energy really. The Twelve Tribes weren't getting such great support in Jamaica at first and so we give them more profile at that time. Bob was a member and always gave them his support. And yes, I was expected to be a member as well. It was nice in them days. Everyone was talented generally, but as the old time people say, a good t'ing doesn't last forever and it wasn't long before it turn and the tide start to change. It's like we have a rise and fall along the way, but in those early days we were just sending people a message, and letting them know that we're standing up and fighting for our rights. We deserved them, so we must demand them and that is what we learn."

Little Roy was another early recruit who joined in a spirit of optimism, but then grew disenchanted.

"When I was 17, I start going amongst the Ethiopian World Federation, which then became known as the Twelve Tribes of Israel," he explains. "There was this belief that things could change and it was exciting to we, because I was one of those youths who go to their meetings on a Sunday evening, even though I have school the next day . . . Looking back, we had a fellowship between us and I don't know what changed it, except some artists don't have that love for you again. Now it's more like a money t'ing and a man want to be above you, rather than say you and him is brethren. He wants to be on top of you and don't want you and him to tread the same road.

"I was still writing songs back then, but I was mostly involved with the group, doing purely Twelve Tribes work and no pay, so I said I had to see if I could earn some money. Well a lot of their other artists weren't up for that. They do what the organisation tell them, but we did a lot of shows all over Jamaica to raise money, only to find out we were raising money for the organiser!"

With their own label, the Twelve Tribes produced a lot of recordings, although these were only circulated among the membership, therefore artists like Little Roy, Brigadier Jerry, and Fred Locks suffered from a lack of exposure. This didn't apply to bigger names like Marley and Dennis Brown, who continued with their professional careers regardless. In their case, celebrity endorsement was enough, although they were expected to attend meetings and make substantial financial donations. Despite their patronage, the Wailers never performed any stage shows for the Twelve Tribes, although they lent them some of their equipment on one occasion and Family Man recalls going to their band's rehearsals at Hope Road every so often, just "to feel the vibes". The Jah Love sound-system, featuring MCs Black Skin The Prophet and Brigadier Jerry, was also closely affiliated to the Twelve Tribes. Their founder, Belcher, and people like Asher T were both good friends of Family Man.*

Thanks to popular singers like Marley, Rastafarians had become

---

* Family Man still attends Jah Love dances occasionally and has fond memories of visiting Twelve Tribes dances with Marley in the early days.

transformed from folk devils into torchbearers for positive change, and were now playing a significant role in Jamaican national affairs. Rasta delegations from Bull Bay were being granted audiences with Prime Minister Manley and hopes of a theocracy one day ruling the island were beginning to stir the faithful, as rival Rastafarian groups jostled for political influence. Just a year ago, the Chi-Lites had made a record called, 'There Will Never Be Any Peace (Until God Is Seated At The Conference Table)' and in Jamaica at least, this was a distinct possibility.

CHAPTER TWENTY-TWO

Rastaman Vibration

THE first few months of 1976 were taken up with finalising the Wailers' new album *Rastaman Vibration*. While life was almost leisurely around 56 Hope Road, Marley had changes of personnel to think about. Anderson said he was leaving, and after the comments he'd made in the British press it still wasn't clear whether Downie would be touring with the band again.

Family Man Barrett: "Tyrone wasn't around for a while, because he'd been caught up in this backstabbing. We were getting ready to go on the road, then out of the blue, here comes Touter! And though him already know the programme, we just break him in. It took some time, but we do some session in Jamaica and then we go to Criteria studios in Miami to do some overdubbing. I want to tell you, Tyrone never even play on the sessions at Harry J's, because we just carry him and Chinna over to Miami to do the overdubbing."

Don Taylor claims Al Anderson left the Wailers because he was always asking for more money, despite Marley's practice of fairly rewarding his musicians. Anderson denies this.

"After I'd become a full-time member of Bob Marley & the Wailers, I asked Bob if I could have a contract for security," he explained in his 2006 court evidence. "Bob was absolutely against any form of written contract and he actually took it very personally that I should have asked him. Matters were dealt with by way of trust in Jamaica, but I was not Jamaican and the way things were done there was very different to my experience in the USA and UK. Bob told me that there were no agreements and that I would get my share of the money from touring and recording. This would be discussed and agreed upon between him and Family Man and then shared out under what was well known between all of the band members to be a partnership. That's what Bob called it. He told me there was one agreement and one agreement only and that was the one he and Aston and Carly Barrett had with Island Records. There were no other contracts and he would not contemplate entering into written agreements with all of us. My own view of this from my observations and conversations with Bob over the years is that he was a man who really didn't like contracts, and wanted to avoid them as much as possible.

"He told me that he'd been stung by a number of Jamaican producers early in his career. Don Taylor was the paymaster and I would ask him if I could see royalty statements or the books so I could check what percentage I was getting, but he was not prepared to let me see them. That was the reason I was always pushing for a contract. Don Taylor controlled our money because Bob didn't want to be responsible for it. Bob was not capable of calculating what was due to each of us, or dealing with the complex issues of finance and offshore banking. That's because he didn't have any form of education in legal or financial matters, or anything else like that."

While he was happy with the Wailers' musical direction, Anderson remained uneasy about his position in the band and, of course, he hadn't always seen eye-to-eye with Taylor. The guitarist had been approached by Peter Tosh who'd survived a recent near-fatal car accident on November 11, 1975, caused by a head-on collision with another vehicle on the Spanish Town Road, at Six Miles. Yvonne Whittingham, who was in the passenger seat, went into a coma from which she never recovered.

Tosh warned Anderson that if he stayed with the Wailers, Marley would treat Anderson in the same offhand manner as he had done with him and Livingston.

Al Anderson: "Peter was a great guitarist. He was out of this world. I loved his songs, really wanted to play with him, and gave him everything I had from the first time I played with him. He said he'd give me production points on his first two albums and an advance to set myself up, so I felt I didn't have much choice but to leave Bob at that point."

Family Man Barrett: "I don't know why Al left when he did, but it surprised me. I guess him just a move round the island and get to know t'ings, y'know what I mean? He never had no contract in those early years, so he was free to leave and though him young, I guess him never understand too much things."

Anderson claims he stuck around long enough to play guitar and also percussion on several tracks from *Rastaman Vibration* (not just 'Crazy Baldhead' as stated on the sleeve). With Anderson's bluesy lead guitar now synonymous with the Wailers' sound, the other band members recognised the need to replace like with like. Earl "Chinna" Smith again breached the gap when accompanying the Wailers to Miami, but prior commitments (with Soul Syndicate and also the High Times label) meant he could only be a temporary substitute. It was at this point Marley recruited the Wailers' second American lead guitarist, 23-year-old Donald Kinsey, who they'd met at an Island press party. Kinsey, who played with the emotive blues feel Marley liked, officially joined the band in March.

Family Man Barrett: "We first run into [Kinsey] whilst we were touring in the Chicago area. He said he was a bluesman, but he liked our vibes and was freelancing at the time. I make him play lead on the *Rastaman Vibration* album, whilst Chinna played rhythm. Though him know how to ride the rhythm and how to fill in, he get the basic of it, and feel man enough to do the work, y'know? This other guy from Trinidad, he love to play with us too, except him couldn't manage it and so we have to let him go."

Kinsey's father was blues singer Lester "Big Daddy" Kinsey, who was to Gary, Indiana, what Muddy Waters was to Chicago, i.e. a blues patriarch. Big Daddy would take Donald and his brother Ralph to local nightclubs, where all the top R&B artists performed, which was how the Kinsey brothers found out the Devil had all the best tunes, although Sundays were a different matter altogether. Reverend Lester Kinsey Senior was pastor of Gary's Chase Street Church of God for nearly 50 years – a place of worship that was known as "the Powerhouse Church of God" because of the spiritual energy generated there.

Encouraged by Big Daddy, Ralph began playing the drums, and Donald, guitar. Donald was so good, he toured as Albert King's rhythm guitarist while still a teenager, even playing on some of King's classic recordings for the Stax label, and performing alongside him at Wattstax. After returning to Indiana, he, Ralph and their younger brother Kenneth formed a blues rock trio called White Lightning and signed to Island Records. They were in the process of folding when Donald met Marley and the two of them clicked straightaway. As usual, it was Family Man's responsibility to ensure the new recruit's playing gelled with the rest of the band. "We rehearse hard, regular, every day for three or four weeks," Marley told interviewer Rob Bowman, who then asked if he did most of the production work himself, to which Bob replied that it was the whole band, "especially Aston Barrett.

"All of us are involved in it and do it together. With reggae music, it's never one man, because reggae music is a thing that comes together and becomes a round ball. Even in mixing, the vibrations you have . . . If you go into the studio and you don't carry the right vibration, then you get fucked. One man alone can't do it, so you know it's all these things we have to understand before we can even start doing the right type of reggae music. The vibrations. There's plenty of things people have to learn and it's one of them type of things."

In the same interview, Marley declared, "The bass is the root. You've got to have a strong foundation. The strongest foundation you can have is a formation like drums and bass. That's why you need a good bassline, to get a good groove . . . [the drummer and the bass] . . . is really where the whole thing starts from . . . Family Man takes care of the bass." After crediting Jackie Jackson with controlling rocksteady, he says, "Family Man controls reggae, so you get a difference. This was in 1968, '69, '70 . . . before Carly, the drummer not really a musician. Carly is really a unique drummer. He can play any type of our music."

As well as supervising the overdubs, Family Man mixed *Rastaman Vibration* alongside Blackwell. Marcia Griffiths had returned to the fold, singing most of the backing vocals, despite Rita and Judy being present as well.

Family Man Barrett: "The first time, when we decide to groom the three of them together, we were working on *Rastaman Vibration* in Miami. That's when we discover Marcia was the only one who could manage the first harmony to Bob, so we double-track her and let Rita do one and Judy do one. That sound good, so we get Marcia to do two tracks again and Rita and Judy one each, just like before. We used eight voices, and then mixed them down to two-track to get that sound. That's where the sound of the I-Threes was born."

Griffiths says that whenever Marley had an idea for a song he'd say, "Get Fams!" telling her that, "Fams knows everything," evidently trusting him with all aspects of his musical production. Marcia put her solo career on hold to tour with the Wailers, but the quality and depth of their music easily outweighed any financial considerations.

"Working with Bob and the Wailers changed me in many, many ways," she told Roger Steffens. "For example, knowing Bob and seeing what he stood for, because when I started out as a young girl, I was singing because I loved to sing. I enjoyed what I'd do and had fun. After I met Bob, my life started to change when I saw how deeply he was involved in music and how serious he took it. It was his life and I started to realise that this whole thing is much deeper than what I thought. You're responsible for your utterances to the world. It turned me around and allowed me to look at things more deeply. And reading the Bible and seeing God calling upon the singers and players of instruments. We are blessed and can communicate with the world easily through the medium of music, which everyone relates to. This was one of the positive changes about working with him and seeing how he did his songs with such conviction.

"From I started with Bob I realised he was a special man on a mission and I found myself as a missionary out there too, spreading the gospel, the word and message to the people. The gospel of the music is the part that touches the soul we cannot see. We teach, educate and uplift, and no matter what you call yourself, the whole thing comes down to livity."

While in Miami, Marley and Taylor visited NORM (the National Organisation of Record Merchants). Family Man and Marley wished to change engineers at Criteria and asked King Sporty if he could recommend anyone. Sporty put them in touch with Alex Sadkin, who was later hired on a regular basis by Blackwell.*

Around the same time as Marley celebrated the birth of his son Kymani (born February 26), stories began circulating around Kingston of a scam at the Caymanas Park racetrack. As Jamaica's best-known footballer, Skill Cole was selected for the island's national squad in February, prior to the team travelling to Cuba in preparation for their World Cup qualification campaign. Marley's friend wasn't having an especially good season. His team Santos were third in the league, his goal scoring had dried up and in January, the quarter-finals of the Allan Cole football competition had been postponed over security fears. Cole had sponsored football tournaments since 1971, but on this occasion, all the teams had been from ghetto constituencies in west Kingston and violence erupted at some of the games. Cole's reign as National Juveniles soccer coach ended after bitter confrontations with former National Sports chairman William Isaacs and acting chairman J. D. Hall, who reported Skill to the police.

Two months later, attendances at Caymanas Park slumped because of further security fears. Armed thugs prevented punters from buying tickets for the eighth and ninth races at the Double Events windows and odds-on favourite Native Prince, who'd finished second, was mysteriously disqualified. Suspicions of foul play were rife and one of the jockeys involved had been kidnapped and threats were being made on both sides.

---

* According to Taylor, Marley handed a cheque for $40,000 to a group of unspecified dissidents during this visit so they could buy arms, although this seems unlikely given Marley's Rastafarian beliefs.

Marley and Taylor returned to Jamaica from Miami just as things were hotting up. Taylor alleges the scandal had been hatched at 56 Hope Road, so those who'd lost out thought Marley should make up the shortfall, which probably explains why he was robbed at gunpoint in the ghetto around this time. Cole, meanwhile, decamped to Ethiopia.

"It was some bandulo shit that caused Skill Cole to leave, because he ended up being wanted by bad men and the police and so had to run," claims Family Man, who scarcely disguises his dislike of Marley's former adviser. "All the while he's amongst us, he's gambling and carrying on and it start to reflect badly on Bob, too, because things get real hot around him, through [Bob] can't control what a gwan. [Cole] used to take away Bob's car and get involved in some bandulo business, where pure shot get fired, because one time I meet this driver. He's like a small island man, a rootsman, and he came to check us in Hope Road, but through Bob have so many men in the yard, it's like some of them are informer, y'know? One day, me and him are reasoning and he say, 'Bwoy, last night me haffi drive someplace me is not supposed to, because me see these guys fire shot and kill off this man.' That's what he said to me and then shortly after that, this same youth die because he knew too much of what a gwan.

"Bob's car get real hot from that time there, because I remember him suggesting I get a BMW just like him but I told him no, I'm not ready for a car like that just yet . . . It's true what Bob said in 'Man To Man', that your best friend can turn out to be your worst enemy."

Lee Jaffe, who referred to Skill as a "combination street hustler and prophet," says that while the other Wailers had a lot of respect for him as an athlete, they couldn't always understand why Marley used him as a business advisor.

"In the early days, when Skill Cole joined Bob, he got the Wailers airplay and Bob did love football," says Bunny Lee, "but that changed later on down the road."

The credits appearing on the back cover of *Rastaman Vibration* contained lines of scripture taken from Genesis, Revelations, and Deuteronomy, headed the Blessing of Joseph. It was the first public indication of Marley's allegiance to the Twelve Tribes of Israel and included a sentence – "The archers have sorely grieved him, and shot at him, and hated him" – that suggested he was facing difficulties of some kind.

There were a number of reasons why Marley was feeling under pressure. After he'd assumed ownership of Island House and invited friends from downtown to share in his new surroundings, charismatic yet potentially troublesome heavies from both sides of Jamaica's political divide had begun hanging out there, as well as a coterie of shady characters and people looking for handouts. Family Man didn't recognise half the sycophants milling around, waiting on Marley's every pronouncement, and while he and Carly were generally welcoming to those who walked through the gate, they now viewed newcomers with caution and spent most of their time hidden away in the music room.

As the Wailers' figurehead, Marley couldn't escape the attention. He had a growing number of media people to contend with, as well as representatives from various religious organisations, or those wanting help or advice with personal difficulties. Each of the ghetto areas had a "don" or gang leader who residents could turn to for help, but it seemed Marley was now "don" for the whole of Kingston. He hadn't sought this role but because faith in Manley was fading fast and Marley had money, influence, and a reputation for caring about injustice, there was a growing sense he should be doing something about the state of Jamaica. Being seen as a symbol of the Rasta movement didn't help and this was a contradiction in any case, since self-reliance and individuality were valued far more importantly by Rastafarians than any ruler, book, or ritual.

"Me no leader," Marley told a journalist that year, "just an ordinary sheep in the pasture. All I know is that Rastaman is of the Twelve Tribes of Israel and that they're coming back together. And people don't like that. They're vexed."

It was the idea of Rastafarians attaining political influence that some found worrying, and for a time it really looked as if the balance of power might swing in their direction. Manley was known to sometimes call in on Marley for late night meetings in an attempt to gauge the people's mood.

Neville Garrick captured an image of a pensive-looking Marley in his soul brother cap and then did a painting of it for the front sleeve of *Rastaman Vibration*. The backdrop not only looked like a crocus (sackcloth) bag but also had the same rough texture. The gatefold sleeve was designed so that herb smokers could rub their ganja on it, cleansing it of seeds and stalks, or use the surface to roll spliffs on. Inside, the lyrics were printed alongside a hand-coloured shot of the band onstage, with Marley, his Gibson at the ready, pointing at Downie like the conductor of some dread orchestra.

The now prosperous Marley wasn't living in Ghost Town any more, so rather than singing about poverty or revisiting Concrete Jungle, he used *Rastaman Vibration* to comment on the political violence afflicting Jamaica and the human tragedy it caused. As well as the tribulations of surviving an unjust system and how he felt betrayed by so-called friends, Marley also talked about the healing power of music and Rastafari.

"That's what makes it work. That's reggae music," he said. "You can't look away because it's real. You listen to what I sing because I mean what I sing. There's no secret, no big deal; it's just honesty, that's all."

The opening rallying call, 'Positive Vibration', was a continuation of 'Jah Live' in a sense, since it rewrites the common perception of Rastafari and rescues it from negative associations. "Rastaman vibration. Positive," he announces, asking, "Are you picking up now?" Marley sounds exultant, infused with the joys of religious certainty as he sings of a "new day, new time, new feeling."*

"Reggae is what you call international music, complete music," he told an interviewer. "Any music you want to play inside of reggae, you can put it here, but it's the rhythm now that is reggae. Proud rhythm and that can't end. It has a different touch. It's earth rhythm. Roots! So you find it can't go out. It's like from the beginning of time, from creation. And you're getting a music that's three in one. You're getting a happy rhythm with a sad sound with a good vibration. That's roots music."

Such an irresistible combination is celebrated to the full on 'Roots, Rock, Reggae', which brushes aside all cultural boundaries for an international audience. "Hey Mister Music, sure sounds good to me," he tells his muse. "I can't refuse it, what to be, got to be. Feel like dancing, dance 'cause we are free." Tommy McCook's rasping sax brings to mind King Curtis, while the rhythm lopes along, inveigling the listener to sway and move in unison, as if possessed by a snake charmer's wiles.

Junia Walker: "That Christmas [1975], I'd wanted to do something for the people in the ghetto and so I just take the sound-system to [the Wailers' shop at] 127 King Street, right there on Beeston Street, and start to play. Keith Hudson was upstairs and downstairs was empty, so that's where we string up the set. Being as it was a holiday that whole downtown area wasn't busy like in the week, so we just take it over! My style of playing was different from what they were used to and it came from playing at these bank parties, where I'd play soul, funk, and R&B, as well

---

* Brazilian singer Gilberto Gil sang a marvellous version of 'Positive Vibration' on her album *Kaya Ngan Daya*.

as some real, off-the-wall reggae. At one point, I played Eric Clapton's 'I Shot The Sheriff' and then Bob's version. Well, Bob was in the vicinity and it was funny, because soon after that I hear this song 'Roots, Rock, Reggae' with the line, 'Play I on the R&B. Want all my people to see. We bubbling on the Top 100, just like a mighty dread,' and to me, that was like him putting it all together. Because in the ghetto, a man has to struggle for respect, so for me now, as a man coming from the bank world and yet coming into the ghetto, playing the two versions of 'I Shot The Sheriff' . . .

"I'm telling them this is what he is and I'm convinced those lines come from that experience. It's like that line, 'Play I some music. It sure sounds good to me,' because we played the whole day! Everybody gathered round and they were surprised at the music I played. They weren't used to hearing that type of selection, because I play Randy's, Tuff Gong, and some tough reggae, as well as the soul and the R&B. Anything I hear Selwyn play downstairs and that sounds good to me, I'd have to get it by the weekend. I'd just weave all those different types of music together, because a good selector takes you on a journey. That's how we used to operate, and it came like an eye-opener to them, because I'd never had that opportunity before."

'Johnny Was' documents a mother's grief over her son, who's been hit by a stray bullet in a shootout. The inference is that he died as the result of a political turf war, fought over some unnamed ghetto community – the kind of sorrowful incident that happens when youths are given weapons and poisoned with a form of tribalism that brings only death and fleeting illusions to those at the sharp end. Here lies the very human cost of political rivalry, Jamaican style, and the mother – comforted by a passer-by, just like the Good Samaritan in the Bible – is left tormented, trying to reconcile her loss, except Johnny died "because of the system" and not because he did anything wrong. Places like Trenchtown witnessed thousands of similar instances after guns flooded in from third world countries.

Some Marley commentators cite Delroy Wilson's brother, Trevor "Bat Man" Wilson, who wrote the Slickers' 'Johnny Too Bad', as the inspiration for 'Johnny Was'. Whatever its origins, the song is another moving docudrama, opening with the shuffle of the drum machine and choir-like harmonies from the I-Threes, before Kinsey's bluesy guitar and sweeping keyboards from Downie add to the atmosphere. The latter made a surprise appearance at a show in Kingston during February, playing jazz piano with the Carlton Samuels Quintet. Samuels had played flute on Burning Spear's *Marcus Garvey* and trumpeter Dave Madden, moonlighting from the Zap Pow horn section, also played with the Quintet that night. Versatile musicians like these were highly valued by Marley, whose quest to cross roots reggae over to a global audience had yet to be fully realised.

Of the more personal tracks on *Rastaman Vibration*, 'Cry To Me' was the kind of song the Wailers sang at Studio One. It's addressed to a newly departed lover and expresses all-too-familiar emotions arising from infidelity. "You're gonna walk back through the heartaches, you're gonna walk back through the pain," Marley warns. "You're gonna shed those lonely teardrops, the reaction of your cheating game."

The hurt doesn't stop there as Marley sings of betrayal in 'Want More', which sizzles with resentment. "You think it's the end, but it's just the beginning," caution the I-Threes, as a rock-solid slice of drum and bass powers beneath them.

Family Man Barrett: "The lyrics and melody [for 'Want More'] were created in the music room, by me playing and singing lyrics I had thought up. Peter and Bunny leaving also inspired it, because they get what they want [the Island contract] and leave but still want more. Bob, Carly and I, we jammed together to finish it and then went to the studio."

"Now you get, what you want, do you want more?" Marley asks on the chorus, after making reference to backbiters who'll "stab you in the back and claim you're not looking, but Jah have them in the region, of the valley of decision."

If 'Want More' was incandescent and uncompromising, the most militant song on the album was 'Crazy Baldhead'. "We're gonna chase them crazy baldheads out of town," Marley told an interviewer in 1976. "That's about the system and the things that happen around here. Like for instance, we build the cabin, we plant the corn, and our people slave for this country. Now you know what I mean, today they look pon me with scorn, yet them eat up all our corn, so we have to chase those crazy baldheads out of town. Ain't nothing else we could do. We can't stand and let them bury us. Enough of that shit! Because we plant the corn, we build the cabin and we build the country, yet you have guys who look for Rastaman and say, 'You know Rasta deh no good.' It's our sweat that's walked on every day; our blood and our sweat."

"We build your schools. Brainwash education, to make us the fools," he sings, before dismissing organised religion with the lines, "Hatred your reward for love, telling us of your God above."

Family Man Barrett: "I co-write 'Crazy Baldhead' and a tune named 'Roots' with Bob. Those things were like me and his t'ings what nobody else know about, because we work on them together on a two-track machine in Chris Blackwell's apartment in Essex House in New York. Then when they come out, I see Bob's name on them alone and them t'ings hurt me inna my stomach, I tell you . . ."

Apart from these two tracks, the Wailers recorded an early version of 'Natural Mystic' and at least three other songs in readiness for *Rastaman Vibration*, but after giving the mastertape to Blackwell in order for him to transfer it from 16 to 24-track, it went missing. In its absence, the Wailers re-recorded 'Crazy Baldhead' and 'Natural Mystic', only hearing back the other tracks, including 'Roots' and 'Wounded Lion In The Jungle', during a later visit to Essex House.*

By now, it was commonplace for the Wailers to reclaim past songs and re-energise them, and 'Who The Cap Fit' and 'Night Shift' were two further examples of this.

Family Man Barrett: "'Who The Cap Fit' was co-written by Carly and I. It's based on a song called 'Man To Man' that Bob wrote. We had written and recorded a version of it when we recorded for Lee Perry as Upsetters, but then we rewrite it, me and Bob, as 'Who The Cap Fit', and we put in lines like, "throw me the corn, me no call no fowl. I'm saying coop, coop, coop, cop, cop, cop." We take that from another song called 'Throw Me Corn', produced by Rannie Bop and myself with a guy named Shaun from Spanish Town. There was a space in the bridge of 'Man To Man' and when Carly changed the rhythm, this was a significant improvement. I also changed the song so as to produce what I call the international sound by adding other instruments such as strings, extending the chorus, and arranging the tempo. That was also the first time Ian Winter played on a session with Bob, because he was always in the music room with us."

Framed by Downie's almost orchestral organ riffs, the opening statement, "Man to man is so unjust, you don't know who to trust," speaks volumes. Not for the first time, Marley had betrayal on his mind as he weaves a cautionary tale containing the prophetic line, "Some will hate you, pretend they love you now, then behind try to eliminate you."

---

* Family Man describes another as a "rude boy song" and the follow-up to 'I Shot The Sheriff', referring to it as 'Old Bill Is Going To Shot Up The Town,' but he's never heard it since.

Referring perhaps, to the unsavoury types now hanging around 56 Hope Road, he describes how, "hypocrites and parasites will come up and take a bite. And if your day should turn to night, a lot of people would run away." By their actions all will be revealed and so if the cap fits, "let them wear it." A song of almost unrelenting gloom, the mood is brightened only by the line, "Who Jah bless, no one curse. Thank God, we are past the worse."

'Night Shift' – titled 'It's Alright' when the Wailers recorded it for Lee Perry – was reputedly written while Marley was working in a Delaware factory during 1966. Despite "working on the forklift, in the night shift, from am to pm" and still "a baldhead", he already shares a righteous outlook, since everything he does "shall be upful and right." Other lines hint at a growing sense of injustice such as "by the sweat of my brow, eat your bread," referring to his employers eating *their* bread, off the sweat of *his* brow. While not an especially great song, 'Night Shift' adds a splash of gritty, everyday realism to an album that's otherwise painted in broader brushstrokes or consumed by fierce, personal troubles.

The lyrical theme to 'Rat Race', recorded during the *Natty Dread* sessions, could scarcely be more relevant, with the political situation in Kingston worsening daily. "Political violence fill ya city," Marley tells Jamaica's heads of state, before spelling out his own position loud and clear with the lines, "Don't involve Rasta in your say–say, Rasta don't work for no CIA," warning that, "when you think is peace and safety, a sudden destruction. Collective security for surety, don't forget your history. Know your destiny." It's as if Marley is summoning the ghosts of slave rebellions long since past, except the song is not just about Jamaica, as the parameters are flung wide open by references to the entire human race.

Perry claims to have arranged 'Rat Race', but Family Man disputes this.

"Scratch wasn't there when we were doing this session for *Natty Dread* and start to play 'Rat Race'. Bob had brought Tommy McCook to Harry J's, so he's there and when him hear me play 'Rat Race', him say I have to change the bass, because it's not in tune. I say, 'What you mean, tune the bass?' And he said the note isn't moving with the chord. I say I'm conscious of the fact, but it's the concept of the tune. It's rat race, so I'm trying to give the rhythm a t'ing and a magic to match it. 'Im say he don't understand, so I say, 'All right. I'm going to move the bass note with the chords and then do it my way, and when we're done, you can listen to them both and tell me which one have the right vibes.' After we're done, I tell the engineer to play back the two of them and when 'im hear them, he's convinced by what I say and can hear the difference. Everybody dance to the second one, but when the note's not there, it didn't have the same effect and that get him at first, but then even the great Tommy McCook can hear the swing in it."

McCook's acknowledgment meant a great deal, considering the scornful remarks Family Man and Carly received from him as youngsters while recording at Treasure Isle.

'Rat Race' wasn't the most profound song on *Rastaman Vibration*, nor the most revolutionary; 'War' held that honour. It differed from the other tracks on several counts. Firstly, it was recorded (with Ian Winter on keyboards) at Joe Gibbs' studio, instead of Harry J's, and with Errol Thompson engineering, rather than Sylvan Morris. Family Man had wanted a change of sound and after vacillating between Channel One and Joe Gibbs, he chose the latter due to factors only he could detect. The result was electrifying, anchored by a bassline that strolls around the aural landscape, shepherding the other instruments into place as they lay down a throbbing groove.

"The lyrics for 'War' were taken from a speech by Emperor Haile Selassie of Ethiopia that we had up on the wall in the music room," says Family Man, who was unlikely to have read it due to his poor schooling. "We had this picture of His Majesty and some writing hanging up there and Bob said the words were from an important speech, made by His Majesty in the early Sixties. Skill suggested putting the speech to music. Carly selected parts of it and created the basic melody and then Carly, Ian, and I laid the basic tracks, drum, bass, piano and organ. Bob played rhythm guitar and I overdub anything that didn't sound right. We decided we were going to give the speech a militant rhythm, a one-drop still, but a more militant rhythm than usual.

"We used to listen to a lot of soul, funk, and jazz, so we wanted to put that concept in it also, because that tempo we start off with, it's not strictly reggae if you notice. It's more like a march, as if the soldiers are going off to war and the bomb's about to drop! Carly created the drumbeat which give it that feel, although we vibe the song together as a group. With some of these rhythms, I'd hum it first and then get the musicians to jam around that and take it from one stage to another 'til we can decide on the chords."

'War' was adapted from a speech Emperor Haile Selassie I gave on

October 6, 1963 at the United Nations in New York.* The Emperor had addressed the League of Nations 27 years earlier, after Mussolini had invaded Ethiopia. His plea for help had gone unheeded, yet he praised the United Nations for providing an "essential escape valve, without which the slow build-up of pressures would have long since resulted in catastrophic explosion." He then talked about the need for countries to entrust their security to a larger entity to create a climate of mutual trust. "Until this is accomplished," he said, "mankind's future remains hazardous and permanent peace a matter for speculation." He called disarmament "the most urgent imperative of our time," and named "true equality among men" as another issue of vital importance. He declared the sacred duty of the United Nations was "to ensure the dream of equality is finally realised for all men to whom it is still denied." After praising John F. Kennedy's efforts to tackle racial discrimination, he referred to the meeting of African heads of state he'd convened in Addis Ababa the previous May.

"On the question of racial discrimination, the Addis Ababa Conference taught to those who will learn this further lesson that until the philosophy which holds one race superior and another inferior is finally and permanently discredited and abandoned, that until there are no longer first-class and second-class citizens of any nation, that until the colour of a man's skin is of no more significance than the colour of his eyes, that until the basic human rights are equally guaranteed to all without regard to race, that until that day, the dream of lasting peace and world citizenship and the rule of international morality will remain but a fleeting illusion, to be pursued but never attained."

The remaining paragraph talked of the need for an end to bigotry, "malicious and inhuman self-interest," and the "unhappy and ignoble regimes" that continued to oppress people in Angola, Mozambique, and South Africa. "Until that day, the African continent will not know peace," he warned. "We Africans will fight, if necessary and we know that we shall win, as we are confident in the victory of good over evil." He concluded by asking how mankind would secure its survival and then furnished the answer. "We must look first to Almighty God," he told the assembled dignitaries. "We must put our faith in Him, that He will not desert us or permit us to destroy humanity. And we must look into ourselves, into the depth of our souls. We must become something we have never been and

* Not California in February 1963, as previously documented.

for which our education and experience and environment have ill-prepared us. We must become bigger than we have been, more courageous, greater in spirit, larger in outlook. We must become members of a new race, overcoming petty prejudice, owing our ultimate allegiance not to nations, but to our fellow men within the human community."

Leaving all matters of divinity aside, it's easy to see from these extracts why Marley and other band members should hold Emperor Haile Selassie I in such high esteem. His Majesty's vision of racial harmony, a nuclear-free world, collective security and the rights of every African nation to self-governance would continue to have a powerful influence on Marley.

Rastaman Vibration appeared on April 30, 1976 to mixed reviews. "Some say it's the group's best and others their worst," said the *Gleaner*. A New York reviewer said it, "falls a little short of the mark set by previous albums," but "seven out of 10 cuts are fantastic." Balfour Henry titled his article "Marleymania explodes on *Rastaman Vibration*," calling Marley "reggae's first superstar," and "a musical genius of the Seventies."

"The Wailers' real success has rested on the fact that they, more than anyone else, have been able to touch the pulse of the masses," he wrote, "to carry forward through music the latest developments in the consciousness of the people."

Many view *Rastaman Vibration* and *Natty Dread* as the Wailers' best-ever albums, and with hindsight the band never again balanced the twin peaks of raw, Jamaican roots and a more international worldview with quite so much vibrancy. Both are powerful, revolutionary works, soaked in the sufferers' blood and besieged by difficulties. When not bathing in the glories of Rastafari and music, Marley sounds embattled and alone. Love is only represented by its absence and even comradeship is bedevilled by betrayal. Both albums' greatness resides in a triumph of the spirit and a readiness to embrace forces beyond their control.

The business issues enveloping Marley and the Wailers were now growing complex with the stakes raised higher with every subsequent album and tour. Taylor claimed there was now "continuous pressure" from Blackwell, who would "keep two or three people constantly purveying rumour and carrying news."

The songwriting credits on *Rastaman Vibration* would cause much duress. Vincent Ford (the writer of 'No Woman No Cry') is credited with writing 'Positive Vibration' and 'Roots, Rock, Reggae', and a co-write with Rita Marley on 'Crazy Baldhead'. Rita herself is credited for 'Johnny

Was' and 'Rat Race'. Carly is named as co-writer (with Family Man) on 'Who The Cap Fit' and 'War' (with Allan Skill Cole), while Marley is solely credited for 'Cry To Me' and 'Night Shift'.

In the 2006 High Court case, Blackwell claimed he was unaware the Barretts had written any of these compositions or had any abilities in this regard. Rita has said the brothers' role was nothing like that of Tosh or Livingston and that Marley wrote all the songs to which the others occasionally made contributions. While she accepted that songs were developed in the studio, she didn't agree they were created in the music room. Instead, Marley wrote his songs "whenever he got the feeling, or felt the vibration." Rita admitted Family Man was the Wailers' band-leader, but only in the sense of getting everyone to turn up on time and telling them what the set list would be, and insisted the Barretts weren't creative. In a witness statement, she said they were "incapable" of writing a song.

While Fams suspected there was something duplicitous going on, he didn't say too much about it at the time.

"No, because I just wanted to see how it would work out," he says. "Except I realised pretty quickly how Don Taylor had come with some diverse doctrine, because one of the first thing he did was to cut myself and Carly's share from two-thirds to 50 per cent. He tried to trick us with that, although it was still 50 per cent of what came in from all areas, like publishing, merchandising, tour support, and different kinds of royalties. The next thing he did was to set up some offshore account and to arrange an extension to our contract, although as far as we were concerned, that still didn't change the 1974 one, because we never made any agreement to alter that."

In a witness statement given in 2006, relating to Family Man's law suit against the Marley estate, Ray Tisdale pointed out how Island "paid mechanical royalties in respect of compositions performed by the band to Bob Marley or one of Marley's companies on the basis that Bob Marley owed the copyright in these songs." He says that to the best of his knowledge, the Barretts never claimed to have owned any of these compositions prior to the (then) current legal action and that Island "had no reason to believe any of the mechanical royalties paid to Bob Marley should have been paid to the Barretts." He denied there was any form of partnership between Marley and any of the other band members, including the Barrett brothers, and says the money Marley gave to his band members "did not take the form of formal royalty payments."

He also denied there was a contractual relationship between Island and any of the band members. "Artist royalties were always paid by Island to Bob or one of his companies and I believe he made ad hoc payments to the other band members as he wished. Where Island did make payments to the other band members, it was specifically at Bob's direction and any such payments were deducted from Bob's royalty account. Island have never accounted to the Barretts for any mechanical or record royalties."

As the Wailers prepared to start touring again, Family Man busied himself with several side projects and made further improvements to 56 Hope Road. "There was this little room around the back, but we couldn't use it for a period of time because Miss Gough lived in it." Fams recalls with a chuckle. "Sometimes she'd ask us to turn down what we were doing, but other times she'd say, 'That's very nice . . .' After she left, I took over that room and even before we kit it out, I hear the volume of noise she'd been getting and think, 'What? This lady really has been getting some grooves!' I realise then how loud it must have been. I think she was from some family related to Chris Blackwell and although we'd soundproofed the rehearsal room, it wasn't until I go in there that I realised that Miss Gough get the bass *hard*, because I have two 18 inch acoustic and a Peavey inside there and used to play them every day. Me don't have my little family with me, because it's just me who live there alone, but me put in new window frames, new windows, and replace all the glass so it look like French windows."

Family Man and Carly featured on Augustus Pablo's 'King Tubby Meets The Rockers Uptown' single and album. Despite its lack of promotion, this collection of rhythms – recorded at Randy's, featuring Chinna and Robbie Shakespeare, plus Pablo on organ and piano, and a horn section – quickly became a cult classic and is still regarded as one of the best ever dub albums. Pablo had been working with Jacob Miller, whose fractured vocals can be heard in places, including the title track, which is a cut to 'Baby, I Love You So'. King Tubby's mixing was inspired as ever but his job was made even easier by the quality of the rhythms, which pour out of the speakers like molten lava. The musicians all knew each other well, of course, and swing like crazy, especially on tracks like 'Keep On Dubbing' (which the Heptones' Leroy Sibbles voiced as 'Keep On Knocking'), 'Stop Them Jah', and a stubborn but ethereal cut of the Abyssinians' 'Satta Massagana'.

Family Man was still visiting Black Ark on occasion, where the Heptones were busy recording a new album and Junior Murvin was putting the finishing touches to 'Police And Thieves', featuring Rannie Bop on wah-wah guitar. Perry was working at full stretch, and looking to follow in the Wailers' footsteps by licensing music to Island, who'd already agreed to release Max Romeo's *War In A Babylon*. In the meantime, Lloyd Willis had released Dean Fraser's 'Concrete Castle King' – the rhythm for which had been rescued from the same tape as Shinehead's 'Billie Jean' – on the Black Explosion label. Fraser was a younger singer and instrumentalist who became Jamaica's most prolific saxophone player over the next two decades. Willis, who played guitar alongside Family Man on 'Watch That Sound', later joined Sly & Robbie's Taxi Gang, playing on dancehall hits like Chakademus & Pliers' 'Murder She Wrote'. As a member of Lloyd Parkes' We The People Band, Fraser toured and recorded extensively with Dennis Brown, who was arguably more popular than any other Jamaican artist, including Marley.

Fraser introduced the singer to 'Concrete Castle King', which Brown included on his *Visions* album, produced by Joe Gibbs. The song quickly registered with the reggae audience, although Parkes' backdrop was nowhere near as majestic as the original, which rested upon a typically heavyweight bassline by Family Man. This same rhythm underpinned Lee Perry's 'Dread Lion' on *Super Ape*, and benefitted from extensive overdubs as Perry balanced power with remarkable delicacy. On his version, it's as if the notes made by the flute are animals scattering for cover in the undergrowth. Prince Jazzbo used it for 'Natty Passing Through Rome' but it's Perry's own cut that stands out, thanks to the bedrock he inherited from Family Man, who named his sound-system after it.

Family Man Barrett: "Dread Lion was the name of my discotheque in Jamaica, too, and any time I used to play out in St Ann's district, a man say it was the only sound that play like it a studio playback, clean as a whistle! And yuh hear everyt'ing, 'cause with sound-system in them days, yuh only hear bottom and tops usually, the big boof, y'know? But some of the guys who work in the fields, grazing their cows, say they can hear it ringing out all around the hillsides, 'cause me go thumping in there a couple of times, me tell you! Although more time me string it up at Hope Road, round the back, or at Marcus Garvey Lawn, which is Burning Spear's place near Ocho Rios."

Legon Coghill painted the Dread Lion speaker boxes in red, gold, and green, just like the artwork he'd created at the Wailers' shop in King Street. Plans were under way to move the record shop into 56 Hope

Road, and so Family Man and Selwyn started to put up shelves, turning one of the rooms by the front entrance into a retail space. The name of the shop would be Tuff Gong, and that too, would be decorated in Rasta colours, declaring that Rastaman Vibration was not only the title of an album, but also the Wailers' way of life.

CHAPTER TWENTY-THREE

Smile Jamaica

WITH the Rastaman Vibration tour scheduled to begin in April, Downie was brought back into the fold at the last minute. Clive Chin asked to become the Wailers' sound engineer, but because his father objected, Dennis Thompson was hired instead. The Wailers already had experience of the US circuit but were determined to make an even bigger impression this time round.

Family Man Barrett: "We had to work out the whole layout of the band onstage so there's no feedback. We work it out with Dennis Thompson and use this PA owned by a lady in Florida. Her company was called Cameron Sound and she build up that particular set to our own specifications. Her speaker cabinets held 21″ speakers and not the regular 18″ ones. We had two doubles like that, plus some 18″ and 15″ speakers. The way we arrange it, it was like an early version of sub-bass and in those days, at some of the concerts we did, you'd see people being carried out on stretchers after the sound had hit them. The sound of the bass and drums would knock them out!"

The tour started at Philadelphia's Tower Theatre, where Marley's mother saw her son perform for the first time, while Bob's nine-year-old son, David "Ziggy" Marley sang onstage with the band during one number. After Georgetown University in Washington DC, the Wailers played two nights at Boston Music Hall, followed by four nights at the Beacon Theater, New York City. Monty Lufter, the president of Ariola Records, distributors for Island in Germany and other territories, attended one of these shows to present a Deutsche Schallplatten Award for special achievement in Ariola's black music division. Photos of the presentation, with Marley flanked by Taylor and Cole, were printed in Jamaican newspapers, reinforcing the singer's growing status.

That same month, *Playboy* ran a piece under the heading 'Bob Marley The Prophet', which began, "Let's say this right upfront and underline it twice, Bob Marley & the Wailers seem to have finally emerged as the finest rock'n'roll band of the Seventies and what's more, they're as heavy a group as we've heard in the 22 year history of the music. They're right up there with any of the giants you care to name, from Chuck Berry, through to Sly Stone. And that includes the Beatles, Otis Redding, and the Stones, all of them. That's how good they are."

The writer likened Marley to Dylan and Jagger, describing him holding his brow in concert, as if "suffering from an extremely soulful headache . . . The music speaks of real and present dangers, of righteous, religious faith, of not giving up the fight. It has the power to play upon an audience's emotions as no music has in years." Describing the sold-out Beacon Theater shows, the article ended with, "there is a Rasta tidal wave building in the Third World, aimed this way, and Marley is its prophet."

In May, the tour continued through Montreal, Toronto, Buffalo, Cleveland, Detroit, Chicago, Minneapolis, St Louis, Houston, and Denver. By the time the Wailers reached San Diego and Los Angeles, *Rastaman Vibration* had entered the UK album charts, remaining there for three months and peaking at number 15. Their return performance at the Roxy Theatre on May 26 was broadcast on local station KMET-FM and taped copies quickly began to circulate, further fuelling excitement about "Bob Marley & the Wailing Wailers" as they were introduced. Captured on two-track tape by Ray Thompson, who was parked outside on Sunset Strip in Wally Heider's Mobile Recording truck, the show was nominated as one of the most important and influential rock concerts of all time by *Rolling Stone* magazine, whose contributors had seen enough of them to know.

As on previous visits to the Roxy, backstage was crowded after the show but Family Man says the band always looked forward to meeting other musicians. "In the early years, some of these guys used to come in the dressing room and say, 'I want a job with you man!' Rick James once brought his bass to show me when we play at the Roxy, 'cause he want to know how I get that particular sound and what bass I play, 'cause I had a Fender Jazz at that point. We used to see this trombone player with Earth, Wind & Fire too, who used to come around us, rapping. I remember [at the July 11, '75 gig], this guy from the Rolling Stones [Ron Wood] come there, 'cause their concert was earlier than ours and so the guitarist come up and jam with us and that was real nice for sure, 'cause 'im fit right in.

"We were attracting a lot of attention at that time and we enjoyed it, because we felt it was overdue in some ways. It was what we'd been working towards for so long and that was the feeling we were generating. Everything was going down nice and we weren't letting anything come

Bob Marley, 1978. Thanks to impressive record sales, he had become Jamaica's first reggae superstar but his health was starting to deteriorate. (LAURENS VAN HOUTEN/FRANK WHITE PHOTO AGENCY)

Peter Tosh, with Mick Jagger, performing in the promotional video for '(You Gotta Walk) Don't Look Back', a minor hit in 1978 and (below) with his band, Word, Sound and Power. Tosh's time with Rolling Stones Records label was fraught with tension. (URBANIMAGE.TV/ADRIAN BOOT)

Marley, flanked by his musical lieutenants, the Barretts on the Exodus tour, 1977. (URBANIMAGE.TV/RICO D'ROZARIO)

Bob Marley's body is interred in the mausoleum at Nine Miles, Jamaica, during the summer of 1981
(URBANIMAGE.IV/56 HOPE ROAD MUSIC/ADRIAN BOOT)

Marley's funeral service at National Stadium, Kingston, 1981. (URBANIMAGE.TV/56 HOPE ROAD MUSIC/ADRIAN BOOT)

Carlton Barrett, master drummer of the Wailers from 1969 until his tragic death in 1987. (URBANIMAGE.TV/LEE JAFFE)

A militant-looking Tosh, with rifle. Ironically, his life was to end at the hands of gunmen in 1987. (URBANIMAGE.TV/LEE JAFFE)

The Wailers Band in 1989, pictured shortly after recording the *I. D.* album for Atlantic. Left to right: Al Anderson, Junior Marvin (seated), Irvin "Carrot" Jarrett, Earl "Wya" Lindo, Mikey "Boo" Richards, and Family Man Barrett. **(DALLE/IDOLS)**

Rita, Damian, Stephen, and Julian Marley, pictured at the MOBO awards in London, September 22, 2005. **(GARETH DAVIES/GETTY IMAGES)**

Family Man Barrett, pictured outside of the British High Court, London, in 2006 during his case against Universal and the Marley estate. (BEN GRAVILLE/REX FEATURES)

Chris Blackwell around the time of the trial. The judge presiding over Family Man's case preferred Blackwell's evidence on several points. (MARK SULLIVAN/WIRE IMAGE)

Rita Marley, dressed in African garb, after her victory at the trial. (EDDIE MULHOLLAND/REX FEATURES)

A defiant Aston "Family Man" Barrett, 2005. (TIM BARROW)

between us, like management or anything like that. We were just trying to hold it down and we'd have an extra amplifier in the dressing room with keyboards and a guitar, so we'd be in there; just jamming and getting those warm vibes before the show. We were ready to go, I tell you!"

The band played LA's Shrine Auditorium the next night, Oakland's Paramount Theatre on May 29 and 30, promoted by Bill Graham, with Little Anthony & the Imperials as opening act, winding up the West Coast leg at the Santa Barbara County Bowl. After a show in Miami at the beginning of June, the Wailers flew to Europe for dates in Dusseldorf (where Marley was briefly detained by customs officials), Offenburg, Hamburg, Amsterdam, Paris, and then six shows over four nights at London's Hammersmith Odeon, beginning June 15. These shows were marred by sound problems and also security scares as hundreds of people knocked over barriers in front of the stage area.

"Rastamania hit Britain tonight with the opening of Bob Marley's British tour," the *Gleaner* wrote on June 18. "Fans swayed, they shouted, they cried. Four thousand converts crowded into the Hammersmith Odeon, London to hear the message of Marley. The security thrown around the Jamaican superstar was total. Hundreds of security officers, many with dogs, guarded every possible entrance to the venue and stage." The report went on to say that Marley arrived onstage "to a screaming and roaring welcome," and that "every expression he made was greeted with shouts from the capacity audience." After Hammersmith, the Wailers played at the West Coast Rock Show in Cardiff's Ninian Park, where they shared a bill with Country Joe McDonald and Eric Burdon. Concerts in Wolverhampton, Birmingham, Bristol, Exeter, and Leeds followed, before they ended the tour at Manchester's Belle Vue on June 27.

London was in turmoil over that notoriously hot summer of '76, and tensions were running high after the introduction of the SUS (Stop Under Suspicion) law. A disproportionate number of blacks were stopped by the authorities as a result, leading to growing unrest on the streets. A massive police presence at the Notting Hill Carnival in August ended in running battles between the law and black and white youths. Up to 60 people were arrested and over 400 were injured either by the police or in the hail of stones and bottles. The nascent punk rock group, the Clash, wrote their first single, 'White Riot' after the Carnival events which had 'War', 'Crazy Baldhead', and Junior Murvin's 'Police And Thieves' (also covered by the Clash) at the heart of its soundtrack. British youths were becoming increasingly politicised and their feelings of injustice worsened after a young Asian boy died as the result of a racist attack in June, resulting in a mass demonstration in Southall. Rock Against Racism formed two months later after Eric Clapton expressed support for Enoch Powell's racist policies, at a show in Birmingham.

The arrival of Bob Marley & the Wailers into such a cauldron served to galvanise several groups of people at once, especially British reggae acts such as Steel Pulse and Aswad, who'd passed the fledgling stage, and were making vibrant, militant reggae music that was the equal of anything heard from Jamaica. The Wailers were their mentors, but activists also admired the band for advocating truth and rights. The burgeoning punk scene, who despised the bloated, complacent rock superstars and whose pent-up energy was fuelled by a decidedly non-Rasta mix of amphetamine and glue, was quick to connect with Marley's rebellious, anti-establishment stance, although the media furore surrounding punk was still some months off.

In Jamaica, Prime Minister Michael Manley declared a State of Emergency (SOE)* amid rumours of a CIA conspiracy to destabilise his government. As Manley strengthened Gun Court law, violence and unrest continued to rise, despite Jamaicans now facing a life sentence without appeal for unlicensed firearm offences. In the meantime, political groups set fire to tenement yards in rival areas, leaving many people dead and hundreds homeless. Some JLP supporters even shot at fire fighters attempting to put out the blaze, prompting Marley to tell a British journalist that, "We trying to make things easier, but the politics keep its teeth. You have two parties fighting each other so we come like nothing, because them guys always fighting and claiming to be the big guys. Plenty people in Jamaica fight for jobs, so the only way to get a job is to be on one side or the other, otherwise you suffer and they hurt you bad. They burn houses with people in it, babies in it, in Jamaica. I don't really understand it. Bwoy, I can't understand that, and I know it's the politicians doing it. It's the youths that catch the place afire, but it's the politicians' influence, so you can see how nasty it is. You can't burn houses and burn babies. That really doesn't look good and politics nasty."

* A State of Emergency suspends some of the fundamental rights and freedoms guaranteed under a nation's constitution and can only be imposed for a limited period (up to a year). It is designed so that the forces of law and order can get to grips with situations threatening national security.

Manley's uncompromising stance on crime was tempered by his socialist ideals, but such dual thinking ultimately left him struggling to convince people of his real intentions. Marley and the Wailers certainly paid heed when Manley opened discussions with representatives from the Divine Theocratic Government of Rastafari, who believed the state apparatus to be temporal instruments of Babylon, created to "obstruct natural livity, empower evil, and oppress the holy." Nothing came of these talks but Manley's willingness to speak with such groups was nothing if not fortuitous; after all, he'd taken office after wooing Rastafarians and brandishing Joshua's "rod of correction." Manley promised more public housing, a minimum wage, increased health and education budgets, literacy campaigns, and fairer distribution of land to small farmers, but had sought to fund these changes through increased taxation on the wealthy, who either scaled down their operations or left the island in droves, just when their skills were most needed.

The oil crisis of 1973–4 had only compounded the situation, and after Manley forged alliances with other Caribbean leaders such as Fidel Castro, who was suspected of providing the PNP leader with arms and trained military personnel, America imposed sanctions. In July 1975, the Prime Minister visited Cuba with the Minister for Foreign Affairs, Dudley Thompson, and called Castro "a peerless example to all those who seek a better world." In return, Castro conferred upon him Cuba's highest honour, the Order of José Martí.

Family Man Barrett: "In Manley times, they were training all these guys with some heavy artillery. We see it after we come back from tour and they were some dangerous guys! We hear the opposition was having them tracked down, but that wasn't what they were trained for. They were trained for the security for the country, but it was getting out of hand and people were saying, 'Why this society need so much armed force? And what is going on?'" The CIA mention in the lyrics to 'Rat Race' caused further controversy as tensions grew in the build-up to Jamaica's next elections.

In January '76, violence broke out in Trenchtown when killings were timed to coincide with over 300 journalists being in the country to cover the IMF conference. Also that month, there had been reports that the CIA was involved in funding opponents of the MPLA (Popular Movement for the Liberation of Angola). The bureau had already orchestrated successful coups in Brazil, the Dominican Republic, Guatemala, Ecuador, Bolivia, Uruguay, and Chile, installing regimes that were friendly to America. It also admitted making agents out of numerous journalists, who could then disseminate the organisation's ideas in the free press while denying they represented official policy. A television programme documenting the CIA-financed overthrow of Dr Cheddi Jagan's Marxist government in Guyana was shown on the CBC (Caribbean Broadcasting Company), just as Manley began claiming American intelligence forces were at work in Jamaica.

On June 13, he gave a speech at Kingston's Ward Theatre lashing out at the CIA and "right wing forces inside and outside of Jamaica." Manley couldn't legally accuse the CIA of attempting to destabilise his government but said, "Strange things have been happening in Jamaica that haven't happened before," and recommended that people watch a film called *The Rise And Fall Of The CIA*.

"Violence without motive is a myth," he said. "Where there is violence there is a reason and somebody has a motive. We have declared our friendship with Mexico, Venezuela, Guyana, Cuba, Trinidad, and Barbados, and all of them have progressive governments. Which one has a motive to hurt us?"

It's worth noting that others in the Jamaican press put a different spin on events, suggesting Manley's government needed the G-Men as a bogey to deflect attention from its political failings, and that tales of CIA interference in Jamaica were merely a cover-up. The *Gleaner* said that if the Prime Minister knew something or had positive evidence, then he should make a formal protest to the US ambassador and "stop the public innuendos". This bold statement came as a result of Dudley Thompson's claim that "there were more CIA agents in Jamaica than Rastafarians in New York." Manley was accused of "bedazzling the nation with sensation upon sensation," despite claiming there had been attempts on his life. The PM responded with a State of Emergency, stating that he was satisfied that action had already been taken against the government, "and is now threatened on such a scale as to endanger public safety."

Soon after the SOE was imposed, a public service announcement spoke of a planned campaign of violence and terror to undermine confidence in Manley's administration. The government carried out raids on 31 JLP candidates, destroying their offices while some of the party's more prominent supporters were detained. There was an escalation of violence in places like Tivoli, where over 40,000 people attended a rally in support of the JLP. Edward Seaga's supporters accounted for most of the 600 people arrested during the SOE, but not one CIA agent was uncovered. A

Newsweek article suggested the Cuban Intelligence Agency (the DGI) was at fault, but then in September, rogue CIA man Philip Agee visited Jamaica for two weeks at the invitation of the Jamaica Human Rights Commission and identified several agents living on the island, all of whom worked for the US Embassy. Agee was quoted as saying that America had an interest in destabilising Jamaica because the island was "a prime supplier of strategic bauxite." Manley would later strike a deal ensuring the Jamaican government retained ownership of several large bauxite concerns, which must have dismayed the spooks even further.

Trenchtown MP Anthony Spaulding had also accused the CIA of meddling in the country's affairs, but seemed to confirm Seaga's talk of communism by saying that Jamaica "was riddled with classes," and the Manley government wanted "one class, a class of one nation, one people." "We say more for the poor," he told an audience in Kingston, stating that socialism must reach down to the masses, "so that every man can regard himself as a man."

Such talk was in complete accord with Marley's own world view, but yet he couldn't openly show allegiance, despite his longstanding relationship with Spaulding, who would soon be accused of rigging housing allocations. Spaulding's right-hand man, Tony Welch, was a "fixer" for the PNP and a close friend of Marley's as was Claudie Massop of the JLP, who'd known the musician since childhood. Marley and Cole often hung out with Massop at the Dizzi Disco in Northside Plaza, Liguanea (where Cindy Breakspeare worked for a time) or at the Turntable Club in New Kingston. Despite their ideological differences they were friends and, besides, such liaisons might one day prove valuable. To some, it looked as though Marley was playing both sides, although he consistently brushed aside politics and spoke only of a desire to unify the two parties.

Marley arrived back in Kingston, later than the other band members, on September 24, the same day it was announced that white rule was about to end in Rhodesia. Manley's slogan, "Heavy Manners", was scrawled on walls throughout the city, while kerbside sound-systems pumped out the latest hits by Leroy Smart ('Ballistic Affair'), Tapper Zukie ('MPLA'), and Freddie McGregor, who'd joined up with musicians from the Twelve Tribes at Studio One to record conscious, Rasta songs like 'I Man A Rasta', 'Rastaman Camp', and 'I'm A Revolutionist'. Marley especially liked the Meditations' 'Tricked' and 'Woman Is Like A Shadow', but balked at the outpouring of Wailers' cover versions. The Gladiators and U

Roy had success with covers of 'Soul Rebel' for Prince Tony, while Delroy Wilson sang over 'I'm Still Waiting' for Lloyd Charmers.

"Bob's own song never even got close to sounding as good as that," says Charmers, laughing. "That was the time people realised that Bob Marley's songs could sound so. It was a monster and when it came out in Jamaica, it exploded!"

The main culprit, however, was Bunny Lee who'd capitalised on Island's reluctance to release too many Wailers tracks as singles. Lee produced covers of Marley songs by virtually everyone in his stable, including Cornel Campbell, Max Romeo, Jackie Edwards, and Johnny Clarke. Just to confound the issue, the sound of these productions was very close to the Wailers' own, thanks to the original bassist's involvement.

Johnny Clarke: "Family Man would come around when we do over a lot of Bob Marley stuff like 'Crazy Baldhead', 'Bend Down Low', and 'No Woman No Cry'. Most of the Bob Marley songs that we covered, Family Man play them twice, because the first time round he played them for Bob Marley, and then he came and played them for Bunny Lee too. No one else knew those songs better than Family Man and that's why Bunny bring him round. Family Man, he was always brilliant, but when Striker call him, it's like he don't know how to say no."

Bunny Lee: "Only a man like me could call Family Man and get him to do something. After Peter and Bunny left, he and Carly concentrate solely on their career as Wailers, building new rhythms with Bob and rehearsing with him. Being in the Wailers became a full-time job, and it's only when they're not touring and I'm running a session would Family Man drop by, and I'd ask him to play one or two bass lines, or maybe play guitar alongside Robbie. Bob, he wouldn't like that, because he was a man who'd say to me, 'Bwoy, me don't want you to get these guys you have to sing any more of my songs,' and I'd say, 'But it's a form of promotion for you.'

"Bob was a funny man when he was ready, too, because he do over a whole heap of Curtis Mayfield songs like 'Keep On Moving', and a good few of the hits he did for Coxsone were cover versions too, so when we did one of his songs and him screw up his face, I'd give him the same argument. And Bob couldn't send over none of his boys to me, because I know everybody and they'd be saying to him, 'Bwoy, a Striker that, y'know? So let him go hustle.' After that now, we'd just wait pon Bob, and when him come with a tune, we'd just gang it. Because one time I form this group called Bob Morley & the Railing Railers and it was a t'ing, y'know? Every producer would just do their own version, but that help popularise him, and so him should have been glad!"

In addition to recording for Bunny, Fams produced the I-Threes' debut single, 'All I Have To Do Is Dream', and also some solo tracks with Rita.

Family Man Barrett: "I play all of them tracks on Rita Marley's first solo album *Who Feels It Knows It*, including the hit single, 'Rastafari Know Everything'. Every other studio was booked up full, so we go straight over to Joe Gibbs, and she never sound so good again. This radio deejay Errol Thompson and I, we used to tape a Tuff Gong radio programme from Hope Road that go out on JBC and RJR, and we start it with 'Rastafari Know Everything'. Then we'd lift it up with some echo and Errol would be around the mic now, saying 'Every Saturday morning at this time. Tuff Gong International Records presents.' Then I put on 'Eastern Memphis' and every time we go on air, we interview somebody on there for every show, whether it used to be a musician, a singer, or someone who work in the record shop or the office. From you work at Tuff Gong, and even if you sweep the yard, then you'd be on it. That goes to show you Wailers value the ordinary man amongst us and we're not into being stars, y'know? Duke Reid and Coxsone had their own radio programme and Miss Pottinger used to have her Tip Top radio programme too, just like some other people, but that Tuff Gong show was the best they've ever had in Jamaica."

The Wailers wanted to extend the studio at 56 Hope Road by equipping it with the latest technology and producing other local acts, once time and finances permitted. A meeting deciding on this course of action was held soon after Marley's return, but he had other things on his mind. It was Taylor's job to collect the rent from the other tenants, including Cindy Breakspeare. A few months after the arrangement came into force, Breakspeare told Taylor she'd already given the money to Marley, which confirmed they were an item. Taylor alleges Marley funded her appearance at the Miss World finals in London through a local PR company, since there were insufficient funds available through the Jamaican authorities. Breakspeare insisted she'd been privately sponsored by Air Jamaica and a local firm called Ammars Ltd. Marley's decision to woo a fashionable model upset certain sections of the Rasta fraternity, since she didn't conform to their idea of a conscious roots daughter.

Real name Cynthia Jane Breakspeare, the 21-year-old worked as a physical fitness instructor at the Spartan Health Club on Lady Musgrave Road in New Kingston. She had won Miss Jamaica Body Beautiful at the

Sheraton Hotel in August, where the judges awarded her special prizes for "best figure and best condition", and Miss Universe Bikini in London during September, after competing against 25 girls from 13 countries. She received a personal invitation from Mecca to compete in the Miss World finals, although the Jamaican government decided there would be no further official participation in Miss World that year because of South Africa's decision to send two contestants, one black and one white. Nine delegates had already withdrawn from the competition in protest at South Africa's stance and Breakspeare was urged by at least one black political organisation to do the same. She considered withdrawing but then discovered the previous year's competition had raised more than two million pounds for charities benefiting handicapped and underprivileged children. "I am strongly opposed to apartheid," she said, "but South Africa had come to this agreement with Mecca that although this year they would send one white and one black girl, next year they would make their contest a truly multi-racial one and this seemed to me quite fair."

On November 18, after coming first out of 60 contestants, Breakspeare was crowned in front of 25 million television viewers. In a *Gleaner* article (dated December 27), she claimed she would not have participated had the Jamaican government asked her not to and further denied having received a telegram from a women's organisation, pressuring her to withdraw. Breakspeare's involvement with Marley didn't go unnoticed for long and the British tabloids were quick to comment on their relationship. "Will Miss World marry the Prince of Wails?" asked *The Sun*, while others made reference to "beauty and the beast" and the Jamaican star's prodigious ganja intake. If Marley was riled by such unwanted attention, he didn't show it, as his writing reflected a growing infatuation with his new muse.

In April 1976, Virgin Records announced they'd signed a deal for Tosh's *Legalise It* together with albums by Keith Hudson, and the Mighty Diamonds.* The credits for *Legalise It* stated that, "Bunny Wailer, Carlton Barrett and Aston Barrett appear courtesy of Island Records." Livingston had signed his own solo deal with the label by this time and Family Man and Carly were clearly considered to be part of the Wailers' agreement. However, when later asked by a London High Court judge whether Island thought they had the exclusive recording services of the Barrett

---

* *Legalise It* was distributed by CBS in America.

brothers, Blackwell disagreed, saying the credit was a mistake made by Island employees *assuming* the brothers were part of the deal.

His denial is interesting when taking into account a letter Sire Records addressed to Island's Robert White that stated: "You have informed us that Bob Marley, Carlton Barrett and Aston Barrett (hereinafter called 'the Artists') whose recording services are exclusively contracted to Island Records Ltd have performed on an album." White is referring to Martha Velez's *Escape From Babylon*, which was finally released shortly after the letter's date of January 29, 1976.

In the *New York Post*, Dave Marsh called *Escape From Babylon* "the oddest recording project of the year . . . it would be extremely ironic if Bob Marley, the most charismatic foreign performer to appear in America since Rod Stewart, should make his initial mark on the American market as a producer rather than as a performer." Balfour Henry wrote in the *Gleaner* that, "[Velez's] album has become the first attempt by a major Jamaican recording artist to make a reggae star out of a basically pop/rhythm and blues singer who has no local roots."

The same description hardly applied to Tosh, who formed a touring band, Word, Sound & Power, in support of *Legalise It*. Alongside Anderson and Lindo, Mikey Chung played rhythm guitar, Errol "Tarzan" Nelson, keyboards, while Sly & Robbie provided the rhythm section. Word, Sound & Power debuted in August at the Jamaica Arts Award show held in the National Arena, before leaving for Miami to rehearse at the Golden Strand Hotel. Their US tour ended in late November with a triumphant performance at Sanders Theatre in Cambridge, Massachusetts. Soon after returning to Jamaica, in a session at Randy's with Anderson, Downie, Shakespeare and Carly, Tosh recorded three tracks, 'I Am That I Am', 'Jah Guide', and 'African' which eventually appeared on his *Equal Rights* album.

Around the same time, Downie, Seeco, the Barretts and the I-Threes took part in a session co-produced by Marley and Lee Perry at Black Ark. The three songs recorded were 'I Know A Place', 'Who Colt The Game' and 'Smile Jamaica'.

Family Man Barrett: "We thought we'd go and test Lee Perry's studio in Washington Gardens. Lee Perry, he was there, but we just use his place, which was a four-track at the time, and he never produced them. He just turn knob and record them, because they were our own productions really. That's it, because we'd already recorded 'Smile Jamaica' at Harry J's. That's the version with the horns, which I arranged, but me just allow

Scratch to oversee the other one, since it wasn't a regular session and he and Bob had a vibes going at the time. The version we do at Harry J's, it's classic, and nuff gunshot we get for that! We do that version one day, go to Black Ark the next, and then just couple them together on the same single, with the classic one on the A-side and the slower one on the B-side."

Perry was now increasingly involved with Island, who'd just released Max Romeo's *War In A Babylon*. Members of the Wailers had played on tracks from Romeo's *Revelation Time*, but it was the title track of 'War In A Babylon', describing the political climate in Jamaica, that proved the biggest hit. Marley had wanted to sing it originally, but Scratch insisted that as Romeo had written it, he should also voice it. Perry was fast gaining a reputation for eccentricity by this stage, although people who worked at Black Ark say he was actually well organised. Marley certainly enjoyed his company and also admired his creative abilities.

Max Romeo: "Everything start falling into place when Lee Perry start up Black Ark. He had this lime tree on the right as you came into the yard, and me, him and Niney used to sit under it regular. As a matter of fact, Bob Marley used to sit under that lime tree too, with his guitar. It gave us a vibe, 'cause from the moment you sit there, the songs start coming to the head. That's when we wrote 'Rasta Bandwagon' and most of the songs on *War In A Babylon* were written under that same tree, but then Scratch decided to cut it down and put a urinal there. I say, 'Scratch, you cannot cut this lime tree down. Find another corner to put your urinal in, 'cause the vibes nah run again.' But he went ahead and cut the lime tree down and that was the end of that. And from the day he cut it, there was this big green lizard that take up residency in that urinal and nobody would go in there! After that, all hell broke loose. The studio burnt down and Scratch becomes the great Pipecock Jackson, but in those earlier times you nah 'ave no money. You just buy a bun and some sugar or a cheese. You pick two limes from the same tree, suck a little ice with it and that's lunch, so it was that type of situation."

After its release on Tuff Gong, 'Smile Jamaica' stayed on the Jamaica charts for five months, but never reached number one, despite becoming one of Jamaica's top 10 best-selling singles over the next year. Marley told a visiting journalist he'd written the song because the country was "too vex", but emphasised the song's non-partisan nature. "I said, 'Smile, you're in Jamaica.' I didn't say, 'Smile Jamaicans, be a Jamaican.' I don't deal with that. A whole bag of fuckery that."

Marley was planning a free concert in Kingston, intended as a goodwill gesture towards the Jamaican people that would hopefully soothe the tense national mood. He wanted it to be held at a venue where Jamaicans of all classes could go, so Taylor suggested the grounds of Jamaica House, near the Prime Minister's official residence. When calling the Prime Minister's office, Marley was immediately put through and invited over to discuss his plans. Upon their arrival, Marley and Taylor were introduced to the Minister for State, Arnold Bertram, who was firmly told there were to be no political affiliations. Artist and manager called a press conference at Hope Road soon after, announcing the concert would take place on Sunday, December 5. In late November, at a PNP rally in Sam Sharpe Square, Montego Bay, in front of 120,000 people, Manley announced the general election date as December 15. It was the largest gathering in recorded Jamaican history. The JLP had recently voted against extending the State of Emergency, but Manley was compelling as ever, despite having no positive manifesto.

Because of the close proximity of the dates, Marley had been used as a political pawn. JLP supporters like Claudie Massop (who was in prison, but sent a letter voicing his opposition), Tommy Cowans, and Harry J all warned Marley against continuing, especially since the choice of venue would also be seen as endorsing Manley. The decision was made to change the venue to the National Heroes Circle in Edelweiss Park, with Marley covering all expenses, but the atmosphere around Hope Road soon became charged as a result of this activity. Warnings were sent to Marley that "certain parties" seriously disapproved of the concert, regardless of the venue, but he and Taylor ignored them, saying they would only respond if those issuing the messages delivered them in person.

In the meantime, the PNP used 'Smile Jamaica' as one of their campaign songs and posters went up all around Kingston stating, "Bob Marley Presents in Association with Cultural Section of Prime Minister's Office . . ." which again made it look as if Marley was endorsing the PNP. He and Taylor had other problems to contend with when Coxsone Dodd attempted to cash in on the Wailers' fame by reissuing tracks they'd recorded a decade or so earlier.

Birth Of A Legend, a double album of Studio One recordings credited to Bob Marley & the Wailers, was released on the Calla label and then reissued into two separate CBS albums, *Birth Of A Legend* and *Early Music.* It was the first time Marley's earliest recordings had been made commercially available outside of Jamaica, but the albums were a blatant cash-in and released without any of the Wailers' endorsement. Dodd had made a habit out of the practice of waiting for others to make his former acts popular and then reissuing old material to capitalise on their success.

"I had to take a lawsuit against Coxsone Dodd," Taylor told listeners to Irie FM in 1994, "because he had a cousin called Nat Calla, who lived in New York, although he was from Chicago originally and a kind of wise guy. He was putting out two records and we weren't getting paid for them, so in order for me to get CBS to pay Bob, I had to take an action somewhere and then notify all the distributors so they would stop selling it. I had a lawyer at the time called Tony Nuñez, who filed the action against Coxsone. This enabled us to notify people around the world that there was an action against these masters and if they continued to sell them or manufacture them, they would be named in a lawsuit. That enabled David Steinberg and myself to sit with CBS and arrange a deal whereby CBS would pay Bob his royalties on that particular album directly. Well, I understand that didn't sit well with Coxsone, and it caused a political situation I was barely aware of. I was new back here [in Jamaica] at the time, and when I look back, I didn't know what I was getting involved in, in terms of political things."

Marley was unaware of any far-reaching consequences as he held court at Hope Road, overseeing rehearsals and fending off threats from political gangsters. Two of Seaga's men warned Al Anderson that Marley would be shot if he went ahead with the show, since his appearance might influence voters towards the PNP. Marley informed the guitarist to tell those concerned that he was "showing the other cheek", and remained outwardly impassive, despite the uncertainty gathering around him.

Family Man Barrett: "Yes, Bob hold it, but something was going down for sure and t'ings get really topsy-turvy. We were trying to do something for the people by playing that concert, but others see it differently and that's why we get these problems. It was like we were having too much of a strong influence on people, or at least that's what I hear, but we were only trying to do what's good for them, and not try to destroy anything."

In late November, Taylor left for New York to hire a film crew in readiness for the Smile Jamaica concert. He began to worry when told that, while he was away, a white man who claimed to represent the US Embassy but could well have had CIA connections, visited Hope Road, saying that if Marley didn't tone down his lyrics, he would not get another visa to enter the US. Marley cursed the man and ran him off the property.

On Friday December 3, at around nine in the evening, Taylor drove through the gates of Hope Road to meet with Marley. He'd arranged to pick up Blackwell from the Sheraton Hotel but the Island boss was at Black Ark, where Perry was voicing 'Dreadlocks In Moonlight', a song he'd originally earmarked for Marley. As Taylor got out of his car he could hear the band playing and went around to the back entrance. Marley was in the kitchen area with the door open, eating a grapefruit. When Taylor asked for some, he smiled and held out a slice, but as Taylor walked towards him, shots rang out. Taylor stumbled and fell onto the floor, dragging Marley with him. As they tumbled over, he heard Marley call out, "Selassie I. Jah Rastafari," but then lost consciousness.

By the time the gunfire ceased, Taylor had been shot three times, once in each thigh and in his side. Marley received wounds to his left arm while another bullet grazed his chest just below his heart. Band assistant Louis Griffiths was shot in the back while a bullet had grazed Rita's head. All were taken to the University Hospital at Mona, not far from Hope Road. Taylor, who'd lost a lot of blood from a bullet severing a main artery, was thought to be dead at first. In fact, his body was on the way to the morgue when Dr Philip Thompson discovered he was still alive. Because a bullet had lodged in the spine, both sides of his body were paralysed. Taylor spent the next six weeks in hospital before being transferred to Miami in a charter plane, paid for by Blackwell, after Taylor's wife Apryl got in touch with the US Veterans' Administration there. The Marleys were both released the same night and taken to Blackwell's estate on Strawberry Hill, in the Blue Mountains. The other band members escaped unhurt apart from cuts and bruises. Marley remarked it was a miracle no one was killed.

"It strengthened me, this experience," he said. "Me feel the vibes and know something was going to happen. I didn't know exactly what, but one night I vision me in a barrage of gunshot. I can't see who fires the shot and me is against the wall amid pure gunshot, but me not get shot. When me wake up, me start to think about my vision and realise it was very serious, so me talk with the brethren about it. Here I was, and when I first heard gunshot outside, me jump and think to run, but I remember the vision and in the vision, I didn't run. I must stay and not run."

Marcia Griffiths' reaction to the tension surrounding the Wailers' camp was even more extreme. "Yes, because I left that day of the shooting, and so they all said I knew something about it. Like I knew about the plans and what have you, but believe you me, all I was going by was the inspiration from God, and it's not like I didn't pass it onto Bob, because I said to him, 'Bob, please don't do that concert, otherwise something terrible is going to happen.' Also, Judy dreamt about throwing a stone at a fowl, but she missed the big fowl and hit three little chickens instead. When she said that, I said the big fowl was Bob and those three little chickens is we. When I told him I was leaving, I lied, because I'd been at the rehearsals every night, and all the time I was in there, I was just nervous, 'cause I was expecting something. I could feel it in the air and I was just so tense. Oh Lord, it was just like God had shown me something, which was to pack up and move, so I tell him I have a show to do and he tell me I should go back to my house and tell the promoter in New York that I cannot make it because I have to perform in Jamaica with him.

"I say I can't do that, because my spirit was just saying to move. I end up travelling that day and from I land in my sister's house that night, Mrs Pottinger call me and say, 'Marcia, they've just been to Hope Road and shoot up the place. They've shot Bob and they've shot Don Taylor' and I couldn't even move from my chair for hours. And because I was there every night at the rehearsals, but then on the one day I leave, everything happen, Bob took that to mean I knew something. And also, because I'd been telling everybody something is going to happen, but I have to follow that inner voice every time and we should always listen to it."

That day's rehearsal had been called for five o'clock, although Family Man didn't turn up until past eight as he had been overseeing some building work. He'd rolled a huge spliff before arriving, but felt he should stay vigilant, so he only took two draws and passed it to Sticko. When the shots rang out, his guitar lead caught round Carly's drum stool, sending his brother sprawling head over heels. All Fams remembers was everyone scrambling for the bathroom and as they dived in, a bullet hit a pipe and everyone got soaked. Marley was last in, bleeding profusely. When the panic subsided, Family Man found that Louis Griffiths, who'd been standing by the mixing-board, where Fams had originally stood before moving, had taken one of the first shots.

The assassination attempt was too amateurish to be the work of the CIA, although a government security team called the Echo Squad, who were supposed to have been guarding Hope Road, mysteriously went missing that night. The gunman apparently had two .38s, one in each hand and fired them indiscriminately without taking aim. All 56 of the bullets used in the shooting had been homemade, and while a white Toyota car carrying four men had been seen entering No. 56 shortly after Taylor's arrival, no one had thought to write down the licence number. Consequently there was little evidence to help the police with their enquiries.

The assassination attempt on Marley would be the talk of the island for months. Manley, who'd visited the singer in hospital with his wife Beverley, called for an investigation, but no one was ever charged in connection with it.

"When them shoot up Hope Road," says Bunny Lee. "It was Tivoli Gardens the man them come from . . . They just go to warn them from doing the Smile Jamaica show, because it looked as though Bob lean too much towards the PNP side. The Labourites, they never like it, although nobody ever hear the full story about those things, because they cover it up."

"When Bob got involved with politics now, that's where the Mafia came in," adds Al Anderson. "It became life threatening being in the Wailers because people wanted us to be leaders and players of instruments at the same time, but you can't be into politics and be a musician. I learned that from those times, but Bob just turned his cheek and ended up getting shot. I'd quit the band by the time they did that concert, because I'd been told he was going to be assassinated, and me too, if I'd have been there as well. That's why I left. I was told that Bob was going to get shot if he continued to endorse Michael Manley as Prime Minister, because certain people obviously wanted the opposition to win. They thought he was a better figure and so did the Americans. Michael was too Communist and he was down with Castro's programme, whilst Eddie Seaga was for Reagan. Bob went against the wishes of the prominent powers and so they were coming to wipe him out, because they killed the Kennedys too, remember?"

When the day of the show arrived, few believed the Wailers would actually perform, despite announcements that Smile Jamaica was going ahead as planned. Family Man certainly didn't, because he'd left Kingston the day before. "I thought they'd cancelled it," he says, "so I just go to Bull Bay, because there was a nyahbinghi session going on over there on the beach. I was there until the morning, eating roast fish, drinking some tea, smoking chalice and giving thanks and praise to the Most High, Jah Rastafari. I wasn't hiding, but the Jamaica Defence Force and local police were instructed to pick me up anywhere I'm spotted and then ferry me to the stadium. This was a long time before we have mobile phone and beeper, so them never manage it and I hear Al played bass for me that night."

The show was supposed to start at five o'clock, but it was around seven when comedian Prince Edward took to the stage in front of 50,000 people to introduce Third World. Marley kept in touch with developments at the stadium via a two-way radio. By the time Third World finished their set, Spaulding had talked the injured star into journeying down from Strawberry Hill. He finally arrived at the National Heroes Circle at 10 pm, intending to sing just one number, but ended up performing for 45 minutes, dancing and singing on a tiny strip of stage lined with hangers-on and musicians. Marley showed no trace of fear as he lead the ad hoc ensemble (including Rita with her head still bandaged) through a set including 'Smile Jamaica', 'Rat Race', 'Keep On Moving', 'Want More', 'Jah Live', and a defiant 'Rasta Man Chant'. At one point, Manley walked onstage to shake Marley's hand, although whether this was a show of solidarity or self-promotion was hard to tell. The 'Smile Jamaica' concert was a momentous event in Jamaican musical history with MC Elaine Wint confirming everyone onstage was there to put their lives on the line for Marley. Significantly, there was no sign of either Tosh or Livingston.

Shortly before the 15th, Manley gave a speech in which he praised Marley for his courage, saying the way he'd "resisted terrorism in Jamaica was a lesson for us all." In the meantime, two former JLP gunmen appeared on British television, saying they'd been paid $150 a week to wage war on PNP supporters who they'd been told were communists, intent on turning Jamaica into another Cuba. Over 250 JLP followers were still in detention by the election, which Manley won with a 57 per cent majority.

On December 6, Marley and a few others flew to Nassau to recuperate in West One, a group of townhouses owned by Blackwell. Spaulding had passed on an invitation from Castro to recover in Cuba but Marley, understandably wary of such affiliations, chose the Bahamas instead. Family Man stayed on at Hope Road for a while longer, where he carried a gun at his waist, like a sheriff from one of his favourite westerns. By mid-December, Downie, Garrick, the Barretts, Seeco and the I Threes had arrived in Nassau, where Breakspeare joined Marley for a spell. The group were understandably still shaken by what had occurred, but preoccupied their time with sightseeing, the odd spot of gambling, and making music.

Family Man Barrett: "We wrote 'Time Will Tell' in this apartment Chris Blackwell had given us. We took over the man's living room, set up some mics and a tape recorder. My brother and Seeco were playing drums, Bob was playing his acoustic guitar and I was playing another guitar and the bass. We create the music and work out the lyrics and that was also the time we discover $10,000 had gone missing from Bob's room. None of us in the band had taken it and we never did find out who took it. We'd been paid the money through Chris Blackwell and were getting ready to go over to Paradise Island and play the Casino. That was around the same time I suggested Chris build a studio on Nassau, because of [the 1971 song by Beginning Of The End] 'Funky Nassau'.

"He said it didn't make sense, but I say, 'Did you ever drive through the ghetto of Nassau?' He say no, so I say, 'Well, Nassau got soul,' because me and Neville Garrick go and check out some of the roots people on the island and see it for ourselves. Chris Blackwell, he actually took my advice and set up this studio called Compass Point. I've never been invited there, although we did pass through later on. I was hoping to see a brass plaque on the wall saying, 'inspired by Aston "Family Man" Barrett,' but no . . ."

CHAPTER TWENTY-FOUR

Exile In London

BOB Marley and the Wailers' exodus to London took place in January 1977. The Wailers were housed at 1 Harrington Gardens, near Earl's Court, although Marley also stayed at 42 Oakley Street, just off the King's Road, when he wanted more privacy. After her two-week tryst with Marley in Nassau, Breakspeare arrived on January 6 and spent the following year touring the world, fulfilling engagements in her capacity as the reigning Miss World. The band soon struck up a routine, leaving mid-afternoon for Island's studio at 22 St Peter's Square, staying there late into the night while finishing off tracks destined for the *Exodus* and *Kaya* albums.

Family Man Barrett: "We were in one hotel and Bob was in another, right across the street and we check him morning, noon, and night. Before breakfast, after breakfast, before lunch, after lunch, before dinner 'til bedtime, I tell you. We were there all together. A so we live. Tight! There was nobody who could separate us, and we work hard, around the clock sometimes. Finish the programme; go home and then let another man take over. Sometimes I'd go to Vyris [Edgehill, the mother of his two daughters, Madeline and Pepsi], fall asleep, then back again to spend all 10 more hours in the studio. It's like that, y'know? We have to stay there until we get it right."

In the absence of Donald Kinsey, who'd joined Tosh's band, the Wailers were in need of a new guitarist. Blackwell came to the rescue when he introduced the Wailers to Junior Marvin.

Marvin was born Donald Hanson Marvin Kerr Richards, Jr in Kingston and lived in Russell Road as a child, before his family moved to England when he was around five years old. Every week his mother would organise house parties to raise money for the family to buy their own home. Junior followed his family to London when he was nine, by which time they had moved into a large, five-storey house in Stoke Newington.

Junior Marvin: "My mother knew this hairdresser called Thelma, who

426

was from Trinidad. She had two brothers and one of them, Keith, became the manager of Ronnie Scott's. Anyway, at the time they used to take us to all these auditions for theatres, television commercials and shows like *The Saint* and *Danger Man*. We ended up performing in a West End musical from South Africa called *King Kong* alongside this guy called Lemmy, who played a great penny whistle. He was the only one they could bring over from South Africa because of the laws there governing black people, so we black British kids got all the parts. We were there six or seven days a week and had tutors and everything. It was great and that's how I got into the business, although my family had made sure I could play the piano, because I'd started to learn that from the age of about two. My grand aunt, she was a piano teacher, but she was also a Garveyite and very militant. She was really strict, because she had this long cane and would hit you on the fingers if you did something wrong."

Growing up in the same area were fellow musicians Calvin 'Fuzzy' Samuels (who later played bass with Crosby, Stills, Nash, & Young) and Conrad Isadore (whose drumming credits included Stephen Stills, Manfred Mann Chapter Three, and Joe Cocker). Marvin and Samuels' first group was the Blue Ace Unit.

Junior Marvin: "I heard 'Green Onions' by Booker T & the MGs, [released in 1962] and thought, 'This is great. I want to play Hammond organ,' but it was so heavy and every time Blue Ace Unit went to do a gig and I wanted to move it, everyone disappeared. I'd be stuck with this organ and couldn't go anywhere with it, so eventually I put a big board on the bottom and I used to slide it everywhere."

After Blue Ace Unit, Junior joined mid-Sixties London club band Herbie Goins & the Nightimers. "This was in the mid Sixties. My manager at the time was an Irish guy called Laurie O'Leary. He used to work for the Krays and he also managed the Speakeasy. I was under age, but he'd get me into all these clubs where musicians like the Beatles and the Rolling Stones hung out, such as the Speakeasy, Bag O' Nails, Marquee, and the Flamingo . . . As soon as I saw Jimi Hendrix at the Bag O' Nails, I thought, 'This is it!' Hendrix was phenomenal. I met him at a party once and he was so shy. I was thinking, 'This can't be the same guy I saw onstage,' because once he started performing, it was like he went into a trance and the spirit took over. I learnt a lot from him."

As well as Hendrix, Marvin was inspired to start playing guitar after hearing Cliff Richard & the Shadows, "and thinking, 'I can do that,' because their guitarist was Hank Marvin and I had the same name."

Around late '67, he joined White Rabbit, featuring lead singer Linda Lewis, who played mainly covers of well-known pop and R&B hits and toured in countries like France and Italy. Marvin also continued to do various theatre work, joining the cast of *Hair* at London's Shaftesbury Theatre in 1968, which also featured singer Marsha Hunt. After a stint in her backing band, he played with the Keef Hartley Band, appearing on several of their albums under the name Junior Kerr.

In 1973, Marvin got a solo recording deal with Emerson, Lake & Palmer's Manticore label, which was distributed by Atlantic.

Junior Marvin: "I was known as Junior Hanson then. When I first looked at my birth certificate, it said Donald Howard Kerr, which is my father, but they'd crossed out the Howard and put Hanson. That way I had the same initials as him, but not the same name. It was my Garveyite aunt who'd changed it to Hanson. I could never figure out why, but she obviously changed it for a reason and that was okay by me. Anyway, I decided to use Junior Hanson as my professional name, because it had that rock sound, and I was playing in a three-piece band doing Hendrix-type stuff."

Based in New York, two Junior Hanson albums were released: *Now Hear This* (featuring Conrad Isadore, Chris Wood and Rebop of Traffic, and Bobby Tench and Clive Chaman, who later played with Jeff Beck) and 1974's *Magic Dragon*.

Junior Marvin: "The record company thought I was American, because there were so many other blues players called Junior at that time, and were so disappointed to find out I was British! Emerson, Lake & Palmer were planning a tour and I was supposed to be opening for them, but that never worked out."

After Hanson split in 1975, Junior played on various Island artists' sessions. The young, confident guitarist could play in a variety of styles, although it was his purity of tone and lyrical expression that stood out. Marvin says Blackwell treated him like a son and would send a Rolls Royce to collect him for sessions. It turned out that Marvin knew Al Anderson, as both men were mutually acquainted with Chris Wood and used to hang out together on the London club scene during the early Seventies.

Family Man Barrett: "Al wasn't there, so none of us know Junior. Him just come in the studio and I see this Ethiopian, Indian looking guy wearing some tight jeans and all of that, and then him show us an album of himself where him named Handsome Junior, or something. He said he'd played on some tracks for Chris Blackwell, who must have told him we don't have a lead guitar. The thing is, we never say we want a lead guitar, because we were going to make Bob play them same style like him when we record *Natty Dread*, so me just hear him make some little comments and I say to Bob, 'Who's this brother here?' He was talking to Bob so loud, he disturb the vibes around the place. I never like how him a chat at first, because him talk so much, but him play for a while and Bob say, 'What you think?' I say, 'Him sound like Al and Al good already. Him says him ready, so there shouldn't be any problem.'"

Being already familiar with some reggae, Marvin immediately fell in love with the Wailers' sound. While not present for the majority of the St Peter's Square sessions, he put in endless hours rehearsing with the band as they schooled him in the nuances of their music. Marvin says they all played each other's instruments which helped them to appreciate each other's contributions.

Family Man Barrett: "We thought Junior was the right man and him give us a good impression the way he play around with this effects box shaped like a spaceship, where you can change the pitch and create all these different moods."

The effects pedal Family Man is referring to was designed by Roger Mayer, who patented the first fuzzbox which Jeff Beck and Jimmy Page were among the first guitarists to help popularise in the mid-Sixties with the use of electronic feedback and distortion. Mayer, who worked at the Royal Naval College in Greenwich, had also assisted Jimi Hendrix with the groundbreaking electronic effects on the guitarist's *Are You Experienced* album in 1967. In the early Seventies the technician had been working on Stevie Wonder's trailblazing albums, including *Talking Book* and *Innervisions*, when he met Marvin for the first time.

Roger Mayer: "I'd just finished working with Stevie at Electric Ladyland and was helping Ernie Isley of the Isley Brothers improve his guitar sound on songs like 'That Lady', when I saw Junior perform at a club one night. We started hanging out together after that and he suggested we do a rock guitar style reggae album. This was in 1976, so we decided to do covers of some of our favourite songs for this album that was never released called *Bionic* . . . A little after that, Junior returned to London and was playing with Traffic and a bunch of other people. He played on Stevie Winwood's album and then Chris Blackwell recruited him for the Wailers."

Family Man Barrett: "It was Junior who brought [Mayer] to the studio

. . . [Mayer knew] about playing instruments and harmonics too, because he would tell you when you're a half tone or semitone out and make our instruments sound quite different. Bob and I like what him a do, because it was like having some technician in the band. What him do sounds like World War III sometimes, but we put all of that in the music and we see the improvements. It makes the sound more sensitive where the instrumental's concerned, y'know? Him just give it a little extra mileage, take it to new levels, and from the minute he talk, we know his worth, because he keep us up to date with hi-tech inventions from there."

Marvin's playing on 'Waiting In Vain' (influenced by the clinical technique of George Benson), the Hendrix-like solo on 'Heathen' and James Brown-like hook on 'Exodus' memorably enhanced each track, thanks to the various technical innovations he and Mayer brought to the band.

Roger Mayer: "Junior was using guitars I'd modified for him and I modified some special pedals for him too. Whatever he used would be appropriate for the songs. We didn't have any specific pedals or equipment. That's the way I work. We obviously had all the different distortions, and whatever echo's going to be used in the studio, but it was all done on a song-by-song basis, just like with Hendrix. There are no rules, because if you're going to create something new, then it has to be new, doesn't it? With the Wailers, most of the tracks had been recorded beforehand and might just be waiting for a solo from Junior. We'd walk into the studio, have a listen to a track and then Junior would play the rough guitar line before we got down to perfecting what he was going to do. It all results from communicating with the guitarist and him having the confidence to put everything into motion. That's what I used to do for Jimi on a lot of the records, because he'd choose the electronics, but I was there in the studio to supervise the sound.

"When I first went to have to have a listen, the band sounded a bit raggedy so I asked Bob what he wanted me to do and after we'd spoken about Jimi Hendrix and all that, he said they wanted to sound international. He said it with a smile, but I understood what he was saying, because I'd been working with black bands to help break them into different markets and had the sound remained like it was before Junior came aboard, the band wouldn't have sounded so international. It would have sounded like a Jamaican band and it couldn't have been marketed internationally like it was. That's the way I saw it and it was the same thing with Stevie Wonder and the Isley Brothers, because they changed what they were doing from a mainly black sound into something more international. The music can travel after that, but if you haven't got the quality in the recordings, then it's not going to happen."

In the wake of 'Jah Live', Marley was now writing more discursive, almost messianic material and the level of his and the Wailers' artistry is more pronounced on *Exodus*.

"We were trying to set a new standard in the music on *Exodus* and of course we have to improvise along the way," says Family Man, who felt immensely proud when *Time* magazine awarded *Exodus* as its Album of the Century in 1998. "At the time we recorded it, everybody try to get smart by crossing over to the R&B or white market, so Island say we 'ave to follow the same trend, which is just what Bob warned about in 'Rat Race' and them other songs. We say 'What are you trying to do? Are you trying to go back?' We tell them, 'Forward ever, backwards never,' because it was the one-drop roots music that take us to the heights and we know it can take us even higher, no matter what other kind of music come in. Because what we notice after a while is that some of these acts get carried away and their music end up sounding too much like pop. Them stray from the roots, which is why we tell them that 'some is roots, an' some is branches, but I an' I is the roots.'"

Exodus opens with a re-recording of 'Natural Mystic', which starts stealthily as if its steady, throbbing backbeat, crying lead guitar, and portentous horns were a page from Revelations put to music. According to Fams, for the re-cut the Wailers "just jammed on it, because we couldn't remember all of it. We'd play eight bars and then start again. That's why you hear it start with the fader coming up, because we're trying to catch back the original magic and feel back the groove before we can start cooking. It took us a good while and then when we get it tight, that's when the drum roll come in and Bob starts to sing from there."

Marley told Rob Bowman the reason 'Natural Mystic' never made it onto *Rastaman Vibration* was because "the record was never really good. We never did it in the right studio. We did it in a two-track studio for just to listen to. Then during the time we did the album, we forgot about it."

After the attempt on his life, Marley had become a real-life outlaw and the imagery he used so effectively on songs like 'Duppy Conqueror' and 'I Shot The Sheriff' resurfaced in more personal form on 'So Much Things To Say'. After noting the mistreatment of Jesus Christ, Marcus Garvey, and Paul Bogle, he sings, "I and I don't expect to be justified by the laws of man. The jury found me guilty, but truth shall prove my innocence."

Marley's bid to bring unity to Jamaica had failed and his honourable intentions had been misread. "I and I no come to fight flesh and blood," he reminded, "but spiritual wickedness in high and low places."

The first side of *Exodus* has a completely different feel to the second, thanks to uncompromising songs like 'The Heathen', evident in its lyrics which offer the type of affirmation that had now become Marley's trademark ("Rise all ye fallen fighters, rise and take your stance again, he who fights and runs away, lives to fight another day") and 'Guiltiness', which rails against social injustice and warns of the futility of unrighteous endeavour. The phrase "bread of sorrows" is borrowed from Psalm 127, which counsels that, "It is vain for you to rise up early, to sit up late, to eat the bread of sorrows, for so He giveth his beloved sleep."

Marley's Bible studies had already inspired so many great songs, and the title track would provide him with another. Family Man says 'Exodus' was initially conceived as a one-drop but soon evolved into the rousing clarion call it became.

Family Man Barrett: "If you notice, nothing is rushed on that track. Everything is spaced and it takes quite a while for the momentum to build up. That's the magic of that song and it's all in the rhythm. It's almost like ska, but we do it in such a way that the suspense is killing you. Bob and myself always have the idea to do a song about exodus, movement of Jah people, because the Bible talks about this. Bob was more hip to that side of things than me, but I still know about the Biblical Exodus, so I always have that in mind and visualise it in sound. I just imagine how people were in those ancient days. I'd seen the [1960] film *Exodus* as a teenager in Jamaica, and the music from it had really turned me on. That's why when I travel to London I hear this track 'Exodus' on an album called *Great Movie Themes*.

"Yeah so, we were all sitting around listening to it, Bob, my brother, and myself and we set it with just the one chord, but it a militant riff for sure. Bob, he takes up his guitar and he started to scratch out this groove like some James Brown, funky kind of sound, whilst I played acoustic. We get the feel and the timing playing those lines together like that.

"After that, I take up the bass and I am the one who set the rhythm as usual, then I also play the acoustic piano myself too. Everyone who plays that piano part, they play it different but the way we do it originally, we add a little effect, like with some reverb, only we add it in the mix and that's what give it that special vibe. From there, we build it up until we're ready to put on the percussion and arrange the horn section. I get ideas for that from the Memphis horns and also Earth, Wind & Fire, because one good artist always inspire another and through all of those acts are from this same concept of music, that's why we catch onto them."

One of Marley's most euphoric songs, 'Jamming', which opened the second side, was designed to have crowds dancing and singing along, while containing a subliminal spiritual message.

Family Man Barrett: "On those songs like 'Jamming', Bob would play the guitar and if it turned out okay, we'd leave it in, but if not, then we'd correct it. We were always jamming in the name of the Lord and searching for that spiritual vibe, coming from nyahbinghi, jump up, poco, and kumina. It's just that we're taking it to the next stage on 'Jamming' and that song was very much loved by Stevie Wonder, because after we'd met with him in Jamaica, he said, 'Why don't you put this song on a 45 because that's a single!' But we wanted to keep the strength of the album, and after we tell him that, he said, 'OK, but if you don't do something about it, then I will.' And that's how come he wrote this song 'Master Blaster'.

"That's probably why Stevie Wonder liked the song so much, because it was disco, coming from funk and I think they called that style of music boogaloo one time as well. We just incorporate those kinds of sounds and build them into the song without disturbing the message at all. We just curve the melody line around the chords and then stick to the original concept of the reggae heartbeat and the backbone."

"The best way to get an important and heavy message across is to wrap it up nicely," Wonder told Craig Werner. "It's better to try and level out the weight of the lyrics by making the melody lighter. After all, people want to be entertained, which is all right by me, so if you have a catchy melody instead of making the whole song sound like a lesson, people are more likely to play the tune. They can dance to it and still listen to the lyrics and hopefully think about them."

Marley was thinking along similar lines, telling one journalist that he wanted to write songs in such a way that even babies could understand them. Such simplicity is clearly evident on his love songs from the period like 'Three Little Birds', 'Turn Your Lights Down Low', 'Is This Love', 'Could You Be Loved' and 'Waiting In Vain'.

Family Man Barrett: " 'Waiting In Vain' was another of those songs that we work out in the rehearsal room. I can't remember whether we use Harry J's or Dynamics for that one, because we always look to get the Jamaican bottom before we head for England and sort out the foreign top.

But we say we want that song to be right there in the relay and I recall one time when we came off tour, Bob went to look for his mother in Delaware, and when he came back he said, 'This is the vibe that I'm working on now,' and it had this "scoop, scoop" sound . . . Doing that song was so cool, because you had some people who were saying that we were two-chord musicians and I would say, 'Yes that might be true at times, but which two chords? And in what tempo or using what riff?' Because sometimes we might use some minor seventh chord to give us that mournful feeling and of course 'Waiting In Vain' was a beat song, written by a man who'd fallen in love for sure.

"People have said that song's about Cindy Breakspeare and I would guess that's true, y'know? But the man need a change because we all serve this thing through thick and thin and we all stick together, so I think he was trying to get some peace of mind by that stage."

Island released 'Waiting In Vain' as a single in September, although it hardly dented the UK Top 30 and barely registered at all with American record buyers. This must have proved disappointing considering the song was carefully tailored for the charts, with its commercial arrangement and catchy melody.

The final song on *Exodus* was an amalgamation of 'One Love', which the Wailers had originally recorded for Coxsone, and a cover of the Impressions' 1965 soul classic, 'People Get Ready'. Curtis Mayfield had long been a favourite of the Wailers and the lilting civil rights anthem dovetailed perfectly with its gospel-infused counterpart.

Family Man Barrett: "Bob had voiced 'One Love' earlier on in Jamaica, but then after we reach London, he get the right inspiration to deliver it, just like 'The Heathen'. We record back some of those songs two or three different times, because we were always trying to improve them. The version of 'One Love' Bob did in the ska era have a lighter step to it than what we wanted, because everybody was dancing differently back then. We wanted to do it in a more universal form too, and so we break it down to what it become on the *Exodus* album, with that catchy piano riff. That was Tyrone playing it too, but it was Bob's idea to do it over, because he said it's one of those classics that need a new treatment, so we give it that extra perfection. And of course, Bob wanted to own a piece of the action and make it part of our own t'ing, 'cause it's nice for us to have everything like that inna the camp."

Marvin claims to have convinced Blackwell to spend an additional £60,000 and have the *Exodus* album remixed, as he felt the initial attempt lacked depth and brightness, but Family Man, who shares a mixing credit with Blackwell, disputes this.

Family Man Barrett: "I play the bass line on all the tracks from *Exodus* and assist with the percussion and some of the keyboards too. Because even though we have Wya and Tyrone, I still bang some as well, and that's a proper grand piano I use on *Exodus*, y'know? Carly, he would set the pattern for some of these songs and I would say that 'Jamming' was one of those and also 'Exodus', because when we were recording it first, the true feeling and the concept was coming from the one drop. We add another track and then when we get ready to mix it, we speed it up a little, just to get that Top 10 feel. We often did things like that to bring a little extra vibes and sometimes we might even record using one of the instruments in a different key, just to give it that individual sound."

Some of the last elements added were the horns – played by Zap Pow's Glen DaCosta and Dave Madden, plus trombonist Vin Gordon – and the backing vocals. Soon after Miss Pottinger released her *Naturally* set, the I-Threes travelled to London, but the night they arrived, Bob and Rita had a big fight. Mowatt sided with Rita and so Griffiths ended up doing all of the harmonies herself. "It was I and I and I," she quipped years later, after paying tribute to Family Man and Karl Pitterson's patience in meticulously overdubbing her vocals.

Although now safe from harm and surrounded by his closest associates, Marley was no longer in touch with the same forces that had inspired the songs on *Natty Dread* and *Rastaman Vibration*. The estrangement from Tosh and Livingston was now compounded by his physical separation from Jamaica, which meant no more drives through the winding roads or visits to old friends in Trenchtown and no more solace from the soothing, natural beauty of Negril or Nine Miles. London was cold, flooded in places after a succession of storms, and riven by social unrest. There was also the fact that for all the plaudits heaped upon them, the majority of songs on *Exodus* (and its successor, *Kaya*) were conceived before the Wailers' journey to London, and weren't so much written in response to his personal odyssey, as merely finished during it. Marley would have to draw deep from his inner reserves of strength for new material while recharging his creative batteries amid an alien landscape.

Then there were the women in his life. He enjoyed Breakspeare's companionship, despite the difficulties this presented whenever he decided to entertain others like Princess Yashi, who was the daughter of the Libyan oil minister and Lucy Pounder, who had given birth to Marley's son, Julian, on June 4, 1975.*

While in London, Marley met Emperor Haile Selassie I's son, the Crown Prince of Ethiopia, and in return for funding the family's flight from Ethiopia, the singer was given a ring which he wore to the grave. Marley and a recovering Taylor also met with Michael Manley who said he'd uncovered evidence of CIA involvement while investigating the Hope Road shooting. Although he'd won the election by such a wide margin, Manley was still under pressure. In February, PNP councillor P. J. Patterson had to refute claims the party were training a 20,000-strong militia and that Cubana, the Cuban Airline were loading and unloading crates round the clock with airport staff turning a blind eye. He also denied that Jamaican intelligence officers were being trained in Guyana by Cubans, that no Cuban Peace Corps or DGI operatives were on the island, and that the PNP had no plans to form a Marxist government. Despite persistent rumours, there was no split between pro-Cuban hardliners and moderates within the party and the PNP hadn't financed Philip Agee's trip to Jamaica.

By March, Agee was facing deportation from Britain, telling reporters that "the CIA programme in Jamaica was designed to destroy the government and lead to a conservative victory. The PNP victory when that election took place in December 1976 was a tremendous defeat for the CIA."

Taylor freely admitted to having been manipulated by Jamaica's politicians, and Marley was typically forthright when asked about his affiliations.

"We are not part of the political thing in Jamaica. Whatever I say in London, for English people to read, when they read it in Jamaica, people might think I want to come back and take over the place, but I don't want to be a leader."

He denied the JLP were responsible for the attempt on his life and said it could have been either one of the political parties, or "even a rival record company. The gunmen get clean away, so them say, but me know them couldn't shoot the Prime Minister or the Chief of Police and just disappear. That could never happen." He concluded by saying the incident was now in the past and that he wished to move on.

---

* Bob bought a house in Cherry Gardens, an affluent area of Kingston near Hope Road, after she became pregnant with their son Damian. In 2007, Damian had become the biggest name in reggae with hits like 'Welcome To Jamrock' to his credit.

Shortly before the incident, Marley and Taylor had requested a replace-ment contract be drawn up between Island and Media Aides Limited, replacing the 1975 Recording Agreement. Island had sent Marley a letter dated 15 December, 1976, agreeing to terminate the 1975 contract, and obtained inducement letters signed by him authorising this new arrange-ment. They were therefore unconcerned by this change. Blackwell later confirmed Island didn't request inducement letters from the Barretts and reiterated there was no reason why they should have done, since the label had signed Marley alone. Yet Family Man remembers being treated as if he was contracted by Island during Marley's lifetime and says Vyris Edgehill would sometimes collect money from Island on his behalf if she needed it.

"This happened on several times between 1974 and the end of the Seventies," he wrote in an affidavit. "Having spoken to Vyris, I would then telephone the Island offices and arrange for her to pick up cash, and on each occasion the sum involved was around £2,000. It was agreed this money would be deducted from my royalties. I can't recall the name of the person I spoke to the first occasion, but after that, it was always Denise Mills. I also remember that whenever I left my car at the Island Records car park in London, a representative would always see to it that it was taxed and insured, ready to drive for whenever I visited London."

That the company would treat a hired sideman with such courtesy is highly commendable but the Media Aides Agreement effectively ruled the Barretts out of any claims to Marley's assets and eliminated all further doubt they were still contracted parties.

By the time *Exodus* was completed, Island had re-released *Catch A Fire* using different artwork. The first edition with the distinctive Zippo lighter design had been replaced by more conventional packaging, featuring Esther Anderson's close-up of Marley smoking a giant spliff. Also, the album was now credited to Bob Marley & the Wailers, as opposed to the Wailers alone, which meant the re-branding process had been backdated to include Tosh and Livingston-era recordings. Was this an accidental slip-up or a deliberate attempt to elevate Marley and rewrite the band's history?

By 1977, Island had added Burning Spear, the Heptones, Toots & the Maytals, and Third World to their roster. Blackwell's label was now the leading outlet for reggae music and, having facilitated the Wailers' crossover success, it was ideally positioned to attract and sign other top acts from the genre. Max Romeo, who had left Jamaica for New York the year before to work with Melvin Van Peebles on a Broadway play called *Reggae*, suspects that Island engineered Marley's success even while signing other reggae artists to the label.

"Chris Blackwell came to Jamaica with his cheque book," he said. "At the time he came, it was 75 US cents that make one Jamaican dollar and so when Lee Perry and I did the deal for *War In A Babylon*, I'd never seen so much money in my bloody life! The trick was, anything that sound good, or appears to be sounding good for the future, Island Records make sure they sign them and they did. But after they do that, they put the rest of us on the shelf so that nothing can go beyond Bob Marley. I was the first one to rebel, but everyone get caught up in it. Third World, you name them, because all the concentration was on Bob Marley and getting him that rock star status. Bob Marley was marketed with that image as a rock star and the rest of us were confined to Mango, which is what [Island] call their reggae label. As soon as I realise what was happening, I rebel. I say I prefer to starve and to set me free, but Bob become the richest Jamaican artist after that, and the rest of us were still deep in the pit."

Despite Romeo's protestations, Marley's success motivated large numbers of other reggae bands, unlocking the doors for such acts as Peter Tosh, Toots & the Maytals, and the Mighty Diamonds, who were generating rave reviews for their sell-out performances at the Bottom Line in New York's Greenwich Village. The latter two acts also sold out the Schaeffer Festival in Central Park, where Marley and the Wailers had so memorably performed two years earlier during the Natty Dread tour. Reggae had finally arrived as a visible force and Island could take a lot of the credit for making it happen. "It's all happening now," crowed Island Vice President of Sales Herb Corsack in the *Gleaner*. "The time is right. We've laid the foundations for the last 14 months and this is the time to strike."

The writer of that same article reported that, "You can almost feel the reggae excitement in New York, all over, in the offices of the music magazines and the big record companies and booking offices in downtown Manhattan. Driving through rush hour traffic and hearing Marley's incisive vocals, or talking to the Jamaican artists, disc jockeys, and record shop owners and producers in Brooklyn and the Bronx who can feel it too and want in on some of the action."

In the early hours of March 10, the Wailers' party had been visiting friends in Ladbroke Grove, west London. Family Man had told Garrick to go out

438

and warm up the engine of their white Ford. Garrick either refused or forgot and when the band prepared to leave, the engine kept stalling. A policeman noticed them, radioed ahead, and as the car drove past Notting Hill Gate police station, they were pulled over and searched. The passengers were taken into the station and searched more thoroughly after a small quantity of herb was found in the vehicle. Family Man had a spliff hidden in his sock, and when the Wailers' living quarters were consequently turned upside down, the police found a chalice in his drawer and a pound of ganja in the room Marley shared with Garrick. Island hired lawyers to defend Marley and Family Man, who both pleaded guilty when their case was heard at Marylebone Magistrates Court on April 6. After telling the judge he'd smoked cannabis "for about four or five years, because I don't drink," Marley was fined £50 for possession. Family Man was fined £25 but wisely kept quiet about his personal consumption.

A month later, the Wailers' second European tour, supported by Steel Pulse, began on May 10 at the Paris Pavilion, attended by 12,000 people.

Junior Marvin: "That was my first show with Bob Marley. A whole heap of celebrities came, and during the show, Bob gave me five and said to me that he liked my style. I remember the first reviews tried to put me to shame. They said I was a disgrace by playing rock style guitar and then on top of that, I was dancing and doing all these Jimi Hendrix style licks. They slagged me off big-time, plus Bob had other people around him saying I was trying to upstage him and so he made a point of coming up to me and said, 'I love what you're doing, because it gives me chance to take a break.' I told him I do what I do for the sake of the show and if the band looks and sounds better, then everyone's going to benefit, because I want to entertain and to give the audience their money's worth. I want to keep them satisfied and he agreed with me, so every time someone came up to him after that, saying I was trying to upstage him, he'd just wink as if to say, 'I'm not listening to them, so don't worry.' I was told that I brought this international dimension to the band, but I never took that for granted, because Bob Marley was already a star when I joined the band and he was going to get bigger and bigger anyway. I just wanted to make sure that whatever I contributed would be remembered."

While in Paris, the band attended a celebrity party hosted by Island. Bianca Jagger, Sandra Kong and the Jamaican ambassador to France were among the guests.

Don Taylor: "Once we were in Paris, we all checked in at the Eiffel Tower Hilton. As usual, Bob had the Presidential suite because of the cooking facilities. It was a three-bedroomed suite and I was in my room there, sleeping. Bob had gone across the street to play football and then Rita Marley woke me up, saying something is wrong with Bob's toe. Bob had taken off his football boots from sweating and she's seen his toe looking funny. He said nothing was wrong and to leave him alone. She insisted, but he said it was a buck toe he'd had from a long time and every time he played football it would sweat, but then heal again. Rita said she didn't like it and it looked like it was going rotten."

Taylor asked a doctor to examine Marley's foot and an in-growing toenail was diagnosed. He arranged to come back the following day, gave the singer an injection and removed the toenail. Marley completed the rest of the tour wearing a special slipper, although he was back in shoes by the time the Wailers returned to London.

Wailers concerts were now a rallying point for thousands of fans, and the larger European venues reflected the band's growing popularity. Marley was now the "world's most visible Jamaican," according to the *Gleaner.* "He's attained the status of the third world's Bob Dylan, part poet, mystic, outlaw, and prophet", and when he took the stage, "even young whites felt a vicarious tingle, whilst black youths idolise him." After Paris, the tour stopped at Brussels, the Hague (where Rico Rodriguez was the opening act), Munich, and Heidelberg, where Marley visited a factory that manufactured artificial limbs. Photographer Kate Simon captured him looking utterly dejected, as if contemplating an amputee's fate. After dates in Hamburg and Berlin, the band travelled to Gothenburg on May 19, followed by Stockholm and Copenhagen, before heading back to London to appear on *Top Of The Pops.*

Island had released 'Exodus' as a single which had duly soared into the UK charts, but failed to breach the Top 10, which remained the preserve of Rod Stewart, Barbra Streisand, and the Sex Pistols, who'd hijacked the Queen's Silver Jubilee celebrations with an electrifying slice of proletarian bile called 'God Save The Queen'. The Wailers weren't too sure about punk, but were amused by the Sex Pistols' boldness and sympathised with their vilification in the tabloids. Britain's gutter press had been sensational-ising the Pistols ever since their appearance on the Bill Grundy show the previous December, where they had been goaded by a soused Grundy into swearing. Newspapers like *The Sun* called them "foul mouthed yobs", running the infamous headline "The Filth and the Fury". The Sex Pistols had become a national obsession, heroes to thousands of youngsters with no hope of a proper education or job and who suffered from a chronic lack of self-esteem; "No future", as the Pistols raged on 'God Save The Queen'. Such feelings bred anger and disillusionment and an army of bands, record labels and DIY fanzines sprang up in the Sex Pistols' wake.

Because there were few record releases by British punk bands in the movement's earliest days, deejays such as Don Letts span reggae records to illustrate the common ground between Rastas and punks. Thanks to the rebellious nature of songs like 'Burnin' And Lootin'' and 'Crazy Baldhead', Bob Marley & the Wailers were hailed as being among the spiritual forebears of this British cultural revolution.

Exodus was released in the UK on June 3, peaking at number eight a week later, and staying on the album charts for well over a year. Balfour Henry described it as Marley's best album yet, commenting on how the singer had moved away from local political issues. "His melodies smack of thoroughbred professionalism and sheer genius," Henry wrote. *The New York Times* dubbed Marley "the Third World's first musical superstar," but others weren't so sure. "Although *Exodus* does not rank as Bob's best work or even come close to *Rastaman Vibration*, there are, however, a few exceptions," wrote a Jamaican reviewer, "notably the title track and the exultant 'Jamming'. Otherwise, there is an air of staleness, of lethargy and formula. The rhythms sag and the lyrics sound mechanical. Quite simply, *Exodus* plods." However, the reviewer conceded that, "whatever its musical failings the album keeps bulleting the charts. Pop lives off image and timing, not masterworks, and Marley's time, it seems, has come."

The Wailers gave proof of this with their four-day stint at London's Rainbow Theatre, beginning on June 1. After the previous year's Hammersmith Odeon shows, the Wailers were the hottest draw in town and tickets had sold out weeks in advance.

Junior Marvin: "The show at the Rainbow Theatre was best, because I'd grown up in the area, so all my schoolfriends, my family, and my teachers came, and they couldn't believe that this kid they'd known since I was little, was up there playing with Bob Marley. Everybody thought it was my show, because there were all these people calling out my name and my cousins were all laughing at me from the front of the stage. Growing up in the theatres and all that, I was used to dancing onstage and so when I play, I dance. The thing was, no one else in the Wailers would dance with Bob, because the rest of them would just stand still like Family Man. Tyrone might do a little bop now and then, but I was up and down the stage."

One of the concerts was filmed and later issued on DVD. Marvin, whose playing is tight, soulful and expressive, gestures to the crowd as he drops to his knees in mock ecstasy while unleashing a solo and generally revelling in the spotlight. Dressed in his familiar denim and facing Carly, Marley gave another inspired performance, jamming on rhythm guitar or dancing by himself at the rear of the stage. The I-Threes are resplendent and the combination of Tyrone, Seeco, the Barretts and Marvin was both visually and musically arresting. Despite, or possibly even because of, their change of line-up and the fresh emphasis on showmanship, the Wailers could justify claims of being the best live act around. "Forget your sickness and dance," Marley sang on 'Them Belly Full', heeding his own advice as the pain from his foot injury was brushed aside.

CHAPTER TWENTY-FIVE

Kaya

WHILE Marley was in London, Lee Perry arrived and, according to [reggae promoter] Tony Owens, wrote 'Punky Reggae Party' on the journey from Heathrow airport into central London. Scratch contacted Marley and the pair voiced it almost immediately at Island's Basing Street studio, using whichever musicians were available at short notice. Alongside Marley on guitar, Aswad's Angus "Drummie Zeb" Gaye played drums, Third World's Ibo Cooper and Richard Daley handled bass and keyboards respectively and Candy McKenzie and Aura Lewis provided backing vocals. Lewis, who had been in the crowd the night Marley and the Wailers played Max's Kansas City, was taken to the studio by Jimmy Cliff, who had hired her as a backing singer. An alternative cut of 'Keep On Moving' (with a built-in message to young Ziggy Marley) was recorded at the same session and Scratch and Marley also worked on the lyrics for 'Babylon System', although nothing was actually captured on tape.

Perry later recut sections of 'Punky Reggae Party' at Joe Gibbs' with Val Douglas, Sly Dunbar, Tyrone Downie, and the Zap Pow horn section. He also got the Congos' Watty Burnett and the Meditations to add harmonies to fill out the sound. It's doubtful whether Marley – who later revoiced his vocals at Criteria – would allow anyone else to take such liberties with his music. "Punk love reggae and some of them say things that Babylon no like," Marley told a British reporter. "I thought them was badness at first, but now me give them 900 per cent right. Them resist the society and say, 'Me a punk 'cause I don't want you to shove me where I don't like it.' Because him nah feel like we inferior. White man feel inferior to the black man and that's why him try and kill the black man and the punk say, 'No! We wanna join with the Rastaman and get something out of life.'"

Don Taylor claims that Marley's interest in punk rock met with resistance from the other Wailers, especially Family Man, who conceded that some of the punk artists had energy and spirit but frowned at their anti-social behaviour and lack of professionalism.

Island coupled 'Punky Reggae Party' with 'Jamming', and the single climbed to number nine in December. 'Punky Reggae Party' is hardly a masterpiece; the words are trite and inconsequential, a rare example of Marley responding to fashions, although working with Perry had lifted his spirits and the song was a good PR exercise. Punk was having a rejuvenating effect on a record industry that had grown stale and complacent. People had begun exploring their potential, and bands like the Clash followed Marley's example by writing message songs, commenting on things happening around them. American punk poetess Patti Smith had invited Tappa Zukie onstage with her at the Hammersmith Odeon the previous year, and in July Johnny Rotten appeared on Capital Radio, playing host Tommy Vance a selection of his favourite records. It was an eclectic mix including Dr Alimantado and Augustus Pablo's *King Tubby Meets Rockers Uptown*. Reggae had already been endorsed by the rock and soul fraternity, and now it was being given the stamp of approval by the new wave. 'Punky Reggae Party' simply returned the compliment.

If the song called for all to congregate in one hearty communion, the reality of the outside world was rather different. In September, a month after Elvis Presley was found dead in his Memphis mansion, black activist Steve Biko died in police custody. The South African police were cleared of his death two months later, despite overwhelming evidence that he'd died of injuries sustained in repeated beatings. There'd been demonstrations against the racist National Front in London, leading to the formation of the Anti-Nazi League. In New York, during one of the hottest summers on record, there was a power failure in the city which had led to widespread looting, and a Puerto Rican terrorist group bombed the Chrysler building in New York where the FBI had their headquarters. Martin Luther King had called riots "the language of the unheard", but those voices were growing louder by the hour.

An article in the *Gleaner* revealed that Marley still owed $250,000 to his backers (Island), who faced collapse unless his record sales improved. The writer pointed out that, for some time, Marley's progress had been painfully slow. The first two albums hadn't sold, they'd lost money on tours, and while *Natty Dread* had been hailed as a critical triumph, it wasn't until Eric Clapton's success with 'I Shot The Sheriff' that things had started to turn around. *Rolling Stone* had just voted Marley Best Performer of the Year, but if the Wailers had conquered Los Angeles and New York, middle America remained relatively unmoved, and that's where potentially the largest sales lay. *Rastaman Vibration* had entered the Top 10 of the US album charts, but it still hadn't been certified gold. The article noted that as Marley's international fame had spread, feelings were hardening against him in Jamaica, where people saw him preaching revolution and Jah, while driving around in a BMW. Some criticised him for not financing schools, while others wanted him to endorse various revolutionary groups, not realising the minefield this would entail.

There were also those who thought Marley had nailed his political colours to the mast by involving himself with the Smile Jamaica concert, but then backed down after the shooting incident. Taylor made things worse when he announced that Bob would get "80 per cent" of the vote if he ran for office, which prompted the *Gleaner* to comment, "Whether he chooses to think so or not, Marley is a powerful political voice in Jamaica. And it's this, together with his Rastafarian beliefs and his criticisms of his country that instigated 'the incident' last December."

Whereas some may have harboured mixed feelings towards Marley, there were no complaints when Family Man began supplying some of the local sound-systems with dubplate mixes of songs like 'War', 'So Much Things To Say', 'Running Away', 'Guiltiness' and 'Want More'. Fams was selective about who he gave these dubs to.

"They were the only three sounds in Jamaica that have them, which was Soul To Soul, Jah Love and Socialist Roots, then in England you have Lloydie Coxsone, Sufferers' Hi-Fi, and a next one too, called Jah Shaka. There were one or two soundmen from America who used to fly out and come to Hope Road as well, but we try and keep it exclusive really. Socialist Roots used to be called King Attorney, and before that, Sir Patrick. It became Socialist Roots during Manley's time, so all socialists could be happy. And them was radical too, y'know? U Brown was with them at first of course, and also this other fellow who turned into Eek A Mouse. Things change after King Attorney change into Socialist Roots, because politics start to come in. The owner get a contract to work fi the Government and people start to brand it as being a politics sound, so one night they shoot up a dance in Barbican and one of the guys get shot in his mouth real bad."

Despite such violent outbreaks from firebrands, the local music scene was vibrant. Filmmaker Jeremy Marre celebrated it as part of a series called *Beats Of The Heart*, which generated widespread interest after it was shown on British television that summer. The reggae edition, 'Roots, Rock Reggae', opened with a terrific live cut of 'Want More', played almost dub style, dominated by Family Man's earth-shattering bass. The music pounding out of the speakers was set to images of fires burning in Kingston and people rummaging for food on a refuse tip. It made a stunning and powerful introduction to one of the few credible documentaries on Jamaican music.

Sly Dunbar and Robbie Shakespeare played on a slew of hits coming out of Channel One and Joe Gibbs' studio. Apart from Dennis Brown, Gibbs was producing artists like Prince Far I and Culture, whose *Two Sevens Clash* embraced the zeitgeist with such fearful, yet joyful exuberance. Marcus Garvey had predicted the world would end when "the two sevens clashed," and on July 7, 1977, Jamaica came to a virtual standstill as people braced themselves against the workings of prophecy. Sly and Robbie were also working with a group from Waterhouse called Black Uhuru, who included moody versions of the Wailers' 'Sun Is Shining' and 'Natural Mystic' in their repertoire. Not to be left out (and ably assisted by Family Man), Johnny Clarke, Leroy Smart, and Dillinger each covered 'Waiting In Vain'. The Wailers' bassist then turned his attentions to Burning Spear, who'd recorded further albums for Island and Jack Ruby in the wake of *Marcus Garvey*, but now wished to produce himself.

Family Man Barrett: "Spear would regularly call me for sessions. He'd left the other two singers behind by then, so it was for solo tunes like 'Social Living' and 'Going From Bad To Worse', and tracks for his *Dry And Heavy* album. In those times, I just play fi him like a session musician. Just play and collect and gone. I don't know where them going to be mixed. I don't know the whole structure, but I make sure that every track I play on has that winning touch."

After his first UK tour Spear was advised by Fams to form his own band. The two began working on Spear's next album, *Marcus' Children*, which Spear again produced and initially released on his own label before Island picked it up and retitled it *Social Living*. Members of Aswad also played on it, including Family Man's friend Brinsley Forde, while Donald Kinsey, Touter, and Wya Lindo all contributed to 'Dry And Heavy'. Lindo had recently played on tracks intended for Bunny Wailer's second album *Protest*. Tosh also contributed, but there was no sign of the Barretts, since Livingston still hadn't paid them for the *Blackheart Man* sessions, or credited Family Man with co-writing tracks like 'Armagideon'. Instead Fams worked with Niney and Dennis Brown on a track that would become one of Brown's biggest ever hits.

Castro Brown had released 'Here I Come' on his Morpheus label in

March, just prior to Joe Gibbs issuing the *Visions* album. The song had proved a sensation since its arrival on pre-release two months earlier, and formed the centrepiece of Brown's *Wolves And Leopards* album, released in August.

Family Man Barrett: "We did that track up by Randy's. That was like Dennis Brown and Niney's personal stuff, 'cause I map it out and do some arranging on it too; get the musicians them. That was the time I was bringing Robbie Shakespeare in on bass, so I let him play that and I play the organ. I play the intro on the solo too."

The Wailers had wanted to build a proper studio at Hope Road before the shooting, but had understandably been distracted. In Marley's absence, Family Man discussed this with Diane Jobson and the two decided the studio should be built downstairs. While Fams organised its construction (helped by a consultant who'd worked at Criteria), Jobson began supervising additional office space. Marley, meanwhile, was struggling with his foot injury, which had been aggravated during a visit to his mother's house.

Don Taylor: "After the tour, we came back to London and everyone started to disperse now, before we were due to meet up again for the US tour. Bob took off his bandage and the top of the toe was healed. Everything was okay, and he'd started wearing shoes again. I went home to Miami, and he went to Delaware, where he waited for the US tour to start. Whilst he was in Delaware, Bob called me to say the toe hurt up again after playing football and this time the toe won't heal. He then gets a call from his friend Claudie Massop, talking about a Peace Concert. Bob told me to arrange a ticket for him and he left to go meet up with Claudie in London. While he was there, a lady who worked for Island called Denise Mills took Bob to see a doctor. All I know is that I get a call from Bob and he said he wanted to come to Miami, because Denise had taken him to this doctor, and he'd taken her into a room on her own for a while, talking about 'toe or tour.' Bob said he was trying to hear what they were saying by listening at the door, but they were whispering.

"He didn't like how the doctor was talking to Denise and not him, but then when the doctor came out, he told Bob he had melanoma cancer and recommended they cut off his foot. Bob repeated that he wanted to come to Miami, but I told him to stay where he was, then got in touch with an African-American doctor in Miami called Dr Bacon, who'd operated on my spine after I'd been shot. I told Dr Bacon the situation and he said to tell Bob not to let anyone touch him, since it's impossible for a black man to have melanoma cancer. Now remember, Bob had that injection in France. Anyway, Bob went to see Dr Bacon, and came to stay with me at my home in Miami . . ."

The Wailers were scheduled to play three nights at the Palladium in New York during late August, but these dates were cancelled. The announcement was only made a month beforehand, after thousands of tickets had already been sold.

"They don't want to run this thing like I want to run it," Marley commented. "Them want to run me on a star trip, but I realise my structure run down. I must rest, but they are not concerned with my structure. Them run and plan a North American tour. I watch Muhammad Ali and Allan Cole and I see how these athletes take care of their structure, but the people who set up the tour don't work. Them just collect the money and when night come you find them in bed with two girls while you bust your rassclaat and work all the time. When my toe was injured, they didn't even know my toenail had just come out and the bwoy them still set up a North American tour. They had planned to cut off my toe just so I could make the tour. *Exodus* was a bubble, and if I make the tour, *Exodus* would sell over a million. His Majesty [Crown Prince Asfa Wossen, the son of Haile Selassie I] said to me in London, 'Is what sin do you agree to cut off your toe?' so I just say to them, 'Fuck off and go away,' and decide to take a rest."

Still determined to make a positive difference in Jamaica, in February Marley met with Claudie Massop and two PNP enforcers, Aston "Bucky" Marshall and Tony Welch, to discuss ideas for a free Peace Concert. Massop and Marshall had shared a jail cell in Kingston and called a peace treaty after realising they had a great deal in common. Both had grown up in the ghettos of west Kingston and were tired of being used by politicians. They also knew a lot of singers between them, especially Marley and Tosh. A new mood of optimism greeted their decision to call a truce and in typically Jamaican fashion, songs commemorating the event had already been making their way onto the local sound-systems and into stores like Randy's on North Parade.

After the Peace Concert meeting, Taylor and Marley flew to Miami for more consultations with doctors. Dr Vernon Carrington visited the singer and pronounced he had "buck toe" because "Rastas can't get cancer," yet cancer was confirmed. Carrington advised Marley to send for Pee Wee, Dr Carl Fraser, a member of the Twelve Tribes, who acknowledged the diagnosis. Doctors were able to save some of the toe rather than amputate. Marley spent a week in hospital and then stayed in Miami for nearly three months, recuperating at Taylor's house, pushing a stroller around and arranging to buy a house in the area for his mother.

In the meantime, leftover tracks from *Exodus* were being mixed at Criteria under Marley's supervision, although not by Alex Sadkin, who had tragically died in a car accident on Nassau a few months earlier.

In January 1978, all the talk around Jamaica centred on 'the Green Bay Massacre'. Agents from the Military Intelligence Unit which was, and still is, a covert operational wing of the Jamaica Defence Force, had offered members of Chubby Dread's JLP 'POW Posse' guns and jobs if they co-operated with the government. Over a dozen men agreed and an army ambulance drove the men out to the Green Bay artillery range near Port Henderson, where a team of snipers awaited them. Five were shot dead and the remainder fled into bushes or swam out into the Bay, where they were rescued by a passing fishing boat. The victims came from a JLP stronghold called Southside in downtown Kingston.

Official sources claimed the men had been shot after being surprised by soldiers doing target practice. In the end, no one was held responsible for their deaths, despite protests from the people of Southside. "No angels died at Green Bay," said the PNP's Minister for Security, Dudley Thompson. The incident is considered one of the worst acts of brutality in Jamaican history and news of it stiffened Marley's resolve to attempt to bring peace to the island.

In February, following the messy demise of the Sex Pistols in America the previous month, John Lydon and Don Letts arrived in Kingston to act as A&R consultants to Virgin Records, who were looking to add to their roster of reggae acts. Virgin boss Richard Branson knew that the Pistols frontman had a genuine love of reggae, from hearing his Capital Radio guest appearance. Like Blackwell, Branson enjoyed hanging out with his artists (with the notable exception of Keith Hudson, who'd tracked the Virgin boss down to his London home and threatened him over disputed royalties). Branson's party booked a whole floor at the Sheraton, and with a suitcase full of money as an incentive, signed an incredible wealth of talent to Virgin's Frontline label, including Johnny Clarke, the Abyssinians, U Roy, Culture, Gregory Isaacs, and Big Youth. Virgin became serious rivals to Island virtually overnight, although their involvement in reggae music would prove to be temporary.

Most of the above acts were making rockers music, chanted over a rubbery, spring-heeled backbeat, designed to summon fire and brimstone in their fight against Babylonian oppression. It was the kind of sound that had made *Natty Dread* and *Rastaman Vibration* so exciting, but the Wailers' career was now headed in a different direction. As a taster for the next album, Island chose to release 'Is This Love', which became the band's second UK Top 10 hit in February. On the 26th, Marley made an impromptu appearance at the National Stadium, where he led the crowd in a chanting session. Two minor earthquakes reverberated around Kingston soon afterward but despite Marley's iconic stature, the Wailers' impact upon Jamaican music continued to diminish.

Kaya was released on March 23 and went to number 4 at the beginning of April, giving Marley and the Wailers their highest ever placing on the UK album charts, staying on there for six months. Since the album contained an acute shortage of rebel anthems and reality songs, with several of the tracks being reworkings of old material, the reviews were generally disappointing.

"Kaya means herb," Marley said by way of explanation. "It's a password some of the brethren use in Jamaica, so Kaya is really dealing with togetherness and humanity and peace, because the thing of peace travel through the earth now. *Rastaman Vibration* and *Exodus* were harder, but this time we're dealing with something softer. You have to be you and make the crowd follow you. When we were doing *Kaya*, we knew that plenty of people were going to say, 'Kaya, blah, blah,' but we still do it, y'know? Everyone must take the pressure some time.

"Maybe if I'd tried to make a heavier album than *Kaya* they would have tried to assassinate me again because I'd come too hard. I have to know how to run my life, because that's what I have and nobody can tell me to put it on the line, you dig? People that aren't involved don't know it, but it's my work and I know it inside out. I know when everything is cool and I know when to tremble, y'understand?"

By now, Marley had developed the knack of writing catchy pop songs built around a righteous framework and 'Is This Love' was the perfect example. A simple love song, written by a man who can barely disguise his good fortune, 'Is This Love' is utterly without pretence. "We'll share the shelter of my single bed," he cajoles, whilst entrusting Jah to "provide the bread." According to Family Man, the rhythm's "all on percussion. Big bass, small bass, two funde and repeater, two maracas, tambourine, and triangle . . ."

The inclusion of 'Easy Skanking', which the Wailers were in the midst of recording when Taylor first appeared on the scene and was also one of the last tracks Lindo played on, helped bring a degree of lightness to an album that is a little too introspective in places. The mournful 'She's Gone' is almost a throwaway by Marley's own standards and he continued the theme of loss on 'Misty Morning', with its refrain of "I want you to straighten out my tomorrow."

Now in his early thirties and the father of several children, Marley was hinting that he might want to settle down. Despite being apart for long periods of time, Marley admired Cindy Breakspeare's intelligence and good business sense which could help him in his career. The fact that she was the reigning Miss World and being fêted by practically all red-blooded males didn't hurt either. After agonising in 'Misty Morning' over having given of himself, only to receive little in return, Marley adopts a more world-weary philosophy on 'Crisis', which couches a devastating critique on international (and of course, Jamaican) affairs, in a quirky delivery that's among the most uncharacteristic of his entire oeuvre. The leaders are still killing the people, he says, but living it up at the same time and although they say the sun shines for all, "in some people's world, it never shines at all."

On 'Running Away', Marley slips into a similar, semi-comic delivery which could easily be construed as an address to the Jamaican people. "I'm not running away. Don't say that," he admonishes. "I've got to protect my life, and I don't want to live with no strife. It's better to live on the housetop, than to live in a house full of confusion so I made my decision, and I left you. Now you're coming to tell me that I'm running away, but it's not true." Because there are unreleased versions of both tracks that are sung in his regular style, it's as if Marley adopted another style of voice to lessen the seriousness of what he was singing. "It's written about what they ask Bob after they shoot us with intent and we were protected by His Majesty," confirms Family Man, who played rhythm guitar and piano on 'Running Away' and praises Seeco for "playing from the heart."

The final track, 'Time Will Tell', written in Nassau immediately after the shooting, starts with Marley's guitar picking, which almost transforms it into a bluegrass tune. The chorus of "Think you're in heaven but you're living in hell," is repeated so many times it becomes a mantra. "Jah would never give the power to a baldhead, run come crucify the dread," he warns. The Wailers originally recorded 'Sun Is Shining', 'Satisfy My Soul' (a.k.a. 'Don't Rock My Boat') and 'Kaya' for Lee Perry.

Family Man Barrett: "We wanted to give them that progressive, Island sound. Those versions we did with Scratch represented an early stage, and by the time we did *Exodus* and *Kaya* we had better equipment, use of a better studio and better knowledge too. We knew we could record them so they would have more impact and take on that international sound."

'Sun Is Shining' has what Fams calls "a chanting vibes." Family Man played the bluesy lead guitar on this track, as well as bass, while 'Satisfy My Soul' and 'Kaya' are both uptempo and again serve to lighten the mood. Marley's cancer was still being kept secret from the media and he was determined not to dwell on his condition, but continue with the band's mission. There was no stopping God's will, although the vibes around Hope Road had changed considerably since the days when the members would climb onto the roof, watching the night sky and dreaming of spreading the Rastafarian message "to the four corners of the earth."

Family Man Barrett: "It was in everybody's mind that we needed more security and we weren't really rehearsing in the same spot any more. We were using a smaller room before, but I decide we need to spread out and find a different spot to rehearse. We were still rehearsing all the time, but we'd often go up to Strawberry Hill and run through our music up there, instead of staying at Hope Road. One time, we even go over to Nine Miles and rehearse in a basement over there, but eventually we made another rehearsal space at Hope Road, once there was extra security in place. We had the pressing plant round the back, but after we decided to move everything out to Three Miles, then I use the whole of that area for rehearsals. That's when we got a dress rehearsal space, with a stage, because we built a drum riser round there too. But the truth is, there was a whole other consciousness going on after the shooting . . ."

Lindo rejoined them for these rehearsals and was welcomed back into the fold as if he'd never been away, although he was a different person to the one that left for San Francisco. The bright, inquisitive keyboard player now had mental health problems and his condition meant the other band members had to look out to ensure he wasn't having a panic attack or forgetting where he was and wandering off alone.

"I don't know where else he go. I don't know what kind of thing he believe or what company he keep, but him nah return the same," says Family Man, who acted as Lindo's protector for the next two decades. "I'm not blaming anybody or saying certain people hurt him, but whatever happened to him took place in the time when him run off and forget about the mission. He got hurt because there wasn't anybody there to watch him, but him still play good."

It was announced that the One Love Peace Concert Marley planned with Massop in London would now take place in the National Stadium on

Saturday, April 22. It would be the Wailers' first proper Jamaican concert for nearly 18 months, and after his meetings with Crown Prince Asfa Wossen, the posters offered evidence of Marley's revised religious beliefs, since they announced he and the Wailers would be appearing "courtesy of the Ethiopian Orthodox Church." Over 20,000 people attended the nine-hour event, which had two main objectives – to celebrate the 12th anniversary of Emperor Haile Selassie I's state visit to Jamaica, and to raise funds for deprived ghetto areas in Kingston. Admission charges were kept low and there was increased security with no "bottles, oranges, or potential missiles" allowed in the venue, by order of Dudley Thompson.

Family Man Barrett: "Police and soldiers had encircled the arena, because memories of the Smile Jamaica were fresh in their minds, I guess. We went to prepare for the show and to gather round in a meditation, but it was like being in a war zone, because Swallowfield was right next door, and that was the place Marcus Garvey had said would be the battlefield! We were right in the middle of a PNP area and had a special group of police and soldiers guarding us but everything was cool and they weren't too obtrusive in the end. When the National Arena was first built, they used it for the birthday night of Norman Manley, the father of Michael Manley, and I opened it with my band, the Hippy Boys, so I always feel there's something significant about playing there. I also played at the wedding party of Edward Seaga, so it's like my bands play by royal appointment!"

Acts appearing that day included Culture, Big Youth, Ras Michael & the Sons of Negus, Junior Tucker, Althea & Donna, Trinity, Beres Hammond, and the Mighty Diamonds. All were relatively young acts and most were Rastafarians, which meant they brought a crowd to match, although the event also attracted large numbers of foreign press and overseas visitors, including a few rock celebrities. The show began at five with Lloyd Parkes & We The People Band. Dillinger took the stage looking like Mr Punch in his gaily-striped suit and Jacob Miller threatened to steal the show by openly smoking a spliff after jumping down into the VIP section next to Manley. He then seized a policeman's helmet, which he wore while racing around in his Wellington boots, his fat belly wobbling and glinting under the lights. Miller's latest hit was 'Peace Treaty Special', for which he invited Massop, Marshall, and other gang leaders up on to the stage. Tosh almost caused a riot during his set when he lambasted Manley with a withering, verbal outpouring, accusing him of failing the sufferers. "I don't want peace, I want justice," he demanded.

Tosh, too, defiantly smoked a spliff onstage, which led to warnings by police that artists would be prosecuted for this in future. "One may well ask whether our new breed of 'entertainers' are exempt from the social disciplines which the rest of us must adhere to," wrote an angry *Gleaner* reader. "And does identification with our 'new roots culture' make us immune from civil accountability?"

Following such controversy wasn't going to be easy, but Marley and the Wailers' homecoming provided abiding images that would come to symbolise the power of music in effecting real, social change, even if only for a frozen moment in time. The stage was bathed in a full moon when the band appeared soon after midnight and opened up with the unreleased 'Conquering Lion'.

Marcia Griffiths: "People from all walks of life came to witness this event, because remember, this was Bob's return, and his first performance there for a long while. Because he had to leave Nassau when too many people found out he was there and leave for England, so it had been a year and a half since he'd been in Jamaica, and everybody came to see what would take place. Most of the songs Bob did that night related to what had been happening, like the shooting and all of that. He chose most of them to speak out, 'cause I remember he did another version of 'Keep On Moving' where he changed the lyrics around."

In the middle of 'Jamming', Marley invited the leaders of Jamaica's two political parties to join him onstage. Claudie Massop helped up Seaga and then Manley appeared, flanked by top ranking PNP hit men. In a historic action, Marley took hold of their hands, lifted them above his head with one hand and then stretched out his other straight in front of him, as if blessing the crowd, while chanting, "Jah, Rastafari." Neville Garrick likened this scene to Jesus Christ on the cross, flanked by the two thieves, but an editorial in the *Gleaner* gave a less poetic interpretation. "Imagine," it asked, "Mr Callaghan and Mrs Thatcher [the two leading British political figures] emotionally shaking hands with each other, stood onstage with Johnny Rotten at a rock charity concert organised by the Krays."

Marcia Griffiths: "Bob was really, really hurting from that shooting. I think his soul was damaged, so all of that must have convinced him to top it off with a performance like that. I think the whole thing was ordained, because before the shooting, he never dreamt anybody in Jamaica wanted to hurt him, and so after returning to Jamaica now, it could never have been better when he brought those two political leaders onstage with him. That was the highlight of that concert, seeing Manley and the Opposition leader joined together like that. Nobody else but Bob could have done that, so it was like him to just use that concert to bring everything back to normal, so we could all just live peacefully, and everything nice. It was one of the most beautiful moments ever captured in Jamaica, because things had been really terrible before that. Something strange happened that night too, because that concert started from like twilight, when the sun was going down, and I remember my children's father, Errol Thompson, was onstage introducing one of the acts, like maybe Junior Tucker, and a shaft of sunlight came across and hit the chrome around the mic, causing a flash of light. It didn't make a sound, but you could just see that lightning right on Errol's face. It was frightening, as if there was some force there with us in the stadium."

Around the time of the Peace Concert, Taylor claims that one of Massop's right-hand men, Tek Life, took him and Marley to a spot near MacGregor Gully, where three men were held captive. All admitted they'd been commissioned by the CIA to kill Marley and issued with guns and cocaine. Two were hanged on the spot, the third shot in the head, out of his and Marley's sight, but not earshot. A fourth, who wasn't present, later died of a drugs overdose. These reports are unconfirmed but, if true, they would have made Taylor and Marley accomplices to murder.

A month after his militant display at the Peace Concert, Tosh was brutalised at a police station by 10 men who beat him for an hour behind closed doors until he pretended to be dead. They then left him bleeding in the reception area, in full view of passers by. Tosh, who'd signed to the Rolling Stones' label and had been entertaining Mick Jagger in Kingston, argued with Marley after Jagger had described Marley as "his friend" on Jamaican radio. All things considered, Tosh's tenure with Rolling Stones Records would not prove a happy one. He was an opening act for the Stones on their US tour that summer and had also accompanied them to the tour rehearsals at Bearsville Studios in Woodstock, where Keith Richards allegedly co-produced an album's worth of tracks featuring himself, Ronnie Wood, and members of Word, Sound & Power, separate from the material included on Tosh's *Bush Doctor*.

"I'm drawn to reggae because there's nothing happening in black American music," Richards told biographer Victor Bockris. "They're going through the disco phase. It's very popular and no wonder people are drawn to it. The temptation to make those records is strong. Reggae took off because there are more Jamaicans in Britain and America than there are in Jamaica! Bob Marley has created an international status for reggae and now Africa will be a big market for the music too. Trouble is, I don't know if roots reggae is what people want to hear from me. When I've got an album's worth of material in front of me, then I'll think about releasing it. I've got Robbie Shakespeare on bass, Sly Dunbar on drums and Robert Lyn on piano. I've been going to Jamaica for over 10 years."

Richards' relationship with Tosh ended dramatically in the summer of 1981, when Tosh refused to leave Richards' villa after staying there for an extended period, claiming it was his owing to the fact that the Stones' label hadn't promoted his albums properly. Tosh accused them of failing to deliver him a mainstream audience and then trashed the place before Richards' return. That summer, Max Romeo released an album (*Holdin' Out My Love To You*) the Stones' guitarist had played only a minor part in. When his name appeared emblazoned all over the sleeve, Richards sued and another friendship ended.

The Kaya tour, scheduled to begin in Tampa, Florida, on May 4, was postponed due to Junior Marvin either falling ill or being convicted for smuggling cocaine in the States, resulting in his deportation back to Jamaica.* Al Anderson, who played with Tosh at the Peace Concert, was asked to rejoin the Wailers.

Al Anderson: "Peter Tosh was great, but by then he'd got a manager named Herbie Miller. Peter was in a bad position financially after he'd left the Wailers and because he was wanting to go out on his own as a solo artist, he needed money to record and so he went to Herbie Miller, who had this reputation as a bad guy. You don't loan money from somebody like that and then make him your manager. You appoint a manager who wants to invest in your career, because it's important you know he's managing your career for the right reasons. Sure, you want to pay him back the money that you owe him, but at the same time, you want to be sure he's looking out for your interests. Well Herbie Miller became powerful when he started working with Peter, so he decided to crush all of us little people who Peter was close to. Peter was with the Rolling Stones and they weren't exactly the greatest people to be around sometimes, since they've got their problems too. I mean Keith and Mick don't get along at times and I really didn't want to be around all of that, so I just backed out.

"Bob asked me if I was happy working with Peter, or did I want to come back into the band, and I told him yes. I'd had other offers, because the Rolling Stones' lawyer had asked me if I would replace Ron Wood for

---

* Marvin refuses to confirm or deny either explanation.

a month whilst they did something about his cocaine addiction. I asked him what my position would be and he said they were going to put Ronnie in rehab, and I could play guitar if I was interested but I turned it down because Ronnie's my friend, and I was looking forward to playing with Bob again."

The tour finally began on May 18 in Ann Arbor, moving on to Cleveland's Music Hall the following day followed by four days off. Over the course of the next month, the band performed in Columbus, Wisconsin, Chicago, Milwaukee, Minneapolis, Pittsburgh, Syracuse, Detroit, Philadelphia, Boston, Toronto (where their Maple Leaf Gardens appearance was described as "a night of magic"), Montreal, Buffalo, Poughkeepsie, Connecticut, and Maryland. On June 17, they played at Madison Square Garden, supported by jazz/funk bassist Stanley Clarke. While in New York, Marley would often visit Club Negril on 2nd Avenue where the speakers attacked your central nervous system thanks to the deejays playing the latest reggae, punk, and hip-hop. However, there was no time for such frivolities on this trip. The night before the concert, a press conference was held at the Waldorf Astoria, where Marley was awarded the Third World Peace Medal on behalf of "500 million Africans" by Mohmmadu Johnny Seka, the Senegalese Youth Minister to the United Nations.*

"How does it feel being a Third World hero?" a reporter asked Marley immediately after the ceremony. "We don't deal with hero," he said. "And what are your thoughts on being called a black Bob Dylan?" another asked. Marley replied that he didn't listen to such talk and only listened to God. He lamented the fact that developed nations continued to supply Africans with guns, rather than "food and justice", and hinted that Ethiopia's difficulties had resulted from the people "fighting against Rastafari." Over the course of the following half hour, he admitted he only recorded 'Punky Reggae Party' because Lee Perry was "his good brethren", and expounded on herb's role as "the healing of the nation."

"When you smoke herb, it makes you meditate," he explained. "If you meditate, then you can pause everyday things. You can have all seven years in the one day, but the system set it so that every day you haffi go to work and come home and the government, scientists, and doctors know that if we smoke herb, then we the people are all going to think alike and they don't want that. That is dangerous for them, because as long as we all think differently, them a get control."

---

* Seka would also die of melanoma cancer at an early age.

On June 18, the first leg of the tour finished at the Music Inn, Lenox, Massachusetts. The band then flew to Britain to play the New Bingley Hall, in Staffordshire. Island had invited a handful of journalists to attend the show, who endured a horrendous coach journey from London, which prompted Penny Reel to call his *NME* article 'Babylon By Bus'. The pace was unrelenting but still no one outside of Marley's inner circle knew he was suffering from cancer. 'Satisfy My Soul', with 'Smile Jamaica' making a belated appearance on the B-side, had narrowly failed to enter the Top 20, despite a wonderful picture sleeve portraying a lion in Rasta colours. After a day in London, the Wailers then boarded a flight to Paris for a four-day stint at the Pavilion. Shows in Ibiza, Stockholm, Denmark, Norway, Rotterdam, Amsterdam, and Brussels followed, before the entourage headed back to London. The band then returned to North America, for dates in Vancouver, Seattle, Portland, Santa Cruz, and Berkeley's Greek Theatre, before a prestigious show at the Starlite Amphitheatre, Burbank, on July 22. Mick Jagger and Diana Ross were backstage, and so, too Tosh, who joined Marley onstage for a rousing duet on 'Get Up, Stand Up'.

"The Pope felt that one!" Marley exclaimed, as the pair triumphantly slapped hands.* It would be the last time Marley and Tosh performed together. Tosh's latest album, *Bush Doctor*, had been recorded at Dynamic and Joe Gibbs, and finished off at Bearsville. The title track featured Keith Richards on guitar, while the lead vocal on Tosh's cover of the Temptations' 1965 hit, 'Don't Look Back' was shared with Mick Jagger. Jagger appeared in the accompanying promo video and also joined Tosh in singing it on *Saturday Night Live* in December. Tosh's movement in rock royalty circles was of little interest to Marley, who remembered Jagger's claims of them being friends, so turned down the Stones singer's offer of guesting with the Wailers that night.

The next show in San Diego was followed by the Santa Barbara County Bowl (which was filmed) and the Starlite Bowl, and the Roxy Theatre in Los Angeles. Two days later, on the 27th, the tour continued in Austin, Fort Worth, Houston, New Orleans, and Atlanta, before fulfilling one last engagement in Miami on August 5. It had been a gruelling tour, compounded by Marley's steadily worsening condition and an expanded

---

* Rastafarians are no respecters of Papal doctrine but their influence must have been exceptionally strong that year as Pope Paul VI died within two weeks of this concert on August 6. His replacement, Pope John Paul I, also died just over a month later.

retinue. Island compiled a double live album from shows in Paris, Copenhagen, London and Amsterdam, but *Babylon By Bus* barely made the Top 40, staying on the charts for just two and a half months, Marley's worst chart placing for an album since *Natty Dread* three years earlier (although *Catch A Fire* and *Burnin'* hadn't charted at all.) The decision to release another live album, thus inviting comparisons with the Lyceum set, proved disastrous. *Babylon By Bus* suggests a degree of raw excitement had been lost from the band's act although they were as rigorously rehearsed and professional as ever. However, that vital spark and blinding intensity, generated by the shows on the Natty Dread and Rastaman Vibration tours, was missing.

The sound quality wasn't great either. Jack Nuber, who got a co-production credit alongside Blackwell, mixed it at Criteria, and the non-involvement of Family Man and other members of the Wailers is evident. Taylor has said Marley resented how Blackwell awarded himself production credits, since it made him appear more involved with the Wailers' music than was strictly true. Al Anderson agrees with him.

"Chris Blackwell would wait for Bob to finish a record after working on it for four or five months straight," he claims. "We'd be working on it every day and every night. We would finish the record, ring him and say, 'Chris, we have the record finished,' then he would fly from England and all of a sudden, it's like the Queen is coming to Jamaica. Then, when he arrives, there's all this big fanfare going on. It was like a big psychological thing, because Chris majored at college in psychology and economics. It had nothing to do with music or art or nothing. He's always been involved with finances. He might tell somebody to put an overdub here or there and so he became the producer . . .

"Family Man, Tyrone, Karl Pitterson, and Alex Sadkin were the key people involved in that and all the engineers we had were very instrumental in producing Bob's music as well – especially Karl Pitterson and Alex Sadkin, because those guys were great at knowing exactly what to put on tape for us. They knew our minds and they were just friends. We lived in the studio, and yet Chris would come to show off, to tell everybody what to do, take the credit and go back to London. Because from the minute his name was put on the record, he was getting paid as if he was in the band. Chris wanted to be in the Wailers, indirectly, and he got paid as a producer and he also got Bob's publishing, so he *was* like a band member, except I feel he didn't deserve it."

CHAPTER TWENTY-SIX

Tuff Gong Uprising

B Y the time *Babylon By Bus* was released in November '78, Marley was enjoying success on the Jamaican charts with a wonderfully understated singalong, 'Blackman Redemption'. "No need to get jumpy," he tells the Rasta brethren, over a lazy, undulating reggae groove. "Cool runnings, can you dig it?" he asks cheekily. The similarities between this track and 'Rastaman Live Up' are striking but then both were originally recorded at the same session and convey a simple yet deep message in the most delightful manner. "Bingy man don't give up. Keep your culture. Grow your dreadlocks, don't be afraid of the wolf pack," he chants on the latter, while reminding the faithful of how David slew Goliath. The rhythm's again irresistible, with Marvin adding delicate touches on lead guitar. Both songs went through significant changes before being released. In fact, both were later re-recorded in different studios and the I-Threes' harmonies replaced entirely.

Marley was friendly with the Meditations, who the Wailers backed on Tuff Gong productions like 'War Monger', and it was their three-part harmonies heard on 'Blackman Redemption' and 'Rastaman Live Up', which are little known outside Jamaica, yet would have made fine additions to the Wailers' next album had Island not declined to release them. Perhaps Blackwell considered the tracks unfinished or too simplistic, because there was now a sub-genre called "international roots reggae", that the Wailers themselves had pioneered with a more refined style of production, as heard on *Exodus* and *Kaya*. This more mainstream form of presentation was mirrored on Third World hits 'Cool Meditation', 'Journey To Addis' and 'Now That We've Found Love', and also the Royal Rasses, with songs like 'San Salvador' and 'Unconventional People'. Bunny Wailer was another exponent, and had recently taken Lindo and Chinna in the studio for the grandiose 'Rockers', celebrating a genre as well as a movie starring Leroy "Horsemouth" Wallace (filmed during Marley and the Wailers' time off the island).

While reggae music had now gone uptown in more ways than one, 'Blackman Redemption' and 'Rastaman Live Up' found Marley returning to basics and addressing a specific section of the black audience. Downie, who'd provided the driving force behind these songs, was now an integral part of the Wailers' set-up, although he wasn't nicknamed 'Jumpy' for nothing.

Family Man Barrett: "Well, they push it, because we didn't have a tour coming up, so we could have just waited for the studio to be finished before doing more recording. It's just that Tyrone wanted to force the issue and maybe make some extra money so he could buy nose candy. He and Don Taylor rent some time at Dynamic and took Wya and the horn section over there. That caused a vibes 'cause Bob get vexed and bring everybody together for a meeting. He lick out at us and get miserable and accuse Tyrone and Don Taylor of being insolent. He said our own studio will be ready in two weeks' time and that no studio in the world is supposed to get the sound we'll have there, so why go ahead with some little booga-booga t'ing, when we can take everything to a higher level?

"No other tunes were recorded at Dynamic after that. Tyrone and Don Taylor, they were into the nose candy and there was this segregation t'ing going on because of that. It was a speed up t'ing, but if the bird wants to learn and fly too fast, then it might fall out the nest. I have to keep reminding them that it was our plan to build a studio and to take up all of these artists who had been mistreated, and put them on the right track. That we'd set the inspiration for the studio from a long time ago, and so why rush it?"

Family Man says Tyrone was valued for his musical abilities and knowledge of electronics, which made putting up with his drug habit a little easier. Weak links were appearing in the chain, nevertheless, and the unity the Wailers were preaching in their music was now rapidly coming apart. Cocaine is no respecter of diligence or forbearance, and even the loyalty between Marley and the Barretts would be tested because of it. Family Man remained steadfast, but he was beginning to worry as the band's collective ambitions entered a new phase.

"My brother and I were committed as ever and just trying to make everything strong and effective," he confirms. "We were only thinking to get everybody together and then turn Tuff Gong into a little Motown, just like we'd always talked about. We also wanted to set up a workshop, 'cause not everyone can make it in music, so we needed to think about providing something else for those who failed. We thought we could help teach them a trade like ironwork, woodwork, and things like that, 'cause we love engineering. Bob was a welder, I do some welding too, and we'd been talking about branching out into some masonry work as well and dealing with it like a contract t'ing."

The Wailers gave consideration towards such things because they were not only concerned with music, but also the Rasta lifestyle. Their art wasn't just about creative expression, but spreading awareness, based on righteousness and spiritual truth, which made Marley and the Barretts so different from their contemporaries in other musical fields. While they had attained a degree of wealth, material gain wasn't considered important and the songs were almost secondary to the messages contained within them. Marley reiterated this in countless interviews. He was an evangelist and his Rastafarian beliefs informed everything he did, from the way he handled his business affairs, to how he spoke, ate, and presented himself. Tuff Gong was to be an empire, built upon Rastafarian precepts, and the Barretts embraced that concept totally, having already sacrificed a great deal of time and energy in helping to see it reach fruition. While Family Man found the actions of certain band members troubling, he was delighted with the new studio, which now took up half the ground floor.

"First we lick out all the doors and windows and strip it back to the concrete walls," he describes, "then we build a box inside of it. We sound-proof all the corners with foam rubber, then we lift up the board and put it on a platform, so it have a little bounce to it. That's how we set it. We had a computer board where we could mix, a 24-track MCI tape machine and two MCI quarter inch, plus various effects for the guitarists, and these boxes we line up perfectly, 'til they hit just the right spot. It's quite small in there, so that means we can just voice, or set up some instruments like electric keyboard and guitar in the room itself. Outside you have the piano room, or the drum room and the bass room, and we sometimes put the organ in a corner with this sheet behind it. That was the live section, y'know? We have the best sound in Jamaica and that's because the board was like a sample. They'd only built two of them. Criteria studios in Miami had one and we had the other. That give us analogue and computer, so we'd use both and they sounded good, I tell you!"

Island wanted an album to coincide with another lengthy US tour booked for the summer and autumn, so sessions at the studio got under way in earnest during the New Year. Apart from the two tracks at Dynamic, the Wailers hadn't recorded in Jamaica for over a year, so Marley had a storehouse of songs he wished to try out, most of which were inspired by cultural issues affecting black people and thoughts of Africa. He felt less vulnerable than when writing and recording *Exodus*, and was driven by the nagging realisation that his illness might immobilise him in future. Sadkin was drafted in to oversee the recordings, although he was helped out by several other engineers, including Dennis Thompson and Errol Brown, who'd been introduced to Marley by Marcia Griffiths.

'Ambush In The Night' was one of the first tracks to come out of Tuff Gong. In addition to documenting the Hope Road shooting, the lyrics made explicit references to the political schisms that had begun to tear Jamaica apart once more after the dissolution of the peace treaty. "They bribing with their guns, spare parts and money, trying to belittle our integrity," Marley informs. "Every time they can reach us through political strategy, they keep us hungry. When you gonna get some food, your brother got to be your enemy." The message is implicit: Jamaica's poor were victims of colonial-style, divide-and-rule tactics, designed to benefit the business classes and politicians. While no solutions were spelled out in 'Ambush In The Night', the *Survival* album would be rife with them.

"Give us the teachings of His Majesty, for we want no devil philosophy," Marley chants on 'One Drop', which talks of death from starvation and hardship over the most delectable chorus and arrangement. Because of this, 'One Drop' is undoubtedly one of the sweetest songs of resistance ever recorded, and arguably the most accessible since Bob Dylan's 'Blowing In The Wind'. Above all, *Survival* concerned itself with Rastafari, placing it at the forefront of the struggle for black liberation in all of its forms. "Dready's got a job to do and he's got to fulfil that mission," Marley declares on 'Ride Natty Ride', which again combines a revolutionary sentiment with an exquisite melody. "All you see a gwan, is to fight against the Rastaman," he continues, "but the stone that the builder refuse, shall be the head cornerstone." It wasn't that long ago when Rastafarians were reviled in Jamaica, yet their influence was now infiltrating the middle classes and spreading worldwide. The fire, Marley explains, burns inside, and that can never be taken away, so "no matter what they do, natty keep on coming through."

It's songwriting like this that made Marley such a global icon, because he communicated a serious message directly from the heart, and in such a way that people from all areas of society could rally to his cause, without fear or uncertainty. And nor did he water down what Rastafarians stood for, since his comments about oppression and social injustice were as uncompromising as ever; perhaps even more so. "All they want us to do is keep on fussing and fighting," he warns in 'Top Ranking', named after the term given to a high-ranking gang member or political gunman. In a direct reference to the failed peace treaty he asks, "Are you fooling one another when you say you wanna come together?"*

Reggae artists grew increasingly wary of voicing political or cultural opinions, so the material Marley and artists like Tosh, Livingston, and Burning Spear were recording in early 1979 represented the last, great flowering of roots reggae music (from the pre-digital era at least). The same themes heard in songs like 'Crazy Baldhead' resurface on 'Babylon System', which is set to a swaying, nyahbinghi backbeat that went through numerous changes before Marley was satisfied. "We refuse to be what you wanted us to be. We are what we are. That's the way it's going to be," Marley sings, before comparing the complicity of organised religions and leading educational institutions to a vampire "sucking the blood of the sufferers" and "deceiving the people continually." His analogy of treading the winepress is not only Biblical, but indicates just how long these deceptions have been occurring. "Rebel," and "tell the children the truth," he urges, as Rasta drums cascade around him.

'Survival' was similar to 'Exodus' in its anthemic chorus, uplifting lyrics, and the kind of arrangement that contains such in-built momentum that it threatens to overwhelm the listener. "How can you be sitting there telling me that you care when every time I look around, the people suffer?" When asked if Marley wrote that defiant opening statement soon after meeting with Manley in London, Family Man couldn't be sure.

"Well Bob and I work on that song together in London for sure," he recalls. "We set up a little tape recorder in the basement of Harrington Gardens and sat around playing guitars, just like we did for 'Time Will Tell'. We didn't start by building rhythm tracks for those, but then after that I put in a piano. You can hear it come in half way down the music, but I had it set like a rhythm box, a bit like how Fats Domino would have played it, because I used to listen to a lot of Fats Domino songs at school. But I play most of the instruments on 'Black Survivors' and it was my arrangement, bass line, and t'ings that give it the thumbs up. We'd often get ideas along the way, while we were on tour. We'd watch how the people rocked to certain kinds of rhythms and that would give us ideas of what to hit them with next. Sometimes, like with 'Black Survivors', we'd

---

* Massop wouldn't hear Marley's plea because he was shot dead by Kingston police in February '79. Bucky Marshall was gunned down in Brooklyn the following March.

make recordings in hotel rooms and then take them back to Jamaica with us, so that we can work on them later. A lot of tracks on *Survival* and one or two other songs were done like that."

Marley wrote another song of protest, 'Zimbabwe', a few months earlier while visiting Ethiopia where he spent four days in Addis Ababa with Skill Cole, who was coaching the national airline's football team. Mugabe's victory had come as the result of an armed struggle, and the song's lyrics left no doubt that Marley believed in Malcolm X's maxim of "by any means necessary," if it involved fighting for God-given rights. "Every man gotta right to decide his own destiny and in this judgment there is no partiality, so arm in arm, with arms, we will fight this little struggle." Island angered Marley when issuing it as a single in a sleeve depicting the singer with Robert Mugabe, who'd toppled Ian Smith and brought an end to colonial rule in Rhodesia. His objection to the picture wasn't due to a lack of admiration for the rebel leader, but because he didn't want the song's meaning to be overshadowed by other considerations, least of all political.

Infused with the spirit of Marcus Garvey (who was quoted on the *Survival* sleeve) and by what he'd seen in Ethiopia, Marley was now passionate about repatriation back to Africa and the unification of the black race. On several occasions he related the story of Noah's three sons, Ham, Shem, and Japheth to journalists saying that each represented a race of people and had been given a special gift by their father. Shem, representing the Asian peoples, had been given wealth; Japheth, representing the white man, technology; while Ham had been gifted with knowledge, wisdom and understanding and was therefore superior, since all other races looked to him for enlightenment. According to Rastafarians like Marley, the world was in such confusion because black people had lost their way and hadn't yet attained their rightful place in the scheme of things, as ordained by God. Only if the black race were united could there be lasting peace.

"How good and pleasant it would be before God and man, to see the unification of all Africans," Marley sings on 'Africa Unite', summoning thoughts of Emperor Haile Selassie I's efforts to create an African League of Nations and Garvey's own attempts at Pan-Africanism. Ironically, while Marley focused on unification, members of his organisation were being ostracised from what they'd strived so hard to build alongside him. Family Man and Carly didn't play on 'Africa Unite', 'Wake Up And Live' or 'So Much Trouble In The World', due to a rift between them and their leader that would last, on and off, for the rest of Marley's life.

Sidney Guisse: "I played on a couple of songs from *Survival* like 'Africa Unite'. Bob get the inspiration for that song whilst we were sat at Hope Road and I even throw a few words in as well. We built up the song under the mango tree out the back whilst I was waiting on [Burning] Spear to come and record his album, *Hail H.I.M.* We get it sounding pretty good, so Bob said, 'Let's go in the studio and cut the song.' We go in there, just me and him, and Sangie Davis came in and Santa Davis, the drummer, he was around, so Bob told him to come in as well. I play the bass on it and then Tyrone came in later and put his stuff on top of it. I didn't get any playing credits for it, due to the record deal and all of that, but I get a special thanks to Sidney Guisse.

"As it turns out, I didn't play on *Hail H.I.M.* Spear was mad that I'd gone in the studio with Bob. It really upset him, so he called Family Man and said, 'You come and play with me, since he's gone in there with Bob!' A few of the musicians who were there got riled up about the whole thing but I said, 'Look here. I'm not trying to take your jobs.' Family Man and I were friends from way back, so we never had any animosities over it. We just stay cool, y'know? But he and Bob had a big falling out because Bob asked me to tour with him after that but I was advised not to. I took that advice, so when Spear came and asked me to play in his group I went along with him instead. But that whole incident arose because I'd been one of Bob Marley's root players from back in the day, during Randy's times, and so Bob felt comfortable with me already. Because whenever he's going to feel out a song, he'd call us in and jam, even though him usually record it with his regular musicians."

Family Man Barrett: "Even the Gong himself get crushed by certain antics too, because him never stick to what we started. It was Jah's work we say we a do and it start from the time he get miserable pon me, when we a work pon the *Survival* album. Then me realise it there again, after we start work pon *Uprising*. Bob look pon me and chat about devilism, and me say, 'What you say 'bout devilism? A me you a talk to 'bout that?' He say everything round there is all right and me is the problem, so after him stop talk, I just walk round the back and leave him to spar with Skill Cole and some other people. That's when Bob come and say he wants me in the studio, and I listen to some of the tracks he'd done without me, like 'Jingling Keys'."

Cole and Lee Perry (who was in a local mental hospital at the time) had recommended Sangie Davis since he was a talented all-rounder who could sing, arrange, and produce. He'd sung hits with the Melody Enchanters back in the late Fifties and formed the Gatherers, whose biggest hit, 'Words Of My Mouth', was produced by Perry. Davis later wrote hits for Judy Mowatt, Marcia Griffiths, Tinga Stewart, and Sophia George, among others. By 1979, Marley made him head of A&R at Tuff Gong and encouraged him to contribute towards studio productions, in addition to auditioning new talent for the Wailers' label, which they planned to expand as soon as other commitments allowed. The songwriter was an active member of the Twelve Tribes and hence wove spiritual conviction into his life and music, something that appealed to Marley. Davis' influence at Tuff Gong would prove effective right from the start, and it was Sangie who wrote 'Wake Up And Live', 'Jingling Keys', and 'Babylon Feel This One', which Jah Love would regularly play on dubplate.

Family Man Barrett: "'Babylon Feel This One' was recorded using the Twelve Tribes band. It was them who play on that one and 'Jingling Keys', because Carly and I were staying away at the time. We were originally going to put them on the *Survival* album and felt they might work because of the vibes they portray and everything. Bob come with a bag of weed and rap with me at the studio one Sunday, saying how he wanted me to hear what these guys can do, but then Tyrone arrive with Mikey Boo, and this bass player called Val Douglas. That meant two different sets of musicians come and play. I listen to them both and say to Bob that 'Jingling Keys' and 'Babylon Feel This One' can go on a different album or a disco 45, but the concept of the *Survival* album was better suited to the ones that Tyrone, Mikey Boo, and Val Douglas play on. Me still haffi fix them up after that session, because it was me who played the lead guitar and also rhythm on tracks like 'So Much Trouble'. If you notice, I get real funky like the Bar-Kays or James Brown when I reach the bridge on that one, but Val Douglas and Mikey Boo are the rhythm section. Tyrone, he was always a problem from them times there. He would keep on trying a t'ing, but it can't complete unless I fix it."

'So Much Trouble In The World' had radically different lyrics at first and started with a computer drum. The brighter album version warned of getting involved in a space race when there were more pressing concerns closer to home. Downie's production helped elevate the Wailers' sound so that it could stand alongside the sophisticated disco and funk emanating from America. UK journalist John Williams visited Marley at Hope Road around this time and found him listening to the *Saturday Night Fever* soundtrack. The singer brushed aside Williams' disbelief by explaining he wanted to find the music's ability in connecting to the millions of people who had gone out and bought it.

There were several other tracks that never made it onto *Survival*, including 'Mix Up, Mix Up' (eventually released on the posthumous *Confrontation*), the lyrically threadbare 'Soul Shake Up Party', and 'Wounded Lion In The Jungle', which spoke of impending revolution, but again sounded unfinished. Others found Marley sketching out ideas over rhythms that were more or less complete after Family Man presented him with ready-made backdrops needing just lyrics, vocals, and horns. This style of working wasn't uncommon but for Marley then to claim sole authorship was a travesty.

The *Survival* sessions had coincided with the emergence of a young trio of Jamaican horn players called Rass Brass, who made their debut on Dennis Brown's *Visions* album. Dean Fraser played sax, Junior "Chico" Chin trumpet and Ronald "Nambo" Robinson, trombone. After Marley invited them over to Tuff Gong, the three took the bus to Hope Road as none of them had cars or could afford taxis. Rass Brass appeared on 'Ambush In The Night', 'Survival', 'Ride Natty Ride', and 'Wake Up And Live', which sounded as if it was recorded outside the walls of Jericho, so inspirational is their playing. With the session rate at that time being JA $100 per track, Marley paid Rass Brass $2,000 each for the session. The musicians immediately contacted him, thinking he'd made a mistake. Marley's gratitude extended to asking Rass Brass to tour with him soon afterwards, except they had already promised to tour with Dennis Brown.* Consequently Glen DaCosta (sax) and Dave Madden (trumpet) took their place on the Wailers' US tour.

Madden was from Papine, in an area of St Andrews called Newcastle. His family's house was destroyed during the 1951 storm, so he was sent to Alpha Boys' boarding school, where he learnt trumpet, Johnny Moore of the Skatalites being one of his tutors. Madden then joined a military band before playing with Lynn Taitt & the Comets. Tommy McCook invited him to play sessions at Treasure Isle and from there Madden approached Coxsone, who teamed him with Cedric Brooks for a spate of hit instrumentals recorded under the name of 'Im & Dave. After Brooks left to join the Mystic Revelation of Rastafari, Madden joined Zap Pow,

---

* Rass Brass never did another session with Marley nor played live with him, although Chico Chin and Nambo Robinson would tour extensively with the Wailers' band in later years.

taking with him an unreleased track, 'Mystic Mood', which became Zap Pow's debut recording and first hit.

DaCosta, who joined Zap Pow a few months later, had also been sent to Alpha Boys' School, where he studied clarinet and saxophone while playing with local dance bands. Like Madden, he learnt the classics as well as more commercial forms of music, before joining Zap Pow and specialising in reggae.

Glen DaCosta: "Zap Pow had some very talented musicians. The drummer, Max Edwards, he left pretty early, and so Cornell Marshall from Third World took over after a while. As a matter of fact, Ras Karbi used to play drums for us and then, before the Wailers got big, we had people like Wya Lindo on keyboards and Carly Barrett on drums. Mikey Williams, who we called Mikey Zap Pow, played bass and shared lead vocals with Beres Hammond, but Dave and I had started to do sessions long before that, because we'd do things for Treasure Isle, Studio One and all over. A lot of us were coming from the big jazz bands, because that's what had attracted me to music in the first place. I ended up doing all the horn arrangements for Zap Pow, but then everyone in that band wanted to be as creative as possible and so we were a complete package. The only thing was, we were always in the studio working on other people's records instead of our own, because sometimes we'd record maybe two albums a day and I can't even recall the names of most of them!"

Zap Pow, whose other major hits included 'Last War' and 'This Is Reggae Music', signed to Island in 1975 and became the unofficial house band at Harry J's. It was therefore inevitable they and the Wailers would work together. Their first session resulted in 'So Jah Seh', and Zap Pow would play on the majority of Wailers' songs featuring horns, except for those on *Survival*.

Despite Marley's wish to tour with a horn section, the Wailers travelled without them when heading for the Far East in early April. It was virtually unheard of for reggae bands to tour so far afield, but this was a band intent on making converts wherever they went, and Marley saw such pioneering exploits as further opportunities to spread the Rasta gospel. The audiences in Tokyo (where they performed six shows in total) and also Osaka were ecstatic, clapping along to every song, and cheering every guitar solo. The Wailers then left for Auckland, New Zealand on April 16, where the band received a traditional Maori welcome. There had been torrential rain for three days beforehand, but the sun beat down on the day of the concert at Western Springs, an open-air venue in a natural valley.

"Reggae music's only purpose is to carry a message," Bob told local TV reporter Dylan Tait, "and that message is Rastafari." When asked if he saw himself as a revolutionary, he said, "Yeah, I see myself as a revolutionary. One who don't have no help and don't take no bribe from no one. Me fight it single-handed, with music."

While in Auckland, Marley and the Barretts were presented with gold discs (signifying one million sales) for *Natty Dread*, *Live*, *Rastaman Vibration* and *Exodus* and a platinum disc (signifying two million sales) for *Kaya*. Family Man looked quietly pleased while his brother's expression was one of bemusement, as if he couldn't believe how popular the band was in this far-off land (whose native Maori and Pacific Islands population identified strongly with Rastafari). Australia followed with shows in Brisbane, Adelaide, Perth, Melbourne, Sydney, and Melbourne again on May 1. The entourage stopped off in Maui and Honolulu before returning to Jamaica. The band members had talked about increasing security at Tuff Gong while on tour and decided to fence off certain sections of the yard to afford them more privacy. Family Man, who had a farm in St James, near to where his mother came from, cut down armfuls of bamboo to use as fencing. He also provided fruit and vegetables whenever members of various Rastafarian organisations visited Tuff Gong for meetings with Marley.

"56 Hope Road was a welcoming place for everybody in those days," says record producer General Lee, "and Bob used to be sat under this big tree out in the front yard, listening to music. You'd go there and hear certain songs playing over and over again, sometimes for days at a time. In those days, Bob wasn't with Rita as far as anyone could see. He was with Cindy Breakspeare and he just kept Rita around because she had kids with him. Across the road, there was this girl called Minnie, who was a friend of Rita's. When you leave from Bob Marley's house, her stall was on the corner of Lady Musgrave Road. It was this little ghetto place where she'd sell bun and bread. Bob used to send youths like me over to Minnie's to buy him a brown bread. In those days, bread used to come in a brown paper bag, except he wouldn't want the bread to eat. He only wanted the bag, so he could roll a spliff in it. As he sat there smoking, he'd listen to whatever was playing and say to one of the musicians, 'Me want you to change that part,' or whatever. That's how some of these songs were written and I'd see that for myself.

"But everyone knew that Bob was a man who took his time when it came to doing things, and you could never rush him. Ansel Creigland of the Meditations told me that, because he and Bob used to sit down and write songs together. Bob used to say the Meditations were one of his favourite acts, and told Ansel he was going to produce them after the Wailers came back from that last tour. Even now, when you look at Ansel onstage, you'd think it was Bob Marley; not because he's trying to copy him, but the two of them used to be so close, they have the same style."

Rita and her friend Minnie opened a restaurant called Queen of Sheba's at Tuff Gong in order to cater for visitors, since there was no other source of food and drinks available for some distance. The premises were now anything but residential apart from Marley's single room upstairs and Family Man's quarters around the back. In addition to a studio, record store, restaurant, and weekly radio programme, Tuff Gong even had its own newspaper for a time, called *Survival*. Inspired by the *Coptic Times*, it featured articles relevant to black people from around the world, especially Africa. This wasn't a first, since the Rastafarian Movement Association had been organising youth programmes and printing its own newspaper, *The Rasta Voice*, for several years. Nevertheless, such organisations pointed the way forward, demonstrating how Rastafarians could play a constructive role in national and international affairs, rather than remaining detached from them.

Marley's status within the social and religious fabric of Jamaican society, as well as his musical success, meant he was now expected to assume responsibility for the island's underclass.

"They'd be hundreds of people come to Hope Road for payment every Friday," continues Lee. "Bob would give them money like he was a bank and that's what Hope Road was about. When you came into the yard, you'd see artists like Israel Vibration sat around, reasoning and smoking their herb. It was like a Twelve Tribes place really, because if someone had a problem, they'd come and ask his advice. It was an open house and yet ordinary Jamaicans can't afford to go into the place now it's been turned into a museum. That's because it's four or five hundred Jamaican dollars to go in, and that's not what Bob wanted. Hope Road is supposed to be free."

This Christlike image of Marley, distributing alms and words of wisdom, is unparalleled anywhere else in popular music. The amount of money Marley gave away during the last two years of his life is incalculable, until Taylor eventually warned him he was in danger of going broke.

★   ★   ★

On July 7, Marley and the Wailers played at Reggae Sunsplash in Jarrett Park, Montego Bay. It was only the second such event, but Synergy's annual mini-festival was already establishing itself as Jamaica's foremost showcase for local music. The band's performance was marred by poor sound in places, and by Anderson's absence. However, a smiling Bob and Rita stood and watched as their two sons Ziggy and Stephen got up and danced merrily around the stage. 'Ambush In The Night', 'Rastaman Live Up' and 'Blackman Redemption' were previewed. The way the crowd sang along to the latter suggested it could have been a hit outside of Jamaica if Island had afforded it an official release. Two weeks later, the Wailers were in Boston, participating in a benefit show, the Amandla Festival of Unity, held at Harvard University. Among the other guests were Patti Labelle, Nigerian drummer Babatunde Olatunji and comedian Dick Gregory, who introduced Marley as a man "who shares his spiritual power with the world." Neville Garrick stood behind Marley, playing triangle and percussion, and Babatunde Olatunji replaced Seeco on congas in a blistering demonstration of African-style drumming. Although the new album still hadn't been released, 'Africa Unite' was played during the encore, along with a storming 15-minute version of 'Wake Up And Live'.

After the show, Marley and Downie participated in a press conference. When asked why he was paid $23,000 for expenses in a benefit show, Marley looked concerned, saying he didn't know anything about it. Gregory then leapt to his assistance, saying the question was an insult. It was a tawdry moment in an otherwise honourable event, which the organisers filmed and hoped to issue on video.*

The pro-black stance of *Survival* and the complete absence of any love songs made it a tough sell for Island as far as the mainstream market was concerned. Family Man confirms *Black Survivors* was the original title for the album, but the label vetoed this on the grounds of it being, "too black, so we called it *Survival* instead." Garrick, who had designed all of the Wailers' sleeves since *Rastaman Vibration*, told Chris Morrow that *Survival* was his favourite.

"The album was going to be called *Black Survival* [sic], but in discussing it, we felt that it might alienate some people who weren't black, so I tried to come up with a visual way of saying black without using the word. The idea of flags came up, so I got information about all the flags of free black Africa and then I painted them using real flat colours. Zimbabwe hadn't

---

* Chris Blackwell has so far declined to sanction its release.

been declared a nation and so it didn't have a flag yet (and I wouldn't use Rhodesia's), so I used the flags of the groups that were fighting, ZAPU and ZANU. But the blacks in America, England and all over, they don't have a flag, and then I got a mindflash, because anybody who's in the diaspora from Africa came out through slavery, so what I did was reverse the word *Survival* out of a slave ship plan. I was really excited, but unfortunately, it was the most under-promoted album that Bob put out, because it was so political. I figured it would make a great billboard and it was supposed to be distributed to schools in the US, but it never went as far as we wanted."

Judy Mowatt's *Black Woman* was the first non-Wailers album to be recorded at the new Tuff Gong studio. After Skill Cole left for Ethiopia, she had started a relationship with Freddie McGregor and bore his child, a daughter called Yeshemabeth. McGregor helped out on the album, in between writing songs of his own like 'Joggin''. Mowatt's version of 'Put It On' ended up among the year's most popular tunes in Jamaica, as was Marley's 'Blackman Redemption', the I-Threes' 'Many Are Called' and Marcia Griffiths' 'Steppin' Out Of Babylon'. Griffiths (who was absent from the Survival tour) had played the rhythm track to Marley, thinking that the beat was too rootsy for her. He danced to it but never got around to writing any accompanying lyrics.

After reading an article on child poverty in the *Jamaica Daily News*, Marley wrote 'Children Of The Ghetto' for the Melody Makers who comprised his and Rita's four children, Ziggy, Sharon, Stephen, and Cedella. In a fitting gesture, he donated the royalties to a Nassau-based children's charity. Anderson says Marley's paternal instincts didn't extend to the record's production, most of which was handled by himself and Family Man. The latter also produced Cedella Marley's earliest singles-covers of the Wailers' 'Baby, Baby I Got A Date' and a new song called 'Zion Train'.

Apart from an occasion when Jeremy Marre was shooting footage for his *Beats Of The Heart* series, Family Man and Burning Spear hadn't met since the *Social Living* session.

Family Man: "I used to go and check Jack Ruby and Burning Spear whenever I was in Ocho Rios, because they'd be chilling over at Marcus Garvey Lawn, and one night when I go there, there was some filming going on. It was Third World they were filming, but I'd already set up the Dread Lion, so it was me playing the sound-system that night. I never want them to film me at the time because I was thinking of the contract with Island, so I keep in the background with my bushmaster hat pulled over my face. Except a man come up to me and say the music lick him inside his head and that he knows Jack Ruby Hi-Fi, but he never heard a sound-system play that sweet before. That's because I'd set up the EQ and tune my mid-range and tweeter just right, so wherever you're standing on the Marcus Garvey Lawn, it's like the music is ricocheting against the sky, before it heads back to earth! People used to say that my set-up sounded just like you were standing in a studio, listening to a playback . . ."

Spear had been unhappy with Island's lack of interest in *Social Living* – or *Marcus Children*, as the album was first known – and was scouting around for another label when preparing to record *Hail H.I.M.* EMI eventually released the album to critical acclaim on the strength of tracks like 'African Teacher', 'Cry Blood Africa', 'Christopher Columbus', and the title track, although Family Man still awaits his production fee.

Family Man Barrett: "Things weren't looking so bright for [Spear] it seems. He wasn't in such a good spirit because there were tape shortages in Jamaica, so I say, 'Bwoy, me have some tape, so better me produce you.' We do some rough mix so we can feel comfortable with the t'ing, I cut some dub and say, 'Don't worry man. I'm gonna set it for you.' When he was writing those tracks, I listen to his soul, y'know? I see where him trying to reach and bring it out. I make sure 'im float and then just build the rhythm around him so that everything's precise, so it was like a Bob Marley, structuring kind of thing and no other Spear album sounds like that one. We don't work together too much after that. I just record one bass line and overdub some other t'ing on *Farover* like 'Jah Is My Driver', which wasn't too bad."

Together with a handful of others, Burning Spear has maintained his reputation for serious message songs in an unbroken continuum dating back to the late Sixties. He and Marley shared the same kind of approach, based on truth and integrity.

"It's very important to live the way you think and to think the way we live," Spear says. "You've got to be really involved in what you believe in, and the way you live should reflect what you really believe in. That's very important and I always believe in creating a lot of strong fans, so I don't want them to get downhearted with me and to start walking away, or failing to get any understanding from my songs. I try to base my career in music around educating people and to make songs that people can relate to, no matter where they come from. Bob did the same thing, since we

474

both make songs people can play when they're down and get some understanding from so they can rise up again."

The other album Family Man produced at Tuff Gong, in between touring, was *Unconquered People* by Israel Vibration, a vocal trio attached to the Twelve Tribes. Cecil "Skelly" Spence, Lascelles "Wiss" Bulgin, and Albert "Apple" Craig were all polio victims who'd met at the Mona Rehabilitation Centre, near the University of West Indies and had lived rough before making their breakthrough with songs like 'Why Worry' and 'Same Song'. The latter became the title track of their debut album, released in 1976, produced by Tommy Cowans. Cowans had been a singer himself (with the Jamaicans) and worked at Dynamic before forming, with his wife Valerie, Talent Incorporation – a Kingston-based label and promotions company at 1c Oxford Road. Cowans produced sides by Jacob Miller, Inner Circle, Ras Michael, and others before working with Israel Vibration and Junior Tucker ("Jamaica's Michael Jackson").

"We were one of the first artists to record at Bob Marley's studio, along with the Melody Makers and Nadine Sutherland," explains Apple, "and we recorded *Unconquered People* using the Wailers' band. That was an incredible experience, 'cause Bob was right upstairs when we were doing it and he really enjoyed it. We were one of his favourite groups."

Nadine Sutherland had been taken to Tuff Gong by Sangie Davis, who spotted her singing at the age of 11 in a Tastees talent competition. The diminutive singer recorded her debut single, 'Starvation On The Land', under the watchful gaze of Tosh and Marley, who ordered that a stool be brought in for her since she couldn't reach the microphone. 'Starvation On The Land' duly went to number one on the local charts. Sutherland stayed at Tuff Gong for several years and remains a highly rated singer in Jamaica, where she hosts a popular talent show on local television.

Marley bought a pressing plant on Orange Street from Sonia Pottinger's husband Lindon. The machinery was located in familiar territory, right near the Wailers' old shop on Beeston Street, and its acquisition was another vital step towards the autonomy Tuff Gong craved. With coloured vinyl being all the rage at the time, the label's releases appeared in a range of different colours, especially red, green, and gold.

Family Man Barrett: "Yeah, we used to put out some lovely pressings, even some looking like tie-dye, and we always tour with some vinyl, because many a time, even with Island, we have to sell these other pressings to eat food, y'know? Yeah man, I always remember carrying them. We never feel too good about it but the people never say no, 'cause we meet all these sound people along the way and their boss deejays. Yeah man, we all have to live pon earth."

Ernest Wilson, Earl 16, Michigan & Smiley, Fred Locks, and another young female singer called Alicia Barnes all recorded at Tuff Gong, as did Jimmy Riley, Little Roy (with alternative cuts of 'Bongo Nyah' and 'Jah Can Count On I'), and revolutionary dub poet Oku Onoura. Onoura, whose real name was Orlando Wong, had befriended activist Walter Rodney and, inspired by Rodney's teachings, he helped distribute radical newspaper *Abeng*. After being shot, arrested and incarcerated, he wrote poems and prose that would be printed in *Echo* in 1977. Two years later, Onoura released his debut record, *Reflection In Red*, with lyrics about the peace treaty. Although not a singer, his anti-establishment views made him a favourite of Tuff Gong stalwarts like the Barretts, who also played on tracks from Tyrone Taylor's *Cottage In Negril* and *Jamming In The Hills* albums.

Tyrone Taylor: "I wasn't signed to Tuff Gong, but they and Love Time, which was my company, decide to stick together, because Bob, Family Man, and myself were friends and a set of rebellious guys that fight against the imperialist. That's what Tuff Gong was all about when it started. It was a home for revolutionaries, so I'd rather Tuff Gong release my t'ings than any imperialist label."

To coincide with the release of *Survival* on October 2, the Wailers' next US tour began almost immediately afterward with a show at Madison Square Garden, followed by three consecutive days, playing early and late shows at Harlem's famed Apollo Theater from October 25 to 28, with soul singer Betty Wright as support act.* While reggae was popular with white rock fans, it still hadn't made too many converts among traditional soul, jazz, and blues fans in America, or even the newly emergent hip-hop kids, come to that. Jah Mel (Melvin Glover), who saw one of the Apollo shows, says the audience was restless, since people weren't familiar with the new songs. "What you gonna play next?" someone shouted, not out of curiosity but scorn.

Mel, who had extended family in Kingston, spent three months in Jamaica at the beginning of 1980. As well as hanging out at Tuff Gong, he got to know Tommy Cowan and Jacob Miller, who encouraged Mel to

* Betty Wright was managed by Danny Sims and would later marry King Sporty.

play guitar, and 25 years later he became the resurrected Wailers' rhythm guitarist.

Following the Apollo residency, the band played at Colgate University in Hamilton and Toronto's Maple Leaf Gardens, before passing through Montreal, Ottawa, and Burlington. In Philadelphia, Stevie Wonder jammed on 'Get Up, Stand Up' and 'Exodus' at a Black Music Association convention at Penn Hall on November 7. The tour then proceeded on to Detroit, Madison, Milwaukee, Chicago, Minneapolis, Edmonton, Portland, Seattle, and Vancouver, with scarcely a day off in between. On November 23, the band performed to 14,000 people at the Pauley Pavilion on the UCLA campus and over the following days they appeared at the San Diego Sports Arena and Santa Barbara's County Bowl, before returning to LA for a benefit at the Roxy Theatre, with the proceeds going towards the Sugar Ray Robinson Foundation.

During the Apollo residency, Marley and Taylor were introduced to Charles Bobette, a business associate of James Brown's, by Betty Wright, who had known Bobette since her teenage years touring with Brown. Bobette turned up at the Roxy with two daughters of President Omar Bongo of Gabon, who invited the Wailers to perform at their country's New Year celebrations. Marley was constantly hearing about how well his songs were being received in Africa, especially new tracks like 'Zimbabwe' and 'Africa Unite', so the idea of performing there intrigued him. However, the rest of the US dates had to be completed, namely Oakland, Sacramento, Santa Cruz (where Donald Kinsey joined them), Denver, Kansas, and Dallas. The band then flew down to Trinidad for a poorly promoted show requiring Taylor to move swiftly in order to secure the band's money. Just to compound their difficulties, the entourage were taken off the plane the next day and told to stay on the island while proper tax clearance could be authorised.

The next week was taken up by shows in Nashville, New Orleans, Atlanta, Tampa, and Nassau, where they performed another benefit show at the Queen Elizabeth Sports Centre on behalf of a charity representing the United Nations International Year of the Child. By the time they flew home to Jamaica on December 16, Marley and the Wailers had played almost 50 shows in as many days.

CHAPTER TWENTY-SEVEN

African Skies

"WE come from Africa and none of the leaders want fi accept it," Marley told a reporter. "They want us to think we are all Jamaicans. The majority of Jamaican people want fi go home to Africa but the leaders say you must stay and die here."

In early January 1980, the Wailers travelled to Gabon in West Africa for two weeks as guests of President Omar Bongo, who invited the Wailers to perform at their country's New Year celebrations.

Family Man Barrett: "We have a chartered flight and I recall it was the first place I've ever been where the people tell me, 'Welcome home,' even though it Jamaica me a born, but them never tell me that yet."

From the minute they arrived the local people mobbed the Wailers, fascinated by their locks. One day, after some of the crowd got a little too enthusiastic, Marley, Marvin and a pregnant Griffiths hid in the back of an equipment truck. After a while, they felt stifled and Griffiths began to complain. Against Marley's wishes, Marvin opened the back doors for air. Marley pushed him out, keeping hold of a fistful of his locks. The guitarist tried to punch him as he swung from the back of the truck and the incident resulted in the pair not speaking to each other for three days after. However, the worst disagreement on the visit was between Marley and Taylor.

"There was a guy called Charles Bobette who I'd heard of but didn't know," Taylor explained. "He'd been involved in some payola business in the United States and testified against a friend of mine, Frankie Crocker. Bobette, he was working for James Brown, and he came to a show [at the Roxy, LA] with these two girls, who turned out to be the President of Gabon's daughters. He then came back and said one of the girls [Pascalene] had asked if Bob would play at her birthday [in Libreville on January 5] and he wanted to negotiate a deal. We'd just left the Apollo, where I'd used Betty Wright as the opening act. Bobette said he wanted the same package because he was a friend of Betty's, so I went along with it. We negotiated a deal for Bob and also Jimmy Cliff, because I was managing Jimmy at the time. I took deposits for both artists and wrote two separate receipts, which plainly stated that one deposit was for Bob and the other for Jimmy.

"When we got to Gabon, there was a lot of confusion about the money Bobette had spent putting the show together. First, Bob and myself were summoned to the President's palace. I explained our part in what had happened to the President and everything was fine. I came back and said to Betty Wright that Bobette was in a lot of trouble. I guess she told it to Bobette in a different way, because he came to me and said he wanted me to pay back the deposit for Jimmy Cliff. I said I couldn't do that and so he said if I didn't, he was going to go to Bob Marley and tell him the money was supposed to be for him, instead of Jimmy Cliff. Yet both receipts were there, but that's how the whole thing blew up and those are the facts."

Taylor was known to have accumulated heavy gambling losses and also had a cocaine habit, which is why he immediately came under suspicion. In addition, Marley was embarrassed when asked by the President why there had only been one Wailers show instead of two. Taylor tried to explain the deposit situation and that Jimmy Cliff had been booked to perform separately (rather than the Wailers support). Marley, who had been known to beat Rita, Jaffe, Garrick (after he'd been caught leaving Rita's room one night) and Diane Jobson, became increasingly bad-tempered as his illness took hold. On January 14, Garrick hurried into Family Man's room, looking for a baseball bat. Gillie Dread and Fams followed him to Marley's room, arriving just as an argument between artist and manager threatened to rage out of control. Taylor told Marley he was being "presumptuous", and at this point Gillie lunged towards the table, where there were two bottles of water, one glass and the other plastic. Family Man quickly snatched up the glass out of harm's way, while Gillie seized the other and threw it at Taylor's head. According to Family Man, the bottle hit the side of Taylor's face and "burst like a grenade."

"Don Taylor, he wasn't on the road with us from that time. Him and Bob move away and that spoil their relationship. The whole thing create an embarrassment, but he should have known what he was doing when 'im try a t'ing in those days, because something had gone down for sure. I'm not too certain what exactly happen, but where discipline's concerned, t'ings really go down, I tell you."

After their adventures in Gabon, the Wailers returned to Jamaica and began recording material for their next album, *Uprising*, although Marley wasn't around for long, as he left for Miami in early February to meet with Danny Sims. Family Man suggests this was a case of "better the devil you know," since there was a queue of first-rate professionals wishing to manage them at the time. However, Marley chose Sims and Cole, who'd returned from his spell of exile in Ethiopia. Marley made it back to Kingston in time for his 35th birthday on February 6 and an all-night party thrown in his honour. He was now the best-selling entertainer in Jamaican history, although this counted for little after neighbours complained about the noise. The *Gleaner* ran reports about how the activities at Tuff Gong were causing disruption in the once-exclusive section of town.

"I want to disturb my neighbour, 'cause I'm feeling so right. I want to turn up my disco, blow them to full watts tonight," he sang on 'Bad Card'. "You go tired to see me face, can't get me out of the race. Oh man, you said I'm in your place and then you draw bad card . . ."

Just over a month later, on March 18, Marley flew to Brazil with Marvin, Blackwell, and Jacob Miller to plan a series of concerts scheduled to take place at the end of the year. Jimmy Cliff was already very popular there and had even lived in Brazil for a time, while Gilberto Gil had achieved a local hit with his cover of 'No Woman No Cry'. The Marley party entered a six-a-side football competition, which they won. As Marvin says, they had to let them win, otherwise "Bob would have got mad." They returned to Jamaica two days later, armed with their trophy, but then on March 23, Miller was killed in a car accident. Inner Circle had been scheduled to open for the Wailers on the South American dates, which were immediately cancelled. The atmosphere was understandably muted around Tuff Gong. Not only had the singer's presence seemed to energise Marley, but he'd also died just down the road, after his Datsun span out of control and hit a lamp post, killing him instantly. Fortunately, the three children in the back seat received only minor injuries. The funeral service, conducted by Archbishop Yeshaq of the Ethiopian Orthodox Church, took place on Sunday March 30 in the National Arena, where Miller's body lay in state until it was taken by motorcade to Dovecot cemetery.

Marley's new songs were tinged with melancholy and the vibrancy of his earlier works was tempered by reflection. "It's worse in Jamaica than it ever used to be in the sense of political pressure," he explained. "A lot of people dying every day, some of them I know. People know say where those things are leading and that them have an alternative, Rasta. Them cause so much fight against Rasta because Rasta is the only redemption to fight. But this pressure, it's not Rasta's fight. We're not fighting a revolution down there, because when two people fight, it's madness. Double wrong. People in Jamaica, them have guns. Where people get the guns? The government give people guns and right now, it explode and something bad have to happen."

The political violence in Jamaica would reach a crescendo in the run-up to the 1980 election scheduled to take place in October, and the brief flurry of optimism created by the peace treaty two years earlier now seemed "but a fleeting illusion," to quote one of Marley's own lyrics. "Would you let the system make you kill your brother man?" he asks on 'Coming In From The Cold'. "No, dread, no," comes the response. "Would you make the system get on top of your head again?" It's as if Marley was struggling to convince himself of a way forward, because for every upbeat track on *Uprising*, there's another written from a despairing viewpoint, such as 'Real Situation'. "Ain't no use, no one can stop them now," he says of world leaders. Marley said that the song was inspired by a recent hurricane that headed for Jamaica, but veered away at the last minute.

"We were lucky for sure," he said, "but the hurricane was to show the Jamaicans that God is God and yet them still go on like them don't believe. That's why I wrote, 'It seems like total destruction is the only solution.' Which means that it seems like total destruction is still what these people want."

This same air of resignation is repeated in 'We And Dem', on which Marley questions whether mankind will ever transcend their inner demons and create lasting peace. "We no know how we and dem a go work this out," he laments, attributing the deepening crisis to a lack of faith, and warning that someone will have to pay for the slaughter of innocents. Biblical scripture demanded it, although there is also an undercurrent of powerlessness when he refers to not having friends "in a high society." Rastafarians might have the vision for a better tomorrow, but Marley himself could only achieve so much and still his best chance of affecting change was with his music. Happily, that crusading spirit returned on tracks like 'Work', 'Zion Train', and 'Forever Loving Jah', on which he announced, "We have found a way to cast away the tears."

'Forever Loving Jah' was another song to undergo a process of evolution before Marley was entirely satisfied. In the end, Family Man handled all the keyboard parts, as he did on 'We And Dem'. The rock-solid groove was versioned by a succession of other reggae artists and musicians over the years. Marley's vocals and lyrics particularly stand out, especially after the growing sense of doom hinted at on other tracks from *Uprising*. "Old man river, don't you cry for me," he sings. "I have a running stream of love you see, so no matter what stages they put us through, we'll never be blue."*

'Zion Train' heralded a return to the type of traditional gospel imagery Tosh was fond of. "Where there is a will, there is always a will," Marley sings, reminding us that "two thousand years of history, black history, could not be wiped away so easily." The idea of black unification, which lay at the heart of *Survival*, resurfaced most strongly on 'Work'. "We Jah people can make it work," he addresses the Rastafarian community, "come together and make it work." Marley counts the days down, singing, "one day to go, working for the next day, every day is work" which sums up the Tuff Gong ethos; if people hadn't got anything to do, then "we got some work for you."

Family Man Barrett: "Some of those tunes from *Uprising*, like 'Forever Loving Jah', it was just me, Bob, and Carly alone who make them. And even when other musicians are there, I give them ideas about the tone and the best way of playing the lines. In the early years, songs and rhythms would just come to us in the studio, but as time went by we did things properly and rehearse them thoroughly first, because them haffi be right, y'know? All of the fine tuning would take place there and since I was the musical director, I would dictate the sound and tempo of the guitars and chose the instruments and where they would come in, because they all had a different flavour. If you notice, listening to all of the Bob Marley & the Wailers' tracks we make over the years, each one is in a class by itself. You're supposed to hear each and every instrument clear in the mix as well and as soon as we pay all this attention to detail, we get the people them hyper and so they were always listening out for something new from us after a while.

"The record company, they couldn't say anything to us, because we just give them our material and it was always up to international standard. We'd started out doing this work with that in mind and we listen to everything else coming out, so we know we're doing it the right way. For the

---

* Marley's friend Desmond "Desi" Smith has claimed that 'Zion Train', 'Coming From The Cold', 'Redemption Song', 'Real Situation' and 'Pimpers Paradise' were all written in Miami, while Marley was recuperating from his toe operation. This might well be the case, except the tracks didn't appear on *Survival*, and nor were they recorded until after the Wailers returned from Gabon.

second album running, love songs were conspicuous by their absence on *Uprising*. Marley's romance with Breakspeare hadn't ended but nor had his interest in other women, such as Pascalene Bongo and Yashi. The only *Uprising* song even to mention a woman was 'Pimper's Paradise', a crushing admonishment of a flighty party girl. "She loves to smoke, sometime shifting coke. She'll be laughing when there ain't no joke . . . a pimper's paradise, that's all she was."

While *Uprising* was full of memorable songs, its contents were over-shadowed by two outstanding contributions, 'Redemption Song' and 'Could You Be Loved'. 'Redemption Song' transcends both genre and time, telling the story of the black race with parable-like economy and eloquence. It talks of being sold into slavery, and then rising from "the bottomless pit", strengthened by faith in the Almighty and the ability to express (and therefore cleanse) suffering with music. Marley knew that, post-emancipation, black people had to free themselves from mental slavery, and delivering it semi-a capella only added to its potency.

In September 1979, South Africa exploded a nuclear device to serve as a warning to the country's freedom fighters. Some claim this is what inspired Marley to write the line, "Have no fear for atomic energy," whereas others say the song dates from two years earlier. " 'Redemption Song' have meaning and I would love to do more like that," he said. "What was the lyric in 'Redemption Song' about atomic energy? 'Have no fear for atomic energy, 'cause none a them can stop the time?' Time is where we are, what we have, and no one can stop the time, so to those who would put the fear into mankind that everything must be destroyed, I say have no fear for atomic energy, because man has hopes. No one can stop the time and you have to live within time, so time is important."

Marley had initially struggled to finish the song and asked Lindo to help him, saying that no other band member would have understood what he was doing. The keyboardist confirms he more or less worked out all the chord changes and arranged the subsequent band version, a claim backed up by Al Anderson.

"If you want to hear Bob Marley by himself," he says, "the perfect example of his ability as an artist would be 'Redemption Song', except Bob didn't write it. Wya Lindo wrote 'Redemption Song', which he never received credit for, and when you consider Bob didn't have any great ability to sing and play guitar at the same time, it was terrible. He was a great songwriter, everybody knows that, but he was not a dynamic guitar player, and what he had to offer by himself wouldn't have necessarily worked, had he not got together with us all as a band, because with Peter and Bunny, it was too competitive and they were way ahead of him. I mean, all the individual members of the Wailers were way ahead of him as a musician."

A cultural anthem, 'Redemption Song' went on to be covered by a significant number of artists outside of reggae, including Santana, Jackson Browne, Johnny Cash, Joe Strummer, and Stevie Wonder. 'Could You Be Loved' became Marley's most enduring crossover hit. As well as being a great dance track, it has an infectious melody and wonderfully inspirational lyrics of holding fast to spiritual and moral values. "Don't let them fool you, or even try and school you . . . don't let them change you, or even rearrange you." There's another word of advice to people trying to accommodate those lusting for power, because "No matter how you treat him, the man will never be satisfied."

When asked about the disco influence in 'Could You Be Loved', Marley replied, "Naturally, if I go to America and hear that type of music, the music is in the air there. If I pick up the guitar now, I have a choice. You can try something with that music and that music has root too. You can try something, or you can try the other thing and go deeper."

Family Man says 'Could You Be Loved' originally started as a slower, reggae cut, but then the Wailers let loose with a funkier style of playing.

"Well, I was listening to what Bob and Tyrone were saying because Tyrone, he was the youngest out of all of us, coming from the Youth Professionals," he recalls. "I'm used to him from those times and Bob, he came to like him too and we really want to feature some of this musical ability that him have. I myself am always interested in what [Tyrone's] hearing on the radio, on record, and also what's playing in these nightclubs and bars that he's going to in Montego Bay and on that side. He was up there, soaking up a lot of the foreign music and concepts, so he was right there in this little hyper t'ing . . . Him and Bob, they want to get that lively t'ing across, so I say, 'OK,' but I soon realise I don't have to play much, but just put in those little rhythm parts. I then start layering it piece by piece and getting everybody coming together with something until it make one big impact and that was it.

"It was much loved by people at the time and it's aged well, I think, because the sentiment expressed in it hasn't changed at all. But that song was the turning point of the whole t'ing, and it seemed to put a seal on the Seventies in many ways, because it's coming from a wide variety of different influences and not just disco, but Fela Kuti and all kinds of people.

That song, it was like another creative source. Some people said it was too commercial, but we knew already the music has no limits, and no matter how high you go with it, there are always gaps, y'know? That's why you got to be flexible, have an open mind and take on new ideas, so the people can have greater expectation and never know what's coming next."

Marley had discussed how reggae and funk were closely inter-related during Rob Bowman's interview in the summer of 1976. Certainly, Jamaican musicians like the Barretts and Downie could easily slip from one to the other, or incorporate elements of each within the same track. 'Could You Be Loved', together with Stevie Wonder's 'Master Blaster (Jammin')', would prove the apex of this style and both became Top 5 hits respectively in the summer and autumn of 1980.

In Africa, reggae was more popular than ever. As a mark of the resonance that 'Zimbabwe' had in the country, Robert Mugabe invited Marley to attend the independence ceremony, due to be staged in Salisbury during April. Marley insisted the invitation be extended to the whole band and suggested they play at least one concert, even agreeing to cover most of the expenditure himself, although Island – who'd initially seen no promotional benefits in the Wailers performing there – eventually contributed US $90,000 and also paid for some press representatives to attend the event.

Marley reputedly spent US $250,000 flying the Wailers and their equipment to Zimbabwe for two concerts, held at Salisbury's Rufaro Stadium on April 18 and 19. At first, the Wailers were taken to a hotel 12 miles outside the city, but this turned out to be unsuitable (as did the pork they were served in a local restaurant!) and so they returned to town. A friendly club owner called Job offered them the use of his home, complete with swimming pool and staff, but there was no telephone, which made communications difficult. During the week they spent there, Marley apparently became quite emotional as he watched 300 former ZANU rebels arrive at the stadium for a rehearsal, dressed in the colours of the new Zimbabwean flag, which were the same as Rasta colours, i.e. green, red, yellow and black.

The Wailers' performances turned out to be something of an ordeal. On the night of the first concert, with 40,000 people in attendance, their set was disrupted for 15 minutes while police tear-gassed sections of the crowd. Apparently, a gate had been opened for some soldiers, who were due to march inside the stadium as part of the ceremony, but large numbers of people had surged through the opening with them. Shots were fired, and tear gas drifted over to the stage, causing the band members some distress.

Family Man Barrett: "We stopped playing for a while, because I notice my eyes were burning me and my nose too. I say to myself, 'How come there's so much smoke in here?' Then when I look around, I notice the people beginning to get flat and lying there on the ground in front of us. Ziggy, Stevie, Cedella, and them were backstage, but luckily we have water and towels there, so we wipe everyone down, and then after we go out there again, we get like a 21-gun salute! Bob say, 'Wow!' They had these cannons they use for Prince Charles and even though they don't have any live ammunition in them, they were licking hard, I tell you! All of that happen before Prince Charles arrive and he was on a different stage to us, so he didn't get any tear gas. Only the rootsman get it."

After restarting, Marley had to sing alone since the I-Threes had gone back to their lodgings, taking his children with them. When the show had finsihed, the Wailers were left stranded without a driver. Because none of them knew the address of Job's house, or even which district it was in, they had to drive round for hours even after they'd found someone willing to help them look. The show the following day was a free event for the poorer classes since 60,000 had camped outside the stadium the day before because most were unable to buy tickets. The venue wasn't so well lit this time and the crowd was smaller. African audiences weren't used to encores, so when the band came back onstage, the majority of the crowd had already dispersed. The Wailers' party moved to the St James Hotel in downtown Harare after the second concert and spent the next few days sightseeing and meeting various people, including former rebels.

Family Man Barrett: "When we went to check the rebel camp in Zimbabwe, the army sent a bus for us and it had no windows. The glass lick out and the raw wind a blow pon me and by the time I go back on the plane, I take sick, and my eyes get full of water. I feel it on my chest, so they give me like these two little tablets."

The Marley entourage arrived in London, where Adrian Boot photographed the band in an elevator (with Fams wearing thick shades as a result of the eye infection he'd contracted in Zimbabwe) at the Kensington Hotel on Bayswater Road – a shot that would be used on the back cover of *Uprising*. The front had been reserved for an illustration of Marley stretching out his arms and awakening, Kraken-like, from a tangle of dreadlocks that resembled the roots of a tree, while in the background, the rising sun peeps over green hills. While not especially well drawn, it was highly evocative all the same.

Having heard a preview of the album (which was recorded prior to the Zimbabwe trip), a reporter asked Marley if he'd felt recharged after returning from Africa. "You can say that again," he said, "but I really get the recharge from Ethiopia because that song 'Zimbabwe' was written in a land called Shasamane in Ethiopia, so you can say it's a full recharge that and when the song come out, it just happen. You can imagine if I wrote all my songs in Ethiopia, then maybe somebody would say, 'Boy, he's a prophet or something.'"

The band continued recording tracks after returning from Zimbabwe. 'Jungle Fever' had a spring in its step and a rhythm similar to 'Could You Be Loved', with Carly in especially good form. 'Give Thanks And Praise', 'Burn Down Babylon', 'Trench Town', 'Chant Down Babylon', 'Jump Nyahbinghi', and 'Stiff Necked Fools' were all recorded during or just after the *Uprising* sessions, but either remained unfinished or discarded when the album was being compiled. Marley also voiced an early take of 'Buffalo Soldier' in Miami with King Sporty's band, a version which Family Man describes as "some hip hop, disco type of thing."

Marley used to drop in to the QUAD Radio recording studio in Miami from time to time, where Sporty and his wife-to-be Betty Wright worked on their own productions. Sporty had been covering Marley's material for years, both on record and onstage. One night, Marley heard him sing 'Buffalo Soldier' at the Les Jardines nightclub in Miami and expressed an interest in recording it. According to some sources, the recording dates from the night before the Peace Concert, at Harry J's, where Sporty was recording with his band of US musicians. Family Man disagrees with this, saying the first version was recorded in the little demo studio at King Sporty's house.

Family Man Barrett: "The version we did at Tuff Gong was done much later. It was like a bonus track left over from *Uprising*. Before we actually record it, we were in Miami talking about the tune, and then out of the blue, here comes King Sporty. It's like he get the vision at the same time, because he drive back to his house and come back with the demo version for me, so that's why when Diane Jobson come and ask me about it, when they had the dispute going on, I tell her that it's supposed to be 50-50 between him and Bob. After that, I hear he wanted two-thirds because he recorded it first, but that wasn't right, y'know? And I keep myself out of it, because otherwise I could have claimed a third for myself as well."

Sylvan Morris mixed it at Harry J's, but Family Man was adamant that Marley should voice it over so the Wailers re-recorded it at Tuff Gong, with Errol Brown engineering. The lyrical theme to 'Buffalo Soldier' told the story of a black soldier – a "dreadlocked Rasta" and a former slave – who fights for the Union in the American Civil War against the racist south. It was the perfect riposte for those black Americans who derided reggae as "island music", since it situated Rastafari at the very place where their freedoms began. Here was Marley recast as a soldier, fighting for survival, and who'd helped "win the war for America", set to a jaunty arrangement and infectious chorus.

Marley also voiced specials for Kilimanjaro in the summer of 1980, singing adaptations of 'Bad Card', 'Get Up, Stand Up', 'Redemption Song', and 'No Woman No Cry' for them to play on their sound-system. He transformed the latter into 'No Sound Boy No Cry', treating the entire episode as a bit of fun, rather than a money-spinner. By now, sound-systems had been battling each other with exclusive dubplates for over two decades, but it was the beginning of a new Jamaican dancehall era, heralded by singers like Sugar Minott, Barry Brown, and Barrington Levy, who got their break by performing on sound-systems, rather than auditioning for studios like Treasure Isle or Studio One. They were like deejays in this respect, because rather than writing songs with musicians, they would often sing over ready-made backing tracks instead. Record producers welcomed this, since it meant fewer studio costs, and audiences seemed to be tiring of the international roots reggae sound in any case. Cassette tapes of live dancehall sessions became popular, and deejays like General Echo rose to popularity by reviving the kind of lewd rhymes ("slackness") that Lloyd Charmers and Max Romeo once specialised in.

Ghetto audiences weren't as enamoured with cultural lyrics as before, feeling they couldn't relate to the island's leading roots artists and musicians in their fancy cars, although 'One Drop' was a hit and so, too, another Tuff Gong production, Junior Tucker's 'One Of The Poorest People'. It had also become increasingly dangerous to venture an opinion about social issues now that members of the Eradication Squad (a specialist police division) were patrolling the dances. At grassroots level, the dream was all but over and this impression had been reinforced by the actions of dreadlocked criminals, masquerading as Rastafarians. Even the local herb trade would soon come under threat, when government forces started to spray the hillsides with Paraquat, a deadly defoliant that had first been used in Vietnam and was already banned in the US.

Marley's favourite singer, Dennis Brown, was now a rival in the local popularity stakes as Brown delivered hit after hit like 'Sitting And Watching', which he voiced for Sly & Robbie's Taxi label. Sly & Robbie were also busy producing hits with Black Uhuru, Jimmy Riley, Gregory Isaacs, and the Tamlins, in addition to playing a hard-edged hybrid of funk and reggae behind Grace Jones at Compass Point studios in Nassau, owned by Blackwell. Sly & Robbie, who provided the axis of the Compass Point house band, were already well on their way towards usurping the Barrett brothers as reggae's most celebrated rhythm section.

On the world stage, Marley and the Wailers were still streets ahead of the competition and looked forward to consolidating their position during the course of the next American tour. The previous Survival trek had been gruelling and the Uprising tour was likely to prove just as daunting due to increased public demand and the organisers' determination to book as many shows as possible. Stevie Wonder would be sharing some of the dates and the Wailers' long-awaited mainstream success Stateside (where 'Could You Be Loved' hadn't done as well as expected) was now definitely within their sights.

Before leaving for America, Marley had an encounter with a young man called Dennis Thomas, who was living out in the countryside with his cousin Neville, who grew fine ganga as well as an assortment of foodstuffs.

Dennis Thomas: "One day this white Volkswagen drive up with a Rastaman in it. I tell him I have a pound of herb to sell, show him a sample, and we made a deal. He gave me a pair of shoes and said I must come to see him in Kingston, at 56 Hope Road, so I decided to go. The first time I went there, I carry two bags full of herb, and walked straight through the gate. There was this man sitting on a doorstep looking at me, but I decide to act tough, so I just passed him by. He was staring at me as I walked by, but I was so happy in my heart to know I was there at 56 Hope Road, a place I had always dreamt about, and that was close to what I loved best, which was music.

"First of all, I went around to where the Rastaman food place was and saw these people talking about a blocked drainpipe, so I went on my hands and knees and cleared it. As I was about to rise off the ground I heard a voice say, 'Who are you?' And then because I was wearing army clothes, the voice said, 'Are you a soldier?' and 'Where yuh come from?' As I looked around, I saw this same man who'd been sat on the doorstep and see it was Bob Marley. I was shocked! A man called Black Barry told him I was a weed man from the country, but the Gong say, 'You there in the soldier suit. Come make me see if you is a soldier,' and then ordered Gillie Dread to get some boxing gloves. When I heard that, I get afraid. I knew it was nothing serious, but if I fight with the Gong and hurt him, I couldn't live with that, plus the brothers around him would have dealt with me, fi real. Luckily, as it was about to start, I was saved by this man called Rats And Bats coming into the yard. He'd stolen some money from a visitor and they hold him and beat him up bad, so he won't steal any more. I never got the opportunity to be so close with Bob again, although I later went to live at 56 Hope Road for a while, because I was one of the youths there who sweep the yard, or wash cars for the Wailers."

Thomas recorded two tracks for Tuff Gong under Family Man's supervision, including his debut single 'Pink Eye'. He then spent 11 months in Kingston's General Penitentiary before reinventing himself as King Kong, recording early digital reggae hits for the late King Tubby. His story refutes the popular image of Marley as some benign, peace loving Rastaman, and reinforces one of him as some kind of "don". Marley had promised to loan Lee Perry a thousand dollars for car parts before going on tour, but by the time Scratch arrived at Hope Road, the Wailers party (which now included Tommy Cowan) had already left. The producer became bitter about this, darkly muttering about all the past favours he'd done for Marley. While in New York, Marley asked Ansel Creigland of the Meditations to collect the tapes of 'Who Colt The Game' and 'I Know A Place' from Scratch, but he refused to hand them over. The reality is that Marley had probably forgotten, preoccupied with the tour through Europe, America, the Far East, and Africa.

The I-Threes now doubled as Marley's opening act, which meant the Wailers were onstage much longer than usual. They'd open with a nyahbinghi chant before moving briskly through numbers like 'That's The Way Jah Planned It' and 'Stepping Out Of Babylon', trading lead vocals as they went.

Beginning on May 30 in Zurich, the Uprising tour played Munich, Grenoble, Dijon, Cologne, Kaiserlauten, Strasbourg, Orleans, Bordeaux, Dortmond, and a return to Munich, before playing Hamburg, Oslo, Stockholm, Copenhagen, and West Berlin, where Marley received first-hand evidence of his fans' loyalty. After getting out of the car, he saw a group of a dozen or so youths standing nearby and so went over to talk to them. He discovered they'd risked their lives to see the concert, having sneaked across the border from East Berlin with no money. Marley immediately asked for them to be given tickets and money for food. The Eissporthalle in Kassel was next on the itinerary, followed by Brussels, Rotterdam, Lille, Toulon, and Milan, where they filled the 100,000-capacity San Siro Stadium, home to the Inter Milan and AC Milan football teams, on June 27. It was the largest crowd for a reggae concert anywhere, including Reggae Sunsplash, and a milestone in the Wailers' careers, since none of them had ever witnessed anything like it before. The Italian excursion ended in Turin.

Griffiths remembers hundreds of disabled people seated in wheelchairs at some of these European shows, and wondered if they'd come thinking Marley's music had magical healing powers. The band then journeyed to Barcelona's Plaza de Toros Monumental, where they were filmed during the soundcheck, and Marley was subjected to yet another round of questioning. *Rolling Stone* journalist Fred Schruers, who'd first met the singer in 1976, joined the tour in Barcelona and described Marley's unerring command of the crowd as "completely entrancing". From Barcelona, they travelled to France. The small charter plane flying between Nantes and Paris hit turbulence, but Schruers says the Wailers took no notice and "glared silently, Rasta-style, at the weather just outside the windows that was soon rattling the plane." Soon after arrival, they were due to play an open-air show in a field on the outskirts of Le Bourget Airport. Schruers described the Marley entourage, "with their dreadlocks, their red, gold and green satin tour jackets," being treated as if they were royalty. They were given a 20-strong motorcycle escort into the city centre after the show, although an incident that happened in the lobby of the Hotel Nikko offered the most insight into Marley's character.

"I was saying farewell to Bob, whom I wouldn't see for almost three months, as Rita Marley and her fellow I-Threes came off the elevator heading for the narrow, steep escalator that led to the street," Schruers wrote. "Rita was wrestling her bulky, rolling suitcase. There was a moment of hesitation. Bob was not a faithful husband and Rita was not an easy wife but there was much history and respect between them. With one of his easy smiles sent over his shoulder by way of goodbye, Bob Marley, Rebel Superstar, hastened as inconspicuously as possible across the lobby, wrangled the suitcase onto the escalator and glided out of view."

After a final French date in Dijon, the band played Dalymount Park in Dublin on July 6 and the gardens at south London's Crystal Palace (supported by the Average White Band), the following day. The Wailers' London performances were invariably special occasions and this was no exception when the small lake in front of the stage gradually began to fill with people, much to the the group's general bemusement and the consternation of the security. Two nights apiece at the Brighton Centre and Glasgow Apollo were followed by the Deeside Leisure Centre, with the tour ending at Stafford Bingley Hall on July 13.

The European leg involved six gigs a week for six weeks in 12 different countries, which Family Man confirms the whole band thought excessive. "After we start to play for some big money, it's like some people want to mash up everything we start," he laments. "But we weren't interested in all that big money; we just want to buy our little studio and pressing plant. And that we a do, but them other people get seduced by big money and switch pon that, but me and my brother, we're not going nowhere."

As in Jamaica, reggae was undergoing changes in England, where a multi-racial band from Birmingham, named after an unemployment benefit card (UB40), would eclipse the Wailers' meagre tally of chart hits. A romantic strain of rub-a-dub called lovers' rock was popular in blues parties, and Franco Rossi's film *Babylon*, starring Aswad's Brinsley Forde, opened in cinemas. Its riveting portrayal of life for black British youths in and around the London reggae scene was the British equivalent of *Rockers*, and won hands-down in the realism stakes. Radical dub poet Linton Kwesi Johnson was expressing political commentary in his records to a degree few Jamaican artists would dare match, including Marley, while Matumbi's Dennis Bovell was a latter-day reggae renaissance man, building important bridges between reggae, punk and pop, in addition to producing dub and lovers' rock.

No fashion stayed still in London for long, which is why the Wailers liked it so much, but they must have been surprised when learning that the latest trend was in reviving Sixties' Jamaican hits and adopting a style of dress first associated with the Kingston rude boys. Acts on the 2-Tone label like the Specials were multi-racial and had grown out of the collision between punk and reggae, whereas the Police leaned more towards rock, yet still included a touch of reggae on hits like 'Roxanne', 'Can't Stand Losing You' and 'Walking On The Moon'. There was an everpresent undercurrent of social unrest as tensions continued to rise between immigrant populations and right-wing groups, and between youth and the authorities. Riots would break out the following year in depressed areas of England, especially those where large numbers of black people lived, such as Brixton, Moss Side, and St Paul's in Bristol.

While in London, Marley met up with his old friend Delroy Washington and together they wrote a song called 'Slogans'. "Can't take these slogans no more," Marley sings, referring to the slogans painted on walls across the world. The lyrics spoke of segregation, frustration, and riots. "Oh, when will we be free?" More of a sketch than a finished song, taped onto a cassette, Marley never recorded the track professionally.*

While the rest of the Wailers returned to Jamaica, Marley flew to Miami to confront Don Taylor about certain financial matters that remained unresolved. Taylor claimed Marley and Skill Cole drew guns on him during this meeting, and called the police.† In the meantime, Sims warned his charge against returning to Jamaica, since the political violence there had now reached boiling point. Marley never saw his homeland again.

Prior to the start of the US leg of the Uprising tour, the Wailers' rehearsals at Criteria studios were filmed. Marley is rarely animated, except when making up lyrics, or trying out new songs. He looks gaunt for the most part, as if the life is slowly draining out of him, and yet he doggedly puts the band through their paces while standing centre stage, his mane of dreadlocks stuffed into an outsize red and green tam, which balances precariously on his head. Downie interjects a few backing vocals in the absence of the I-Threes and even sings lead at times, as on 'Zimbabwe', which he embellishes with synthesiser drums. He appears more like a bandleader than Family Man, who stands quietly in the background, apart from when trading instruments with Anderson. Marvin's presence barely registers until he takes hold of Marley's guitar and strums a few chords as Marley improvises on an unreleased (and unrecorded) track called 'Real Good Time'. There's no trace of Marvin's showmanship, but then every one of these rehearsals is lacklustre, despite Downie's best efforts to lift the band's spirits.

The young keyboard player orchestrates the crescendos at the end of 'Sun Is Shining', sings call and response with Marley on 'So Much Trouble', and adds bright, synthesiser riffs to 'Work'. With Downie utilising all the latest technology, there would have been little chance of Marley's music sounding dated as reggae music entered the digital era. On September 16, the band performed at Boston's J B Hynes Auditorium. It

* Marley's children later asked Eric Clapton to overdub guitar on the track which became the centrepiece of an album called *Africa Unite*, released in 2005.
† Taylor later sued Marley for $500,000, but ended up settling out of court after the singer's death.

was not until well over half an hour into the set that anything from *Survival* or *Uprising* was played, adding credence to the suspicion that some of the newer songs weren't that well suited to the dynamics of a live show, lacking the effect of Marley's earlier hits. The exceptions were inevitably 'Redemption Song' and 'Could You Be Loved', which proved a show-stopper right from the outset.

Following a gig in Providence, Rhode Island, the band had a day off on September 18 and then opened for the Commodores over two nights at New York's Madison Square Garden. Ras Karbi says that Family Man's bass reverberated around the venue at such volume, some people instinctively clutched at their stomachs and had trouble staying on their feet and that the venue emptied after the Wailers' performance, which proved highly embarrassing for the headliners. 'Could You Be Loved' brought the house down and Marley's performances were remarkably coherent, considering the ravages cancer was doing to his body.

"The evident energy and fire he brought to those gigs now seems heroic," wrote Schruers. "Perhaps he had a foreboding sense that these would truly count. The day after the second, I was scheduled to accompany Bob and the band out to the annual West Indian Day Parade in Brooklyn. The plan was for the band to travel the parade route on a flatbed truck, waving and grooving to their own recordings played through a sizeable speaker set-up. I met Lister, the Island aide who had promised 'soon come' to a generation of journalists, downstairs in the Essex House [Hotel] lobby and we rode up to the room with its view all the way north up Central Park to Harlem.

"Once again, I found myself in the doorway of his suite, and again there was that smile – one I appreciated all the more because of the obvious effort it cost him. Bob was wearing one of his concert outfits, a tight denim suit with bell-bottoms, but the dreadlocks he liked to unleash with a flourish were gathered under a tam and his face looked drawn. He was seated in a stiff-backed wooden chair immediately beside the door, as if he'd diligently brought himself that close before sitting back down. He seemed to be gathering himself for a moment. Finally, he looked up. 'Lister,' he said, with real regret in his voice, 'Nah cyan do it.'"

While in New York, Marley hosted a press conference in which he could barely summon the energy to reply to questions. His mind was still sharp when it came to music however, as Family Man discovered soon after their arrival.

"Bob said to come over to Chris Blackwell's apartment in Essex House, so me and him alone go over there and he goes over to this reel-to-reel tape recorder that's kept in there," Fams recalls. "Well, Bob started to play this tape and that's when I hear this song, 'Wounded Lion In The Jungle'. I say, 'Wait, that's the same tape I look for!' Chris, he started to laugh, so I tell him he was supposed to get it transferred. That was the final time we go there, but we all wonder why Bob alone was staying there, whilst we're being kept elsewhere. I remember saying to Dennis Thompson, 'Who's idea was it to put Bob alone up in there?' And he said, 'Allan Cole.' I knew it was going to be pure trial and crosses from the minute he come back, and Gillie didn't like it either, because I remember him saying how Skill had come back to 'kill the Gong'. Bob was never right from deh so and then we hear about that party them have . . ."

The party in question was thrown for the Wailers at the Negril by Frankie Crocker, who was the promoter for the Madison Square Garden shows. Family Man, Carly, and Gillie weren't invited, since they opposed cocaine use. Family Man later saw several photographs taken at the party, which confirmed his suspicions that there'd been some kind of foul play, since Marley looked disturbed and ill at ease. One depicted a girl with long, painted fingernails, draping herself over him, while handing him a drink. Her attentions seemed to worry Marley.

"All I know at the time is that the man was a hard worker and through him work so hard upfront onstage . . . because those lights, they can drain you sometimes," says Family Man, who hadn't been told his bandleader had cancer. "I saw all of that, and we know say him have some foot injury, but him have a great spirit and keep going, just like before. After we do that second show at the Madison Square Garden, we have a day off and this brethren ask me if I hear about how Bob faint [in Central Park]. I say, 'How can Bob faint? Because Bob is one fit man and that can't happen,' but him say the man them training, running up and down, and then Bob collapse. So I think maybe Bob is overhung and him a try to jog it off, y'know? That's how I was checking t'ings."

Vivian Blake, leader of the infamous Shower Posse, visited Marley at the Essex House Hotel, whose room was now peopled by hardcore hustlers. Marley had fallen ill after the first New York show, but revived before collapsing again. Dr Pee Wee Frazier took him to see a neurologist, who diagnosed he had two or three weeks to live. Marley insisted on continuing performing and played his last ever concert at the Stanley Theatre, Pittsburgh, on 23 September.

Family Man Barrett: "It's like him run out of gas, because then him faint up onstage. That was in Pittsburgh and I say to myself, 'Wait. Is this really a Wailers thing up here?' 'Cause them expect something powerful from we, better than that . . . You see I never know too much about his condition. There were other people who him talk to 'bout that and who were trying to influence Bob in a different direction, so I and I move away really, because it's only musically we know each other towards the last part. Musically we can still grow too, but through some other people want to come in pon some other level, whether them friends or whatever, they spoil up the programme, and that's what happened."

The tour was cancelled the next day. Marley was taken to Cedars of Lebanon hospital in Miami and then flown to a specialist cancer hospital in New York, where he was diagnosed as having cancer of the lungs and stomach and also a malignant brain tumour, which required chemotherapy treatment. Family Man visited Marley almost by accident, which would be the last occasion the two saw each other.

"After they stop the tour, I walk around New York and run into Lee Jaffe who say, 'What? You still in town?' He said Bob was at some hotel and to check him out, so we went over by Bob's room, knock on the door, and I hear his daughter Cedella say, 'Who is it?' I tell Lee to answer, him say, 'Lee Jaffe and Family Man,' and we hear the chain begin to pull off the door and when the door open, man I see Bob for the first time without him dreadlocks, looking just like Telly Savalas! The man was completely bald and I was so surprised, I couldn't even say anything. I think to myself, 'How the Gong going to go through all of these treatments and we don't even discuss it among ourselves? And if it was that bad, then why weren't we told about it sooner?' All these things were running through my head, but I still couldn't really believe what I'd seen."

CHAPTER TWENTY-EIGHT

Harbour Sharks

O N November 4, Bob Marley was baptised Berhane Selassie in the Ethiopian Orthodox Church. Five days later, he was flown out to a Bavarian clinic to see Dr Josef Issels, who specialised in cancer treatment. Island Records continued to deny there was anything seriously wrong with their artist, apart from "exhaustion". Marley spent his 36th birthday in Germany, surrounded by friends and most of his immediate family, including Rita and Cedella. The majority of his close associates had been sent tickets, although there was no sign of the Barrett brothers. According to Anderson, Marley kept asking for them, but no one heeded his wishes.

Family Man Barrett: "After Bob took sick, I hear the family send tickets for lots of people, but they don't send any for me or my brother. They don't send one for Wya either, yet we are the three chief musicians, who were with Bob the longest . . . We're just so laid back I guess, but I still don't know why them never send for us. He was asking for me and Carly up to the end and I'm told Bob was in tears two or three times."

Things might have been different had Marley been in his homeland, where he'd just been awarded Jamaica's Order of Merit. Says Anderson: "Bob just made the decision to go to Germany and deal with it."

The guitarist remained until four days before Marley left for Miami and would carry him to another part of the clinic for his daily chemotherapy sessions, although he says Marley had lost so much weight, there wasn't much left of the man by this stage.

Al Anderson: "He was just lying there in his own shit and piss by then. It was tragic and he could see the tears in my eyes, but then got angry and said not to 'Pussy claat cry.' It was so upsetting, and I remember Mrs Booker saying, 'Haven't you had enough of seeing him like this yet?'"

By May 3, Dr Issels had given up, saying Marley couldn't be saved. Anderson claims when Marley asked the doctor how long he'd got and was told three or four days, the stricken singer asked to be taken home to Jamaica. In his autobiography, Don Taylor claims Marley repeatedly told him and Diane Jobson how important it was for him to write a will, but had delayed doing so until it was too late. Marley phoned from Germany to say he was leaving for Miami and wanted to see Taylor, confirming he hadn't signed any will by that stage, despite being asked to do so by Rita and representatives of the Twelve Tribes. He asked to meet at the Cedars of Lebanon hospital, so Taylor left Los Angeles and went straight to his Miami office, where Rita phoned him to say that Bob's health had deteriorated and to hurry. It was the afternoon of May 11, 1981, but by the time they got to the hospital, he had already passed away.

Neville Garrick said that Marley hadn't written a will because that would have meant he'd given up his fight to live. Garrick also made the observation that the absence of a will had caused everyone in Marley's circle "to reveal who they really were." Bob died intestate and under Jamaican law, Rita would get 55 per cent of the estate and all of his children, whether born within wedlock or not, the remaining share. Marley's assets were valued at $30,000,000, but only Taylor had intimate knowledge of what form they took and where they were located.

"Bob Marley didn't trust anyone and always believed someone was trying to get something over him," Taylor wrote in his autobiography. "He died mentally aware of everything and chose not to make me resign from the company and put Rita Marley or someone else in charge. He left me to deal with it and that should show you that anything else people may say is stupid. The fact is he left all this vast amount of money in my control. All he had to do was take my name off, but he didn't."

For advice regarding the estate, Rita contacted Taylor who in turn approached Diane Jobson. Wisely, she recommended they turn it over to the Jamaican Attorney General, although this didn't happen until later and only then by default.

Family Man had been keeping busy, playing bass alongside Sly Dunbar on a session for Tosh, recording 'The Poor Man Feel It' (Robbie Shakespeare went back the following day to play on 'Wanted Dread And Alive'). Livingston meanwhile, was over at Channel One with the Roots Radics, recording songs for his *Rock And Groove* album. The Barretts were working at Tuff Gong when they heard Marley's death announced on the radio. Fearing looters, they immediately closed down the studio and also the pressing plant on Orange Street.

Taylor spoke to JLP Minister Babsy Grange about arranging a state funeral, which took place in Kingston on Thursday May 21. Neither Tosh nor Livingston attended the funeral; Rastafarians believe in letting "the dead bury the dead." However, there was a sadness that several of Marley's closest musical associates weren't there to bid him farewell. As expected, the Twelve Tribes and Ethiopian Orthodox Church shared the ecumenical service between them. Marley's body, with a Bible and guitar nestled in his arms, lay in state at the National Arena throughout the day, and thousands of people came to pay their final respects before his casket was taken by motorcade to a mausoleum in Nine Mile.

"His body was transported, often on single-lane roads, in a winding caravan to his mausoleum near his birthplace in Nine Mile in St Ann's Parish," wrote Fred Schruers. "As he was put in the tomb, I found myself as one of many white faces that had made the pilgrimage. Next to me was Chris Blackwell, certainly sombre but as usual attentive to the tenor of the assemblage, and at the same time offering comfort with personal and private grace. Afterwards, [photographer] Kate Simon and I found ourselves at an impromptu memorial at Tuff Gong Studios, where Cedella Booker, swaying at the centre of a small gathering of musicians, powerfully sang a hymn. We had put aside our work implements in that sacred space. As I was phoning in the story of the day's events to the *Washington Post*, I could hear the repeated, gently rocking refrain spilling through the open studio door: 'And I say, hail, hail, hail . . .'"

Taylor returned to Miami after the funeral. Marley's mother was the legal guardian of Rohan and later insisted Yvette Morris' daughter get a share of the legacy. The battle for control over Marley's fortune had now begun in earnest. Rita, however, held all the aces, and was advised by Taylor to open accounts for each of the children with banks in the Bahamas, appoint their mothers as trustees and then transfer their fair shares into them. About two months after the funeral, she and Taylor went to Nassau and put $10,000 into each of the children's accounts, while Taylor began the process of familiarising Rita with her late husband's assets, which took about six months.

For starters, Taylor ensured that Rita receive approximately $400,000 from the Island Records account in New York. She then asked for another $1,000,000, which Taylor ordered to be transferred from the Tortola account. At Rita's request, he set up an offshore bank account for her at the Bank of Nova Scotia in Nassau. Taylor knew the rights to Marley's publishing had expired prior to his death, so he took Rita and David Steinberg to Los Angeles to meet the head of A & M, who arranged for her to get a $1,000,000 advance. This came with the proviso that each time the company released a record and the advance was recouped, they would re-advance her another large sum, depending on the actual sales. A & M recouped this initial advance within a month, thus underlining Bob Marley & the Wailers' strength in the marketplace.

Taylor said Steinberg worked closely with Rita during this stage and she paid him large sums of money, although lawyer George Desnoes eventually oversaw transferring control of Marley's affairs over to Rita. Taylor gave Rita, Desnoes and two other lawyers a list of Marley's estate holdings, but when Desnoes said they needed a banker, they brought in Louis Byles, who worked for the Mutual Security Merchant Bank in Jamaica. The initial meetings went well, so the lawyer in Tortola was contacted and told to draw up papers so that Taylor could hand over control of Bob's assets to Rita. Her signature would be the only one required on the Tortola accounts from now on. However, no sooner was the transfer completed than Rita, Steinberg, and the original accountant Marvin Zolt distanced themselves from Taylor, who had also played a key role in getting the Melody Makers a record contract with EMI in the US with a $250,000 advance. Taylor later found out that Steinberg had recommended Rita form a company called Rita Marley Music and register it in the Dutch Antilles (Curacao) at a cost of $30,000. The majority of income owed to Marley would be channelled into this account from then on.

Taylor had set up the original Island recording agreement so that if Marley died, the contract would expire, leaving Island with the 10 albums as stated and nothing more. Under its terms, Rita would have to give Blackwell the first album released after Marley's death and also the rights to all unreleased material, for which she was paid a $1,000,000 advance. The question of publishing rights had played a part in Marley's renewed friendship with Sims, prior to the Wailers' last US tour. Having dispensed with the services of Taylor, Marley consulted him about management issues but also wanted help refinancing Tuff Gong, so he could take the organisation on to the next level. His ultimate goal was autonomy from labels like Island, while having the freedom to strike his own distribution deals, since he already had the facilities required for production and manufacturing. The newly restructured Tuff Gong would have made the Wailers relatively self-sufficient, brought them economic independence, and allowed them to provide other artists with a safe haven from exploitation.

Al Anderson: "Danny Sims decided he could come and give Bob the publishing money he needed to develop his company and Tuff Gong. Danny was connected to CBS and I heard that Walter Yetnikov offered

Bob $10,000,000 for a contract. Blackwell was only offering around £2,000,000 and yet Bob didn't want to be cast immediately as this huge megastar, which Walter and CBS would have done instantly. Bob wanted the Wailers to build a studio complex and have publishing companies and pressing plants, and Blackwell wasn't into that. That's why I was hoping we'd go to CBS, draw a big bag of cash and open up our own production company so we could start developing other acts. We would have had facilities for artists, singers, and dancers . . . We were planning to develop kids in Jamaica. That's what we really wanted to do."

Family Man Barrett: "We were definitely thinking about other labels, because I remember hearing something about Warner Brothers and then CBS before Bob pass. CBS had released 'Reggae On Broadway' in the past and it looked like things were going to happen with them for a while. That was in the making, and after we'd finished doing this tour with Stevie Wonder, we were going to buy out the whole front part of the beach near Runaway Bay and then sort out the accounting between Bob, Carly, and myself or any other unfinished business we had. Bob would often fly over to Tortola with Cindy Breakspeare and meet with this dread from over there who wrote songs for him, because some of those songs they say Bob Marley wrote, he bought them off this brother and we wanted to take care of him officially. When Bob died, people like him got forgotten, because Rita never listened to anything I said . . .

"I met with this lawyer and the bank manager over there one time and they mentioned one of the beneficiaries was listed as Skill Cole. Imagine that! Because how can it get there? It must have been Don Taylor and Bob who arranged that, so he could get money after he'd gone on the run, hiding from his gambling debts. I asked the bank manager if my name was mentioned anywhere and he said no."

Family Man and Carly had shared Marley's vision and worked hard in helping to establish Tuff Gong. Without their leader, the dream of transforming Tuff Gong into "a little Motown" was effectively over, and on December 17, 1981, the deeds to 56 Hope Road were transferred to Byles at the Mutual Security Merchant Bank. The band members were now loose ends, to be tidied up as Rita saw fit, which is exactly what happened on December 2, when they signed an agreement defining their future involvement with the estate.

Family Man Barrett: "After Bob died, Rita told me there would be a delay in receiving royalties while Bob's estate was sorted out. At the end of 1981, we were all summoned to a meeting in Philadelphia by Mr David

Steinberg, who was Rita's lawyer. I couldn't make it, but I recall my brother and Junior coming back and being very upset and they explained that they'd [signed] an agreement and that Rita had said the agreement was meant to save the estate tax, so there would be more money for all us. I did later sign the agreement, though I don't recall having done so. From that time on, I received cheques from Marvin Zolt until 1986, when the royalties stopped."

In this 1981 contract, Rita agreed to pay the Wailers royalties on the recordings they'd made with Bob Marley. On December 17, letters of administration were sent to the Mutual Security Merchant Bank, advising them of these changes. The contract with the Wailers pre-dated Rita's appointment as administrator of the estate, and would not therefore be bound to it. Despite Family Man's assurances to the contrary, legal records show that Rita paid the Wailers in the region of £1.2 million between 1981 and 1986. Family Man alone is listed as having received $344,000.

Being working musicians, the ex-Wailers couldn't stay inactive for long, despite the heavy aura of loss and disbelief hanging over the camp. However, there seemed little incentive for them to go out and play since, thanks to Rita, they were getting paid without having to do much. One or two were struggling with the effects of serious drug use, while another had mental heath problems. Rita, on the other hand, was busy recording; her song, 'One Draw', (recorded with other musicians) proved a massive Jamaican hit in 1982, despite being banned for its exuberant herb lyric. Her other cause for celebration that year came after releasing a single by the Melody Makers, 'What A Plot' b/w 'Children Playing In The Streets', on her own Rita Marley Music label.

Island took their first steps towards building the Marley myth, after news began circulating that there were plans for a film called *Marley*, directed by Gary Weis, to be completed in time for the Cannes Film Festival that year. Island planned to issue an accompanying soundtrack album, but while neither the film nor the album materialised, the project marked the beginning of Island's bid to accumulate and ultimately control everything to do with the late superstar, including images, press clippings, and film footage.

Rita consulted with Tosh and Livingston in the period immediately following Bob's death, but Family Man says the pair got excluded after power struggles developed and outside advisers made their presence felt. The two ex-Wailers performed at the Youth Consciousness Festival, held

502

in Kingston over the 1982 Christmas period, performing a number of Wailers songs together, including 'Get Up, Stand Up', 'Soul Rebel', 'Run For Cover', 'Hypocrite', 'No Woman No Cry', and 'Keep On Moving'. It seemed as if Marley's passing had energised them, since both appeared ready and willing to fill the post he left behind as reggae music's leading figurehead.

Livingston, in particular, was on a run of form. He'd already released two albums of Wailers songs (*Sings The Wailers*, *Tribute To The Hon Nesta Marley*) and followed them with a set entitled *Rock And Groove*, recorded with Sly & Robbie and a fresh, new band working out of Channel One called the Roots Radics. By November 1982, he'd issued such tracks as 'Collie Man' and 'Trouble Is On The Road Again', which number among the strongest of his career.

Tosh, too, had not stopped working since signing with the Rolling Stones' label. After being badly beaten by Kingston police on several occasions, he sought the help of traditional healers while he was in Nigeria with master drummer Babatunde Olatunji. The visit inspired the title track of his next album, *Mama Africa*, recorded with members of the Soul Syndicate. Prompted by Donald Kinsey, he also recorded a rip-roaring version of Chuck Berry's 'Johnny B Goode', which some of his Jamaican fans derided, but Tosh himself defended. "Because what's wrong with telling people to be good?" he asked them.

Livingston produced Marcia Griffiths after becoming intrigued by the drum machine she'd bought on a trip to Canada. The single that resulted from this session, 'Electric Boogie', became an instant success when Island finally released it in 1983 and it even gave birth to a popular dance craze, called the Electric Slide. The single marked the commercial zenith of both Livingston's and Griffiths' careers and said a great deal about the depth of talent among former Marley associates.

Not that Marley's own career was now over; far from it, in fact. Island reissued the Lyceum live version of 'No Woman No Cry' as a single in June 1981, and while it reached number eight in the UK, America's record buyers again resisted. Island followed it with a previously unreleased track, 'I Know', although this reflective but happy affirmation of Rastafari failed to chart, despite a bright, contemporary mix and some engaging melodies.

Family Man Barrett: "'I Know' was one of those early crossover, hip-hop tracks we did with Bob. It was ahead of its time so we hadn't put it out yet, because it was recorded soon after we'd finished the studio at 56 Hope Road, at the end of 1978, coming into 1979. I play keyboards, rhythm guitar, and lead guitar on it and then do a computer mix of it, except we didn't use up the full 24 tracks. We just use 22 and then we use the remaining two to mix down with. We wouldn't do that with every track. It was just certain music we'd record like that, like some disco, funky type of tunes. I have the mix down tape up until now and a lot of people don't even recognise it as the Wailers! But I mix it and then fly up to Miami where Ken Khouri master it and then I send it to Dynamic to cut the stamper and I pay for all that out of my own pocket, never to be reimbursed yet. We were all so dedicated in my time, I tell you . . ."

Marley had sent word for Family Man to prepare it for release before his death, so 'I Know' was the last Wailers track to be sanctioned by Marley himself. In May of the following year, to commemorate the second anniversary of his passing and also to coincide with a BBC 2 TV documentary on Marley, Tuff Gong released *Confrontation*, a collection of former singles, demos and rehearsal tracks, some of which had been reconstructed using new rhythm tracks. The album's credits list Bob Marley & the Wailers and Errol Brown as producers, with Rita named as executive producer. Rita and Garrick have said that Marley had wanted to call his next album *Confrontation*, while Family Man says the last songs he wrote were in a nyahbinghi style, based around the sound of Rastafari drumming, and that subsequent recordings would have reflected this quest for a deeper, more authentic form of expression.

"As we'd finished recording *Uprising*, and were heading for *Confrontation*, we were thinking of turning our music into a kind of more Afro-Jamaican style, taking it closer to nyahbinghi, cah we knew it was time to come with that pattern. Bob and I used to discuss it, saying how people were going to come for the reggae, but after they do that now, we were going to move into the nyahbinghi, so it was going to take on more of those same chant vibes you hear on songs like 'Running Away', 'So Much Things To Say', and 'Guiltiness'."

Marley once described nyahbinghi as "the highest form of music" and likened it to Christian hymns. He said it was "beyond reggae," and you can only do it well when "you really know what you're doing." Leroy "Horse Mouth" Wallace agreed, telling Penny Reel that, "there's a basic truth behind playing reggae music and there's a purpose why the drummer play. It's a revolution, because drum is the language we used to speak a long, long time ago, and everything about it has meaning. It's a revolution, you no see it? And it informs the people's minds to get strong towards Babylon."

While not a nyahbinghi track, the opening 'Chant Down Babylon' encapsulates the same mindset and dates from the *Survival* sessions, since 'Santa' Davis plays drums. Jack Ruby had been playing it on a dubplate for years, although his version was not as light and breezy. The gospel influence appears on 'Jump Nyahbinghi', another of Marley's celebrations of music, herb, and the simple joys of the Rastafarian lifestyle. 'Give Thanks And Praises' is more downbeat and austere, while the poignant 'Trenchtown' pays further tribute to the singer's origins. "Up a Cane River to wash my dread, upon a rock I rest my head," he sings, referring to the times when he, Jaffe, and Esther Anderson would go and visit Livingston in Bull Bay. Marley lashes out at the vainglorious on 'Stiff Necked Fools', with its telling line of, "You think you're cool, to deny me for simplicity." It was Marley's down-to-earth philosophy and his identification with what was real that had imbued some of his best songs with greatness, and while none of those are on *Confrontation* – although Island included alternate mixes of his two Jamaican hits, 'Blackman Redemption' and 'Rastaman Live Up' – it's clear that fame and fortune didn't affect him in the least.

Although broadly welcomed by critics and fans alike, *Confrontation* failed to take the market by storm and ranks as the most dispensable of the Island albums. "We try and make it so it sounds like Bob was still alive," says Family Man, in the album's defence. "Nothing has changed, because we show the full energy of it and I'm not sure that anyone else could have made things look this way, not with their beat. They don't know anything of that. But there were enough tracks to make two more albums. I don't know whether they can ever heat them up to the fullness though, because only I can do that with Bob's things.

"Some of the tracks on *Confrontation* were just his voice and guitar alone, from the music room he set up at his mother's house in Miami and some from my rehearsal room also. 'Mix Up Mix Up' started like that, because I have to overdub the drum, the bass line, and also the guitar on that one, and then put everything around the voice, which was recorded on just two-track originally. Tyrone, he added that keyboard phrase, which sounds like some little boogaloo, funk thing. But there were several tracks like that, so I do a lot of work on them, because Bob's voice sounded a little tinny in places, before I fat it up and round it up."

The week before *Confrontation* was released, Island issued the most outstanding track, 'Buffalo Soldier', on a 12″ single and it was an immediate hit, streaking to fourth place on the UK charts, Marley and the Wailers' highest-ever chart position. This wasn't the version recorded with King Sporty in Miami in 1978, but the later interpretation, recorded at Tuff Gong during the following 18 months. King Sporty's mix was originally scheduled for release at the same time as Island's re-recorded version, but then came out on a white label with little or no promotion once Island had offered Sporty $150,000 for joint ownership of the masters and publishing. Taylor had opened the negotiations with him, but his task wasn't made any easier by Rita contesting the fact that Sporty had written the song. Legal action ensued which was eventually settled out of court.

Enthused by the success of 'Buffalo Soldier' in August, the Wailers performed at Reggae Sunsplash which was devoted to Marley's memory and starred Stevie Wonder, who sat in with the band for a couple of numbers. To mark what would have been Bob's 39th birthday Rita hosted a tribute show on February 6, 1984 at Nine Mile, where a new incarnation of the Wailers' Band, with Marvin on lead vocals, made its entrance. Family Man, Carly, and Lindo were still there, but Seeco had disappeared, Downie was touring with Grace Jones, and Anderson was back in New York, so Stephen Stewart played organ, Neville Garrick, percussion, and Nadine Sutherland joined the I-Threes on harmonies. The previous year, Downie had sung a techno-pop version of 'Jamming' on an album called *Pecker Power*, featuring members of the Wailers, Yellow Magic Orchestra, and Sly & Robbie, and would also play occasional sessions for both Tosh and Livingston during 1984/85. The former was recording at Music Mountain by this time, with Dennis Thompson engineering. Most of these tracks remain unreleased, as do the Wailers' dub mixes Thompson had worked on soon after Marley's death.

It's somewhat of a puzzle why Island never released a Bob Marley & the Wailers dub album, given the Barretts' pioneering exploits on *King Tubby Meets The Rockers Uptown*, *Pick A Dub*, and other classics of the genre. The closest in a strictly reggae style was by a Canadian group called Chalwa, who re-recorded the entire *Exodus* and *Uprising* albums in instrumental form. Their efforts are dismissed as "terrible" by Family Man, who is still the most qualified person to oversee such a project in future. Apart from backing Rita and overdubbing old tracks, the Barretts played a few sessions for producers like London based singer Trevor Bow, whose group the Sons of Jah had recorded their 1982 album, *Universal Message*, at Tuff Gong. Trevor's label, Natty Congo, had already released a number of other Sons of Jah albums featuring the Barretts, including *Bankrupt Morality*, *Burning Black* and *Reggae Hit Showcase*.

Jamaican producer Roydale "Andy" Anderson also hired the Wailers to play on tracks behind his nephew Jah Mel, who'd been born in Kingston, but then moved to Rochester as a young man, where he formed a band called Rhythm Factory. Anderson took them down to Jamaica in the summer of 1983. He had originally wanted to use the Roots Radics on their album but then discovered they were on tour. It was Prince Jammy who recommended Anderson check out the Wailers. Family Man liked what he heard, so Anderson booked Harry J's for three days, where Family Man, Carly, Lindo, Ian Winter, and Leroy "Gitsy" Hamilton laid tracks for Jah Mel's debut album, *Watchful Eyes*. Dean Fraser, Nambo Robinson, and Bongo Herman added horns and percussion the following day. A couple of Rochester musicians then added further overdubs once Jah Mel returned home, but that essential, Wailers one-drop groove remained. The standout tracks include 'Homesick', 'Sufferers' Song', 'Never Be Over For Me', and a cover of the John Holt hit 'Left With A Broken Heart', with Twelve Tribes singer Judah Eskender Tafari on backing vocals.

Jah Mel sounded a little like Sugar Minott, but the Wailers' next frontman couldn't have been more different. John Denver, or "Johnny Denver", as Family Man calls him, was a MOR singer/songwriter who specialised in country-tinged, folk homilies woven around environmental themes. His two best-known hits, 'Leaving On A Jet Plane' and 'Take Me Home Country Roads', had both proved popular in Jamaica and he'd been one of America's top-selling acts during the mid-Seventies. It was the Wailers' universal message and roots-based rhythms that had inspired him to recruit them for a track on his 1983 album, *It's About Time* – an experience Family Man still treasures to this day.

"Yes, we did it at Criteria in Miami and spent two nights in there where everybody a jam," he recalls. "It wasn't the same Criteria where we worked on *Rastaman Vibration*. This was a new studio and as soon as we light a spliff in there, we saw some of the people in there just a screw up their face at the fragrance, y'know? They don't smoke so them can't understand it, but from we start to play music now, their faces light up like a Christmas tree! Johnny Denver, he came out to us and says he's got his own band, but this particular tune sound so much like us, they figured we should play it. That song is called 'World Game' and there was this part he kept repeating that go, 'You and me, you and me,' so I say to him, 'Why don't you say 'I and I' because it's the same as you and me.' He work that in, and then after that now, he put some harmonies on it by Rita Marley, Marcia Griffiths, and Judy Mowatt, and the tune sound nice. Later on I hear that Rita do some business behind my back by getting the I-Threes to do those harmonies, but I never make the deal for them. They make it into a monetary t'ing and what I get for the whole band I think that's what the three of them get. I don't question them and from Rita's involved, you know something like that has gone down for sure. But it was a thrill that day there, I tell you! It was a good feeling and me give him a dub mix of it too . . ."

The idea of a John Denver dub track, languishing in the RCA vaults, blessed by Bob Marley's rhythm section, may seem far-fetched, but it's definitely out there somewhere. However, other musical irregularities concerning Marley didn't prove as amusing.

Family Man Barrett: "After the passing of Bob, I go to Mrs Booker's house to secure these tapes, 'cause we'd set up this four-track machine in there, so he could voice songs with just his guitar. I wasn't in any rush at the time to go to Bob's house. His mother lived there and other members of his family and no one else should have had more respect for his things, but by the time I decide fi go up there and check, it's like a tornado had passed through there and torn up everyt'ing. All the sheets come off the bed and everything we set up was torn down. Me see the empty table with not even a mic, so me say, 'That shouldn't have been moved. That's supposed to be there same way,' but every piece of equipment we'd set up had gone. All the drawers, they pull them out and take out certain t'ings. And when my eyes rest upon them, everybody's face look solemn like bullfrog, as if them just come fi realise what they've done, so I turn from there and left. It took me 10 years before I go back to that place, and to see how them disrespect we like that . . ."

CHAPTER TWENTY-NINE

Bad Card

RELEASED in May 1984, the Bob Marley compilation *Legend* stayed at the top position of the UK album charts for 13 consecutive weeks and became a fixture of the *Billboard* charts for some years, going on to become the biggest-selling reggae album of all time. Compiled by Island's Trevor Wyatt, *Legend* cleverly mixed Marley's more commercial, sing-along tunes like 'Is This Love', 'Could You Be Loved', 'Three Little Birds', 'Waiting In Vain' and 'One Love'/'People Get Ready', with the message-based 'Get Up, Stand Up', 'Exodus' and 'Redemption Song'. Alas, nothing was included from *Natty Dread*, *Rastaman Vibration*, or *Survival*, to cast Marley in a more rebellious light. By early the following year, *Legend* had sold over six million copies.

Island released an accompanying home video, consisting of a collection of clips mirroring each track. Most were taken from the 1977 Rainbow show during the Exodus tour; others were drawn from television appearances or filmed at Tuff Gong, such as the one for 'Could You Be Loved', showing Marley sitting in the vocal booth wearing football boots. Specially commissioned videos accompanied 'Is This Love', featuring Bob dancing with children at a west London day centre; 'Buffalo Soldier', portraying images from the lyrics with various members of Aswad and King Sounds & the Israelites; and 'One Love'/'People Get Ready', starring a boy with dreadlocks and a roll call of personalities like Madness, and Paul McCartney. The Don Letts-directed video for the latter helped push the 'One Love' single to number five in the UK charts.*

In support of the compilation, during the summer of 1984 Rita contacted Taylor to help put a *Legend* tribute together. Taylor says he was paid $40,000 for organising the 30-date tour in the US and Canada for October

---

* Island wouldn't have the same degree of success with follow-up singles, 'Waiting In Vain' or 'Could You Be Loved'; in fact, Marley's music wouldn't feature in the singles chart again for almost a decade, despite the continuing sales of *Legend*.

and November. "The costs were extravagant," he claimed, although there appeared to be no obvious reason for this since it was little more than an extended Marley family outing featuring the Wailers, the I-Threes, and Ziggy Marley, with Marvin and Downie sharing lead vocals. Rehearsals took place at the Cultural Arts Centre on the University of West Indies' campus at Mona, north-east Kingston, where Carlton's young son Akila (alias Errol) watched as the Wailers went through their paces.

"Every day they'd start at about four o'clock in the afternoon and go on 'til late at night, because I'd often drop to sleep by the time they'd finished," Errol recalls. "People always talk about Bob Marley, but to see the way that band played his music was so amazing. Sometimes I'd see my father and when he roll that snare, my heart leap inna me chest like it wanted to jump right out! He didn't play like any other drummer, because he'd bounce in his seat and lean forward, like he's riding a horse. He hit the drums with precision, like there was no doubt in what he did and I'd love watching him tape up the bottom skin on the tom tom, or put some chamois leather in the bass drum, just to dampen the sound. He did some things that were ahead of his time, and up until today there's no other drummer like him. It wasn't just about having rhythmic sense either, because it was quite scientific how he approached it. For instance, he'd tune his drums to different keys, just like how you'd tune a guitar."

A typical set would open with the I-Threes, backed by the Wailers. Marvin and Downie would then share vocals on songs including 'Positive Vibration', 'Is This Love', 'Jamming', and 'Three Little Birds', before Cedella Booker joined them for 'Redemption Song'. Ziggy would take over for 'Lively Up Yourself' and 'Get Up, Stand Up', and returned during 'Exodus', after the Wailers and I-Threes brought the house down with 'Buffalo Soldier'.

Al Anderson maintains he had no idea that Marley's mother and son were going to be on the tour but conceded that, "It was the real deal. No bullshit at all. The magic was still there."

That August, Mrs Booker had gone into Tuff Gong with Family Man to record her debut album, *Redemption Songs*, written during and after her son's illness. The collection included 'Mother Don't Cry', which she claimed were Bob's final words. The album, on which Cedella's niece Gloria and daughter Pearl (half sister to both Bob and Bunny) sang backing vocals, was later re-released as *Awake Zion* by Danceteria Records, followed by a gospel set and also an album of children's songs shared with Taj Mahal. It's a measure of the reverence in which Bob Marley is held that many fans accepted the emergence of his mother as a singer, although it's doubtful that the man himself would have countenanced sharing a stage with her.

On November 23, the Wailers played the Los Angeles Amphitheater, and during their time in the city, the entourage performed in front of a small crowd at Universal Studios (just as Marley and the Wailers had done in the Capitol Records Tower over a decade earlier), which was videotaped.

Family Man Barrett: "We had two screens set up behind us, left and right, showing movies like the 'Buffalo Soldier' video. I remember there was all this talk of paying the band $500,000, because that money was supposed to pay the musicians, the engineer, and the people who take care of the visuals. That was the first Legend tour in 1984 and everything sound good. They make a film out of it that hasn't been seen yet. I've seen pieces of it, but they mix parts of these different shows all the while, for use in their marketing strategies."

Anderson spoke to *Black Echoes'* Simon Buckland in February 1985. "We went on a tour in October just to see if we could still maintain the band and stay together. We went to California and did a few gigs throughout the States and it came out pretty well, but we're always doing sessions and playing on other people's records. Basically, everybody's been working on an album of their own, as well as trying to get an album out as the Wailers, because most people don't know us, and I think the Wailers were pretty much faceless until a couple of years ago. It was always Bob, Peter, and Bunny, but there are more of us than just those three, so we've all been real busy and we've got a Wailers' album ready to go. The only problem with it is there was this crazy director down at Tuff Gong, because at one time, Tuff Gong was trying to enlist proper administration to get the company moving, and get artists coming in with the ability to chart.

"We had this guy there who thought he knew the business, Jim Terrell, who used to be Vice President for black music at CBS years ago. He thought he had it all figured out for the Wailers, but he knew nothing about what was going on in the reggae market in Jamaica, let alone outside of it. Anyway he heard this album of 10 songs we'd done, with everybody contributing maybe a song or two each. We were pleased with it and looking for a deal, even though we probably weren't as far ahead of the game as we should have been, but things had come to a close with Bob and we were ready to go right out there and project ourselves. Others wanted to hold us back for some reason and a lot of it had to do with this guy Jim Terrell, who didn't know his arse from his elbow! He left Tuff Gong after a while and the album's still there, although we're not too interested in looking for a deal for that material now. What we want to do is go back in the studio and do another album with the I-Threes and just get back out there."

"We used to have separate accounts for the studio, the record shop, and the pressing plant," Family Man told web journalist Bones. "The next thing you hear is that [a lot of cash has gone missing]. . . I am one of the official directors of Tuff Gong, but they start to work around me now like I don't exist and [from then on] everything start to go wrong. I point out these things to people at Tuff Gong, but they don't really listen becah them just there, looking after them own best interests . . ."

When Federal studio on Marcus Garvey Drive came up for auction, Rita bought it, thereby extending Tuff Gong's operations to include another studio (one well suited to "live" ensemble recordings) as well as manufacturing and mastering facilities. Family Man's Uncle Boysie had built the original Federal studio for the Khouris, and despite a growing dis-illusionment with the management of the business, Fams felt proud in upholding the family tradition. For her part, Rita was determined to make a break with the past by achieving Marley's vision of competing at the highest level. That meant restructuring the company, reassessing people's worth, and gaining the Melody Makers a record contract with Virgin in the UK. Since Family Man's relationship with Rita was deteriorating fast, the boys embarked on their Hey World tour with a different set of musicians.

In 1984, Brazilian singer Gilberto Gil recorded his *Raca Humana* album at Tuff Gong. Family Man had an instinctive feel for Latin music and the two sets of musicians gelled beautifully as Gil wove reggae into his shim-mering, samba backdrops on tracks like 'Indigo Blue', 'Vamos Fugir', and the title track.

Gilberto Gil: "After samba and balao [a folk rhythm from the north-east of Brazil], the thing I like most is reggae. It is a black thing. Black people like percussion, there is no way out! In fact, I found a kind of similarity between the Cangaceiro [a bandit from the north-east of Brazil at the beginning of the last century] and the Rastaman. Both impressed on me the strangeness, beauty, and grandness with which they view their life processes and projects."

In the absence of Downie, Anderson, Marvin, and Seeco, Family Man brought Chinna Smith and Lloyd "Gitsy" Willis back into the fold on lead and rhythm guitars respectively, and then augmented the Zap Pow duo of Glen DaCosta and Dave Madden with the Mystic Revelation's Calvin Cameron on trombone. Loyal as ever, Carly and Lindo both played on these sessions, as did organist Stephen Stewart and nyahbinghi drummer Ras Michael.* Justin Hinds' album for Jack Ruby, *Travel With Love*, was another to benefit from the Barretts' magic touch as they were forced to redefine their musical direction. Although an infrequent visitor to Kingston, Hinds was an old friend from the Duke Reid Treasure Isle days. Downie and Chinna joined them for the sessions at Tuff Gong, although the finished tracks were mixed at Aquarius with help from Nighthawk's Leroy Pierson, who'd made the project possible.

The tracks, including 'Miss Wendell', 'Book Of History', and the country-tinged 'Weeping Eyes' were classical roots reggae – well-sung and arranged, with lyrics that spoke eloquently of nature, black history and the human condition and provided a more valid continuation of what Marley had represented than most other projects emanating from the new-look Tuff Gong. While most recognised its spiritual and musical value, *Travel With Love* unfortunately failed to sell in vast numbers.

The Tuff Gong administration didn't appear all that interested in promoting or utilising what was left of Marley's former rhythm section, now that the roots reggae the Barretts had helped to popularise over the past decade was being swept away by digital rhythms voiced by dancehall artists like Tenor Saw and Paul Joseph, a.k.a. Paul Plummer, who recorded a number of tracks with the brothers during 1984.

"Family Man lived out the back of 56 Hope Road so it was no problem to actually meet him," Joseph told Simon Buckland. "He's a very humble man, so we made an arrangement to get together for a rehearsal in the music room and then laid down five or so of my original songs, including 'Love Revolution'. I picked out that song for my first release because of the message. The message is very important. It's all right having nice melodies, but through the spirit quickens the flesh, the right lyrics go a long way towards uplifting the mind."

The gentle, rub-a-dub strains of 'Love Revolution' and follow-up single 'Always Loving You' hark back to the arrangements Family Man used on Marley classics like 'Turn Your Lights Down Low', but the

---

* Gil later returned to Jamaica to record an entire album of Marley songs.

material itself wasn't of the same calibre.* British dub poet Benjamin Zephaniah also passed through Tuff Gong during this time.

Benjamin Zephaniah: "It was Bill Gilham of Upright Records who suggested I should go to Jamaica and record my album. In those days we had these big master tapes that were about four inches wide, so I put a couple of them under my arm and went to Jamaica. I was thinking of recording with Burning Spear, so I went round to Tuff Gong and just missed him . . . There were a few other people I had in my mind, like Fred Locks, but then the keyboard player from Third World, Ibo Cooper, suggested I go and work with the Wailers. People in the business knew the Wailers weren't really active at that stage because they were too busy arguing over Bob's money and all of that. There seemed to be all kinds of things going on with them, but Ibo put me in touch with Family Man. I spoke to him on the phone and he said they knew about me. Also, I'd met Bob some years earlier, even though I'd only glimpsed Family Man at the time.

"Anyway, I played him a very rough demo of a track called 'Free South Africa' I'd recorded using just a bass line and my voice and he said there were two ways of doing it. One, we could go in the studio and do it with his brother on drums and they can play everything themselves, or they could put the Wailers back together. He said I wouldn't get the modern Wailers, but they still had Wya Lindo on keyboards and him and his brother on bass and drums, which sounded good enough for me. Rita was running the studio at the time, so he went to see her and I heard there was a bit of a heated argument about it and the rest of the staff were told to leave the room after some big row had developed. I was surprised as anything when Family Man called me back and said, 'Yeah, we're on.' He told me afterwards that he'd been arguing with people who said they weren't going to play until they'd got their money and so he'd said, 'Listen to the brother's track, because it's about South Africa and it's about Mandela, yet here we all are, arguing about money.' He said they should unite for the cause of the record, because it was saying something meaningful and that Bob would have been proud of.

"It was a freedom fighter, conscious lyrics, so they came together and did it. The other thing they said what swung it was the fact I'd come to them with something completely different. I mean there were lots of people

---

* The Barretts are also rumoured to have worked with Lee Perry during this period, although this seems unlikely given the producer's dubious mental state, and Family Man has no recollection of this session ever taking place.

Bad Card

queuing up to front the Wailers back then, but these were all Bob Marley impersonators, y'know? They'd all come and do their versions of 'Is This Love' or 'No Woman No Cry', whereas there was no way anyone could say I was trying to imitate Bob! When I came back, I told Bill the Wailers were playing on the record and he said, 'Are you for real?' Then from I put it on, everyone knew immediately because only Carlton Barrett plays drum rolls like that and to this day, they haven't even got a computer that can sound like him! That whole experience was a really proud moment in my life, but I'd had dealings with Bob already, because when I was a young boy, I sent him a letter that went, 'Dear Bob Marley, I am a poet . . .' I addressed it to 56 Hope Road and he wrote back; can you imagine? He wrote something like, 'Yeah man, nice lyrics, keep it up.' I was just blown away and then to actually work with his band, that was really something . . ."

Jimmy Riley was now well established as a solo act in Jamaica, after recording hits for Sly & Robbie. Having been friends for over 15 years, since Riley's days with the Uniques, he and Family Man began work on an album.

Family Man Barrett: "We decide to work together again and said we'd do an album and then a tour, because he'd never been on tour in his life before! We went out on tour with him a year after the Legend tour. Some of the tracks on that album were done before we left and then we finish it off in early 1985, although we had some little falling out after the tour, so he finish the album with some other musicians, and that spoil what we were originally trying to do with him."

World For Everyone, released by Blue Mountain in 1985, contains several tracks recorded with the Wailers, augmented by another veteran from the 'Watch This Sound' session, guitarist Lloyd Willis. 'Trigger Happy' is one of the standouts as Riley comments on Jamaica's rising level of gun crime, "trigger happy recruits". The songs featuring the Wailers are properly constructed, combining Downie's progressive use of synthesisers with a more old-school flavour, as typified by the Barretts' sensuous, one-drop rhythms and Marvin's bluesy lead guitar. On the evidence of songs like 'Trigger Happy', 'The Little Boy Is Lost', 'You Don't Love Me', and the title track, it would have been interesting to hear an entire album featuring just the Wailers, but Riley fleshed it out with material recorded elsewhere and the opportunity was lost.

Jimmy Riley: "I did lot of great music with the Wailers that still hasn't been released to this day. When Bob died, they asked me to join with the Wailers and I fronted them right through the States. We did shows on

515

both coasts and they all sold out. It was like Bob Marley was there and even Carly start tease me by saying how them think I'm Bob Marley. Fi real! But Rita Marley didn't like that so it had to end because she wouldn't hear nutten about Wailers and Jimmy Riley. It wasn't like I was trying to be Bob, because we didn't even use the name Wailers. We call ourselves the Jimmy Riley Experience, but everybody knew it was them playing, because the sound they get was heavyweight. Those shows were awesome and it was all Jimmy Riley stuff we were doing like 'Majority Rule', 'This Little Boy Is Lost' and 'Tell The Youths The Truth', but because the Wailers were there, people would call out for one or two Bob Marley songs, y'know? That's when I usually do 'Three Little Birds' or 'Jamming' and they would cause havoc 'cause we get five, six encores every night and people couldn't believe it, serious!"

Family Man Barrett: "Yes, because when we were about to do the tour with Jimmy Riley, he tell me the booking agent was getting worried and that Rita had tried to blacklist us. He said the man [Steve Martin] had received a threatening letter from Rita Marley saying we can't use the name Wailers, but we are the Wailers! So we have to fly to New York and when I come in to sign the document, I tell the man, 'Let Rita Marley sue me if she wants, because I cannot impersonate my own self.' The plan was to play one month on the West Coast and another month or so on the East Coast, but then as soon as we get ready to move off, our father went missing. He'd been missing for two days and then they find him dead, chopped up into pieces. He'd been dismembered and decapitated and we still don't know the reason for it. His eyes were bad, but he'd been beaten up physically and then kidnapped. All I know is that our father's death affected Carly and I greatly."

The tragedy of the Barretts' father's death was never solved as the police investigation came to nothing. There was no apparent motive for anyone wanting to brutally kill and butcher an elderly, frail man, who lacked wealth and had no enemies.

While events in the Barretts' personal lives were now taking precedent, the brothers still found time to record several tracks for Munchie Jackson before leaving for New York. Jackson had a 24-track studio in the Bronx, where Peter Tosh and Jacob Miller sometimes used to hang out, and so too Wailers engineer Dennis Thompson. Family Man and Carly laid down a number of tracks there for Keith Hudson, who died of lung cancer in November 1984.

★   ★   ★

Around the same time, Cayman Music Inc brought proceedings in New York against the estate for unpaid royalties relating to certain songs off the *Natty Dread* and *Rastaman Vibration* albums that Danny Sims alleged Marley had credited to various individuals and friends, to avoid them falling within his music publishing agreement with the company. The estate denied these allegations yet Marley's extended contract with Cayman lasted from October 1973 until October 1976, so if the credits listed on the albums in question were to be taken at face value it would appear Marley didn't write any songs during this period.

Allegedly, this process started prior to the release of *Natty Dread*, hence the confusion over the authorship of songs like 'Talkin' Blues', 'Natty Dread' and 'Rebel Music'. The writers would not be awarded the copyrights of these songs, since Tuff Gong Music Co retained ownership and the composers were termed "employers for hire".

Blackwell sided with Marley in his contractual difficulties, saying he understood at the time that Marley had put these songs into other people's names because Sims wasn't paying him royalties. Island, who simply paid mechanical royalties to Tuff Gong for the songs in question, weren't the publisher of the songs (A & M were).

In his autobiography, Don Taylor admitted the credits were "fictitious", as he had assigned the authorship on *Rastaman Vibration* so that Marley (under the guise of Bob Marley Music and Media Aides Ltd, Tortola) would retain the publishing rights while the other names were gifted the performing rights. He and Marley also credited certain songs to "R Marley," which could refer to either Robert or Rita.

For the case, Rita asked for legal assistance from Taylor, who roped in Dick Griffey, the owner of Solar Records and head of the Black Music Association. He, Taylor, Rita and Sims met in Hollywood, where it was agreed that Rita could settle the claim with Cayman and Sims for $900,000. Rita agreed to this at first but then changed her mind.

According to Taylor, it was Rita's generally obstructive attitude that helped Sims get such close friends of Marley's as Skill Cole, Mortimer Planno and Tartar Ford to give depositions against the estate. Cole claimed Marley had been advised by David Steinberg to credit other people with his songs and this is also consistent with others' statements, although there's no proof.

In September 1986, the Mutual Security Merchant Bank approached J. Reid Bingham to represent them and he was duly appointed ancillary administrator and ancillary personal representative of the Marley estate by the courts in New York and Florida. Reid Bingham investigated Cayman's claim on behalf of the estate and termed the wrongful credits "a matter of convenience". He also accepted that Marley had collected and kept the royalties derived from these songs during his lifetime as if they were his own, and because of this the estate considered them part of its assets and not the assets of those individuals Marley had credited them to.

Sims flew Family Man to Los Angeles for a meeting before the trial began but he was soon flown back to Kingston once Sims ascertained the bassist wouldn't be of much help to his case. Family Man admits to becoming interested in songwriting credits only once Rita stopped the Wailers' payments in 1986. If Marley thought someone merited a credit, then Fams didn't question his decision and wouldn't necessarily have known if someone else had made a genuine contribution in any case.

When the Cayman case was brought to trial, Sims gave evidence in both pre-trial depositions and at the trial itself, claiming to have been told of the false crediting in discussions with Rita, her attorney and her accountant, as well as with representatives of Island Records and Almo Music, and Taylor, who testified on behalf of the estate.

The presiding judge summarily dismissed some of Cayman's claims, with the only issue for the jury to determine being whether Sims had learnt that the potential fraud had been committed in or before 1980, since this would affect the question of whether the claims were time-barred or not. The jury decided Sims had known of them previously and so his case was dismissed in January 1988. The judge also ruled that while Marley may have attributed certain compositions to deserving causes – like Tartar, for example – this didn't mean to say that all of the disputed songs had been awarded in a similar fashion.

The confusion surrounding certain songs from the two albums in question continued to resurface, as when Legon Cogill wrote to Zolt and Loomis in November 1988, demanding to know why he wasn't receiving any royalties. Zolt and Loomis referred him to J. Reid Bingham, to whom he wrote a similar letter in February 1989. Reid Bingham replied in April, refuting the claim, pointing out how the copyrights of the songs had been assigned to Marley during his lifetime. Legon didn't pursue the matter any further but Reid Bingham later conceded that his application had been an honest claim.

Life for the Barretts took a serious turn for the worse. During the Legend tour, Rita had asked Family Man to hand over his keys to 56 Hope Road, the studio and pressing plant but he said to wait until they were back in Jamaica. Shortly after returning, Louis Byles, representing the estate's administrators, visited Hope Road and asked why Family Man hadn't replied to his letters. Bearing in mind Family Man's reading difficulties, he may have been confused by any detailed communication, although he had expressed his fears to Rita and been assured he had nothing to worry about. The brothers argued with Byles, questioning his right to address them in such an officious manner and sent him away.

Family Man Barrett: "Louis Byles said to me, 'Your experience here is the past.' So I say, 'No, my experience at 56 Hope Road could never be the past. My experience here is history because I'm the man who set up the deal then work and pay for the place. You may not see my name up there alongside Bob Marley or in the deeds, but we all sacrifice and work on it over the years.' Louis Byles didn't just walk in unannounced or fall out of the sky. It was the government who'd appointed him and Rita . . .

"The arguments had started through Gabby [Williams] really. I wasn't there because I was abroad, but Gabby must have let them know it was Family Man who built this t'ing here with Bob, but they fail to hear, and through Gabby a rage pon them, they ban Gabby and ban me too. Rita sent a message to say I must come and take away all of my things from Tuff Gong. Then, as I make the first trip with my things when I leave there, some people broke in and took away all of my tapes and my car parts. Everything just went missing . . .

"As I leave there, all these thoughts run through my head, like the time Bob was ill in Germany and he ask people all the while to send me and my brother tickets to come visit him, and yet these same people do nothing about it and don't tell us anything. And, meanwhile, I was back in Jamaica at 56 Hope Road, holding the fort otherwise it would have been captured."

Family Man was eventually evicted and barred from 56 Hope Road, where he and Marley had conceived some of the world's best-selling popular music.

Al Anderson: "It's cruel and ridiculous. Family Man lived in the back yard of Hope Road for 10 or 12 years, so how can you take away the man's home? Not only that but they bulldozed where he'd been living. They knocked it down because they wanted to get rid of him, so that he wouldn't be looked upon as a permanent fixture there, which he was. Georgie, Lar, Rennie and Family Man were the essential people around Hope Road because that meant there was always food and also the bass man, who produced all of Bob's music . . ."

It took Family Man three trips to move all of his belongings. He left clutching a cheque and bought a place on Waterloo Avenue, not far from Hope Road, where he lived for the next 20 years. "Then the year after I settle in, that's when I went and did that Reggae Sunsplash tour Synergy promote in Europe," he says. "When I rope back in Al, Tyrone and even Junior Marvin because I say to them, 'When did you last take a vacation and have all of your expenses taken care of? Get a pocket money, go places to play some music, and meet up with people in the business again?' As the Wailers, we couldn't do any better for ourselves at the time and that was a nice tour too, with Black Uhuru, Cornel Campbell, and one or two other artists."

The Wailers weren't the only ones to perform in 1986. Bunny Wailer, who was notoriously reluctant to perform outside of Jamaica, ventured to Los Angeles that summer for a show in Long Beach that had reviewers positively drooling. Rumours that he, Tosh, Constantine "Vision" Walker and Junior Braithwaite were collaborating on new material, were confirmed in December, when 'Music Lesson' b/w 'Nice Time' was released as a Tuff Gong single, credited to the Original Wailers. An album, *Together Again*, was in the offing, arranged by Livingston, who stripped the rhythms from a handful of JAD recordings, got Sly & Robbie to re-record them, then overdubbed new vocals by himself, Tosh, Walker, and Braithwaite, alongside the existing voice of Marley. It was a similar process to the one Sims had used on *Chances Are* – an album of late Sixties tracks overdubbed and released soon after Marley's death, featuring a deceptive recent picture of the artist on the cover. *Chances Are* caused an outcry, and what the Original Wailers had done really wasn't much better, despite Tosh and Livingston's involvement.[*]

Alongside this, Marley's demo recordings of 'Rainbow Country' and 'Natural Mystic' were released on Daddy Kool 12″ singles, courtesy of Lee Perry. Marley's still-growing legions of fans were grateful, but his legacy was being cheapened nonetheless, and Island and the estate took every opportunity to clamp down on similar future ventures.

With Family Man out of the way and the other members all but marginalised, 56 Hope Road was renamed the Bob Marley Museum and officially opened to the public on May 11, 1986, the fifth anniversary of the singer's death. Advertised features included a video room, listening

---

[*] Temporarily shelved amid various legal disputes, *Together Again* wouldn't resurface until 1993, when it was released as *Never Ending Wailers*.

booths, an archive room with library, and a permanent exhibition of photographs, guitars, clothes, tour memorabilia and posters. There was also a separate merchandising section, which sold records, badges, T-shirts and other items (none of which featured the Wailers). The Rastafarian ideals of reggae's first superstar were severely compromised when his music was used to advertise washing powder, alcoholic drinks and even sanitary towels. The Marley rebranding process had begun in earnest.

CHAPTER THIRTY

Hurting Inside

BY 1986, Island's roster of reggae acts had dwindled to just Ini Kamoze and Sly & Robbie. The label developed a passion for African music, releasing albums by the likes of King Sunny Ade, but overlooked Alpha Blondy's *Jerusalem* which became the most artistically successful collaboration between African and Jamaican musicians for some years. Blondy was schooled in Liberia and New York and had fallen under the spell of roots reggae after spending two years recuperating from a nervous breakdown. In 1983 he launched his musical career with songs outlining the political and social struggles in his country and soon developed a reputation for being the Ivory Coast's own Bob Marley. After moving to Paris the following year, he signed to EMI, stirring up controversy with his song 'Apartheid Is Nazism', which likened South Africa to Hitler's Germany. Blondy had jammed with the Wailers in Tel Aviv, and Family Man loved his spirit and readily agreed to back him on sessions, accompanied by a reduced Wailers' line-up of Carly, Lindo, and Marvin, whose lead guitar can be heard wailing passionately on tracks like 'Bloodshed In Africa' and the title track.

Family Man also journeyed to King Jammy's studio during 1986, where he played on two tracks by Michael Rose. Born in Waterhouse, Rose began his career with Jammy, before joining Black Uhuru. Jammy's set-up on St Lucia Road was a hotbed of activity in the wake of hits like Wayne Smith's 'Under Mi Sleng-Teng', which helped to bring Jamaican music into the digital age. The arrival of "the Butcher", as Jammy called Rose, wasn't the event it might have been a few years earlier, but the songs themselves couldn't be ignored quite so easily. 'Can't Be Like Me' (which Rose later re-recorded as 'Be Yourself') was a scathing attacking on Junior Reid, who'd taken over from Rose as Uhuru's lead singer. '(Duck Duck) A Who You', aimed straight at Uhuru founder Duckie Simpson's head, eventually reappeared, completely reworked, on Rose's album for Niney the Observer.

On July 16, Don Taylor sent letters to Mutual Security and also the Jamaican Administrator-General, Edward Seaga, outlining his concern that 1978 documents authorising the transfer of Marley's chief assets to Rita were fraudulent, in that she had actually signed them in 1981. According to an official affidavit, Rita confessed to signing the backdated papers under the direction of Steinberg and Zolt.

Faced with an order from Jamaica's Supreme Court insisting that she should resign her position as head of the estate until the investigations were complete, Rita drafted a formal resignation letter addressed to Louis Byles dated September 11. She was officially dismissed as estate administrator on February 3, 1987.

On December 16, in its capacity as administrator of the estate, the Mutual Security Merchant Bank filed an eight million dollar lawsuit in New York against Steinberg and Zolt, alleging infringements under the RICO Act,[*] claiming the parties "developed and engaged in a pervasive and continuous conspiracy and scheme" to defraud the estate. In March 1987, ancillary administrator J. Reid Bingham was then substituted as the plaintiff in what lawyers refer to as "the 1986 New York action." Additional defendants were named, consisting of companies and individuals connected to either Steinberg or Zolt. Meanwhile, back in Jamaica, Byles had started to think about how he could best convert Marley's assets to cash and even contemplated selling 56 Hope Road, despite the fact it now housed the Bob Marley Museum. The trial itself wouldn't take place for another three years.

Family Man Barrett: "As soon as Rita resigned from her position of administrator, there was a lot of litigation. Our payments suddenly dried up, so I discussed the matter with the other Wailers, and Junior Marvin in particular, because Junior was brought up in England and was well-educated. He became the spokesman for the band during this period, because he had a much greater understanding of these things. Musical matters were left to me, but we knew we had to do something about this latest development, as we had no money."

The Wailers duly applied to intervene in the course of the estate's claims against Steinberg and Zolt. Somewhat ill-advisedly, they claimed they'd been partners with Marley and were therefore entitled to 50 per cent of his earnings. Their application was refused on June 18, 1987 and an appeal dismissed the following January.

---

[*] The RICO Act deals with fraud, negligence and breach of fiduciary duty.

The Wailers toured the Far East in early 1987, and on their return from New Zealand on February 14, they stopped off at Roger Steffens' house in Los Angeles, where they were shown his Marley memorabilia archives and conducted filmed interviews. During the course of these conversations, each was asked to name their favourite Marley song. 'War' was Carly's choice, Downie selected 'Forever Loving Jah', "because we have to", Anderson plumped for 'Roots', because he was there when Marley wrote it. Fams liked "a wide range", although when pressed further, he named 'So Much Things To Say', 'Guiltiness', and 'Get Up, Stand Up'.

Six weeks later, on Good Friday, April 17, Carlton Barrett was murdered at the gate of his Kingston home, at 12 Bridgemount Park Avenue, Kingston 8. Albertine had sent Carly out for some jerk chicken, although since it was a public holiday, this meant he'd had to drive some distance to find any. The gates to his house had to be manually locked and unlocked, requiring getting out of the car. That day, he'd left them open so he could drive straight back in. Carly and Albertine also kept four Dobermans to guard the property, although they were locked up and nowhere to be seen. Bridgemount Park Avenue was a cul-de-sac, so there was no passing traffic. The gunman had therefore either lain in wait by the house, or followed Carly as he drove up Stony Hill Road. Carly's distinctive silver BMW had a rainbow sticker and picture of Haile Selassie I on the rear. As the drummer approached the gate, he saw it was locked. Carly stopped the car to get out, just as the gunman appeared by his side and shot him twice in the head. Albertine's daughter, who was a year younger than Carly's first son, Errol, heard the gunshot and after looking out of the window, cried out that someone had shot "Daddy".

Family Man Barrett: "I was up in the hills in Mount James. I just sit up there, smoke a little spliff, drink some juice and then just crash. I drop asleep by the radio and me hear the name Barrett mentioned, but me never hear the first name them a call through me half asleep, so me haffi listen out fi it again. When them repeat it again and say, 'Carlton Barrett was shot and killed,' me sit up straight away, and when I go to stand up, I fall straight back down, 'cause my arms and legs, them a lock up, y'know? This happened just two years after my father was murdered. I was in a state of shock, deep depression and fear, because my brother and I were extremely close. Carly was irreplaceable, not only as a brother, but also as the drummer for the Wailers. We formed such a strong team and there is a constant void without him in the music now that I am alone."

Within two weeks, Albertine and her lover Glenroy Carter, a 34-year-old taxi operator, would be charged with murder. The man suspected of committing the killing, Junior Neil, a.k.a. "Bang", was still at large.

Family Man Barrett: "I had to go to the police station and become a detective myself, 'cause the police couldn't find out what was going on and didn't know how to deal with these things. Most of the cops don't know to investigate. I went to the police station one morning at 10 o'clock and didn't leave there 'til 3.30 the following morning. When I left there [Albertine] was in jail and also the guy who it was claimed planned it with her and it was only the hit man who wasn't there yet. I went into his neighbourhood with a cop, thinking maybe we could dust him out, but I wasn't really meditating on it so much."

Family Man returned to the house on Bridgemount Park Avenue to safeguard Carly's belongings, but found his brother's room locked.

"I go round there and tell whoever's there that I am Carly's brother and ask them if they have the keys to his room," he continues. "They say [Albertine] has it, but the police didn't find any key pon her and nobody at the house knew anything, so I walk into the kitchen and see a whole bunch of keys hanging up there. I take them up, and then go to his room, open the door and when I click the light on, I see this doll sat in a rocking chair with pins sticking out of it, like some voodoo business. I see another doll with pins in it on the bed and also candles, incense, and more pins lying about. It was pure obeah in there and so I build a fire out back and burn the whole lot of it."

Carly had met Albertine shortly after Errol was born in the early Seventies. "Derrick Harriott had a shop called One Stop in King Street, and that's where he see her for the first time," says Family Man. "I remember [Carly] say how good she look in her pants suit an' t'ing. After a while, I see her come around the shop in Beeston Street and discover it's Bob she come for, but it's like Bob make a one move with her and then he shun her quick! I still see her around after that and I remember buying her some food one time, and then another time I go to buy her another food when I realise it's my brother she come for. I was surprised, because he'd already seen how Bob never treat her too good. It was shortly after that some guys tell me she is nothing but trouble and through I notice how she is always out there on the street, I don't contradict none of them."

After the Barretts' father died, the whole family rallied round to help, but Family Man had to shoulder most of the responsibilities alone after Carly was killed, due to in-fighting between various relatives and discrepancies in distributing his assets. In addition to playing detective,

Family Man had to surrender the deeds to his farm in St James in order to pay for the funeral and was deeply saddened by the reaction of Island Records and the Marleys.

"Island Records never even call me," Fams says, shaking his head. "They give me nothing! Rita says she nah have any money either, and Ms Booker gave me a hundred dollar. I can remember that one hundred dollar, because I just take it and give it to the bus driver who carried people to the funeral at Dovecote. Me never want it, because me done borrow money from the bank already, y'see?"

Family Man says there wasn't a great deal of attention paid to his brother's death in Jamaica, apart from one or two radio tributes. There was no stage show and the Marley estate didn't do anything to commemorate his passing either. In fact, there's still nothing in the Bob Marley Museum to mark his important contributions, some 20 years later.

In an obituary for *Echoes*, Ian McCann wrote that Carly's "syncopated playing added a new dimension to the music. His one drop was steadier than anyone else's, somehow he could play less than anyone else and still make it sound like more, keeping you waiting for the rim shot that resolved the rhythmical puzzle. There will never be another drummer exactly like Carly, or another rhythm section like the Barrett brothers. With Carlton Barrett's death, a certain part of reggae, a certain sound has died."

Anderson, who calls Carly, "the best reggae drummer on the planet," feels the balance and the sound of the Wailers changed out of all recognition after his death and that the band has never been the same without him. He pertinently adds that since Carly was more outspoken and articulate than the other band members, he therefore constituted more of a threat to anyone wishing to exclude the Wailers from Marley's legacy, in both the monetary and musical sense.

The three charged in connection with Carly's murder were remanded in custody, although Albertine would soon be granted bail. Her first court appearance was on September 16. On April 6, 1988 (the same day an official representing the Reagan administration commended Jamaica's efforts in eradicating the ganja trade, singling out Edward Seaga for special praise), she had her bail extended to June 20. On June 16, after Miss Justice McKain granted an adjournment following a joint application by the Crown and the defence, it was announced that the trial would start on July 26. By this stage, Albertine was being represented by attorney-at-law Tom Tavares Finson, who was now married to Cindy Breakspeare. The quest for justice would prove lengthy and convoluted. The trial date was further adjourned to October 5, then November 21. On that date, the Deputy Director of Public Prosecutions informed the court there was a new indictment in respect of Junior Neil, who had been charged with the actual murder, but would now be indicted for conspiracy to murder and tried at a later date. Neil was duly remanded in custody until January 9, 1989.

The defence had objected to cautioned statements by Albertine and Glenroy Carter being tendered as evidence. The pair had given these statements to police officers immediately after the shooting and, in them, confessed to having plotted Carly's death. The judge was asked to rule on their admissibility (they were refused) and the announcement was made that the trial would take place behind closed doors. The jury failed to arrive at a unanimous verdict at the first trial and so Mr Justice Patterson ordered a retrial and remanded Albertine and Carter in custody, although Albertine was later granted bail of JA $25,000 on condition she surrender her travel documents to the police and report to Constant Spring police station twice a week. The retrial then commenced on December 23, 1988, more than 18 months after the murder. The crown alleged the two accused had made plans to kill Carly and, while they admitted to being lovers, both denied having committed the offence. In the end, Albertine and her boyfriend escaped the murder charge and were convicted and sentenced to seven years each for conspiracy to murder. After spending just over a year in prison, they were acquitted and released in December 1992.

Family Man Barrett: "The gunman, he was a fool but his days were already numbered because I heard that someone got him later. He gave my brother two bullets and he got 16. Live by the sword and die by it."

Carly's last recording session was with Robbie Shakespeare on a song by Dennis Brown and Gregory Isaacs called 'Let Off Supm', produced by Gussie Clarke at Music Mountain. Carly also played on other Brown tracks at the studio, including some for Trevor Bow's Natty Congo label. His final recording with the Wailers, apart from a rehearsal session on April 10, was the appropriate 'Have Faith In Jah'. Shortly after, Brent Clarke released the Wailers' *Tribute To Carly Barrett* on Atra, which was little more than a rehash of the *Kingston Rock* album, remixed by Fat Man, Ribs from Unity, and the Mad Professor. It wasn't all that characteristic of Carly's talents, but since the Marley estate chose not to get involved, Carly's contributions to Marley's legacy would go relatively unheralded.

On September 11, 1987, the Wailers arrived in London from Jamaica to the news that Peter Tosh had been brutally murdered in cold blood. Tosh lived in a large house on Plymouth Avenue in the Barbican district of Kingston. That evening, he'd been relaxing and watching television in an upstairs living room with his common law wife Marlene Brown, Carlton "Santa" Davis, the herbalist Wilton "Doc" Brown, and friend Michael Robinson. There was a knock at the door at around 7.30 pm. Robinson went downstairs and let in three men, since he recognised one of them, Dennis "Leppo" Lobban, as being an old friend of Tosh's from Trenchtown and a regular visitor to the house. Much to his surprise, Robinson was led up the stairs at gunpoint and motioned, ashen-faced into the sitting room, whereupon the three men pulled out their guns and told everyone to "belly it", i.e. lie face down on the floor. Santa thought they were joking at first, but was soon jolted out of his complacency.

Leppo asked about money, saying, "Oonu just come from foreign and have nuff foreign currency," but Tosh insisted there wasn't any in the house. As the men began snatching up whatever money and jewellery they could find, there was another knock at the door. Local radio deejay Free I and his wife Joy had come to visit Tosh, and they too were escorted upstairs and robbed. In the meantime, Leppo had gone into an adjoining bedroom, found a machete, and held it to Tosh's throat, demanding money and threatening to kill him. Marlene started protesting and was told to shut up, while Free I's wife was hit over the head with a gun butt as she panicked in fright. One of the men told Tosh he was about to die. There'd been rumours the police had stopped the singer and found a weapon on him, but that Leppo had taken the rap, although none of the men made any mention of this and seemed only to be interested in money. Threats turned to direct action when Tosh, Doc Brown, and Free I were each shot in the head as they lay face down on the floor. As soon as the men fled, Marlene called for help. Tosh was rushed to University Hospital at Mona, but died shortly after arrival, Doc Brown died at the scene and Free I died three days later, having received two bullet wounds to the back to his skull.

The circumstances surrounding Tosh's funeral and burial arrangements proved almost farcical, since a court had to decide who should take responsibility for his body after his mother Alvira Coke, his estranged father Alfred McIntosh, and Marlene all claimed rights to it. In addition to this, a man called James McIntosh appeared on the scene, alleging he was Tosh's real father, although Alvira disputed this claim, saying she'd never seen him before. Mrs Coke was finally granted custody of her son's body and a thanksgiving service was held on Saturday, September 26 at the National Arena, where Tosh lay in state from noon until four in the afternoon. The Reverend Kes Estafanus of the Ethiopian Orthodox Church officiated at the ceremony. The body was then driven to Tosh's home town of Belmont in Westmoreland, for burial in the family plot. Alfred, who hadn't met with his son until long after Peter had become an adult, then objected to the gravesite, because he claimed Alvira had kept pigs on the plot. Alvira admitted to keeping pigs in the near vicinity but insisted they'd been kept some distance away. Peter was thus laid to rest, as Kingston police examined the circumstances of his death.

They couldn't establish a clear motive for the killings, but were working on the premise "that it was the result of a feud between some of the victims and the gunmen." Forces had been mobilising against Tosh a while before his death and it wasn't just repercussions from the past that brought him closer to danger. Peter and Marlene, who was handling Tosh's affairs by this stage, had been warned that people were out to kill them. Tosh had become obsessed by evil spirits and claimed to have seen 49 ghosts, or duppies in his house. Such visions had led him towards seeking protection, although since "Rasta nuh fear," he'd declined to do this by more conventional methods, like informing the police (whom he believed wanted him dead anyway) or putting additional security measures in place. Tosh had expressed these concerns to a bush doctor he'd consulted in Nigeria and been given a roots drink that was supposed to grant him the power to change his form and thus escape bullets. The visit changed him. People say he grew more sombre and increasingly distant from friends and colleagues after returning to Jamaica, and that he'd "lost the mystic." Tosh complained he was tired of the music business, of being used, and talked of forces plotting to "assassinate those who speak the truth."

"Peter went off the rails when him get mixed up with the underworld," claims Alton Ellis, "and when it came out, it came out too drastic, 'cause 'im lose his life, y'know? But he was in touch with the underworld, selling out those guys who do things to other people, and you can't be mixed up in those things y'understand? But it was the vanity what came in between, and it just diminish people's true desire really . . ."

"To have the truth in your possession, you can be found guilty and sentenced to death," Tosh proclaimed, after announcing that he'd been sent "to help alleviate the dirt, filth, and corruption" promoted by the system. He claimed his people had been inoculated with a powerful virus that had brainwashed and corrupted them, and that "it's only the truth that can set a man free and let a man live."

Like Tosh, Free I believed in upliftment and black consciousness. Tosh had supported his friend's bid to launch an independent radio station for the express purpose of promoting black music and culture. Many still believe this was the cause of their deaths, as Jamaican society wasn't ready for such a station as the authorities believed it would create unrest. Tosh knew that Jamaica's ruling elite was scared of Rastafarians gaining influence over the country's poorer classes, but had remained staunchly defiant.

"I'm going to kill the fuckery out there and people are going to be demanding the truth," he told a group of reporters. "People are sick and tired of hearing bumbaclaat get down shit and shake your booty. People are sick and tired of hearing, 'Darling, I bloodclaat love you.'"

Radio was the ideal medium for disseminating ideas and information via speech based programmes, as well as music. Despite its popularity overseas, reggae music still wasn't being played to any great extent on Jamaica's two existing radio stations and certainly not Rasta music like that of Tosh, which, in his own words, was intended to "stir and strengthen the oppressed and to take away all pain and sorrow." He and Free I knew that the large numbers of black Jamaicans that couldn't read or write would immediately benefit from programmes informing them about their own cultural history and the ideas of men like Emperor Haile Selassie I and Marcus Garvey. Their station would thus offer an antidote to the propaganda spread about Rastafarians by those in authority, who regularly used violence against them.

Tosh lived according to his beliefs, and the central tenets of his music never changed. During his adolescence in Trenchtown, he came to believe the system was designed to keep Rastas down. Word, sound, and power were thus key weapons in mounting a challenge to Jamaica's leaders, whom Tosh considered little different to Jamaica's past colonial rulers.

Such thinking made him a threat to the Jamaican political establishment, just as Marley had been in the run-up to the 1976 election. After the devestating loss of his partner Yvonne Whittingham, he became more emboldened than ever. The relentless pursuit of his convictions brought Tosh problems all the while, even when signed to the Rolling Stones' label. Like Marley, he felt his music deserved parity with white rock music, especially since it dealt with moral upliftment and cultural values. When it wasn't promoted to his liking, he became outspoken, since he refused to compromise his ideals in order to make money or pursue fame. "I come with earthquake, lightning and thunder to break down these barriers of oppression, drive away transgression and rule equality between humble black people," he railed. No one could accuse him of having ever done otherwise.

Shortly before his death, Tosh recorded a number of private, devastatingly honest monologues which would later form the basis of a film *Red X: Stepping Razor*, directed by Wayne Jobson. He talked about his illegitimate birth and his mother being too poor to give him a proper education, "but my ambition and determination, my hopes and my aspirations, and my inner concept of creativity that was born in me showed me to help myself, and I did." Tosh's ghetto education had taught him to "multiply nothing with nothing and get something; zero with zero and get one," and how Jesus was white and, because he was black, this meant Tosh had been born into sin and iniquity. Eventually, after moving from rural Westmoreland to Kingston, he saw through the lies and hypocrisy and realised how black history had been suppressed. Such knowledge was gained the hard way, since "the most dangerous things I ever see or heard in my life is when I find myself in Trenchtown," he said. "I see many youths become victims of the shit-stem. I see them die, I see them cry." Many became lost in fantasy and, like Leppo, grew increasingly unhinged as they entered a life of crime and drugs.

On September 17, news reports suggested two men had been detained in connection with the murders, but their names weren't released. Police issued a warrant for a third suspect, who they named as Dennis "Leppo" Lobban of Ninth Street, Kingston 12. He was described as 33 years old, 5′ 8″, and "scarred on the left forearm and left cheek." A police spokesman said he was considered armed and dangerous and to be approached with caution. Fearing for his safety, Leppo gave himself up the following day and went to the offices of the Jamaica Human Rights Council in Kingston, claiming he'd been at a shop in Jones Town on the night of the murders. The police disagreed and in the presence of a lawyer, formally charged him with three counts of murder, robbery with aggravation, illegal possession of a firearm and four counts of shooting with intent at Marlene, Yvonne Dixon, Michael Robinson and Santa. Lobban was found to have eight previous convictions stretching back to 1971, including vagrancy, robbery with aggravation, assault with intent to rob and wounding with intent. On his last visit to court, in July 1974, he was sentenced to 25 years' hard labour, although he'd only served 12 years and five months of this sentence before being paroled in October 1986.

Leppo's trial was initially scheduled for April 19, 1988, but the defence experienced difficulty in preparing witness statements and were duly granted more time. A new trial date of June 13 was set in the Home Circuit Court, where Lobban – described as a "dub poet and haggler" – was jointly charged with 26-year-old Steve Russell, also known as "Honey". Russell worked as a purchasing clerk for a firm in Spanish Town and in a statement made at the Gun Court he admitted taking Lobban and two others to the house on the evening in question. He said a co-worker had asked him to give three men a ride and, after pulling up outside a house in the Barbican, the men had requested he wait for them while they ran an errand. Russell said he started to drive away after hearing shots coming from the house, but the three men ran outside and forced their way back into the van before ordering him to drive off. Russell's story was obviously believable, since he was freed on June 16, after the judge upheld a no-case submission made by his attorneys.

Eleven people testified during the five-day hearings. The judge had denied press permission to report the trial, although Lobban's lawyer made several complaints about breaches having taken place. Such protests fell on deaf ears and he was referred to the Director of Public Prosecutions on each occasion. On June 17, the jury took just six minutes to reach a verdict of guilty. Mr Justice Patterson sentenced Lobban to hang after imposing the death sentence on him, informing the court, "I would have arrived at the same verdict. I have no doubt in my mind that he went there that night and killed Tosh and the others. It was just by chance that the other four survived or we would have had seven people lying dead."

Leppo was taken to Spanish Town prison and left to await his fate on death row, although he later appealed to the Privy Court in London and had the sentence commuted to life imprisonment. The other two killers were never identified, although friends of Tosh say the men were subsequently shot and murdered by unknown assailants.

CHAPTER THIRTY-ONE

Fussing And Fighting

IN the Wailers' absence, Tuff Gong's roster of artists continued making records under the stewardship of Sangie Davis and Bob Andy. The latter joined the label in November 1987 as their A&R and Promotions Director, and represented Tuff Gong Music at many industry functions in Jamaica and abroad, in addition to producing music by such artists as Nadine Sutherland, Ernest Wilson, and Tyrone Taylor. A cultured singer/songwriter in his own right, Andy made an articulate spokesman for Tuff Gong and helped raise standards at the company, both in its business operations and in the quality of its musical output.

Family Man was forced to watch from the sidelines, as he was still devastated by the loss of his brother. The Wailers went into a tailspin for a while. There was talk of them touring with Lee Perry, after Family Man visited him at his girlfriend's house in London. On that occasion, Perry gave Family Man some money for his children back in Jamaica but legend has it that Scratch then cancelled plans for the tour after a CD Family Man had given him jammed in his player. Two years previous, the increasingly eccentric producer had released a track, 'Judgment In A Babylon', with lyrics accusing Chris Blackwell of being a vampire and claiming Blackwell had given Marley cancer, killing him "for telling the truth." Tosh would have no doubt approved, but most onlookers merely shook their heads and deliberated over the decline of a once-mighty talent.

In 1988, Family Man and Downie went into the new Tuff Gong studio on Marcus Garvey Drive with Little Roy and contributed several tracks to his *Live On* album, namely 'Without My Love', 'Jamming To Jah Music', 'Hobby', and a recut of 'Mr T'. Family Man was rejuvenated by the experience, but his joy was shortlived when yet another death within Jamaica's musical fraternity cast a pall. In February 1989, King Tubby was gunned down in the driveway of his home in Duhaney Park, not far from where Fams had once shared a house with Niney the Observer. His killer robbed Tubby of his watch, gold chain and licensed gun, and with one senseless act of violence, ended the life of Jamaica's greatest-ever mixing engineer. His passing marked the closing of an era, as did the sale of Island Records to Polygram for an estimated £272 million. Blackwell stayed on as director for a further eight years and while Island's reputation as a home for off-the-wall, innovative acts was diminished, his interest in cementing Marley's legend status continued unabated.

Jamaican law makes no provision for the assets of an intestate's estate to be held upon trust for sale, so in October 1987, the Mutual Security Bank had applied to the Jamaican court for directions as to whether it was legally required to sell whatever belonged to the Marley Estate. The court informed the bank that it was their duty, and so on April 27, 1988 Mutual Security entered a conditional agreement to offload certain assets, including various music rights, to Island Logic Inc. This company, like Island Records, belonged to Island International Limited, based in the Bahamas. Mutual Security issued an originating summons on May 5, seeking an order that this conditional agreement be confirmed, subject to any modifications the court saw fit.

Blackwell says that there were many discussions regarding the best way in which to safeguard Marley's legacy, and that several parties had expressed interest in buying the estate's assets. His original proposal was for Island to purchase the estate outright, as outlined in the agreement he'd presented to Mutual Security in 1988, before the sale to Polygram.

When this proposition met with a number of legal challenges (including one from the Marleys) he reopened discussions with the Marley family and proposed that Island lend them the money to purchase the assets themselves. In essence, the agreement provided that Island would manage the catalogue for a specified period and thereafter the assets would be owned and managed by the Marley beneficiaries. The latter had initially objected to the sale, and when their objections were overridden in December 1988, they appealed to the Privy Council, which referred the matter back to the Jamaican courts who would not announce their decision until December 1991. This in turn resulted in the 1992 Sales Agreement, naming the joint purchasers of the estate as Island Logic and the adult beneficiaries of the Marley estate.

Meanwhile, on December 19, 1989, the Mutual Security Bank assigned such title as it had to the writer's share, performance royalties, and copyright in compositions originally attributed to the Barrett brothers to Island Logic, meaning that Blackwell once again controlled a significant chunk, even before the sale went through. Taylor was furious that Rita had effectively handed the estate back. According to his former manager, Marley's goal was to honour his commitment to Island and he had been on the brink of achieving this when he died, so the rights to his music would have reverted back after a period of so many years. Marley was set to prosper as an independent recording artist and producer and had left a generous enough legacy for all of his dependents, including former band members. It was Taylor's belief that had the estate's affairs been administrated properly from the beginning, then the Marleys wouldn't have had to ask Blackwell for financial aid in acquiring it.

Once they'd absorbed what was happening between Mutual Security, Blackwell, and the Marleys, the Wailers consulted their lawyers and began two legal actions of their own. The first took place in Jamaica during January 1989, over Mutual Security's attempt to sell the estate's assets without the band's involvement. Like their previous action, the suit alleged that the members had been in a partnership with Marley ("Bob Marley & the Wailers") and were therefore due a share of all recording and publishing rights, product licensing, merchandising, performance rights, and any profits and losses arising from these. In his affidavit, Marvin, who'd led this latest action, stated that, "most of the songs performed by the partnership were written by Bob Marley, but some were co-written by members of the Wailers and this entitled those members to songwriting royalties as well." Marley had managed this partnership and also negotiated and executed contracts on their behalf. Mutual Security denied this and reasserted their bid to sell the estate's assets.

In April, the Wailers applied for a freezing order preventing Mutual Security from doing so, but the latter countered that Marley had paid the band "such remuneration as their services had warranted" and "without complaint from any of them." Mutual Security also counterclaimed for the monies paid to the Wailers under the terms of the 1981 agreement.

The freezing order was granted on an interim basis and was renewed from time to time, but was ultimately discharged in favour of a replacement order restraining the estate from disposing of half the proceeds derived from record royalties for a certain period. The Wailers weren't claiming 50 per cent of the assets on this occasion but just a share of the proceeds from any sales.

The Wailers' other legal action commenced in New York's US District Court on August 9, 1989. The defendants were Island Logic Inc and Island Inc. By now, Island Logic had provisionally acquired certain assets of the Marley estate from Mutual Security by conditional agreement.

Island Inc had been party to the 1975 Recording Agreement, which Marvin stated was "exceedingly significant" in determining the relationship between Marley and some of the Wailers, i.e. Family Man. This latest action again claimed there was a partnership and therefore they were entitled to royalties generated by record sales and other sources of music-related income. On November 2, the 1989 New York Action was stayed pending the outcome of the 1989 Jamaican Action, which prompted a frustrated Louis Byles to request the Jamaican courts reach their decision with due haste.

Taylor, who watched such manoeuvrings with interest, mentioned the pertinent fact that although Marley had controlled a great deal of money during his lifetime, he'd aroused few conflicts. He'd kept his business simple and paid out very little money to lawyers and accountants, while treating his associates generously. Taylor also expressed the opinion that Marvin had acted hastily by dragging Family Man and Carly into the latest legal actions, because Rita disliked him, and so refused to play ball. Despite his views, Taylor testified on the Wailers' behalf, since he thought it wrong they should be deprived of a share in the Marley millions. Blackwell disagreed and said as much in his witness statement.

"Following Bob's death, my firm view, which I expressed to the surviving members of the band, was that they should disband and get on with their own careers, rather than trying to keep touring and recording under the Wailers name. In my view, Bob was the key person behind the band's creativity and popularity. I expressed this view to the band and said that the Wailers were like a frame with the picture removed, although this view was not well-received at the time."

Although Family Man was getting performance royalties from ASCAP for the songs Marley had credited him with, he found the blizzard of litigation confusing and, to complicate things further, Bunny Wailer also entered the fray by contesting their right to call themselves the Wailers, just as Rita had done when the members first toured with Jimmy Riley.

Family Man Barrett: "The whole of them give us problems because both Rita and Bunny Wailer were against us at that time. I remember going to Studio One and Mr Dodd asking me what was going on. I tell him we are still on the road and trying to put out an album just to let the people know we are still about as Wailers, but that Bunny Wailer is giving us a real fight about it and he said, 'What? But you have even more right than Bunny, because it's you who take the name international.' I was surprised when he said that, but one of his brethren get up and say, 'Fams, it was a different set of guys we had with us here, training to be a success in the business, because when they were introduced to us, they'd never had a hit yet, and it was Coxsone who called them Wailers.' That's how come I get the blessing from the man himself and from I hear that now, I get strong . . ."

The album Fams is referring to was *I.D.*, the debut album by the Wailers Band, released on Atlantic courtesy of Oscar Cohen, who'd been Marley's booking agent in the US. Most of it had been recorded at Kashif's Marathon Studios in New York and the remainder at Dynamic, since both Tuff Gong studios were now out of bounds. The band financed more than half the £150,000 recording costs out of their own pockets before signing the Atlantic deal. Mikey "Boo" Richards took over from Carly on drums while Seeco and Downie were replaced by Martin Batista and Third World's Irvin "Carrot" Jarrett on keyboards and percussion. Marvin sang the majority of lead vocals and wrote or co-wrote all but one of the 12 tracks that featured a bright, modern, electro-reggae sound. Wailers originals like 'Irie', 'Reggae Love', 'Rice And Peas', and 'Solutions' did the band's reputation no harm since they were squarely aimed at a multi-racial, international audience and skilfully tailored for playing live.

In an interview with *Echoes*' Ian McCann, Marvin said the band had spent the last seven years organising the album, "trying to get our writing ability to as high a standard as possible. Apart from legal things, we spent much of the time trying to choose from 300 songs. The thing is, when Bob died it was a big lull both for us and for reggae. We missed him a lot and didn't know exactly where to turn, or what direction to move in. Bob's wish was for us to stay together and so we did that by doing tribute gigs and the Legend tour in 1984; also Reggae Sunsplash in 1986. This was without a record label and it was very difficult for us, because we had to prove ourselves all over again. People felt that Bob was everything in the band even though he himself used to say 'I'm a Wailer. I'm not Bob Marley & the Wailers.'"

A similar line-up with Boo on drums, Carrot on percussion, and Downie back in the fold, played on Joe Higgs' album *Blackman Know Yourself*, recorded at New York's Green Street Studios and released on Shanachie in 1990. Lee Jaffe was credited as co-producer along with Higgs, although Family Man claims Jaffe never showed up while they were in the studio. Writer Randall Grass commented on "the rightness" of these sessions, describing the music as flowing "like vintage wine – pure, easy, and fine."

Higgs chose to cover songs by the Gladiators and the Wailers (including 'Small Axe' and 'Sun Is Shining'), as well as reworking several of his own compositions, most notably 'Sons Of Garvey', 'Wages Of War', 'Steppin' Razor', and the title track. The result is one of Higgs' best albums, on which "simplicity", as Grass so accurately points out, "yields eloquence."

As well as playing guitar on *Blackman Know Yourself* Marvin also began work on another album with Roger Mayer, over a decade after their aborted *Bionic* set. Some of the tracks were laid at Music Mountain with Sly Dunbar, before Mayer overdubbed them at New York's Electric Ladyland. Despite his multiple roles as the Wailers' lead singer, chief song-writer, and acting manager, Marvin occasionally harboured thoughts of a solo career, but increasingly devoted himself to the Wailers' cause.

As expected, the I-Threes aligned themselves with Rita, although Mowatt was notching up solo hits like 'Guilty' for Mikey Bennett's Two Friends label and Griffiths released her *Carousel* album on Island. The label teamed her with the Miami Sound Machine in the wake of 'Electric Boogie' and it was the closest she came to making outright pop music but after failing to engage with the crossover market, Griffiths soon returned to Donovan Germain's Penthouse label and her more familiar reggae style. Rita, meanwhile, was finishing tracks for a new solo venture and continued to oversee the Melody Makers, who'd just released their debut album, *Play The Game Right*, on EMI.

In 1990, Island embarked on a reissue and remastering programme of the entire Bob Marley catalogue that took a year to complete. Blackwell had recently installed Neville Garrick as head of the Bob Marley Foundation, which had been set up to look after the interests of the estate, and to prevent lawyers from growing rich off it. The Foundation's aim was to gather all Marley-related merchandising under one legal banner and to halt all unofficial and unlicensed use of the Marley name. In support of this, Bob Marley Music Inc, the company responsible for licensing his image to outside retailers, would soon include the following message on their advertising material: "Portions of the proceeds from sales will go to help preserve and support Bob Marley's personal, musical and social legacies in Jamaica and around the world." Marley's business interests were being given an ethical spin, convincing consumers that the activities of his estate reflected Marley's ideals, despite the wealth of moneymaking schemes that would soon engulf his legacy.

One of the first projects from the new arrangement was the release of *Talkin' Blues*, a live studio album recorded in San Francisco during 1973, when Joe Higgs was a member of the Wailers, released to coincide with what would have been Marley's 46th birthday on February 6, 1991. After attending the Namibian independence celebrations with the Melody Makers, Rita flew to Los Angeles for the city's annual Bob Marley Day festivities, while taking the opportunity to promote her new album *We Must Carry On*. Concerts had been held in Los Angeles to commemorate Bob Marley Day ever since his death and the 1991 event lasted two days, drawing crowds of over 20,000 people. Ragamuffin Promotions agreed to use the profits to fund a Bob Marley star on the Hollywood Walk of Fame. This involved potential candidates being nominated by a business associate or family member, then voted on and approved by the Hollywood Walk of Fame Committee. Once accepted, a star could cost thousands of dollars to have installed, although there was no shortage of supporters, since Ragamuffin soon gathered over 40,000 signatures in support of Rita's application.

February 6 was also declared Bob Marley Day in Jamaica that year, marked by Governor General Sir Florizel Glasspole presenting Rita with an official proclamation at a special ceremony held in Kingston. Things had certainly changed from the days when Marley and Cole would have to threaten radio deejays before they'd play Marley's songs, and while he probably wouldn't have welcomed the Governor General's attentions, Bob would have been heartened by the news that the Foundation had begun donating funds to the ANC and the Ethiopian Orthodox Church. A television special featuring star guests in concerts was also planned, the proceeds of which were intended for a Bob Marley Scholarship Fund which would enable two Jamaican students a year to avail themselves of a US college education. Unfortunately, because the affairs of the estate were still unsettled during this time, plans for a music school were rejected on the grounds that day-to-day administration costs would prove expensive.

Bunny Lee caused a stir when he issued an album entitled *All The Hits*, containing early Wailers self-productions like 'Hypocrites', 'Nice Time', 'Thank You Lord', and 'Mellow Mood'. Production was credited to Bunny, as "licensed from Rita Marley." In addition to reissuing 'One Love'/'People Get Ready' on a 12″ single, Island organised a major collection of Marley-related artwork at the Special Photographers Company in Kensington Park Road, London, on April 10, called simply Bob Marley: An Exhibition. Featured photographers included Adrian Boot, Dennis Morris, and Kate Simon while Garrick was among those contributing graphics. After its premiere in London, the exhibition travelled to various US cities, including New York and Los Angeles, then headed for Japan and galleries in Europe, including an appearance at Expo 92 in Seville. It then returned to the UK later that year and was shown in several cities throughout Britain before ending up at the Bob Marley Museum in Jamaica, where many of the exhibits remain.

As the exhibition travelled across the States, the Marleys launched an official Bob Marley clothing line and, at a press conference in Rome, Rita, Cedella, Mrs Booker, Julian, and Stephen Marley made public their decision to bid for the Marley estate. Cedella Booker had recently under-taken a promotional visit to the UK to announce her forthcoming book and an album of songs recorded in Paris. The previous year she'd almost been evicted from her house in Miami which Marley had bought for her in 1978. He'd argued with Taylor over the terms of its purchase since he'd wanted his manager to pay for it in cash, so his mother owned the property "free and clear". Taylor arranged a mortgage instead. Apparently, Rita had been giving Mrs Booker money for its upkeep, but the payments had ceased after she was deposed as administrator of the estate. Blackwell stepped in and paid off the outstanding mortgage costs, totalling some $60,000.

On July 16, 1991, a panel of judges met in Jamaica to decide who would own the Bob Marley estate, since while his immediate family had become beneficiaries, they weren't inheritors. Three years earlier, Blackwell offered $8.2 million for the estate and had effectively been managing it ever since, but the Privy Council instructed Mutual Security to re-advertise for bids on appeal by members of the Marley family, who considered Blackwell's initial offer too low. The new date for the Jamaica Supreme Court ruling was October 28, 1992. MCA and several of the Marley children (including Cindy Breakspeare's son Damian) duly offered $15.2 million for the assets, which included publishing rights to Marley's Island work, the property at 56 Hope Road, and the Tuff Gong label and pressing plant. Blackwell, now in collaboration with the Marley family, then matched this offer, although not in straight cash terms. Blackwell managed to reinstate his company's offer after threatening Mutual Security with legal action, since the bank had initially refused to present his bid to the Jamaican Supreme Court.

Pascalene Bongo, daughter of the President of Gabon, also made a bid for the estate, supported by Marley's mother, who invited her to Jamaica for that purpose. When the bid failed, Mrs Booker shifted her allegiance to Blackwell, who was high in her estimation after he'd saved her home. At one stage, she also sided with Yvette Morris after Morris claimed one of her children was Marley's.* Blackwell's bid was finally accepted, a decision that prompted yet more legal action after it was questioned why the lesser bid won. Blackwell had managed to convince the adjudicators that the MCA bid would take ownership of the estate out of Jamaica, whereas he would not only keep it in Jamaica, but also within Marley's family. The issue was further complicated by the fact that since Island took control of the estate, their reactivation of Tuff Gong and reissue programme had increased the estate's value (in Blackwell's own estimation) by at least $3.5 million.

Plans had already been announced for a film celebrating Marley's life with a working title of *Catch A Fire*. Island had wanted Billy Wilmot (lead singer with the Mystic Revealers) to play the lead role, but he reportedly turned down the offer after learning he wouldn't be allowed to perform his own songs.† A 90-minute documentary, directed by Declan Lowney, called *Time Will Tell: The Life And Music Of Bob Marley* was first screened at London's Bijou Preview Cinema on Wardour Street on March 30, 1992 and opened at the Prince Charles Theatre just over a fortnight later. Shortly before its US premiere in Santa Monica, May 11 was declared Bob Marley Day in Toronto, where Mrs Booker accepted the proclamation at the city hall and appeared on Canadian television, singing 'Selassie Is The Chapel'. Her latest album, *Smilin' Island Of Song*, a collection of "favourite children's songs of Jamaica and the Caribbean", appeared soon afterwards. Around the same time, Heartbeat Records released a double CD anthology of Wailers Studio One material, including such rarities as 'Diamond Baby'.

Meanwhile, Blackwell turned his attention to Marley's publishing rights, and that spring he bought the Cayman Music catalogue (including a good many Marley compositions) for $1.2 million (recorded materials such as demo and master tapes remained under Sims' control). Blackwell also persuaded Don Williams to sell his Number Eleven Music publishing interests.

"I get angry every time I think about the situation with Chris and what I call the 1992 transfer," says Williams. "Back then, I thought the best place

---

* On the strength of Mrs Booker's support the child was officially added to the list of beneficiaries, even though another man came forward claiming to be the father.
† Rumours suggested the script was poor and all talk of a biopic was shelved until 1998, when the Fugees' Wyclef Jean was briefly considered for the role.

for Bob Marley copyrights was with Blackwell, but I was wrong and I made a serious error of judgment. There'd been this big fight over the estate and I can't remember why it took so long after Bob's death to resolve certain ownership issues, but then Chris suddenly wanted to acquire all of Marley's publishing rights. Chris never had any publishing rights up until then, and so when those rights came up for sale . . . Anyway, I made a mistake and it was a big one . . . I grew up with that legacy and I guess that's why I took it so personally."

Williams wasn't the only one left rueing an error of judgement, since the trial investigating Mutual Security's claims against Steinberg and Zolt began on August 5, 1992 in New York, lasting three months. The administrator's lawyer Robert Brundige claimed in his opening statement that Rita had been "misadvised and misdirected by her lawyers and accountants" and that Steinberg and Zolt had raked off about £1 million in fees. The defendants "were found liable for funnelling millions of dollars in royalty payments out of the estate through various schemes. Companies and contract rights were fraudulently transferred out of the estate in order to facilitate the diversion of many royalty cheques into defendants' bank accounts."

Zolt and Steinberg argued that their activities in creating new corporations and transferring funds from the estate were aimed at minimising the estate's tax liabilities, leaving more to be distributed to Marley's beneficiaries. Marley's three British Virgin Island companies (the ones registered in Tortilla) continued to receive royalty payments and income from various recording and publishing contracts. These sums would have become estate property, except Zolt and Steinberg were found to have advised Rita to forge Bob's signature on three documents, transferring ownership of the companies to her. The papers were pre-dated in 1978 to make it appear that Marley had made the transfers during his lifetime. Steinberg signed the documents as a witness, and ownership of the companies transferred to a company owned by Rita registered in the Dutch Antilles. Bob's three former companies were then liquidated and all payments diverted to accounts set up by Zolt.

In addition, for a period of around two years after Marley's death, Zolt and Steinberg did not report to the estate Marley's personal share of royalty cheques totalling approximately $1 million dollars received from a company called Almo Music, which administrated his song publishing activities.

Thirdly, Rita forged Bob's signature on a document, again witnessed by

Steinberg, that had been backdated to August 13, 1980, which assigned Marley's individual rights under contracts with Island Records to one of the Tortilla companies and hence the one owned by Rita in the Dutch Antilles. Finally, Rita again forged Bob's signature on a document assigning the assets of Tuff Gong Productions Ltd (Tuff Gong-Delaware) to one of the three Tortilla companies, which she again funnelled into the Dutch Antilles account. This document was dated November 30, 1980, although it was actually signed after Marley's death. These latter assets (mainly music copyrights) were valued at $100,000, but are thought to have generated millions in royalties between the years 1980–1985.

The estate estimated that it had lost a total of approximately $13.4 million between 1981 and 1986, but after crediting the defendants for funds recovered by the estate and for payments acknowledged to be legitimate, the estate sought $9.7 million in compensatory damages, plus $1 million in consequential damages. After deliberating for nearly two weeks, the jury found Steinberg and Zolt liable and found the other law firm defendants not liable for any of the estate's damages. The amounts awarded to the estate were amended by the court after various post-trial motions and on 21 July, 1993 an amended judgement was entered, awarding the estate $2,861,409.79 in damages against the defendants, $3,029,428 in attorney fees and disbursements and $250,000 in punitive damages against Steinberg.

Both unsuccessfully appealed against the verdict. Although legal fees incurred by the estate passed the $4 million mark, Rita's lawyer, Kaare Phillips, called the verdict "a complete vindication" of her client.

In September, Island rush-released a previously unreleased Bob Marley & the Wailers track 'Iron Lion Zion', originally recorded around the time of *Natty Dread*. The tape, discovered in the basement of Rita's Kingston home and overdubbed by musicians like Downie and British jazz saxophonist Courtney Pine, was remixed by Trevor Wyatt and Ingmar Kiang at the Fallout Shelter in London. Issued on a 12" single with 'Smile Jamaica', 'Could You Be Loved' and a previously unreleased mix of 'Three Little Birds', the newly crafted 'Iron Lion Zion' flew to number five on the UK charts on the crest of excitement surrounding the critically acclaimed *Songs Of Freedom*, a four-CD boxed set of Marley tracks. Released on Tuff Gong in late September, it contained 78 tracks ranging from 'One Cup Of Coffee', Marley's solo debut for Leslie Kong, to a version of 'Redemption Song' from his last-ever concert in Pittsburgh. As well as 'Iron Lion Zion', two other previously unreleased studio recordings, 'High Tide Or Low Tide', and 'Why Should I' rubbed shoulders with 12″ mixes of 'Jamming', 'Ride Natty Ride', 'Could You Be Loved' and 'One Love' as well as a seven-track acoustic medley recorded during Marley's Swedish sojourn with Sims and Nash.

The packaging was suitably impressive, including a 64-page booklet featuring contributions from Rita and Marley biographer Timothy White. There were plans to simultaneously release *Songs Of Freedom* in 30 countries, backed by a Wailers Family tour featuring the Melody Makers, I-Threes, Cedella Booker and the Wailers Band, although this never came to fruition. Instead, Cedella visited London to assist with promoting the album and also her acting debut in the film *Joey Breaker* (she'd previously appeared as an extra in *The Mighty Quinn*, starring Denzil Washington). Also known as *Agent Breaker*, the film was written, produced and directed by former Melody Makers agent Steven Star and co-starred Richard Edson. Cedella played a girl from St Ann's who gets funded by her local community to move to New York to train as a nurse. She enters a relationship with a white gay man who asks her to stay in America, instead of returning to her community as promised, but then dies from AIDS. Cedella predictably came under fire from Rastafarians for acting in a film portraying homosexuality but her response was typically forthright.

"A lot of Rastas would condemn me, and do, but that's another prejudice to keep us separated," she said. "It's just like slavery trying to hold us down and this chauvinistic thing, it's bullshit! They say I'm an embarrassment to my father and his family and the memories, but I say kiss my fucking ass!"

In an interview with *Etna* magazine, Cedella confessed to receiving angry letters concerning her manner and appearance and said that certain proceeds from the *Songs Of Freedom* box set would be donated to a school in Ethiopia, chosen by her mother and Neville Garrick. She also pleaded poverty, on the grounds that her family's share of the inheritance had been forfeited in order to throw in their lot with Blackwell.

"Understand that we're set up as a charity. We give to Amnesty, take care of certain schools in Jamaica, give musicians on hard times money but yes, we do have to be careful and make sure that we preserve the Marley image and that we get our proper percentage and royalties. We're doing a line of Tuff Gong clothing; we've got the Museum but having said all that, I don't like what my grandmother did at Nine Mile. She's turned his mausoleum into a tourist attraction and I did think that was the one place we could have kept for ourselves. Basically, we're there to protect anything to do with Marley and to make sure that he's exploited in the right way. Because we don't want him to end up on beer commercials, feminine protection ads, or whatever.'"*

Just two months after 'Iron Lion Zion', Island released 'Why Should I?' (from *Songs Of Freedom*), remixed by Trevor Wyatt, Ingmar Kiang, and Errol Brown, featuring overdubs from Downie, Sly & Robbie, and trombonist Rico Rodriguez, with a Rebel MC remix of 'Exodus' named the 'Kindred Spirit Mix'. Wyatt, who supervised its reconstruction, said that Family Man was invited to participate but he was busy touring with the Wailers, promoting their second album, *Majestic Warriors*, issued on the French label Tabu. Neither Anderson nor Downie played on the album, although Seeco returned and Marvin again sang lead on all but one track, in addition to contributing the majority of songs. While retaining a contemporary feel, *Majestic Warriors* is a more rootsy set than *I.D.* Highlights include the opening track, 'Liberty', 'Sweet Cry Of Freedom', and two songs, 'My Friend' and 'Out Of Exile', featuring Carly on drums, which reinforces Anderson's view that Carly's murder dealt the Wailers' sound a deathblow.

Another piece of the legacy the Wailers worked so hard for passed out of their reach on November 15 when 56 Hope Road was sold to the Bob Marley Foundation for $3,750,000. There was no mention of injustice within the official book *Bob Marley: Songs Of Freedom*, published on February 6, 1993 by Bloomsbury. Many such cosmetic, albeit well-written, Marley biographies followed over the years but it fell upon Taylor's autobiography *So Much Things To Say: My Life As Bob Marley's Manager* (issued by Blake Publishing at the end of February) to challenge some commonly held beliefs about Bob, Blackwell, and Rita Marley. Its arrival was met by threats of legal action from members of Island and the Marleys' inner circle, including Neville Garrick, who clearly anticipated stories far worse than being accused of spying for Blackwell or having his drug-related activities revealed.

At the end of 1993, having endured several years of non-stop litigation, the Marley estate prepared legal action against tobacco giant Philip Morris, who had filed a trademark application for registration of the name 'Marley' in France. The range of their intended goods included tobacco, matches,

---

* Ironically, that's just what happened. 'Lively Up Yourself' was used to sell an alcoholic beverage, 'Stir It Up' could be heard in advertisements for Columbian coffee and 'Three Little Birds' promoted deodorant.

and smokers' papraphernalia. Bob Marley Music Inc demanded an immediate cancellation of the application, since such a move by Philip Morris would provide the company with marketing opportunities, including (should marijuana ever be legalised) the sale of ready-rolled spliffs. Bob Marley Music Inc claimed that as a Rastaman, Marley only used marijuana for spiritual and medicinal purposes and that "to have the Marley name registered and used by a third party in such a manner is unacceptable." A Philip Morris spokesman argued they weren't seeking to register the name "with Bob Marley in mind, or with any other Marley, like the famous Dickens' character by that surname," claiming that, "consumers just would not associate a Marley tobacco product with Bob Marley."

This was obviously disingenuous, and by mid 1996, Marley's Superior Dutch Blend hand-rolling tobacco appeared throughout Europe, packaged in the traditional Rasta colours of red, green, and gold. The momentum of Bob Marley as a brand name was unstoppable, as shops and traders' stalls groaned under the weight of unlicensed T-shirts, posters, albums, tapes, cards, cigarette papers, mugs, ashtrays, scarves, and badges. Six years after Balfour Henry wrote of 'Marleymania', the evidence of his statement was more widespread than ever.

CHAPTER THIRTY-TWO

Real Situation

EFFORTS in 1991 and 1992 to settle the litigation between the Wailers and the administrators of the Bob Marley estate had come to nothing. The Wailers' Jamaican lawyer, Mr Gordon Robinson, asked what sort of deal the estate would offer the band for a world tour as well as advances and royalties on a future album. The reply hadn't been encouraging, so Robinson wrote back on 20 May 1992, suggesting a settlement in the region of $500,000, together with a four-album deal and payment for performances on a world tour. When these negotiations again broke down, exacerbated by the release of *Time Will Tell*, featuring unauthorised footage of Marley and the Wailers in concert, preparations were made for the case to be taken to the High Court. In his 2006 court action, Family Man claimed he met with Blackwell to try and resolve the Wailers' difficulties.

"During this time I felt incapable of doing anything much and felt paralysed by all the personal tragedies . . . I was really desperate for money, as were the rest of the surviving Wailers. I met Diane Jobson at 56 Hope Road one day. Diane worked at Tuff Gong and is a lawyer. I believe this was in the middle of 1993, but cannot be sure, though I remember what happened. Diane was pleased to see me and I told her it had been a long time since I'd seen Chris Blackwell. She said he was on the island and asked if I wanted to see him and I said yes. She was going up to see him and she gave me a lift to his home in Strawberry Hill. Chris and I discussed the past and the litigation in a very general way and I told him I had no money. Diane was present at this meeting.

"He said that he would like to put together a Legend 2 tour to celebrate the 50th anniversary of Bob's birthday. He also wanted to put out another *Legend* album of Bob Marley & the Wailers recordings, pay us royalties on that and said we should look at this as a positive way forward. This was not enough for me. I said that for me, the case was about royalties on all of the work Carly and I had done with Bob, about the money due to Carly and I for the sale of records with our performances on, and to get what was due to me and to Carly's children. I told him I wanted royalties going forward and that the settlement would have to include acknowledgment of the royalties due and there would have to be payment on all future sales as well. Chris accepted that and said he had no problem paying royalties to myself, for my brother's work and, as he put it, to 'those he knows', referring to Tyrone and Seeco. He said that he would start the royalties after the release of the new *Legend* album. We discussed how a tour could put the Wailers back on the map and get us working for at least a year and it was all very exciting. I gave Diane Jobson my account details and US $10,000 was later transferred into my account.

"I heard nothing for several months, then I got a message that Chris wanted to see me at his resort in Jamaica. I arrived around 6.30pm. He said Rita was coming too. We waited and she eventually turned up at 9.30pm with her daughter Cedella. She took Chris away and after waiting over an hour for them to return, I felt embarrassed so I left. Something similar happened on another occasion, after my earlier meeting with Chris at Strawberry Hill, when I went back there. I did not know there was a party going on. I approached Chris and he told me to come back early the next morning and speak to him then. I wanted to get his reassurance about the royalties he'd promised me. I did go back the next morning and spoke to Chris. He was about to leave in his helicopter. I asked him whether he remembered what he had said about paying the royalties going forward and he said, yes he did, and indicated this would be okay."

When giving evidence, Blackwell had no recollection of any of this. However, he insisted he did not say (and would not have said) that he could keep the litigation going for 20 years. He did accept that money was paid to Family Man but that, he said, was because the bassist was broke and needed help. Jobson recalled taking Family Man to see Blackwell for the same reason but she claimed not to have heard any threats involving legal action or promises regarding royalties because, according to Jobson, the Wailers had never received royalties, but only regular, gratuitous payments by either Bob or Rita. "Chris could not be promising any royalties," she said, "because he had no authority to do it. If there [were] any new recordings, then they would probably be entitled to royalties. As for what happened in the past, he could not have been in a position to offer Family Man royalties from Bob's estate."

The judge, Mr Justice Lewison, preferred the evidence of Blackwell and Jobson on the basis that Carly's estate was not a party to the proceedings and the case was not about recovering funds for his estate; Family Man was not the kind of person who negotiated on business matters, as he repeatedly emphasised in his evidence, so it was more plausible that he went to Blackwell for financial help; Blackwell had no interest in Marley's estate and it is implausible that he would have promised to pay royalties (as it was not a matter for him); it was in the estate's interest to bring the proceedings to a quick conclusion so as to be able to make undisputed title to the musical assets. It would not have been in the estate's interest to prolong the litigation. Nor would it have been in the interest of any purchaser of those assets to have done so.

Family Man went on to describe another alleged meeting which he claimed took place outside Kingston courthouse after Don Taylor had sworn an affidavit on 18 February 1993.

"I remember we were attending a hearing where Don Taylor gave us an affidavit confirming [his alleged understanding of] our business arrangements, saying that he'd always paid 50 per cent to Bob and the other 50 per cent to myself, my brother and the Wailers . . . Chris and Rita persuaded us to have a meeting [at 56 Hope Road later that same day]. We went to the meeting, but no progress was made and it broke up quickly. I can't remember the exact timing, but some time during early 1994 we all attended another meeting at 56 Hope Road. [The members couldn't agree how long this meeting lasted when questioned. Some said it broke up quickly, while others remembered the discussion dragging on for some time.]

"There were no lawyers present as far as I was aware and certainly not our lawyers. I remember Diane Jobson was there and so was Rita. The situation of my brethren Wailers was not good. It was well known that we were all short of money, particularly as none of us had been paid any royalties or had done any really profitable touring since 1986. We all had families with children and attendant financial responsibilities. During that meeting, Chris made it very clear he would be happy to pay us $1 million, or if he did not pay us $1 million, he would pay it to his lawyers who would keep the litigation going for 20 years. As far as I was concerned, Chris had promised me we would get royalties and the money we were receiving was what I called 'back pay'. I always thought I would be getting royalties going forward. Al said that he didn't want to sign without a lawyer but that was refused. Tyrone also said that he didn't want to sign. The atmosphere got very tense. Diane Jobson had the cheques for all of us.

I can't recall whether by Chris, Rita, or Diane, but it was made plain that if we didn't sign there and then, we would get nothing.

"I remember signing a document, which I assume was the Settlement Agreement, outside at the back of 56 Hope Road in front of Diane. I did not read the document. I was not given a copy at the time. I can confirm that our lawyer, Gordon Robinson, was not at the meeting and did not witness my signature. I recall the pressure at the meeting. I could not go on with litigation hanging over my head for 20 years. My head was numb. I had no space in my head. I thought if we got back on the road and toured and royalties started coming in again then things may get back to normal.

"I thought that the settlement agreement I signed would give me and the other Wailers money for back royalties, that the litigation would be finished, and that I would get royalties going forward, as Chris had said I would, for Carly's children and I. I did not know until very recently that the settlement agreement said that I had agreed to testify that Carly did not have certain claims. I am unhappy about that. As far as I am concerned, Carly's death means that nothing has been paid for the work he did since 1986, when the cheques stopped.

"The rest of 1994 we spent rehearsing for the Legend 2 tour and I remember we were paid part of the money under the Legend Tour Agreement up front and the balance was going to be paid during the tour. I do not now recall signing that agreement but the signature on it is mine. I know from discussions with Junior Marvin that he tried to get the rest of the money but the response he got was 'If you want it, sue us.' At that stage, we really had had enough of litigation."

When testifying, Marvin recalls Blackwell saying that it was in everyone's interest to reach a settlement, echoing Family Man's claims that he could either split a million dollars between them, or give it to lawyers, so they could spin proceedings out for another two decades. Marvin also claimed a settlement was discussed on the basis of a lump sum for back royalties, a lump sum for a tour, a sum for legal costs, and payment of royalties going forward for both work on previous albums and also the forthcoming *Legend 2* set.

Again Blackwell had no recollection of any such meeting and denied that he said (or would have said) that he could keep the litigation going for 20 years. Jobson also said that she could recall no meeting on the courthouse steps. Rita also backed up Blackwell's assertions – "The conversations that are alleged to have taken place between me, Chris Blackwell and the

Wailers at 56 Hope Road never happened. I do not recall ever meeting the Wailers together with Chris Blackwell" – and dismissed allegations of threats to Wailers members as "ridiculous."

Blackwell denied all knowledge of Rita making threats, and further claimed he didn't broker the 1994 Settlement Agreement and had no recollection of meeting with Family Man at Strawberry Hill. He also refuted having decreed that only Family Man should have royalties, since he was always of the view that if payments were to be made to one Wailer, then they should be made to the others as well, as this was the rationale behind the 1994 Settlement Agreement.

Once again the judge unhesitatingly preferred the evidence of Blackwell and Jobson. He had difficulty accepting the account of a meeting because as Jobson pointed out, there did not appear, on the evidence, to have been any reason for both sides to have gathered at the courthouse in 1993. A procedural hearing relating to the Wailers' legal action, not requiring their presence, nor Rita's and Blackwell's, took place on 18 February that year (the same day on which Taylor's affidavit was sworn) but no other trial activities, apart from a date-fixing session in November took place that year. Taylor wasn't subpoenaed to give evidence until October 1993 and none of the Wailers would have needed to attend in any case. The lawyers requested a meeting in June, but Blackwell turned this down on the grounds that the two sides "were so far apart there is little likelihood of our arriving at a settlement."

The correspondence between the lawyers at the time makes no mention of any meeting or settlement talks having taken place between the two sides' legal advisers, apart from a solitary complaint, made in December 1993 by the Wailers' US lawyers, that Blackwell had approached the band without counsel, and offered them "a side record deal and payment of a relatively small, token amount of cash."

This was inconsistent with any understanding on the Wailers' part that they were being offered royalties on past recordings. Moreover, had Blackwell threatened to keep the litigation going for two decades (contrary to the interests of the estate and any purchaser from the estate), then the letter of complaint would have mentioned this. The making of such a threat struck the judge as inconsistent with the conduct of both sides' lawyers in pressing the court for a trial date in February 1994.

Serious settlement negotiations began in earnest towards the end of 1993, when Mr Michael Hylton, the lawyer acting for the estate, sent Robinson a draft settlement offering the Wailers $500,000, to be apportioned between the six plaintiffs, and also $60,000 for the estate of Carlton Barrett.

Junior Marvin, who dealt with the Wailers' lawyers, said he was unaware of what was passing between the lawyers and that he did not receive correspondence copied to him or, if he received it, did not read it. The judge did not accept this evidence. On 13 January 1994, Hylton wrote to Robinson, proposing as terms of settlement that $500,000 be paid to the Wailers, shared as they saw fit, half payable immediately and the remainder after 12 months. A contribution of $100,000 was to be set aside towards the Wailers' legal costs and, in return, the band members would relinquish all their claims on the estate. Hylton also mentioned that a new compilation, *Legend 2*, was to be launched and that the Wailers' involvement in its promotion would guarantee them no less than $500,000.

Robinson replied on January 24 to inform Hylton that the schedule of payments was not acceptable. He requested accelerated payments and a greater initial advance. On 28 January, Hylton wrote to say he had met with two of the Wailers in New York and that the estate had agreed to pay $400,000 immediately and a further $200,000 within four months. Robinson's reply (on 31 January) stated that "Our clients have instructed us to accept the offer as set out in your letter of January 13, 1994, subject to an improved scheme for payment which, in part, seems to be reflected in your latest letter."

Robinson sent a copy of this letter to Marvin, with a reminder that he wasn't acting for Carlton Barrett's estate. On February 10, he again wrote to Hylton, asking if the Marley estate would reconsider the matter of royalties regarding *Legend 2* and pay the Wailers four percentage points. The answer was unequivocally no. On March 2, an agreement ("the 1994 Settlement Agreement") was made between Island Logic Limited, the Marley adult beneficiaries (including Julian Marley) and the six plaintiffs in the 1989 Jamaican Action, i.e. the Wailers (excluding Neville Garrick and the estate of Carlton Barrett) and the I-Threes.

The 1994 Settlement Agreement, which had the effect of settling the 1989 Jamaican action and the 1989 New York Action, was in the form that had been agreed between the parties' respective lawyers. The fifth point was the most important, by which the Wailers agreed to: "hereby jointly, severally, unconditionally, irrevocably, and absolutely release and discharge" all interested parties. They also agreed to cause the 1989 New York Action to be removed from the Courts and to testify according to the terms stated in the Settlement in the event of any claim being made on behalf of Carlton Barrett's estate. Each of the Wailers' signatures was appended in the presence of Robinson, who also helped draw up another agreement that same day, confirming that the Wailers would take part in a concert celebrating Bob Marley's 50th anniversary and also in a tour to promote an album provisionally entitled *Legend 2*. The terms of the agreement included a "buy out" of the Wailers' rights arising from their performances on that tour.

When *Legend 2* was eventually released as *Natural Mystic*, two of the tracks included were 'War' and 'Who The Cap Fit'. On March 13, 1994, Hylton sent Robinson a cheque for $400,000, as required by the agreement, with Family Man being paid $80,000 of that sum. In accordance with clause six of the Settlement Agreement, the 1989 New York Action was "dismissed with prejudice" on October 14.

Accounts of the actual signing widely differed. Family Man, Marvin, and Anderson all claimed it took place at 56 Hope Road in the presence of Rita and Blackwell. Marvin has said that the two spoke individually and secretively to the Wailers, with Rita warning how "things could get very bad" if they did not sign. He felt intimidated as a result, as did Anderson who said he was threatened by Rita that he would be "done in" if not complying. Anderson wanted to show the document to his own lawyer, Michael Guido, but was refused.*

In his judgement, Mr Justice Lewison again utterly rejected allegations that the Wailers were forced into signing the agreement under pressure or duress.

In his written evidence, Michael Hylton, who by 2006 was the Solicitor-General to the Jamaican government, said that his opposite number Gordon Robinson was an experienced litigator and "extremely competent Counsel." After hearing about Family Man's allegations of being threatened, Hylton stated that as far as he was aware, it was the first time "it has ever been alleged that the 1994 Settlement Agreement was entered into by certain Wailers under duress as a result of threats made against them. No threats were made by anyone, including Rita Marley, at any meeting I attended in connection with that agreement . . .

"The reason we entered into that agreement was because everyone who had ever been involved with the band was making claims against the

---

* The guitarist later claimed he had shown the agreement to Guido, who told him not to sign under any circumstances. Anderson therefore didn't add his signature until almost a year after the others.

estate. It was clear that the administrators wanted to settle every possible claim that might be made."

Rita denied having threatened anyone or having spoken to the Wailers individually at any settlement meeting. She, Blackwell and Jobson all denied that Anderson was refused permission to show the agreement to his personal lawyer. Jobson said that the 1994 Settlement Agreement was in fact signed at Robinson's offices and that she was driven there by Family Man in his car. Since Robinson witnessed the Wailers' signatures and none mention him being present at 56 Hope Road, the judge concluded that this had to be the true version of events. It also seems highly unlikely any threats would have been made in Robinson's presence, and nor is there any evidence to suggest the Wailers' lawyers were angry with them for signing the document, as some members claimed. Significantly, the judge noted that Robinson ("who is still alive and active") was not called to give evidence by the claimants.

Jobson also noted it would have been impossible for her to have prepared individual cheques as Family Man stated, since the settlement terms provided the payment for a lump sum, unapportioned between the individual Wailers, so she would not have known who was supposed to get what. Moreover, the amount was paid to Robinson's firm and not to the Wailers personally. In actual fact, the settlement was worth $2 million to the Wailers, since the 1981 agreement with the estate had been invalid, so if their litigation had gone to trial and been unsuccessful – a distinct possibility – they would have had to repay the $1.2 million that Rita paid them between 1981 and 1986.

The I-Threes signed a separate settlement agreement in January 1994, each receiving $100,000 in exchange for dropping any claims they might have against the estate. "In reality, I only wanted what everybody else was getting," Rita said, "and particularly as I had put my heart and soul and many years of my life into the band."

By now, it was clear that individual members of the Wailers were in desperate financial straits. Marvin was facing drug charges and alimony suits and needed money fast. Family Man had a growing army of children to support, Downie was struggling with drug problems, and Lindo's mental state was precarious. The estate had needed the Wailers immediately following Bob's death, but the Melody Makers' emergence had changed the situation. Anderson suggests the younger Marleys could be more easily controlled.

"Before that, the Marleys were very instrumental in letting us believe that we were a part of the Tuff Gong organisation and we were going to receive royalties and percentages from all of these videos, albums and remixed tracks they'd been putting out, because that was the music we'd created," he asserts. "Rita had so many people coming at her with lawsuits at the time, including Danny Sims, various songwriters, and Allan "Skill" Cole. We were in the process of filing as well. They had made offers, but we were going to stay united and go the long route towards getting what we [believed we] rightfully deserved.

"Rita, she never had a great lifestyle, and I think she was really unhappy being an I-Three and working with the whole Tuff Gong programme, because Bob always had other women and children round him and that must have been upsetting to her. There were all these things going on and no one really knew what she was going through so everyone decided Rita was dirt and they'd go after her. She in turn was trying to protect what she was eligible for. Chris Blackwell decided the best thing to do was to glorify Bob and erase the Wailers entirely, including Peter and Bunny, Carly and Family Man, and whoever else had anything to do with Bob. Take them out of the picture and just make Bob the functioning part of what people imagined the Wailers to be. It went from Bob Marley & the Wailers to just Bob Marley and that's a travesty."

Ultimately, Anderson blames Marley for not having left a proper will and it's difficult not to agree with him. Instead, everyone was left to fight it out, with Rita – no doubt harbouring grievances – in the driving seat. The signing of the 1994 Settlement Agreement would prove a major turning point for the Wailers. "None of us were in our right senses when they draw up a t'ing like that," Family Man admits. Somewhat predictably, the Legend 2 tour spluttered to an unhappy conclusion after just two weeks.

"Each of the 1984 shows were great and we thought they were going to extend it to Europe, but they had it shut it down until 1995, which is when we did the European one for like 10 days, so that was for even less time," he says, shaking his head.

Shortly after the settlement, Bunny Wailer released a track, 'False Beneficiaries', which was clearly aimed at those he felt were benefiting from the Wailers' music. The title, credit (the Wailers) and label (a facsimile of the original Tuff Gong design depicting Marley, Tosh and Livingston) all constituted a flagrant challenge to the estate (which had been issuing records on Tuff Gong since Marley's death), but it was the lyrics that reverberated most. "False beneficiaries, they have come to reap what they have not sown," Livingston sang. "Them nah plant nuh corn but them run control it. Them bake no cake at all but them nah even want fi share it. And all who lay the foundations, them nah want them to live under a roof. Like rats, they've joined together with one intention but them have no proof . . ."

Livingston then started work on a 50-track collection to mark Marley's half century. The majority were covers of songs Marley wrote with the latter-day Wailers' line-up, which could be interpreted as either a tribute to his departed friend's songwriting or an attempt to co-opt the work of the post-Livingston era Wailers. Family Man helped his old bandmate select the songs and also put together a band to play on five of the cuts but claims, in a predictable state of affairs, he still hasn't been recompensed for his services.

The Grammy-winning double set was entitled *Hall Of Fame*, a reference to yet another milestone in Marley's canonisation, when he was inducted into the US Rock and Roll Hall of Fame on January 19. U2 lead singer Bono presented the award to Rita, who accepted it on behalf of her late husband. No mention was made of the Wailers, despite the credits on all of his hit albums and singles clearly stating "Bob Marley & the Wailers," the clear inference being that Bob Marley achieved his success in the manner of artists like James Brown or Miles Davis, i.e. hiring sidemen to carry out their musical visions. According to the Hall of Fame's own publicity material, "Reggae's loping, hypnotic rhythms carried an unmistakable signature that rose to the fore of the music scene in the Seventies, largely through the recorded work of Marley and the Wailers on the Island and Tuff Gong labels. Such albums as *Natty Dread* and *Rastaman Vibration* endure as reggae milestones that gave a voice to the poor and disfranchised citizens of Jamaica and, by extension, the world.

"In so doing, he also instilled them with pride and dignity in their heritage, however sorrowful the realities of their daily existence. Moreover, Marley's reggae anthems provided rhythmic uplift that induced what Marley called 'positive vibrations' in all who heard it. Regardless of how you heard it – political music suitable for dancing, or dance music with a potent political subtext – Marley's music was a powerful potion for troubled times."

It would be fair to think that Aston Barrett, a principal architect of these "reggae milestones" (and many more by the likes of Burning Spear, Bunny Wailer, Peter Tosh, and innumerable others) would merit some credit, or at the very least, an invite to the ceremony. Unfortuntely, this pattern would keep on being repeated at Marley honourings and not one of the musicians or award committees queuing up to pay tribute seemed to notice.

In the aftermath of the settlement, the surviving Wailers released their third album, *Jah Message*, first issued on a German label, Red Arrow, although distribution problems led to RAS reissuing it two years later. Recording took place at Mixing Lab and also Peter Couch's studio up in the hills overlooking Kingston. Junior and Family Man shared production, while the contributing musician line-up of Carrot, Seeco, Lloyd "Gitsy" Willis, Marcia Griffiths, the Zap Pow horn section, and Peter's former backing singers, the Tamlins, lent a family atmosphere to the sessions. Lindo was present, although Martin Batista played the majority of keyboards, since Downie only appeared on two tracks. Two old friends of Marley's, Desmond Smith and Joseph "Bragga" Russell, co-wrote most of the songs, including 'Miracle', which could have easily been written about the Wailers, with lyrics like, "It's a miracle we reach this far, against all odds, to stay on par. And so we fight with all our might to keep Jah love in our sight."

Jah Message was another fair attempt to try and establish the Wailers' own identity, but its poor visibility and competition from a wealth of newer, Jamaican roots reggae acts meant it struggled to gain a hearing. This fresh wave of cultural singers and deejays was led by Garnet Silk, a quietly spoken Rastaman from the country parish of Mandeville, whose soaring, spiritually charged vocals and deeply felt, Rastafarian lyrics had earned him the title "Reggae Messiah" among cognoscenti. By 1994, he'd signed to Atlantic subsidiary Big Beat and was looking to create wholly original material, rather than sing over ready-made or "do-over" rhythms. Family Man played on four of his tracks, only two of which – 'Consider The Garden' and 'Slave' – have been released to date. The contrast between these tracks and those of the Wailers – or Canadian act Andru Branch, whose album *What If I Told You* also features Family Man and Downie – accentuated what keen-eared listeners had known all along. Family Man was best heard working behind inspirational singers like Marley and Burning Spear. 'Slave' is certainly the equal of many Marley tracks and Fams and Silk would clearly have made a formidable team. However, in December 1994, the singer tragically perished in a fire at his mother's house.

In 1995, numerous events held to commemorate Marley's 50th birthday included a concert at Hope Road (which again left certain musicians complaining they hadn't been paid). Most notably, the Jamaica Post Office issued a set of special Bob Marley stamps and the Bank of Jamaica announced limited runs of silver JA$50 and gold JA$100 coins, each carrying Marley's portrait. Any of those that remained unsold after June 30, 1996 would be melted down, thus increasing their value to collectors.

In May, Rita proclaimed her husband's spirit was responsible for two minor miracles involving his life's work. Firstly, an electrical fire which gutted three bedrooms in her Jamaica home, stopped only a few feet away from where her irreplaceable Wailers archive material was stored. That very same week, halfway across the world in Croatia, a lorry carrying a Marley photographic exhibition suffered a direct hit from a Serbian rocket. Fortunately, the two passengers were unhurt and their cargo of Marley memorabilia spared from damage. Rita's revelations were well timed, since Tuff Gong had just released *Natural Mystic: The Legend Lives On*. The collection largely featured Marley's rebel and reality songs and so provided an ideal foil to the more commercial aura that *Legend* presented. The remixed, hit version of 'Iron Lion Zion' was included, as was a cut of 'Keep On Moving' recorded in London during the summer of 1977, co-produced by Marley and Lee Perry. Issued as a single, backed with a Sly & Robbie remix and 'Pimpers Paradise', 'Keep On Moving' went to number 17 in the UK charts.

The release was followed by another 12″ single, this time containing 'Easy Skanking', the band version of 'Redemption Song', an extended mix of 'Punky Reggae Party', and the previously unreleased 'All Day All Night'. It failed to chart, although *Natural Mystic* peaked at number five in the UK album charts during June, its success reflected in a glut of Marley magazine articles and radio tributes. RAS issued *The Bob Marley Interviews: So Much Things To Say* CD around the same time, while Rita, Ziggy and the Melody Makers, Jimmy Cliff, and the Wailers were all scheduled to tour throughout the summer under the Natural Mystic banner, yet it was the Melody Makers' band – featuring Chinna Smith – that finished the tour. Growing in confidence all the while, the Melody Makers had recorded their latest album, *Free Like We Want 2 B*, at the original Tuff Gong studio inside 56 Hope Road.

Members of the Marley clan regularly used the studio from then on, including three of Bob's sons – Kymani, Julian, and Damian – who released debut albums recorded at Tuff Gong during 1996. The Marley brothers now had their own label, Ghetto Youths International, reserved for their own recordings, while sister Cedella was A&R director at the other Tuff Gong on Marcus Garvey Drive.* All three brothers sustained successful solo careers, while Stephen came into his own as a producer, as well as a recording artist. He sang alongside the Fugees (whose singer Lauryn Hill was in a relationship with Stephen's brother Rohan) on their hit cover of 'No Woman No Cry' – a record that raced to number two on the UK charts in November 1996, and which inspired the contentious television spectacle of a New York hip-hop group performing in front of the Jamaican flag on *Top Of The Pops*.

Apparently it was the "Marley boys", together with Richard Booker, who developed plans for a Bob Marley Pavilion in Universal's Entertainment Zone in Orlando, Florida. Rita and Mrs Booker duly sanctioned these plans, with the Pavilion to include exhibits, reconstructions of rooms at 56 Hope Road and stage facilities. The accompanying press release made allusions to the family now being free of legal entanglements, hence the flurry of commercial deals taking place. The Pavilion was an idea on the grand scale, but smaller deals continued to proliferate, such as the sets of Bob Marley legend collector cards issued in 1996, under the auspices of yet another new company, Island Vibes Publishing Ltd.

Mrs Booker – or "Miss B" as she prefers to be known – was now firmly established as a recording artist in her own right after the release of a third album, *My Altar*, the previous December. A collection of gospel songs, production was handled by her grandson Stephen, since Family Man quit the project after apparently being insulted by members of her household. In September, Miss B flew to London to promote the publication of *Bob Marley: An Intimate Portrait By His Mother*, a book she wrote with help from Jamaican author Tony Winkler. Winkler hadn't been her first choice by any means, as she'd fallen out with three previous collaborators. Unfortunately, the book revealed little that wasn't already known. The October 6 *Observer Review* referred to Miss B as "Reggae's Queen Mother", describing how she'd "become a celebrity in her own right" since her son's passing.

In the meantime, the Wailers picked up the pieces by organising their own tours and Mark Miller, a Wailers roadie during the last three years of Marley's life, played a key role in this process. Miller rejoined the Wailers in 1995 when he was hired to work in a management capacity alongside

---

* One of her first signings was talented Jamaican singer/songwriter Yvad, who fronted the Wailers for a short time in 2007.

Junior Marvin. He told *Wailers News* that Junior had done a fabulous job of keeping the band going for so long after Marley's death, "because no matter what anyone thinks, they would have gone down the tube sooner without him. Unfortunately, promoters were pissed off because there were constant changes in the band's line-up and they never knew who was going to show up. The originals were constantly at each other's throats. Al hated Junior, then he hated Fams, and then it was Tyrone who got into a fight with him. It was reported that Al broke Tyrone's jawbone, but that was bullshit. I walked onto the bus just as they were punching the fuck out of each other. Tyrone went to hospital, but he only had a badly bruised ego, and a lot of dislike for Al, who is a great guitarist, but has a lot of inner demons. They all do . . ."

CHAPTER THIRTY-THREE

Who The Cap Fit

IN February 1997, Bob Marley received a Lifetime Achievement Award, which Rita accepted on his behalf. In a statement on its website, the Recording Academy referred to Bob Marley as, "reggae's most transcendent and iconic figure." No mention was made of the Wailers, who continued to promote the music that was being honoured, and which had their name emblazoned all over it. Family Man, who watched the awards on television, since he wasn't invited to the ceremony, surely deserved some recognition for his contributions to the legacy of Bob Marley & the Wailers. Out of all the surviving Wailers and Marley dependents, he best fulfilled the criteria outlined in a speech made by Michael Greene, President and CEO of the Academy.

"The recipients of these awards are among the most important architects and builders of many of the most distinctive and seminal recordings of this century. Their outstanding achievements have left a timeless legacy of innovative and powerful music that has changed the world socially, politically and given a voice to our cultural condition. They exemplify the highest creative and technical standards by which we all must measure our own personal and professional contributions."

The following month, the Wailers began a world trek taking in South America, Europe during April, May and June, and US dates over the summer. The tour formed the basis of a live album called *My Friends* which demonstrated the extent to which the band blended their own material with Marley originals. By now, the line-up had changed again, with Claudio Peppe replacing Carrot on percussion. Marvin left after the tour to pursue a solo career, paving the way for Downie's return as lead singer. Meanwhile, old acquaintances were scouring the archives and repackaging old material, as when Danny Sims announced he was re-issuing over 200 Marley tracks recorded for his JAD label during the late Sixties. The first box set from this collection (which included the ultra-rare 'Selassie Is The Chapel'), *Complete Bob Marley & the Wailers*

1967–1972, was heavily promoted at 1997's MIDEM festival, prompting several other titles to appear before they were all mysteriously withdrawn. Several months later, Island courted further controversy by releasing the album *Dreams Of Freedom: Ambient Translations Of Bob Marley In Dub*, featuring remixes by Bill Laswell.

Despite the band's close links with the likes of King Tubby, Errol "E T" Thompson and Lee Perry, Island had failed to commission a Bob Marley & the Wailers' dub album during Marley's lifetime, so for the label now to release such a leftfield album angered many old-time fans, prompting Laswell – who'd already worked on a similar project with Miles Davis – to say that it wasn't reshaping Marley's music that had intimidated him but the size (and, presumably, expectations) of his audience. The effect Laswell created was ethereal, like hearing Marley's music in a dream – hence the title – although the deciding factor of each suite of songs is the bass, which rises majestically from Laswell's overdubs.

In November 1997, Chris Blackwell left Polygram, six months before Seagram, owner of MCA/Universal, acquired it for $10.7 billion. Polygram had been one of only two globally significant media companies not to be owned by trans-national conglomerates.* Their roster of artists included Elton John, Luciano Pavarotti, U2, and Sheryl Crow, in addition to which they also owned the Motown, A & M, Def Jam, and Mercury labels, as well as a film division. By this time, Blackwell had formed Islandlife, a New York-based holding company incorporating hotels and resorts in the Caribbean and Florida, plus several entertainment subsidiaries involved in video, CD-Rom, and animation, such as Palm Pictures. Unfortunately, Blackwell's companies were highly leveraged with debts to banks and a private investor group. Shortly after leaving Polygram, he sold them to Ryko Corp, an independent recording company. From its base in Salem, Massachusetts, Ryko had grossed over $50 million the previous year and could offer Blackwell's business interests better access to distribution.

In 1999, Blackwell joined the board of Listen.com and prophesised that "downloadable music is going to revolutionise the recording industry." A fellow board member described him as "a visionary", and "an extraordinary identifier and developer of music talent."

If Family Man and the other Wailers were being cold-shouldered by sections of the industry, they had made some friends outside of the reggae fraternity. Lauryn Hill invited them to join her at the Grammy Awards

* The other was EMI, which Seagram had also expressed an interest in buying.

and recruited Anderson to work on her classic *Miseducation Of Lauryn Hill* album. The guitarist accompanied her onstage for the next two years, including at the 1998 Bob Marley Festival in Miami. After Downie left the Wailers, Anderson suggested they hire Elan Atlas, a 22-year-old, half-Jewish kid from LA, as their new singer. A week after joining them, Atlas performed in front of 100,000 people in Paris, singing 'No Woman No Cry' in Arabic to tumultuous applause. He later signed a six-figure deal with Interscope and was replaced by City Heat singer, Gary Pines. Over the next few years, the Wailers line-up, now clearly revolving around Family Man, became a movable feast as Anderson, Marvin, Lindo, and Seeco all came and went, as well as Marcia Griffiths, Nambo and Chico from Ras Brass, drummer Nelson Miller, Glen DaCosta, Dave Madden, and former Tosh sideman Keith Sterling.

These Jamaican veterans were augmented by the likes of Christian Cowling, Melvin "Ras Mel" Glover, Ernest "Drummie Zeb" Williams, Rannie Bop, Senya, Ian Winter, backing singers Marie Do and Kali, and several others, as Family Man strove to keep the band working. The Wailers had become his only source of revenue, with few sessions of note to bolster his income.

In June 1999, one of the original Studio One-era Wailers, Junior Braithwaite, was shot and killed in Kingston. The news filtered through as Livingston and representatives of Tosh's estate did battle in the law courts with Island Logic Ltd and the estate over unpaid royalties relating to Tuff Gong. Livingston also challenged the estate's continuing use of the Tuff Gong label, logo, and early recordings. The Bob Marley Foundation, Tuff Gong International, and another of the estate's companies, Fifty-Six Hope Road Music Ltd, launched a petition in 1996, asking the courts to decide as to the rightful owners. Legal action commenced in both Jamaica and the UK, with an out-of-court settlement finally being agreed on June 28, 1999. Livingston and Tosh's estate were both given six months to file certain documents but didn't comply. It was therefore considered "just and equitable" that the original company be wound up. Jamaica's Supreme Court gave an order winding up Tuff Gong on Thursday September 28, 2000, relegating yet another milestone in the Wailers' lives to history.

Under the terms of the settlement, about $2 million would be shared between Livingston and Tosh's estate. This amount was intended to cover royalties from earlier and also more recent Tuff Gong titles. Both Livingston and the Tosh estate would still be entitled to use the logo depicting three fists, but not the one portraying Marley, which was to be retained for the exclusive use of his estate, and nor would the Court's decision affect the operations of Tuff Gong International, based on Marcus Garvey Drive. The end of the dispute was described as "a healing and re-allegiance between the Marley, Tosh, and Wailer families. They will now be able to act in unison in promoting the products and to help stamp out the piracy of these products," said Mr Kendall Minter, the lawyer representing Livingston and the Tosh estate. No sooner said than done, as Livingston and members of the Marley family embarked on a number of joint ventures, including recordings and tours.

Members of Tosh's family also looked at ways in which to raise awareness of his contributions. After a meeting at Peter's grave in Belmont during October 2001, the family made the decision to resurrect the Intel Diplo label and to form a Peter Tosh Foundation. It had taken years of litigation, but the Wailers family had grown one step closer.

Meanwhile, the younger Marleys were making their own bid to uphold their father's tradition so as to appeal to urban music fans. In 1999, *Chant Down Babylon*, originally known as *Black Survivors,* was released. The brainchild of Stephen Marley, it featured the vocals of hip-hop and R&B artists overdubbed onto extensively remixed Marley tracks. "Though black people in the United States would seem to be the natural recipients for Bob Marley's message of peace, unity, and race liberation," wrote former Public Enemy "Media Assassin" Harry Allen in the liner notes, "in his lifetime, he never reached African American audiences in the way he'd truly felt possible." Despite the Grammy-nominated 'Turn Your Lights Down Low', featuring Lauryn Hill, which was a hit on both sides of the Atlantic, reaction to *Chant Down Babylon* varied enormously. It wasn't just the choice of artists that aggravated purists (whoever thought they'd hear Aerosmith's Steven Tyler and Joe Perry on a Marley release?), but the fact that Stephen had taken liberties with his father's original work by completely reconstructing it.

Bob and Rita's youngest son defended himself by explaining he'd attempted to broaden reggae's musical horizons, as his father had done, which is why he'd recruited the likes of Baby Face, Erykah Badu, Guru, Busta Rhymes, Chuck D, the Roots, Rakim, Jazzy B, Brandy, and Lenny Kravitz to sing on the album, over Jamaican acts. The Marley brothers themselves joined forces for 'Kinky Reggae'.

Family Man Barrett: "They are not following in their father's footsteps of roots, culture, and reality. They are trying to do other things like hip-hop and don't even know what direction they are going in. They don't have any culture. They look like roots Rasta, but they are in no way praising Jah or the orthodox. They make some big offers in the church, yet they still love their fancy clothes and cars, and that's not it, because what about the people who started it, who made it possible? None of these youths have to work and that's because the cash is set already, through the work of I and I. They take away what we do many years ago and try to put some other tune around it, but it's an inborn concept they're messing with. You can't imitate it and you can't grab Bob's spirit in another belly. Bob is rotting in himself right now and until he show himself to them, they wouldn't realise how mad he is."

Despite Family Man's gripes, the Marleys were at least reminding people of their father's greatness and this in turn, somewhat ironically, helped increase attendances at Wailers gigs. As the band members became ever more disillusioned, recognition of Marley's achievements continued to grow. As the turn of the century approached, the BBC announced that it had made 'One Love' their official anthem of the Millennium. A new version of the song, featuring Ziggy Marley, the Gypsy Kings, and Boys Choir of Harlem, was played throughout the BBC's live broadcast on Millennium Eve. Another excellent Jeremy Marre documentary, *Rebel Music*, was screened in the summer of 2000, by which time US network TNT had underwritten a stage show-cum television feature on Jamaica's north coast, featuring many of the artists heard on *Chant Down Babylon*, as well as others such as Tracy Chapman and Queen Latifah.

"That show wasn't a tribute to Bob Marley, that was just so the Marleys and TNT could make some money from Bob Marley," opined Carly's son Errol, who was living with Rita when it took place. "I was broke at the time and yet them never give me a ticket at first, let alone a VIP pass! Eventually they give me a one ticket, but I just rip it up and don't go and then when they see me they say, 'Oh, you should have come and everything would have been alright.' Except me never had anywhere to sleep or anything like that and the whole thing was too hurtful for me, as Carlton Barrett's son because I knew them already and had a good idea of how it would have gone. I would have reached there, had nowhere to sleep and nobody would have paid me any attention. I would have had to go through the normal gate just like everybody else and then I would have had to struggle to get through security to see my uncle and the other Wailers and so that's why I decided to forget it.

"When I was living with Rita, it was at the house in Jack's Hill. There's no good time I can recall because I was just there to do an endless succession of chores about the place and yet I was the most intelligent person there, because I was the only one who'd been to high school. When Rita wanted something, like some recording, she'd say, 'Errol, go look for that tape,' because she never even know what's in the vault. When Chris Blackwell sent a man down there to get stuff for *Songs Of Freedom*, I was the one who find him all the tapes, because I was the only one who knew what was on them. Those tapes were in the worst condition you could imagine. Water was leaking onto them and lizards and cockroaches run up and down pon them. The room itself stink through disuse.

"I had no influence, but I tried in my own little way to care for [the tapes]. I remember one time I tell [Rita] she need to build some shelf for them, because the tapes get wet up and she said, 'Oh, we'll deal with that a next time.' Except there never was a next time, because there was always something else and all that great history just continued to deteriorate . . ."

Rita claimed she "made a personal commitment to take care of Errol because Aston, his uncle, was not doing so. In effect, I adopted Errol by taking care of him, sending him to school and giving him a job. I treated him as a member of my family. Errol was employed by Tuff Gong as a handyman on and off from the late Eighties until about 2002, when he began failing to show up for work."

She recalled discussing with Errol, "how Aston wasn't paying him his dues in terms of the ASCAP royalties payable to his father's estate." She says Errol got annoyed about this and so she recommended he get a lawyer to look into it. She suggested he speak to Michael Hylton about recovering the monies due to him, saying she was unaware that he and Carlton's two other children, Carlton (Jermaine) and Jacqueline, "had assigned their rights to those royalties to Aston in 1999."

Errol Barrett: "I was expected to go to [Rita's] lawyer, who was going to help me remove my uncle as the executor for my father's estate. But at the same time, I'd already started to learn about the music business and none of them knew that, as I'd been doing it secretly, so I went along to him and say, 'Well alright, how much money is there?' He said there was $300,000, so I said, 'Okay, show me from what period of time that money accumulated to the present and where that money supposed to have come from.' He said I am very smart and that he will get back to me. A little after that, I see a copy of the settlement agreement signed by everybody in 1994, but guess whose signature wasn't there? My father's because he had died in 1987 and so I knew this agreement [wasn't applicable]. As far as I could see, my uncle wasn't a wealthy man, so I just take my time and learn what I can about the whole situation little by little, until he and I finally got to talking, and him start to show me some things.

"I went on tour with him to see how it worked and could see he'd got nothing. I see him make the sacrifice and I see how all the Wailers are suffering, even though they still try and keep strong to the public and within themselves. That's when my doubts about him fell away, because it's Family Man who keeps Bob Marley's music alive and who was responsible for those tracks on the *Legend* album that's sold so many millions. The Marleys don't even play Bob Marley's music, because I live with them for six years and don't hear them play it hardly at all and I'm including his children in that too."

In a court document, Hylton confirmed that Errol Barrett contacted him in March 2000 to discuss his entitlement (if any) to monies due to his father's estate. He stressed that Errol wasn't his client, although he admits to having sent him a copy of the 1994 Settlement Agreement and also contact details of a lawyer in the US "who claimed to act on behalf of Carlton Barrett's estate and Aston Barrett."

Family Man Barrett: "At some time in 1999, Errol asked me where his dad's money was. We had an enormous row because since Carly's death, his estate had never been sorted out. Despite this row, Errol and Carly's two other children wanted me to become the administrator of the estate and to consider how best to get their father's money. Errol said that since I was around during his father's life and shared his working life, I would be in the best position to administer his estate. He told me that he had met with Rita's lawyer and that Mr Hylton had given him a copy of the 1994 Settlement Agreement. He went on to the internet, put in a track written by his father and the search said the publisher was Bob Marley Music . . .

"I later accompanied Carlton's three children to see lawyers about becoming the administrator of my brother's estate, and this was made official on May 16, 2001. I'd already engaged Alex Hartnett, a US attorney who was working on his own in New York, in early 1999, and the Jamaican lawyers, Haughton & Associates. Alex went to work for Greenberg Traurig, and organised the only asset of Carly's we knew was producing money, i.e. his ASCAP income, and this was assigned to me by my niece and nephews, as I was to administer the estate. Soon afterwards, I decided it was time to sort out matters for myself as well and I therefore instructed Greenberg Traurig to start and make the requisite enquiries.

"In the meantime, my English solicitors, Charles Russell, wrote to the

Legal Department of Island Records on 9 March, 2001. The letter they wrote on my behalf refers only to the recording contract with Island Records made in 1974. Until recently, I'd believed the 1974 agreement signed by Bob for all three of us was the only contract with Island Records and covered all the recording work we did for Island. It was only after Charles Russell wrote to Island that I became aware there were other recording agreements with them, and also other contractual documents relating to the work my brother and I did with Bob. As far as I was concerned, Bob agreed to take care of the business side of things for Carly and I after we'd had our discussions in 1974. He did that by getting us our recording contract and generally dealing with Island Records. Carly and I believed we three were the ones contracted to Island Records and Bob always treated us as if we were, until his death."

On March 1, 2001, Family Man announced at a press conference his decision to sue the Marley Estate and Island Music for breach of fiduciary duty for royalties received, contractual disputes and defamation of character. His lawyer claimed there had been a failure to attribute copyright of certain songs to Family Man and his brother and that despite his huge contributions to Bob Marley & the Wailers, "there has been a systematic exclusion of Aston 'Family Man' Barrett; explicitly in terms of the failure to credit him with his work and, more generally, the rewriting of history to remove his name from the credit of the works."

In February 2000, Family Man had sat down with the Wailers' then manager Bill Reid and drafted a letter outlining his grievances to the Marley children, who were each rumoured to be receiving an allowance of $40,000 a month. Reid delivered a copy of the letter to various members of the Marley family at Universal's Entertainment Zone in Orlando, which contained facilities owned by the Estate.*

"These people only look out for themselves and aren't interested in spreading the wealth to certain individuals who Bob Marley looked up to," commented veteran reggae deejay Dennis Alcapone. "I'm sure that if Bob Marley was here today, he would see to it that something was done about it, y'know? There were plenty of little people who Bob helped, but

---

* These included a live reggae venue and restaurant called A Tribute To Freedom, serving "authentic Jamaican and Caribbean cuisine." As well as buying a selection of Marley-related merchandise, diners could order such dishes as Belly Full (Jamaican beef patties), 'Stir It Up' (a smoky white cheese fondue), Jammin' (a plantain dish) and a portion of Trenchtown Rock (island fish chowder).

it's been a completely different ball game since he's gone. Now it's all about people grabbing onto whatever they can get and without showing any love to anyone. It's like they don't want anyone else to come up to the same heights as Bob Marley. It's sad though, y'know? It's sad how a man like Family Man has to be going through all this right now, because the relationship can never be the same any more."

Al Anderson: "It's a really pathetic situation . . . I mean Bob Marley shouldn't be in the Hall of Fame without the Wailers. Chris Blackwell should definitely have nothing to do with the Hall of Fame, because the Wailers put him there.* How come Chris Blackwell is in the Hall of Fame and the Wailers aren't? That's just not fair. I mean this guy's earned off all these talented Jamaican people and they don't have anything. Yet without them, he'd be nothing . . ."

Blackwell was inducted into the US Hall of Fame in 2001, joining other record label inductees such as Berry Gordy and Ahmet Ertegun (who once described the Jamaican-born producer as "the baby-faced killer"). In 2003, he went on to receive the Musgrave Medal – a Jamaican award commemorating outstanding artistic achievement – and in 2004, the Order of Jamaica for "outstanding contributions to the entertainment industry." On February 6, 2001 (what would have been his 60th birthday), Marley received a star on the Hollywood Walk of Fame. Members of his family and also Lauryn Hill were present at the ceremony but none of the Wailers were invited. That same year, *Forbes* revealed Marley was the seventh highest "dead" earner, with annual earnings of over $10 million. "Whilst the majority of Marley's earnings are from record royalties," said a *Forbes* spokesperson, "15 per cent is 'from sales of over-the-top trinkets like Bob Marley soccer shoes and knapsacks of hemp.'"

---

* Anderson's rather one-sided opinion fails to reflect that Blackwell's label introduced the world to such important acts as U2, Traffic, Grace Jones, Fairport Convention, etc.

CHAPTER THIRTY-FOUR

Who Colt The Game

IN 2002, Tuff Gong remastered several Marley albums and also issued a Deluxe Edition of *Legend*, featuring remixes by Julian Mendelsohn and Eric Thorngren, which were widely condemned, arguably representing the nadir of Marley's musical legacy. An American compilation, *One Love: The Very Best Of Bob Marley and the Wailers* served up yet another collection of hits. In June that year, Cedella Marley launched Catch A Fire, a fashion range promising designs that were "fresh and funky", but which turned out more expensive and tacky. Her brother Robbie managed a store called Vintage Marley, incorporating the Original Rude Bwoy clothing line based on his father's informal dress style.

As part of the Wailers' own range of merchandise, Family Man sold T-shirts depicting himself and Marley sitting together backstage, sharing a spliff. While the Wailers were performing at New York's B. B. King's club during the summer of 2002, US officials raided their tour bus searching for contraband merchandise and periodically checked up on the band at dates across America, where the Wailers were touring as support to Santana. Carlos Santana apparently tried to intervene on their behalf but to no avail.

"The police asked me if we're selling drugs because that was just a week or so after they hold Julian and Stevie for weed," says Family Man, referring to an incident in Tallahassee where the two Marley brothers were jailed overnight for ganja possession.

In January 2003, Universal-Island Records and UMG Recording tried to get Family Man's court action struck out as an abuse of process of the courts, but British High Court Judge Mr Justice Laddie granted the go-ahead on March 28, after four days of deliberation.

"They tried to bury us, which I find really ironic considering that Universal has been talking about artists' rights so much in regards to passing legislation in California and with file-sharing," commented Family Man's US attorney, Stewart Levy. "These two men [the Barretts] made huge contributions to the world of music and just seek the credit they deserve."

Universal-Island Records declined to comment on the matter, or on Graham Strong's documentary, which examined the circumstances behind Marley's fortune since his death. The film, broadcast by the BBC in September as part of a series called *Can't Take It With You*, told the story in some detail. Mrs Booker, J. Reid Bingham, Michael Hylton, Neville Garrick, Wailers' attorney Stuart Levy, and Arthur Kitchin (who represented two of the mothers of Marley's children), all contributed. Levy gave eloquent testimony on Family Man's behalf, saying, "I think the legacy of Bob Marley has been irreparably harmed by the way Aston Barrett has been treated. Aston Barrett is the person who's a link with Bob Marley, who goes out there to promote the songs and promotes his world view of love, peace, and harmony; one love and one people, crossing all ethnicities. Instead, what you have here is both Island Records and the Bob Marley estate taking a very hard, legalistic position. They're looking at technicalities available to them under the law, but they're not focusing on what fairness dictates. It's like the Pharisees in the temple and that's what the legacy's become. It's become Babylon."

Although he didn't appear in the documentary, throughout the build-up to the trial Family Man remained adamant he wasn't being driven by greed but the same quest for truth and rights that had motivated so many Wailers songs.

"When we started out there was no money at all. Bob didn't even have a bicycle, whereas I had three cars and stopped what I was doing with the Hippy Boys and Lee 'Scratch' Perry to do the thing with Bob, Bunny and Peter together as Wailers. That was through we were giving praise to the Almighty. It was a God works, a Rasta works, human rights t'ing we were doing and we sing and play music like 'get up, stand up for your rights' and 'how good and pleasant it would be to see the unification of everyone.' It seems the Marleys have forgotten these words of wisdom, and because of the cash, they got blindfolded. Now they're trying to make us look like we are the bad guys for taking them to court."

Chris Blackwell started 2003 by fending off reports he was selling his interests in Compass Point for undisclosed millions. Blackwell owned other properties in the Bahamas, such as Pink Sands on Harbour Island, which formed part of his Island Outpost chain of resorts. His interest in acquiring such properties started in the early Nineties, with the purchase of the Marlin Hotel on Miami Beach. Within 10 years, Island Outpost owned six hotels and resorts in Jamaica and a similar number in Miami's South Beach, including the Tides Hotel and Kent Hotel, in the heart of Miami's Art Deco district. Island Outpost's roster of properties – most of which can be described as "celebrity getaway places" – also includes Cuckoo's Nest in the mountains of Provo, Utah, which Blackwell designed himself.

Meanwhile, the estate announced it was going to sue Sanctuary, the owners of Trojan Records, for £100 million in a joint lawsuit under the Tuff Gong banner, shared with Bunny Wailer and the estate of Peter Tosh, seeking an end to the "continuous illegal distribution of the Wailers' products in the international marketplace." Livingston said it was an attempt to recover royalty payments after "28 years of bootlegging and piracy of recordings, starting with *Soul Rebel*, *Soul Revolution*, and *Best Of The Wailers* . . . Along with over 25 songs recorded on the Wailers' own labels, this has resulted in over 700 products being exploited worldwide." As of 2007, this action remained unresolved. Livingston had assumed the role of elder statesman with some conviction and continued making his opinions felt, as Rita Marley was about to find out.

In April 2004, she launched her autobiography, *No Woman No Cry*, in which she alleged her late husband "wouldn't take no for an answer . . . so he forced himself on me and I call that rape." A British newspaper, the *Daily Mirror*, gave this accusation maximum coverage which angered Livingston, who demanded she apologise. "That to me is disrespect and she owes the world, Bob Marley and their children and grandchildren an apology," he railed to the *Jamaican Observer*. "Why would she wish to taint him at a time when he is being treated as a saint?" Livingston pointedly asked. "This individual, who the world is now seeing as an icon, a prophet, and a spiritual leader because of the legacy he's left us and the legacy that he's also left her?" Rita countered by saying the *Mirror* had taken her words out of context and that she'd never intended to give the impression Bob had been a habitual rapist.

The timing of the book coincided with Rita's exodus from Jamaica to a mansion in Ghana overlooking Accra, in the village of Aburi-Akwapim, near Koforidua, along with various other Marley clan members, including 37 of her grandchildren. Since becoming attracted to Ghana, the family matriarch established a day-care centre in the village, adopting at least 30 children, as well as founding the Rita Marley Foundation. In 1999, the organisation began remodelling Konkonuru Basic School, which caters for

85 children, funding local irrigation projects and "distributing to villages". By 2004, the emphasis had shifted, after Rita announced plans to build a recording studio and a hi-tech computer centre. Such activities had earned her the title of "Nkosohene" or "Queen of Development" in the area, even as rumours began to circulate that she was fearful of being poisoned by people from her village, who felt envious or resentful towards her.

In November 2004, she attended a ceremony inducting Bob Marley as one of the first 10 entrants to the British version of the Rock 'n' Roll Hall of Fame. A week later, an announcement was made that Rita and Universal had struck a deal with American entertainment giant Clear Channel, the company behind the West End blockbuster, *The Producers,* for the production of a Bob Marley musical. The following month, an initiative to accord Marley the status of national hero was launched in Kingston with February 6 to be declared a national holiday. The PR disaster that followed could have only been caused by overweening self-interest.

Rita had declared plans to host a concert in Addis Ababa to commemorate Bob's 60th birthday, but in January 2005, she told the *Associated Press* of her plans to remove his remains from the mausoleum in Nine Mile and rebury them in Ethiopia. "He has a right for his remains to be where he would love them to be. That was his mission," she said, declaring, "the impact is there and the time is right." Rita claimed that both the Ethiopian church and government officials had expressed support for the reburial and that "Bob's whole life was about Africa and not Jamaica."

Her announcement caused waves of protest as Marley had obviously wished to die on the island, since he tried making a heroic effort to return there after discharging himself from Dr Issels' clinic. On one hand, the Jamaican authorities were hoping to enshrine Marley as a national hero and on the other his widow was planning to take his remains elsewhere. Rupert Lewis, a political science professor in Kingston, warned that, "Marley is a crucial part of Jamaica's identity and any attempts to move his remains would be met with serious hostility." The following day, a spokesperson for the Bob Marley Foundation denied the reports, claiming Rita's words had "been twisted". The free concert in Addis Ababa attracted 200,000 people, but few of Marley's old friends were there to celebrate his 60th year, since the line-up comprised various Marley family members, plus guests such as Lauryn Hill and Angelique Kidjo. Reflections on the event inspired Stephen Davis, author of *Bob Marley: Conquering Lion Of Reggae*, to write an open letter, which first appeared in US publication *The Beat.*

"Bob, I guess the worst news I have to break to you in this letter is about what your family has done with your legacy. It was recently reported that your estate is worth an estimated $100 million. An album you never saw called *Legend* is one of the best selling records in history. You're a T-shirt, a comic book, a line of footwear, a theme park, a stage musical, and soon to be a major motion picture.

"Bob, I hate to be the one to tell you, but your family is blowing it. I'm sorry to be the one to tell you that your wife is building a Bob Marley resort, not in teeming and violent Jamaica, but in the placid Bahamas, which is barely a real place at all. Hey, Bob. Where is the Bob Marley Hospital for the Poor that should be operating in Spanish Town? Where is the Bob Marley orphanage that should be the pride of St Ann's Bay? What about the Bob Marley Home for the Aged in Negril, or the Bob Marley Early Childcare Centre in Sligoville and Port Antonio? These institutions don't exist because your family has other priorities, which seem to be mostly themselves. That your wife is using your legacy to build a tourist resort is beyond disgraceful. I'm sure that if you were alive, she would be totally out of the picture and that you would be using your immense fortune the way you did when you were walking among us. As a river of resources to help those that depended on you, which back then numbered in the thousands and today could number many times more than that. It's hard to believe that you, Bob Marley, ever had cause to rape your wife. But it's clear to me that she must believe it, because now she's raping you."

Davis signed off with, "If you were here with us today, and had a clear view of the runnings, you would be mad as hell at what is, and what is not, being done in your name."

Contrary to what the writer estimated, Rita has been quoted that the estate is worth in the region of $600 million. Certainly, its value kept increasing, as did the fortune amassed by Blackwell, who announced Island Outpost's exclusive One Love holiday package in March. "It's all about spirit, sensibility, and heart," he gushed. "Like Island Records, Island Outpost is about feeling the bliss of authenticity. This is a chance to encapsulate the life of Bob Marley and share the vision with travellers the world over."

Most of the Island Outpost locations, including Strawberry Hill and Goldeneye, offered accommodation at rates averaging around $375 per night. As part of the One Love experience, tourists were offered trips to Kingston locations associated with Marley, such as his mausoleum in Nine

Mile, Coxsone Dodd's studio on Brentford Road, the National Stadium, and the Bob Marley Museum at 56 Hope Road. The latter attracts hundreds of thousands of visitors a year, who can marvel at Bob's favourite jacket or the many press clippings from around the world, pasted, rather than mounted, onto the walls. They can then eat at the Queen of Sheba restaurant or buy Cedella's fashion items. The Lifetime Achievement Award takes pride of place in a downstairs room, where gold discs proliferate, although there are no photos of the Wailers line-ups anywhere to be seen. In fact, there's no evidence to suggest Marley ever had a band at all.

Admission to the Bob Marley Museum costs JA $500, making it out of the financial range of many ordinary Jamaicans. One can only imagine what Marley would have thought about a significant part of his legacy becoming the preserve of the wealthy, let alone an incident that happened in April 2005, when a BBC researcher sent an e-mail to the Bob Marley Foundation, saying a planned documentary on the song 'No Woman No Cry' "would only work with some participation from Bob himself." The corporation admitted to being "very embarrassed".

Harking back to their Ethiopian venture, the estate's final act of 2005 was to issue an album entitled *Africa Unite: The Singles Collection*, previewed by a previously unreleased track, 'Slogans'. The press release claimed Ziggy Marley had unearthed the song – which had been extensively overdubbed – in the family's vaults. This was untrue because Marley collector Roger Steffens had discovered it, along with eight other songs (or rather aural sketches, sung to the accompaniment of an acoustic guitar), during a visit to Cedella Booker's house in May 1989.* After asking to borrow the tapes for the night, Steffens had taken them to Miami radio station WDNA where he duplicated them and later presented Ziggy with cleaned up copies as a gift. Universal were reputed to have spent a million pounds on advertising *Africa Unite* which, like 'Slogans', sold disappointingly, suggesting the public were no longer willing to keep shelling out for the same material.

Family Man's search for witnesses in his upcoming High Court case took him and his lawyers to California, New York, Miami, and Jamaica,

---

* Steffens has made repeated attempts to house his vast collection of Marley memorabilia in Jamaica where he feels it belongs. He claims Rita Marley once tried to buy it from him but describes her offer as derisory.

where they registered at their hotel under assumed names after being advised to proceed with caution. Some of Family Man's old associates asked for money (and were declined) before they would give witness statements, while others refused point blank, professing their fear of repercussions. Downie spoke at length to Family Man's lawyers but then withdrew his statement after further deliberation. It was said he gave the impression of being "a broken man".

Three weeks before travelling to London for the trial, Rita performed at Bob Marley's birthday celebrations in Accra, where the International Fair Conference Centre hosted the Africa Unite Symposium. The theme of the event was "Bob Marley, the Man and his Music" and various professors from Africa, the US, and the Caribbean gave speeches. *Africa Unite*, a documentary based on the 2005 Ethiopian stage event featuring Lauryn Hill and actor Danny Glover, as well as various Marley family members, made its US debut in April at the New York African Film Festival. Glover is also a UNICEF Goodwill Ambassador and his company, L'ouverture Films, shared production of the film with Tuff Gong Pictures. Director Stephanie Black (*Life And Debt*) issued a statement saying it had been her aim to "further Bob Marley's eternal message of hope and struggle across continents and generations," adding that, "We know that change occurs when we refuse to be silent in the face of injustice and inequality."

A week after Family Man left Jamaica, his son Kymani was murdered when gunmen broke into his apartment and dragged him to a nearby gully, where he was shot eight times. Fams was understandably not in the best of spirits when the trial finally opened in March 2006 amid a blaze of publicity. All the press and radio reports quoted figures and information provided by sources close to the estate, much to Fams' displeasure.

Family Man Barrett: "What people have read about me in the press so far, it's the [estate] who supplied the information. They say I am suing the Bob Marley estate for £60 million but I really don't know who came up with the figure. I was so surprised when I read that and it was quoted in every newspaper I saw . . . It's like they were trying to paint me blacker than I am and portray me as someone who's greedy and corrupt, in the international press, which is such a shame."

The trial, described as "the reggae trial of the century" lasted for three weeks and was presided over by Mr Justice Lewison. A spokesperson from Universal told *Music Week* that Family Man's case would quickly unravel once proceedings got under way and their lawyers even insisted there wasn't a case to answer in their opening remarks. Family Man, represented by his counsel Mr Stephen Bate, testified over two days. The contrast between this unassuming musician and his cross-examiner, Ms Elizabeth Jones QC, couldn't have been more pronounced, yet he stood up to her line of questioning with remarkable fortitude. Punctuating his version of events with the occasional humorous remark, Family Man delivered the most memorable soundbites from the entire trial, such as when he was asked to define his and the Wailers' relationship with Blackwell. "He was the plantation owner," he explained, "and we were the musical slaves."

Blackwell took to the stand for his two lengthy stints looking dishevelled in baggy corduroy trousers, with no socks, and an open neck shirt. Vivian Goldman, who was there to testify on behalf of the prosecution, greeted Blackwell with pity in her eyes as he left the stand. ("He was my mentor," she later wailed, back at the hotel.) In his testimony, Blackwell admitted to being unfamiliar with Sixties reggae hits like 'Return Of Django' and 'Liquidator' and claimed to have gifted 56 Hope Road to the estate *after* Marley's death. However, the judge found him generally to be a reliable witness.

Rita was on the stand only half a day rather than the anticipated two. Her testimony was vague in parts, particularly relating to the authorship of certain songs. She denied seeing important documents and letters relating to ASCAP payments and claimed some of them had been destroyed when her house had subsequently "burnt down". Rita, who left the court sobbing after taking the witness stand, gave the impression of having been overwhelmed by events after her husband's death, especially as she'd had 11 children to care for. The judge found her to be a reliable witness, concluding: "Over the years she has, I accept, tried to do her best for the Wailers and for the estate, even though, at times, their respective interests have been in conflict." Despite retracting claims in her statement that the Barretts were mere sidemen, incapable of writing music and lyrics, Rita didn't look or speak to Family Man once during the trial.

Diane Jobson was the defence's most impressive and cogent witness, striking an incongruous figure in her pinstripe suit and huge, woollen tam. The testimonies of assorted Island attorneys proved mildly diverting, since their memories of events from over three decades ago ranged from crystal clear to non-existent. Lee Jaffe was a late addition, having bumped into Cedella Marley by accident, while visiting London on business. When Cedella had told him about the trial, he'd immediately offered to testify on the Marleys' behalf.

Anderson appeared wary and uncertain, while Marvin, looking scholarly in his grey suit and glasses, spoke at considerable length. Both were adamant that Marley had treated all of the Wailers as members of a partnership, but that the Barretts were senior to everyone else, even though they weren't necessarily involved with business discussions.

The three Wailers had left to go back out on the road by the time the trial finally wound to a conclusion on April 7. Mr Justice Lewison was asked to make findings on 23 main points; one required him to decide that if the Barretts were parties to the first Island contract, but not the 1975 Recording Agreement or the Media Aides Agreement, then did their contractual recording rights continue under the 1974 Recording Agreement, and, if so, in respect of which albums? The most likely contenders were *Natty Dread, Live,* and *Rastaman Vibration,* which although not released until 1976, had been recorded in 1975. If the decision was affirmative, then Family Man and Carlton's estate would net a tidy fortune in back-dated royalties and see revenue streams reinstated that had been denied them for more than 20 years.

The judge was also asked to rule on whether the Barretts actually wrote the disputed songs on *Natty Dread* and *Rastaman Vibration,* or whether Marley wrote them alone. His findings would determine the rightful copyright owners, and ascertain if and when the Barretts ever assigned them to Tuff Gong Music, which had been in possession of them for over 30 years. His decision regarding those half dozen tracks could again net the Barretts a considerable sum, in addition to which, he was also required to determine if the brothers had given Island the right to exploit their performances on the best-selling DVD and video compilation, *Legend.*

It cost Family Man in excess of $1.2 million to bring the case to trial and so he obviously hoped to receive a good deal more in recompense once his grievances had been resolved. Having weathered personal tragedies and all manner of indignities in his search for justice, this was his last throw of the dice, since at 60 years of age, with nearly 40 children to support – three of them under school age – he wouldn't have the energy or finance to pursue his claims any further.

The decision, announced in May, took the form of a highly detailed written judgement running to 401 paragraphs. Mr Justice Lewison ruled against Aston Barrett on all 23 points, a decision that left the musician penniless and probably wishing he'd never contested the estate in the first place. Not only had he lost his claim for a share of the Marley fortune and song credits, but also recognition for having helped create so many famous tunes. Marley's poetic genius was unquestionable, yet his musical abilities were limited, which is why he'd enlisted gifted musicians such as the Barretts in the first place.

"When you consider that Fams' brother made up his own drum kit out of paint pans and Family Man's first bass had just the one string, I would say it's ordained for them to come so far," notes Ian Winter, who'd studied the Barretts' working practices at Hope Road more closely than most. "They created a sound that became universal and could be understood in any language, because people from all over the world can feel the vibe and relate to it and yet most reggae music tends to have very few chords. It's how you play them that matters. It's all about timing and a certain kind of riff that cannot be written down. The dynamics of reggae music, I would say is totally down to Family Man. The way he plays the bass isn't like anyone else. It's a different instrument him play, because the way the rhythm a drop just right, it's like him play every note with nuff experience behind it.

"This man is the foundation of our music and he's been my teacher in all sorts of ways, including some little technical things other people would overlook, but which made all the difference to Bob's music. His genius is in the details, because the man will spend hours onstage just making sure everything's in order, or he'll take three or four hours in the studio setting everything up so it'll give you exactly the right sound. Family Man, he's inimitable, because no matter how good you're playing, if the sound is not coming across in this right form, then it's not happening. Family Man and Carly's contributions have been essential in helping make Bob Marley's music stand the test of time and I don't think anyone can dispute this."

Family Man's lawyers lodged an appeal on the grounds that since *Natty Dread* was released in February 1975, either the Barretts *had* signed the 1974 Recording Agreement, or the need for their signatures had been waived, because the album couldn't have been issued and the advance paid without one or other of these conditions being met. They also argued that the 1994 Settlement didn't cover any of the assets after the date of the Settlement, only prior to it. As of June 2007, no date for the appeal hearing has been set and there is no clear indication whether it will even be allowed to proceed.

Within weeks of losing the case, Family Man's wife and her five children were threatened with eviction from the house Fams bought on Waterloo Road after being forced to leave Hope Road. In paying for the trial, he'd already lost his other home in Florida and with most of his belongings in storage he became a wandering minstrel, pursued by creditors with a massive debt hanging over him. Despite the hurt, Family Man continued to respond in a most dignified manner. He didn't sell his story to the media but consoled himself with messages of support that flooded in from all quarters of the reggae business.

Fams wasn't the only former Marley associate to fall on hard times. Georgie, Marley's friend from Trenchtown and Hope Road, was now almost blind, while the elderly Seeco, who the singer had viewed as a father figure, suffered respiratory problems. His wife reported that they couldn't afford to pay his medical bills. The same is also true of Lindo, whose mental condition prevents him from touring. Alva "Reggie" Lewis is destitute while Carly's two children live in abject poverty in Brown's Town.

Family Man, and occasionally Anderson and Marvin, derive their livelihood from performing with the Wailers, who continue to enrich the estate by promoting the Bob Marley catalogue. In a Catch-22 situation, the members are unable to capitalise on their Marley association with CD or DVD projects, since the estate won't grant them licensing rights, yet all around them the relentless marketing of Marley's legacy continues apace.

Four months after the verdict was announced, Marley was in the charts again with the most ghoulish use of his music yet, 'Hold Ya Head', a record sampling 'Johnny Was', made to sound like a duet with the equally deceased rap star, Notorious BIG. This was followed by the news that Jamie Foxx, who had portrayed Ray Charles in the award-winning biopic *Ray*, was to play the lead role in a similar venture focusing on Marley's early life. Filmmaker Rachid Bouchareb acknowledged the project was the brainchild of Rita, saying he "wanted to look at him as a child, growing up to be a young man, and at how he became interested in Africa."

In January 2007, Blackwell launched another addition to the portfolio of Island Outpost – a multi-million dollar resort development on one hundred acres of land adjacent to James Bond beach in Oracabessa, on Jamaica's north coast. Situated next to Goldeneye, once owned by James Bond author Ian Fleming, it would include approximately 90 "rustic villas and cottages in a lush tropical setting." The resort will have its own marina, spa, swimming pools and natural secluded lagoon. Just outside the front entrance is the coastal road stretching from Negril to Port Antonio, which the Jamaican authorities are planning to call the "Bob Marley Highway". Blackwell's fondness for such ventures has clearly rubbed off on the Marleys, who announced the opening of the Marley Resort and Spa on Cable Beach in the Bahamas during March. Rooms there cost $450 per night with suites from between $600–$1,500 per night. All 16 rooms are named after Bob Marley songs like 'Lively Up Yourself' and 'Positive Vibration', apart from the Royal Rita, in deference to the self-styled "Queen of Reggae". Visitors to this luxury pit stop can immerse themselves in the 'Natural Mystic' spa or dine at the 'Simmer Down' restaurant, in between buying Cedella Marley fashion wear and the usual array of Marley memorabilia.

In June, a deluge of product commemorating the 30th anniversary of *Exodus* arrived, including a book, DVD, and reissues of the original album on vinyl, CD, micro SD memory card for use in mobile phones, and also a limited edition USB memory stick. Anthony Wall, the director of the commemorative *Exodus 77* documentary, considered Marley to have two sets of peers: black, political leaders like Malcolm X, Martin Luther King, and Nelson Mandela, together with third world revolutionaries like Che Guevara; and white musical and cultural icons like Bob Dylan and John Lennon, whose lyrics have had a sizable impact upon 20th century culture. Wall found that the Wailers' essential mission had triumphed – despite all the hurt and greed in the wake of Marley's passing.

"When we asked everybody from 18 to 70 what the message of Rastafari was," says Wall, "they all said the same thing, which is that it's a message of peace and harmony. Somehow, Marley got that message across to people from all over the world, and it went deep. And it's only 25 years since he died so the fact it's drilled itself into people's minds to that extent is a really impressive achievement. Then again, it accords with what he always said, which is that his music's principal function was to spread this kind of message. Well I think he did it, against all the odds, and the more you think about it, the more amazing it gets . . ."

ACKNOWLEDGMENTS

In writing any book, one incurs debts that can never be repaid. Literally hundreds of individuals have helped me with research and interviews, and I thank them all. The following are just some of the people who helped in this project. To those I've missed, I extend sincere apologies.

This book could not have been written without the involvement of Family Man and Jennifer Miller, whose input was invaluable. Thanks also to Catherine Gillo, who arrived just in time.

Glen Adams, Dennis Alcapone, Al Anderson, Roydale Anderson, Susan Andrews, Bob Andy, Sadek Asha, Dave Barker, Elizabeth Barraclough, Akila Barrett, Tim Barrow, Dennis Bovell, U Brown, Lloyd Charmers, Clive Chin, Junior "Chico" Chin, Leonard "Santic" Chin, Chuck in Hawaii, Johnny Clarke, Jimmy Cliff, Christian Cowling, Richard Cupidi, Glen DaCosta, Junior Dan, Desmond Dekker, Junior Delgado, Errol Dunkley, Sly Dunbar, Murray Elias, Alton Ellis, Claude Evans, Brinsley Forde, Hugh Francis, A. J. Franklin, Dean Fraser, Laurence Gilmore, Melvin "Ras Mel" Glover, Olive "Senyah" Grant, Marcia Griffiths, Leon and Maurice Hamilton, Toots Hibbert, Joseph Hill, David Hinds, Justin Hinds, Ray Hurford, Gregory Isaacs, Jackie Jackson, Kali, King Kong, Larry Lawrence, Sandra Lawton, General Lee, Bunny "Striker" Lee, Roger Lewis, Earl "Wya" Lindo, Little Roy, Fred Locks, David Madden, Marie Do, Chris Markland, Damian, Julian, Kymani, Stephen and Ziggy Marley, Gaylene Martin, Junior Marvin, Roger Mayer, Freddie McGregor, Count Prince Miller, Derrick Morgan, Niney the Observer, Augustus Pablo, Lloyd Parks, Alvin "Seeco" Patterson and Willie Pep, Lee "Scratch" Perry, Phil Pratt, Janis Punford, Penny Reel, Jimmy Riley, Peter Roberts, Ray "Shorty" Robertson and family, Ronald "Nambo" Robinson, Tony "Gad" Robinson, David Rodigan, Winston and Sonia Rodney, Max Romeo, Devon Russell, Lister Lowe Smith, Keith Sterling, Nadine Sutherland, Tyrone Taylor, Linval Thompson, Prince Lincoln Thompson, Karl Toppin, Junia Walker, Don Williams, Ernest "Drummie Zeb" Williams, Rannie "Bop" Williams, Anthony Wall, Tony "English" Welch, Yabby You, and Benjamin Zephaniah.